RUSSIFICATION IN THE BALTIC PROVINCES AND FINLAND, 1855-1914

The Western Borderlands of the Empire.

RUSSIFICATION IN THE BALTIC PROVINCES AND FINLAND, 1855-1914

EDITOR
EDWARD C. THADEN

COAUTHORS
MICHAEL H. HALTZEL
Aspen Institute for Humanistic Studies

C. LEONARD LUNDIN
Indiana University, Bloomington

ANDREJS PLAKANS
Iowa State University

TOIVO U. RAUN
California State University, Long Beach

EDWARD C. THADEN
University of Illinois, Chicago Circle

Princeton University Press
Princeton, New Jersey

CONTENTS

Contents

PREFACE

THIS BOOK is a byproduct of the sessions on elites, modernization, and Russification in which we participated between 1972 and 1974 at the Third and Fourth Conferences on Baltic Studies in Toronto and Chicago and at the International Conference on Slavic Studies in Banff, Canada. In 1975 I drafted a proposal on the behalf of our group in response to the Ford Foundation's International Research Competition in Soviet/Russian and East European Studies. It has been largely because of the generous support we received from the Ford Foundation that we have been able to complete our project.

In our proposal to the Ford Foundation we listed the following questions among those with which we were attempting to deal. To what extent was Russification the result of the rationalization of the basic legal-administrative order that emerged in Russia during the era of Great Reforms? Was there ever a real possibility of political cooperation between the Baltic Germans and Estonians and Latvians? What were the effects of Russificatory changes in elementary education for Estonians and Latvians? How rapidly, for example, and to what extent was Russian really used as the language of instruction? What effects did administrative changes have, especially those in municipal government and the administration of justice? And how was the manner in which Estonians and Latvians responded to Russification affected by the level of cultural, social, and economic development they had already reached before 1880? With regard to Finland, what circumstances and conditions enabled her to grow into a modern country with a high degree of self-consciousness and a set of institutions and values that differed markedly from those of Russia? What effect did various internal conflicts have on the response of the Finns to Russification between 1899 and 1914?

In attempting to answer these and other questions we have viewed Russification in the context of what was happening both in the interior of the Russian Empire and in its borderlands. We have been particularly interested in determining the effects this policy had on the lives of the inhabitants of the Baltic Provinces and Finland. We have, therefore, undertaken to write as much an ethnic, social, economic, and intellectual history of this area between the Crimean War and World War I as a history of Russian nationality policy.

We have tried to base this study of Russification in the Baltic

Provinces and Finland on the best sources available in the United States, Finland, western Europe, and the Soviet Union. Unfortunately, none of us has been able to work in the archives of the Soviet Baltic republics, although several of us have visited these republics and discussed our research with Soviet Estonian and Latvian scholars. A good part of the memoirs, letters, fiction, newspapers, journals, and historical materials published in the Baltic Provinces and in independent Latvia and Estonia before 1940 is available outside the Soviet Union. Such Baltic and, of course, Finnish materials are to be found especially in the libraries of Helsinki and Turku universities and the Åbo Akademi in Finland. The valuable papers of the minister state secretaries for Finnish affairs and of the Russian governors-general (as well as other pertinent papers) can be consulted in the Suomen Valtionarkisto (Finnish State Archives) in Helsinki. Additional pertinent manuscript materials are deposited in the Bremen Universitätsbibliothek and in the Hessisches Staatsarchiv in Marburg, Germany.

A problem all scholars working on Russification have encountered is the difficulty of gaining access to the principal Soviet archives and manuscript collections located in Leningrad and Moscow. The subject is one that Soviet archival and other authorities obviously consider sensitive. Soviet scholars have treated it only peripherally; foreign scholars wishing to work on it specifically have, to the best of our knowledge, never been accepted as participants in the official exchanges between the Soviet Union and foreign countries (the only way to gain entry into the archives). Certain pertinent Soviet archival materials are, however, available for the use of non-Soviet scholars, and in this study such materials have been very useful for the clarification of important points in regard to the formulation of government policy on nationality during the 1860s.

This study has benefited from the assistance of a number of institutions, libraries, archives, and individuals. The importance of support from the Ford Foundation has already been mentioned. We also appreciate the financial assistance, conference and research facilities, and library, cartographic, and administrative services made available to us by the institutions at which we teach or for which we have worked: the Aspen Institute for Humanistic Studies; Hamilton College; the California State University, Long Beach, and the CSULB Foundation; Indiana University; Iowa State University; and the University of Illinois at Chicago Circle. The Iowa State University Graduate College provided assistance with preparing the maps, and the chart in Part Three; the University of Illinois, indispensable secretarial and administrative services for the Ford Foundation grant between 1975 and 1978. The International Research and Exchanges

Board (IREX) made possible research in Soviet archives. In addition, thanks are due to the staffs of many libraries in this country and abroad: The Finnish Literary Society, Helsinki; the Institute of History at Helsinki University; the Institute of History of the Soviet Academy of Sciences; the J. G. Herder Institute in Marburg, Germany; the Hessian State Archives; the Finnish State Archives; the manuscript divisions and reading rooms of the Lenin and Saltykov-Shchedrin libraries and the Pushkinskii dom in Moscow and Leningrad; the Library of Congress; the New York Public Library; and the university libraries at Berkeley, Bremen, Chicago (University of Chicago), Columbia, Göttingen, Harvard, Helsinki, Los Angeles (UCLA), Seattle (University of Washington), and Urbana-Champaign, Illinois.

Professors Alfred Levin of Kent State University, Barbara Sciacchitano of North Central College, Illinois, and Valters Nollendorfs, President of the Association for the Advancement of Baltic Studies, made useful suggestions for revision of the original draft of the proposal we submitted to the Ford Foundation early in 1975. Dr. Marianna Thaden prepared the final version of the proposal and successfully completed the negotiations with the Ford Foundation. Several of us benefited greatly from discussions with Professor Peter Scheibert of Philipps Universität, Marburg, Germany, who brought to our attention collections of Baltic materials in the Hessian State Archives. Problems concerning the period of Alexander III were clarified thanks to discussions with and critical comments received from Professor Theodore Taranovski of the University of Puget Sound. Last but not least, the five authors of this book have helped each other, profiting especially from the analysis of texts and discussion at three meetings that took place during 1976 and 1977 in Chicago, Dallas, and Aspen, Colorado.

In order to avoid possible confusion, something must be said about the transliterations and the place and personal names that will be encountered in this work. Russian names and words have generally been transliterated according to the Library of Congress system. In referring to the three Baltic Provinces we have used, with a few exceptions, the pre-1917 German place names and territorial designations. We have done this largely because of the need for uniformity of usage among four authors dealing with a multilingual Baltic society. With regard to Finland, on the other hand, Finnish place names have been used because they are fairly familiar to today's English-speaking reader and because there is a degree of continuity in Finland's historical development absent in that of the Baltic Provinces.

We have tried to give personal names in the form that the person in question would seem to have preferred. Russian names are trans-literated, as well as those of persons of foreign origin who clearly considered themselves to be Russians. The names of Baltic Germans, Estonians, Finns, Latvians, and Swedes are given in their original German, Estonian, Finnish, Latvian, and Swedish forms. Baltic Germans in Russian state service who maintained their ties with their native provinces have not been Russified in our text. We do, however, refer to Eduard Frisch, a Riga-born Baltic German, as E. V. Frish; Frish, by all accounts, was a completely Russified tsarist *chinovnik*. On the other hand, Minister of Justice Konstantin von der Pahlen does not become fon der Palen; he retained close ties with his native Kurland and lost neither his German accent nor his Baltic loyalties despite more than fifty years of service in the Russian bureaucracy. F. L. Heiden (or in German: Friedrich Graf von Heyden) really should be F. L. Geiden if we were entirely consistent, for, even though his grandfather is listed in the *Deutschbaltisches biographisches Lexikon,* he did not speak German fluently and was unmistakably a Russian. Here we have deferred to the wishes of our expert on Finland and to common usage in Finnish historical literature.

In certain instances we have given two versions of controversial names (e.g. Heiden-Geiden, Zein-Seyn, Gerard-Gerhard, and Shvarts-Schwarz). The Estonian, Latvian, or Swedish names for the towns and geographical and administrative units we have referred to in their Finnish or German variants can be found in the glossary at the end of Part Five.

In Part Five on Finland dates are given according to the Gregorian Calendar; in the other sections, according to the official Julian Calendar of the Russian Empire (twelve days earlier than the Gregorian in the nineteenth century and thirteen in the twentieth).

Chicago
August 1979

ABBREVIATIONS

For additional details concerning the asterisked archival collections, see Part I of the bibliography. For published books and articles (with the exception of certain journals and reference works listed here), see Part III of the bibliography.

AS   Shakhovskoi, S. V., *Iz arkhiva kniazia S. V. Shakhovskogo*, 3 vols.
BM   *Baltische Monatschrift*, Riga, 1859-1913, vols. 1-76. The volumes for 1914-1915 and 1927-1931 are referred to by year of publication, not volume number. The BM was continued under the title *Baltische Monatshefte* between 1932 and 1939.
Brokgauz-Efron   *Entsiklopedicheskii slovar'*, 41 vols. in 82 (Leipzig: F. A. Brokgauz; St. Petersburg: I. A. Efron, 1890-1904).
Buchholtz   [A. Buchholtz], *Deutsch-protestantische Kämpfe in den baltischen Provinzen Russlands*.
*Bunge   "Zapiska naidennaia v bumagakh N. Kh. Bunge," in Harvard Law School Library.
*CAAK   C. A. Armfelt collection, in VA.
Chteniia   *Chteniia v imperatorskom obshchestve istorii i drevnostei pri Moskovskom universitete*, 1846-1918, vols. 1-264.
DBL   *Deutschbaltisches biographisches Lexikon 1710-1960*.
Engelhardt   Roderich von Engelhardt, *Die deutsche Universität Dorpat*.
Estlander   B. Estlander, *Elva årtionden ur Finlands historia*, 5 vols.
*GBL   Moscow, Gosudarstvennaia biblioteka imeni V. I. Lenina, otdel rukopisei.
*GorK   Ivar Gordie collection, in VA.
*GPB   Leningrad, Gosudarstvennaia publichnaia biblioteka imeni M. E. Saltykov-Shchedrina, otdel rukopisei.
*HjK   Edvard Hjelt collection, in VA.
*HomK   Viktor Theodor Homen collection, in VA.
*IgAn   Ignatius, notes on negotiations, 1892, in IgK.
*IgK   K. F. Ignatius collection, in VA.
*IgMi   Ignatius, notes on political events, 1899-1909, in IgK.
*IgPo   Ignatius, notes on several political figures, in IgK.
*IgSj   Ignatius, autobiography, in IgK.
IMM   *Izglītības Ministrijas Mēnesraksts* [The Monthly of the Ministry of Education], Riga, 1920-1939.

Isakov S. G. Isakov, *Ostzeiskii vopros v russkoi pechati 1860-kh godov.*

JäK A. A. Järnefelt collection, in VA.

KanEl *Kansallinen elämäkerrasto,* 5 vols. (Porvoo: Söderström, 1927-1934).

Katkov M. N. Katkov, *Sobranie peredovykh statei Moskovskikh vedomostei, 1863-1887 gg.,* 25 vols. Referred to as Katkov, *1863 god, 1864 god,* etc.

*KKK Kenraalikuvernöörinkanslian arkisto [Archives of the Chancellery of the Governor-General], in VA.

KM S. M. Seredonin (ed.), *Istoricheskii obzor deiatel'nosti Komiteta ministrov,* 4 vols.

Langhoff A. Langhoff, *Sju år såsom Finlands represant inför tronen,* 3 vols.

Manasein N. A. Manasein, *Manaseina revīzija.*

*Materialien R. Staël von Holstein, "Materialien zu einer Geschichte des Livländischen Landesstaates," Welding collection, in Bremen, Germany, Universitätsbibliothek.

*Mek Leo Mechelin collection, in VA.

Obozrenie rasporiazhenii Kratkoe obozrenie pravitel'stvennykh rasporiazhenii o vvedenii v upotreblenie russkogo iazyka v Pribaltiiskikh guberniiakh.

*PD Leningrad, Institut russkoi literatury Akademii nauk SSSR, otdel rukopisei (Pushkinskii dom).

Petukhov E. V. Petukhov, *Imperatorskii Iur'evskii, byvshii Derptskii universitet,* 2 vols.

Polovtsov A. A. Polovtsov, *Dnevnik gosudarstvennogo sekretaria A. A. Polovtsova,* 2 vols.

*PoTi Political information collection, in VA.

*Procopé collection V. N. Procopé collection, in VA.

PSZ *Polnoe sobranie zakonov Rossiiskoi imperii,* 3 series (St. Petersburg: 2-oe Otdelenie Sobstvennoi ego Imperatorskogo Velichestva Kantseliarii, 1830-1916).

Rozhdestvenskii S. V. Rozhdestvenskii (ed.), *Istoricheskii obzor deiatel'nosti Ministra narodnogo prosveshcheniia.*

Samarin Iu. F. Samarin, *Sochineniia,* vols. 1-10, 12.

*SetK E. N. Setälä collection, in VA.

SIRIO *Sbornik imperatorskogo istoricheskogo obshchestva,* St. Petersburg, 1867-1916, 148 vols.

*SoSa Soisalon-Soinen collection, in VA.

*StaK K. J. Ståhlberg collection, in VA.

Tobien A. von Tobien, *Die livländische Ritterschaft in ihrem Verhältnis zum Zarismus und russischen Nationalismus,* 2 vols.

Toimetised Eesti NSV Teaduste Akadeemia, *Toimetised*, Ühiskon-
nateadusted [Akademiia Nauk Estonskoi SSR, *Izvestiia*, Ob-
shchestvennye nauki], Tallinn, 1956-.

TRÜT Tartu, Riiliku Ülikool, *Toimetised* [Tartu, Gosudarstvennyi
universitet, *Uchenye zapiski*], 1941-.

*TsGIAL Leningrad, Tsentral'nyi gosudarstvennyi istoricheskii
arkhiv.

*TuK Sten Carl Tudeer collection, in VA.

*VA Helsinki, Valtionarkisto [State Archives].

*ValAs State documents collection, in VA.

Valuev P. A. Valuev, *Dnevnik P. A. Valueva ministra Vnutrennikh
del*, 2 vols.

Vēstis Latvijas PSR Zinatņu Akademija, *Vēstis* [Akademiia Nauk
Latviiskoi SSR, *Izvestiia*], Riga, 1947-.

*VSV Valtionsihteerinviraston arkisto [Archives of the State Secre-
tariat], in VA.

Wittram R. Wittram, *Baltische Geschichte 1180-1918*.

*YKK Yrjö-Koskinen collection, in VA.

Zinātniskie raksti Riga, Universitāte, *Zinātniskie raksti* [Riga, Gosudarstvennyi universitet, *Uchenye zapiski*], 1949-.

RUSSIFICATION IN THE BALTIC PROVINCES AND FINLAND, 1855-1914

INTRODUCTION

O NE OF THE EVIDENT GAPS in the historiography of modern Russia is the lack of a thorough and systematic study of Russification in the Baltic borderlands during the period 1855-1914. Without such a study it is difficult to see in proper perspective the complexity of the inter-action before World War I of Russians with Germans, Estonians, Latvians, Finns, Swedes, and the other nationalities living in the Baltic area. Historians, in trying to understand the rationale of the Russian government's efforts to integrate these nationalities and to bring them closer to the empire, and resistance of the various na-tionalities to this process, are still obliged to turn to the emotionally charged terminology and selected facts offered by polemics of sixty to over a hundred years ago concerning the so-called Finnish and Baltic questions. Or they must rely on works written since 1917, which—both inside and outside the Soviet Union—tend to be marred by the excessively national or ideological preoccupations of their authors.

This study of Russification will focus on Finland and, especially, the three Baltic Provinces of Estland, Livland, and Kurland. Until the mid-nineteenth century even Russians generally agreed that the area's level of cultural and social development compared favorably with that of other parts of the empire. Partly for this reason, Russian tsars let it have a considerable degree of autonomy and granted to its traditional elites well-defined rights and privileges. Eventually, this special position of the Baltic Provinces and Finland came to be questioned. Russian attitudes toward the elites of this area changed largely because of fears generated by the unification of Germany and because of the gradual systematization of government and moderniza-tion of society in Russia, especially during the period of reform and counterreform that followed the emancipation of the Russian serfs in 1861. German- and Swedish-speaking elites continued, however, to perform many useful services for Russia. Unlike the Polish *szlachta*, clergy, and townsmen of Lithuania, the right-bank Ukraine, and Congress Poland, they remained steadfastly loyal to the Russian throne until the twentieth century. This may explain why the German nobility of the Baltic Provinces retained certain of its special rights and privileges until 1917 and why Finland was never fully integrated with the rest of the Russian Empire.

Introduction

Although Poland and Lithuania are Baltic states, they will be considered only incidentally in this study. The Baltic region consists of several areas that are distinct in terms of historico-cultural evolution. In the nineteenth century Russians made a distinction between Poland-Lithuania and the other Baltic areas within the Russian Empire, and they looked at the Polish question as being quite different from that of the Baltic Provinces and Finland. In this study our primary concern will be to examine the impact of Russification on the Baltic Provinces and Finland. Here, in contrast to Poland-Lithuania, the common people were both literate and exposed to a process of comparatively rapid social and economic modernization, and there was no rebellion against Russia. The Polish insurrections of 1830-1831 and 1863-1864, the presence of millions of socially and economically disadvantaged Orthodox Eastern Slavs in historic Lithuania and the right-bank Ukraine, and the dominant position locally of the *szlachta* and Polish civilization influenced Russifying officials to pursue policies in the lands of the former Polish-Lithuanian Commonwealth that differed from those they employed in the Baltic Provinces and Finland. But the lessons Russia learned in Poland-Lithuania had obvious applications to other parts of the empire. Events occurring in Congress Poland and Lithuania will, therefore, be discussed in this study insofar as they help to explain changes in Russian attitudes and in the general direction of official nationality and borderland policy. These events are of intrinsic interest and importance, and we hope that our study of Russification in the Baltic Provinces and Finland will encourage others to undertake similar studies not only of Poland and Lithuania but also of other parts of the Russian Empire.

The Baltic Provinces and Finland occupied about 2 percent of the land area of the Russian Empire, and by the end of the nineteenth century their 5 million inhabitants accounted for approximately 4 percent of its population. The majority of Finland's 2.5 million inhabitants then lived in coastal regions and in the southwestern section of the country, while the greater part of Finland's 144,253 square miles of territory (located in the center and north) was either uninhabited or very sparsely settled. Finland was mainly of interest to Russia for strategic reasons: the defense of St. Petersburg and naval control of the Gulf of Bothnia. The Baltic Provinces (Estland, Livland, and Kurland), being located on the Baltic Sea between St. Petersburg and Germany, also had strategic importance for Russia. In addition, they were the natural outlet for a vast Russian hinterland connected with the Baltic by the Western Dvina River and (beginning in the 1870s) a railway network terminating in the ports of Riga, Reval (Tallinn), Windau (Ventspils), and Libau (Liepāja). In 1897 Liv-

4

land, the largest and most populous of the three Baltic provinces, with 18,160 square miles of land and nearly 1.3 million inhabitants, was among the leading industrialized and urbanized regions of the Russian Empire. Kurland (10,535 square miles and 674,437 inhabitants) and Estland (7,818 square miles and 413,747 inhabitants) were smaller, but they ranked with Livland among the most highly developed provinces of the Russian Empire.

The political frontiers of the Baltic Provinces and Finland were shaped by the conquests, wars, and political rivalries of Scandinavians, Germans, Poles, and Russians over a period of centuries. In the thirteenth and fourteenth centuries the Estonian and Latvian indigenous population of Old Livonia was brought under the rule of the Teutonic Order and of German nobles and townsmen. Successive Polish, Swedish, and Russian domination of the area divided it into three provinces but left the Germans in control of religion, courts, trade and commerce, the land, and institutions of self-government. The physical boundaries of the three provinces did not follow ethnic lines, for the Estonians in Estland were separated from their co-nationals in northern Livland, while the Latvians were divided into three segments: their people lived in southern Livland, Kurland, and Lettgallia,—the Polish province of Inflanty—which in the nineteenth century formed the western part of the Russian *guberniia* of Vitebsk.

The Reformation was an important landmark in the history of the Baltic Provinces. The establishment of Lutheranism as the official religion of Estland, Livland, and Kurland strengthened their ties with Germany and Sweden and tended to cut them off culturally from Orthodox Russia and Catholic Inflanty and Poland (even though Kurland remained part of the Polish-Lithuanian Commonwealth until 1795). The extent to which Lutheranism influenced the daily lives and moral outlook of the Baltic peasants is debatable, but there can be no question about the significance of the work of Lutheran pastors in developing the Estonian and Latvian languages and spreading literacy among the peasants. By the 1880s, thanks to the combined efforts of the Lutheran Church, large landowners, and the peasant townships, elementary education was almost universal in the Baltic Provinces. In the rest of the Russian Empire a comparable elementary educational system existed only in Finland.

Until the nineteenth century the overwhelming majority of Latvians and Estonians were serfs living on the estates of the German nobility. The emancipation of the Baltic serfs between 1816 and 1819 left them economically dependent on the German landowners. During the 1850s and 1860s Latvians and Estonians obtained the right to own land. This benefited a minority, who gradually became successful

5

peasant proprietors. The bulk of the Latvian and Estonian population remained tenant farmers, landless peasants, or urban workers. In the second part of the nineteenth century about 15 percent of the Baltic peasants lived on lands formerly owned by the Swedish or Polish crown. Until the mid-century the affairs of these peasants, who came to be known as state peasants (*gosudarstvennye krest'iane*), had been controlled by Baltic Germans, but beginning in the 1860s the Russian Ministry of State Domains took a number of measures to promote their welfare. How successful these measures actually were is a matter of interpretation, but toward the end of the nineteenth century conditions among the former Baltic state peasants do not seem to have differed appreciably from those among the former serfs of the German landowners.

Finland was part of Sweden from the thirteenth century until her annexation by Russia in 1809. Unlike the Baltic Provinces, Finland's historic boundaries did more or less correspond to the facts of ethnography. Finnish was spoken or understood in all parts of the country except for the Åland Islands and the narrow strip of Swedish coastal settlements along the Gulf of Finland and the Gulf of Bothnia. Finland's peasants had never been enserfed. They had independent institutions, local self-government and rights protected under Swedish law, and even sent representatives to the Riksdag in Stockholm. Like the Baltic peasants, they benefited from the efforts of the Lutheran Church to develop for them a written language and to spread literacy. In the eighteenth and early nineteenth century, the use of Finnish was confined largely to the peasants; officials, the nobility, townsmen, and even the clergy generally spoke Swedish. But an increasing number of Swedish speakers, many of whom had descended from Finnish-speaking families, began to view Finland as an embryonic, Hegelian nation-state and to identify themselves with the nationality of the peasant majority of the population. Finland's society was always less rigidly organized than that of the Baltic Provinces; the willingness of a significant number of individuals from the Swedish-speaking middle and upper strata of the population to join forces with the Finnish national movement tended to alleviate national, class, and economic tensions. It made possible at the beginning of the twentieth century the cooperation of Swedes and Finns in a common struggle against Russification. In the Baltic Provinces similar cooperation among Germans, Estonians, and Latvians did not and perhaps could not have occurred.

In the second part of the nineteenth century Finland also differed from the Baltic Provinces and the other western borderlands in being governed separately from the rest of the empire. Thus, in Finland the authority of the Russian Ruling Senate, State Council, and ministries was not exercised directly, but indirectly through the emperor and the State Secretariat for Finnish Affairs; internally, Finland was governed by an administrative Senate and a Diet representing all four estates (including the landed peasants); and her religious affairs were not subjected to central bureaucratic control and supervision as had been the case elsewhere in Russia's western borderlands since the first part of the nineteenth century. It was the extent and apparent certainty of Finland's autonomy that made certain measures of administrative Russification—which were mild in comparison with its practice elsewhere—seem so outrageous and unjustifiable at the beginning of the twentieth century to the vast majority of Finns and significant segments of public opinion in western Europe and the United States.

The Baltic Germans reacted with similar indignation when the introduction of Russian reforms and institutions first came under serious consideration during the 1860s. The Baltic Germans feared not so much the actual measures introduced by the government at the time as what seemed to be their long-term implications. Although they did not know exactly what the government intended to do, their publicists of the sixties did not hesitate to ascribe to the government the goal of forcibly making Russians out of non-Russians.[1] By the beginning of the twentieth century this definition of Russification came to be generally accepted by liberal and radical political leaders and journalists. In Soviet times the notion of Russification as a "forcible great-power-colonial policy" (in tsarist Russia only, of course) has been enshrined lexicographically as historical fact.[2]

But did Russian officials and nationalistic publicists understand the word in this sense? It would not seem so. Until the mid-nineteenth century the intransitive form of the verb Russify (*obruset'*) was generally used, meaning "to become Russian," as contrasted with the later and more active form of *obrusit'*, or "to make Russian."[3] Catherine II used the verb *obruset'* as early as 1764, to mean centralizing and unifying the empire's administrative and legal structure to assure government control over society and the interests of the Russian state in the Ukraine and the Baltic Provinces. Nicholas I, who was no nationalist in the modern sense of the word, seems to have meant much the same thing when he asked his son in a testament prepared in 1835 to complete the work of Russification (*obrusevanie*) in Congress Poland.[4] In the 1860s Russian officials and publicists employed the term sparingly because they realized how well it served the purposes of anti-Russian publicists. Thus, as early as 1864 the leading Russian nationalistic journalist, editor of *Moskovskie vedomosti* Mikhail N. Katkov (1818-

1887), derisively dismissed as fantasy the talk in the French press about his newspaper's reliance on Moscow merchants who wished to Russify not only Riga, Vilna, and Warsaw but also the entire world.[5] Toward the end of the sixties the famous Slavophile and Baltic polemicist Iurii F. Samarin (1819-1876) did cautiously advocate the Russification of the Estonians and Latvians, but he made this recommendation defensively and as a means of putting an end to what he considered the alarming and progressive Germanization of these two small peoples, who were "obviously not intended for an independent political development" and who would voluntarily become Russians if only given some encouragement.[6]

Official circles observed similar caution in the use of the word Russification. It was only toward the end of the nineteenth century that it gained wide currency as a convenient expression of the government's desire to extend Russian political and judicial institutions to the borderlands and to make Russian the language of the schools and local officialdom throughout the empire. But no less an authority than Holy Synod Procurator Konstantin P. Pobedonostsev (1827-1907), in speaking of Congress Poland, pointed out that it would be futile to try to transform Poles into Russians. He denied that the Russian government had any such intention, adding that the word Russification had so many different meanings that much confusion and error would be eliminated if it were not used at all.[7] Another would-be Russifier, Nikolai I. Bobrikov (1839-1904), the Russian governor-general in Helsinki between 1898 and 1904, stated categorically that he had no plans to Russify the Finnish and Swedish-speaking inhabitants of the Finnish Grand Duchy.[8] If Russian officials were less categorical in their statements about the Estonians and Latvians, they realized by the beginning of the twentieth century that these two small peoples were determined to defend their own national identity. In any case, it is dubious that there was at that time a coherent tsarist policy aiming at making Russians out of the Estonians and Latvians.

In this study we will employ the word Russification in three senses: unplanned, administrative, and cultural. The verb *obruset'*, or "to become Russian," suggests unplanned, voluntary Russification. Since the sixteenth century countless Tatars, Chuvashes, Mordvinians, Belorussians, Ukrainians, and other non-Russians had naturally and voluntarily adopted Russian customs, culture, and language as a result of serving in the army or bureaucracy, marrying Russians, or simply by residing and working where Russian was spoken. In the period inaugurated by the emancipation of the serfs and the Great Reform, the rate of unplanned Russification was no doubt accelerated. The building of railways and economic expansion and modernization brought the borderlands closer to the Russian interior. Development of industry and of the internal market and the improvement of communications and of professional and social services created new opportunities for Russians and non-Russians alike. Impressive achievements in literature, the arts, science, and scholarship made the Russian culture, language, and way of life more attractive than ever before. Finland was the least affected by this form of Russification. In the Baltic Provinces, on the other hand, a number of Baltic Germans seem to have responded positively to the allures of Russian nationality. If the Latvians and Estonians who remained in the Baltic Provinces proved to be surprisingly resistant to Russification and insistent on the retention of their own nationality, hundreds of thousands of individuals from among their ranks sought economic opportunity outside the Baltic Provinces. In the interior of the empire, the majority of these Baltic emigrants were, sooner or later, Russified.

Administrative Russification, on the other hand, was a more deliberate and conscious policy and began with the reign of Catherine II. It aimed at uniting the borderlands with the center of the empire through the *gradual* introduction of Russian institutions and laws and extension of the use of Russian in the local bureaucracy and as a subject of instruction in schools. This was the form of Russification that generally prevailed in the Baltic Provinces and Finland.

The advocates of cultural Russification believed that it was not enough for the borderland peoples to be integrated into the political and administrative structure of the empire. Russia, in their opinion, could only become a modern national state if her borderland minorities accepted the language and cultural and religious values of the Russian people. Samarin was the most effective champion of this form of Russification. During the 1860s and early 1870s his sharp criticism of official Baltic policy and his advocacy of the Russification of the Latvians and Estonians, Orthodox proselytizing, and the restructuring of Baltic society greatly disturbed Alexander II and St. Petersburg officialdom. Alexander III disagreed with his father and took Samarin's views on the Baltic question seriously, even trying in the latter part of the eighties to put them into practice.

Problems of definition and sources and the need to work with the six principal languages spoken in the Baltic Provinces and Finland during the nineteenth century (Estonian, Finnish, German, Latvian, Russian, and Swedish) make the study of Russification there a difficult one for the isolated scholar who works by himself. For this reason, the

five authors of this study decided as early as May 1972, at the Third
Conference on Baltic Studies in Toronto, to pool their knowledge of
languages and skills in such areas as literature, demography, and the
behavioral sciences (we are all historians) to undertake a group study
of Russification in the Baltic region.

The nature of the subject and our own respective interests have
convinced us that the most appropriate approach to the organization
of our study would be one suggested by the German novelist Karl
Gutzkow in 1850. In the introduction to the first volume of the novel
Die Ritter vom Geiste, Gutzkow then referred to two principles for
the organization of a novel: *das Nebeneinander* as opposed to *das
Nacheinander*. What Gutzkow proposed to do was to write a new
sort of novel that would no longer revolve about sequential and uni-
linear deeds and actions of a single hero (*das Nacheinander*) but
would place kings alongside beggars in order to reflect the most varied
viewpoints of people from all walks of life (*das Nebeneinander*).[9]

We propose to place Russian bureaucrats and publicists alongside
various strata of the German, Estonian, Latvian, Swedish, and Finnish-
speaking population of Finland, Estland, Livland, and Kurland. We
will endeavor to bring out the manner in which the Baltic peoples
were affected by that peculiar combination of reform, Russification,
and compromise so characteristic of Russian borderland policy. The
response to Russification of each of the Baltic social strata and nationalities was conditioned by its material interests, traditional role
in local society, prospects of social mobility, and the level of development it had reached by 1855. These are all factors that must be taken
into consideration if one is to understand Russification in the Baltic
Provinces and Finland between 1855 and 1914.

Aware of the perils of the *Nebeneinander*, we have made a special
effort to achieve a proper division of labor. Some repetition is unavoid-
able, for we are dealing with a single subject viewed from a variety
of group and national perspectives. The main outlines of Russification
as a policy and its impact on privileged groups in the Baltic borderlands are sketched in the first two Parts of this study. In the first Part
I discuss the gradual emergence of a policy of administrative Russification before 1855, the duel between advocates of administrative and
cultural Russification in the post-emancipation period, and the incon-
clusive outcome of this contest. Emphasized here is policy formulation (as opposed to policy implementation) in two separate periods:
1855-1895 in regard to the Baltic Provinces and 1890-1910 in regard to
Finland. In the second Part Michael H. Haltzel describes the traditional world of the Baltic Germans, shows how a new particularist

ideology took shape during the 1860s, and concentrates on the Baltic German reaction to the implementation of Russification during the period 1881-1905. Russification was a threat to the dominant position of the Germans in Baltic society. Symbolically, it pointed to the gradual transformation of the old and familiar Russian Empire into a Russian nation-state in which there would be little room for loyal, non-Russian landowners from the Baltic Provinces.

In the third and fourth Parts Andrejs Plakans and Toivo U. Raun view Russification through the eyes of the Latvians and Estonians. The attitudes and objectives of these peoples are somewhat more difficult to document than those of Russian and German publicists and leaders, as they were dominated for centuries by the Baltic Germans and had no political and national elites of their own until the second part of the nineteenth century. But Plakans and Raun, by supplementing textual analysis of contemporary accounts with a prosopographical study of intellectual leaders, have succeeded in showing a wide range of responses to Russification among Estonians and Latvians. Social, cultural, and economic progress produced a new system of social stratification and a greater degree of social mobility, permitting the gradual rise of Estonian and Latvian elites who aspired to a leading role in local Baltic society. They were primarily concerned with the social and economic advancement of their own national communities. Russification (but only of an administrative kind) was first seen as a desirable curb to Baltic German influence and later as something that was irksome but not necessarily a threat to their own cultural and economic future.

Finland was the last important area of the Russian Empire to be affected by Russification. In the fifth Part C. Leonard Lundin discusses in detail the response of the Finns to Russification between 1881 and 1910. By then Finland was a modern country with a high degree of self-consciousness and a set of institutions and values that differed markedly from those of Russia. Russians understandably did not look kindly on the alienation of Finland from the rest of the empire; Finns, in their turn, were disturbed by Russian efforts to alter the special relationship Finland had had with the empire for about a hundred years. The actual impact of Russification on Finland was not great, but before 1914 certain danger signs indicated that those elements in the bureaucracy which had, since the sixties, advocated moderation in the practice of Russification in the Baltic Provinces and Finland would perhaps no longer prevail. The fear that this would happen helped to unite Finns at a time of considerable internal and national tension.

11

Notes to Introduction

1. F. I. Fircks [*pseud.*: D. K. Schédo-Ferroti], *Études sur l'avenir de la Russie*, VIII: *Que fera-t-on de la Pologne?* (Berlin: E. Bock [B. Behr]; Bruxelles and Leipzig: Aug. Schnee, 1864), pp. vii-viii, 151-55; C. Schirren, *Livländische Antwort an Herrn Juri Samarin* (Leipzig: Duncker und Humblot, 1869), pp. 41-42, 110-12.

2. "Obrusitel'nyi," "obrusit'," "russifikatsiia," *Tolkovyi slovar' russkogo iazyka*, ed. B. M. Volin and D. N. Ushakov (Moscow: Gosudarstvennoe Izdatel'stvo Inostrannykh i Natsional'nykh Slovarei, 1938), II, 705; III, 1407.

3. Akademiia Nauk SSSR, Institut Russkogo Iazyka, *Slovar' sovremennogo russkogo literaturnogo iazyka* (Moscow-Leningrad: Akademiia Nauk, 1950-), VIII, 410-11.

4. Catherine II to A. Viazemskii, 1764, SIRIO (see List of Abbreviations), VII (1871), 348; "Zaveshchanie Nikolaia I synu," ed. V. I. Picheta, *Krasnyi arkhiv*, III (1923), 293.

5. Katkov, *1864 god* (see List of Abbreviations), p. 551.

6. Samarin (see List of Abbreviations), IX, 468.

7. *Svod vysochaishikh otmetok po vsepoddanneishim otchetam za 1896 g. general-gubernatorov, gubernatorov i gradonachal'nikov* (St. Petersburg: Gosudarstvennaia Tipografiia, 1898), p. 35.

8. *Vsepoddanneishaia zapiska finliandskogo general-gubernatora 1898-1902* ([St. Petersburg]: Gosudarstvennaia Tipografiia, [1902]), p. 13.

9. Karl Gutzkow, *Die Ritter vom Geiste*, I (Leipzig: F. A. Brockhaus, 1850), pp. 6-8.

PART ONE

THE RUSSIAN GOVERNMENT

EDWARD C. THADEN

CHAPTER 1

REFORM AND RUSSIFICATION IN THE WESTERN BORDERLANDS, 1796-1855

Essentially, the Russian government's relations with the empire's borderlands is to be seen as an aspect of local government. Russia was an undergoverned country, and even in the Great Russian center of the empire the lack of appropriate institutions, the absence of satisfactory legal and administrative order, and the insufficient number of competent and trained officials made it difficult for the government to rule effectively outside St. Petersburg and the *guberniia* capitals. However, Russia, like other European states, often tried to impose her own religious and political norms on national and religious minorities living within her frontiers. This was particularly the case in the eastern borderlands and the left-bank Ukraine, where the local elites were either easily assimilated or had weakly developed institutions of self-government. In the western borderlands, on the other hand, the local administrative, legal, and social institutions often seemed to be superior to those of the Great Russian center. These institutions were the product of a long historical development that had permitted Polish *szlachta*, German burghers and nobles, and Swedish estates either to win new rights and privileges or to defend old ones in a secular struggle with relatively weak Polish or Swedish kings. Russia, a much more powerful monarchy than either Poland or Sweden, initially confirmed these rights and privileges because it was expedient for her to try to assure for herself the cooperation of the Polish, German, and Swedish upper classes in newly conquered areas during wars with Sweden and France in the eighteenth and at the beginning of the nineteenth century. Although no Russian ruler seems to have considered these promises to have been of the binding contractual nature assumed by certain Baltic German and Finnish publicists, a sufficient number of well-educated and competent borderland nobles performed useful services for the Russian state to incline Russian rulers up to Alexander III to confirm the autonomy and special rights of the upper classes in the western borderlands as long as they re-

15

mained loyal to Russia. Furthermore, because Russian law was neither uniform nor codified before the 1830s and because there was a shortage of trained jurists and officials, defenders of local privileges easily found arguments against the wisdom of introducing Russian laws and institutions. Only after Russian society had been profoundly altered by the reforms of the sixties and seventies did it seem appropriate to proceed systematically with programs of Russification in the western borderlands.

NEITHER RUSSIFICATION nor the reforms of the 1860s and 1870s can be properly understood without some reference to earlier efforts to centralize and rationalize government and to apply in Russia what George Yaney has referred to as "legal-administrative system."[1] These efforts affected the eastern borderlands of the empire and the left-bank Ukraine as early as the sixteenth and seventeenth centuries. The Baltic Provinces, Old Finland, and the lands acquired from Poland between 1772 and 1795 were brought directly under the supervision of the central government during the eighteenth century. Interference in the local affairs of the Baltic Provinces began in the mid-eighteenth century, when agents of the central government suggested the introduction of measures based on seventeenth-century Swedish legislation in order to increase government revenues and to protect Estonian and Latvian peasants from arbitrary treatment at the hands of their German masters.[2] Catherine II, as is well known, viewed borderland privileges with particular suspicion and favored from the very beginning of her reign a basic "Russification" of their administration and political institutions. During the latter part of her reign Russian forms of taxation (especially the head tax) and the Russian *guberniia*, nobility, and town institutions provided for in the Provincial Reform of 1775 and the Charters to the Nobility and Towns of 1785 were introduced throughout the vast area that had been annexed from Poland and Sweden during the seventeenth and eighteenth centuries.[3]

In November and December of 1796 five decrees of Paul I set Livland, Estland, Old Finland, and the former Polish lands apart from the rest of the empire, declaring them to be *gubernii* administered on "special foundations according to their rights and privileges."[4] But Paul believed, no less than did his mother Catherine, in the need to keep the provinces under the control and supervision of the central government and its agents. It was chiefly in the areas of strictly local affairs, courts, and the administration of law that he willingly permitted the western borderlands to deviate from the norms observed elsewhere in the empire. He continued to collect the head tax throughout this region, whereas in the Baltic Provinces he introduced the

Russian recruitment system—something from which Estonian and Latvian peasants had been spared before 1796. In addition, despite Paul's restoration of privileges, governors-general, civil and military governors, boards of public welfare, and *guberniia* financial and treasury offices continued to represent the authority of the central government in the western borderlands on the basis of Catherine II's Provincial Reform of 1775.[5]

After 1796, however, representatives of the authority of the central government in the western borderlands found it difficult to do anything that affected the interest of the local privileged estates without securing the cooperation of their assemblies of the nobility and town councils and of the German and Polish officials who took care of the everyday administrative, police, and court affairs of this area. To a considerable extent the administrative Russification undertaken by Catherine II seems to have been premature. Officials from the Great Russian center of the empire usually lacked the requisite knowledge and expertise to deal effectively with the local affairs of the western borderlands. This was especially the case in Belorussia, Lithuania and the right-bank Ukraine.[6] In Estland and Livland the rapid introduction of the head tax and of Russian legislation and institutions that sometimes protected the rights of the lower classes disturbed the equilibrium of a traditional society based on hierarchically arranged estates.[7]

The annexation of Finland in 1809 (augmented by Old Finland in 1812) and of Congress Poland in 1815 created another category of privileged provinces within the Russian Empire. Granting concessions to the wishes of the upper classes in Finland and Congress Poland was one way of securing their support during and immediately following the Napoleonic Wars. Traditional religions, laws, customs, and political institutions were retained, and the Russian Provincial Reform of 1775 was introduced in neither Finland nor in Congress Poland. Alexander I placed Finland directly under his own personal supervision and specifically instructed the Russian ministers and the Senate in St. Petersburg not to interfere in Finnish affairs. At the Porvoo (Borgå) meeting of the Finnish Diet in 1809 Alexander promised to respect Finland's existing laws and "constitutions" and announced the establishment of a Government Council consisting exclusively of inhabitants of the Grand Duchy. The major purpose of this Council, or the Finnish Senate after 1816, was to direct and coordinate the operation of Finland's internal administration. A Committee for Finnish Affairs (the State Secretariat for Finnish Affairs after 1826), staffed largely by citizens of Finland, was established in St. Petersburg as a coordinating office through which all matters pertaining to Finland had to go.[8] Similar arrangements were made for Congress Poland after 1815, including a Polish minister secretary who resided in St. Petersburg and served as a representative of Polish interests and as an intermediary between the emperor and Russian officials in Warsaw and St. Petersburg. Furthermore, in one respect Polish autonomy seemed to be more satisfactorily guaranteed than that of the Finns: Alexander I granted the kingdom of Poland a Constitutional Charter that provided for regular meetings of a Polish Sejm, local self-government, a separate army, and civil rights for Polish subjects of the Russian Emperor, who ruled as king of Poland.[9]

Elsewhere in the western borderlands privileged German and Polish elites gained new ground, especially in the areas of peasant reform and education. Peasant reform did not become a serious issue in Lithuania, Belorussia, and the right-bank Ukraine, where the land-owning Polish *szlachta* shared many of the social attitudes of Great Russian landowners. But local leaders of Polish society endeavored to use education as a means of isolating these areas culturally and linguistically from the rest of the empire. The Polish Commission of National Education, founded in 1773, had already laid the foundations for a viable network of schools. During the first third of the nineteenth century these schools contributed significantly to the re-Polonization of the middle and upper classes in the very area where Catherine II had recommended Russification in the latter part of the eighteenth century.

In the Baltic Provinces, the emancipation of the Estonian and Latvian serfs between 1816 and 1819 provided an essential point of departure for a social and economic development quite different from that of the Great Russian center of the empire. During the ensuing half century a system of elementary education with Estonian and Latvian as the languages of instruction, a rudimentary form of peasant self-government, and an agricultural economy based on free labor and the principle of private property gradually evolved. By the 1860s the progressive accentuation of the differences separating the organization of the society and economy of the Baltic Provinces from that of the center of the empire had greatly complicated the task of administrators hoping to extend to the region the Russian Great Reforms.

The terms of serf emancipation in the Baltic Provinces were worked out early in the reign of Alexander I by committees representing the local nobility. These committees studied peasant obligations and landholding and compiled new and more reliable inventories of obligations (*Wackenbücher*). Committees representing the Livland *Ritterschaft* were particularly important. Initially, the Russian government exercised some influence over this work, but its attention was soon drawn away from Baltic peasant questions by war and other more pressing affairs, while the few Russian officials attached to the local Baltic committees had little first-hand knowledge about Baltic affairs and generally accepted the advice of the Germans with whom they worked. This advice, of course, usually favored the interests of the local landowners. The peasant was emancipated without land and remained economically and socially dependent on the Baltic German nobility. He was a free man and a member of a self-governing rural community that now elected its own officers; he was called upon to help organize and support rural elementary schools and to participate in the administration of local affairs. However, if he desired to leave his native province he had to obtain permission from the local landowner and from officers of his local peasant community, who carried out their duties and functions under the watchful eye and supervision of the nearby nobility and officials working for the organs of the Baltic *Ritterschaften.* And, to some extent freedom became a mixed blessing, for the landowner no longer had the legal and moral responsibility to take care of the peasants in times of need.[10]

For all its shortcomings the emancipation of the Baltic peasant did provide Estonian and Latvian peasants with opportunities for elementary education that existed for few peasants in other parts of the empire during the first part of the nineteenth century. The Russian government of that time did little to promote the dissemination of literacy among peasants, and the social structure and values associated with serfdom discouraged the Russian clergy and nobility from taking the initiative in founding schools. In the Baltic Provinces, however, many peasants had been taught reading under the supervision of the Protestant clergy even before the emancipation. Beginning in 1819 legislation, approved separately in each of the three Baltic Provinces, opened the way for the establishment of an elementary educational system that spread literacy among Baltic peasants several generations earlier than elsewhere in the empire (with the exception of Finland). What was achieved by this educational system, it should be noted, depended on the commitment and supportiveness not only of the German clergy and nobility but also of the Estonian and Latvian peasantry. Local authorities controlled and supervised the rural school. The Russian Ministry of Education, as its official historian sadly commented, "was altogether eliminated from the business of elementary, popular education in the Baltic region."[11]

In regard to secondary and higher education, the system of national education established in 1802 was a highly decentralized one. The actual administration of school affairs was centered in six educational regions located in Dorpat (Tartu), Vilna, Kharkov, Kazan, Moscow, and St. Petersburg. Liaison between them and the Ministry of Education was maintained through curators who resided initially in St. Petersburg. In the Dorpat and Vilna regions German and Polish were the respective languages of instruction, and textbooks and educational programs were determined by local German or Polish professors and administrators.[12] The educational affairs of Finland and Congress Poland were then administered in almost complete isolation from those of the rest of the empire. Four of the eight universities in the Russian Empire between 1816 and 1830 were located in the western borderlands, their languages of instruction being Polish (Warsaw and Vilna), German (Dorpat), and Swedish (Åbo/Helsingfors).

A thorough reconsideration of educational and other aspects of borderland policy began under Nicholas I, especially after the Polish insurrection of November 1830. During the 1840s attention was drawn to the Baltic Provinces because of the failure of the local German landowners to prevent serious social unrest among the Estonian and Latvian peasantry. The efforts under Nicholas I to codify Russian law, to draft new municipal legislation, to deal with the problems of the empire's peasant population, and to centralize and standardize bureaucratic controls over society pointed in the direction of lessening the dependence of the Russian government on borderland nobles. Nicholas' minister of the interior during the forties, L. A. Perovskii (1792-1856), advocated for Poland, Finland, and the Baltic Provinces the introduction of Russian laws, administration, and municipal institutions as well as the establishment of Russian as the official language of the local administration and as the language of instruction in schools.[13] Nicholas I, despite his interest in unifying and centralizing the empire's administrative and legal system, did not accept these proposals in their entirety.

He did, however, act firmly in Congress Poland after the uprising of 1830-1831. Thus, he replaced the Polish Constitutional Charter of 1815 with the Organic Statutes of 1832, which abolished the Polish Sejm and army. Dictatorial power was concentrated in the hands of Prince Field Marshal I. F. Paskevich (1782-1856), the new viceroy of Poland. Paskevich, with the apparent approval of Nicholas I, opposed the introduction of Russian laws and institutions into Poland, arguing that not the slow-moving Russian bureaucracy but an exclusive power that stood outside the law was needed to deal with the special conditions and problems obtaining in Russia's borderlands.[14]

Other Russian officials, especially those employed by the Second Section of His Imperial Majesty's Own Chancery, worked systematically to prepare the groundwork for the very thing against which

Paskevich had warned, namely, the introduction of Russian laws and institutions into the borderlands. Within the Second Section, which was concerned with the codification of Russian law, such officials as M. M. Speranskii (1772-1839), D. N. Bludov (1785-1864), and D. V. Dashkov (1788-1839), soon realized that the codification of local laws in the Caucasus, Poland, Finland, and the Baltic Provinces was a necessary step preliminary to the establishment of general legal norms for the entire empire. In the borderland regions existing laws and court procedures represented an extraordinarily complicated mosaic of differing and often conflicting traditions written down in a variety of languages ranging from Latin, German, Polish, and Swedish to Arabic and Georgian. Russian legal experts were obviously not in a position to gain much insight into the nature of the actual legal conditions and laws in the borderlands without simplified and systematized collections of local laws in the original and in Russian translation. Because of the importance attached to bringing local laws into conformity with the general laws of the empire, it was prescribed that all codifications of local laws should be modeled after the Russian *Svod zakonov* and that they should in no way be in conflict with the rights and prerogatives of the autocratic power and with Russian fundamental laws. Work was commenced on law codes for all the major borderland areas, but it was only in the Baltic Provinces that a local code received official sanction, an action which the Baltic Germans interpreted to be a confirmation of their traditional rights and privileges. In the western *gubernii*, on the other hand, the traditional Lithuanian Statute was abolished, and local Polish law was replaced by the Russian *Svod zakonov* between 1831 and 1840.[15]

In Finland, in contrast to the Baltic Provinces, Russian-sponsored codification of local laws at the beginning of the forties was seen by Finnish State Secretary Alexander Armfelt (1794-1876) and other Finnish officials as a threat to the Finns' privileged position and rights within the empire. They found an ally in Prince A. S. Menshikov (1787-1869), the Russian governor-general in Finland, who, though not particularly opposed to the codification of Finnish laws, was very concerned about the maintenance of social order and stability in Finland. Having been told about the Finns' apprehensions concerning Bludov's plans and reminded about the role Russia's respect for Finnish traditions had played in making Finland's union with Russia popular, Menshikov used his influence to convince Nicholas I that great caution had to be exercised in dealing with the Finns. As a result, the Second Section's work on the codification of Finnish law was, in effect, suspended by the beginning of the fifties.[16]

Peasant problems provided reform-minded Russian officials with another pretext to intervene in the affairs of the western borderlands. Latvian and Estonian peasants had been emancipated, but they remained dependent on the Baltic German landowners. Between 1842 and 1863 social unrest among the Baltic peasants convinced the three provincial Diets of the need to discuss legislation to permit the former Estonian and Latvian serfs to acquire and own land. Problems of Baltic agriculture were also studied by Russian officials, but the possibility of unilateral intervention on their part in Baltic peasant affairs was practically ruled out through the creation of the Baltic Committee (*Ostseekomitee*). This committee met in St. Petersburg and presented its views on almost all projects of Baltic reform between 1846 and 1876. Consisting as it did of a majority of Baltic nobles or sympathizers, it never seriously challenged the German landowners' control of the Baltic countryside.[17] Nevertheless, Russian officials did exert some influence on Baltic peasant reform during the 1850s and 1860s, as will be discussed in connection with the Russian reforms of the sixties.

The government acted somewhat more vigorously in regard to education, language, and religion. But it only did so in the western *gubernii* and the Baltic Provinces, and not in Poland and Finland. In the western *gubernii*, in particular, the government made every effort to separate this formerly Polish area from Congress Poland, where cultural and educational Russification had been largely limited to abolishing the University of Warsaw and encouraging young Poles to learn Russian and to seek career and educational opportunities in the center of the Russian Empire. In the western *gubernii*, on the other hand, the government made a special effort to Russify law, education, and religion. The former Polish-language university at Vilna was moved to Kiev, where it became the Russian-language St. Vladimir University. Russian replaced Polish as the language of instruction in state-supported elementary and secondary schools, and as much education as possible was taken out of the hands of the Catholic clergy and entrusted to the care of teachers "selected by the government and acting according to its instructions."[18] At the same time, increasing pressure was put on the Uniate clergy to separate from Rome, to remove themselves from the tutelage of Polish Catholicism, and to bring their flocks back into the Orthodox Church that their ancestors had gradually left during several centuries of Polish rule. In 1839 the reunion of 1.5 million Uniates with the Russian Orthodox Church was officially proclaimed.[19]

Similar but less drastic measures were taken in the Baltic Provinces. Here new emphasis was placed on the teaching of the Russian language, geography, and history in secondary schools. Competency in

Russian became a condition for obtaining academic degrees at the University of Dorpat. By the beginning of the forties, all students matriculating there were required to pass a rigorous entrance examination in Russian. In 1850 the use of Russian was decreed obligatory for the official business of all branches of the state bureaucracy in the Baltic Provinces.[20] Meanwhile, the Russian government, after some initial hesitations, allowed tens of thousands of impoverished Estonian and Latvian peasants to leave the Lutheran Church and to convert to Orthodoxy so that they could, in the words of Minister of Education Sergei S. Uvarov (1786-1855), "enter into a more intimate union with our faith, with our ideas, our way of life."[21] Other influential figures in the government, such as Minister of the Interior L. A. Perovskii and Synod Chief N. A. Protasov (1798-1855) shared this view. Nicholas I, however, feared all popular movements among the empire's peasant majority and was easily frightened by Baltic German warnings about the social unrest and confusion likely to result from allowing peasants to leave the Church of their landowners and social superiors.[22]

During the fifties official efforts in the Baltic Provinces to promote Orthodoxy and Russian language and culture slackened. For one thing, the revolutions of 1848 in western and central Europe seemed to illustrate the importance of reinforcing traditional order in all parts of the empire. In the Baltic Provinces official encouragement of the conversion movement was abandoned, and the new Germanophile governor-general, Prince Aleksandr A. Suvorov (1804-1882), prevailed upon Nicholas I not to insist on immediate enforcement of the language law of 1850, for otherwise some 300 Germans in Baltic state service, whose knowledge of Russian was inadequate, would have to be forced into retirement. Following the Crimean War, uncertainty about how peasants and landowners would react to emancipation and a general atmosphere of reform and relative liberalism helped Suvorov, who remained governor-general until 1861, to persuade Alexander to agree to further concessions to the Baltic Germans. As a result, less emphasis was placed on Russian-language instruction in Baltic schools, and a high degree of competency in Russian was no longer required for graduation from secondary schools. In 1858, Alexander II agreed to delay indefinitely the implementation of the language law of 1850.[23]

The spirit of reform in Russia during the late fifties and early sixties had similar effects in Poland. The western borderlands in general then benefited from proposals for administrative decentralization. Many Russians in intellectual and official circles saw Russia's recent setbacks as the consequence of shortcomings of Nicholas I's rigid, overly centralized, and ineffective bureaucracy. Influential figures in the all-important Ministry of the Interior accepted this indictment of Nicholas' system and, therefore, took measures to give governors more powers and a greater degree of control over their own provincial bureaucracies.[24] Given these new circumstances, it was important for the Poles that after 1856 both the new viceroy in Warsaw, Field Marshal M. D. Gorchakov (1793-1861), and the new general-governor in Vilna, V. I. Nazimov (1802-1874), were on good terms with the *szlachta* and favored leniency in dealing with the Poles. In the Russian capital, there was no agreement about how the Polish problem should be handled, but fear of peasant unrest and the need to concentrate on the central task of reform argued in favor of detente and compromise in the borderlands. This was indeed the policy Alexander II and his advisers pursued during these years, culminating in 1862 with the appointment of Grand Duke Konstantin Nikolaevich (1827-1892) as the viceroy and the Polish Marquis Alexander Wielopolski (1803-1877) as the head of the civil administration of the Kingdom of Poland. This experiment in Polish self-government was, however, a rather short-lived episode in the history of Polish-Russian relations.[25]

DILEMMAS OF BORDERLAND POLICY IN THE ERA OF GREAT REFORMS: POLAND AND FINLAND, 1855-1881

During the sixties and seventies the Russian government clearly had no fixed and well-articulated plan for the Russification of the empire's western borderlands. Initially, as has been pointed out, preoccupation with internal reform produced a rather conciliatory policy toward them, a policy continued in regard to Finland throughout these two decades. But the Great Reforms of the sixties and seventies provided Russia for the first time with institutions and laws that seemed to compare favorably with the traditional ones of the western borderlands. Had not, therefore, the time come to introduce into this region zemstvos, reformed courts, and peasant and municipal reforms similar to those that had just been promulgated for the interior provinces of the empire?

High-ranking officials debated how fast and to what extent the Great Reforms should be extended to the western borderlands. This area, Third Section Head Petr A. Shuvalov (1827-1889) once remarked to a marshal of the Livland nobility, was essentially a battleground on which Russian conservative, liberal, and nationalist officials fought over questions of Russian internal state policy.[1] The major combatants were the so-called aristocratic or German party as opposed to the so-called democratic, patriotic, or even anarchistic party. The "German" party, which included Shuvalov, successive Ministers of the Interior Petr A. Valuev (1814-1890) and Aleksandr E. Timashev (1818-1893), and Baltic Governor-General Petr P. Al'bedinskii (1826-1883), tended to doubt the ability of Russian and non-Russian peasants to assume an independent role in society, and supported measures that would assure the continued social and economic predominance of wealthy, landowning nobles in the countryside of both the Russian interior and the borderlands of the empire. Although this "party" favored reform in the western borderlands and their integration with the rest of the empire, it wanted to proceed with such reform and

25

integration gradually and in a manner that would enable borderland nobles to retain their leading position in local society.[2]

The "democratic" party, which included the brothers D. A. and N. A. Miliutin, Grand Duke Konstantin Nikolaevich, and Minister of Education A. V. Golovnin (1821-1886), sought a somewhat broader base of public support for the government than the nobility. The members of this particular group of officials felt that the peasants should be encouraged to play a more independent role in local affairs, disapproved of current projects of "aristocratic" reform, and distrusted the borderland nobles as likely allies of their opponents at home. Viewing the Baltic "barons" with particular suspicion, they wanted the government to deal firmly with problems of social, political, and economic reform in the Baltic Provinces. In regard to Finland and Poland, however, they were willing in the early sixties to allow the leaders of local Finnish and Polish society to operate within the framework of autonomous institutions. In Poland this conciliatory policy lasted only until 1863, when Nikolai A. Miliutin (1818-1872) undertook the laying of the groundwork for the Russification of the Congress Kingdom. This new policy in Poland was not accepted by all members of the democratic party. Konstantin Nikolaevich could not accept it because of the close association of his name with the experiment with Polish autonomy after having so recently served as viceroy in Warsaw during 1862-1863; and after 1863 Golovnin, Konstantin Nikolaevich's friend and former associate in the Naval Ministry, loyally tried to defend the policy the grand duke had followed in Warsaw.[3]

Two important figures who stood apart from both the German and the democratic parties were Dmitrii A. Tolstoi (1825-1889), the minister of education and chief procurator of the Holy Synod, and Aleksandr A. Zelenoi (1819-1880), the minister of state domains. The democratic party could usually count on their support for Russifying reforms designed to undermine the predominant position of the Germans in the Baltic Provinces.[4] Otherwise, Tolstoi and Zelenoi did not champion the causes of liberal-minded bureaucrats within the government.

Something also needs to be said about a third party, one that the journalist Katkov liked to refer to as the "national" party. According to Katkov, this party only wanted what was "useful for Russia"; it opposed the "non-Russian" policy and Polonophilism of the cosmopolitan and antinational Russian intelligentsia.[5] Another influential Russian publicist who insisted on the importance of Russian nationality as the basis of the empire's spiritual unity and of borderland policy was the Slavophile Iurii Samarin. He was N. A. Miliutin's co-worker in Poland during 1863-1864 and the most renowned of Russia's Baltic

26

polemicists of the sixties and seventies. But borderland and western European historians and Russophobe journalists have exaggerated the influence Katkov and Samarin had on official Baltic and Polish policy. On the whole, discussion of sensitive issues was allowed only when the Russian government felt it needed public support. Whenever journalists became bold enough to attack established government policies, Russian officials were quick to take repressive measures against the press.[6]

A borderland policy based on considerations of Russian nationality was, however, no novelty. As we have already seen, there was evidence that such a policy existed at the time of Nicholas I and even earlier. In the western *gubernii*, it is important to note, the government continued during the 1850s and 1860s to follow a more or less Russificatory policy. The Ukrainian and Belorussian majority of the population of this area was, to be sure, considered by the government to be Russian. Although certain concessions were made to the wishes of its most influential minority—the Poles—Russian remained the official language of its schools and local administration. Its courts and municipal and *guberniia* institutions continued to operate as part of the general legal administrative system of the Great Russian *gubernii* of the empire established by Catherine II's Provincial Reform of 1775. In the early 1860s Russian officials saw no reason not to proceed with plans to extend Russian peasant, judicial, and other reforms to the western *gubernii*.[7]

It was in the western *gubernii* that the reassessment of Russia's conciliatory borderland policy of the 1850s began. Disturbed by the rebellious mood of local Poles at the end of the fifties and in the early sixties, Alexander and his advisers outlined a program to curtail the anti-Russian activities of the Poles and to increase Russian influence in this area. Some of the measures considered were reinforcement of police controls, support of the Orthodox Church and parochial schools, the establishment of Russian landowners in the area, and the weakening of the dependence of local Ukrainian and Belorussian peasants on the Polish *szlachta*. After the January insurrection of 1863 these measures were carried out with ruthless severity by Mikhail N. Murav'ev (1796-1866), the Russian governor-general in Vilna. In addition, Murav'ev, the famous "hangman of Vilna," executed, exiled, imprisoned, and confiscated the estates of thousands of Poles who had been involved in the insurrection.[8]

Between 1863 and 1866 the direction of the Congress Kingdom's affairs lay above all in the hands of N. A. Miliutin, who introduced into that unfortunate province a steadily increasing number of Russian officials for the implementation of social, bureaucratic, and agrarian reform. These men were known to Miliutin either personally or they were carefully selected by him from among young officials or recent graduates of Russian universities. On the whole, these appointees had very little or no experience with Polish affairs and approached Polish problems from a distinctly Russian point of view. Their control over Polish affairs could only mean that Polish interests would almost always be subordinated to what Russian officials narrowly interpreted to be the interests of the empire.[9]

Since Russians could only function effectively in their own native tongue, in 1868 Russian became the official languge of all *uezd* and *guberniia* offices in Poland. At the same time, the procedures and organization of these offices were brought into line with those prevailing elsewhere in Russia. In 1871 the *Dziennik praw*, the bulletin of Polish laws, ceased to be published, being replaced by the Russian-language *Sbornik zakonov*. In 1875 the Russian legal reform of 1864 was extended to Poland. Persons who neither spoke nor understood Russian were still permitted to testify in Polish, but court proceedings were exclusively in Russian.[10]

Russian officials, administration, and law meant, in the final analysis, that Russian had to be taught in the schools of Congress Poland, for now the tsar's Polish subjects could neither communicate with the officials who governed them nor understand the laws and administrative rules that so profoundly affected their lives unless they were competent in the official language of the empire. Russian administrators in charge of Polish affairs had little understanding or sympathy for Poles and Polish society. They ignored, or may have been unaware of the sensible advice Miliutin offered in 1864: that it was impractical and futile to force the Russian language of Polish schoolchildren.[11] These officials assumed, for example, that since Polish was similar to Russian there was no good reason why Russian should not be made the language of instruction in Polish secondary schools and at the University of Warsaw. Russian officials who controlled elementary schools also began to introduce Russian as the language of instruction in schools for Polish peasants. By the mid-eighties the use of Russian became obligatory in all Polish elementary schools.[12]

Meanwhile, the Finns, located but a few miles from St. Petersburg, retained their autonomy and even gained new concessions from Russia. Clearly, the events in Poland did not mark an unequivocal victory for the so-called national party and bureaucratic centralizers in St. Petersburg. A policy of Russification had been applied to Congress Poland above all because of the crisis in Polish-Russian relations resulting from the insurrection of 1863-1864. Elsewhere in the western borderlands, especially in Finland, Russia was still inclined to pursue a more traditional policy based on the cooperation of the non-Russian privileged strata of the population with the Russian Emperor and his officials.

In the years immediately following the Crimean War, Finnish spokesmen urged the Russian Emperor to convoke the Finnish Diet (*lantdag*), which had not met since Alexander I addressed it at Porvoo (Borgå) in 1809. Alexander II first reacted cautiously, because granting Finland the right to have a Diet was likely to provide the Poles with an argument to ask for the convocation of the Polish Sejm. However, the same considerations that had persuaded many government officials in the late 1850s and early 1860s to question the wisdom of continuing a policy of bureaucratic centralism in Poland, the Baltic Provinces, and elsewhere in the empire made them view sympathetically the special needs and desires of Finland. There seemed every reason for them to do so. Both the dominant Swedish-speaking conservative bureaucrats who governed Finland and the so-called Fennomans (who also generally spoke Swedish but desired to build a Finnish nation based on the language and culture of the Finnish-speaking majority of Finland's inhabitants) believed that Finland's future depended on good relations with Russia. Some Russian officials feared that if the Finns were not encouraged by timely concessions, they might soon look in the direction of Sweden for their spiritual—and even political—guidance.[13]

The three men who occupied the post of governor-general in Helsinki between 1855 and 1881—that is, Generals F.W.R. von Berg (1794-1874), P. I. Rokasovskii (1800-1869), and N. V. Adlerberg (1819-1892)—had considerable influence at Court and were well disposed toward Finland. Berg did much to stimulate the development of Finland's economy and society by building railways and supporting Fennoman demands for extending the use of the Finnish language. His popularity, however, declined because of differences of opinion and bad relations with the circle of Suecoman (i.e. pro-Swedish language and culture) liberals and intellectuals in Helsinki.[14] Berg also had difficulties with Alexander Armfelt, the Finnish minister state secretary, and other influential Swedo-Finnish administrators in St. Petersburg. Armfelt scored an early victory over Berg in 1857, when he persuaded Alexander II to restore the Committee for Finnish Affairs in St. Petersburg, an advisory body designed to enable the Finnish minister state secretary to take over some of the functions of the governor-general and to assume a more active role in the relations of central government with Finland than had been the case between 1826 and 1857.[15]

It was, however, only in 1861 that Berg's Finnish opponents man-

aged to have him replaced by General Rokasovskii, who had served
previously in Finland between 1848 and 1855 and who had been a
member of the Committee for Finnish Affairs in St. Petersburg since
1857. During his first three years in the post of governor-general he
enjoyed great popularity in Finland as a stalwart and dependable
defender of the Finnish point of view, but by 1864-1865 he, too,
decided that the plans of Finnish political leaders did not coincide
with the interests of the empire. Of particular concern to Rokasovskii
was a Finnish project for a new Form of Government, which he
labeled a "constitution" and considered to be above all an attempt to
limit the power of the governor-general and of the Russian Emperor
in Finland. Alexander II replaced Rokasovskii with General N. V.
Adlerberg in 1866, but the new governor-general joined his predecessor in opposing the Finnish project.[16]

General Adlerberg, the son of Minister of Court V. F. Adlerberg
(1791-1884), always took great pride in the Swedish and Swedo-
Finnish origins of his family. For fifteen years the cosmopolitan resi-
dence of Count Adlerberg and his German-born, Catholic wife was
the center of the social life of high-ranking Swedo-Finnish and
Russian officials and army officers in Helsinki. Among themselves
Russian army officers and administrators in Helsinki, of course, spoke
their own native tongue, but the languages of Adlerberg's social and
official world were French, Swedish, and—especially—German. Of all
the Russian governors-general in Helsinki, Adlerberg perhaps came
closest to being an ideal representative of Russian state power in
Finland—at least from the rather subjective point of view of Swedo-
Finnish political leaders and administrators. Only during his first
several years in Finland did Adlerberg continue his predecessors'
policy of opposing projects that seemed to diminish the influence of
the Russian central government in Helsinki. Later, Finnish political
leaders could almost always count on Adlerberg as a friend and as
someone who would support their projects for reform and who would
present to the emperor all that pertained to Finland in a most favorable light.[17] The Russian nationalist and specialist on Finnish history
M. M. Borodkin said of Adlerberg:

> During fifteen years he remained the only influential representa-
> tive of the authority of the Russian government in Finland and
> was of no benefit whatsoever to the interests of the Russian state.
> On the contrary, during his administration of the country took
> place all those major reforms which led to the manifest aliena-
> tion of Finland from the Empire.[18]

The reforms that alienated Finland from Russia had commenced, however, several years before Adlerberg arrived in Helsinki. In April 1861, before Berg's departure from the Finnish capital, Alexander II summoned a commission representing the four Finnish estates to enact provisional laws until circumstances would permit a regular Diet to meet. Vociferous elements in Helsinki thereupon protested vigorously, interpreting this action to be a violation of Finnish rights. Alexander gave way before these protests, first by reassuring the Finns concerning his intentions and then, at the height of the Polish crisis in June 1863, by consenting to the convocation of the Finnish Diet. The Diet's powers and functions were defined somewhat later, namely, by a statute passed by the Diet in 1867 and confirmed by the emperor in 1869. The Diet met regularly after 1863, and enacted legislation during the next several decades that accentuated the differences setting Finland apart from the rest of the Russian Empire. Thus, the franchise was gradually extended, the principle of freedom of worship affirmed, and education expanded more rapidly than in any other place in Russia outside the Baltic Provinces. In 1865 the Bank of Finland received the right to issue quarter-ruble notes, or marks. In 1878, when Finland went on the gold standard, she achieved complete monetary independence from Russia. That same year the Finns also received, despite the objections of Minister of War D. A. Miliutin (1816-1912), the right to maintain a separate army, which was to be commanded by Finnish officers and serve only in Finland. Miliutin pointed out quite correctly at the time that a "completely separate, independent [Finnish] army within the empire's borders" was incompatible with general military reform and made it difficult to integrate the Finnish armed forces into the Russian army.[19]

An important factor in the Finns' success in achieving their objectives was most assuredly timing. They had obtained from Alexander II the original concession upon which their expanded autonomy depended before Russian political leaders decided definitely to return to the bureaucratic centralism so recently (and ineffectively) practiced by Nicholas I. During the years immediately preceding their uprising, the Poles, too, had briefly benefited from the efforts of certain influential St. Petersburg officials to decentralize administration and to encourage local self-government. However, these officials gradually lost influence in government circles, because between 1861 and 1863 growing tension in Poland coincided with disturbing signs of serious social and political crisis in Russia. Student unrest closed universities and manifestoes urged soldiers, peasants, and the younger generation to prepare for revolution. A Russia-wide revolutionary organization, the first *Zemlia i volia*, was discovered by the police, and a gentry constitutionalist movement aspired to assume a role of political leadership.

P. A. Valuev, minister of the interior, and other high-ranking officials in St. Petersburg reacted to these challenges to their authority by affirming the unity of the Russian state and the need for firm central government control over Russian society. This attitude was already clearly reflected in the zemstvo statutes of 1864 and the censorship law of 1865, and became even more evident after D. V. Karakozov's attempt on the life of Alexander II in 1866.[20]

This tendency in government circles to reaffirm principles of bureaucratic centralism affected Russian policy in Congress Poland and the Baltic Provinces but not in Finland. Until the 1880s the official evaluation of Finnish affairs continued to depend largely on information obtained from either a Finlandophile general-governor in Helsinki or from two able and successive Finnish minister state secretaries in St. Petersburg, Alexander Armfelt and G.E.K. Stjernvall-Walleen (1806-1890), both of whom were linked by close ties of friendship with Alexander II and other influential figures at court and in St. Petersburg high society.[21] Even War Minister Miliutin was seldom critical of Finland. It is to be noted that the newspaper his ministry published, *Russkii invalid*, ran in the early sixties an entire series of friendly and informative articles about Finland.[22] As a whole, the liberal and Slavophile press approved the convocation of the Diet and the internal reforms proposed by Finnish political leaders at the time. Only M. N. Katkov's *Moskovskie vedemosti* sounded the alarm about Finnish "separatism" in a newspaper debate with the *Helsingfors Dagblad* toward the end of 1863. Few Russians, however, seemed to take the danger of Finnish "separatism" very seriously. The government, disliking newspaper polemics on the Finnish question, resorted in the beginning of 1864 to indirect pressures to put an end to the *Dagblad-Moskovskie vedomosti* debate. From this time until the late 1870s the theme of Finnish "separatism" disappeared from the Russian press. Occasionally during these years Katkov did voice disapproval of Finland's status as a "neighboring state," but he did so carefully and in moderate language. Otherwise, the infrequent references to Finland made by liberal and Slavophile journalists and writers were usually in a friendly tone, and Finland's right to internal autonomy was not questioned.[23]

CHAPTER 3

ADMINISTRATIVE RUSSIFICATION IN
THE BALTIC PROVINCES,
1855-1881

ALEXANDER II, in addressing the representatives of the Baltic estates at Riga in June 1867, urged them to become an integral part of the "Russian family" and cooperate with his officials in carrying out reforms he considered to be "necessary and useful."[1] By this time Alexander and his principal advisers on Baltic affairs, who consisted mainly of such members of the so-called German party as Valuev, Shuvalov, and Baltic Governor-General Al'bedinskii, had decided on a policy of gradual administrative Russification in the Baltic Provinces. This policy aimed at bringing these provinces closer to the rest of the empire on the basis of the "fundamental principles of the unity of the state."[2] However, Alexander and his advisers disagreed with certain nationalistic and Slavophile journalists who demanded that Russian land reform be introduced in this area and that the Orthodox Church be used to bring the local Estonians and Latvians into closer contact with the Slavic majority of the empire's population. Alexander and his advisers considered it impractical and unwise to tamper with the existing structure of the agricultural economy and system of land ownership in the Baltic Provinces and felt that Russian interests would be better served by a policy of religious tolerance than one of Orthodox proselytizing. They hoped to bring all elements of the Baltic population closer to Russia through the establishment of Russian as the official language of the local state bureaucracy, the introduction of Russian municipal, judicial, and educational reforms, and the development of railways and economic ties linking this region with the rest of the empire. Organized resistance on the part of the privileged German minority to the government's program of reform was not to be tolerated; the stirring up of national hatreds and animosities through unnecessary newspaper polemics in the Russian press was considered equally undesirable, for such polemics could only, in the opinion of Alexander II's advisers, give birth to misgivings on the part of the Baltic peoples in regard to Russian intentions and impede and delay the work of economic and political integration.[3]

Such integration, of course, had been already delayed by the policies pursued in the Baltic region from 1848 to the end of 1864 by Riga Governors-General Suvorov and Baron Wilhelm Lieven (1800-1880). Suvorov, as Valuev once aptly put it, was "more the permanent representative of the Baltic region in St. Petersburg than a representative of St. Petersburg in that region."[4]

Lieven, who replaced Suvorov in 1861, was a Baltic German. His continued presence in Riga during the Polish insurrection of 1863-1864 indicates that the government still had not definitely decided on giving a new direction to its Baltic policy. In the first part of 1865, however, Lieven was replaced by an ambitious native Russian, Shuvalov, who immediately began what Valuev has referred to as "almost feverish activity"[5] in all major areas of Baltic reform. Shuvalov considered the Riga governor-generalship as merely a stepping stone to a higher post in St. Petersburg and remained only briefly in the Baltic Provinces, but the moderately Russificatory program he instituted in 1865 was continued by his successors. Therefore, it is clear that by the end of 1864, when Shuvalov's replacement of Lieven became known, the government had already decided to proceed with one form or another of Russification in the Baltic region.

It would seem that the government made this decision essentially for two reasons: (1) a renewed wave of social unrest in the Baltic Provinces and (2) uncertainty in the minds of Russian leaders after the Polish revolt concerning the security of the empire's western frontier.

In the early sixties the Baltic religious and social unrest of the forties was still a fresh memory for many Russian officials and publicists. Golovnin, Valuev, and Samarin all had served during the forties as young officials in the Baltic Provinces. In the fifties Golovnin was Konstantin Nikolaevich's personal secretary, and in 1852 he had read to the grand duke detailed official reports he had prepared in the latter part of the forties on the historical, economic, and social reasons for peasant discontent in Livland.[6] Peasant unrest resumed in the Baltic Provinces after the Crimean War, and assumed a particularly alarming character during the so-called Mahtra War of 1858. This began with a bloody encounter between armed soldiers and 700-800 peasants on an estate near Reval (Tallinn), and eventually involved about 20-25 percent of the peasants of Estland *guberniia* in demonstrations and attacks against local German judges, officials, and landowners.[7] It was, in all probability, these events that influenced V. T. Blagoveshchenskii (1801-1864), a Russian-language teacher and educational administrator who had spent his entire professional career in the Baltic Provinces, to publish anonymously, and abroad, the book *Der Ehste und sein Herr* in 1861. In this book he painted a very unflattering picture of the legal, economic, and social situation of the Estonian peasant. The general nature of its contents and conclusions became known to a wide circle of Russian readers at the end of 1862, when the naval officer V. V. Ivanov (1836-?), who was the Reval correspondent of Konstantin Nikolaevich's publications *Morskoi sbornik* and *Kronshtadtskii vestnik*, published his article "The Estonian and his Master" in Ivan Aksakov's newspaper *Den'*.[8]

The theme of the dangers of German unity and aspirations for hegemony in central and eastern Europe, and what it meant for Russia, was developed as early as 1863 in a memorandum submitted by Latvian nationalist leader Krišjānis Valdemārs (1825-1891) to Minister of Education Golovnin.[9] Valdemārs found ample opportunity to sow further seeds of dissension between Russians and Baltic Germans as a contributor to Katkov's *Moskovskie vedomosti* and as one of the editors of the newspaper *Pēterburgas avīzes*, which he and other Latvians managed to publish in St. Petersburg between 1862 and 1865, thanks to the patronage of Konstantin Nikolaevich and other Russian friends. He warned about the threat the progress of Germanization among Latvians and Estonians represented for Russia, and he provided Russian officials with detailed (though perhaps not entirely reliable) statistics concerning the acceleration of Germanization in the Baltic Provinces during the 1860s.[10]

In the first part of 1864 Lutheran General Superintendent Ferdinand Walter gave a rather naive sermon before the Livland Diet on the moral responsibility of the Baltic educated classes to Germanize and improve the lot of the local peasant population. This sermon provided Katkov, Valdemārs' Russian ally, with an occasion to discuss publicly the implications of Germanization and "separatism" in an area bordering on Prussia, "that advanced post of German nationality which, in its expansion, has been involuntarily gravitating toward the east."[11] During the remainder of the sixties Katkov and other Russian journalists continued to comment on the meaning for Russia of repeated Prussian military victories and of evidence of increasing nationalism and Russophobia in both Germany and the Baltic Provinces.[12]

Government officials did not question that it would be folly to allow local German political leaders to reinforce the separate identity of the Baltic Provinces through the Germanization of the Estonians and Latvians. Nor did they ignore any more than did Russian journalists what Prussian victories and the unification of Germany implied for the security of Russia's western frontier; but until the 1890s it seemed to them to be in the best interest of Russia to base her European diplomacy on friendship with Germany. At the same time, they were reasonably confident that improvement of Russian-language facilities in the Baltic Provinces would attract the socially mobile, educated minority of Estonians and Latvians to the Russian language and culture. During the 1860s Russian officials do not seem to have had plans to Russify the entire Baltic population. They rejected the advice of extremists like Samarin who recommended a counter-program of Russification as a means of halting Germanization; and they saw no reason why ordinary Estonian and Latvian peasants could not keep their own native languages and popular culture.[13]

The resistance of the Baltic Germans, however, to even moderately Russificatory measures irritated officials in St. Petersburg. They also considered Baltic German attempts to defend and even extend the provinces' privileges and autonomy to be contrary to the general interests of the empire. Consequently, they welcomed at least some affirmation in the press of Russian national interests and critical commentary about what was happening in the Baltic Provinces. As the director of the Ministry of the Interior's Chief Administration on the Press pointed out in 1865, such discussion was useful because it affirmed the "necessity of state unity" and the "inviolability of the state and the rights of Russian nationality." Baltic polemics, however, assumed a too virulent tone for the tastes of Russian officials after the publication in the late sixties of the first issues of Samarin's *Okrainy Rossii*, Woldemar Bock's *Livländische Beiträge*, and Carl Schirren's *Livländische Antwort an Herrn Juri Samarin*. Additionally, they now found themselves accused of not having defended Russian national interests in the Baltic Provinces. In 1870-1871 polemics on the "Baltic question" (or *ostzeiskii vopros*) were halted for a period of about a decade.[14]

High-ranking Russian officials in Riga and St. Petersburg were especially offended by the insinuation that they had failed to defend Russian national interests in the Baltic Provinces. In their view these interests had never before been so energetically and effectively defended as during the period 1865-1870.[15] As has already been pointed out, a new Baltic policy began with the arrival of Shuvalov in Riga early in 1865. It aimed at the political, administrative, and economic integration of the Baltic region with the rest of the empire and touched upon almost all major areas of Baltic reform: peasant-landowner relations, peasant self-government, the Baltic state peasants, the use of Russian in the bureaucracy, Russian language instruction in schools, the position of the Orthodox and Lutheran Churches, and the bringing of Baltic municipal and judicial institutions into a greater degree of conformity with those of the other *gubernii* of European Russia.[16] Shuvalov, however, only remained in Riga until the spring of 1866, and his immediate successor, Eduard Baranoff (1811-1884), until the fall of the same year. The principal architect of the new policy to be implemented in the Baltic Provinces was P. P. Al'bedinskii, who served as governor-general between 1866 and 1870.

The most sensitive area of reform was the Baltic peasant question. Since the 1840s the provincial Diets and the Baltic Committee in St. Petersburg had been working on legislation that would gradually eliminate the corvée and enable a minority of the Estonian and Latvian peasants to become a class of independent proprietors. By the end of the fifties work on a somewhat more liberal peasant reform for the Russian interior of the empire posed an obvious threat to the existing economic and social status quo in the Baltic countryside. At that time the ministers of the interior, justice, and state domains criticized the final draft of new agrarian legislation prepared by the Livland Diet and the Baltic Committee, arguing that it left the peasants economically dependent on the landowners and made it unnecessarily difficult for peasants to purchase land. When this draft was discussed in the State Council in January 1860, its president, A. F. Orlov (1786-1860), questioned the wisdom of giving final approval to special legislation for the Livland peasants that differed in important respects from the peasant statutes the government was about to promulgate for the rest of the empire. As a result, the proposed Livland legislation was referred to the combined Legal and Economic Departments of the State Council for further study. The representatives and friends of the Livland *Ritterschaft* in St. Petersburg strongly advised, of course, against further delay, and by November 1860 they managed to persuade Alexander II to approve the Livland project. This was only three months before the Russian peasants were emancipated on February 19, 1861. It was a narrow escape for the Baltic nobility.[17]

After 1861, therefore, new Baltic peasant legislation continued to be considered by the provincial Diets and the Baltic Committee, separately from the peasant affairs of the rest of the empire. In 1863, it is true, Prince P. P. Gagarin (1789-1872), the chairman of the State Council's Department of Laws, frightened the Baltic nobles by proposing referral of the question of passports for Estonian and Latvian peasants (many of whom wished to emigrate out of the Baltic Provinces in search of land elsewhere in the empire) to the Chief Committee for the Organization of the Agricultural Estate (*Sostoianie*). Until 1882 this committee dealt with carrying out the statutes of February 19, 1861, in the Great Russian and western *gubernii* of the empire. But friends and representatives of the *Ritterschaften* in St. Petersburg successfully opposed referral of the Baltic passport question to the Chief Committee and on July 9, 1863, obtained Alexander II's approval of new passport regulations that took into account the interests of the Baltic nobles by retaining certain restrictions on the right of Estonian and Latvian peasants to leave the Baltic Provinces.[18]

The Baltic nobles also felt threatened by numerous peasant petitions asking for the extension of the principles of Russian emancipation to the Baltic Provinces. These petitions, which were often drawn up with the assistance of Estonian and Latvian nationalist and intellectual leaders, clearly reflected the peasants' impatience with the persistence of the corvée system, their desire to obtain land on the same terms that Russian peasants did in the interior of the empire, and to have rents and redemption payments regulated according to norms prescribed by the state. The most famous of these petitions was the one presented to Alexander II in November 1864 by a delegation representing twenty-four Estonian-speaking settlements in northern Livland. This petition and the many grievances of the Baltic peasants against their German landowners received wide publicity and general support in the Russian press, especially in such influential newspapers as Katkov's *Moskovskie vedomosti*, Aksakov's *Den'*, and D. A. Miliutin's *Russkii invalid*. Alexander II, however, sided with Valuev, Baltic Governor-General Wilhelm Lieven, and representatives of the Baltic *Ritterschaften* in exiling to the interior of Russia a number of Estonian and Latvian intellectual leaders who had helped draft or translate peasant petitions. Minister of War Miliutin was obliged to discontinue the publication of articles in the *Russkii invalid* about Baltic agrarian problems and the plight of landless Estonian and Latvian peasants.[19] Furthermore, on several occasions in late 1864 and early 1865 the emperor personally assured the marshal of the Livland nobility, Prince Paul Lieven (1821-1881), of his continuing goodwill toward the local nobles and his approval of the existing form of landownership in the Baltic countryside. When Shuvalov arrived in Riga at the beginning of 1865 he carried with him the promise of Alexander II that there would be no obligatory, regulated sale of land to the Baltic peasants.[20] In this way the Russian government unmistakably dissociated itself from the Baltic agrarian policy advocated by the Russian liberal and nationalist press. The Livland *Bauernverordnung* of November 13, 1860, not the statutes of February 19, 1861, remained until the February Revolution of 1917 the basic document upon which the agricultural order of the Baltic countryside rested.

For Shuvalov and his immediate successors in the office of governor-general peasant reform was, therefore, confined to such matters as abolition of the corvée and corporal punishment, the removal of peasant self-government from the control of the local nobility, and the improvement of conditions among state and Orthodox peasants. The government, however, as both Alexander II and Shuvalov made clear in early 1865, expected the Baltic nobles to cooperate in carrying out this rather modest program of peasant reform.[21]

The ending of the corvée had been favored by more progressive-minded Baltic German landowners for a number of years, and in Kurland 80 percent of the peasant farmsteads had been transferred to money payments by 1860.[22] In Livland during the 1850s most landowners thought their interests could be better served by delaying the introduction of money rents, but in the early sixties the government, disturbed by widespread social and agrarian unrest in Livland, put pressure on the local nobles to abandon their delaying tactics. Thus, in March 1865 the Livland Diet finally agreed to terminate all corvée contracts by no later than St. George's Day, or April 23, 1868, when all obligatory labor services were scheduled to end in Kurland. An order of the Baltic governor-general of March 25, 1868, also abolished the corvée in Estland *guberniia* as of that same date.[23]

The need to moderate the rigors of corporal punishment was understood by both the government and local Baltic German society. In 1865 for example, Shuvalov experienced little difficulty in prevailing upon the Livland Diet to bring the norms regulating corporal punishment into a greater degree of conformity with those that had been in effect in the interior of the empire since 1861.[24] During 1865 and 1866 corporal punishment in the Baltic provinces was further limited through action of the local Diets, the Baltic Committee, and the central government. Certain St. Petersburg officials were still, however, not satisfied with what had been accomplished, as is indicated by Alexander II's confirmation on November 20, 1866, of the opinion of the Department of Laws of the State Council that the court and police institutions of the Baltic Provinces were to conform as closely as possible with those of the rest of the empire.[25] But it was easier to affirm the principle of administrative uniformity in St. Petersburg than to apply official policy locally in the Baltic Provinces. Russian police and court reform came to these three provinces only at the end of the 1880s. Instances of excessively severe corporal punishment in the Baltic Provinces were observed by Senator N. A. Manasein as late as 1882-1883, when he conducted his famous senatorial inspection in Kurland and Livland.[26]

On the lowest level police and court institutions formed a part of peasant self-government. At the time no effort was made to apply the Russian zemstvo statute of January 1, 1864, to the Baltic Provinces, for, as Valuev pointed out in 1870, the German nobles were then in a position to control Baltic zemstvos organized along the lines of those

39

in the interior of the empire.[27] The influence the local German landowners still had over the affairs of the peasant communities and township courts had been one of the major complaints made by peasants in their petitions of the early sixties.[28] Both the government and the Baltic Germans recognized that new legislation had to be drafted to ensure that the peasants' institutions of self-government would be freed from the tutelage of the large landowners. The government, however, did not undertake to work out this new legislation but, instead, entrusted the task to the Baltic Diets. The *Ritterschaften* acted with dispatch in early 1865 and, within a few months, formulated detailed proposals that met with the general approval of Shuvalov in Riga and the Baltic Committee in St. Petersburg, and became law on February 19, 1866, the fifth anniversary of the emancipation of the Russian serfs.[29]

The new law forbade direct interference on the part of the local noble landowners and agents of the *Ritterschaften* in peasant self-government and in the work of the township's police and court institutions. A new function taken on by the peasant community in 1866 was that of tax collector, the members of each community being made collectively responsible for taxes owed to the state. Owners or leaseholders of peasant land (*Bauernland*) had the right to participate directly in the meetings of the township assembly; landless agricultural laborers could do so only indirectly. The chairman and two members of the township committee, which supervised the local police, courts, and administration, were elected by the township assembly from among its own regular members. On the whole, the new law was an important step in the direction of making the Baltic peasantry an independent force in local society. But as long as district and provincial court and police institutions remained organs of the *Ritterschaften*, it was extremely difficult for township officials to avoid some outside interference in the discharge of their duties. In the 1880s Manasein still easily found for his senatorial report many illustrations of the continued dependence of peasant officials on the local Baltic German nobility.[30]

Only in regard to the Baltic state peasants did the government rely primarily on its own officials, not the Diets of the Kurland, Livland, and Estland *Ritterschaften*, to draft new peasant reform legislation. The direct involvement of Russian officials in the lives of Estonian and Latvian state peasants, who made up almost 15 percent of the total male population of the Baltic Provinces, began with the establishment in 1841 of local organs of P. N. Kiselev's Ministry of State Domains. From the very beginning certain efforts were made to regulate the relations between state peasants and members of the

Baltic German nobility who leased state lands, but German nobles continued to staff the ministry's local organs and interfere in the local affairs of peasants living on lands owned by the Russian state in the Baltic Provinces. At the very end of the 1850s and during the 1860s, however, the Baltic German nobility began to take alarm as the Ministry of State Domains developed plans for the redemption of land by state peasants on terms similar to those offered, or under study for the central and western provinces of the empire.[31]

In 1868 Minister of State Domains A. A. Zelenoi and his assistant P. A. Shul'ts (1831-1905), a young official who sympathized with the position of Iurii Samarin and other anti-Baltic-German publicists, defined their principal task as that of determining the extent to which the general regulations for state peasants elsewhere in the empire could be applied to the Baltic Provinces.[32] An *ukaz* of November 24, 1866, had established such regulations for the thirty-six interior provinces of European Russia, and at the end of March of the following year these regulations were extended in modified form to the western *gubernii*. The latter form seemed particularly relevant to the Baltic Provinces because of the absence of the repartitional peasant commune and the similarly structured economies and societies in these two areas. All peasants in the western *gubernii* had received preferential treatment for political reasons after the Polish insurrection of 1863-1864, and state peasants throughout the empire were emancipated under more advantageous conditions and with larger land allotments than was the case for the serfs who had formerly belonged to private landowners.[33]

The reform proposal worked out by Zelenoi and Shul'ts placed prospective owners of land among the Baltic state peasants in a position considerably more favorable than that of their counterparts on the private estates of the Baltic landowners. Governor-General Al'bedinskii, Minister of Finance M. Kh. Reutern (a Baltic German by birth), and Minister of the Interior A. E. Timashev criticized this proposal, pointing out that it prescribed procedures contrary to Baltic private law and allowed state peasants to redeem land at prices appreciably lower than the local market value of land. This, they warned, would certainly give rise to harmful rumors, endless disputes over the inheriting and mortgaging of land, and a substantial loss of revenue for the state treasury.[34] Such criticism obliged Zelenoi to reconsider certain features of his proposal, but its final version, which became law on March 10, 1869, following discussion in the Baltic Committee, still discriminated in favor of state-peasant purchasers of land. Zelenoi defended his proposal by emphasizing the importance of promoting the well-being of a class of prosperous peasant farmers as the basis

Edward C. Thaden

of conservative social order.[35] Unquestionably, the legislation he sponsored did increase the number of Estonian and Latvian state-peasant proprietors. State peasants were, however, but a minority among Baltic peasants, and even among the state peasants the agricultural laborers with little or no land continued to outnumber by far the owners and lessees of full-sized peasant allotments.

Any basic change in the structure of Baltic society obviously depended as much on court and legal reform as it did on peasant and agrarian legislation. Baltic German liberals, Russian publicists, Latvian and Estonian nationalists, and conservatively and liberally inclined Russian officials all agreed that the antiquated laws and courts of the three Baltic Provinces needed reform. Baltic Germans, of course, wanted a reform that would be based on modern European principles of law and justice without destroying the autonomy and historical continuity of traditional Baltic legal order. Estonian and Latvian leaders, on the other hand, emphasized the urgency of eliminating what they considered the evils of Baltic justice, its class-based nature, its lack of adequate controls over the actions and decisions of judges, and its failure to safeguard the rights of non-German peasants and workers. Liberal and Slavophile Russian publicists and officials felt that these shortcomings could best be corrected either through introduction of the Russian judicial statutes of November 20, 1864, or, at least, through a basic and far-reaching reform made in the spirit of these statutes.

Conservative-minded Russian officials responsible for Baltic policy, especially Valuev and Shuvalov, did not deny the need to introduce Russian legal norms and institutions into the Baltic area, but they wanted to proceed gradually and to take into account its existing laws and local particularities.[36] This policy did not come under concerted attack in the liberal and Slavophile press during the 1860s, but in 1871 Katkov called attention to the fact that the government had not announced concrete plans to introduce the judicial statutes of 1864 into the Baltic Provinces, as it already had done with regard to Congress Poland and the western *gubernii*.[37] Iurii Samarin, to be sure, continued to criticize this and other aspects of official Baltic policy from abroad.

Baltic German legal experts only began to work seriously on judicial reform after Alexander II announced on September 29, 1862, that the principles of Russian legal reform would be extended to "all regions governed under special institutions." For the leaders of Baltic German society the acceptance of these principles as the point of departure for Baltic legal and court reform appeared to be a dangerous precedent that could easily be used as a justification for the introduction of other Russian reforms. The principles in question were part of the Basic

Principles for the Reform of the Courts, which had been prepared during 1862 by young legal experts attached to the State Chancellery and working under the direction of V. P. Butkov (182?-1881).[38] Although Alexander II approved the Basic Principles, the manner in which they were implemented in the Baltic Provinces depended very much on the advice he received from senior officials of conservative inclinations in St. Petersburg and from his governors-general in Riga. In 1865, for example, Shuvalov and Valuev helped the *Ritterschaften* to overcome initial opposition in Russian official circles to the retention of the elective principle (*Wahlrecht*) in the selection of the Baltic judiciary.[39] Elsewhere in the empire judges were appointed.

This concession was part of the general compromise on problems of Baltic reform reached in government circles in the mid-1860s. But conciliatory gestures toward the *Ritterschaften* did not mean that the government had abandoned its intention to introduce in the Baltic Provinces, sooner or later, the judicial statutes of 1864. Indeed, it reaffirmed this intention at the end of that same year. Russian legal experts then realized, however, that the great differences separating Russian from Baltic civil law, peasant legislation, and judicial procedure made the task of introducing the Russian judicial reform into the three Baltic Provinces an extraordinarily complicated one. Only a week before Alexander II promulgated the judicial statutes of November 20, 1864, he approved the third volume on civil law of the *Provincial Law of the Baltic Provinces*, which had been worked out over a period of years under the direction of F. G. von Bunge (1802-1897) in the Second Section of His Imperial Majesty's Own Chancellery.[40]

Several years later it was decided not to proceed directly with the introduction of the Russian 1864 judicial reform in the Baltic Provinces. In February 1867 Alexander II approved Governor-General Al'bedinskii's proposal of a partial and gradual reform of the Baltic court and legal system. Generally speaking, the government was to follow the same policy it did in the western *gubernii*, where the separate introduction of the institution of the justice of the peace marked the initial stage of judicial reform. But in the Baltic Provinces, in contrast to the western *gubernii*, the local estates were allowed some say in the matter. For this purpose a special commission attached to the Baltic governor-general and consisting of representatives of the *Ritterschaften* and of the major Baltic towns, Reval, Riga, and Dorpat, was created.[41]

In the fall of 1867 Alexander II appointed the Baltic German Konstantin von der Pahlen (1830-1912) to the post of minister of justice. Whether or not Pahlen's close personal associations with the Baltic *Ritterschaften* and property interests in Kurland influenced his actions as a Russian minister is difficult to determine, for very complicated legal and political considerations undeniably played a major role in delaying the introduction of Russian legal institutions into both the western and Baltic Provinces. Reform moved ahead particularly slowly in the Baltic Provinces, for it was only in 1875 that Pahlen's ministry completed the first stage of its work on special legislation concerning the introduction of the institution of justice of the peace. By the time the final legislation was approved on May 28, 1880, justices of the peace had already functioned in the western *gubernii* for a number of years; and that same year the government completed the work of judicial reform in these provinces by opening higher judicial chambers and regional (*okrug*) courts provided for in the judicial statutes of November 20, 1864.[42] In the Baltic Provinces, however, discussion of judicial reform was still limited to the institution of justice of the peace. And even in the project under discussion, unlike the practice in the western *gubernii*, the use of the Russian language was not required, meaning in effect that German would be the language used by Baltic justices of the peace. Otherwise, the rules and regulations governing the actions of these justices deviated very little from the pertinent paragraphs in the statutes of November 20, 1864. Where they did, this was largely because of differences between Russian and Baltic civil and property law. Such differences proved to be particularly troublesome with regard to local legislation applying to the Baltic peasants. Indeed, it was partly because of problems caused by this legislation that the 1880 law on the Baltic justices of the peace was never implemented.[43]

The third aspect of Baltic policy about which the government and its Slavophile and liberal critics disagreed concerned the interests of the Orthodox Church. These critics, the Slavophile Iurii Samarin in particular, wanted the government to act firmly and resolutely in advancing the cause of Orthodoxy and enforcing laws favoring the interests of Orthodoxy as opposed to those of Lutheranism. Baltic governors-general, however, then felt that the religious policy advocated by Samarin would serve mainly to alienate the Lutheran majority of the local German, Estonian, and Latvian population.[44] This view of the Baltic religious situation was reinforced by the report Count V. A. Bobrinskii (1824-1898) presented to Alexander II on April 18, 1864. Bobrinskii, who had just completed an on-the-spot official study of religious conditions in Livland, confirmed in many respects what German pastors and landowners had said for some time about the superficiality of the religious convictions of a large proportion of the Orthodox Estonians and Latvians. He also commented on what he and others considered the questionable methods used during the 1840s to convert these Baltic peasants to Orthodoxy.[45] At the same time, bad publicity abroad concerning the alleged persecution of Lutherans in the Baltic Provinces did not accord very well with Russia's European diplomacy, which then aimed at pursuing Russia's Balkan interests and revising the Black Sea clauses of the Treaty of Paris on the basis of cooperation with Prussia in Europe. Russia, of course, rejected Prussia's right to interfere in Russian internal affairs, but it is noteworthy that Alexander II's secret order of 1865 releasing parents in mixed Orthodox-Lutheran marriages from the obligation to baptize their children in the Orthodox Church was made soon after the one serious attempt Bismarck ever made to speak out in support of the religious rights of the Baltic Lutherans.[46]

Two of the most effective and persistent defenders of a conciliatory Baltic religious policy were Governor-General Al'bedinskii in Riga and Third Section Chief Shuvalov in St. Petersburg. In 1874 it seems to have been above all Shuvalov who managed to persuade Alexander II to yield to organized and world-wide pressure of the Evangelical Alliance to drop all pending court cases against Baltic Lutheran pastors accused of having received into their churches Estonian and Latvian Orthodox peasants. During the sixties and seventies the conciliatory Baltic religious policy resulting from Alexander II's decisions of 1865 and 1874 allowed from 30,000 to 40,000 Estonians and Latvians, or up to one-fourth of the entire Orthodox peasant population, to revert to Lutheranism.[47]

The government no less than its critics, however, wanted to strengthen the Orthodox Church and to support its activities in the Baltic Provinces. Serious consideration of appropriate measures to improve the position of Orthodoxy in this region began with a report Riga Archbishop Platon (1803-1891) made after a visitation of Orthodox parishes in Livland in the late summer of 1864. In 1866 S. N. Shafranov (1820-1888), the director of the Baltic Chamber of State Domains, proposed to use available state lands in the Baltic Provinces as allotments for landless Orthodox peasants and as a source of financial support for Orthodox schools. This proposal was supported by Alexander II and a majority of the members of the Council of Ministers.[48] In 1868 the initiative of Riga Archbishop Veniamin (1822-1874) and Governor-General Al'bedinskii resulted in the government's decision to appropriate 10,000 rubles annually to assist Baltic Orthodox communities to develop and improve their schools. Al'bedinskii, though he opposed Orthodox proselytizing in the Baltic Provinces and therefore had arranged to have Veniamin's predecessor, Platon, transferred to the Don region in 1867, was determined to demonstrate his own commitment to promoting the well-being of Orthodoxy in the provinces he administered. Thus, in October 1868 he supported a comprehensive program for the reorganization of the Orthodox Church's elementary school system in the Baltic Provinces, the establishment of Orthodox Estonian and Latvian teachers' seminaries, and the shortening of military service by two years for those who could pass an examination in the Russian language after having studied it in Baltic Orthodox Church schools. These proposed measures were approved by Alexander II in 1870. That same year the not inconsiderable sum of 800,000 rubles was made available for the construction and repair of Orthodox churches and school buildings in the Baltic Provinces.[49]

For such critics of the government's Baltic religious policy as Archbishops Platon and Veniamin and Iurii Samarin, these measures were woefully inadequate. Samarin, of course, could do openly in the polemical works he published abroad what Platon and Veniamin, two churchmen in the official service of the state, could not do inside Russia: that is, argue the necessity of uniting the Estonian and Latvian peasants with the rest of Russia through all-out support of the Orthodox Church in the Baltic Provinces. The government, Samarin pointed out, had no right to enjoin the Orthodox clergy to abandon proselytism, for the very nature of religion obliged every creed to seek new followers to join it in a community of faith.[50]

As the official representatives of Orthodoxy in the Baltic Provinces, Platon and Veniamin did, however, influence both the government and public opinion with regard to the needs of the Orthodox Church in this area. It was largely their description of the meager financial and material resources of the local Orthodox Church and of the poverty and economic dependence of Orthodox Estonians on Baltic German landowners that persuaded the government to take measures to halt the decline Baltic Orthodoxy had experienced since the 1850s. They also succeeded in inducing private Russian well-wishers inside and outside the Baltic Provinces to contribute generously to its support. By 1870 nine Orthodox brotherhoods worked in the Baltic Provinces, and supporting religious societies were organized in Moscow, St. Petersburg, and Saratov. Iurii Samarin was among the more generous donors to Orthodox brotherhoods. In 1867, for example, he gave 10,000 rubles to the Riga Peter-Paul Orthodox Brotherhood for the exclusive purpose of supporting schools and scholarships for the education of Latvian Orthodox children. Among the brotherhoods organized outside the Baltic Provinces, the St. Petersburg Christ the Savior Baltic Orthodox Brotherhood was especially important. As early as 1873, two years after its foundation, it spent almost 8,000 rubles on elementary education and the building and equipping of Orthodox churches.[51] Such activities supplemented those of the government and contributed to improve the position of Orthodoxy within the Riga

Eparchy. By the 1880s the Orthodox Church once again began to attract converts from among the Lutheran majority of the population of the three Baltic Provinces.

In the three remaining areas of Baltic reform—the introduction of Russian as the language of the state bureaucracy, Russian instruction in schools, and town reform—liberal and Slavophile journalists found less reason to criticize official policy, especially on the first item. As has already been pointed out, Russian had been proclaimed the official language of state officials in the Baltic Provinces as early as 1850. To be sure, former Governor-General Suvorov had neglected to enforce the law of 1850, and, as Al'bedinskii once noted in a report, in 1865 Governor-General Shuvalov almost accidentally ran across this law and called it to the attention of his superiors in St. Petersburg on several occasions before he left Riga to become chief of the Corps of Gendarmes. After this almost everyone in official circles faulted Suvorov for having failed to carry out the language law of 1850, which Alexander II reaffirmed on June 1, 1867.[52]

During the next three years Al'bedinskii studied the original intent and scope of the law of 1850 on the basis of the best expert opinion available. He then proceeded to introduce it in as orderly and systematic a manner as possible. German-speaking officials were allowed several years of grace to study Russian and to adjust to the new situation. The police, court, and other special institutions of the nobility and the religious and self-government organs and institutions of the local population were not affected by the law other than in their official communications with the Russian authorities. The use of Russian, however, was prescribed for all branches of the administration subordinated to the Ministry of the Interior and for *guberniia* financial and treasury offices, the Chambers of State Domains, the Riga Orthodox Ecclesiastical Consistory, the military, excise offices, customs offices, the Riga Office of the State Bank, and all assay and post offices. The continued use of German in the organs of local self-government was considered to be a personal decision of the emperor, not the legal right of the *Ritterschaften* sanctioned by history and eternally guaranteed. A number of German protests and petitions were firmly rejected between 1867 and 1870, and Shuvalov and Valuev worked closely with Al'bedinskii to thwart well-placed Baltic Germans in their efforts to influence Alexander II to abandon enforcement of the law of 1850.[53]

For the successful implementation of this law the instruction of Russian in Baltic schools obviously had to be expanded and improved. A. V. Golovnin, who was minister of education between 1861 and 1866, knew quite well the special conditions prevailing in the Baltic

Provinces because of his study of Baltic peasant affairs as a young official during the 1840s and because of his personal contacts with Latvian nationalist Krišjānis Valdemārs. Although he was mainly concerned with educational reform in the interior of the empire, from 1862 Polish unrest and, then, insurrection obliged him to take special measures to ensure the predominance of Russian education, language, and culture in the western *gubernii*.[54] With regard to the Baltic Provinces, in 1863 his ministry published a study it had commissioned S. N. Shafranov (then a Russian-language teacher in the Riga gymnasium) to do on the previous and largely unsuccessful efforts of the Russian government to make a mastery of Russian a sine qua non for graduation from Dorpat University and Baltic secondary schools.[55] On a number of occasions during the next several years the Committee of Ministers studied general problems of Baltic education as presented by Archbishop Platon, Baltic governors-general, a special committee of 1864-1865, the Russian press, and representatives of the Ministry of Education. The most comprehensive proposals resulted from the special Baltic missions of 1865 and 1867 undertaken by Ministry of Education officials M. M. Mogilianskii and A. N. Tikhomandritskii, who recommended a significant increase in the supervision and hours of Russian instruction in Baltic secondary schools as well as the introduction of Russian instruction in Estonian and Latvian Lutheran schools. Modilianskii, in particular, emphasized the need for a considerable expenditure of money and effort to teach Russian in village schools in order to prevent the Germanization of the Latvians and Estonians and to "attach to the Russian family more than a million and a half of the native population."[56]

On the whole, government officials accepted the premise that the danger of Germanization was a real one and that it could be best combated through the introduction of more and better Russian-language instruction in Baltic schools. More extreme proposals for the rapid Russification of the entire Baltic school system were, however, rejected. Here the compromise position of Shuvalov, Al'bedinskii, Valuev, and Alexander II prevailed: the existing German-language secondary and higher educational system was to be retained; but new Russian-language gymnasia were to be established in Riga and Reval; the teaching of Russian was to be introduced gradually into the instructional programs of Latvian and Estonian elementary schools and improved and expanded in the German secondary and higher schools.[57] Minister of Education D. A. Tolstoi, the Russifier of the Kingdom of Poland's schools, opposed this program, as he wanted to concentrate available resources on the Russification of the existing secondary and higher schools rather than on the establishment of separate Russian gymnasia. He also wished to subordinate all elementary schools in the Baltic Provinces to the direct control of the Ministry of Education. Others pointed out that the quality of education in the German schools would be impaired by too radical changes in their instructional programs, and that the Russian state still lacked the resources to fund Baltic elementary schools if the German nobility withdrew all financial support, which they certainly would do if these schools were subordinated directly to the Ministry of Education. Such subordination did not take place during the 1870s, but beginning in 1874-1875 new statutes regulated the governance and teaching programs of these schools; and opportunities for Latvians and Estonians to attend schools in which Russian was taught were significantly augmented during the same decade.[58]

Tolstoi and others continued, however, to complain throughout the seventies and into the early eighties about the unsatisfactory progress of the Russian language in Baltic schools. In secondary and higher schools Tolstoi did manage to have Russian established as the obligatory language of all their official correspondence, but his efforts to increase the amount of Russian instruction did not appreciably improve the Russian-language skills of their students. Indeed, his measures tended to stimulate resistance to so-called Russification and to intensify anti-Russian feelings among both students and teachers.[59] In the elementary schools the situation was somewhat better, for part of the financial support for them came from the peasants, who often sought work or land in the interior of the empire and who could shorten their term of service in the army if they could demonstrate knowledge of Russian. Even German landowners sometimes felt that prudence dictated cooperation in introducing Russian instruction into Lutheran schools—if for no other reason than not to provide enemies in Russia with ammunition to attack the existing status quo in the Baltic Provinces. The rural Lutheran school statute for Kurland and Estland of April 25, 1875, provided that Russian instruction was to be compulsory in parish schools and introduced as far as available resources would permit over a period of five years. In Livland, according to the official statistics, by 1882 Russian was taught in 790 of 1,085 Lutheran parish and peasant community schools.[60]

But the teachers of Russian in these schools were often badly prepared. Even the minority of them who had come from the regular teachers' seminaries at Irmlau in Kurland, Riga, Dorpat, and Walk (Est.: Valga; Lat.: Valka) in Livland, and Paschlep (Passlepa) and Kuda (Kuuda) in Estland had received too few hours of Russian instruction to master the language and to converse in it freely. The standards of Russian instruction in the parish schools, where such instruction was obligatory after 1874-1875 and where most Russian teachers for the rural schools received their training, were even lower.[61] And, once employed, these teachers could only be supervised with difficulty by the Ministry of Education, for the Baltic elementary school legislation of 1874-1875—much to the regret of Tolstoi—regulated their activities but did not place them directly under the control of the Ministry of Education.

The inhabitants of the three Baltic Provinces could, however, learn Russian well in Russian-language schools organized since the late 1860s. These schools were particularly well developed in Latvian-speaking southern Livland and Kurland, where there were thirteen of them by 1882. As early as 1870 a considerable number of Latvians received a Russian education in eight Russian-language elementary and secondary schools located in Riga, Mitau (Jelgava), Jakobstadt (Jēkabpils), and Tukum (Tukums). In Riga Latvians then made up 32 percent of the boys in the Alexander Gymnasium, 93 percent of the girls in the Lomonosov Gymnasium, and 45 percent of the pupils in the Russian elementary school, while in Tukum, Kurland, 48 percent of the Orthodox school's students consisted of Latvians. By the beginning of the eighties the number of Russian-language schools had increased to a total of thirteen among 137 town and *uezd* schools in Kurland and Livland. In addition, the children of some 50,000 Latvian Orthodox peasants received some instruction in the Russian language from Orthodox Church parish and auxiliary schools that had been organized since the 1840s.[62]

During the 1870s considerable improvement took place in the administration and quality of instruction in Orthodox elementary schools for both Latvians and Estonians. Russian-language and religious instruction, for example, benefited from the establishment of Russian-language Orthodox teachers' seminaries in Riga. In 1873 the administration and supervision of all Baltic Orthodox Church schools were brought directly under the control of the Ministry of Education. Until then the quality of Orthodox schools had compared unfavorably with neighboring Lutheran ones, but henceforward they assumed an increasingly important role in the education of Baltic peasants, particularly the 100,000 Estonian-speaking ones in northern Livland. On the eve of the Russification of Baltic education in the late 1880s, 18 percent of Estonian elementary schools in northern Livland and Estland were Orthodox. The teaching of Russian in these schools also attracted many Lutherans, who made up 13.4 percent of their pupils in 1881.[63]

The last Russian reform introduced into the Baltic Provinces during the reign of Alexander II was the Municipal Statute of 1870. Russian municipal legislation had not applied to the Baltic Provinces since 1796, when Paul I restored to the nobles and burghers of the western borderlands the rights and privileges they had lost under Catherine II. Between 1846 and 1848, however, a Russian investigatory commission working in Riga seriously questioned the justice and utility of the rights and privileges of Baltic townsmen. Attached to this commission was Iurii Samarin, who then prepared a history of Riga for the Ministry of the Interior and, unofficially, wrote the first important polemical work directed against the Baltic Germans. In 1849 Samarin was briefly incarcerated for having circulated the manuscript of his "Letters from Riga" among friends in Moscow.[64] During the 1850s projects for both Baltic and Russian municipal reform had been shelved because of Nicholas I's distrust of reform after the events of 1848, and at the end of the fifties the emancipation of the serfs took priority over all other reforms. In 1862, however, work resumed on municipal reform, beginning with the collection of materials concerning the history and organization of town government in Russia and western Europe and the formation of town committees to advise the Ministry of the Interior about local wishes and problems.

Baltic town committees also participated in this preliminary work. Two successive Baltic governors-general, P. A. Shuvalov and P. P. Al'bedinskii, criticized these committees for not trying to limit the power of German patricians in town government and for not including in their proposals provisions that would assure the equality of the Russian language with German in the conduct of town affairs. In 1867 Al'bedinskii argued for the introduction of a "general town statute" into the Baltic Provinces. He pointed out Riga's commercial and economic importance, and the role railways would have in bringing the Baltic region closer to Russia and in linking its ports with the provinces of the interior. It was, he emphasized, "advantageous for the interests of neither the government nor the local citizens" to preserve "medieval," German forms of municipal government that were burdensome and stifled the initiative of the majority of the inhabitants of Baltic towns.[65]

The Russian Municipal Statute was approved on June 16, 1870. A measure which greatly encouraged self-government and stimulated economic and social development in Russian towns, it specifically instructed Minister of the Interior Timashev to prepare proposals for the application of Russian municipal legislation to the western and Baltic Provinces. He was to take "local conditions" into account and to consult with the respective governors-general. A detailed proposal for the introduction of the statute into the western provinces was ready as early as December 1873 and given final approval on April

29, 1875.[66] The preparation of rules governing the application of the statute to the Baltic Provinces took somewhat longer.

The advice, petitions, and other information received from Baltic Governor-General P. R. Bagration (1818-1876), the three Baltic governors, and local Estonian, German, Latvian, and Russian leaders and residents of the Baltic Provinces were referred to a special commission chaired by Timashev. On it sat representatives of the Ministries of the Interior, Justice, and Finance, the Second Section of His Imperial Majesty's Own Chancellery, the State Chancellery, the Russian higher administration of the Baltic Provinces, and the Baltic towns of Riga, Reval, and Mitau. The representatives of the central government on the commission included Second Section Head S. N. Urusov (1816-1883) and Director of the Ministry of the Interior's Economic Department A. D. Shumakher (1820-1898), both of whom had taken leading parts in the preparation of the Municipal Statute of 1870.[67]

Urusov, Shumakher, and other experts on municipal affairs from the Second Section and the Ministry of the Interior insisted on the principles of the 1870 law and saw to it that only minor concessions were made to placate local Baltic interest groups. But local interests and conditions were taken into consideration in the rules of March 26, 1877, which applied the Russian municipal law to the Baltic Provinces. These rules did not abolish the town magistrates altogether, allowing them to continue to perform their previous judicial functions until general court reform would be introduced; neither did they abolish the guilds, which were left with a number of social and welfare functions; they permitted the town literati—certain educated Germans who did not always meet the property or city tax qualifications required to vote—to participate in town elections, although only under the rubric of "temporary regulations"; and they specified that German, Russian, or, where appropriate, the "local dialects" could be used in conducting town business until the preparation of "special regulations."[68]

The isolation of Baltic town life from that of the rest of the empire had clearly come to an end. For the first time since the days of Catherine II they again had basically the same laws and internal organization as the towns of the Russian interior.[69] On the whole, the change was a beneficial one: it weakened the stranglehold a handful of privileged Germans had had on Baltic towns, made it easier for local Russians, Estonians, and Latvians to compete with Germans for the control of town government, and marked the point of departure for the rapid growth of Riga and other Baltic cities at the end of the nineteenth and beginning of the twentieth century. These beneficial results will again be noted in other sections of this study.

The firm, matter-of-fact manner in which Russian officials proceeded with Baltic municipal reform in the seventies contrasted strikingly with their hesitant policy in the sixties with regard to peasant, judicial, and religious affairs. No longer did they consider it necessary to seek the advice about new reforms from such formally constituted Baltic bodies as the institutions of the *Ritterschaften* and the Baltic Committee. Local views and conditions were taken into account, but the concrete details of Baltic town legislation were worked out by a government commission dominated by Russian experts on municipal affairs. The administration of the towns, like other aspects of Baltic administration, was to be Russified. Thus, there was no longer any place for such symbolic expressions of Baltic unity and particularism as the Baltic Committee and the office of Baltic Governor-General. The Baltic Committee met for the last time on April 11, 1875, and the Baltic *general-gubernatorstvo* was abolished on January 25, 1876.[70] The completion of this process of administrative Russification was only a matter of time. That it would not be too long was suggested by the *ukaz* of May 20, 1880, which concerned the institution of the justice of the peace in the Baltic Provinces and announced publicly for the first time that the government also intended to impose upon them the entire Judicial Statute of 1864. "In political terms," Katkov wrote in his editorial of April 3, 1880, "this information was the most outstanding feature of the Law of May 20."[71]

CHAPTER 4

THE ABORTIVE EXPERIMENT:
CULTURAL RUSSIFICATION IN
THE BALTIC PROVINCES,
1881-1914

DURING THE LATTER PART of the 1880s it seemed for a time that the Russian government had finally decided to go beyond mere administrative Russification and to act energetically and resolutely in carrying out a policy of cultural Russification in the Baltic Provinces. Pro-German governors-general no longer resided in Riga, and in St. Petersburg Alexander II, Valuev, Shuvalov, Reutern, and von der Pahlen had been replaced by a new emperor and a new generation of officials who had read approvingly Iurii Samarin's *Okrainy Rossii* and the many critical newspaper editorials on the "Baltic question" written by Katkov, Aksakov, and other Russian journalists during the 1860s. Emperor Alexander III, Minister of the Interior D. A. Tolstoi, Chief Procurator of the Holy Synod K. P. Pobedonostsev, Minister of Justice N. A. Manasein (1835-1895), and Minister of Education I. D. Delianov (1818-1897) then set the tone of Russian internal policy. They all were men who believed that Russia had to be ruled with a firm hand and that her borderlands and national minorities had to be made a more integral part of the general political and cultural life of Russia. These notions were inculcated in the mind of Alexander III above all as a result of the influence of Pobedonostsev, his former tutor. Pobedonostsev seems to have passed on to his pupil certain quasi-Slavophile ideas about the close relationship between Russian nationality, political authority, and the Orthodox Church and to have introduced him to the writings of Samarin on the Baltic question.[1] In this regard Alexander III was a good pupil, for he was the first Russian ruler who deliberately withheld confirmation of the privileges and special rights Peter the Great had granted to the Baltic Germans some 170 years before.

In practice, however, cultural Russification in the Baltic Provinces tended to conflict with other policies and objectives of the Russian government. All three Russian tsars who ruled between 1855 and

54

1917 accepted the necessity of overcoming the military, economic, and organizational weaknesses of Russia that were so graphically illustrated by military or diplomatic setbacks experienced in connection with the Crimean War of 1853-1855, the Russo-Turkish War of 1877-1878, and the Russo-Japanese War of 1904-1905. Unable to ignore the importance of developing the Russian economy and transportation system as a basis for military power and a successful foreign policy, Russian rulers became increasingly dependent on the advice of experts in the Ministry of Finance, the Second Section, the Senate, and the State Council, who could help to make use of Russia's human and economic resources in a somewhat more orderly and rational manner than had been the case in the past. Such experts were inclined to be critical of borderland and other policies of their colleagues in the Ministry of the Interior and the Holy Synod. Frequently, in the Committee of Ministers and State Council, they succeeded in watering down or substantially modifying projects of counterreform or cultural Russification introduced by Tolstoi and Pobedonostsev, in this way giving rise to what Heide W. Whelan has referred to as the "politics of equilibrium."[2]

A particularly good formulation of the attitude of economic and legal experts toward cultural Russification is contained in the memorandum ex-Minister of Finance N. Kh. Bunge (1823-1895), then chairman of the Committee of Ministers, prepared for Alexander III and Nicholas II during the first part of the 1890s. Bunge was quite aware that the nineteenth century was an age of nationalism, and he defended Russia's right to take measures to assure a dominant position for Russian state institutions and the Russian language throughout the empire.[3] He warned, however, that forcible administrative and police measures to discourage the use of local languages or to eradicate the historically developed forms of life among non-Russians could only be counterproductive. Instead, Bunge wanted a "cautious and well-considered policy" that would introduce reforms gradually, avoid giving the impression that the government acted under "the pressure of the Russian press" and in accord with the "pretensions of Russian chauvinism," win the "respect and sympathy of the local population," and convince non-Russians of the advantages to themselves of learning the Russian language and establishing closer relations with the rest of the empire.[4]

In the long run, time was against the advocates of cultural nationalism in the Baltic Provinces. By the end of the nineteenth century it was clear that their Orthodox proselytizing and Russified schools had had very little impact on Estonians and Latvians. Economic progress, on the other hand, had a major impact. The high level of literacy in the Baltic Provinces, the skills and practical knowledge of their bourgeoisie, workers, and farmers (especially the German landowners and independent Estonian and Latvian proprietors), the building of railways, Russian financial policy, and various administrative measures aimed at uniting this area with the rest of the empire, all contributed to stimulating the rapid growth of agriculture and industry. Markets were readily found in both Russia and abroad. By 1914, 40 percent of the Latvian and more than 20 percent of the Estonian population of the Baltic Provinces was urban (compared to 15 percent for European Russia as a whole), and Riga had become the fourth city of the Russian Empire (after St. Petersburg, Moscow, and Warsaw) with a population of 520,000. The ports of Kurland, Livland, and Estland handled 30 percent of Russian foreign trade and in 1913 the volume of such trade for Riga exceeded that of St. Petersburg by 77 million rubles.[5] Thus, on the eve of World War I the Baltic Provinces formed an integral part of Russia, and the interests and problems of their inhabitants were often very difficult to separate from those of Russians living in Baltic cities or elsewhere in the empire. The principal common denominator uniting Latvians and Estonians with Russians was not the Orthodox Church or Russian culture but economics.

In the short run of the 1880s, however, Minister of the Interior Tolstoi and Holy Synod Procurator Pobedonostsev had an opportunity to experiment with cultural Russification. The operation of tsarist central government was never very well coordinated, and the influence of individual ministers was generally limited to activities and concerns falling within the jurisdiction of their respective ministries. As influential as the Russian minister of finance became toward the end of the nineteenth century, he could not challenge directly the authority the minister of the interior and the procurator of the synod had in regard to the activities of policemen and Orthodox priests in the Baltic Provinces. He was all the less likely to do so in view of the personal interest Alexander III had in ending Baltic German particularism and in winning over the Latvians and Estonians to Orthodoxy and Russian nationality.[6]

The point of departure for the measures of Russification introduced under Alexander III was the senatorial inspection N. A. Manasein conducted in Kurland and Estland between May 5, 1882, and August 31, 1883. This senatorial inspection was organized in response to widespread peasant unrest, Estonian and Latvian petitions for reform, and Baltic German complaints about "social democratic" agitation. Senator Manasein was apparently selected to head the investigation because of his reputation for being not only a Russian nationalist but also an energetic and highly competent government official.[7] The emotional fervor with which he defended the Orthodox Church and criticized the University of Dorpat and the Baltic German landowners and *Ritterschaften* in the report he submitted to Alexander III in 1884 indicates that he was a natural ally of the advocates of cultural Russification. The most convincing sections of the report, however, concern the structure of Baltic courts, administration, and agriculture, where Manasein based his recommendations on a detailed and careful review of the available evidence. On these subjects his advice was, generally speaking, sound and prudent, as one would expect of a graduate of the School of Jurisprudence who had served for many years in courts and in offices of the Senate and the Ministry of Justice and who had a wide range of competence and experience with judicial, administrative, and peasant affairs.[8] Not surprisingly, therefore, the principal achievement of Manasein's report was to provide St. Petersburg bureaucrats with the "incontrovertible facts" about the "true state of things" in the Baltic Provinces.[9] In his capacity as minister of justice after 1885, Manasein, himself, worked out the final details of extending the Judicial Statute of 1864 to the Baltic Provinces, which was one of the most important measures of administrative Russification in that region.

The detailed instructions given to Senator Manasein early in 1882, the responses he made to the questions contained in these instructions, and the manner in which the government acted on his recommendations shed considerable light on the theory and practice of Russification under Alexander III. By that time, as has already been shown, the government had decided on a fairly ambitious program of administrative Russification. The outlines of this program were clearly reflected in the instructions Manasein received from the ministers of justice and of the interior. Cultural Russification, on the other hand, was suggested by the questions asked by the procurator of the synod. Lists of additional questions for Manasein to investigate came from the ministers of finance, state domains, communications, and the navy.[10]

All senior officials seem to have then agreed that every effort had to be made to assure more general use of the Russian language in the Baltic Provinces. In 1882 the Ministry of the Interior specifically instructed Manasein to clarify to what extent the language law of 1850 and Al'bedinskii's measures of the late sixties had actually been carried out.[11] Manasein was not satisfied with the progress that had been made. He recommended that the exclusive use of Russian in government offices and in the relations of the population of the Baltic Provinces with officials should be made obligatory by no later than 1885. He made an exception, however, for peasant township institutions, and allowed for the use of translators, or translations by natives of the Baltic Provinces whose inadequate knowledge of Russian did not permit them to communicate otherwise with government officials. Generally speaking, he felt that because many local people did know Russian there was no longer any reason to hesitate about making it the language of all official business transacted in the Baltic Provinces above the level of the peasant township. All that was necessary to overcome local resistance to the general official use of Russian, he concluded, was "the firm will of the government."[12]

Two years later Manasein's recommendation for the obligatory use of Russian by Baltic officialdom received imperial sanction in an *ukaz* of September 14, 1885. This was the first Russificatory act of Alexander III resulting directly from Manasein's senatorial inspection. In 1889 the language *ukaz* of 1885 was also applied to the official proceedings of Baltic municipal governments.[13]

Baltic education represented a second area in which Russian officials considered reform to be urgently needed. Manasein received no instructions in 1882 from the Ministry of Education, although later he did consult with Dorpat Educational Region Curator M. N. Kapustin (1828-1899) about problems concerning secondary and higher education. The Ministry of the Interior, on the other hand, which exercised indirect and rather ineffective control over the Lutheran rural elementary schools in the Baltic Provinces, did give him instructions. This ministry was most concerned about how little influence it actually had on elementary education in this region, where the teacher seminaries and elementary schools for the overwhelming majority of the population were controlled by the Baltic German nobility and the Lutheran Church. Manasein was, therefore, asked to determine to what extent an imperial order of April 25, 1875, concerning the introduction of Russian-language instruction in the teachers' seminaries and rural schools of Kurland had been carried out. Manasein's instructions also raised the question of whether or not the Lutheran elementary schools in the Baltic Provinces should be placed under the administration and direct control of the Ministry of Education.[14]

In his report Manasein regretted that education had failed to unite the Baltic Provinces with the rest of the empire by instilling in their inhabitants respect and understanding for the Russian language, history, and literature.[15] He, therefore, recommended that Russian be made the language of instruction in teachers' seminaries and a subject in the instructional program of all elementary schools; that it replace German as the language of instruction at Dorpat University; and that by 1885 it be made the language of instruction in all public and private secondary schools. To assure more effective control by the government over Baltic education, he advised placing parish and other elementary schools and teachers' seminaries directly under the control of the Ministry of Education. Dorpat University and secondary schools had been administrated by the Ministry of Education since the beginning of the nineteenth century, but the location of the administration of Baltic education in Dorpat, the center of Baltic particularism, was, Manasein felt, unfortunate. Thus, he proposed moving the administrative headquarters of Baltic education back to Riga, where it had been located briefly between 1870 and 1876 and where the influence of Russian officialdom was much more firmly established.[16]

Manasein also commented on conditions at Dorpat University. No doubt influenced by the newspaper polemics of the sixties, he castigated the students and professors at Dorpat for being a corporate brotherhood that accepted the teachings of Carl Schirren and lived in a private world of Baltic privileges and special rights, cut off from the rest of Russia and culturally and intellectually linked with Germany.[17] This university, therefore, had to undergo fundamental changes: Russian had to be made its language of instruction; the curriculum of the Juridical Faculty brought into conformity with the requirements of the Russian legal system established in 1864; the Dorpat Theological Faculty closed and replaced by an Evangelical Ecclesiastical Academy located in St. Petersburg; and stricter control by the curator of the educational region established over the activities of the student corporations.[18]

On the whole, Manasein's proposals for educational reform were accepted by the government. By the early 1890s Russian had been established as the language of instruction in Baltic schools, including Dorpat University; the headquarters for the Baltic educational region had been moved to Riga; elementary schools and teachers' seminaries had been placed under the direction of the Ministry of Education; the curriculum of the Dorpat law faculty had been brought into conformity with that of law faculties of Russian universities; and Dorpat professors and students were subjected to stricter control by agents of the central government. In 1893 both the town and the university at Dorpat were renamed Iur'ev, but the university's Theological Faculty was not abolished and, as an exception, retained German as its language of instruction.[19]

Of particular interest to Manasein personally was Baltic court reform. The instructions he received from Minister of Justice D. N. Nabokov (1826-1904) were of a detailed, technical nature, asking him to concentrate on questions concerning how Baltic law and civil and criminal procedures could be brought into a greater degree of conformity with those of the rest of the empire. These instructions permitted Manasein considerable latitude and did not rule out the possibility of retaining some features of traditional Baltic law. The question of the language in which proceedings and investigations were to be conducted—Russian, German, Latvian, or Estonian—in courts on various levels was left open,[20] indicating that in 1882 the Ministry of Justice still had not decided definitely that Russian had to be the language of all courts.

Manasein found only negative features in the existing system of Baltic justice. Courts were either directly controlled or excessively influenced by the nobility; they were unduly slow in processing cases, especially those involving the interests of the peasants; they were particularly severe and even arbitrary in dispensing justice to the lower classes; and their proceedings could be followed only with difficulty by the majority of the population because they were conducted in German mixed with incomprehensible Latin legal terms and citations.[21]

Alexander II, Manasein pointed out, had approved as early as 1862 the extension to the empire's borderlands of the principles of the judicial reform then under consideration. Since 1864 the new court institutions had been introduced not only in the central *gubernii* of European Russia but also in the Kingdom of Poland, the Caucasus, and even areas annexed to Russia following the Russo-Turkish War of 1877-1878. Manasein regretted that application of the 1864 judicial reform to the Baltic Provinces had been limited to the approval in 1880 of legislation for the introduction of but one aspect of this reform, namely the institution of justice of the peace. He noted, however, that the State Council had then recommended to the minister of justice the taking of further measures to extend the entire 1864 legal system to the Baltic Provinces.[22]

The carrying out of the recommendation made by the State Council in 1880 was the simple remedy Manasein prescribed to eliminate the inadequacies and inequities of the existing Baltic legal system. He argued at considerable length against limiting Baltic judicial reform to introduction of the institution of justice of the peace, for these justices were elected officials who would certainly represent the interests of the Baltic nobility and, therefore, lacked the objectivity required to serve the interests of all classes of the local population. Only full application of the judicial reform of 1864, Manasein believed, would guarantee the elimination of antiquated and "medieval" German legal procedures and the proper administration of justice in the Baltic Provinces independent of narrow class interests.[23]

In 1884, when Manasein submitted his report to Alexander III, few high-ranking officials in St. Petersburg disputed the necessity of basic legal reform in the Baltic Provinces. Manasein's specific contribution at the time was to provide detailed information about the inadequacies of Baltic justice and convincing arguments for the legal experts in the Ministry of Justice who wished to make Baltic laws and legal practices conform as closely as possible with those of the rest of the empire. After Manasein became minister of justice in 1885 he applied himself energetically to the task of completing several decades of work on Baltic court reform. By the latter part of 1888 he had ready for the State Council a final project for the replacement of the traditional Baltic judicial system with Russian court procedures, judicial chambers, district courts, justices of the peace, and peasant township courts. The project was confirmed by Alexander III on July 9, 1889.[24]

Baltic courts were subordinated to the St. Petersburg Court Chamber. Thus, Manasein rejected the advice of the Baltic *Ritterschaften* to establish a special court chamber in Riga. Such a high court of appeals, he argued, would not act independently of local influences and, therefore, would not contribute to "political objectives of paramount state interest"—that is, to ending the isolation of this region and uniting it with the empire's "inner *gubernii*."[25]

Certain deviations from the 1864 reform were, however, allowed in the Baltic Provinces. Because Russian was the language of court proceedings above the township level, the jury system was not introduced into the Baltic region as there still were too few Russian-speaking Baltic candidates for jury service. Justices of the peace appeared in the Baltic region at a time when they disappeared elsewhere in the empire. Realizing that the local Germans were in a position to control elective judicial posts, the government introduced *appointed* justices of the peace into the Baltic Provinces, not elected ones as had been the practice in Russia between 1864 and 1889. In the general area of civil law, the government hesitated to tamper with local legal traditions. Thus, Volume III of the Baltic Provincial Code remained in effect, for the cautious and thorough bureaucrats of the Ministry of Justice feared that supplanting it with Russian civil law would have a disruptive effect on local commerce, property relations, and agricultural production. They had been equally cautious, it should be pointed out, in dealing with the civil law of Congress Poland during the 1860s and 1870s. In all, the reform had been worked out with great care, and improved the administration of justice in the Baltic Provinces, although it did cause much inconvenience and added expense for local inhabitants because of its requirement of Russian as the procedural language of Baltic courts.[26]

Baltic police institutions represented another area in which Russian officials considered reform to be urgently needed. In March of 1882 the Ministry of the Interior asked Manasein to try to answer two important questions: had Baltic society and officials impeded putting into effect the recommendation of the State Council, which Alexander II had confirmed on November 20, 1866, that police institutions in the Baltic Provinces should conform as closely as possible to those of the rest of the empire; and to what extent did the existing organization of the district (*uezd*) and town police correspond to the "needs of the time and the interests of the local population"?[27] Manasein answered the first question affirmatively and the second negatively. The class organization of Baltic society and institutions, he pointed out, had definitely impeded the development in that region of a police system designed to protect the rights of all its inhabitants on the basis of the principle of equality before the law, as was supposedly the case elsewhere in the empire. The existing police system in the Baltic Provinces did not meet the "needs of the time and the interests of the local population" because it was controlled by a small group of Germans and functioned independently of the control and supervision of representatives of the central government. Such a situation, Manasein emphasized, easily led to arbitrariness and abuse of police and judicial authority. It was obviously contrary to the interests of the government and of the overwhelming majority of the local population.[28]

Russian police institutions, however, were not organized as satisfactorily as the empire's judicial system. For this reason Livland Governor Mikhail A. Zinov'ev (1838-1895) suggested in his 1885 report modification, not abolition, of the existing Baltic police system as the best way to assure the interests of the government in regard to the administration of police affairs in the Baltic Provinces. In the spring of 1886, when Minister of the Interior D. A. Tolstoi first developed in detail his ideas on Baltic police reform, State Secretary Aleksandr A. Polovtsov (1832-1910), the chief administrative officer of the State Council, tried to persuade Alexander III that the existing defects of Russian police institutions had first to be corrected before they were introduced into the Baltic Provinces.[29] Although this advice was not accepted, Russian police institutions were substantially modified upon being extended to the three Baltic *gubernii* in 1888. Thus, the Baltic German manor police (*Gutspolizei*) was retained, for neither Alexander III nor the State Council could see any other way to maintain order on the greater part of the agricultural land in these *gubernii* still controlled by German landowners. But the authority of the manor police did not extend beyond the confines of each landowner's estate, and Russian police institutions replaced the traditional ones of the

Baltic *Ritterschaften*. Although a number of Russian police officials were imported into the Baltic Provinces, a large part of the staff of the district (*uezd*) police continued to consist of Baltic German noblemen. They worked, however, under the direct control and supervision of the Ministry of the Interior, not the Baltic *Ritterschaften*. Many Estonians and Latvians occupied the lower ranks of the district police. The peasant township police was not affected by the police reform of 1888.[30]

More than 40 percent of Manasein's report was devoted to an analysis of peasant conditions in Kurland and Livland.[31] Around 1880 Estonian and Latvian unrest seriously threatened the peace of the Baltic countryside. Local Baltic Germans attributed peasant restiveness to revolutionary agitation. Russian officials, on the other hand, tended to find the root of the evil in shortcomings in the existing social and economic organization of rural life in the Baltic Provinces. Thus, the ministers of the interior, justice, and state domains instructed Manasein to study carefully the measures the government might take to improve the economic, legal, and social position of the peasantry in Baltic society, and Alexander III personally asked him to pay special attention to the problem of landless Estonian and Latvian peasants and to investigate the possibility of settling them on state lands.[32]

Manasein was an experienced and enlightened Russian *chinovnik*. He had served as an arbitrator in carrying out the emancipation statutes in Kaluga *guberniia* and then participated, as a legal specialist, in the complicated work of adapting the court reform of 1864 to local conditions in various parts of the Russian Empire.[33] In his report of 1884 he made skillful use of information obtained not only from official sources but also from Latvian and Estonian leaders and 20,000 peasant petitions. With this information he convincingly documented the chronic social and economic injustices and tensions that plagued the Baltic countryside. He recommended a review in the near future of existing laws concerning the Baltic peasantry, pointing out that violent social upheaval could occur unless the government took action to further the peasants' welfare and assure them some of the advantages he believed to have been obtained by the Russian peasants in 1861.[34]

Despite his obvious sympathy for what he considered an exploited Estonian and Latvian peasantry, Manasein refrained from proposing a detailed program of radical Baltic agrarian reform. Indeed, his instructions scarcely authorized him to do so. The government, after all, was in no position to consider the restructuring of Baltic agriculture and society as long as it continued to recognize the validity of the special Baltic agricultural laws of the 1850s and 1860s, which provided the legal basis for the separation of the agrarian affairs of the Baltic Provinces from those of the rest of the empire.

The government, however, did make at least a token effort to help Baltic peasants during the following decades. After 1889 two commissars for peasant affairs (*kommisary po krest'ianskim delam*) worked in each Baltic *uezd* to watch over peasant affairs and township government. In some respects the office of the commissar for peasant affairs resembled that of the land captain (*zemskii nachal'nik*) in the interior of the empire. Both offices were created in July of 1889. But the commissar, as Toivo Raun points out in Part Four of this study, did not function as justice of the peace. It was the concentration of judicial and administrative functions in the hands of a single official from the nobility to which Manasein had particularly objected when the law project to create the office of land captain was discussed in government circles.[35] This feature of the land-captain law of July 12, 1889, the first important counterreform introduced during the reign of Alexander III, was avoided by establishing the office of commissar for peasant affairs in the Baltic Provinces, and was never introduced, apparently because St. Petersburg officials feared that it would only serve to increase the influence of the Baltic nobility over the police, administrative, and court affairs of the local peasants.

The commissars for peasant affairs generally held service rank and were appointed by the government and supervised (after 1893) by *guberniia* boards of peasant affairs chaired by the respective Baltic governors. Inasmuch as they lacked sufficient independent authority and were largely local noblemen and Russian or German officials with *chin*, it was hardly to be expected that these commissars would effect fundamental changes in the arrangement of things in the Baltic countryside. But, as Raun shows, many of them took their responsibilities seriously and were of considerable benefit to the peasants. In addition, the government continued to make state-owned lands available to Estonians and Latvians. Unfortunately, the amount of such lands offered for purchase or lease was limited and did not contribute significantly to solving the problem of the Baltic agricultural proletariat.[36]

Meanwhile, Baltic farms, whether owned by German nobles or Estonian or Latvian peasant proprietors, compared favorably with those of the Russian interior with respect to productivity and the efficiency of their operation. Since the 1870s Russian officials had worried increasingly about what seemed to be the deteriorating economic condition of the Russian peasantry but found it difficult to agree among themselves about what should be done. In regard to the Baltic

Provinces, they decided not to disrupt the existing patterns of agricultural production. The Baltic agrarian legislation of the 1850s and 1860s remained in effect until 1917.[37]

Manasein also proposed the radical reorganization of provincial government in the Baltic Provinces: that is, two new *gubernii* divided by the language frontier and centered in Riga and Reval. His instructions from the Ministry of the Interior did not authorize him to make such a proposal. As Raun and Plakans mention in their respective sections, it was apparently Estonian and Latvian petitions presented to the Russian government in 1881 and 1882 that suggested to Manasein the possibility of creating two new *gubernii* to replace Estland, Livland, and Kurland. As did the Estonian and Latvian leaders, Manasein saw in this new territorial division a means of ending the predominance in the Baltic area of the local Germans.[38] And, he pointed out in his report, the proposed territorial reorganization would simplify the administration of the Baltic Provinces by reducing the number of *gubernii* and by making it possible to conduct administrative and court affairs on the lower, local level in a single language: Latvian in Riga *guberniia* and Estonian in Reval *guberniia*. Excluded from his proposed Riga *guberniia* was Illuxt (Ilūkste) *uezd*. This was the most eastern part of Kurland, a narrow wedge-shaped area that projected eastward between Vitebsk and Kovno *gubernii*. A substantial proportion (but not a majority) of this *uezd*'s population consisted of Old-Believer Great Russians, Orthodox Belorussians, and Catholic Belorussians and Poles. Russian, Manasein averred, was generally understood in the area, yet the local landowners conducted public affairs in German and did their utmost to use the school system as an instrument of Germanization. It was to eliminate this danger once and for all that he recommended annexing Illuxt *uezd* to Vitebsk *guberniia*.[39]

In addition, the proposed Riga and Reval *gubernii* provided a convenient framework within which Baltic zemstvos could be organized. The memorandum representatives of the Estonian intelligentsia presented to Alexander III on June 19, 1881, asked for the extension of zemstvo institutions to the Baltic Provinces. Alexander III approved in principle the introduction of zemstvos into the Baltic Provinces on September 14, 1881. In March 1882 the Ministry of the Interior instructed Manasein to investigate to what extent the zemstvo statutes of January 1, 1864, needed modification in their application to the "local peculiarities" of the Baltic Provinces.[40] In his report Manasein chose to ignore this question, preferring to emphasize the role they could play in ending the predominance of the Baltic Germans in local affairs. For, within Latvian and Estonian zemstvos organized on an

65

all-class basis in two new *gubernii*, Baltic German landowners would obviously be a minority. Once these zemstvos began to function effectively, the *Ritterschaft* institutions of the Baltic Germans would by necessity lose their control over local society, and the activities of these institutions would thenceforth be largely limited to the corporate affairs of the nobility.[41]

The government did not follow Manasein's advice to deprive the German nobility of its dominant position in Baltic society by introducing zemstvos and creating two new *gubernii*. By the 1890s an era of counterreform had begun. In St. Petersburg political circles zemstvos, liberal bureaucrats, and Estonian and Latvian nationalists lost ground, while conservative bureaucrats and nobles, even if they were Baltic Germans, gained in favor. Estonians and Latvians then came under suspicion because they clearly displayed more interest in developing their own respective national movements than in establishing more intimate contacts with Russian society and culture.[42]

Russian officials soon came to have second thoughts about introducing zemstvo institutions into the Baltic Provinces. Implementation of the project was first postponed in 1886, when Minister of the Interior Tolstoi decided that Russia's zemstvo institutions were deficient and in need of basic reform. Then, in December 1887, a special conference chaired by Assistant Minister of the Interior Viacheslav K. Plehve (1846-1904) concluded, as P. A. Valuev had done once before in 1870, that there was no way to prevent the German nobles from dominating zemstvos in the Baltic Provinces. Plehve's conference recommended, however, thorough reform of the institutions of local self-government in the Baltic countryside to make certain that they would have "a governmental character with the participation of representatives of the nobility," but this advice was never acted upon.[43] The Russian zemstvo reform of 1890, which further strengthened the position of the nobles in the zemstvos of the interior of the empire, made it all the more unlikely that these institutions would be introduced into the Baltic Provinces.

Meanwhile, Tolstoi and Plehve frightened the Baltic nobles by raising the specter of the possible abolition of the separate institutions and special rights of the *Ritterschaften*. This threat, however, was not carried out, perhaps because Tolstoi died in 1889 and perhaps because Livland Governor Zinov'ev, who in some respects was an energetic Russifier, saw much that was worth preserving in the Baltic nobility's institutions of self-government. About this time he began to cooperate with the *Ritterschaften* in opposing those in the bureaucracy who favored the introduction of Russian institutions of local government into the Baltic Provinces.[44] Other reasons for dropping the project of applying the Russian Charter to the Nobility to the Baltic Provinces are discussed in Part Two.

Manasein's report to Alexander III also contained a lengthy discussion of fifty-seven pages on promoting the interests of the Orthodox Church in the Baltic Provinces. Although this discussion is not included in the version of Manasein's report published at Riga in 1949, Soviet historian E. Laul's brief commentary concerning it clearly establishes that Manasein wanted the government to act firmly and resolutely in this matter.[45] Holy Synod Procurator Pobedonostsev hardly needed to be convinced of the merits of this argument, for this same point had been argued previously on a number of occasions in detailed reports made since the 1860s by Riga bishops, Orthodox priests, and Synod agents. The most important Synod agent working in the Baltic Provinces during the 1880s was Efim M. Kryzhanovskii (1831-1888), a graduate of the Kiev Academy who, before he was attached to the Holy Synod in 1883, had taken an active part as an educational administrator in the Russification of education in Congress Poland. Pobedonostsev sent Kryzhanovskii to the Baltic Provinces twice during 1883-1884 to study on-the-spot legislation and problems affecting Orthodox Latvians and Estonians. Kryzhanovskii's recommendations for a more vigorous defense of Orthodox interests in the Baltic region were contained in a *Memorandum on Mixed Marriages* and an essay entitled "The Baltic Question and Orthodoxy," both of which he completed in the latter part of 1884.[46]

Beginning in July 1885 the empire's laws concerning mixed marriages, which had not been enforced in the Baltic Provinces since 1865, once again obliged local parents of mixed Orthodox-Lutheran backgrounds to bring up their children as Orthodox Christians. In November of that same year Minister of Justice Manasein and Pobedonostsev argued before representatives of the departments of the State Council that the recent successes of the Orthodox Church in the Baltic Provinces, as well as the obstructionist tactics of German landowners to prevent the Orthodox Church from obtaining land needed for churches, schools, and cemeteries, made it necessary to give the local governors and the Ministry of the Interior the power to expropriate such land. The major objection in the State Council to these proposed expropriations was that they would violate the property rights of the German landowners. On February 10, 1886, however, rules were approved to permit the expropriation of plots of land up to five desiatins. Three months later a statute of the Committee of Ministers forbade the further use of local taxes collected from Orthodox Latvians and Estonians as contributions to the support of Lutheran pastors and churches.[47]

The question of punishing Lutheran pastors who violated the religious laws of the Russian Empire was raised by Zinov'ev in his annual report for 1885. In 1887 Tolstoi and Pobedonostsev defended new proposed rules before the State Council designed to enable the minister of the interior to remove from their posts pastors against whom court proceedings had been initiated. Although a majority of the State Council did not approve these rules, they were confirmed by Alexander III on March 22, 1888. By the early 1890s almost all Lutheran pastors in Livland were involved in one form or another of criminal proceedings. A number of them were even tried under provisions of the Russian criminal code that permitted banishment to Siberia, their "crime" having been the administration of confirmation or other Lutheran rites to those who were officially registered as Orthodox Christians. Zinov'ev, in his report of 1890, approved of severe penalties for uncooperative pastors, arguing that sternness on the part of the government would help to restore religious peace in the Baltic Provinces by discouraging the pastors from further interference in the affairs of Estonians and Latvians who wished to leave the Orthodox Church.[48]

In other words, during the late 1880s and the early 1890s the Russian government gave every indication of a determination to follow Iurii Samarin's advice: to act energetically in promoting the cause of Orthodoxy in the Baltic Provinces. Such action then seemed appropriate and well timed, for the conversion of more than 15,000 Latvians and Estonians between 1883 and 1887 suggested that a mass conversion movement comparable to that of the 1840s was about to begin.[49] For the first time thousands of Baltic peasants were attracted to Orthodoxy not only in Livland but also in Kurland and Estland. The greatest number of new conversions took place in Estland, where Governor Sergei V. Shakhovskoi (1852-1895) optimistically viewed them as a means of separating the Estonians from the local German nobility and Lutheran Church and uniting them with the "great, Orthodox Russian family."[50] It was also in Estland that the Russian state supported with particular generosity the building of new Orthodox churches and the activities of Orthodox brotherhoods and priests in meeting the religious needs of the new converts,[51] in this way satisfying another requirement of the church policy Samarin had recommended for the Baltic Provinces a generation earlier.

By the mid-1890s, however, the Russian government had weakened in its resolve. During 1894-1895 it dropped the pending court cases against the Baltic Lutheran pastors, and after that legislation concerning mixed marriages and the reconverts in this region was no longer vigorously enforced. This marked an important turning point in the government's Baltic religious policy, although religious tolerance was not proclaimed for the Baltic Provinces—and the rest of the empire— until 1905.[52]

Disapproval in the Senate, State Council, and Committee of Ministers of Pobedonostsev's interpretation of Russian state interest in the Baltic Provinces was at least one factor in this change of policy. Committee of Ministers Chairman Bunge, for one, considered the threat Lutheran propaganda posed to Orthodoxy to be exaggerated, and criticized the excessive attention paid to the prosecution of pastors.[53] In the State Council State Secretary Polovtsov, among others, did what he could to oppose projects that increased the arbitrary power of Russian agents in the Baltic Provinces to expropriate land for Orthodox churches and schools and to deal with other problems caused by uncooperative landowners, pastors, and reconverts.[54] In the Senate Anatolii F. Koni (1844-1927), the procurator (*ober-prokuror*) of the criminal appeals department stubbornly refused in the early 1890s to cooperate with higher political authorities in what he considered improper application of the Russian criminal code to the cases of Baltic pastors. The banishment of pastors to Siberia, Koni commented later, was not only unlawful but also imprudent and even "unpatriotic," for this made religious martyrs of the pastors, won for them the sympathy of the local population, and served to alienate the Baltic region from the rest of Russia.[55]

Although Alexander III was personally interested in winning the Estonians and Latvians for Orthodoxy, he does not seem to have favored active proselytism in the Baltic Provinces. Thus, when Kurland Governor Konstantin I. Pashchenko recommended in 1886 the taking of measures to prepare the Latvians for union with Orthodoxy, the Russian Emperor commented as follows:

> All this is like some kind of Orthodox propaganda; I do not allow that this is a good thing. The movement to Orthodoxy must be spontaneous, on the personal initiative of the Latvians, without any pressure of the government. . . .[56]

And, inasmuch as Alexander III believed in a well-ordered society in which the family played a prominent role, he surely must have been troubled by the argument of *Ritterschaft* representatives that the enforcement of Russian religious legislation in the Baltic Provinces undermined faith in the authority of the family by calling into question the validity of hundreds of marriages and the legitimacy of an even greater number of children. Russian court authorities in the Baltic

Provinces, *Landmarschall* Friedrich von Meyendorff stated publicly before the Livland Diet in 1893, were even capable of going so far as to use the laws of the empire to give legal sanction to bigamy.[57]

The consolidation of the position of Orthodoxy had been what Samarin, Pobedonostsev, and others had considered the principal means by which the Baltic Provinces would be united with the rest of the empire. The last outspoken advocate of this approach among the local representatives of the Russian state was Estonian Governor Shakhovskoi. Before Shakhovskoi died in 1894 rumor had it that he was to be transferred to Kursk, which prompted Pobedonostsev to defend him and the "firm principles of the new Russian policy."[58] One reason this policy then came under widespread attack and criticism was the obvious preference of a growing number of Estonians and Latvians to develop their own national movements rather than to merge with the Orthodox Church and Russian national culture. Earlier, many of them had been attracted by the Russian and Orthodox East because they hoped that the tsarist government would introduce reforms into the Baltic Provinces that would weaken the influence of the Germans over local society.

By the early nineties, however, the Russian government had clearly decided not to follow a consistently anti-German line of policy: it introduced neither Russian peasant nor zemstvo institutions and it showed no evidence of an inclination to reconstitute the three Baltic Provinces into a new Latvian Riga *guberniia* and a new Estonian Reval *guberniia*. There does seem to have been some correlation between the declining rate of conversion to Orthodoxy during the 1890s and the growing awareness among Estonians and Latvians that the Russian government had no intention to restructure Baltic society in a manner that would be to the advantage of themselves, the majority of the local population.[59] The decision to drop the pending court cases against Lutheran pastors and the faltering enforcement in the Baltic Provinces after the mid-1890s of the empire's laws on mixed marriages marked, in effect, the abandonment of cultural Russification in this region.

After 1895 the Russian government inclined much more to follow a policy of coexistence with the Baltic Germans than to form alliances with the local Estonians and Latvians. Although many Russians moved into the Baltic Provinces during the eighties and nineties, no attempt was made to eliminate local elements altogether from Baltic schools and administrative offices. By the beginning of the twentieth century Russians still fell short of constituting a majority of the teachers in Baltic secondary schools, and the Baltic Germans continued to participate actively in the administration of education, recruitment, higher peasant courts, social welfare, local taxation, economic and municipal affairs, and road building and maintenance.[60] Witte's powerful influence between 1892 and 1906 certainly helped the Baltic Germans, for Witte was more interested in practical results than in nationalist and religious ideology. Thus, Baltic agriculture appeared in a rather favorable light in the official reports prepared in 1902-1903 by the Estland, Livland, and Kurland local committees for Witte's Commission on the Needs of Agricultural Industry.[61] Following the Revolution of 1905 the Baltic Germans were very much encouraged by the government's decision to reform the agricultural system established in the Russian center of the empire by the emancipation statutes of 1861. The commune, so praised by earlier critics of agricultural conditions in the Baltic Provinces, now fell into disrepute. This made it easier for Baltic publicists to write credibly about the achievements and productivity of Baltic agriculture, pointing to it as a model for the rest of the empire to follow.[62]

Education was the single area in which the Russian government continued to pursue actively a Russificatory policy during the period 1895-1905. Until the nineties the Russification of school administration and of secondary and higher education had affected principally but a minority of the Baltic Provinces' population consisting of Baltic Germans and more affluent Latvians and Estonians who could attend district and town schools. In 1884 Manasein had not recommended the Russification of elementary schools, and M. N. Kapustin, who served as curator of the Dorpat Educational Region between 1883 and 1890, opposed for pedagogical reasons the beginning of the education of Estonians and Latvians in anything other than their own native languages. In 1887, however, new "temporary supplementary regulations" made Russian the language of instruction during the third and final year of the instructional program of Baltic rural township schools for all subjects other than religion and church singing.[63]

In 1890 Minister of Education Delianov replaced Kapustin with N. A. Lavrovskii (1827-1899). A former educational administrator in the Ukraine and one-time professor at Warsaw University, Lavrovskii subscribed to the then prevailing view in Russian educational circles that the Russian language could be taught to non-Russians according to the so-called direct method (i.e. without reference to the native languages of the students).[64] As early as 1887 the Ministry of Education's "temporary supplementary regulations" permitted the use of Estonian, Latvian, or *Russian* "according to convenience" during the first two years of the three-year program of township schools in the Baltic Provinces. During the 1890s the curator of the Riga Educational Region was given the right to determine to what extent it was "convenient" to teach in Russian during the first two years of the instruc-

71

tional program "with a view to gradually preparing pupils in these schools for the instruction of all subjects, with the exception of religion, church singing, and the native language, in the state language during the last winter."[65] There was, of course, little question in the mind of anyone how Lavrovskii and his immediate successors in the office of Riga educational curator would make use of this "right." This is a subject which is discussed elsewhere in this study.

It is doubtful, however, that Russian educational administrators then intended to employ the elementary school in the Baltic Provinces as an instrument to make Russians out of Estonian and Latvian peasants. Russian school authorities would appear to have had a twofold motivation in establishing Russian as the language of instruction in the Baltic township school. First, overlooking the deteriorating demographic position of the Baltic Germans, they continued to fear that the Lutheran township schools could be used as instruments of Germanization unless appropriate countermeasures were taken. Thus, Lavrovskii, according to his one-time University of Warsaw colleague and later University of Iur'ev Rector A. S. Budilovich (1846-1908), had nothing against the Latvian and Estonian languages but wanted only to avoid use of Latvian and Estonian schools as a covert means of Germanizing the local peasant population.[66] Second, Russian educational administrators believed that Russian state interest required the establishment of Russian as the language of instruction throughout the empire's borderlands. This view of the relationship of national school policy to state interest was, of course, not restricted to Russia around 1900. As one Russian educational administrator, N. Ch. Zaionchkovskii, pointed out in a study of 1902 on Baltic rural schools, Russia followed the same policy in the Baltic Provinces that Germany pursued in Schleswig-Holstein, Alsace-Lorraine, and Posen (Poznań), and that France did in Flanders, Brittany and the Basque-speaking area of the western Pyrenees. Although he conceded the non-Russians (*inorodtsy*) freedom of culture and language, he insisted that it was inadmissible to extend such freedom to what pertained to the activities and functions of the state. In the sphere of the state (*oblast' gosudarstvennaia*) and in the school, he concluded, the state language had to prevail in order to make it possible for the *inorodtsy* to participate in "the common national life and culture."[67]

The policy defended by Zaionchkovskii failed to make the Baltic nationalities an integral part of the social and cultural life of Russia. On the contrary, in the Baltic and the other borderlands it was above all against the Russified elementary school that nearly all social groups protested during the period of revolutionary unrest between 1905 and 1907. The pressure of the revolutionary events of these years and the advice of moderates in the bureaucracy, such as D. M. Sol'skii (1833-1910), N. S. Tagantsev (1843-1923), and S. Iu. Witte, soon influenced the government to issue the famous October Manifesto of 1905 and to make other concessions to the wishes of the nonrevolutionary opposition, including the nationalities of the western borderlands.[68] Specifically with regard to the schools of the Baltic Provinces, the Committee of Ministers recommended as early as May 1905 that instruction could take place in the local languages. Beginning in April 1906 it became possible to found private schools in which the language of instruction was Estonian, German, or Latvian; and between October 1906 and August 1913 instruction was once again given in the local languages during the first two years of elementary schools supported by public funds.[69] These concessions, as limited as they may appear, represented a serious setback for those who saw in the Russified elementary-school classroom the instrument that would unite the nationalities of the Baltic Provinces with the rest of Russia.

Somewhat more than a generation earlier Iurii Samarin had urged the government to promote the social and economic interests of the Estonian and Latvian peasants and to take measures to protect them from abuse at the hands of the German landowners. All the government had to do to induce these peasants to "merge with us in unity" was, in Samarin's opinion, to extend a helping hand to them.[70] St. Petersburg officialdom disregarded this advice especially during the revolutionary years 1905 and 1906, when it sent, in response to the appeals of Baltic Germans, punitive military expeditions into the Baltic Provinces to restore law and order. Between December 1905 and mid-1908 thousands of Estonians and Latvians were executed or banished to Siberia. All the representatives of the Baltic Provinces in the first two Dumas were Estonians and Latvians (including one Jewish representative from Kurland in each Duma) and belonged to parties in opposition to the government (the Kadets and Social Democrats) which demanded radical agricultural reform and protested the illegality of the government's repressive measures in the Baltic Provinces and elsewhere.[71]

The government, therefore, favored the Germans rather than the Estonians and Latvians in applying the new electoral law of June 3, 1907, to the Baltic Provinces. As a result, six to seven of the twelve deputies the Baltic Provinces sent to the Third and Fourth Dumas represented the German *Ritterschaften* and townsmen, who then accounted for less than 7 percent of the Baltic population; all the Baltic representatives in the State Council, the upper house of the Russian legislature after 1906, came from the German *Ritterschaften*. These representatives worked, of course, closely with the dominant landowning and propertied elements in both the Duma and the State Council, with which they had a common interest in preventing radical social and agrarian reform in all parts of the empire.[72] For the Estonians and Latvians this meant just one more obstacle that stood in the way of their gaining control of local society and politics in the Baltic Provinces.

Even the Baltic Germans had reason to feel uneasy in the Russia of the Third and Fourth Dumas. They could not complain about being unduly abused in these two Dumas, for, until World War I, the "Baltic question" did not appear on their agenda for serious discussion. But the Baltic Germans could hardly help but notice the excessive nationalism displayed by a Duma majority responsible for giving approval to the introduction of Russian zemstvos into six western *gubernii*, detaching the Chelm region from Congress Poland, and renewing a policy of Russification in Finland.[73] Could not these same nationalistic politicians direct their attention to the Baltic Provinces at just about any time? Furthermore, after experiencing the years 1905-1907, many Baltic Germans wondered about the stability and viability of the Russian Empire; and they were not reassured by the government's obvious disinclination to approve restoration of a permanent Baltic *general-gubernatorstvo* and other reforms they considered necessary to safeguard their position both locally and in the empire as a whole.[74]

Outside the Duma the Baltic Provinces clearly did begin to attract the attention of Russian nationalists. In 1909, for example, *Okrainy Rossii* [Borderlands of Russia], the principal journal devoted to the cause of promoting the unity of Russia, complained about the Baltic Germans' alleged efforts to Germanize the Estonians and Latvians and to enlist the support of the Octobrists in the Duma to undo the educational work of Kapustin and Lavrovskii, obtain special privileges for themselves, and separate the Baltic Provinces from the rest of Russia. That same year began the publication of the papers of former Estonian Governor Prince S. V. Shakhovskoi, whose outspoken advocacy of cultural Russification had met with considerable criticism in government circles for several years before he died in 1894. And in 1910 the editor of the Russian nationalist newspaper in Riga, *Rizhskii vestnik*, came out with his *Studies in the History of the Unification of the Baltic Region with Russia, 1710-1910*. This work not only outlined how the Baltic Provinces were united with Russia but also emphasized the benefits Russificatory reform had brought to the indigenous population throughout the borderlands of the Russian Empire.[75]

As we have seen, however, the spirit of Russificatory reform no longer guided official policy in the Baltic Provinces. Government policy, to the chagrin of many Russian nationalists, confined itself largely to maintaining the existing social and economic status quo and holding fast to the level of administrative and educational Russification attained by the mid-nineties. From an official point of view, to be sure, much had been accomplished: Russian had become the language of the bureaucracy, town government, and the courts; everyone attending school studied the state language, and in secondary schools students seem to have learned it very well indeed;[76] Estonian, Latvian, Jewish, and German politicians from the Baltic Provinces sat in the Duma or State Council and spoke Russian fluently (in certain cases even without accent), often participating actively and effectively in the political life of Russia;[77] and, although not absorbed culturally by Russia, the inhabitants of the Baltic Provinces were linked to her by economic interest and by experiences in the army, factory, and political and social arenas they shared with millions of the Russian tsar's other subjects. With a little more effort and imagination St. Petersburg's officialdom might very well have succeeded in devising a policy that could have won the hearts and sympathies of the Baltic peoples for Russia. But it was highly unlikely that such a policy could ever have emerged from the pleas for national and religious unity as expressed in the printed pages of *Okrainy Rossii* and *Rizhskii vestnik* and in the papers of Prince Shakhovskoi.

CHAPTER 5

ADMINISTRATIVE RUSSIFICATION
IN FINLAND, 1881-1914

By THE END of the nineteenth century, as C. Leonard Lundin brings out in Part Five, the inhabitants of Finland had succeeded in developing a complex society and a sense of national identity that set them apart from the rest of the Russian Empire. Sooner or later the incompatibility of this evolving Finnish national society with firm autocratic government, uniform centralized institutions, and the primacy of the Russian language and culture throughout the empire almost inevitably had to come to the attention of Russian publicists and officials. Fortunately for Finland, in 1881 Governor-General Adlerberg was replaced by Fedor L. Heiden (or Geiden; 1821-1900), who rather consistently opposed any policy designed to integrate Finland with Russia other than gradually and in a manner that would avoid unnecessary confrontations with the local population and Finnish political leaders.

Advocates of a second form of administrative Russification in Finland held that Finnish autonomy was incompatible with Russian autocracy and that the importance of the empire's military and naval security in the St. Petersburg and Baltic regions obliged Russia to defend her national interests in Finland energetically and without compromise. Before Heiden's departure from office in 1897 this point of view had little impact and was held only by certain army leaders and nationalistic publicists and journalists. Between 1898 and 1904 and again between 1907 and 1914 it came to dominate official Russian policy in Finland. Even then, no influential senior official seems, however, to have thought in terms of subjecting Finland to the extremes of cultural Russification like those practiced in Poland and the western *gubernii* after 1863 and in the Baltic Provinces during the late 1880s and early 1890s.

In 1881 Heiden's attention was called almost inadvertently to the question of the relationship of Finnish to general imperial legislation. More than a generation earlier, during the reign of Nicholas I, Russian officials of the Second Section of His Imperial Majesty's Own Chancellery had begun work on a codification of Finnish civil and criminal

76

law that was supposed to be undertaken in conformity with norms established by the Russian *Svod zakonov*. This work, however, was pretty much suspended at the end of Nicholas' reign, and moved ahead extremely slowly in the hands of Finnish Diet and Senate committees during the 1860s and 1870s. In 1881 Heiden and gendarmes stationed in Finland suffered considerable embarrassment in connection with the arrest of a Finnish citizen of Russian origin who allegedly had been involved in the activities of Russian revolutionaries residing in Helsinki. This episode was fairly obscure and inconsequential, but it reminded the Russian authorities that serious work on the codification of Finnish laws needed to be resumed.[1]

In a rescript of September 30, 1882, Alexander III instructed Heiden, "together with the Imperial [Finnish] Senate," to prepare a codification project for Finland.[2] In 1885 Alexander III, following Heiden's advice, appointed a five-member codification committee, consisting of Finnish legal experts and administrators. The committee worked rapidly, and in 1887 Heiden referred its completed proposal for the "Form of Government and the Privileges of the Estates" in Finland directly to Manasein and the head of the Codification Section of the State Council, E. V. Frish (1833-1907), without giving the Finnish Diet an opportunity to act on it.[3]

Official discussions of the codification of Finnish laws and of a new criminal code drew the attention of Russian publicists to unresolved problems concerning Russo-Finnish relations. The first prominent Russian anti-Finnish polemicist was Kesar F. Ordin (1836-1892), who published in 1888 a critically annotated translation of Leo Mechelin's *Précis du droit public du Grand-Duché de Finlande*.[4] Mechelin was the leading Finnish authority on the "constitution" of the Grand Duchy of Finland.

Ordin's point of departure as an expert on Finland was as a member of the sizable colony of St. Petersburg officials who spent their summers in nearby Viipuri *guberniia*. Frequently, such officials were exceedingly irritated by what they considered discrimination at the hands of the local authorities, for, as Russians, they did not enjoy full rights of citizenship within the borders of the Grand Duchy of Finland. Ordin decided to do something about this. During the 1870s he learned Finnish and Swedish and seriously studied Finland's law and history. Using his connections as a government official and chamberlain at the imperial court, he obtained access to Russian military and state archives, devoting the last years of his life to the writing of an impressively documented, but tendentious, two-volume study concerning the conquest of Finland by Russia (*Pokorenie Finliandii*). This book, his annotated translation of Mechelin's *Précis*, and the many polemical articles he wrote for *Moskovskie vedomosti* and *Novoe vremia* had the primary purpose of refuting the arguments made by Finnish historians and legal scholars in support of the constitutional and contractual nature of the relations of Finland with Russia.[5] Between 1891 and 1897 S. A. Petrovskii, the editor of *Moskovskie vedomosti*, republished articles and editorials by Ordin and other writers in a collection entitled *The Finnish Borderlands of Russia.*[6] From this time on the Finnish question came to acquire a significance that one can only compare to the famous Baltic question of the 1860s. Once again, it is clear, powerful figures in the government were willing to relax the restraints of censorship in order to help win battles over borderland policy within the bureaucracy.

Legal experts at universities and in the bureaucracy represented another source of support for high-ranking officials interested in bringing Finland closer to the rest of the empire. Since the 1860s the dominant school of legal thought in Russia rejected the forms of decentralization and self-government that had been so popular at the beginning of the era of Great Reform. During the 1870s and 1880s legal scholars in both Germany and Russia exalted the authority of the central government as the foundation upon which a modern national state had to be built.[7] In Russia Nikolai M. Korkunov (1853-1904), Nikolai D. Sergeevskii (1849-1908), and Nikolai S. Tagantsev attempted to popularize this point of view in the journal *Iuridicheskaia letopis'*, which was published between 1890 and 1893. Several articles on Finnish questions appeared in this journal, including an article by Tagantsev on the Finnish criminal code.[8]

As Russia's most eminent authority on criminal law, Professor and Senator Tagantsev played a major role between 1881 and 1902 as a member of the commission that drafted the Russian criminal code of 1903. In 1890 Alexander III appointed Tagantsev chairman of a special committee formed to review the new Finnish criminal code. Tagantsev then objected to features of this code he considered not in keeping with established principles of Russian criminal law. Although the Finnish code had been approved by Alexander III in 1889 and was supposed to go into effect at the beginning of 1891, its implementation was delayed until certain changes were made in its text to satisfy the objections of Tagantsev and other Russian legal specialists. A separate code for Finland was, however, finally approved in 1898, with only minor revisions and five years before a new criminal code was worked out for the rest of the empire.[9]

Meanwhile, in 1890 the Finnish postal system was incorporated into that of the empire without the consent of the Diet. The efforts of the Russian Ministries of the Interior and Finance during the 1880s to reform certain aspects of the empire's internal administrative and financial systems involved a basic reorganization of the Russian postal system,[10] and such orderly and centralizing bureaucrats as D. A. Tolstoi and I. N. Durnovo (1834-1903) saw little reason not to include Finland. The Finnish authorities then protested what they considered a violation of constitutional legality in Finland. Recently, however, the Finnish historian Kertulli Saarni has convincingly argued that the Finnish Senate and Diet failed to demonstrate the illegality of the Russian postal manifesto of 1890 and that it is by no means certain that the Finnish estates had a constitutional right to protest formally the subordination of postal services in Finland to the Russian Ministry of the Interior.[11]

Similarly, Ministers of Finance I. A. Vyshnegradskii (1830-1895) and S. Iu. Witte were interested in simplifying the administration of the empire's customs and monetary systems. Separate Finnish customs and money had given rise to certain problems and difficulties during the 1880s. Russian ministers of finance tended, however, to lack the centralizing zeal and energy of Russian ministers of the interior. Consideration of the possibility of abolishing Finland's separate monetary and customs systems began in 1889—that is, at the very same time that a third mixed Russo-Finnish commission commenced study of the postal question. Separate Finnish money and tariffs were abolished, however, neither in 1890 nor at any other time prior to 1917, even though the question of their abolition was repeatedly raised during the intervening period of twenty-seven years. Finland retained her separate monetary and customs systems largely because of considerations of practical Russian fiscal policy and because of the fear certain Russian business interests had of Finnish competition in the event that customs barriers between Finland and the empire should be abolished.[12]

What perhaps bothered the Finns more than anything else was the assumption by Russian officials that they had a right to introduce legislation affecting Finland simply because the interests of the empire as a whole necessarily took precedence over those of Finland. This was first adumbrated in discussions of the codification of Finnish law that took place in St. Petersburg and Helsinki during 1890 and 1891. In St. Petersburg, Codification Section Head Frish and Minister of Justice Manasein argued that Finnish laws had but local validity and that the Finnish Diet was no more than a consultative body. The Diet, according to Frish and Manasein, had no right to stand in the way of applying and enforcing Russian laws in Finland that the emperor and the State Council considered to be "fundamental laws" or to involve the interests of the empire as a whole.[13]

In Helsinki the "Form of Government and the Privileges of the Estates" proposal prepared during 1885 and 1886 by an earlier Finnish codification committee was now examined by a new committee consisting of eight Finnish senators and chaired by Governor-General Heiden. Soon, to the surprise of the Finnish senators, this committee was reinforced by the addition of three legal experts from St. Petersburg: P. A. Kharitonov (1852-1916), A. A. Khvostov (1857-1922), and K. I. Malyshev (1841-1907). No agreement was possible between the Russian legal experts and the Finnish senators. Heiden sided with the Russian legal experts in assigning to the Russian autocrat the right to issue laws for Finland in all cases involving common Russo-Finnish affairs without necessarily having to consult the Finnish Diet.[14] The argument was continued during 1892 and 1893 in a new Russo-Finnish codification committee that met in St. Petersburg and was headed by Chairman of the Committee of Ministers N. Kh. Bunge. The Russian majority of this committee then proposed formally for the first time that legislation of general state significance affecting both Finland and the rest of the empire should be examined in the Russian State Council.[15] Alexander III died, however, before this suggestion could come under serious discussion.

Meanwhile, Russian officialdom turned its attention increasingly to the question of how to proceed with the integration of Finland into the empire's general system of military service. As has already been mentioned, D. A. Miliutin was the first outspoken proponent of such integration. In the seventies Miliutin had wanted to bypass the Finnish Diet and to impose on Finland by imperial edict the Russian system of universal service. Finnish Governor-General Adlerberg, who accepted the Finnish view that Russian military reform could only be introduced into Finland with the consent of the Diet, threatened to resign from his post if Miliutin had his way. This threat and the necessity of concentrating on other more pressing matters during the Russo-Turkish War obliged Miliutin to withdraw his opposition to the establishment of a separate Finnish army. One reason he did not pursue this matter more energetically was that the new separate Finnish military system was to be reviewed and possibly revised after a trial period of ten years.[16]

Inasmuch as the separate military law for Finland went into effect in 1881, Miliutin's successor, General Petr S. Vannovskii (1822-1904), began his review of Finland's separate army around 1890. In December 1890 the Russian publicist K. F. Ordin prepared, at the request of Vannovskii, a fifteen-page memorandum on the history of the military question in Finland.[17] In a report of August 1891 Vannovskii recommended to Alexander III that the organization and conditions of military services in Finland be brought more in line with the general system prevailing in other parts of the empire. More concrete recommendations were made in April 1893 at a special conference on the possible integration of Finnish troops into the Russian army, which was chaired by Vannovskii and attended by representatives of the Ministry of War, the assistant commander of troops in the Finnish military district, Finnish Governor-General Heiden, and Colonel Mikhail M. Borodkin (1852-?), then a military judge attached to the Court of the Warsaw Military District. Borodkin, born in the Åland Islands, was the son of a Swedo-Finnish mother and a Russian sea-captain father. The assignment to Vannovskii's special conference marked the beginning of a long and successful career for Borodkin as a Finnish military specialist, member of innumerable committees on Finnish affairs, research worker, senator, and prolific writer on Finnish history.[18]

Initially, work on the drafting of a new military statute for Finland, which was entrusted to a special committee consisting of five representatives of the Ministry of War and one Finnish senator, proceeded rather slowly. Some Russian officials, it is clear, were not enthusiastic about the minister of war's plans for Finland. Heiden, for one, opposed radical reform of the Finnish army, arguing that there was no pressing need for such reform and that Finnish autonomy should not be encroached upon unless absolutely necessary.[19]

Following the conclusion of the Franco-Russian Alliance in 1894, the strengthening of the Russian army and the defense of St. Petersburg assumed a new importance. As France's ally Russia was more likely than before to get involved, sooner or later, in a war with Germany, the most powerful nation on the European continent. Sweden then seemed to be a possible ally of Germany, and Finland a likely route of invasion by Russia's enemies in the event of war.[20]

Vannovskii's 1893 committee had already called for substantial changes in the military relationship of Finland with the rest of the empire. In the second part of the 1890s new military committees continued work on projects that aimed at the extension of the Russian system of military service to Finland. The Finnish representatives on these committees naturally objected.[21] But such objections were no longer very effective, for Vannovskii and Heiden were replaced in 1898 by two younger men who favored a more energetic pursuit of Russian national interests in Finland: Aleksei N. Kuropatkin (1848-1925), the new minister of war, and Nikolai I. Bobrikov. Equally important, in 1899 the first Russian since Speranskii, V. K. Plehve, took the place of Victor Procopé as minister state secretary for Finnish affairs.[22]

Designated already in 1897 as candidate Finnish governor-general, Bobrikov, the former chief of staff of the St. Petersburg Military District, prepared himself diligently for his new position. He studied the history of Finland and carefully examined the proceedings and documents compiled by the various Russian committees that had worked on Finnish problems since the 1880s. In a memorandum he presented to Nicholas at the time of his appointment as governor-general in August 1898, he outlined an ambitious ten-point program of reform for Finland. It included integration of the Finnish army into that of the empire, equalization of the military and fiscal burdens and service obligations of Finns with those of Russians, abolition or limitation of the activities of the State Secretariat, the staffing of more administrative posts in Finland with Russians, the introduction of the Russian language into the Finnish Senate, educational institutions, and administrative offices, the codification of Finnish laws, and the establishment of acceptable regulations and procedures for dealing with legislation of concern to both Finland and the rest of the empire.[23]

On August 2, 1898, two weeks preceding Bobrikov's appointment, a committee chaired by K. P. Pobedonostsev was convened in St. Petersburg to edit the text of legislation on military service for presentation to the Finnish Diet. Although the proposed legislation emanating from this committee differed little from what had been previously worked out by Russian military authorities, Kuropatkin still was not satisfied; for he was determined that the Finnish Diet's role would be no more than a consultative one and that it would have no opportunity to try to revise the project submitted to it.[24] And he did have his way. In January 1899 a new committee was formed to settle once and for all the relationship of imperial authorities and legislation to the local laws and institutions of Finland.

The Grand Duke Mikhail Nikolaevich (1832-1909) chaired the committee on the "order of editing and promulgating general laws for the empire and Finland." Making use of the previous work of the Heiden, Bunge, and other committees on the subject of the subordination of Finland to the empire, this new committee reaffirmed the position taken as early as 1890-1891 by Heiden and Russian legal experts: the Russian Emperor had the right to issue laws of concern to both Finland and the rest of the empire independently of the Finnish Diet.[25] Accordingly, the manifesto of February 3, 1899, proclaimed that the Russian Emperor thenceforth reserved for himself the right to determine the final form of all legislation for Finland in matters of "general imperial concern" while the Finnish Diet only had the right to give its opinion.[26]

This manifesto provided Bobrikov with an apparent legal-constitutional justification to ignore Finnish public opinion and the Finnish Diet in carrying out the program of reform he had presented to Nicholas II only six months before. This is not the place to discuss in detail Bobrikov's extraordinary tactlessness in dealing with the Finns from 1899 up to the time of his assassination in 1904. It will suffice here to mention that he resorted increasingly to harsh administrative and police measures. In March 1903 he was granted dictatorial powers, which he used not only to track down draft evaders and to arrest and exile suspected leaders of the Finnish opposition movement but also to push forward with his program of administrative Russification. Thus, in Finland Russians replaced Finns in a number of administrative posts, the hours of Russian instruction in secondary schools were significantly increased, and Russian was introduced as the language of proceedings in the Finnish Senate, over which Bobrikov could now preside.[27] Obviously, a time of growing opposition to official policy and of intensifying social and political crisis in the urban centers and countryside of European Russia and the borderlands was not well chosen for the implementation of Bobrikov's program.

As early as 1900 moderate elements in the State Council opposed Bobrikov's policy in Finland. These elements, which constituted a majority of the State Council's active members, pointed out that the proposals mooted by Bobrikov and Kuropatkin were bound to give rise to unnecessary fears about Russian intentions and to anti-Russian agitation in a province that had hitherto been peaceful and law-abiding. They recommended substantial modification of Kuropatkin's project for extending the Russian conscription system to Finland. Nicholas II, however, chose to accept the position of the minority in the State Council, resulting in the unfortunate Finnish conscription law of June 29, 1901. Finnish passive resistance to the enforcement of this law contributed significantly to the discrediting of Bobrikov's Finnish policy. Even V. K. Plehve, who served between 1902 and 1904 as minister of the interior in addition to continuing as Finnish state secretary and who had previously supported the projects of Bobrikov and Kuropatkin, favored making at least some conciliatory gestures in order to pacify public opinion in Finland.[28] But it was perhaps too late for such gestures. In 1904 both Bobrikov and Plehve were assassinated.

During the revolutionary years 1905 and 1906 the more gradualist and moderate Finnish program of Chairman of the Council of Ministers S. Iu. Witte and of the majority of the pre-1906 State Council won out over that of Bobrikov. In Helsinki Nikolai N. Gerard (or Gerhard; 1838-1929), who had previously supported Finland in the State Council, became Finnish governor-general, while in St. Petersburg General

August Langhoff, a man of Swedo-Finnish origin, was appointed minister state secretary for Finnish affairs. An act that gained instant popularity for Gerard in Finland was his arranging to have Frants A. Zein (or Seyn; 1862-1918), a faithful follower of Bobrikov and, until then, director of the Finnish governor-general's chancellery, transferred to Grodno, where he served as governor from June 1906 to November 1907.[29] Gerard also interpreted liberally the manifesto of October 22, 1905, which had called into question a number of Bobrikov's special laws and measures and suspended the manifesto of February 3, 1899, "until the matters therein mentioned shall be dealt with by legislative process."[30] In April 1906, for example, he removed the Russian language from the proceedings of the Finnish Senate, in this way making it extremely difficult for himself or any other Russian-born official to participate directly in the deliberations of the body that coordinated the entire internal administration of Finland. At the same time, Langhoff managed to transform the predominantly Russian staff of the Finnish State Secretariat in St. Petersburg into one that was overwhelmingly Finnish in its composition.[31]

The pendulum began to swing in the other direction with the appointment of P. A. Stolypin as chairman of the Council of Ministers in July 1906. Stolypin knew little about Finland, but his own experience as a landowner and marshal of the nobility in Kovno *guberniia* and governor in the western and the Volga provinces predisposed him to be distrustful of non-Russian elites in the empire's borderlands. Furthermore, the restoration of order in a vast empire torn by civil unrest was his primary concern during his first years in office. Evidence of cooperation between Finnish liberals and radicals and the Russian revolutionary movement greatly disturbed him, as did also reports concerning the organization of an armed anti-Russian opposition movement in Finland.[32]

Stolypin had much in common with the admirers and former associates of Bobrikov, who warned during 1905 and 1906 that the autonomist movements that had emerged everywhere in the borderlands represented a serious threat to Russia's very survival as a nation. They demanded that the rights and interests of the Russian state and people be defended in the borderlands.[33] In Finland Bobrikov's policies had to be resumed, a point that General M. M. Borodkin made as early as 1905 in his deluxe edition of the history of Finland during the administration of Bobrikov. Beginning in 1906 Borodkin and other former associates and admirers of Bobrikov met annually at a dinner held in February to pay homage to the martyred Finnish governor-general and to praise, in the most hyperbolic language, his firm defense of Russian national interests in Finland.[34]

The close cooperation of Stolypin with Bobrikov's admirers and former associates began in 1907. In June of that year Stolypin was certainly influenced by their advice in denying to the Finnish Senate the right to work out a new Form of Government for Finland on the ground that proposals for altering Finnish basic laws raised questions about Finland's position within the empire and were therefore not to be decided in Helsinki.[35] In the fall of 1907 F. A. Zein was brought back to Helsinki, where he became assistant to the Finnish governor-general; and a Special Conference for the Affairs of the Grand Duchy of Finland was formed and attached to the Council of Ministers. From the fall of 1907 to the beginning of 1917 all important new legislation worked out in Russia for Finland was discussed by this Special Conference. The chairman of the Council of Ministers, Finnish governors-general and minister state secretaries, and selected other officials participated in its meetings. Its composition changed over the period of a decade, but four or five Bobrikovites always made up what could be described as its permanent membership, including Zein after he became governor-general in the fall of 1909.[36]

Between 1908 and 1910 Stolypin and his advisers on Finnish affairs concentrated their attention on what was then officially called the "order of promulgating laws of general state significance concerning Finland." In 1909 the law project they prepared was referred to a joint Finno-Russian commission chaired by State Comptroller P. A. Kharitonov, a senior bureaucrat who had been a member of several committees on Finnish affairs since 1890. The five Russian members of the commission were all Bobrikovites, who, together with Kharitonov, outvoted the commission's five Finnish members on every issue. It was, consequently, their Russian law project that was presented to the Duma and the State Council in the first part of 1910. Stolypin then delivered a major speech before the Duma on the Finnish question, emphasizing the urgency of defending Russian national interests in the borderlands and of defining properly the relationship of Finland to the rest of the empire. He did so in order to give the impression that representatives of the entire Russian people stood behind the law on the "order of promulgating laws of general state significance concerning Finland" that he and his Finnish advisers had drafted. Actually, the patriotic majority in Stolypin's Third Duma represented but a comparatively small number of land and property owners, and the State Council was even less representative of the entire Russian people. Both bodies supported the proposal overwhelmingly, and it became law on June 17, 1910.[37]

The new law made it clear that Finland had no more than certain rights of local self-government to be determined by Russia. All Finnish affairs affecting the interests of the empire were to be dealt with in a manner prescribed by the June 17 law and general imperial legislation, and the Finnish Diet would have no more than a purely advisory voice in all such matters. Nineteen subjects of general state significance were listed in the law. As comprehensive as this list was, it was not intended to be all-inclusive, for the Russian Emperor was given the right to alter or add to it. In all cases, legislation of general state significance was to take precedence over local Finnish laws, which were to be revised or repealed whenever in conflict with the laws of the empire.[38]

At the time Stolypin forwarded his law project to the Duma and State Council in March 1910, however, he promised that the government would exercise restraint and caution in working out the detailed application of its legislative program for Finland.[39] On the whole, he and his successor V. N. Kokovtsov kept this promise. Thus, Stolypin, who strongly disapproved of Gerard's elimination of the Russian language in the conduct of the internal affairs of the Finnish Senate and local bureaucracy, decided not to impose Russian on Finnish officialdom immediately after approval of the law.[40] Only points one, three, and eighteen of the nineteen items on Stolypin's legislative program for Finland (these points concerned Finnish participation in the military expenditures of the empire, the equalization of the rights of Russians living in Finland with those of Finns, and the subordination of the Finnish pilot and lighthouse services to the Russian Naval Ministry) were actually carried out.[41]

In spite of the relatively restrained and cautious policy of Stolypin and Kokovtsov between 1910 and 1914, they did not win many friends for Russia in Finland. This was largely because of the undiplomatic behavior and impatience of Governor-General Zein and his Bobrikovite allies in St. Petersburg. The existence of a comparatively free press after 1905, a vociferous minority in the Duma and State Council that opposed the suppression of Finnish autonomy, and a Council of Ministers chaired after September 1911 by a man not greatly in sympathy with the Great-Russian nationalism of the Bobrikovites[42] made it difficult for them to exercise the same degree of influence over Finnish policy that Bobrikov had between 1899 and 1904. Frustrated by the government's obvious reluctance to move full speed ahead with the implementation of its legislative program for Finland, the Bobrikovites tried to politicize Finno-Russian relations by leaking information to the Russian nationalist press and by seizing upon every possible pretext to demonstrate the need for extreme measures to defend Russian national interests in Finland.

The first incident occurred at Viipuri in August 1912, some seven months after the promulgation of the equalization law of January 3 of that same year. It involved a jurisdictional dispute between local Russian and Finnish authorities in connection with the application of a Russian to open a butcher shop. The Finnish Court of Appeals (*Hovrätt*) in Viipuri did not cooperate with the Russian authorities. Governor-General Zein saw in the uncooperative attitude of the Viipuri court evidence of a general conspiracy in Finland against the equalization law. He pressed for immediate application of provisions of this law calling for the trying and sentencing in Russian courts of officials who refused to cooperate in carrying it out in Finland.[43] Despite the objections of certain pro-Russian senators in Helsinki who had been appointed by Stolypin and of members of the Council of Ministers, Zein had his way. In January 1913 the twenty-three members of the Viipuri Court of Appeals who refused to recognize the validity of the equalization law were sentenced by the Third Section of the District Court of St. Petersburg to sixteen months' imprisonment and deprived of the right to serve in any state or communal office for a period of ten years. These twenty-three jurists and other uncooperative Finnish officials were brought to the Kresty prison in St. Petersburg during 1913 and 1914.[44]

Another incident, a leak of information concerning secret deliberations in St. Petersburg concerning Finland, occurred on April 23, 1914. On that day *Novoe vremia* published an accurate and detailed report on decisions made only two days earlier by the Special Conference on Affairs of the Grand Duchy of Finland. The first part of the report revealed that the conference had recommended not to annex the parishes of Kivennapa-Terijoki and Uusikirkko-Kanneljärvi to St. Petersburg *guberniia*, because the detachment of all of Viipuri Province from Finland seemed to be a more satisfactory way to safeguard Russian interests in Karelia.[45] The second part reproduced the entire legislative program for Finland that a preparatory commission headed by Nikolai N. Korevo (?-1935), a Bobrikovite who also chaired the Commission for the Systematization of Finnish Laws attached to the State Chancellery, had been working on since the beginning of 1912. The preparatory commission had been formed in delayed response to a letter Zein had sent to Stolypin in October 1910. Pointing to the unreliability and anti-Russian tendencies of Finnish journalists, officials, and judges, Zein had recommended the application of Russian press and public-meeting laws to Finland and the reinforcement there of the authority of Russian policemen and judges in order to deal more effectively with a hostile public opinion and an uncooperative local bureaucracy. Korevo's commission not only endorsed Zein's recommendations but added to them a new and far-reaching program for the administrative integration of Finland with the rest of Russia. The final revised version of the program, which Nicholas II approved in September 1914, contained thirty-seven separate points. On November 4, 1914, this final version of the commission's program was published in newspapers in both Finland and Russia.[46]

In Finnish historiography the point is often made that the resentment and the fear of Russification inspired by the arrest and imprisonment of twenty-three Viipuri judges and by revelations concerning the Finnish program of the Special Conference and the Korevo commission led directly to the wartime resistance movement and independence in 1917. This is a valid point. But one can argue equally that had there been no Russian Revolution in 1917, the pendulum of Russian Finnish policy might very well have swung back in the moderate direction associated with the names of such figures as Heiden, Bunge, Langhoff, Gerard, and Witte. If it had, it is certain that the Finns would not have been entirely happy. For, there was one axiom of borderland policy that Bobrikov, Borodkin, Kuropatkin, Korevo, Zein, Bunge, Heiden, Gerard, and Witte all accepted: namely, that no one and no institution in Finland had a constitutional or legal right to stand in the way of the implementation of policies decided upon in St. Petersburg. In their opinion, the interests of the empire as a whole always had to take precedence over those of Finland or any other province. In the subjective eyes of pre-1917 Finns, there was, therefore, not that much difference between the Finnish policy of the Bobrikovites and the policy of those who preached moderation and restraint in dealing with the empire's non-Russian borderlands.

Notes to Part One

CHAPTER 1. REFORM AND RUSSIFICATION IN
THE WESTERN BORDERLANDS, 1796-1855

1. George L. Yaney, *The Systematization of Russian Government: Social Evolution in the Domestic Administration of Imperial Russia 1711-1905* (Urbana and Chicago: University of Illinois Press, 1973), pp. 10-11.

2. Ia. Ia. Zutis, *Ostzeiskii vopros v XVIII veke*, pp. 275-79, 282-84, 335.

3. Ibid., pp. 292-301, 627-28; SIRIO, VIII (1871), 330-31, 335-39, 348-49; U. L. Lehtonen, *Die polnischen Provinzen Russlands unter Katherina II. in den Jahren 1772-1782: Versuch einer Darstellung der anfänglichen Beziehungen der russischen Regierung zu ihren polnischen Untertanen*, tr. G. Schmidt (Berlin: G. Reimer, 1907).

4. PSZ, 1st ser., XXIV, 20-21, 212-13, 229-33, 251, nos. 17,584, 17,594,

17,634, 17,637, and 17,681, November 28 and 30, December 12 and 24, 1796.

5. M. V. Klochkov, *Ocherki pravitel'stvennoi deiatel'nosti vremeni Pavla I* (Petrograd: Senatskaia Tipografiia, 1916), pp. 115-16, 410-11, 426-27; Tobien (see List of Abbreviations; other works by this author will be cited separately), II, 186.

6. Klochkov, *Ocherki*, pp. 410-11.

7. Zutis, *Ostzeiskii vopros*, pp. 559-66, 608-10, 620-25.

8. I. I. Kiaiviariainen [Käiväräinen], *Mezhdunarodnye otnosheniia na severe Evropy v nachale XIX veka i prisoedienie Finliandii k Rossii v 1809 godu* (Petrozavodsk: Karel'skoe Knizhnoe Izdatel'stvo, 1965), p. 219; M. M. Borodkin, *Istoriia Finliandii: Vremia Imperatora Aleksandra I*, pp. 221-23, 235-50, 320-21; Osmo Jussila, *Suomen perustuslait venäläisten ja suomalaisten tulkintojen mukaan 1808-1863*, pp. 18-21, 73-92, 98, 129-34, 137-40, 147-50; Keijo Korhonen, *Suomen asian komitea: Suomen korkeimman hallinnan järjestelyt ja toteuttaminen vuosina 1811-1826*, Historiallisia Tutkimuksia, no. 65 (Helsinki: Suomen Historiallinen Seura, 1963), pp. 36-41, 229-32, 278-81, 297-328, 373-416.

9. The French original of the charter is to be found in N. D. Sergeevskii (ed.), *Konstitutsionnaia khartiia 1815 goda i nekotorye drugie akty byvshego Tsarstva Pol'skogo (1814-1881)*, Biblioteka Okrain Rossii, no. 5 (St. Petersburg: A. S. Suvorin, 1907).

10. Samarin, x, 71-407; A. Tobien, *Die Agrargesetzgebung Livlands im 19. Jahrhundert*, I, 151-440; Juhan Kahk [Kakhk], *Krest'ianskoe dvizhenie i krest'ianskii vopros v Estonii: V kontse XVIII i v pervoi chetverti XIX veka* (Tallinn: Akademiia Nauk Estonskoi SSR, 1962), pp. 166-216, 302-11.

11. Rozhdestvenskii (see List of Abbreviations), pp. 89-96, 157-58; Helmut Speer, *Das Bauernschulwesen im Gouvernement Estland vom Ende des achtzehnten Jahrhunderts bis zur Russifizierung*, pp. 53-88, 96-132; M. F. Shabaeva (ed.), *Ocherki istorii shkoly i pedagogicheskoi mysli narodov SSSR XVIII v. -pervaia polovina XIX v.* (Moscow: "Pedagogika," 1973), pp. 202, 400, 423-25, 437-38, 469-73, 480-83.

12. Rozhdestvenskii, pp. 52-55, 149-58; Shabaeva, pp. 197-206, 422-26, 436-42, 485-88; Daniel Beauvois, "Les Écoles polonaises de l'Empire Russe: Aspects du centralisme administratif de l'Université de Vilna (1803-1831)," VIIe Congrès International des Slavistes, *Communications de la délégation française* (Paris: Institut d'Études Slaves, 1973), pp. 35-49.

13. [L. A. Perovskii], "O neobkhodimosti vvesti v vsekkh guberniiakh i oblastiakh imperii russkie organicheskie zakony," *Chteniia* (see List of Abbreviations), 1865 (July-September), Kniga Tret'ia, v ("Smes'") pp. 182-83. Perovskii's authorship of this memorandum is indicated by the two copies of it (one a Swedish translation) in VA (see List of Abbreviations): Poliittisia asiakirjoja, no. 73, and L. G. von Haartman papers, Etui 5 (cf. Osmo Jussila, "Finnland in der Gesetzkodifikation zur Zeit Nikolajs I, *Jahrbücher für Geschichte Osteuropas*, xx [1972], 27).

14. A. P. Shcherbatov, *General-Fel'dmarshal Kniaz' Paskevich: Ego*

zhizn' i deiatel'nost' (St. Petersburg: V. A. Berezovskii, 1888-1904), v, 12-13, 390-92.

15. P. M. Maikov, *Vtoroe otdelenie sobstvennoi ego imperatorskogo velichestva kantseliarii 1826-1882: Istoricheskii ocherk* (St. Petersburg: I. N. Skorokhodov, 1909), pp. 222-24, 312-29; R. Staël von Holstein, "Die Kodifizirung des baltischen Provinzialrechts," BM (see List of Abbreviations), LII (1901), 275-78, 353-58; Jussila, "Finnland in der Gesetzkodifikation zur Zeit Nikolajs I," pp. 24-31; D. N. Bludov, "Neskol'ko zamechanii na proekte svoda osnovnykh zakonov Finliandii," in O. Jussila, *Suomen perustuslait*, pp. 260-62; V. Ia. Shulgin, "Iugo-zapadnyi krai pod upravleniem D. G. Bibikova," *Drevniaia i novaia Rossiia*, II (1879), 117-18.

16. Jussila, "Finnland in der Gesetzkodifikation," pp. 35-40.

17. Tobien, *Agrargesetzgebung Livlands*, I, 151-67, 280-88; II, 123-25, 133-41; Tobien, "Das Ostseekomitee," BM, LXV (1908), 73-84; N. Sh., "Ostzeiskii komitet v Peterburge v 1856-57 gg.: Iz vospominanii Pavla Antonovicha Shul'tsa," *Golos Minuvshego*, God III, no. 1 (January 1915), pp. 124-45; no. 2 (February 1915), pp. 146-70; Wittram (see List of Abbreviations; other works by this author are cited separately), pp. 152-62.

18. S. S. Uvarov, *Desiatiletie Ministerstva narodnogo prosveshcheniia, 1833-1843 gg.* (St. Petersburg: Akademiia Nauk, 1864), p. 47; Rozhdestvenskii, pp. 296-310.

19. How this reunion took place is described in detail by Iosif Semashko, a former assessor in the Uniate Department of the Roman Catholic College in St. Petersburg whom the Russian authorities elevated to the position of Orthodox Metropolitan of Lithuania: *Zapiski Iosifa Mitropolita Litovskogo* (St. Petersburg: Akademiia Nauk, 1883), 3 vols.

20. [A. Buchholtz], *Fünfzig Jahre russischer Verwaltung in den baltischen Provinzen Russlands*, pp. 22-23; *Istoricheskii obzor mer pravitel'stva dlia usileniia v ostzeiskom krae sposobov k izucheniiu russkogo iazyka* (St. Petersburg: Iosafat Grizko, 1863; Tobien (*Ritterschaft*), I, 359-60.

21. Uvarov, *Desiatiletie*, p. 55.

22. Wittram, pp. 185-86; Samarin, VIII, 560ff., x, 432-37.

23. Manasein (see List of Abbreviations), pp. 182-83; Tobien, I, 360.

24. S. Frederick Starr, *Decentralization and Self-Government in Russia, 1830-70* (Princeton: Princeton University Press, 1972), pp. 45-47, 51-58, 182-84.

25. R. F. Leslie, *Reform and Insurrection in Russian Poland, 1856-1865* (London: The Athlone Press, 1963), pp. 47-49, chaps. 3-5; Irena Koberdowa, *Wielkie Książę Konstanty w Warszawie 1862-1863* (Warsaw: PWN, 1962).

CHAPTER 2. DILEMMAS OF BORDERLAND POLICY
IN THE ERA OF GREAT REFORMS:
POLAND AND FINLAND, 1855-1881

1. Tobien, I, 372.

2. Ibid.; Isakov (see List of Abbreviations; other works by this author

cited separately), pp. 6, 178-83; Katkov, *1871 god*, pp. 150, 165-66; Katkov, *1880 god*, pp. 193-96; V. I. Lamanskii, "Bezbardis i Nemtsy," *Den'*, 1865, no. 49 (December 4), pp. 1167-73; Samarin, IX, 463-85; M. M. Dukhanov, "Rossiia i Baltiiskii vopros v 60-kh godakh XIX veka" (Candidate's dissertation, Moscow University, 1962), pp. 239-91; Dukhanov, *Ostzeitsy, iav' i vymysel: O roli nemetskikh pomeshchikov i biurgerov v istoricheskikh sud'-bakh latyshskogo i estonskogo narodov v seredine XIX veka*, pp. 22-31, 136-73.

3. Koberdowa, *Wielkie Książę Konstanty*, pp. 215-57; A. V. Golovnin to F. I. Fircks, September 3/15 and 5/17, 1863, GPB (see List of Abbreviations), f. 208, no. 36.

4. Rozhdestvenskii, pp. 576-92; P. P. Gagarin to A. A. Zelenoi, July 18, 1866, GPB, f. 379, ed. khr. 358; A. A. Zelenoi, "Ob okonchatel'nom pozemel'nom i administrativnom ustroistve v Pribaltiiskikh guberniiakh krest'ian, vodvorennykh na kazennykh zemliakh," GBL (see List of Abbreviations), f. 265, op. 93, ed. khr. 2, fols. 45-74.

5. Katkov, *1860 god*, pp. 194-95.

6. E. C. Thaden, "Samarin's 'Okrainy Rossii' and Official Policy in the Baltic Provinces," *Russian Review*, xxxiii (1974), 405-15; Isakov, pp. 153-57; *Materialy sobrannye osoboiu kommiseiu vysochaishe uchrezhdennoiu 2 noiabria 1869 goda, dlia peresmotra deistvuiushchikh postanovlenii o tsenzure i pechati.*

7. KM (see List of Abbreviations), iii-1, 159-89; P. F. Shcherbina, *Sudebnaia reforma 1864 goda na pravobrezhnoi Ukraine* (Lvov: "Vyshcha Shkola," 1974), pp. 86-89; A. F. Smirnov, *Vosstanie 1863 goda v Litve i Belorussii* (Moscow: Akademiia Nauk, 1963), pp. 81-85, 154-59, 300-302.

8. KM, iii-1, 186-227; Smirnov, pp. 51-85, 299-306.

9. I. I. Kostiushko, *Krest'ianskaia reforma 1864 goda v Tsarstve Pol'skom* (Moscow: Akademiia Nauk, 1962); W. B. Lincoln, "The Makings of a New Polish Policy: N. A. Milyutin and the Polish Question, 1861-1863," *Polish Review*, xv (1970), 54-66; S. J. Zyzniewski, "Milyutin and the Polish Question," *Harvard Slavic Studies*, iv (1957), 237-48; A. Leroy-Beaulieu, *Un homme d'état russe (Nicolas Milutine) d'après sa correspondance inédite: Étude sur la Russie et la Pologne pendant le règne d'Alexandre II (1855-1872)* (Paris: Hachette, 1884), chaps. 6-14.

10. N. Reinke, *Ocherk zakonodatel'stva Tsarstva Pol'skogo (1807-1881)* (St. Petersburg: Senatskaia Tipografiia, 1902), pp. 163-72; S. J. Zyzniewski, "Russian Policy in the Congress Kingdom of Poland, 1863-81" (Harvard University Ph.D. dissertation, 1956), pp. 142-59.

11. N. A. Miliutin, "Kopiia so vsepoddanneishei dokladnoi zapiski stats-sekretaria Miliutina ot 22 maia 1864 goda, s predstavleniem proektov po uchebnoi chasti v Tsarstve Pol'skom," *Issledovaniia v Tsarstve Pol'skom po vysochaishemu poveleniiu proizvedennye pod rukovodsvom stats-sekretaria Miliutina* (St. Petersburg: n.p., 1864-1865), iv, 1-22; Zyzniewski (dissertation), p. 110.

12. Zyzniewski, "Russian Policy in the Congress Kingdom," pp. 159-81; Rozhdestvenskii, pp. 587-92; E. Staszynski, *Politika oświatowa caratu w*

Królestwie Polskim (Warsaw: Panstwowe Zaklady Wydawnictwo, 1968), pp. 16-45; D. A. Tolstoi, "Rech' proiznesennyi gr. D. A. Tolstym v Varshave 12-go sentiabria, 1868 g." *Zhurnal Ministerstva narodnogo prosveshcheniia,* cxxxix (1868), Section III, pp. 363-86.

13. L. Krusius-Ahrenberg, *Der Durchbruch des Nationalismus und Liberalismus im politischen Leben Finnlands 1856-1863,* pp. 127-208.

14. Ibid., pp. 118-24, 196-208, 304-11.

15. Ibid., pp. 60-87, 118-24, 196-208, 304-11.

16. M. M. Borodkin, *Istoriia Finliandii: Vremia Imperatora Aleksandra II,* pp. 117-20, 254-60; L. Krusius-Ahrenberg, "Från grundlagskommitté till Lantdagsordning," *Historiska och litteraturhistoriska studier,* Skrifter utgivna av Svenska Litteratursällskapet i Finland, no. 298, xx (Helsinki: Merkators Tryckeri, 1944), 247-50, 324-28, 334-36, 342-43, 354-58.

17. Borodkin, *Vremia . . . Aleksandra II,* pp. 314-15, 493-98; J. Ahrenberg, *Människor som jag känt: Personliga minnen, ur bref och anteckningar,* II (Helsinki: Söderström, 1907), 119-66.

18. Borodkin, *Vremia . . . Aleksandra II,* pp. 493-94.

19. D. A. Miliutin to the Finnish State Secretariat, January 21, 1876, VSV (see List of Abbreviations) 1/1878, pt. 1, fol. 57; Borodkin, pp. 209-425; E. Jutikkala, *A History of Finland* (London: Thames and Hudson, 1962), pp. 211-17; O. Seitkari, *Vuoden 1878 asevelvollisuuslain syntyvaiheet: Suomen sotilasorganisaatio- ja asevelvollisuuskysymys 1860- ja 70-luvulla,* pp. 218-27.

20. Starr, *Decentralization and Self-Government in Russia,* pp. 246-47, 325-26.

21. Krusius-Ahrenberg, *Der Durchbruch,* pp. 80-87; Borodkin, *Vremia . . . Aleksandra II,* pp. 498-500.

22. Especially to be noted are the fifteen "letters" concerning Finland published between October 3 and November 29, 1863: *Russkii invalid,* 1863, nos. 216, 225, 226, 234, 235, 237, 239, 246, 247, 258, 261, 262, 263, and 264.

23. Borodkin, *Vremia . . . Aleksandra II,* pp. 189-95, 240, 246-47, 394-95, 417-18, 426-28; Keijo Korhonen, *Autonomous Finland in the Political Thought of Nineteenth Century Russia,* pp. 50-80; L. Krusius-Ahrenberg, " 'Dagbladsseparatismen' år 1863 och den begynnande Panslavismen," *Historiska och litteraturhistoriska studier,* Skrifter utgivna av Svenska Litteratursällskapet i Finland, no. 346, xxx (Helsinki: Svenska Litteratursällskapets i Finland Förlag, 1954), 170-214; Katkov, *1871 god,* p. 149.

CHAPTER 3. ADMINISTRATIVE RUSSIFICATION IN
THE BALTIC PROVINCES, 1855-1881

1. Tobien, I, 83.

2. Valuev (see List of Abbreviations), II, 430.

3. The best and most complete exposition of the Russian government's Baltic policy during the sixties and seventies is contained in an official report entitled "The Baltic Question from the Government's Point of View,"

which was written during 1870-1871. Unfortunately, while in Leningrad in May 1975 I was not allowed to examine this document (TsGIAL [see List of Abbreviations], f. 908, op. 2, no. 45, pt. 2, fols. 126-76); however, its contents are conveniently summarized by Isakov, pp. 178-83. Since P. A. Valuev participated in the drafting of this document, of particular interest is the long commentary concerning the Baltic question he prepared for insertion in his diary while in Rome during the fall of 1868: Valuev, II, 421-34. Equally important statements of official Baltic policy are the reports of Baltic Governor-General P. P. Al'bedinskii, two of which have been published: Samarin, IX, 342-420; [Buchholtz], *Fünfzig Jahre russischer Verwaltung in den baltischen Provinzen*, pp. 288-97.

4. Valuev, II, 427.

5. Ibid., II, 430.

6. A. V. Golovnin, "I. O volnenii lifliandskikh krest'ian 1841 g.; II. O sobytiiakh v Lifliandii v 1845 g.; III. O polozhenii krest'ian v sobstvenno-russkikh guberniiakh i v Liflandii," GPB, f. 208, d. 6, fols. 2, 28, 99.

7. J. Kahk [Kakhk], *Krest'ianskoe dvizhenie 1858 goda ("Voina v Makhtra")* (Leningrad: *Avtoreferat* of Candidate's dissertation, Leningrad University, 1954), pp. 6-13.

8. V. V. Ivanov, "Korrespondentsiia iz portov: Revel'," *Morskoi sbornik*, LVI, no. 11 (November 1861), "Sovr. obozrenie," pp. 49-62; LVII, no. 1 (January 1862), pp. 62-68, no. 2 (February 1862), pp. 143-54; *Den'*, 1862, no. 50 (December 15), pp. 9-14; R. Wittram, *Liberalismus baltischer Literaten: Zur Entstehung der baltischen Presse*, pp. 15-22; Isakov, pp. 15-20. On V. V. Ivanov, see A. Liubarskii, *Slovo druzhby: Istoricheskie ocherki, materialy* (Tallinn: Estonskoe Gosudarstvennoe Izdatel'stvo, 1956), pp. 304-10.

9. M. M. Dukhanov, "O memorandume Krish'iana Valdemara," *Zinātniskie raksti* (see List of Abbreviations), LXXXII (1967), 44-45.

10. Isakov, pp. 32, 69-74, 178; A. Plakans, "The National Awakening in Latvia 1850-1900" (Harvard Ph.D. dissertation, 1969), p. 129; K. Valdemārs, *Zur Geschichte und Statistik der Gelehrten und Schulanstalten des Kaiserlich Russischen Ministeriums der Volksaufklärung* (St. Petersburg: F. Assmann, 1865); *Ob uchebnykh zavedeniiakh Pribaltiiskogo kraia v otnoshenii k russkomu iazyku*, tr. from the German (St. Petersburg: F. S. Sushchinskii, 1866). No author is given for the last cited work, but the initial "V" at the end of the text and the nature of the factual data and arguments presented indicate Valdemārs' authorship.

11. Katkov, *1864 god*, p. 737; ibid., pp. 257-60, 292-95, 324-30, 342-46, 353, 487-89, 580-84, 786-91.

12. Dukhanov, "Rossiia i Baltiiskii vopros" (dissertation), pp. 207-18, 286-93.

13. Isakov, pp. 178-83; Samarin, IX, 203, 365-66, 419; Valuev, II, 422-23, 428-32.

14. *Materialy sobrannye osoboiu kommisseiu vys. uchr. 2 noiabria 1869 goda, dlia peresmotra deistvuiushchikh postanovlenii o tsenzure i pechati*, I, 3-20, 236; II, 422-23, 428-32; P. P. Al'bedinskii to P. A. Shuvalov, Novem-

ber 19, 1867, TsGIAL, f. 1016, op. 1, d. 968, fol. 18; P. A. Valuey to Al'bedinskii, December 9, 1867, ibid., fol. 24; Al'bedinskii, "O vvedenii russkogo delovogo iazyka v Pribaltiiskikh guberniiakh," written in early 1868, ibid., fols. 90-93; Thaden, "Samarin's 'Okrainy Rossii' and Official Policy in the Baltic Provinces," *Russian Review*, xxxiii, 405-8.

15. *Materialy*, pp. 235-36; Konstantin von der Pahlen, "Zametki K. I. fon der Palena po povodu literaturnei deiatel'nosti Samarina," written after 1867, TsGIAL, f. 1016, op. 1, d. 189, fols. 2-5; Al'bedinskii to E. M. Feoktistov, November 24, 1868, PD (see List of Abbreviations), 9092/L 18.104, fols. 4-6; Feoktistov to M. N. Katkov, September 14, 1868 (?), GBL, f. 120, kart 12, ed. khr. 15. fols. 1-5.

16. Valuev, ii, 430.

17. M. Kozins [Kozin], "Agrarnaia politika tsarizma v Pribaltike v 60-kh godakh XIX v.," *Ezhegodnik po agrarnoi istorii vostochnoi Evropy: 1960 g.* (Kiev: Akademiia Nauk Ukrainskoi SSR, 1962), pp. 454-57, 463; Materialien (see List of Abbreviations), v, 112-25; Tobien, *Die Agrargesetzgebung Livlands*, ii, 234-40. It should be noted that the Estland and Kurland nobles worked out separate regulations for the peasants in their respective provinces: in 1856 for Estland (temporary regulations) and in 1863 for Kurland. These regulations did not differ substantially from those of Livland, the largest of the three Baltic Provinces. Had Alexander II decided not to approve the Livland law project in 1860, it can be assumed that final approval of special legislation for the Estland and Kurland peasants would not have been given.

18. Kozins, "Agrarnaia politika," pp. 457-61; Tobien, *Agrargesetzgebung*, ii, 256-58, 273-81; M. M. Dukhanov, "Ostzeiskoe dvorianstvo i zakon 9 iulia 1863 g.," *Zinātniskie raksti*, CLXXXV (Germaniia i Pribaltika, no. 2, 1973), 65-79.

19. H. Kruus, "Petitsionnaia kampaniia estonskikh krest'ian v 60-kh godakh XIX v.," in *Iz istorii obshchestvennykh otnoshenii: Sbornik statei akademika Evgeniia Viktorovicha Tarle* (Moscow: Akademiia Nauk, 1957), pp. 494-514; V. I. Lamanskii, "Bezbardis i Nemtsy," *Den'*, 1865 no. 49, pp. 1167-73; Dukhanov, "Rossiia i Baltiiskii vopros" (dissertation), pp. 335-36; Iu. F. Samarin, "Delo Bezbardisa i Krauklisa," GBL, f. 265, kart. 93, ed. khr. 3.

20. Tobien (*Ritterschaft*), i, 82-83, 108-10; Tobien, *Agrargesetzgebung*, ii, 272-73, 291; Dukhanov, "K voprosu o politicheskoi platforme tsarizma v Baltiiskikh guberniiakh v 60-kh godakh XIX veka," *Zinātniskie raksti*, xl (1961, no. 3), 271; Kozins, "Agrarnaia politika tsarizma," *Ezhegodnik*, p. 463.

21. Kozins, "Agrarnaia politika," p. 463; Tobien, *Agrargestzgebung*, ii, 291-92.

22. *Istoriia Latviiskoi SSR*, ed. K. Strazdiņš, ii, 41-42.

23. Ibid., pp. 22-23; Tobien, *Agrargesetzgebung*, ii, 272-77, 282-84; Dukhanov, "Iz istorii otmeny barshchiny v Lifliandskoi gubernii," *Vēstis* (see List of Abbreviations), 1973, no. 10, pp. 79-90.

24. Tobien, *Agrargesetzgebung*, II, 278-86; Kozins, "Agrarnaia politika tsarizma v Pribaltike," pp. 458-59, 463.

25. Manasein, p. 75.

26. Ibid., p. 74.

27. Valuev, II, 434; Isakov, p. 183.

28. Kruus, "Petitsionnaia kampaniia estonskikh krest'ian v 60-kh godakh XIX v.," *Iz istorii obshchestvennykh dvizhenii*, pp. 498, 508-9; *Istoriia Latviiskoi SSR*, II, 19-21.

29. Tobien, *Agrargesetzgebung*, II, 292-301; Dukhanov, "K voprosu o politicheskoi platforme tsarizma. . . . ," *Zinātniskie raksti*, XL, 272-73.

30. PSZ, 2nd ser., XLI, 149-60, no. 43,034, February 19, 1866; Manasein, pp. 125-40.

31. Tobien, *Agrargesetzgebung*, II, 326-39; N. M. Druzhinin, *Gosudarstvennye krest'iane i reforma P. D. Kiseleva*, 2 vols. (Moscow: Akademiia Nauk, 1946-1958), I, 313, 468-72, 603-7.

32. Ministerstvo gosudarstvennykh imushchestv, "Ob okonchatel'nom pozemel'nom i administrativnom ustroistve v Pribaltiiskikh guberniiakh krest'ian, vodvorennykh na kazennykh zemliakh," GBL, f. 265, kart. 93, ed. khr. 2, fol. 50.

33. N. M. Druzhinin, "Agrarnaia reforma 1866 g. i ee posledstviia," in *Slaviane i Rossiia: K 70-letiiu so dnia rozhdeniia S. A. Nikitina*, ed. Iu. V. Bromlei (Moscow: "Nauka," 1972), pp. 139-63; P. A. Zaionchkovskii, *Otmena krepostnogo prava v Rossii* (3d ed., Moscow: "Prosveshchenie," 1968), pp. 260-91; Zaionchkovskii, *Provedenie v zhizn' krest'ianskoi reformy 1861 g.* (Moscow: Izdatel'stvo Sotsial'no-ekonomicheskoi Literatury, 1958), pp. 365-78.

34. "Ob okonchatel'nom pozemel'nom i administrativnom ustroistve v Pribaltiiskikh guberniiakh krest'ian, vodvorennykh na kazennykh zemliakh," fols. 61-62, 67.

35. Ibid., fols. 70-74.

36. M. M. Dukhanov, "Ostzeiskoe dvorianstvo i sryv sudebnoi reformy v Pribaltiiskikh guberniiakh v 60-kh gg. XIX v.," *Zinātniskie raksti*, CLXXXV (Germaniia i Pribaltika, no. 2, 1973), 82-92; Dukhanov, *Ostzeitsy, iav' i vymysel*, pp. 17-18; R. Staël von Holstein, *Fürst Paul Lieven als Landmarschall von Livland* (Riga: W. F. Häcker, 1906), pp. 67, 110, 115-16, 130-4, 164; [A. B. fon] B[ushen], "Spravedlivy li tolki o separaticheskikh stremleniiakh ostzeiskogo kraia?," *Russkii invalid*, 1865, no. 13 (January 17), pp. 1-2; Tobien (*Ritterschaft*), I, 488-93; Wittram, *Liberalismus baltischer Literaten*, pp. 36-37, 66, 94-96; *Istoriia Estonskoi SSR*, ed. A. Vassar and G. Naan, II, 57-58.

37. Katkov, *1871 god*, p. 259; Isakov, pp. 126-29, 148.

38. Dukhanov, "Ostzeiskoe dvorianstvo i sryv subebnoi reformy," pp. 82-84; Wittram, *Liberalismus baltischer Literaten*, pp. 36-37; Staël von Holstein, *Fürst Lieven*, pp. 126-30, 176-78; Richard S. Wortman, *The Development of a Russian Legal Consciousness* (Chicago and London: University of Chicago Press, 1976), pp. 257-61; Manasein, pp. 149-50.

39. Dukhanov, "Ostzeiskoe dvorianstvo," pp. 88-92; Staël von Holstein, *Fürst Lieven*, pp. 102-15, 138; Tobien I, 492-93.

40. Dukhanov, "Ostzeiskoe dvorianstvo," pp. 90-94; Staël von Holstein, *Fürst Lieven*, pp. 156-78; A. G. Gasman, "Subebnaia reforma v Pribalti-iskikh guberniiakh," *Zhurnal Ministerstva iustitsii*, xx, 1914, no. 9, pp. 146-56; Oswald Schmidt, *Rechtsgeschichte Liv-, Est- und Curlands* (2nd ed.; Hannover-Döhren: Harro von Hirschheydt, 1968), pp. 249-51, 253-54.

41. Gasman, "Sudebnaia reforma," p. 147; Tobien, I, 494; Shcherbina, *Sudebnaia reforma 1864 na pravoberezhnoi Ukraine*, pp. 106-10.

42. Gasman, "Sudebnaia reforma," pp. 147-57; Shcherbina, *Sudebnaia reforma 1864*, p. 110.

43. Gasman, "Sudebnaia reforma," pp. 155-65; Katkov, *1880 god*, pp. 325-27.

44. Samarin, IX, 203, 257-58, 366-68, 374-87.

45. G. Passit, *K 25-letiiu Rizhskogo Petropavlovskogo Pravoslavnogo Bratstva* (Riga: M. Jakobson, 1892), pp. 72-84; N. A. Leisman, *Sud'ba pravoslaviia v Lifliandii s 40-kh godov XIX stoletiia* (Riga: G. Gempel', 1908), p. 112. The Bobrinskii report was, of course, welcomed by anti-Russian Baltic German polemicists. It was published abroad with a French translation in 1870: *Rapport du général-major à la suite de sa majesté impériale de toutes les Russes, M. le Comte de Bobrinski, suivi d'un mémoire: Documents relatifs à la question de libre confession en Livonie, présentés à s. m. i. le 18/30 avril 1864* (Berlin: B. Behr, 1870).

46. Ia. Ia. Zutis, "K istorii ostzeiskogo voprosa v 60-kh godakh XIX veka," in *Iz istorii obshchestvennykh dvizhenii i mezhdunarodnykh otno-shenii: Sbornik statei v pamiat'* . . . *Tarle*, pp. 479-80; W. E. Mosse, *The Rise and Fall of the Crimean System 1855-71: The Story of a Peace Settlement* (London: Macmillan, 1963); Barbara Jelavich, *The Ottoman Empire, the Great Powers, and the Straits Question 1870-1887* (Bloomington and London: Indiana University Press, 1973), pp. 9, 19, 32-34; Helmut Muskat, *Bismarck und die Balten: Ein geschichtlicher Beitrag zu den deutsch-baltischen Beziehungen*, Historische Studien, no. 260 (Berlin: E. Ebering, 1934), pp. 89-106.

47. Tobien, I, 184-89, 197-98; Samarin, IX, 7-49, 375-87; Woldemar von Bock, *Evangelische Allianz und russische Diplomatie* (Berlin: F. Schneider, 1872), pp. 96, 167-231, Buchholtz (see List of Abbreviations; other works by this author cited separately), p. 356; Leisman, *Sud'ba pravoslavii v Lifliandii*, p. 111; P. A. Shuvalov to P. P. Al'bedinskii, February 18, 1867, TsGIAL, f. 1016, op. 1, ed. khr. 1023, fol. 1; Al'bedinskii to P. A. Valuev, February 1867, ibid., fol. 3.

48. Passit, *K 25-letiiu*, pp. 73-93; P. P. Gagarin to A. A. Zelenoi, July 25, 1866, GPB, f. 379, ed. khr. 358, fols. 1-4; Leisman, *Sud'ba*, pp. 112-13; Samarin, IX, 127-54; KM, III-1, 335-58; III-2, 189; Tobien, *Agrargesetzge-bung*, II, 344-47.

49. P. P. Al'bedinskii to E. M. Feoktistov, April 9, 1869, PD, f. 9092/L 18.104, fols. 9-10; Leisman, *Sud'ba*, pp. 114-15; M. Stoliarov, "Pravoslavnye

shkoly v Pribaltiiskom krae," *Zhurnal Ministerstva narodnogo prosveshcheniia,* cccii, sec. 3 (October 1895), pp. 24-25, 31; Samarin, ix, 379-83.

50. Samarin, ix, 252-60, 367, 441-46.

51. Archbishop Veniamin to Iu. F. Samarin, June 1867, GBL, f. 265, kart. 199, ed. khr. 27, fols. 1-2; *Otchet Pribaltiiskogo bratsva vo imia Khrista Spasitelia za 1873 (tretii) god ego deiatel'nosti* (St. Petersburg: A. A. Kraevskii, 1874), pp. 19-21; Stoliarov, "Pravoslavnye shkoly v Pribaltiiskom krae," pp. 24-27; Samarin, ix, 107-10, 119-21, 185-237, 257-58.

52. Valuev, ii, 427-28; P. P. Al'bedinskii, "O vvedenii russkogo delovogo iazyka v Pribaltiiskikh guberniiakh," TsGIAL, f. 1016, op. 1, d. 968, fols. 77-102; Samarin, ix, 405.

53. P. P. Al'bedinskii to P. A. Valuev and P. A. Shuvalov, October 12 and November 19 and 21, 1867, TsGIAL, f. 1016, op. 1, d. 968, fols. 18-19; Shuvalov to Al'bedinskii, November 23, 1867, ibid., fol. 19; Valuev to Al'bedinskii, November 25 and December 9, 1867, ibid., fols. 19, 24; Al'bedinskii, "Vsepoddanneishii doklad po voprosu ob ispolnenii zakona 3 ian. 1850 g.," 1867, ibid., fol. 23; Samarin, IX, 414-20; Tobien (*Ritterschaft*), i, 362-72.

54. KM, iii-1, 177-89; Rozhdestvenskii, pp. 460-71.

55. [S. N. Shafranov], *Istoricheskii obzor mer pravitel'stva dlia usileniia v ostzeiskom krae sposobov k izucheniiu russkogo iazyka* (St. Petersburg: I. Ogrizko, 1863); S. G. Isakov, *Russkii iazyk i literatura v uchebnykh zavedeniiakh Estonii XVIII-XIX stoletii,* i, 16.

56. Isakov, *Russkii iazyk,* ii, 4-13; *Otchet chlena soveta Ministerstva narodnogo prosveshcheniia tainogo sovetnika Mogilianskogo ob osmotre oseniu 1865 goda uchebnykh zavedenii Derpskogo uchebnogo okruga* (n.p., n.d), as cited by Isakov, ii, 8.

57. Speer, *Das Bauernschulwesen im Gouvernment Estland,* pp. 298-99; Isakov, *Russkii iazyk,* ii, 10-12; Dukhanov, "Rossiia i Baltiiskii vopros" (Candidate's dissertation), pp. 237-38; KM, iii-1, 189; Rozhdestvenskii, p. 579.

58. P. P. Al'bedinskii, "Ob uchrezhdenii v Rige russkoi Aleksandrovskoi gimnazii," TsGIAL, f. 1016, op. 1, d. 968, fols. 69-103; Al'bedinskii to S. D. Sheremetev, 1867, ibid., fol. 150; Al'bedinskii to D. A. Tolstoi, December 6, 1867, PD, f. 16, d. 21; Isakov, *Russkii iazyk,* ii, 9-16; Isakov (*Ostzeiskii vopros*), pp. 179-81; Speer, *Bauernschulwesen,* p. 299; Samarin, ix, 362-66, 372.

59. Rozhdestvenskii, pp. 577-78; Isakov, *Russkii iazyk,* ii, 21; Manasein, pp. 201-91; K. Büchner, *Lebenserinnerungen,* i: 1847-1890 (Tübingen: H. Laupp, 1919), pp. 201-9.

60. Isakov, *Russkii iazyk,* ii, 42-44; Manasein, p. 186; Speer, *Bauernschulwesen,* pp. 287-92, 314-18.

61. Isakov, *Russkii iazyk,* ii, 47-56; Manasein, 192-94.

62. B. F. Infant'ev, *Russkii iazyk v natsional'noi shkole Latvii: Istoricheskii ocherk,* pp. 40-42; *Obzor deiatel'nosti vedomstva pravoslavnogo ispovedaniia za vremia Aleksandra III* (St. Petersburg: Sinodal'naia Tipografiia, 1901), p. 203.

63. S. E. Ernits, "Pravoslavnye sel'skie shkoly v Estonii s 1850-kh gg. do shkol'nykh reform 1880-kh gg.," in Tallinskii pedagogicheskii institut, *Problemy istorii shkoly i pedagogii v dorevoliutsionnoi Pribaltike: Tezisy konferentsii* (Tallinn: "Punane Tiakht," 1973), pp. 24-29; Stoliarov, "Pravoslavnye shkoly v Pribaltiiskom krae," pp. 24-42.

64. B. E. Nol'de, *Iurii Samarin i ego vremia* (Paris: Imprimerie de Navarre, 1926), pp. 46-49; E. C. Thaden, *Conservative Nationalism in Nineteenth-Century Russia* (Seattle: University of Washington Press, 1964), pp. 133-34; [Iu. F. Samarin], *Obshchestvennoe ustroistvo goroda Rigi: Issledovaniia Revizionnoi kommisii naznachennoi Ministerstvom vnutrennikh del, 1845-1848* (St. Petersburg: Tipografiia Ministerstva Vnutrennikh Del, 1852). Samarin's work was republished, with minor editorial changes, as Vol. VII of his *Sochineniia*.

65. P. P. Al'bedinskii, "O Pribaltiiskikh gorodakh," TsGIAL, f. 1016, op. 1, ed. khr. 967, fols. 53, 63-68.

66. Ministerstvo vnutrennikh del, *Materialy, otnosiashchiesia do novogo obshchestvennogo ustroistva v gorodakh imperii (gorodovoe polozhenie 16-go iunia 1870 g.)* (St. Petersburg: Tipografiia Ministerstva Vnutrennikh Del, 1877-1883), VI-2, 1-2; idem, *Izlozhenie dela . . . o privedenii v deistvie novogo gorodovogo polozheniia . . . k gorodam Zapadnykh, a takzhe Pribaltiiskikh gubernii* (St. Petersburg: n.p., 1875), p. 1; PSZ, 2nd ser., XLV, 821-39, no. 48,498, June 16, 1870; Lester T. Hutton, "The Reform of City Government in Russia" (Urbana: University of Illinois Ph.D. dissertation, 1972), p. 103.

67. *Materialy*, VI-2, 3-4; Hutton, pp. 47-48, 52, 121.

68. *Materialy*, VI-2, 51-52, 233-58, 315-23, 337-42, 414-21, 433-34, 490-98; PSZ, 2nd ser., LII, 262-66, no. 57,101, March 26, 1877.

69. For general discussion in English of the municipal law of 1870, see Hutton's dissertation and Walter Hanchett, "Tsarist Statutory Regulation of Municipal Government in the Nineteenth Century," *The City in Russian History*, ed. M. F. Hamm (Lexington: The University Press of Kentucky, 1976), pp. 96-107.

70. A. Tobien, "Das Ostseekomitee," BM, LXV (1908), 81-82; PSZ, 2nd ser., LI, 45-46, no. 55,501, January 25, 1876.

71. Katkov, *1880 god*, p. 325.

CHAPTER 4. THE ABORTIVE EXPERIMENT: CULTURAL RUSSIFICATION
IN THE BALTIC PROVINCES, 1881-1914

1. Robert F. Byrnes, *Pobedonostsev: His Life and Thought* (Bloomington and London: Indiana University Press, 1968), pp. 75-77, 83-86, 303-4, 311-13; Thaden, *Conservative Nationalism*, pp. 135, 185-86; Iu. V. Got'e "K. P. Pobedonostsev i naslednik Aleksandr Aleksandrovich, 1865-1881," in *Sbornik*, published by the Publichnaia Biblioteka SSSR imeni Lenina, II (Moscow, 1928), 108-9, 116; *K. P. Pobedonostsev i ego korrespondenty: Pis'ma i zapiski* (Moscow: Gosizdat, 1923), I-2, 1015.

2. Heide W. Whelan, "Aleksander III and the State Council: The Politics of Equilibrium" (University of Chicago Ph.D. dissertation, 1973).

3. Bunge (see List of Abbreviations), pp. 16-19.

4. Ibid., pp. 18-19, 44-45, 50-55, 65, 70-73.

5. I. M. Bogdanov, *Gramotnost' i obrazovanie v dorevoliutsionnoi Rossii i v SSSR* (Moscow: Statistika, 1964), pp. 58, 61; V. K. Iatsunskii, "K voprosu o razvitii promyshlennosti Pribaltiki vo vtoroi polovine XIX veka," *Vēstis*, 1953, no. 9, pp. 5-12; Iatsunskii, "Znachenie ekonomicheskikh sviazei s Rossiei dlia khoziaistvennogo razvitiia gorodov Pribaltiki v epokhu kapitalizma," *Istoricheskie zapiski*, XLV (1954), 105-47; *Istoriia Estonskoi SSR*, II, 537-45; *Istoriia Latviiskoi SSR*, II, 392-97; M. Kozins (ed.) *Ocherki ekonomicheskoi istorii Latvii 1860-1900* (Riga: "Zinatne," 1972), pp. 226-48, 372-402, 480-86; Bunge, pp. 1-8, 96-137.

6. Byrnes, *Pobedonostsev*, pp. 148-67. The best study of the poor coordination of the operation of the tsarist central government is Theodore Taranovski, "The Politics of Counter-Reform: Autocracy and Bureaucracy in the Reign of Alexander III, 1881-1894" (Harvard University Ph.D. dissertation, 1976).

7. Manasein, pp. 35-38; I. Lepman, "O naznachenii N. A. Manaseina revizorom Lifliandskoi i Kurliandskoi gubernii," *Toimetised* (see List of Abbreviations), X (1961), no. 2, pp. 144-48.

8. *Ministerstvo iustitsii za sto let, 1802-1902: Istoricheskii ocherk* (St. Petersburg: Senatskaia Tipografiia), pp. 174-75; A. G. Gasman, "Nikolai Avksent'evich Manasein (nekrolog)," *Zhurnal Ministerstva iustitsii*, I, no. 10 (October 1895), pp. i-x; G. I. Arsen'ev, *V. A. Manasein: Zhizn' i deiatel'nost'* (Moscow: Gosudarstvennoe Izdatel'stvo Meditsinskoi Literatury, 1951), pp. 9, 21-25, 182; E. C. Thaden, "N. A. Manaseins Senatorenrevision in Livland und Kurland während der Zeit von 1882 bis 1883," *Jahrbücher für Geschichte Osteuropas*, XVII (1969), 46-47.

9. Manasein, p. 35.

10. Ibid., pp. 35-38, 216-32; E. Laul, "O raporte senatora N. A. Manaseina Aleksandru III," *Toimetised*, X (1961), 150-51.

11. Manasein, pp. 225-26.

12. Laul, "O raporte senatora N. A. Manaseina," p. 158.

13. Ibid.; PSZ, 3d ser., V, 413-14, no. 3,194, September 14, 1885.

14. Manasein, pp. 221-22.

15. Ibid., pp. 180, 184-85, 193-97.

16. Ibid., pp. 210, 212-13.

17. Ibid., pp. 200-3, 208-9.

18. Ibid., pp. 212-13.

19. Paul W. Johnson, "I. D. Delianov and Russian Educational Policy" (Atlanta: Emory University Ph.D. dissertation, 1971), pp. 219-28; Wittram (see List of Abbreviations), pp. 219-20.

20. Manasein, pp. 216-20.

21. Ibid., pp. 152-62.

22. Ibid., pp. 149-51.

23. Ibid., pp. 151, 163-67.

24. Gasman, "Nikolai A. Manasein," *Zhurnal Ministerstva iustitsii*, I, no. 10, pp. vi-ix; P. A. Zaionchkovskii, "Sudebnye i administrativnye preobrazovaniia v Pribaltike," in *Problemy obshchestvennoi mysli i ekonomicheskaia politika Rossii XIX-XX vekov pamiati professora S. B. Okunia: Sbornik statei*, ed. N. G. Sladkevich (Leningrad: Izdatel'stvo Leningradskogo Universiteta, 1972), pp. 44-47; Ministerstvo iustitsii, *Vsepoddanneishii otchet Ministerstva iustitsii za 1888-1889 gody* ([St. Petersburg: Tipografiia Pravitel'stvuiushchego Senata], n.d.), pp. 3-6.

25. "Osoboe mnenie chlenov podkommissii po sudebnoi chasti G. G. Tsege fon Manteifel' i baron O. M. Shtakel'berg po voprosu (xii) ob uchrezhdenii osoboi sudebnoi palaty dlia Pribaltiiskikh gubernii," Hoover Institution Archives, Ts Russ B 197: Misc. materials in regard to government of Baltic provinces; Gasman, "Nikolai A. Manasein," pp. vii-viii.

26. *Otchet Ministerstva iustitsii za 1886-1887 gody* (St. Petersburg: Tipografiia Pravitel'stvennogo Senata, 1889), pp. 31-33; A. Gasman and A. Nolcken, *Polozhenie o preobranzovanii sudebnoi chasti i krest'ianskikh prisutsvennykh mest v Pribaltiiskikh guberniiakh i pravila o privedenii oznachennykh polozhenii v deistvie* (St. Petersburg: Tipografiia Pravitel'stvennogo Senata, 1889); *Svod Grazhdanskikh uzakonenii gubernii Pribaltiiskikh*, ed. V. Butkovskii (Riga: G. Gempel', 1914); Zaionchkovskii, "Sudebnye i administrativnye preobrazovaniia v Pribaltiki," pp. 44-47. For further comments on the inconveniences caused by the Russian language in Baltic courts, see the Parts of this study by Haltzel, Plakans, and Raun.

27. Manasein, pp. 224-25.

28. Ibid., pp. 134-39, 154-55.

29. Zaionchkovskii, "Sudebnaia i administrativnye preobrazovaniia v Pribaltike," p. 42; Polovtsov (see List of Abbreviations, I, 408, 539 n. 53; II, 60-61.

30. Zaionchkovskii, pp. 43-44; KM, IV, 233-34; *Obzor deiatel'nosti Gosudarstvennogo soveta v tsarstvovanie gosudaria imperatora Aleksandra III, 1881-1894* (St. Petersburg: Gosudarstvennaia Tipografiia, 1895), pp. 54-56; Lifliandskii gubernskii statisticheskii komitet, *Pamiatnaia knizhka i adres-kalendar' lifliandskoi gubernii na 1894 g.* (Riga: Lifliandskaia Gubernskaia Tipografiia, 1894), pp. 18-27.

31. Of the report's 396 pages, 128, not counting appendices. See Laul, "O raporte N. A. Manaseina Aleksandru III," *Toimetised*, x (1961), 151.

32. Manasein, pp. 35-37, 216-27.

33. Thaden, "N. A. Manaseins Senatorenrevision," *Jahrbücher für Geschichte Osteuropas*, XVII, 46-47.

34. Manasein, pp. 36, 58-63, 113-15, 122-24.

35. Manasein's stubborn resistance to the land-captain law and other counterreforms is discussed in detail by Theodore Taranovski, "The Politics of Counter-Reform: Autocracy and Bureaucracy in the Reign of Alexander III, 1881-1894," pp. 441-518.

36. *Pamiatnaia knizhka i adres-kalendar' lifliandskoi gubernii na 1894 g.*, p. 15; S. Kivimäe, "Riigimaade jaotamine kehvtalurahvale Eestis XX sajandi

algul," *Toimetised*, xxiv (1975), 129-49; Kozins, *Ocherki ekonomicheskoi istorii Latvii 1860-1900*, pp. 289-95; J. Krastiņš [Krastyn'], ed., *Ocherki ekonomicheskoi istorii Latvii 1900-1917* (Riga: "Zinatne," 1968), p. 158.

37. Kozins, *Ocherki . . . 1860-1900*, pp. 227-38, 314-15, 347-48; Krastiņš, *Ocherki . . . 1900-1917*, pp. 40-41, 182-208; V. G. Chernukha, *Krest'ianskii vopros v pravitel'stvennoi politike Rossii (60-70 gody XIX v.)* (Leningrad: "Nauka," 1972), pp. 17-24, 143-64, 185-204.

38. Manasein, pp. 170-71.

39. Ibid., pp. 175-79.

40. Ibid., p. 223. The Estonian memorandum of June 19, 1881, is discussed in Part Four of this study.

41. Ibid., pp. 172-75.

42. KM, iv, 224; Bunge, pp. 43, 71.

43. Polovtsov, ii, 502 n. 52.

44. Materialien (see List of Abbreviations), vi, 270-349; Tobien, i, 438-39.

45. Laul, "O raporte senatora N. A. Manaseina Aleksandru III," *Toimetised*, x (1961), 157.

46. E. M. Kryzhanovskii, *Sobranie sochinenii*, 3 vols. (Kiev: S. V. Kul'zhenko, 1890), i, xxxiv-xxxv; ii, 541-804.

47. *Obzor deiatel'nosti vedomstva pravoslavnogo ispovedaniia za vremia imperatora Aleksandra III* (St. Petersburg: Sinodal'naia Tipografiia, 1901), p. 207; Polovtsov, i, 353-54, 520 n. 22, 531 n. 107; KM, iv, 457-59; PSZ, 3d ser., vi, 50-53, no. 3,507, February 10, 1886; ibid. vi, 191, no. 3,695, May 14, 1886.

48. Polovtsov, ii, 64, 473-74 n. 75; *Obzor deiatel'nosti Gosudarstvennogo soveta v tsarstvovanie . . . Aleksandra III*, pp. 5-6; Tobien, i, 203-5, 209-10; A. F. Koni, *Na zhiznennom puti*, i: *Iz zapisok sudebnogo deiatel'ia* (St. Petersburg: "Trud," 1912), pp. 586-87.

49. *Izvlecheniia iz vsepoddanneishego otcheta ober-prokurora sviateishego Sinoda K. Pobedonostseva za 1883 g.* (St. Petersburg: Sinodal'naia Tipografiia, 1885), pp. 100-108; *Obzor deiatel'nosti pravoslavnogo ispovedaniia za vremia imperatora Aleksandra III*, pp. 203-8; *Svod vysochaishikh otmetok po vsepoddanneishim otchetam za 1881-1890 gg. general-gubernatorov, gubernatorov, nachal'nikov oblastei i gradonachal'nikov* (St. Petersburg: Gosudarstvennaia Tipografiia, 1893), pp. 3-4, 25-26. The number of conversions for the five-year period 1883-1887 were as follows, according to the official statistics at the end of the annual reports of the procurator of the Synod: 1883, 2,243; 1884, 941; 1885, 3,662; 1886, 5,745; 1887, 3,061.

50. AS (see List of Abbreviations), iii, 26-27. On Shakhovskoi, see B. L. Benford, "Tsarist Nationality Policy and the Baltic Germans: The Example of Prince S. V. Shakhovskoi, Governor of Estonia, 1885-1894," *Canadian Review of Studies in Nationalism*, ii (1975), 317-33.

51. *Obzor deiatel'nosti vedomstva pravoslavnogo ispovedaniia za vremia imperatora Aleksandra III*, pp. 123-31, 203-8, 338-51.

52. Wittram, pp. 217-18; Tobien, i, 209-11.

53. Bunge, pp. 44-45.

54. Polovtsov, II, 60-61, 64, 473-74 n. 75.

55. Koni, *Na zhiznennom puti*, I, 575-78, 581-83, 587-89; Koni, *Sobranie sochinenii* (Moscow: "Iuridicheskaia Literatura," 1966-1969), II, 291.

56. *Svod vysochaishikh otmetok . . . za 1881-1890 gg.*, p. 26.

57. Livländische Landtagsrezesse, March 1893, Hessisches Staatsarchiv, Marburg: Livländisches Ritterschaftsarchiv, film no. A15, p. 142.

58. K. P. Pobedonostsev, *Pis'ma Pobedonostseva k Aleksandru III* (Moscow: "Novaia Moskva," 1925-1926), II, 258; Thaden, *Conservative Nationalism*, p. 199.

59. For further development of this point, see the discussions of religious policy during the 1880s and 1890s in the respective Parts of this study by Plakans and Raun.

60. See *Spisok sluzhashchikh v Rizhskom uchebnom okruge: 1900/1901 uchebnyi god* (Riga: L. Blankenshtein, 1900); *Pamiatnaia knizhka i adreskalendar' lifliandskoi gubernii na 1894 g.*, pp. 12-17, 76-92, 100-57.

61. See the pertinent volumes of *Trudy mestnykh komitetov o nuzhdakh sel'skokhoziaistvennoi promyshlennosti*: XVIII, *Kurliandskaia guberniia* (St. Petersburg: Kirschbaum, 1903); XX: *Lifliandskaia guberniia* (St. Petersburg: "Narodnaia Pol'za," 1903); XLVIII, *Estliandskaia guberniia* (St. Petersburg: Tipografiia Shtaba Otdel'nogo Pogranichnoi Strazhi, 1903).

62. For samples of what Baltic publicists then wrote about the advantages of the Baltic agriculture system compared to that of the empire's Russian provinces, see *Baltische Wochenschrift für Landwirtschaft, Gerwerbefleiss und Handel*, XLIV (1906), 79-86, 97-108, 211-13, 271-77.

63. A. A. Borzenko (ed.), *Mikhail Nikolaevich Kapustin i ego pis'ma k A. A. Borzenko* (St. Petersburg: "Obshchestvennaia Pol'za," 1902), pp. 10-11; Isakov, *Russkii iazyk*, II, 205-6.

64. Isakov, *Russkii iazyk*, II, 206.

65. V. Pravdin, *Sbornik postanovlenii i rasporiazhenii po nachal'nomu narodnomu obrazovaniiu v Pribaltiiskom krae* (Riga: F. I. Treskina, 1902), p. 15.

66. A. S. Budilovich, *Pamiat' N. A. Lavrovskogo* (Iu'rev: K. Mattisen, 1899), p. 12.

67. N. Ch. Zaionchkovskii, *K istorii sel'skoi inorodcheskoi shkoly v Pribaltiiskikh guberniiakh i ee reform*, pp. 5-6.

68. Howard D. Mehlinger and John W. Thompson, *Count Witte and the Tsarist Government in the 1905 Revolution* (Bloomington and London: Indiana University Press, 1972), pp. 15-16, 31-46, 72-73, 172-73; N. S. Tagantsev, *Perezhitoe: Uchrezhdenie Gosudarstvennoi dumy v 1905-1906 gg.* (Petrograd: Gosudarstvennaia Tipografiia, 1919): *Materialy po voprosu o poriadke izdaniia kasaiushchikh Finliandii zakonov obshchegosudarstvennogo znacheniia* (St. Petersburg: Gosudarstvennaia Tipografiia, 1910), pp. 61-68 (VSV [see List of Abbreviations], 98/1910).

69. Tobien, I, 271-72, 301-2; *Istoriia Estonskoi SSR, II*, 682; *Zakonodatel'nye akty perekhodnogo vremeni, 1904-1908 gg.: Sbornik zakonov, manifestov, ukazov Pr. senatu, reskriptov i polozhenii Komiteta ministrov,*

ed. N. L. Lazarevskii (St. Petersburg: "Pravo," 1909), pp. 87-90, 340-41.

70. Thaden, "Samarin's 'Okrainy Rossii,'" *Russian Review*, XXXIII, 411-12; Samarin, IX, 249-50, 252, 253-55.

71. Wittram, pp. 231-32, 240; S. Iu. Witte, *Vospominaniia* (Moscow: Izdatel'stvo Sotsial'no-ekonomicheskoi Literatury, 1906), III, 157-60; *Istoriia Estonskoi SSR*, II, 462-69, 473, 488-90; Gosudarstvennaia duma, *Ukazatel' k stenograficheskim otchetam*, vtoroi sozyv, 1907 (St. Petersburg: Gosudarstvennaia Tipografiia, 1907), pp. 11-12, 26, 308-13.

72. Alfred Levin, *The Third Duma, Election and Profile* (Hamden, Conn.: Archon Books, 1973), pp. 50, 89, 104-5, 154 n. 12; Gosudarstvennaia duma, III sozyv, 3-ia sessiia, *Spravochnik 1910 g.*, vypusk vtoroi (St. Petersburg: Gosudarstvennaia Tipografiia, 1910), pp. 14-17, 42-43, 56-57, 60-61, 66-69, 78-79, 84-85, 90-93, 108-9, 119, 429-41; idem, IV sozyz, 1-ia sessiia, *Spravochnik 1913 g.*, vypusk shestoi (St. Petersburg: Gosudarstvennaia Tipografiia, 1913), pp. 16-17, 22-23, 28-29, 30-31, 38-39, 62-63, 64-65, 74-75, 84-85, 104-5, 114-15, 140-41, 151, 311-12, 314, 316, 321, 323; Wittram, pp. 240-41; Eduard von Dellingshausen, *Im Dienste der Heimat!*, pp. 140-79; "Die Memoiren des livländischen Landmarschalls Adolf Pilar v. Pilchau," ed. H. von Foelkersahm, *Baltische Hefte*, XV (1969), 18-30.

73. Even if they disregarded nationalistic editorials in newspapers, the Baltic Germans could not fail to notice the importance the influential Nationalist Party assigned to a vigorous defense of Russian national and state interests in the western borderlands (see this party's official report for the years 1907-1912: *Nationalisty v 3-ei Gosudarstvennoi dume* [St. Petersburg: A. S. Suvorin, 1912]). It was little consolation that they, the Baltic Germans, were not a primary concern for the Nationalists between 1907 and 1912.

74. Tobien, I, 120-21, 442-55; C. Leonard Lundin, "The Road from Tsar to Kaiser: Changing Loyalties of the Baltic Germans, 1905-1914," *Journal of Central European Affairs*, X (1950), 233-40, 248-50.

75. *Okrainy Rossii*, 1909, nos. 15 and 46 (April 11 and November 11), pp. 212-14, 668; I. I. Vysotskii, *Ocherki po istorii ob"edineniia Pribaltiki s Rossiei, 1710-1910 gg.* (Riga: N. A. Nitavskii, 1910), I, 2-12; Benford, "Tsarist Nationalist Policy and the Baltic Germans: The Example of Prince S. V. Shakhovskoi," *Canadian Review of Studies in Nationalism*, II, 317-33.

76. E. V. Petukhov, *Neskol'ko zamechanii po povodu osmotra srednei uchebnykh zavedenii Rizhskogo uchebnogo okruga so storony propodavaniia v nikh russkogo iazyka i slovesnosti v 1910-1911 uch. godu* (n.p., 1911), pp. 1-16.

77. One Livland *Landrat* and representative in the Third and Fourth Dumas, Alexander von Meyendorff, was Orthodox and completely bilingual. He gave his nationality as German in the *Spravochnik* for the Third Duma and as Russian in the *Spravochnik* for the Fourth Duma. Meyendorff was among the most eloquent defenders in the Duma of constitutional legality and the rights of nationalities (see Ben-Cion Pinchuk, *The Octobrists in the Third Duma 1907-1912* [Seattle: University of Washington Press, 1974], pp. 52-53, 95, 117, 119, 122, 196).

Chapter 5. Administrative Russification in Finland, 1881-1914

1. B. Federley, "Storfurstendömet Finlands författninger och de allmänna rikslagarna," *Historisk tidskrift för Finland*, 1969, pp. 41-43.

2. *Finlands allmänna tidning*, October 6/18, 1882.

3. Federley, "Storfurstendömet Finlands författningar," pp. 47-49, 56-58; Federley, *Till frågan om rikslagstifningen: Om den tyska doktrinen och dess betydelse för den ryska politiken mot Finland*, pp. 18-19, 21, 66. For a detailed and scholarly study of the legal position of Finland within the Russian Empire during the second part of the nineteenth century, see the recent (1978) monograph of Robert Schweitzer, *Autonomie und Autokratie: Die Stellung des Grossfürstentums Finnland im russischen Reich in der zweiten Hälfte des 19. Jahrhunderts*.

4. K. F. Ordin, *Sobranie sochinenii po finliandskomu voprosu*, ed. V. K. Ordin, i, 35-36.

5. Ordin's two-volume study *Pokorenie Finliandii: Opyt opisaniia po neizdannym istochnikam* was first published in 1889 by the Imperial Academy of Sciences. It reappeared in 1908-1909 as volumes two and three of Ordin's *Sobranie sochinenii*; in the first volume of this edition V. K. Ordin introduced and edited his father's polemics, letters, and memoranda on the Finnish question. On the Russian colony in Viipuri *guberniia* and Russian Finnish policy, see Vilho Hämäläinen, "Karjalan kannaksen venäläisen huvilaasutuksen poliittinen luonne," *Historiallinen aikakauskirja*, 1969, no. 1, pp. 5-11.

6. S. A. Petrovskii (ed.), *Finliandskaia okraina Rossii: Sbornik statei, ocherkov, pisem, dokumentov i inykh materialov dlia izucheniia tak-nazyvaemogo "finliandskogo voprosa,"* 3 vols.

7. Federley, *Till frågan om rikslagstiftningen*, pp. 7-32; S. A. Korf, "Den ryska statsrättens litteratur," *Tidskrift utgifnen af Juridiska föreningen i Finland*, xlvii (1911), 219-33.

8. The *Iuridicheskaia letopis'* was edited by N. D. Sergeevskii in collaboration with N. F. Deriuzhinskii, A. A. Isaev, and N. M. Korkunov. Concerning its editorial policy, see pp. 3-5 of the first issue, January 1890. Tagantsev's article, "Vysochaishii manifest 1/13 dekabria 1890 g. i finliandskoe ugolovnoe ulozhenie," appeared in *Iuridicheskaia letopis'*, 1891, i, 97-146.

9. Tagantsev, *Vysochaishii manifest 1/13 dekabria 1890 g. i finliandskoe ugolovnoe ulozhenie* (St. Petersburg: Gosudarstvennai Tipografiia, 1910), pp. 3-7; Honkasalo (ed. and tr.), *Das finnische Strafgesetzbuch vom 19. Dezember 1889* (Berlin: de Gruyter, 1954), pp. ix-xii; "Tagantsev, Nikolai Sergeevich," *Entsiklopedicheskii slovar'*," xli, pt. 6 (Moscow: "Russkii Bibliograficheskii Institut Granat," 1938), 678-80; Brokgauz-Efron (see List of Abbreviations), xxxiv, 688-89; Schweitzer, *Autonomie und Autokratie*, pp. ii, 250-56, 321-26.

10. Brokgauz-Efron, xxiv, 803.

11. K. Saarni, "Kysymys postimanifestin perustuslaillisuudesta," *Historiallinen aikakauskirja*, 1965, no. 4, pp. 287-305. VSV 16/1888 and 84a/1890 and KKK (see List of Abbreviations) 33/1890 and 69/1906 IV jaosto con-

The Russian Government

cern the Finnish customs, monetary, and postal questions. Russo-Finnish postal matters are also treated in detail by E. K. Osmonsalo in III: *Ajanjakso 1870-1938 of Suomen postilaitoksen historia 1638-1938* (Helsinki: Posti- ja Lennätinhallitus, 1938).

12. In regard to the problems of Russian monetary and customs policy in Finland between the 1880s and 1917, see I. M. Bobovich, *Russko-finliandskie ekonomicheskie otnosheniia nakanune Velikoi Oktiabr'skoi Sotsialisticheskoi Revoliutsii* (Leningrad: Izdatel'stvo Leningradskogo Universiteta, 1968), pp. 31-94, 130-45; G. D. Kornilov, *Russko-finliandskie tamozhennye otnosheniia v kontse XIX-nachale XX v.* (Leningrad: "Nauka," 1971), pp. 56-212.

13. Frish's memorandum on this subject and a letter Manasein wrote to Heiden on October 11, 1890, are included in *Materialy otnosiashchiesia k proektam form pravleniia i soslovnykh privilegii dlia Velikogo Kniazhestva Finliandii sost. vys. uchr. 9 marta 1885 a takzhe imp. finl. Senatom i finl. gen.-gub. gr. Geidenom 1885-1892* (St. Petersburg: Gosudarstvennaia Tipografiia, 1907). The materials contained in this volume are not paginated consecutively; a convenient summary of the Frish and Manasein documents is provided by Federley, "Storfurstendömet Finlands författningar," *Historisk tidskrift för Finland*, 1969, pp. 56-58. See also Schweitzer, *Autonomie und Autokratie*, pp. 279-85.

14. "Vsepoddanneishaia zapiska finliandskogo general-gubernatora," 1891, with appended "Uchrezhdenie upravleniia gubernii Velikogo Kniazhestva Finliandii," Procopé collection-1 (see List of Abbreviations); B. E. Nol'de, *Ocherki russkogo gosudarstvennogo prava* (St. Petersburg: "Pravda," 1911), pp. 547-49; Estlander (see List of Abbreviations), II, 297-98; Schweitzer, pp. 157-71, 286-99.

15. Estlander, II, 300-1; *Till hundraårsminnet af Johan Philip Palmén*, ed. A. Charpentier and E. G. Palmén (Helsinki: F. Tilgmann, 1915-1917), II-3, 1141-43; Schweitzer, pp. 302-10.

16. Seitkari, *Vuoden 1878 asevelvollisuuslain syntyvaiheet*, pp. 414-15; J. Gallén, "La Finlande militaire au temps du Grand Duché (1809-1917)," *Revue internationale d'histoire militaire*, XXIII (no. 23, 1961), 202; P. S. Vannovskii, report of August 29, 1891: "O peresmotre ustava o voinskoi povinnosti v Finliandii i ob organizatsii finskikh voisk s ikh upravleniiami," pp. 1-29, Procopé collection-4.

17. Ordin, *Sobranie sochinenii*, I, 133-44.

18. "Zhurnal soveshchaniia, sostoiavshegosia 3 aprelia 1893 g. dila rassmotreniia voprosov po ob"edineniia finskikh voisk s russkimi," pp. 27-35, Procopé papers-4; "Borodkin, Mihail," *Kansallinen elämäkerrasto* (Porvoo: Söderström, 1927), I, 314-15.

19. P. S. Vannovskii, "Doklad po glavnomu shtabu 12 iunia 1893, no. 7 po ob"edineniiu voisk s prochimi voiskami imperii," appendix to IV, pp. 38-39, Procopé collection-4.

20. T. Polvinen, *Die finnischen Eisenbahnen in den militärischen Plänen Russlands vor dem ersten Weltkrieg*, pp. 13-21, 261-75.

21. A. N. Kuropatkin, report of May 22, 1898: "II. Ob"iasneniia kom-

missii po peresmotru ustava o voinskoi povinnosti v Finliandii," pp. 23-26, Procopé collection-4; Estlander, III, 8-9.

22. E. Amburger, *Geschichte der Behördenorganisation Russlands von Peter dem Grossen bis 1917*, pp. 298, 437-38.

23. M. M. Borodkin, *Iz noveishei istorii Finliandii: Vremia upravleniia N. I. Bobrikova*, pp. 65-69.

24. Ibid., pp. 77-84; Kuropatkin, report of May 22, 1898: "II. Ob"-iasneniia kommissii po peresmotru ustava o voennoi povinnosti v Finliandii," p. 26; V. Procopé, *Min verksamhet såsom t. f. minister-statssekreterare för Finland 1898-1899* (Helsinki: Söderström, 1923), pp. 36-39.

25. Borodkin, *Iz noveishei istorii*, pp. 98-101; N. D. Sergeevskii, *Finland: The Question of Autonomy and Fundamental Laws*, pp. 22-24, 64-65.

26. "Vysochaishii manifest 3 (15) fevralia 1899 g.," in *Seimovyi ustav dlia Velikogo Kniazhestva Finliandskogo vysochaishe utverzhdennyi 20 iulia 1906 goda*, ed. N. N. Korevo (St. Petersburg: Gosudarstvennaia Tipografiia, 1913), pp. 185-88. For a translation, see Appendix I of Sergeevskii, *Finland*, pp. 73-76.

27. Borodkin, *Iz noveishei istorii*, pp. 119-95, 371-418.

28. Gosudarstvennyi sovet, *Otchet po deloproizvodstvu Gosudarstvennogo soveta za sessiiu 1900-1901 gg.* (St. Petersburg: Gosudarstvennaia Tipografiia, 1902), pp. 37-41, 53-57, 63-68, 75-76; Witte, *Vospominaniia*, III, 268-70; Borodkin, *Iz noveishei istorii*, pp. 231-33.

29. Estlander, III, 357-61; Witte, *Vospominaniia*, III, 273-81; "O sluzhbe Frantsa Aleksandrovicha Zeina," KKK 96a-b 1, Fh 7.

30. *Finland and Russia 1808-1902: From Autonomy to Independence: A Selection of Documents*, ed. D. G. Kirby, p. 115; *Zakonodatel'nye akty perekhodnogo vremeni (1904-1908 gg.)*, ed. N. I. Lazarevskii, pp. 167-69.

31. Langhoff (see List of Abbreviations), I, 42-75; M. M. Borodkin, *Finland: Its Place in the Russian State*, pp. 74-75, 85.

32. A. S. Lande [pseud.: A. Izgoev], *P. A. Stolypin: Ocherk zhizni i deiatel'nosti* (Moscow: K. F. Nekrasov, 1912), pp. 12-24; Mary Schaeffer Conroy, *Peter Arkad'evich Stolypin: Practical Politics in Late Tsarist Russia* (Boulder, Colorado: Westview Press, 1976), pp. 4-12, 111-12, 115, 124-25, 134-35.

33. M. M. Borovitnikov, *Nikolai Dmitrievich Sergeevskii i ego professorskaia, nauchno-literaturnaia i obshchestvennaia deiatel'nost': Biograficheskii ocherk* (St. Petersburg: Tipografiia Odinochnoi Tiurmy, 1910), pp. 105-24; A. S. Budilovich, *Mozhet-li Rossiia otdat' inorodtsam svoi okrainy?* (St. Petersburg: A. S. Suvorin, 1907), Biblioteka Okrain Rossii, no. 4, pp. 12-23, 71-74; "Otkryta podpisi na 1909," *Okrainy Rossii*, IV (1909), n.p.

34. Borovitnikov, *N. D. Sergeevskii*, pp. 115-16; A. Ia. Avrekh, *Stolypin i Tret'ia Duma* (Moscow: "Nauka," 1968), p. 46; Borodkin, *Iz noveishei istorii Finliandii*; Borodkin, *Pamiati finliandskogo general-gubernatora Nikolaia Ivanovicha Bobrikova* (Kharkov: Gubernskoe Upravlenie, 1905).

35. Stolypin to A. Langhoff, June 24, 1907, VSV 143/1910.

36. Avrekh, *Stolypin*, pp. 45-46; Borovitnikov, *Sergeevskii*, p. 96; Estlander, III, 399-400; Langhoff, I, 151-53, 255; III, 65, 71, 75.

37. Langhoff, I, 368-73; Avrekh, *Stolypin*, pp. 64-78; G. A. Hosking, *The Russian Constitutional Experiment: Government and Duma, 1907-1914* (Cambridge: Cambridge University Press, 1973); B. Pinchuk, *The Octobrists in the Third Duma*, pp. 119-23; Komissiia dlia sistematizatsii finliandskikh zakonov pri Gosudarstvennoi kantseliarii, *Zaprosy po finliandskomu upravleniiu: Gosudarstvennai duma, zasedaniia 1, 5 i 12 fevralia, 5, 12 i 13 marta 1908 goda* (St. Petersburg: Gosudarstvennaia Tipografiia, 1910), pp. 35-61; Gosudarstvennaia duma, *O poriadke izdaniia kasaiushchikhsia Finliandii zakonov i postanovlenii obshchegosudarstvennogo znacheniia: Proekt predsedatelia Soveta ministrov i ego rassmotrenie v Gosudarstvennoi dume i Gosudarstvennom sovete* (St. Petersburg: Gosudarstvennaia Tipografiia, 1911), pp. 1-6. The stenographic reports for the sessions on Finland in the Duma of March 17, May 19, 21, 22, 24, 25, 26 and 28, 1910, and in the State Council of April 7, 10, May 26, June 8, 9, 10, 11 and 14 are reproduced in Sections II and III of *O poriadke izdaniia kasaiushchikhsia Finliandii zakonov*. For Stolypin's speech before the Duma of May 25, 1910, see Section II, cols. 2025-2042.

38. The text of the law of June 17, 1910, is contained in Section V of *O poriadke izdaniia kasaiushchikhsia Finliandii zakonov*, pp. 1-6. For an English translation, see Sergeevskii, *Finland*, pp. 77-83.

39. "Ob"iasnitel'naia zapiska k proektu predsedatelia Soveta ministrov o poriadke izdaniia kasaiushchikhsia Finlinadii zakonov," *O poriadke izdannia*, p. 19.

40. *Zaprosy po finliandskomu upravleniiu*, pp. 41-42. During 1909 and 1910, for example, Stolypin avoided conflicts with the Finns over the language question in the Finnish Senate by appointing new senators who could speak Swedish and/or Finnish. The majority of these new senators were, however, men who had served for many years in the interior of the empire. See Estlander, IV, 18-19; *Obzor pechati o Finliandii* (St. Petersburg: Gosudarstvennaia Tipografiia, 1911), pp. 77-78, 83, 91, 101-8.

41. Avrekh, *Stolypin*, pp. 78-89; Langhoff, III, 245; Pinchuk, *The Octobrists in the Third Duma*, pp. 168-71; *Obzor pechati o Finliandii*, pp. 59-60. On the pilot question, see *Kratkii ocherk o sostoianii lotsmanskogo i maiachnogo vedomstva Finliandii posle podchineniia v 1912 godu Morskomu ministerstvu* (St. Petersburg: Gosudarstvennaia Tipografiia, 1912), pp. 1-16; *Kratkii ocherk o sostoianii lotsmanskogo i maiachnogo vedomstva Finliandii v 1913 godu*, vypusk vtoroi (St. Petersburg: Gosudarstvennaia Tipografiia, 1914), pp. 1-12—all three of which are to be found in KKK Hd 21: Seynin asiakirjat, Luotsilaitos 1912-1914.

42. V. N. Kokovtsov, *Out of the Past: The Memoirs of Count Kokovtsov*, ed. H. H. Fisher (Stanford: Stanford University Press, 1939), p. 349.

43. F. A. Zein to the procurator of the St. Petersburg Court Chamber, October 22, 1912, KKK Hd 100; "Spravka o sluchaiakh protivodeistviiakh gofgerikhtov gosudarstvennoi vlasti, 27 oktiabria 1912 g.," in ibid.

44. Estlander, IV, 43-85; "Osobyi zhurnal Soveta ministrov, 2 noiabria 1912: Po voprosu vozbuzhdenii ugolovnogo predsledovaniia protiv chlenov vyborgskogo gofgerikhta," KKK Hd 100.

45. *Novoe vremia*, No. 13689, April 23/May 6, 1914; V. Hämäläinen, "Karjalan kannaksen venäläisen huvilaasutuksen," *Historiallinen aikakauskirja*, 1969, no. 1, pp. 16-19.

46. *Novoe vremia*, April 23, 1914; Avrekh, *Stolypin*, pp. 89-90; V. Rasila, "Vuoden 1914 venäläistämisohjelman synty," *Historiallinen aikakauskirja*, no. 1, 1966, pp. 1-16; "Ett afgörande pa högste ort: Den särskilda kommittens för finska ärenden program fastställdt," *Hufvudstadsbladet*, no. 316, November 4/17, 1914; "Finland i ryska pressen," *Hufvudstadsbladet*, nos. 319 and 321, November 7/20 and 9/22, 1914.

PART TWO

THE BALTIC GERMANS

MICHAEL H. HALTZEL

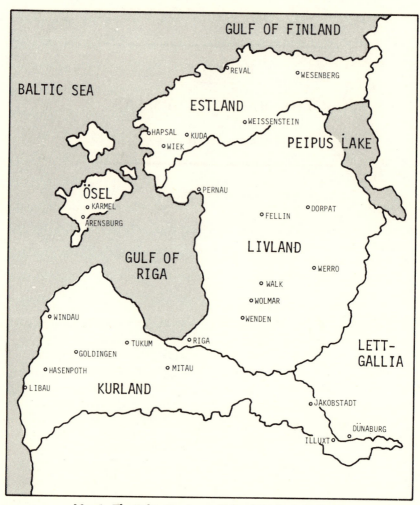

Map 1. The Baltic Provinces: Estland, Livland, Kurland.

CHAPTER 6

BALTIC PARTICULARISM
AND THE BEGINNINGS
OF RUSSIFICATION

The periodical *Soviet Life* reported in October 1973 that gold prospectors had found a salamander-like creature frozen in the tundra in the remote Kolyma region of Siberia. As soon as the ice around the creature melted, the animal came to life after a hibernation of nearly 100 years. Soviet scientists identified it as the small amphibian known as *Hynobius keyserlingii*.[1] The incident, of great interest to zoologists, also has historical overtones, pointing as it does to the scientific contributions of the Keyserlings, one of the many Baltic German families that served the Russian throne for generations. For further evidence of this service one might also look eastward from Kolyma to Alaska where the names Wrangell, Krusenstern, Kotzebue, and Hagemeister adorn mountain ranges, capes, sounds and towns, reflecting past Baltic German involvement in that former Russian territory.

Historians will scarcely need zoological or geographical reminders of the importance of the Baltic Germans to the last 200 years of the empire of the Romanovs. Beginning with the invitation by Peter the Great in 1723 to nobles of Livland and Estland to enter Russian state service,[2] a steady stream of Germans from the Baltic area staffed the military and civil branches of government to a degree surpassing that of all other non-Slavs (witness Bakunin's scathing reference to the Romanovs' Empire "knouto-germanique").

On its part, the Russian government allowed the Germans a wide measure of political and cultural autonomy, first elaborated in a series of capitulations they had made at the time of the conquest by Peter's armies in the Great Northern War. The Baltic governmental system, efficient for its time, was highly esteemed by Russian officialdom. Hence, for more than a century the imperial administrators were not inclined to tamper with it. When, however, in the mid-nineteenth century Russians began to perceive their newly reformed system of government as at least on a par with the Baltic model, the tsar came under pressure to curtail Baltic administrative autonomy. Rising Rus-

111

sian national pride at the same time combined with fear of expansion from Imperial Germany to add a clamor for action against the cultural provisions of the Baltic privileges.

Alexander II did his best to moderate the more extreme government policies, but his son Alexander III gave wide latitude to those imperial officials who saw Russification as a necessary component of modernization. The Baltic Germans—a sociologically diverse group despite their small numerical size—in general viewed the change in government policy with alarm. Led by the nobility, which stood to lose the most from centralization, large segments of the Baltic German community organized spirited, if uncoordinated, resistance. While they achieved some measure of successs, and while Nicholas II proved to be less zealous than his father in pushing for reform, by the eve of World War I it was clear that the Baltic Germans' once-omnipotent position had vanished forever.

The Baltic Germans considered their special position in the empire to be securely established by the agreements they had concluded with the representatives of Peter the Great at the beginning of the eighteenth century. These agreements contained many statements of only momentary relevance, but fundamentally the *Ritterschaften* (corporations of the nobility) received confirmation of nearly unrestricted freedom of action over the land, which in the case of Livland was an affirmation of the *Privilegium Sigismundi Augusti* granted by the Polish king in 1561.[3] The nobles also received the exclusive right to own manors.[4] Politically, the agreements confirmed the German estate self-government together with its German judicial system. In addition, Estland and the city of Reval reserved for themselves a German governor.[5]

The central cultural features of the agreements concerned religion and language. The tsar granted security to the Augsburg Confession and the Evangelical Lutheran *Landeskirche*, and the use of the German language in the provincial government bureaucracy. In the educational sphere, Livland was offered the prospect of an academy in Pernau (Pärnu), to be staffed by professors of the Lutheran faith, as long as one of them would teach the Russian language.[6]

Although Peter had satisfied most of their wishes, the Livland nobles were unhappy with two formal reservations in the tsar's general confirmation of their privileges. Peter had confirmed the statutes, noble rights, immunities and freedoms of the *Privilegium Sigismundi Augusti*, "as far as they are appropriate to the current government and time" (*eliko onyia k nyneshnemu Pravitel'stvu i vremeni prilichaiutsia*), "but granting (them) without prejudice and detriment to ours and our state, highness, and law" (*odnakozh Nashe i Nashikh Gosudarstv Vysochestvo i prava predostavliaia bez pre-dosuzhdeniia i vreda).*[7] These qualifications are not found in the agreements between Peter and the *Ritterschaft* of Estland and the cities of Riga and Reval.

In February 1711 the provincial councillors (*Landräte*) of Livland delivered to the tsar's plenipotentiary, Baron Johann Gerhard Löwenwolde, (?-1723), a memorandum protesting these two reservations. Löwenwolde rejected their protest but was more conciliatory regarding the *Landräte's* request that the provincial administrator be a native Baltic German if possible, and if not, then at least someone with a command of the German language. He informed the tsar of their petition, and formal confirmation of this request was granted in a resolution dated March 1, 1712.[8]

The rights and privileges of the Baltic *Ritterschaften* and burghers received further confirmation in general terms without reservations in two international treaties, Nystad (1721) and Åbo (1743).[9] With the exception of the baby Tsar Ivan VI and the murdered Tsar Peter III, every Russian monarch until Alexander III confirmed the privileges of the Livland and Estland *Ritterschaften* and several confirmed those of Kurland's and Ösel's nobles. Beginning with Alexander I, however, the privileges of the Livland and Estland *Ritterschaften* contained in their confirmations the clause, "insofar as they are in agreement with the general decrees and laws of our state" (*eliko soobrazny oni s obshchimi Gosudarstva Nashego posta-novleniiami i zakonami*).[10]

The Baltic German nobility had developed after the conquest of the Baltic area in the thirteenth century through the coalescence of various vassals of the Livonian bishops and the German Order. Associations of these vassals gained strength as the Order and the Archbishop of Riga weakened each other by frequent battles. Gradually they united into *Ritterschaften*, which began to cooperate in governing the territory. After the collapse of the Livonian Confederation in the sixteenth century they remained—along with the cities—as the major political power, taking control of the countryside. They strengthened this control by creating a complex oligarchic system of government which the rulers of Poland, Sweden, and Russia in turn confirmed.[11]

The *Landtag* (Diet) was the highest administrative organ in each of the Baltic Provinces. It functioned both as a body directing the affairs of the entire countryside and as an assembly of the province's nobility dealing with the nobles' internal affairs. A Council of the Diet (in Livland and Estland called the *Landratskollegium*, in Kurland known as the *Ritterschaftskomité*) acted as the executive arm of the nobles' organization, carrying out most of the essential duties in the province such as maintenance of government highways, mail stations, military conscription offices, police functions, and bridge building.

The single most important position in provincial government was that of marshal of the nobility (*Landmarschall* in Livland and on the island of Ösel [Saaremaa] which had its own *Ritterschaft*; *Landes-bevollmächtigter* in Kurland; *Ritterschaftshauptmann* in Estland). The marshal of the nobility's most important function as the nineteenth century wore on became representing his *Ritterschaft* at Court in St. Petersburg. As a result, diplomatic tact and good connections in high government circles counted heavily as criteria for election to the post. Local government was also highly developed—in the countryside in the form of the parish (*Kirchspiel*), in the cities through a system of guilds and councils solidly controlled by Baltic Germans.

After a few initial rubs with the local power structure the new Russian overlords soon settled into a laissez-faire policy toward the Baltic Germans. The losers in this arrangement were, of course, the Latvian and Estonian peasants. The chronicler Kelch (?-1710) had called Livland, "the heaven of the nobility, the paradise of the clergy, the gold mine of the foreigners, and the hell of the peasants." Estland was no different; Treitschke labeled it "the classical land of peasant oppression." Baltic serfdom saw its heyday during the first decades of Russian rule in the eighteenth century.[12] The situation began to change with Catherine the Great. A friend of Enlightenment ideas, she had read a treatise against serfdom by a Baltic German pastor, Johann Georg Eisen von Schwarzenberg (1717-1779), and after interviewing the author visited Livland and Estland herself in 1764. Perhaps appalled by the conditions she found there or motivated by a desire to reduce the power of the indigenous nobility, the empress had her governor-general browbeat the recalcitrant nobles into agreeing to a mild reform of forced labor, dues, and corporal punishment, but the imperial government soon found that enforcing it was another matter.[13]

Catherine also had the issue of provincial autonomy on her mind. First debated at the Legislative Commission, the question of limiting autonomy had to wait for action until the suppression of the Pugachev Rebellion and the successful conclusion of a war with Turkey. In 1783, Catherine ordered the Provincial Reform of 1775 extended to Livland and Estland. This attempted streamlining of government compelled the Baltic cities to disband their guilds and to hold elections with wider suffrage. The reformed city governments brought into leadership new elements—still German—but regarded by the urban patriciate as demagogues and ruffians. After some initial financial mismanagement in Riga the new administration gained competence, and the change proved to be more one of form than of substance. In the countryside the imperial government convened new Diets which brought together for the first time under the same rights all landowning nobles, not just the registered nobility.[14]

Kurland, which had managed to limp through the upheavals of the eighteenth century as a semi-independent duchy, finally was annexed by Russia on April 15, 1795, just before the Third Partition of Poland. The following November the new province was integrated into the reformed Baltic administrative system and hence, unlike Livland and Estland, did not obtain autonomy from the outset.[15]

In autocratic Russia, however, sudden reversals of policy often swiftly followed a monarch's demise. On November 6, 1796, Catherine died, leaving the crown to her unstable son Paul. Almost immediately the new emperor, as part of a general turnabout from his mother's programs, restored the old governmental system to Livland and Estland and also extended it to Kurland.[16] Catherine's measures, although they had struck at Baltic provincial autonomy by administrative reorganization, had made no attempt fundamentally to alter the dominant position of the Baltic Germans by Russification of language, education, or religion. The sudden about-face in Russian Baltic policy after Catherine's death dramatized the absolute nature of imperial power, which could in the future be turned against provincial autonomy in all spheres of life.

As for the Baltic Germans themselves, in this twilight period of their total dominance, before rapid industrialization changed the ethnic as well as economic character of the area, a *Biedermeier*-like tranquility, broken only by periodic local peasant disturbances, typified their life style. In the countryside and the small towns life centered on the Protestant home. Local newspapers resembled advertisement sheets more than political or literary organs. Foreign newspapers, usually from Germany, arrived late on the heavily laden post carriages which twice weekly traveled back and forth along the main military road traversing the Baltic Provinces between St. Petersburg and Tauroggen. The road also served as a first-hand cultural link to western Europe. Luminaries of the theater and music world such as Franz Liszt, Robert and Clara Schumann, Anton Rubinstein, and Hector Berlioz stopped to perform in Riga, and some leading artists also appeared in Mitau, Dorpat, and smaller towns along the way.

The Baltic Provinces had long had intimate cultural ties with Germany. The movements of the Enlightenment and Pietism both took root in their soil, and the Baltic German poets Lenz and Klinger belonged to the literary circle of *Stürmer und Dränger* which gathered around the young Goethe. Kant had his *Critique of Pure Reason* first published in Riga by Hartknoch, the same publisher who brought out the first works of Hamann and Herder, both of whom had lived and worked for extended periods in the Baltic area. Richard Wagner was the conductor at Riga's municipal German theater from 1837 to 1839. Many professors from Germany taught at Dorpat University after its founding in 1801, and most universities in Germany had at least one Baltic German lecturer on their faculty. In addition, it was customary for young Baltic Germans, particularly Kurlanders, to spend a few semesters at a German university, most often Jena or Göttingen, before enrolling at Dorpat.

Still, the Baltic experience with its harsh climate, subservient non-German population and geographical isolation had created in the Baltic Germans feelings of identity separate from Germany, which they often considered to be more impersonal than their homeland. They also felt scant attachment to the Germans in St. Petersburg, whose outlook was inevitably more urban and cosmopolitan than their own.

Over the centuries a variety of historical experiences had also engendered differences in outlook among the Germans of the three provinces, and because of the poorly developed communications network there was little social intercourse to bridge the gap. The one institution which might have acted as a unifying force for the Baltic Germans, the University of Dorpat, fell short of fulfilling that function. Membership in Dorpat's student corporations was usually based upon one's geographical origin, and despite their participation in a general student government, the corporations tended to reinforce provincial loyalties. Vertical tensions also existed within Baltic German society, especially in Kurland where the particularly powerful nobility faced assertive literati whose pride in intellectual achievement included a certain haughtiness vis-à-vis both the nobility and the rest of the bourgeoisie.[17]

If the Baltic Germans were not a unified group, they had no difficulty agreeing that they were culturally superior to the Latvians and Estonians who comprised more than 90 percent of the area's population. Most Baltic Germans were bewildered at the attempts of some of their own Lutheran pastors to educate the peasant masses and to develop their native languages. Peasants, the manor lords held, were to be treated sternly. The renowned biologist Jakob von Uexküll (1864-1944) recalled his father's advice: "These people have respect only for an angry master."[18] In this case the Baltic German code of honor intervened, and Uexküll's father added, "but one doesn't therefore really have to be angry." Many of the masters would doubtless have been shocked at the results of a private poll about the Baltic Germans which Uexküll took among the Estonians in his neighborhood. The unanimous opinion of the Estonian peasants, Uexküll reported in a puckish way, was: "The Germans are stupid, but honest."[19]

Such mutual misperceptions among the Baltic nationalities persisted into this century. As a result of the German character of higher education in the Baltic Provinces some Latvians and Estonians did become Germans—a process which until late in the nineteenth century was a precondition for upward economic or social mobility. The overwhelming majority, though, held on to its old identity. With the industrialization of the Baltic region in the latter half of the nineteenth century came urbanization and small but active native intelligentsia which propounded the idea of Latvian and Estonian nationalities.[20] The responses of the Baltic Germans to the upsurge in national feeling among these long-suppressed peoples ranged from active encouragement by some pastors to implacable hostility from conservative manor lords and burghers who saw their dominant economic positions threatened. Probably, though, the most characteristic reaction was simply lack of comprehension.[21]

The rigid class structure of society with its formal associations that had prevented the absorption of the Baltic Germans by the local populations also bred a provincialism, arrogance, and intolerance running counter to the liberal spirit ascendant in western Europe. Such traits not only antagonized the Latvians, Estonians, and Russians in their midst but, as we shall see, also prevented the Baltic Germans themselves from uniting to enact reforms necessary for the maintenance of their rule.

During the first part of the nineteenth century neither Alexander I nor Nicholas I put undue pressure on the Baltic Germans to introduce needed reform. These two sons of the unfortunate Emperor Paul were both personally well disposed toward the Baltic Germans. Alexander, despite the fact that he inserted the previously mentioned new qualifying clause into his confirmation of the Ritterschaften's privileges, generally supported the Baltic Germans in their conflicts with his own bureaucracy. Nicholas' behavior was more ambiguous. He once declared to the marshal of the Kurland nobility, "I am just as good a Baltic provincial as you,"[22] and in the 1840s he withheld support from some of his officials who tried to restructure the municipal government of Riga. Yet the drawing together of the huge empire had begun, and during Nicholas' long reign the Russian government

117

commenced its whittling away at the German character of the Baltic schools and gave its blessing to the Orthodox Church's push into the region.

In 1801, at the very outset of Alexander's rule, the young monarch gave official recognition to the special position of the Baltic Provinces by uniting them into a vice royalty under a governor-general with his seat in the great castle in Riga. Several of Alexander's officials in St. Petersburg and Riga struggled repeatedly to restrain, even to reverse, the trends toward greater Baltic autonomy, but the provincial nobility succeeded in thwarting their efforts.[23]

The most serious challenge to Baltic administrative autonomy during the first half of the nineteenth century came from the so-called Stackelberg-Khanykov Commission (1845-1848), directed by Collegiate Assessor Baron Adolf Stackelberg (1807-1865) and State Councillor Ia. V. Khanykov (1818-1862). The commission, which included the young Slavophile Iurii Samarin, wanted to work out a new system of government for Riga and to that end collected a mass of material on all aspects of the city's life. It seemed to be on the road to success when in the revolutionary month of March 1848 the emperor replaced Governor-General E. A. Golovin (1782-1858) with Prince Aleksandr Suvorov, grandson of the great field marshal. Suvorov had studied in German Switzerland and had participated in German student life in Göttingen. He immediately felt that the Stackelberg-Khanykov Commission was a one-sided attempt at discrediting the Baltic German city administration and ordered it disbanded. The commission's proposals were bandied about in the Russian bureaucracy for twenty years until made redundant by the municipal statute of 1870.[24]

Nicholas' choice of Suvorov as governor-general reflected his changing view of the Baltic Provinces. Influenced by Baltic peasant disturbances in the 1840s (to be discussed later) and especially by the European revolutions of 1848, the emperor came to value the stability of the established Baltic German power structure over the potentially negative aspects of provincial autonomy in an ethnically non-Russian region. When Nicholas, for example, read Samarin's anti-German "Letters from Riga," the product of the young official's historical research and observations while serving on the Stackelberg-Khanykov Commission, he had Samarin incarcerated in the Peter and Paul Fortress for twelve days and then personally rebuked him for having denounced the Baltic Germans.[25]

During Nicholas' reign the Second Section under Mikhail Speranskii undertook the collection of Russian laws and also the codification of the local laws of various non-Russian parts of the empire such as Siberia, Bessarabia, the Western Ukraine, Lithuania, the Baltic Provinces, and Finland. Speranskii saw the local laws as only additions to Russian law and, therefore, except in the Baltic Provinces none of the local codes received legislative sanction. For more than a century the *Ritterschaften* had been striving for a codification and sanction of Baltic law, first promised by Peter the Great. After considerable labor begun by Baltic jurists in 1818 and continued successively by a joint committee of the four *Ritterschaften*, a special imperial revision committee, and the Second Section, the codification was finally completed in 1845.[26] Nicholas' confirmation of the "Provinzialrecht der Ostseegouvernements," secured largely by influence at Court, seemed to strengthen Baltic German domination of the area. The Baltic provincial criminal code, however, was supplanted by the first edition of the *Code of the Laws of Russian Empire* (*Svod zakonov*) in 1832 and the Russian criminal code of 1845. In the long run this development was more significant than the confirmation of the "Provinzialrecht," for it was one of the first steps toward the standardization of administrative practice which would mold a Russian *Nationalstaat* by the end of the century.

Centralizing St. Petersburg officials also did not entirely overlook the area's German educational system, which was one of the main pillars of Baltic particularism. The secondary schools with roots deep in the Middle Ages (the Cathedral Schools of Riga and Reval functioned for seven centuries, the former until 1919, the latter until 1939) by the nineteenth century had evolved into various forms, all of which were characterized by an academic excellence and spirit, rare, if not unique, in northeastern Europe. The jewel of Baltic German education was the University of Dorpat. Originally founded in 1632 by the Swedish King Gustavus Adolphus, Dorpat was forced to close its doors during the turmoil of the Great Northern War. After repeated efforts during the eighteenth century to resurrect a university elsewhere in the Baltic Provinces, Dorpat finally reopened during the burst of activity at the outset of the reign of Alexander I, which also saw the establishment of universities in Vilna, Kharkov, and Kazan. For most of the nineteenth century Dorpat remained one of the premier universities of the Russian Empire.

The first hint of regularizing Baltic elementary and secondary education came in 1803 when the three provinces and Russian Finland were united into the Dorpat Educational Region under the general regulations of the recently founded university there. The emancipation of the Baltic serfs after the Napoleonic Wars provided the occasion for the issuance of the special school statute of 1820 for the Dorpat Educational Region, which remained essentially intact until the 1880s. According to the statute there would be three kinds of public boys' schools—municipal elementary schools, township schools, and gymnasia—and two kinds of public girls' schools—elementary schools and municipal high schools for girls.[27] The student body of the elementary schools was overwhelmingly German, that of the gymnasia and high schools completely so.

The Estonians and Latvians populated the township schools, which were now to be maintained jointly by the newly organized peasant communities with the manor lords functioning as honorary officials. These township schools were filled with the spirit and doctrines of the Lutheran Church and staffed by instructors trained in Germanic teachers' seminaries.

Each of the three provincial capitals—Reval, Riga, and Mitau—and the university town, Dorpat, was given one gymnasium. In Reval the Cathedral School maintained by the nobility of Estland retained its status and functioned as a fifth gymnasium. In addition, the district schools in Riga, Arensburg (Kuressaare), Pernau, Libau, and Goldingen (Kuldīga), were gradually converted into gymnasia with the help of subsidies from the cities or the *Ritterschaften*.

As one might expect from the highly stratified class structure in the Baltic Provinces, private schools played an important role in the educational set-up. Especially significant were the boys' boarding schools located in small country towns where classical education and intimate personal living combined to create individual school traditions and loyalties not unlike those of English public schools.[28]

Dorpat University and the Baltic secondary schools were allowed nearly complete pedagogical freedom until the 1830s. In 1833, Tsar Nicholas appointed as minister of education the president of the Academy of Sciences, Count Sergei Uvarov, an extremely well-educated man who had studied in Germany and there come to know Goethe. At first, Uvarov, a leading exponent of Russian nationalism, was preoccupied with measures attacking the language and culture of the rebellious Poles. Late in December 1836, in a secret report to the emperor, he turned to the Baltic Provinces, and proposed the upgrading of the teaching of Russian in the region's secondary schools and at Dorpat, the appointment of Russians or other Russian-speaking individuals as school administrators, the gradual introduction of Russian as the language of business in the gymnasia and schools and as the language of instruction at Dorpat, and the subordination of Baltic gymnasia and secondary schools to the imperial government rather than to Dorpat University. The last proposal mirrored provisions of the 1835 school reform for the empire.[29]

Nicholas agreed with Uvarov's proposals, and the government

swiftly enacted laws denying higher degrees to candidates who lacked a sufficient knowledge of Russian, requiring all new Dorpat professors to conduct their classes in Russian, and centralizing government control over Baltic schools. Soon, however, after news of Uvarov's memorandum had leaked out to the public, protests from influential Baltic Germans began. While certain individuals' careers suffered as a result of their outspoken opposition to Uvarov's suggested measures (Dorpat Theology Professor Ulmann being the most notorious case), the protests—combined with obstinacy—succeeded in making the new laws a dead letter and in frustrating more ambitious plans such as the abolition of Dorpat's theological faculty.[30] The nonobservance of most of Uvarov's educational dicta for the Baltic Provinces presaged his fall from imperial favor, and he was dismissed shortly after the revolutions of 1848.

The Lutheran Church also came under attack during the first part of the nineteenth century. In the eighteenth century it had maintained a privileged position in the Baltic Provinces under Russian political rule. Peter the Great and his successors left intact the Baltic Church structure inherited from Swedish times with its central organ, the high consistory, located in Dorpat. Members of the Orthodox Church could convert to Lutheranism without hindrance, and until 1747 children of Orthodox parents could be baptized as Lutherans upon the desire of their parents.[31]

The first real change in imperial policy toward the Lutherans came in 1819 when Alexander named a bishop for the Evangelical-Lutheran religion in Russia with his seat in St. Petersburg and placed all Lutheran churches and clergymen under the bishop's direction. At the same time the emperor created an evangelical imperial consistory to supervise the fulfillment of Church decrees, corollate religious books and teaching with the fundamental principles of the Church, and oversee the conduct of the clergy.[32]

Nicholas I carried his brother's religious politics much further by codifying Russia's laws and binding the various foreign faiths to them. During the 1830s his government deprived the Georgian Church of its independence, restricted the activities of the Catholic Church in Poland, and persecuted the Uniates. Only the Finnish Church was allowed to preserve its special position.[33]

The Lutherans of Livland, Estland, and Kurland were affected by the altered religious policy. A law dated December 28, 1832 abrogated the autonomous character of the Baltic provincial churches.[34] Henceforth, they would fall into the same category of "tolerated churches" applied to other non-Orthodox Christian churches. The law confirmed an Evangelical-Lutheran consistory in St. Petersburg as the highest central authority of Protestant affairs in the empire, sub-servient administratively to the Ministry of the Interior, judicially to the Ruling Senate. Hence, the Orthodox tsar became able, either by direct intervention or through his ministers, to exert influence on the structure of the Lutheran Church.

One provision of the law, later to be incorporated into the criminal code, would play a crucial role in subsequent Baltic history: the stipulation that a Lutheran clergyman could be removed from his office if he consecrated without special permission a mixed marriage between members of the Lutheran and Orthodox Churches, baptized children of such marriages, or ministered in any way to members of the Orthodox Church. In addition, the Russian law requiring a non-Orthodox subject wishing to marry a member of the Orthodox Church to sign a pledge to baptize and raise all their children in the Orthodox Church was extended to the entire Lutheran Church of the empire.

The government did agree to minor modifications of the first draft of the law, and few Baltic Germans recognized the potential signifi-cance of the final version. In 1832 the number of Orthodox subjects in the three provinces was very small; the possibility of government interference seemed remote.[35]

Meanwhile the Russian Orthodox Church had decided to initiate missionary work among the Latvian and Estonian population in the Baltic Provinces. In 1836 an Orthodox bishopric was founded in Riga to put pressure on its large and influential colony of Russian Old Believers. That same year in the ancient Russian city of Pskov on the eastern border of Livland the Orthodox Church opened a seminary for priests in which the seminarians received instruction in the Latvian and Estonian languages. The new seminary also translated religious materials into Latvian and Estonian for distribution in the Baltic Provinces,[36] a tactic the Orthodox Church used along the Volga in the Tatar language.

Orthodoxy's first opportunity for frequent contacts with the Latvi-ans and Estonians came as a direct result of economic conditions. The liberation of the peasantry in Estland in 1816, in Kurland in 1817, and in Livland in 1819, actually resulted in a worsening of the peas-ants' plight because they were given personal freedom without land. The new "serfdom of the corvée" that resulted was aggravated in the late 1830s by a succession of bad harvests which led in 1841 to famine in Livland.

In the atmosphere of despair, rumors arose that the imperial gov-ernment intended to give Baltic peasants land allotments in "warm" southern Russia. When the Baltic Governor-General Baron Karl Mag-nus von der Pahlen (1779-1863) refused to take the names of thousands of peasants hoping to sign up for land, the crowds turned to Irinarkh (ca. 1790-1877), Orthodox Bishop of Riga, who obliged them in most cases. The authorities sent troops to calm the situation, but order was restored only after a military tribunal meted out stiff punishments and the emperor had recalled Bishop Irinarkh.[37]

Four years later the story repeated itself, but this time the government was more amenable to an active policy by the Orthodox Church, though it never gave full rein to the proselytizers. The Latvians' and Estonians' motives for converting were a pathetic mixture of hope for economic betterment, feeling against the great landowners, and a desire for spiritual fulfillment. The conversion movement assumed mass proportions, with about 100,000 Lutheran peasants in Livland going over to Orthodoxy between the years 1845 and 1847. The exodus from Lutheranism petered out at the end of the decade, partly because the peasants realized that conversion would not bring them economic benefits, partly because the emperor, fearing the unrest generated by the movement, withdrew his hesitant support of the proselytizing.[38]

The conversion movement had several important consequences. First, the peasants' desperation stimulated further agrarian reform during the succeeding fifteen years, culminating in laws enabling them—though not without difficulty—to buy their own land.[39] Second, the unrest had significant religious ramifications. The conversions were legally irreversible, both for the converts and for their descendants. In the 1850s many Latvians and Estonians, disillusioned with their new faith, attempted to reenter the Lutheran fold. The Russian government, true to its principles, strove to enforce the laws binding both converts and children of mixed marriages to Orthodoxy. In response, the Baltic German nobility and clergy began energetically to defend the freedom of choice of the unfortunate souls entangled in the religious confusion, no doubt hoping to prevent an increase in Russian influence in the three provinces as well as to champion a humanitarian cause.[40] This ticklish situation would reach crisis proportions in the 1860s and again in the 1880s, proving to be the Baltic issue most embarrassing to the imperial regime. Finally, the conversion movement of the 1840s underscored a dilemma for the Baltic Germans. They needed Russian power to prevent agrarian crises from degenerating into uprisings, but aid from the imperial government would ineluctibly lead to interference with Baltic autonomy and their own privileged position.[41]

CHAPTER 7

RUSSO-GERMAN POLEMICS
OF THE SIXTIES

THE BALTIC GERMANS welcomed the accession to the throne of Alexander II with a good deal of optimism. Despite occasional difficulties with the sporadic intrusions of Nicholas' officials, the German population of around 125,000 still retained complete control of city and rural politics in the three provinces, exuded confidence in the superiority of its culture, and held the economic levers to benefit from the industrialization which would shortly burst upon the Russian Empire. The imperial governor-general in Riga, Prince Suvorov, moreover, had proven himself most sympathetic to Baltic German interests, and when the new emperor confirmed the Baltic privileges in February of 1856 all seemed to be right with their provincial world.

A new element, however, soon entered the picture. Before the reign of Alexander II all attempts at reducing Baltic autonomy had involved only official government or Church circles. In the 1860s for the first time the Russian public, through articulate nationalistic publicists, joined the debate. Between 1856 and 1860 several Baltic Germans, fearful that the preparations for the emancipation of the Russian serfs might foreshadow the extension to their area of any future reforms, published a spate of articles, brochures, and books portraying their region in idealized terms. The radical publicists Nikolai Chernyshevskii in *Sovremennik* and Alexander Herzen and Nikolai Ogarev in *Kolokol*, along with many Russian liberals vigorously challenged this rosy picture of Baltic life, pointing out how the Baltic peasantry had been exploited since its landless emancipation. The Baltic Germans attempted to gain influence with conservative segments of the Russian press, but ultimately only the right-wing newspaper *Vest'* supported their cause.[1]

Many Baltic Germans were also understandably concerned about their image in western Europe. To attempt to correct what they considered a misunderstanding of the facts, several individuals under the leadership of the publicist Julius Eckardt (1836-1908) set up a Baltic news service in the large cities of Germany, in Paris, and in Brussels.[2] While this move may have had some influence on foreign opinion, at

124

home it proved to be counterproductive because it seemed to lend credence to the Russian nationalists' charges of Baltic German disloyalty to Russia.

The discussion in the Russian press about Baltic social and political issues sharply increased in scope and in emotion after the Polish uprising of 1863 had focused public attention on the western borderlands and had caused an upsurge of Russian chauvinism.[3] The spark which ignited the dry tinder was provided by the Superintendent-General of the Lutheran Church of Livland, Bishop Ferdinand Walter (1801-1869). On March 9, 1864, Bishop Walter delivered a sermon to the Provincial Diet in which he urged the Germanization of the Latvians and Estonians in order to bring these "fragments of peoples vanishing from history . . . to an equal footing of nationality with their masters, like the religious equality they now enjoy."[4] Walter's views had long been known, but in the context of the intensely patriotic mood in Russia at that moment his sermon was monumentally tactless. It mattered little to the Russian nationalists whether the Estonians and Latvians were to become Germans on humanitarian or political grounds; for the Baltic Provinces to become completely German for any reason whatsoever was anathema to them, and the advocacy of such a policy by a prominent Baltic German was certain to enrage them.

The fiery nationalist Mikhail Katkov led the attack on Walter. In an article in *Moskovskie vedomosti* he attacked German cultural pretensions and asked rhetorically whether a German in Russia while "not forgetting his language . . . and not changing his faith," nonetheless ought not to "call himself above all a Russian and value this title?"[5] If the Estonians and the Latvians were to be lifted out of their tribal cultures to one of a great historical people they should go over to Russian culture. In the face of mounting pressure, Walter submitted his resignation as superintendent-general in mid-May.[6]

Walter's departure, however, did not allay the fears of Katkov, who tended to view all events in the Baltic Provinces through the prism of separatism. Seeing a plot whose intent it was to turn the Russian Empire into a more decentralized one of the Austrian or Turkish type, Katkov railed against attempts then underway to unify the three provinces. The ultimate danger to Russia, he warned, was a Germanization of the Baltic region that would lead to annexation by an expansionist Germany. Therefore, there was a pressing need to bring Livland, Estland, and Kurland politically and juridically closer to Russian practice. Other conservative organs such as Mikhail Pogodin's *Russkii* and Ivan Aksakov's *Den'* and *Moskva* tended to support Katkov's general analysis, though not his nearly pathological fear of separatism. The liberal press (*Vestnik Evropy, Golos,* and *Sanktpeter-burgskie vedomosti* among others) was more concerned with the German minority's antiquated medieval privileges than with separatism or Germanization, but as the decade of the sixties progressed, they too tended to gravitate toward Katkov's nationalistic attitudes. Talk of Russifying the area, previously directed only against the Estonian and Latvian population, now was extended by papers like *Moskva, Golos,* and *Moskovskie vedomosti* to include the Baltic Germans. Dorpat University especially roused their ire. V. I. Lamanskii, like Katkov, boasted that Russia did not need a German university and called for Dorpat's Russification.[7]

The imperial government attempted to tone down the debates, chiefly through selective censorship. Although both sides were affected by and complained against this policy, it seems clear that the Baltic German journalists suffered more heavily than their Russian counterparts, particularly after a decree in 1865 abolished preliminary censorship in St. Petersburg newspapers but not in Baltic ones.[8]

Emperor Alexander made no secret of his disgust with the extreme attacks on the Baltic Germans. Addressing (in French) the representatives of the Baltic nobility on October 12, 1867, the monarch castigated the press for trying to divide the nation rather than unite it: "I spit upon this press which tries to put you on the same level with the Poles. I respect your nationality and will be as faithful to it as you. I have always maintained that it is ridiculous to criticize someone because of his origins."[9]

The Baltic German leadership also contributed to this emotional atmosphere. Two of its most prominent spokesmen, Julius Eckardt and Woldemar von Bock (1816-1903), vice-president of Livland's superior court, emigrated to Germany in order to wage propagandistic battles free from the fetters of censorship. Bock's efforts were particularly intemperate. Between 1867 and 1871 he published (until 1869 anonymously) a periodical entitled *Livländische Beiträge* which contained numerous documents full of a mixture of passionate criticism of Russian society and the Orthodox Church, a legalistic defense of the Baltic German privileges, and calls for Finnish-style autonomy for the "United Baltic Duchies." Bock declared that he alone should be held responsible for his journalistic activity, but under intense pressure from Katkov the government in 1868 forced the *Ritterschaften* publicly to disavow him.[10]

The climax of the Russo-German journalistic battles of the 1860s was the remarkable polemic between Iurii Samarin and Carl Schirren. Not only was their writing notable for its biting style and frequent incisiveness (Schirren's *Livländische Antwort*, in particular, has often been called one of the greatest propagandistic works in the German language), but the two adversaries charted the main lines of argument—and action—for the respective camps in Baltic affairs for the succeeding several decades. More fateful for the history of modern Europe was the fact that all the Baltic historians who played a key role in creating Russia's public image in Imperial Germany before World War I followed directly in Schirren's footsteps. For these reasons it is necessary to examine the Samarin-Schirren debate in some detail.

Iurii Samarin, an extremely well-read man, fluent in French and German, had graduated with distinction from the University of Moscow at the age of nineteen. Deeply impressed by Pogodin's nationalistic lectures on Russian history, he subsequently fell under the influence of Slavophilism and became, with Ivan Aksakov, the movement's leading publicist.[11] In the 1850s Samarin distinguished himself in the preparations for the emancipation of the Russian serfs, arguing eloquently for granting land to the freed peasants. His first contact with the Baltic Provinces, as we have seen, occurred in the late 1840s as a member of the Stackelberg-Khanykov Commission. During the 1860s he continued his attacks on the Baltic Germans on the pages of the Slavophile newspaper *Den'*.

Samarin's major work on the Baltic Provinces—*Okrainy Rossii. Russkoe Baltiiskoe Pomor'e* (Borderlands of Russia. The Russian Baltic Coast)—appeared in six volumes from 1868 to 1876. The first volume, entitled *The Russian Baltic Coast at the Present Moment* and published in Prague in 1868, summarized Samarin's opinions of Baltic life and was the only part of the series to which Schirren addressed himself in his *Livländische Antwort*.[12] In it Samarin frequently cited material from Bock's *Livländische Beiträge* and caustically assailed the German culture of the three provinces, the rule of the Baltic nobles and their claims to privileges, and the failure of the Russian government to recognize the serious danger inherent in the situation. The Baltic Lutheran Church, Samarin claimed, bore a heavy guilt for frustrating the attempts of Latvian and Estonian peasants to join the Russian Orthodox Church. The Slavophile ideologist also saw a design to stamp out Orthodoxy in the Baltic Provinces in the persistent attempts to repeal the law requiring children of mixed marriages to be raised in the Orthodox Church.[13]

Samarin perceived a linkage between the Baltic Germans' economic and cultural policies. By aiding in the formation of a small, wealthy native elite which quickly adopted German culture, the Baltic Germans, he felt, were consciously trying to create a group that would lead the rest of the Latvians and Estonians to Germanization.[14] In the face of all the Baltic German behavior hostile to Russian interests, the imperial government, Samarin repeatedly complained, had refused to take a strong, consistent stand. In order to forestall Germanization and to prepare Estonians and Latvians for careers in the imperial civil service he strongly urged the introduction of the Russian language into the Baltic school system and its use in the provincal political administrations and courts of law.[15]

Essentially, Samarin took the Social Darwinist position that it was the right of the more numerous to dispose of the less numerous, hence weaker. Translated into Baltic terms this would necessitate a fundamental change in attitude on the part of the Baltic Germans. It was time, Samarin cried, for the Baltic Provinces to stop trying to isolate themselves from Russia and "to be convinced at last that . . . they are not an advance post of Germany . . . but a western, maritime borderland of Russia, and, therefore, to recognize entirely, unconditionally, and for all time . . . that they are bound now and in the future to the destiny of the latter."[16]

Samarin directed his sharpest attack at the foundation for the German dominance of the Baltic provinces—the privileges granted to the Baltic Germans at the time of the Russian conquest more than a century and a half before. The capitulations, he insisted, had been transactions of the Russian government with the cities and the *Ritterschaften* of conquered provinces, not bilateral treaties between two equal parties. The so-called privileges were unilateral grants of the tsar, given on the express stipulation that they would remain valid only so long as they were in accordance with the interests of the empire.[17] No "treaty" could have been made with the "duchies" of Livland and Estland, as the Baltic Germans claimed, since they never existed as political entities. "Russia," Samarin sneered, "conquered its Baltic coast from Sweden, not from the councillors of Livland or the mayors of Reval."[18]

The retention of the special rights which the Baltic Germans so tenaciously defended could only lead, he believed, to further autonomy, to a "new Baltic Finland."[19] In an emotional call to the Russian public, Samarin asked rhetorically:

Are we then obliged to bow down reverently before antiquated and worthless institutions whose single virtue, according to the assurances of their admirers, consists of the fact that under them our Baltic coast is being preserved for Germany in the expectation of some sort of better times? Is it true, as the Baltic politicians assure, that international treaties and public law have made it necessary for us to preserve and recondition forever an

advanced fortification of Germanism in a border region conquered by our ancestors?[20]

Samarin had an unambiguous answer to the questions he had posed.
Even if one conceded the legality of the Baltic Germans' privileges,
he considered them expendable: "Throughout the world the path of
historical progress is strewn with fragments of privileges, and in this
respect the Baltic region is no exception."[21]

The Russian press instinctively foresaw that the first two volumes
of *Okrainy Rossii*, published in August 1868, would be banned by the
government. Therefore, several papers immediately began to print
extensive sections of its conclusions, often with commentary. Samarin's
work received approval from a wide spectrum of Russian reviewers.
Pogodin compared his former pupil's book with Harriet Beecher
Stowe's *Uncle Tom's Cabin*. In the autumn of 1868 the government's
opposition to *Okrainy Rossii* became apparent as the censor refused
to allow it into the empire and Minister of the Interior Valuev attempted to prevent its dissemination. By November, the press had
been cowed to the point where Nikolai Nekrasov was unwilling to
risk printing an article about it in his journal *Otechestvennye zapiski*.[22]

In mid-November, Samarin was summoned before the governor-
general of Moscow, who voiced the emperor's displeasure with the
book. Undaunted, Samarin replied to Alexander shortly before Christmas 1868 in a letter staunchly defending the principles enunciated
in *Okrainy Rossii*. The author apparently expected to be subjected
to some sort of punishment for his actions, but for reasons still unclear this never occurred.[23]

Several Baltic Germans, foremost among them Julius Eckardt, who
had already emigrated to Germany, were eager to respond to Samarin.
First to begin a reply was Carl Schirren (1826-1910), Dorpat historian
and publicist. When Schirren learned of Eckardt's plans he asked him
to hold off publishing his work until the spring of 1869. Eckardt com-
plied with the request in spite of his reservations about Schirren's
aggressive journalistic style.[24]

Carl Schirren was forty-one when the first two volumes of *Okrainy
Rossii* appeared. Born in a Riga pastor's family, he studied at Dorpat,
then served as headmaster of a boys' school and taught in a gymnasium before returning to his alma mater, where he ably filled the
chair of Russian History.[25] Schirren's *Livländische Antwort an Herrn
Juri Samarin* was published in May 1869 in Leipzig. The book was
immediately forbidden in Russia, but the ban probably stimulated
public interest and helped its distribution more than hindered it. In

St. Petersburg it was sold openly under an altered title, and in Dorpat Schirren himself, as university censor, arranged for its immediate sale.

Schirren pursued several aims in the *Livländische Antwort*. He hoped to influence public opinion in Germany, but the great number of specific details of Baltic issues included in the book indicates that foreign readers were not his primary target. Somewhat more important was the attempt to paint Samarin as an enemy of the emperor as well as of the Baltic Germans. Schirren's chief goal, however, was to bolster the spirit of the Baltic Germans, and in this respect the *Livländische Antwort* had an immediate and striking impact. The historian Theodor Schiemann wrote in his unpublished memoirs: "Like me, most Dorpat students sat up the whole night to read it. Today one can scarcely imagine what a profound impact it had upon us." Georg Berkholz, editor of the periodical *Baltische Monatsschrift*, exulted to Baroness Edith Rahden: "That is a book! I have never experienced such an immediate and general effect from any other."[26]

Such emotional responses were not surprising, for Schirren's dramatic, biting prose was intended precisely to arouse the passions of his readers. The Livlander's opening statement to Samarin rang with the challenge of the medieval knight:

> Herr Samarin! . . . I speak in the name of the land with the same right as you speak in the name of race. You have neither legal authority nor an official mission; nor do I. You have deemed it proper to insult us. I deem it proper not to bear that. . . . Volunteer against volunteer—that makes the match not too unequal.[27]

Using the vague, emotional language of nationalistic polemicists of his age, Schirren labeled his opponent's principles *"Instinct"* and *"Race"* and contrasted them to *"Kultur"* and *"Recht."* He declared, "Race war translated into the language of internal politics is Russification; constructed upon the instinct of the masses it is chaos."[28] To Schirren, bigger was not necessarily better. His own people were few in number, but their quality, he clearly felt, was higher than that of Samarin's. The Dorpat professor theoretically accepted natural Russification if it would come as a result of a peaceful competition of cultures; he considered, however, such a result impossible and saw enforced Russification as an admission of the inferiority of Russian culture.[29]

Basically, Schirren tried to support an eighteenth-century idea with nineteenth-century polemics when he asserted that by defending their privileges the Baltic Provinces were defending the structure of the empire:

Against the instinct of destruction we are asserting the great privileges of law, of freedom of conscience, of human worth, even
if only for three small provinces. Saved in the province, they are
saved for the empire. We are defending them against the domin-
ion of race.[30]

The Baltic Germans in their closed democracy of the nobility had
created a refuge against the mass government that was engulfing
Russia. Tradition of this sort, in Schirren's way of thinking, was far
preferable to progress.

Schirren went to great lengths in attempting to disprove Samarin's
contention that the agreements of 1710 were merely unilateral grants
of the tsar. He held the capitulations of July 4, 1710, to be the basic
agreements and the foundation of Baltic autonomy. The general confirmations of September 30, 1710, he reasoned, were merely ratifica-
tions of the capitulations. Finally, the Treaty of Nystad provided
international sanction to the privileges.[31]

The concepts of culture, rights to land, social class, and political
power were in Schirren's ultra-conservative mind all closely connected. Samarin had charged that the capitulations of 1710 were not
bilateral treaties because the Baltic nobility had not constituted a
nation. Schirren's retort was the tenuous construction that the concept of *Ritterschaft* was inseparable from the concept of land, and
therefore an attempt to isolate social class from land was the same as
advocating starvation. He concluded that the capitulations and the
Treaty of Nystad made the Baltic nobility the representatives and
guardians of the whole land. Such was Schirren's valiant, rather pathetic defense against the decline of aristocracy in his part of nineteenth-century Europe.[32]

Schirren, in fact, evolved a lord-vassal theory of the Baltic privileges which stood the conditional grant formulation on its head; it is
the Russian rule in the Baltic Provinces which is conditional, he
argued, not the Baltic privileges. The vassal (the Baltic nobility)
had pledged loyalty to the lord (Peter the Great) who in return
granted him full rights over the fief (the Baltic Provinces). If, however,
the lord (or his successors) does not fulfill his obligations to his vassal,
then the vassal may consider his pledge of loyalty invalidated.[33]

The qualifying clauses to the privileges presented a ticklish problem
for Schirren. He bravely enunciated the legally dubious proposition,
"It is universally recognized that clauses in general confirmations cannot take the force and validity away from special confirmations," and
then attempted to show that the qualifying clauses were merely for-

131

malities by demonstrating through textual comparison the close similarity between the charter of the Livland *Ritterschaft* of 1710 and a
grant made by the King of Sweden in 1678.[34]

There was no doubt in Carl Schirren's mind about the meaning of
the Baltic privileges: "The German nation and its descendants in
these lands, and these lands for the German nation and its descendants—that is the sum of all the capitulations."[35] The Estonian or
Latvian reader must have wondered how that statement squared
with the idea of the Baltic nobility as the guardian of the whole land.

In direct response to Samarin's justification for breaking the privileges in the future, Schirren warned ominously:

> You may certainly remind us that the highway of history is
> decorated with the debris of privileges; we know that as well
> as you. But we also know that next to the fragile privileges which
> have stood in the way of the development of mankind and lie
> broken, eternal privileges stand erect on the street which runs
> past the rubble of thrones and the ruins of great empires.[36]

Though this admonition bordered on sedition, Schirren had earlier
emphasized that the Russian Empire had always been served loyally
by talented Baltic Germans, and he scoffed at Samarin's allegations
of conspiratorial intentions.[37]

What rankled Schirren most was the fact that, in his mind, an inferior people had imposed its rule on a superior one. The man who
detested "*Race*" in Samarin's thinking revealed an ugly streak of prejudice in his own. "Before one can speak in earnest of a world-his-
torical mission" he mocked, "a people must have taken off children's
shoes and accomplished something." In the Russian's character Schirren found "nothing which entitles (him) to rule: neither seriousness, moderation, perseverance nor a certain proclivity to utilize
skills. . . ."[38] In contrast to the American people, which he saw as
"industrious, practical, full of the liveliest initiative," Schirren considered the Russian "careless, easily satisfied . . . and completely incapable of creating anything significant or permanent by himself."[39]

With ill-disguised contempt the Livlander lectured his adversary:
"No, your people is not mature and not worthy of ruling over us. . . .
Chain up your instinct and teach it to control itself. . . ."[40]

Nothing remained more ingrained in Baltic Germans' consciousness
than Schirren's defiant declaration on the future:

> To stand fast—that will be our action against you, Herr Samarin,
> and your kind; to hold out—that must be the sum of our policy.
> If by doing this we lose the lawful inheritance that our fathers

have left us, at least we will not have cowardly betrayed it. And
if honor is saved, then everything is saved.[41]

Two weeks after the appearance of the *Livländische Antwort* Schirren
was removed from his chair as professor. The removal had been
proposed by Count Alexander Keyserling (1815-1891), the curator
of the Dorpat Educational Region and former marshal of the Estland nobility, as a way of defusing the tense situation. Shortly thereafter, Schirren left Dorpat for Germany to escape possible arrest. In
the autumn of 1869 the Council of the Livland Diet thanked him for
his patriotic defense of the Baltic privileges and granted him a
yearly pension equal to his former salary. In 1874 Schirren was named
professor of history at the University of Kiel, in 1878 rector. He died
there in 1910.[42]

Long after Samarin's death and Schirren's emigration their ideas
continued to have a powerful impact. Most Baltic Germans, mesmer-
ized by Schirren's pugnacious eloquence, turned to the *Livländische
Antwort* for ideological support. In retrospect it seems unwise for
them to have identified so closely with a document oblivious both to
modern political trends and to the existence of the Latvian and Estonian peoples. Edmund von Heyking, editor of the *Baltische Monatsschrift*, sensed this when he complained a decade after the publication of the *Livländische Antwort* that it had ossified the Baltic
Germans' resistance.[43] *Okrainy Rossii*, though essentially disregarded
by Alexander II, did reach—at least in partial form—the future Alexander III through his tutor Konstantin Pobedonostsev. The royal pupil
was told of the potential danger the Baltic Germans posed to Russia
and of the consequent necessity of pursuing a nationalistic course in
Livland, Estland, and Kurland.[44] Alexander III's policy of Baltic
Russification from 1881 to 1894 can thus be traced in some measure
to the teachings of a man whom both his father and grandfather had
reprimanded.

CHAPTER 8

QUARRELS AND ACCOMMODATIONS
WITH RUSSIAN OFFICIALDOM,
1855-1881

ALEXANDER II's accession to the throne and the resulting "New Era" in Russia stimulated hope for change among Baltic Germans who, while generally opposed to social and economic change, nevertheless recognized the need to revitalize the archaic administrative and judicial structure of the three provinces. The more perspicacious among them also realized from the experience of Nicholas' reign that the only hope for saving their institutions from eventual Russification was reform from within. During the quarter-century of Alexander II's reign attempts at reform were not wanting, but class and provincial disunity in most cases prevented meaningful accomplishment.

The major reform project actively considered was the four-point proposal presented to the Livland Diet by Woldemar von Bock in February 1862. Bock called on the Diet immediately to appoint a commission to draw up a plan: (1) to petition the imperial government for the creation of a superior court for the Baltic Provinces; (2) to restore the right of manor ownership to all citizens of Livland; (3) to restore to the small cities of Livland the representation in the Diet which they had enjoyed until the end of the sixteenth century; and (4) to create a united Diet for the three provinces.[1]

Bock's proposal failed miserably. The plans for a united Diet and a superior court both miscarried in preliminary discussions, and in 1864 the Diet denied representation for Livland's small cities. Only after bitter resistance from conservative nobles, which worsened relations between the *Ritterschaft* and the bourgeoisie, was the proposal for manor ownership finally adopted in 1866. The Diets of Kurland and Estland had granted the same right the previous year.[2]

Early in the 1860s the ancient patriarchal Baltic judicial system, in which only nobles occupied the judges' chairs, also came under scrutiny, particularly after the State Council laid down basic principles for judicial reform in Russia.[3] The crucial question was, of course, whether reforms would be part of a remodeled Baltic judicial system or a segment of the new Russian system (which became law in 1864)

134

for Latvian and Estonian participation in provincial government and
to be applied to the Baltic Provinces. The imperial government inclined toward the latter view and said that any special modifications
of the new Russian judicial system would have to be approved by the
Baltic governor-general.

The governor-general in 1864 was Baron Wilhelm Lieven (1799-
1880),[4] the last Baltic German to hold that post. At Court, Lieven and
Minister of the Interior Valuev spoke up for letting the three provinces
work out their own judicial reform proposal. This argument carried
the day, but at the cost of the governorship; though an old personal
friend of the emperor, Lieven had to resign under intense pressure
from the nationalist press, which charged that he was abetting separatism.

Lieven's sin had been the creation of a Baltic central judicial commission composed of members chosen from the *Ritterschaften*, the
large and small Baltic cities, and Dorpat University (but not from
the peasantry). In St. Petersburg and in the Baltic Provinces great
hopes were placed in the commission which was charged with drawing up a reform proposal by November 1, 1865. The commission,
however, proved to be a dismal affair which was unable to come up
with a coherent plan for change. Its members, overcoming internal
dissension, finally were able to unite on matters such as criminal and
civil process and mortgage law, but could not agree on the pivotal
issue: a judicial administration for all three provinces, city and
countryside alike. Ultimately, the imperial government failed even to
put the commission's modest proposals into effect.[5]

The collapse of the Bock plan for Baltic unity and the failure of the
judicial commission killed the last real opportunity for the Baltic
Germans to effect necessary change and concurrently solidify regional
autonomy. It is true that even if either of these efforts had succeeded,
strong pressure from Russian nationalists might have caused their
cancellation. Katkov, for example, in 1864 assailed the proposed united
Diet and superior court in a series of articles in *Moskovskie vedomosti.*[6] Nonetheless, the Baltic Germans' inability to put their own
house in order was a virtual invitation to St. Petersburg to intervene.
Soon thereafter the imperial government decided to introduce the 1864
Russian legal reform into the Baltic Provinces in stages, and in consultation with the local estates—a concession not granted to the western *gubernii* of the empire.

Basic administrative reform within each individual Baltic province
proved as elusive as on the regional level. In Livland alone, between
1864 and 1880 fourteen different proposals for reform were submitted
to and turned down by the Diet. The most significant included plans

for changing the Livland Diet from a body of individual members not responsible to any constituencies into a representative assembly. The story was similar in the ultra-conservative Diet of Estland, while at the opposite extreme Kurland's nobility in 1878 actually considered— and rejected by a vote of only 257 to 190—the idea of introducing the Russian zemstvo, the elective rural council which did have peasant representation.

Aside from moral arguments and the ever-present threat of intervention from St. Petersburg, the rapid growth in population and economic strength of the Latvians and Estonians should have indicated that it was imperative to grant those groups a share in running provincial affairs. But the inflexible argument of die-hard nobles and burghers that any concessions to other nationalities would inevitably lead to the end of Baltic German dominance always won enough support to block any fundamental province-wide political reorganization.[7]

In a sense the Baltic nobles were prisoners of their own creation. Their self-governing *Ritterschaften* were based more on the principle of consensus than on majority—a situation not unlike the Polish *Sejm* until the late eighteenth century. In this preparliamentary system where each member represented himself alone it was far more difficult for an individual to give way than it would have been in a modern representative system. For many nobles, "holding out" was a matter of honor, a moral principle which, though perhaps impractical, it nevertheless seemed essential to try to uphold.

While all attempts at Baltic reform at the regional and provincial levels during Alexander II's reign came to naught, there was significant movement in rural and urban local reform. Largely through pressure from the imperial government, three important pieces of legislation were enacted: the rural community police law of 1866, the Livland rural administrative reform of 1870, and the extension to the Baltic cities in 1877 of the Russian municipal statute.

According to the rural community law of 1866, worked out by the *Ritterschaften* after prodding from St. Petersburg, the manor lord's jurisdiction and police authority over the peasant community were terminated. On the peasant land the community elder would exercise police power with limited powers of punishment. On manor land the manor lord or his agent would retain police power but without powers of punishment. Persons arrested by the manor police were supposed to be handed over to the communal or parish courts or the district police, depending on their class and the nature of their crime.[8] As the Latvian historian Schwabe (Švābe) has said, "The reign of the German master's whip over Latvian and Estonian backs was ended."[9]

The largest of the Baltic Provinces extended this reform into rural administration. In January 1870 the Livland Diet passed an act formally establishing near-parity between manor and peasant community.[10] The basic unit of rural self-government, the church assembly, was divided into church and parish assemblies, the former body retaining control over church and school affairs, the latter receiving responsibility for all other matters. In the new church assembly peasant delegates were given full voting rights; in the parish assembly the peasant community elders were enfranchised. Despite these formal changes, the peasantry in Livland did not achieve real decision-making power.

A thorough overhaul of the medieval system of Baltic municipal government was a matter of first priority. Years later Baltic Germans wistfully reminisced about the pomp and dignity of the old, closely knit government of Riga,[11] but the sad fact was that there, as in the other Baltic cities, only about 2 percent of the inhabitants belonged to the citizenry, and the overwhelming majority of these were Baltic Germans. Members of other nationalities, as long as they were Christians and Russian subjects, were not legally excluded, but usually it was difficult for them to gain the professional training required for admittance to the guilds, and hence they were effectively denied participation in the government of the city.[12]

Reform proposals were bandied about in the Baltic metropolis, Riga, during the 1860s, but the ruling circles stood firm against a move toward cultural autonomy for every nationality, and the imperial government rejected a plan of the mayor's commission since it was itself engaged in working out a new municipal statute for all of Russia.[13]

That new statute, based upon the Prussian Municipal Statute of 1853, became law in 1870 and was put into effect in stages, region by region, coming in 1877 to the Baltic Provinces.[14] In the place of the city council and two guilds, a municipal assembly would henceforth be elected by all male subjects of the Russian Empire, twenty-five years of age or older, who paid taxes on property or trade and were not in arrears on those taxes. The voting lists were arranged in three classes. The wealthiest individuals, whose taxes taken together made up one-third of the total tax sum, were grouped in class I; the moderately wealthy, whose taxes made up another third, in class II; and the remaining bulk of the taxpayers in class III. The classes elected equal numbers of representatives to sit in the municipal assembly. The size of the assemblies varied from city to city, Riga with seventy-two representatives having the largest.

The imperial government granted several special concessions to the

Baltic cities in the new statute. Although the administration of city finances and services was transferred to the new municipal assembly, the former city magistrates remained as the municipal judicial authorities. The government also granted an exception to the voting requirements to the literati, who could receive the franchise by paying an annual tax. Finally, the law permitted the use of the German language, at least temporarily, in the new municipal institutions.

The holding of elections for the new municipal assembly made the Latvians and Estonians urban political forces to be reckoned with in the third electoral class.[15] The electoral campaigns were spirited, and although in Riga a nearly completely German party won victories in all three classes, Mitau's contest demonstrated social rather than nationality conflict, and in Reval nationality cooperation was strikingly successful. There a reform ticket in the third electoral class consisting of twelve Germans, six Estonians, and six Russians handily defeated the conservative former city councillors and guild elders.[16] Against the sorry picture of rancor and intolerance, not to mention ineffectiveness, which the urban patriciates and the *Ritterschaften* exhibited in the 1860s and 1870s, the city voters' first exercise of the franchise was a breath of fresh air and indicated that at least some Russian reforms could benefit the Baltic Provinces.

Meanwhile, the Baltic Germans continued to consider the special position of the German language as the core privilege granted by Peter the Great. Attempts to impose the Russian language on the city administrations of Reval and Riga began after the ink had scarcely dried on the capitulations of the Great Northern War, but these intrusions were short-lived. In 1773, Catherine the Great expressed her desire for local Baltic officials to learn the Russian language. There is no evidence of mass compliance with her wish. The next indication of government concern with the language question came nearly a half-century later. In 1817, in connection with the liberation of the Kurland peasantry, an imperial decree was issued which stated that the reports of the peasant commission to the emperor and to offices in other provinces (except Livland and Estland) were to be in Russian.[17]

Nevertheless, the first part of the provincial law code of 1845 made the primacy of the German language explicit: "In the offices of the Baltic vice-royalty business in general is handled in the German language, except in the peasant communal courts where it is handled in the local Latvian or Estonian language."[18] To facilitate correspondence with the imperial authorities and with authorities in other provinces, special translators were provided to translate the German original into Russian.[19]

The governor-general could correspond with St. Petersburg in

Russian and could converse in Russian with his retinue in the Riga castle, but as soon as he had to deal with the provincial authorities he was required by law to use the German language. When the populace had dealings with the governor-general it was also to use German; Russian was used only if the matter went to the ministries or the Senate. Even the highest administrative body in the province staffed by the imperial government, the so-called Gouvernementsregierung, was divided into two sections, one which conducted its business in German, the other in Russian.[20]

An illustration of the peculiar language situation in Baltic administration is a survey taken in 1849 which showed that of 343 chancellery officials of the imperial authorities in the Baltic Provinces only 80 knew enough Russian to be able to carry on business in that language.[21] In retrospect it seems remarkable that the imperial government was willing as late as 1845 to grant such far-reaching concessions to the German language; and considering the woefully weak position of the Russian language in Baltic administration, it is not surprising that opposition to the policy of deference to German developed very rapidly.

In 1847, Minister of the Interior Perovskii introduced a proposal to require Russian as the language of internal business for all imperial authorities in the Baltic Provinces, and after three years of debate the law was passed by the Committee of Ministers and confirmed by the emperor in January 1850. As usual, though, thanks to intervention by Baltic Germans at Court and sympathetic Russian officials the law gathered dust for more than a decade and a half. Finally, in 1867 the Committee of Ministers called for the carrying out of the 1850 law, and Alexander, perhaps feeling the pressure of the press campaign, confirmed the committee's decree.[22]

A few weeks after this confirmation Alexander visited Riga and received the representatives of the city and of the four *Ritterschaften* in the Riga castle on the bank of the Dvina. Speaking in Russian instead of the French or German that he usually used in the Baltic Provinces, the emperor declared:

> I wish, gentlemen, that you too belong to the Russian family and form an indivisible part of the Russia for which your fathers and brothers and many of you yourselves have spilled your blood. That is why I am justified in hoping that also in peaceful times I will find from you cooperation with me and with the representatives of my sovereign power, in order that the measures and reforms which I consider necessary and useful are carried out.[23]

Despite subsequent assurances by Alexander that existing institutions would be respected and a temporary order postponing implementation from Baltic Governor-General Petr Al'bedinskii, the Livland *Ritterschaft*—unlike its peers in Estland, Ösel, and Kurland—refused to be appeased. The Diet voted to petition the emperor for retention of German as the language of business in the province, choosing to ignore the fact that Alexander had specifically stated he would not accept any petitions for a modification of the language decree. Minister of the Interior Petr Valuev (1814-1890), himself half Baltic German by birth, was appalled at the tactlessness of the Livland nobles. In his diary entry for November 19, 1867 he called the petition "extremely unreasonable" and Livland's Governor August von Oettingen (1823-1908) "a participant and culprit in this unpardonable and unreasonable demonstration."[24] After a short comedy featuring Oettingen and Governor-General Al'bedinskii rushing back and forth between Riga and St. Petersburg, the former received an imperial reprimand and resigned his post as governor.[25]

On November 4, 1869, the Committee of Ministers, chaired by the emperor, definitively decreed that, beginning January 1, 1870, all the business of the crown authorities would be conducted in Russian. Again, the Livland *Ritterschaft* broke ranks with its sister provinces and composed a futile petition cataloging its complaints against the imperial government's intrusion into the administrative, educational, and religious life of the province and asking for a return to the autonomy it had previously enjoyed. The petition was rather self-servingly dubbed the "Great Action," but the greatest thing about it was the resentment it aroused both in St. Petersburg and in the other three *Ritterschaften*, all of which refused to associate themselves with it, although Estland's nobles later did submit a short supplication of their own.[26]

The language edict of 1869 was yet another of the measures designed to standardize governmental operations in the Russian Empire. It was not intended to single out the Baltic Germans for special punishment; in fact, the imperial government had recently acted more harshly in language questions in the Ukraine and Belorussia where in 1863 and 1866 the printing of popular books in the local languages had been forbidden. Similarly, the abolition of the Baltic vice-royalty (*general-gubernatorstvo*) in 1876 followed similar measures taken earlier by Alexander II in Belorussia and Little Russia. More importantly, as comments by Al'bedinskii, a lengthy entry by Valuev in his diary, and a government memorandum of 1870-1871[27] all indicate, the prevailing sentiment in St. Petersburg was still against radical Russification of the Baltic area. While the Baltic

Germans would have to acquiesce in the curtailment of their administrative and judicial autonomy, the government opposed their cultural Russification, reserving that fate for the Latvians and Estonians.

Just at that time events were occurring in western Europe that would have a profound significance for the Baltic Germans: the Franco-Prussian War and the establishment of the German Empire. The Baltic Germans had always taken their ethnic identity more or less for granted. Though they jealously guarded their linguistic, educational, and religious prerogatives, most spoke French at social gatherings until well into the nineteenth century and felt no conflict in serving the Russian Empire. Germany could by definition only exist as a spiritual homeland, since it was a political jumble of nearly forty assorted and competing units.

All this changed in 1871. The German triumph of arms and national unification sent many Baltic Germans into paroxysms of joy. Bismarck had deep sympathy for the Germans on the shores of the Baltic, and he protested in 1865 against the "barbarism" of Russia's religious policy there, but after 1871 he pursued a course of good-neighborly nonintervention.[28] Despite the Iron Chancellor's restraint, suspicion of the vigorous new European power grew in Russia and with it the fear of an eventual German attempt to annex the Baltic provinces à l'Alsace-Lorraine. In a diary entry in 1889, Count Alexander Keyserling, the noted scientist and politician who had been a close friend of Bismarck since university days in Berlin,[29] wrote that he had come more and more to the conclusion that the chief cause for the loss of provincial autonomy was this Russian fear of annexation: "It is a delusion, I feel, but it is futile to preach against it."[30]

Iurii Samarin was among those who had urged a vigorous defense of Russian interests in the Baltic region, warning that otherwise the question of Estland, Livland, and Kurland could easily become at any time "the younger brother of the Schleswig-Holstein question."[31] Samarin demanded promotion not only of the Orthodox Church but also of Russian education in this area. German schools, in the opinion of Samarin, were primarily instruments of Germanization. If the progress of Germanization were to be halted, there had to be Russian schools in the Baltic Provinces.[32]

During the 1860s and 1870s the Baltic school system expanded considerably. Various administrative bodies, dominated by the manor lords but with active peasant participation, directed the rural elementary schools that did not receive any funding from the imperial Russian government. The *Ritterschaften* of Livland, Estland, and Kurland opened teachers' seminaries to train the faculties of these schools.[33]

Baltic municipal education that had consisted of municipal schools and urban gymnasia was supplemented in the 1870s by the secondary *Realschule*, actually a Russian creation (*real'noe uchilishche*), which quickly spread to Reval, Riga, Dorpat, and Libau. Concentrating on nonclassical studies, the Baltic *Realschulen* resembled the Russian model in their organization into six or seven classes with commercial and general divisions. The system of girls' schools also took part in the expansion.[34] Finally, partly through a generous subsidy from Alexander II, Livland received provincial gymnasia which absorbed the two best-known of the private schools. The one new school, named "Gymnasium Kaiser Alexander II," was located in Birkenruh near Wenden (Cēcis) and had its charter confirmed in 1883 as a classical gymnasium with German as the language of instruction. The second provincial gymnasium was located in Fellin (Viljandi).[35]

Many Estonians, Latvians, and Russians resented the fact that the Baltic elementary and secondary schools were dedicated to preserving the societal status quo, but by the European standards of the day they were of high quality. The most convincing testimony to this assessment was the warning against Russifying the Baltic schools, given in 1864 by none other than the Russian nationalist Katkov:

> May God protect us from wishing that any kind of vandalic raids be made upon the school system existing there on foundations common to the entire civilized world, or that their gymnasia be lowered to the pitiful level of our educational institutions. . . . Let the instruction both in the gymnasia and the university there be in German: to raise protests against it would be on our part a false national pride from which, thank God, we are completely free.[36]

During the period of Alexander II's rule modest efforts were made to improve the teaching of the Russian language in Baltic schools and to have Russian used in correspondence between school officials and imperial authorities. These attempts made little progress, largely due to the extreme scarcity of Russian teachers and administrators in the Baltic schools.[37]

At the top of the Baltic educational establishment Dorpat University experienced its "golden age" during Alexander II's quarter-century reign. In 1862 the emperor named as curator of the Dorpat Educational Region—a post with decisive influence on the university—Count Alexander Keyserling, former Marshal of Estland's Nobility and an accomplished geologist. Married to the eldest daughter of former Russian Minister of Finance Kankrin, he possessed numerous ties in the highest circles in the capital. A cosmopolitan, cultivated person, Keyserling felt that Dorpat should not restrict its horizons to being a provincial university with purely Baltic interests. Rather, he held, it should consider the feelings of its financial supporter, the Russian state, and strive to become an international mediator between Western and Eastern culture.[38] While Dorpat never fulfilled Keyserling's dream because of obdurate provincial conservatives like Carl Schirren, it nonetheless functioned as a first-rate academic institution whose graduates performed valuable services for the Russian Empire.[39]

Dorpat, once called by Adolf Wagner "the most German of the German universities,"[40] did differ in significant respects from its peer institutions farther to the west. In an age when German universities gradually turned into specialized professional schools, Dorpat retained within the framework of the Baltic German life style a tinge of humanism, a residue of the spirit of Alexander and Wilhelm von Humboldt. Unlike the aloofness customarily shown by professors in Germany, the Dorpat faculty, which included many individuals of wide reputation, usually maintained close personal relations with the students. As in Germany there were student corporations, but at Dorpat none was exclusively for nobles.[41] Even the fencing duels that were a common feature of German student life were modified in the Baltic; those who chose to duel at Dorpat kept their heads protected, thereby avoiding the worst wounds. The ethos of Dorpat of the 1860s and 1870s resembled that of the University of Berlin a half-century earlier or of the Weimar of Goethe's last years. J. Hampden Jackson has described Dorpat's atmosphere as "reminiscent of Trinity College, Dublin,"[42] while an American who looks at photographs of old Dorpat is struck by the architectural similarity to some of Harvard's nineteenth-century buildings.[43]

Dorpat was by no means without enemies. As we have seen, beginning in the 1860s the Russian nationalist press, recognizing the university as the intellectual wellspring of Baltic German particularism, began attacking it vigorously. As the century drew to a close, Russian critics, including some former Dorpat students, asserted that the university's academic standards were seriously declining.[44] Much of this type of criticism can be dismissed as jealousy or as politically motivated, but beneath the exaggerated rhetoric was an important truth: while undeniably serving the state, Dorpat University nevertheless was alienating itself from Russia. There was no doubting the arrogant attitude of many young Baltic Germans toward the empire of the Romanovs, summed up by Baron Eduard von Dellingshausen (1863-1939),[45] who recalled that he and his comrades felt that "Russia was there in order to be governed and dominated by Balts;

if they didn't desire our services any longer, we wouldn't force ourselves on them."[46] Baltic German students, wrote a Russian Dorpa-
tenser, P. Krasovskii, did not want to learn anything about Russia and
made the atmosphere such that Russian students felt more at home in
France or Germany than at Dorpat.[47]

Reading the memoirs of the novelist and linguist Petr Boborykin, a
Russian who greatly admired many aspects of the "Livonian Athens,"
one cannot fail to note the insufferable behavior of the Baltic German
students toward their Russian comrades at Dorpat. Boborykin, who
had spoken German since childhood, recalled that the Germans
scarcely ever spoke with Russians in classes. "We only came into
contact with the Germans," he explained, "we didn't live with them."[48]
It seems clear, though, that the poor relations—or absence of relations
—between Russians and Germans at Dorpat resulted as much from
class differences as from ethnic ones, the Russians usually feeling
inferior in dress and manners to their wealthier German fellow
students.[49]

The student corporations at Dorpat, granted official recognition in
1855 and permission to wear their colors publicly in 1862, were
profoundly political organizations despite their formally apolitical character. Like the guilds and the *Ritterschaften*, they were set up basically to protect the Baltic Germans' ethnic identity against the non-
German surroundings—to provide a "conscious education for the
nationality struggle."[50] The Dorpat German corporations aggressively
asserted their nationality, singing songs like *Was ist des Deutschen
Vaterland?* and *Deutschland über alles* which were certain to offend
Russian ears, particularly after 1871. There was a Russian corporation
at Dorpat called *Ruthenia*, but it was frequently disbanded and reorganized and had difficulties in gaining full admission to the student
government.[51]

Even the faculty was not above indulging in petty national exclu-
siveness. Pavel Viskovatov, biographer of Lermontov and professor
of Russian language and literature from 1873 to 1895, was a graduate
of Leipzig University where he had studied under Mommsen, Ranke,
and Droysen. Yet his impressive German education and his cultured
and amiable personality did not prevent his nearly complete social
isolation in Dorpat, and Viskovatov could never forgive the Baltic
Germans for it.[52]

On the other hand, the first Russian to hold the position of curator
of the Dorpat Educational Region, the jurist Andrei A. Saburov (1837-
1916), enjoyed great popularity during his five-year tenure, especially
since he moved the region's seat back to the university town from
Riga where his predecessor had transferred it in 1870.[53]

During the reign of Alexander II attempts to increase the compulsory study of the Russian language and to introduce it into the daily business of the university made little headway, as the proposals fell victim to the compromises of the standard "special panel" of the Ministry of Education.[54]

A second Baltic institution of higher education received its charter in 1861. This was the Riga Institute of Technology, which was financially underwritten by the Livland *Ritterschaft*, the Riga business community, and the Riga city council. At its founding the Riga school was the first institute of technology in the Russian Empire to include all the technical disciplines. Its purpose was to train students for all branches of industry, engineering, farming, and trade. As a private school it had only limited rights of state certification, but the burgeoning Russian industrial complex cared more about performance than formalities, and Riga graduates had no difficulty finding employment. By the mid-1870s the Riga Institute of Technology was on firm financial and academic footing.[55]

With regard to the relations of the Lutheran and Orthodox churches in the Baltic Provinces, nothing was more symptomatic of the pre-ecumenical age than the so-called Cathedral Question[56] that made headlines in 1869-1870. It revolved around the Russian government's request that all Baltic officials, including teachers who were Lutherans, attend prayers for the emperor in Orthodox churches on state holidays. The Livland and Estland *Ritterschaften* protested and offered to pray for the emperor in Lutheran churches at the same hour as the Orthodox services. The government refused, so Count Keyserling resigned his post as curator. Following his example, Baron Nikolai von Dellingshausen (1827-1896) resigned as marshal of the Estland nobility; and after an unpleasant feud within the Livland *Ritterschaft*, so did Baron Gustav Nolcken (1815-1879), as marshal of the Livland nobility.[57]

The members of the Kurland and Estland *Ritterschaften* finally agreed to the formal cathedral visits, but even after Count Shuvalov told Nolcken's successor, Nikolai von Oettingen, that the government would be prepared to support the Livland nobles in judicial and agrarian questions and on the matter of the reconverts if their representatives would only appear a few times in an Orthodox church in their uniforms, they still clung to their obdurate refusal. On the surface their tactic seemed vindicated when the government dropped its demand a few years later, but it was a Pyrrhic victory in that it alienated many influential persons in the capital.

The central religious problem in the Baltic Provinces throughout the second half of the nineteenth century was the fate of the so-called reconverts—those Estonians and Latvians who had converted to Orthodoxy during the 1840s and later wished to reenter the Lutheran Church and to bring up their children in that faith. The attempted movement back to Lutheranism began at the end of the 1850s. The Baltic agrarian situation had improved somewhat over the miserable conditions of the previous decade, thereby reducing the expectation of economic gain from membership in "the tsar's faith." In addition, the converts' children were excluded from the Lutheran schools, which were generally of a higher caliber than the Orthodox ones. Another irritant was the obligatory written pledge to raise children of mixed marriages in the Orthodox faith, a requirement seen as coercion by many of the converts whose own attachment to Orthodoxy was tenuous.

Since conversion from Orthodoxy to another faith was prohibited by law in the Russian Empire, the disenchanted peasants took matters into their own hands. Marriages outside of the Church by a simple exchange of vows proliferated, and parents often baptized newborn infants themselves. Passive resistance to the Orthodox clergy was common, and it was not unheard of for peasants to take Lutheran sacraments under false names in distant parishes. The *Ritterschaften* of Livland and Estland and the Baltic Lutheran Church attempted to arrange various compromises with the government,[58] but it was not until religious disorders in Livland took a serious turn in 1864 that the emperor embarked upon the first stage of action.

Alexander dispatched a trusted member of his staff, Count Vladimir Bobrinskii, on a fact-finding mission to the troubled province. On April 15, 1864, Valuev wrote that Bobrinskii, who had just returned, felt that the Latvians and Estonians "are not falling away from Orthodoxy, rather they never belonged to it."[59] Three days later Bobrinskii submitted his report. It was a stinging indictment of the government's religious policy. He estimated that scarcely one-tenth of the official total of 140,000 Orthodox Christians in Livland genuinely embraced Orthodoxy. Labeling the condition there "constraint of conscience," Bobrinskii concluded:

> Your Majesty! It has been painful for me, both as an Orthodox Christian and as a Russian, to see with my own eyes the degradation of Russian Orthodoxy through the public disclosure of this official deception.[60]

When the Marshal of the Livland Nobility Prince Paul Lieven met Alexander two weeks later, the emperor confided that he had been shaken by Bobrinskii's report.[61]

Rural unrest increased during the autumn, and by 1865 it became apparent that some kind of concrete action was imperative to an easing of the religious crisis. Baltic Governor-General Count Petr Shuvalov felt that peace could be restored only by military force or by declaring full religious freedom.[62] The latter course was politically unpalatable, first of all because of the huge loss to the Orthodox Church it would involve, and secondly because a similar freedom would also have to be granted to the Catholics whose Church had played an important role in the Polish uprising two years earlier. Military force in a religious matter would be catastrophic for Russia's already tarnished image in western Europe.

Alexander chose a middle path: a gradual conversion of the next generation to Lutheranism. Influenced by Prince Gorchakov and probably by Bismarck's "barbarism" remark, the emperor on March 19, 1865, issued a secret order which lifted the requirement of the written pledge to raise children of mixed marriages in the Orthodox faith.[63] A publicly announced addition to the *Polnoe sobranie zakonov* was deemed impossible because of public opinion.

The order was communicated to the Lutheran consistories and to the Orthodox clergy, but it soon became clear that the latter group was ignoring it. Thereupon the monarch had Platon, the Archbishop of Riga and Mitau who had previously overseen the repression of the Uniate Church in Poland and Lithuania, transferred to the Cossack center of Novocherkassk on the lower Don. Platon's successor, Veniamin, proved to be more willing to accept the new practice regarding mixed marriages.[64]

Alexander's temporizing half-measure, however, had a bit of "the emperor's new clothes" about it: the problem of adults wishing to reconvert could not be ignored. The Baltic Lutheran clergy was indeed on the horns of a moral dilemma: refuse sacraments to those desiring them on genuine religious grounds and thereby be derelict in its pastoral duties, or give the sacraments and thereby be in violation of the law of the land? The Lutheran Synod decided to meet the issue head-on, as it voted overwhelmingly against secret ministering to those wishing to reconvert. The pastors, left to make personal, open decisions, overwhelmingly chose to give the sacraments openly. Of 105 active Lutheran pastors in Livland, 93 performed functions which were punishable by suspension or removal from office, and some of the other 12 did not do so only because no members of the Orthodox Church resided in their parishes.[65]

As the number of legal proceedings against Baltic Lutheran pastors rose steeply in the late 1860s and early 1870s, protests from abroad were heard. Adolf von Harless, president of the evangelical consistory for Bavaria, wrote a book on the situation,[66] and in North Germany the Baltic Germans found an ally in Adolf Stöcker, who would later rise to prominence as Prussian court preacher and demagogic anti-Semite. The most influential foreign support for the Baltic pastors came from the world-wide Evangelical Alliance, founded in 1846 in London to aid victims of religious persecution. One of its members, Leopold von Wurstemberger, visited the Baltic area in 1870 and returned to write a book on the religious turmoil there. The following year the Alliance sent a hastily put-together international delegation led by an American theologian to meet Imperial Chancellor Prince Gorchakov in the town of Friedrichshafen on the German shore of Lake Constance. One of the American delegates unable to attend at the last minute was Samuel F. B. Morse, the inventor of the telegraph. The Friedrichshafen discussion rapidly broke up after it became evident that Gorchakov and the petitioners had totally different conceptions of religious freedom, but the Alliance circulated its report of the meeting throughout western Europe.[67]

On July 22, 1874, the emperor, influenced by the remonstrances of the Evangelical Alliance and the Livland Consistory and by the advice of Count Shuvalov, ordered the suspension of legal action in still-outstanding cases against Lutheran pastors. Because of the position of Catholicism in Poland, Alexander made no formal declaration in favor of religious liberty, but former members of the Orthodox Church who had subsequently been ministered to by Lutheran pastors were henceforth unofficially to be considered Lutherans.[68]

Alexander's order signified tolerance of conversions in practice, if not by law. Officials began to close their eyes when pastors welcomed peasants back to Protestantism; perhaps 30,000 Latvians and Estonians returned to their old faith during the ensuing period of calm. Many Lutheran pastors abused their new freedom. According to Traugott Hahn (1848-1939), one of Baltic Protestantism's best-known clergymen, these pastors considered the acceptance of reconverts now to be legal and the question of conscience ended for them. They began to admit peasants, in Hahn's words, "because of provincial Church politics, yes even because of German-confessional politics."[69]

The relaxation of the pressure on the Lutheran Church more than any other deed endeared Alexander II to the Baltic Germans. Despite the inroads the Russian language and system of administration made in the three provinces during his reign, Alexander's sense of fairness in the religious question, his sponsorship of secondary education in Livland, and his open affection for the *Ritterschaften* won him great popularity. Moreover, every informed person knew the depth of Pan-

Slavic and anti-German feeling which existed in other circles in St. Petersburg, especially around the heir apparent. It was thus with deep foreboding that Baltic Germans received the news on March 1, 1881, that the Tsar-Liberator had fallen victim to a bomb of the People's Will organization.

CHAPTER 9

TRIUMPHS AND FRUSTRATIONS
OF ADMINISTRATIVE RUSSIFICATION,
1881-1914

THE FRENCH HISTORIAN Victor Bérard told of a Russian peasant prophesy that "as the first Alexander had delivered us from the Frenchman and the second from the Pole, so the third is destined to relieve us of the German."[1] Alexander III had indeed, unlike his father, harbored anti-German feelings,[2] and, as we have seen, his tutor Pobedonostsev acquainted him with Samarin's writings on the Baltic Provinces. Nonetheless it came as an unpleasant shock to many Baltic Germans when Alexander III became the first Russian monarch other than the baby Ivan VI and the ill-fated Peter III not to confirm the privileges which Peter the Great had granted to the Livland and Estland nobility. The nobles never actually received a definitive rejection of the privileges; the closest Alexander came to repudiating them was his statement in 1885 that he regarded the Baltic Provinces as just another part of the empire.

Before we examine the Russification of the 1880s and 1890s let us briefly look at the declining demographic situation of the Baltic Germans. Their number stood at 180,423 in 1881, but by 1897 it had dropped to 152,936[3]—largely because the Russification had induced half-Germans to change their nationality, but also because of the attractiveness of the young national movements to the children of recently Germanized Latvians and Estonians. While the Baltic Germans had lost nearly 28,000 persons, the Latvians and Estonians had gained over 375,000.[4]

During this period there was also a pronounced rural-to-urban population movement as a result of the rapid industrialization of the area. Until 1880 the German population in the Baltic countryside had continued to grow, as natural increase, some immigration from Germany, and the addition of socially aspiring Latvians and Estonians had more than compensated for the incipient migration to the cities. After 1880 the situation changed; nearly all of the Baltic German population decline from 1881 to 1897 was in the rural areas. Whereas

28.5 percent of the Baltic Germans had lived on the land in 1881, by 1897 only 20.3 percent did. By 1897 the rural Baltic Germans—that is the nobility, the relatively few burgher manor owners, country pastors, doctors, and foresters—were isolated islands in a sea of non-Germans. In that year in the rural population of Kurland, for every German there were 32.9 Latvians, 1.7 Russians, and 1.5 Jews; in Livland the ratio on the land was 27.0 Latvians, 29.3 Estonians, and 1.05 Jews for every German; and in rural Estland for every German were 2.2 Russians and the staggering number of 73.3 Estonians.[5]

The Baltic German urban population suffered only a slight absolute loss during the period 1881-1897, but because of the massive influx of Latvians and Estonians from the countryside the percentage of Germans in the city populations declined markedly. In Riga, for example, their actual number continued to increase slowly, but their proportion in the city's total population sank in the following manner:[6]

1867	42.8%
1881	39.4%
1897	23.7%
1913	13.5%

Moreover, when it occasionally appeared that new immigrants from Germany might significantly bolster the Baltic German community, the nationalist Russian press raised an outcry.[7]

Baltic German participation in the imperial government was always vastly disproportionate to its minuscule fraction of the empire's population. The staffing of the Russian officer-corps by Baltic Germans resembled, though on a much larger scale, the important role of the Transylvanian Saxons in the Austrian army. They also became the most important group of non-Slavs in the Russian civil service. The Russian ambassadorship to Great Britain became virtually a Baltic German post; for 93 of the 105 years between 1812 and 1917, Baltic noblemen represented the tsar at the Court of St. James.[8] Erik Amburger's exhaustive study of the Russian bureaucracy from the reign of Peter the Great to 1917 mentions 2,867 officials, 1,079 of them non-Russian. Of these, 355 were Baltic Germans—that is, approximately one-eighth of all officials, and nearly one-third of all non-Russians. Of the 355 Baltic Germans, 243 (68.5 percent) were members of or descendants of families belonging to one of the four *Ritterschaften*.[9]

Russian nationalists tended to exaggerate the number of Baltic Germans in high government posts, though perhaps they—and some historians—gained a distorted impression from the fact that a great many other officials (143 in Amburger's study, for example)[10] who were born abroad spoke German as their mother tongue.

In any event, the number of Baltic Germans in the higher ranks of the civilian and military hierarchy varied greatly at different times. There was, in general, a steady growth in their number and significance until the mid-nineteenth century. Thereafter a decline set in, caused by several factors. First, the anti-German thrust of Pan-Slavism and the policies of Alexander III and Nicholas II made Baltic Germans begin shunning government service, and at the same time the government less eager to employ them. Finally, the better market for agricultural produce and secondary rural products (alcohol, lumber, bricks) demanded more intensive work on the nobles' estates, which did not allow time for imperial service.

Meanwhile, locally, the imperial government enlivened the already heated debates within the Baltic Diets on self-reform of provincial government above the parish level by asking the *Ritterschaften*, in October 1881, how the zemstvos could be accommodated with the constitutions of Livland, Estland, and Kurland. Unmindful of the way St. Petersburg had already circumscribed the power of the zemstvos, many Baltic nobles reacted with alarm. In 1883 and 1884 two conferences of the *Ritterschaften* overcame their differences and sent a reform plan to Governor Zinov'ev of Livland in April 1886. The plan gave participation in economic affairs to representatives of the Latvians and Estonians in the parish and district assemblies in which the manor owners would have the same number of deputies as all the other classes combined; the provincial Diets, however, would remain strictly a noble affair. The government never formally acted upon this reform plan, Minister of the Interior Tolstoi now telling Marshal of the Livland Nobility Baron Friedrich Meyendorff (1839-1911)[11] that since the zemstvos in Russia were by this time themselves in need of reform it would be pointless to extend them to the Baltic Provinces.[12]

The Baltic Germans asserted that the Russian government, fearful of a potential united front of Germans, Latvians, and Estonians, prevented reform as part of its "divide and rule" policy.[13] That analysis is sound as far as it goes, but the Russian government need not shoulder all of the blame for lack of meaningful reform. As usual, the Baltic Germans presented a sorry picture of disunity, with Estland this time playing the role of maverick. More important, the proposed reform was too little, too late. Had the nobles been able to agree on a reform proposal during the 1870s it might have stood some chance of acceptance under the regime of Alexander II. As it was, because of the obduracy of the conservatives within the Diets,[14] reform above the parish level languished until threats from Alexander III's government pushed the nobles into action. By that time conditions had changed, and the Baltic Germans were left holding a halfway measure which pleased neither the imperial authorities nor the local nationalities.

The Manasein Senatorial Inspection is dealt with in detail elsewhere in this volume. Several circumstances surrounding the genesis of the inspection are, however, revealing about Baltic German behavior and, therefore, require our attention. In the first place, Marshal of the Livland Nobility Heinrich von Bock (1818-1903)[15] may have helped bring the inspection about when in an audience with Alexander III in July 1881 he protested government inaction against recent anti-German violence in Livland. The same is true for a delegation of Baltic nobles which insinuated to Minister of the Interior Ignat'ev that Alexander II's assassination could in part be traced to Latvians and recommended delegating the nobility even greater power over the rest of the Baltic populace. Ignat'ev reported this meeting to the emperor and recommended a senatorial inspection to ascertain the real nature of the situation.[16]

When the possibility of an inspection in the Baltic Provinces became known in the capital, Bock and Councillor of the Diet Arthur von Richter welcomed it, since they felt that the Livland nobles had nothing to hide and would benefit from the disclosure of their efficient rule.[17] Considering the anti-German feeling in many government circles, the sentiment for granting the Latvians and Estonians a greater share in Baltic governance, the possibilities for manipulating public opinion, and not least, the depth of hostility of large segments of the native population to the Baltic Germans, Richter's and Bock's judgment was a pathetically naive one.[18]

Baron Wilhelm von Wrangell (1831-1894), the marshal of the Estland nobility, took a more realistic view of a senatorial inspection. The historian Alexander von Tobien had passed along a warning from the former minister of justice, Count Konstantin von der Pahlen, about the potential dangers involved, so Wrangell composed a report to the emperor, recommending that Estland be exempt from any inspection, because Alexander when he was grand duke had often taken the cure in Hapsal (Haapsalu) and hence already knew the conditions in the province first-hand.[19] Apparently Wrangell's flattery worked, for in January 1882 on the recommendation of Ignat'ev the emperor named Nikolai Manasein[20] to lead an inspection of Livland and Kurland, but not Estland. As we have seen in Part One of this volume, Manasein's report to the emperor recommended a complete overhaul of the police and judiciary, a redrawing of the administrative boundaries of the Baltic Provinces, the introduction of the Russian zemstvos, centralization of control over Baltic secondary education, and Russification of

Dorpat University. We shall now turn to the Baltic German response to the centralizing measures which the government of Alexander III undertook in the Baltic Provinces.

On April 13, 1882, a law introduced Russian as the language of business in all provincial, municipal, and district draft board offices in the three provinces. Inductees not knowing Russian could, however, ask questions and receive answers in their native language.[21]

The following January the government compelled all its bureaus, including legal offices, in the Baltic Provinces to accept petitions and other papers written in Russian, Latvian, or Estonian as well as in German. This measure, while safeguarding the rights of all three of these non-German peoples, especially served as another entrance for the Russian language since, as had recently been the case with the Ukrainian language, the law referred to the Latvian and Estonian languages as "dialects."[22]

Many leading Baltic German officials saw the handwriting on the wall but tried to avoid using Russian in communicating with imperial officials nonetheless. The most celebrated case in this regard was that of the Mayor of Reval, Wilhelm Greiffenhagen (1821-1890),[23] who was ultimately removed from his post by the emperor as a result of his dispute over the language of correspondence with the governor of Estland, Prince Sergei Shakhovskoi.[24] Riga's mayor, Robert von Büngner (1815-1892) was also dismissed on similar grounds.[25]

On February 22, 1885, an *ukaz* demanded the exclusive use of Russian in Baltic mixed crown-estate offices.[26] The stage had been set for the introduction of the Russian language into all branches of Baltic administration. The governors of Livland and Estland, Zinov'ev and Shakhovskoi, provided the final push when they described to the emperor the insubordinate behavior of the Riga and Reval mayors and of Count Woldemar von Tiesenhausen (1845-1915),[27] marshal of the Estland nobility. Alexander was reportedly so angry that he instructed the president of the Committee of Ministers to draft a law that would settle the administrative language problem in the Baltic Provinces once and for all.

On September 14, 1885, Alexander, while vacationing in Fredensborg near Copenhagen, confirmed the most extreme language measure yet applied to Livland, Estland, and Kurland. The law made the Russian language compulsory for the business of all mixed crown-estate offices, provincial judicial and police offices, and peasant offices in dealing with higher authorities. For peasant affairs German, Latvian, or Estonian could be used but had to be accompanied by a Russian translation.[28]

With the examples of Greiffenhagen's and Büngner's dismissals fresh in mind, Baltic German officials were not likely to disobey the new law, especially after the penalty for wilful disobedience—exile or even resettlement in Siberia with loss of class privileges—was published in the Baltic German-language press. Aside from a few initial problems, there was general, if grudging, acceptance of Russian as the new official language.[29]

On November 9, 1889, a law ordered the introduction of Russian into the internal proceedings of Baltic municipal governments. Proclamations of the city authorities to the public could also be in any of the other three principal languages of the area.[30] Despite the formal application of this law, delegates to the municipal assemblies of many Baltic cities later circumvented it by meeting for "preliminary consultations" in which the language used was German.[31]

The ultimate effrontery to the Baltic Germans came in 1893 with the renaming of Dorpat "Iur'ev" and Dünaburg "Dvinsk." As a symbolic gesture of defiance the editor of the *Dorpater Zeitung* refused to call his paper the *Jurjewsche Zeitung*, renaming it instead the *Nordlivländische Zeitung*.[32]

The one institution of Baltic German administration in which the Russifiers failed to achieve their linguistic aims was the *Ritterschaft*. In October 1887 Shakhovskoi wrote to the minister of the interior asking for the introduction of Russian as the language of internal business for all *Ritterschaft* organs by January 1, 1888. The request was denied. In June 1890 Shakhovskoi repeated his proposal, but again the Ministry of the Interior refused to act.[33] The Diets and other noble-run bodies, along with the peasant communal administrations, were the only institutions which retained their native languages for internal business until World War I.

The Baltic Germans suffered another defeat locally with regard to judicial reform. Their failure to reform the Baltic judicial system during the 1860s left the region with outmoded and inefficient courts at a time of increasing pressure for the standardization of the branches of government within the empire. The 1864 judicial reform had given Russia a legal procedure among the most liberal in Europe. Inevitably, the Baltic judicial system, symbolized by its noble judges in white waistcoats, became a prime target for the modernizers.[34]

In 1880 the State Council instructed the Ministry of Justice to institute without delay a general judicial reform in the Baltic Provinces, and four successive laws from that year until 1884 decreed, then postponed the introduction of the office of justice of the peace into the area. Manasein's inspection report in 1884, as has been pointed out in Part One, criticized the Baltic judicial system from top to bottom. On June 3, 1886, the emperor confirmed a law drawing the outlines

for a basic Baltic court reform on the Russian model of 1864.[35] Later
that month, Alexander sent his brother, Grand Duke Vladimir, on an
official mission to inspect Baltic military establishments. Actually, the
main purpose of the trip was to inform the leading Baltic German
circles that the emperor was intent on reform and would brook no
opposition to his plans. Vladimir, who was known to be upset about
reports of religious persecution in the Baltic Provinces, had been
warned by State Secretary Aleksandr Polovtsov not to be used by the
local German population to defend its dominant position.[36]

The grand duke was supposed to make a speech about the reforms
in Reval and Riga, but each time decided against it. In Dorpat, the
last point of his tour, immediately after a reception in the great hall
of the marketing center, Governor Zinov'ev instructed the representatives of the city, university, and the nobility who were in attendance
to reassemble in a room on the first floor of Count Manteuffel's house.
Georg von Oettingen described the scene:

> We stood tightly pressed together in the small one-windowed
> room. The grand duke strode into our midst and after a few in-
> troductory words read a rescript (or a speech?) of the emperor
> from 1858 in which the necessity of a closer union of the Baltic
> Provinces with the empire was stressed. He repeated in the name
> of the emperor that from now on things would unquestioningly
> proceed in this way. After he had carried out the task, which was
> visibly unpleasant for him, he bowed, clicked his heels together
> with a clanking of spurs, and quickly left us amidst the oppressive
> silence of his listeners.[37]

There could no longer be any doubt about the crown's intentions.
In 1887 a St. Petersburg newspaper wrote that the lawyers of the
capital were eagerly awaiting the judicial reform in the Baltic Provinces. Permits to practice law were being given so often in St. Petersburg that many of the lawyers were having difficulty earning a living
and hence had decided to leave for the Baltic area as soon as the
Russian judicial reforms were introduced there.[38]

The imperial government soon began to fulfill the hopes of the
eager Petersburg lawyers. Manasein, since 1885 the minister of justice,
put two proposals before the State Council on the last day of 1887.
After nearly a year and a half of debate, in which several Baltic
Germans participated, that body forwarded a draft law to the emperor who on July 9, 1889, signed two orders transforming the Baltic
judicial system.[39] Russian officials named by the Ministry of Justice
replaced the noble judges, and Russian criminal and civil procedure,
including public and oral proceedings, was introduced. Generally, the

courts were put more directly under St. Petersburg's supervision. The municipal judicial councils (*Magistrate*), a vestige of the city councils of pre-1877 days, were abolished. Baltic private law remained in force with minor changes.

In a move which detracted greatly from the beneficial aspects of the reform, the legislation made Russian the official language of legal proceedings with occasional exceptions granted to the native languages in the dealings of the new justices of the peace and some peasant courts. Despite Manasein's stated intention that the presidents of the peasant superior courts must know Latvian or Estonian, few if any did. Hence, as in Russian Poland, the government assigned translators to the courts to enable communication between the judges and the local inhabitants, but unfortunately these poorly paid individuals usually lacked legal training and often misinterpreted the courts' explanations.[40]

The reform of peasant institutions created an important new post called "commissar for peasant affairs" (*kommisar po krest'ianskim delam*). It has been pointed out elsewhere in this study that many of the commissars for peasant affairs did indeed carry out their duties honorably, but there were frequent examples of careerists who flaunted and misused their power. Governor Zinov'ev, one of the more even-handed imperial officials and one who came to respect many Baltic German institutions even as he attempted to modernize the outmoded ones, criticized over-zealous subordinates who were insensitive to local conditions.[41]

The government completed the destruction of the old Baltic judicial system in 1892 when it issued a new edition of the imperial code of laws. The Baltic Provinces were no longer listed among the specially governed areas and would henceforth be administered under the general laws of the empire.[42]

The Russification of the Baltic police system preceded that of the judicial system by a year and resembled it in its genesis and consequences. As early as 1866 the State Council had ordered such a move, but it was only on February 27, 1885, that an imperial *ukaz* finally provided for a thoroughgoing Baltic police reform to be worked out with the Russian system as the model. From 1886 to 1888 the State Council with the participation of the three Baltic governors and representatives of the *Ritterschaften* debated a draft proposal of Minister of the Interior Tolstoi. Largely due to Governor Zinov'ev's insistence, the manor police were retained, though shorn of most of their feudal powers. On June 9, 1888, the emperor confirmed the project as law.[43] Russian became the language of business for the district and city police, and thereafter the government usually appointed Russians as police officials, many of whom did not know the native languages. Predictable difficulties ensued, but the law effectively broke the class character of the Baltic police system.

One measure enacted during Alexander III's reign was clearly advantageous to the Baltic Germans. As part of the conservative counterreforms in the late 1880s and early 1890s the government passed a law on June 11, 1892, which restricted the electorate of the cities throughout the empire.[44] The law scrapped the three-class voting system, raised the property qualifications for the franchise for property owners and institutions, and tightened the guild qualifications for suffrage.

The urban Baltic Germans, therefore, gained in voting strength relative to their less affluent Estonian, Latvian, and Russian neighbors. The law of 1892 proved to be the key factor in maintaining German municipal administrations in Riga, Mitau, Dorpat, Weissenstein (Paide), and Hasenpoth until World War I. In Riga, in order to retain control, the Germans were forced into an electoral alliance by 1901. The world had truly turned, for they made the pact with the Russians of the city in order to block the Latvians from capturing the municipal administration. In 1905, after negotiations with Latvian leaders broke down, the Riga Germans again embraced the Russians and repeated their triumph at the polls. Shady tactics also helped the German cause. Wealthy Germans often parceled up large properties and nominally gave title to many individuals, thereby increasing the number of German voters.[45]

Restrictive laws, ethnic alliances, and electoral shenanigans could not withstand the force of demography in several cities. In 1897 the Latvians captured their first municipal government in Wolmar, their second in Tuckum the following year, and another in Wenden (Cēcis) in 1906. A Latvian-Estonian coalition took the ethnographic border town of Walk (Est.: Valga; Lat.: Valka) in 1901, and in 1904 an Estonian-Russian coalition assumed power in Reval. Thereafter, Estonian slates captured the city government of Werro (Vōru) in 1906, Hapsal in 1909, Pernau in 1913, and Wesenberg (Rakvere) in 1914.[46]

The *Ritterschaften* managed to weather serious threats to their formal control of the provincial governments. Manasein's inspection report proposed redrawing the administrative boundaries of the Baltic area to create two provinces divided along the Estonian-Latvian linguistic border. The imperial government spared the Baltic nobles the trouble of opposing this idea. St. Petersburg knew that a reshuffling of the Baltic provincial borders on ethnographic lines would set a precedent for the Poles whose "By-Vistula" province also contradicted ethnographic realities. Moreover, the earlier sympathy in the capital for the Latvians and Estonians had ebbed considerably as the potential danger to Russia of the nationalist movements became evident.[47] The government dropped Manasein's second major administrative proposal—that of introducing the zemstvos into the Baltic Provinces—after a law in 1890 which by reducing the participation of peasants[48] made certain that the German nobles would dominate these bodies if they were extended to Livland, Estland, and Kurland. Moreover, the imperial government viewed with disfavor an all-class body which would bring together Baltic Germans, Latvians, and Estonians.

The strongest attack on the central governing functions of the *Ritterschaften* came in 1889. A special commission of the Ministry of the Interior chaired by future Minister V. K. Plehve recommended a reform of the land-tax system of the Baltic Provinces and the emasculation of the *Ritterschaften* by substituting the Russian statute of the nobility for the more powerful Baltic one. Concurrently, Governor Zinov'ev was advising the replacement of the Livland Diet and the Council of the Diet by a government body which would better serve the interests of the whole community.

Several events then combined to tip the scales in the Baltic nobility's favor. The Livland *Ritterschaft* agreed to a deal with Governor Zinov'ev in which he would drop his demand for alteration of the provincial government in return for their acquiescence to equal taxation standards for peasant and manor land. Meyendorff and Oskar von Ekesparre (1839-1925),[49] marshal of the Ösel nobility, skillfully presented the *Ritterschaften's* case in special sessions in St. Petersburg, and in 1890 the Ministry of War unexpectedly intervened strongly in favor of maintaining the political status quo in the Baltic countryside in order to keep the excellent mobilization and support system of that strategically crucial area in experienced hands. In the face of all these developments the imperial government decided not to tamper further with the Baltic rural governmental system.[50] The *Ritterschaften*, though they had lost much of their power through the police and judicial reforms, continued until World War I to hold on to the rights of manor policing, taxation, and, in Estland and Kurland, church patronage.

The Revolution of 1905 in the Baltic Provinces will be discussed in greater detail in the Parts of this volume on the Latvians and Estonians. The violence made a profound impression on the Baltic Germans, but it is important to note that their loss of life was relatively small: from 1905 to 1907 only eighty-two of them were killed.[51] While some Baltic Germans began rethinking their relationship to the Russian Empire,[52] most reacted to the revolutionary upheavals by hav-

ing still another go at reforming the untenable governmental structure of the three provinces. Alas, neither the Baltic Germans nor the
Russians had learned from the lessons of the past. Several bodies
heavily dominated by the Baltic Germans debated the issue but once
again could not agree to a fundamental change of the provincial
rural government or to a thoroughgoing land reform. When in 1907
a district government reform proposal was agreed upon, the imperial
government rejected it because of the democratized version of the
zemstvos it advocated. The Latvians and Estonians, considering that
they constituted by far the majority of the rural population, were also
understandably not content to have mere parity with the large landowners in district government. As in the 1880s the Baltic Germans
had offered concessions which several decades earlier might have
been perceived by the Latvians and Estonians as consonant with
their fair share of power but which now fell far short of their rising
expectations.

CHAPTER 10

RELIGIOUS TURMOIL

Iɴ ᴛʜᴇ ʟᴀsᴛ ᴛᴡᴏ ᴅᴇᴄᴀᴅᴇs of the nineteenth century Russian governmental modernizers striving to create a national state increasingly turned to the ancient Muscovite notion of a state-church as one of the vehicles to unify the disparate areas of the realm. When St. Petersburg began energetically to advance the cause of Orthodoxy it inevitably clashed with many of the empire's non-Russian peoples including the Lithuanian and Armenian Catholics and the Tatar and Kazakh Moslems. In the Baltic Provinces the government's activist religious policy of the 1880s and 1890s created a unique situation. Not only did St. Petersburg encourage a conversion movement to Orthodoxy and hinder the activity of the competing faith, Lutheranism, but it also subjected tens of thousands of people—the Latvian and Estonian reconverts to Protestantism—to extreme pressure to rejoin the Orthodox fold while also persecuting the Lutheran pastors who continued to minister to them. This merciless policy stood in stark contrast to the government's behavior toward the other large group of reconverts in the empire—the 40,000 Volga Tatars who had returned to Islam. Though deportations after riots and demonstrations occasionally did occur, the Tatars were usually encouraged to remain Orthodox Christians not by the stick of repression but by the carrot of superior education, and the authorities allowed Moslem missionaries to compete with Orthodox clerics for the allegiance of the Tatars and neighboring peoples.[1]

Systematic Orthodox activity in the Baltic Provinces began in the 1860s and rapidly accelerated. The spearheads of the campaign were groups of Orthodox Brotherhoods which in 1882 were centralized into a single organization directed by the high Orthodox clergy in St. Petersburg. While the consolidated Baltic Brotherhood concentrated on educational and charitable works, it also translated many Orthodox pamphlets of anti-Lutheran character from Russian into Latvian and Estonian.[2]

In the early 1880s churchmen launched an intensive effort to woo the Latvian and Estonian peasantry to Orthodoxy, often stressing worldly benefits to accrue from conversion rather than theological dogma.[3] The proselytizers had but modest success, the number of converts in Livland between 1874 and 1894 being about one-seventh that of the mass movement of the 1840s. Unlike the earlier movement, after 1885 there were also conversions in Kurland. In Estland thousands converted in the mid-1880s, but the flood dwindled to a trickle a few years later.[4] All in all the movement did not begin to alter the area's fundamentally Protestant character. By 1904 there were 282,000 Orthodox Christians in the three provinces, yet they still comprised only about 10 percent of the Baltic population. About one-quarter of them were Russians. To accommodate the increased numbers of the faithful the Holy Synod, aided especially by Governor Shakhovskoi and private Russian contributors, constructed many new churches.[5] The two most noteworthy additions to Orthodoxy in Estland were a convent in Püchtiz and the massive Alexander Nevsky Cathedral atop the Domberg in Reval which to this day adds a discordant note to the city's (i.e. Tallinn's) otherwise Gothic skyline.[6]

Coupled with the upsurge in Orthodox activity, the government undertook a series of measures designed to weaken the Baltic Lutheran Church. In 1885 authorization for the construction and repair of non-Orthodox churches was made dependent on the permission of the Orthodox authorities.[7] The following year Alexander III confirmed two laws detailing the procedure for the alienation and seizure of private property for the needs of Orthodox churches, prayer meetings, cemeteries, clergy and schools in the Baltic Provinces. Shortly thereafter the Senate in St. Petersburg ruled against the centuries-old practice of the Baltic Lutheran clergy's collection of real estate taxes from Orthodox Christians, and in May 1886 it was officially forbidden.[8] Many Baltic German Lutherans, bitter at what they considered a punitive measure, soon began raising the rents on those of their properties housing Orthodox tenants and evicting those who could not or would not pay. They then turned the extra revenue from those tenants who did pay over to the Lutheran Church. Both Governor Shakhovskoi and Governor Zinov'ev complained that they were powerless to halt this tactic.[9]

The government also began interfering in the internal affairs of the Baltic Lutheran Church. From 1885 on the synods had to submit the minutes of their meetings in Russian translation to the minister of the interior, and two years later they were admonished to discuss only questions which had been cleared with the provincial governors in advance. In 1890 and 1891 the government abolished the Lutheran consistories in Riga, Reval, and Ösel and ended *Ritterschaft* rights to appoint the lay presidents of the three remaining Baltic consistories.[10] Another annoyance was a law of June 1891 declaring that the Lutheran Church would have to begin keeping its registers in the Russian language.[11] Finally, as a petty irritation, the minister of the interior forbade collections in Lutheran churches for foreign missions.[12]

As vexing as the harassment of the Lutheran Church was, it paled in comparison to the agony which the government caused by its treatment of the reconverts and Lutheran pastors. On July 26, 1885, Alexander III rescinded his father's ordinance of twenty years before (which had never officially been made a law) and reinstated the requirement of the pledge in mixed marriages. Moreover, the new order had retroactive force: children who had been baptized, raised, and confirmed in the Lutheran Church and knew nothing of Orthodoxy were suddenly claimed by the Orthodox Church and were compelled, in the event they married a Lutheran, to raise their children in the Orthodox faith. From 1865 to 1885 in Livland no fewer than 6,770 children of mixed marriages concluded before 1865 had been baptized in the Lutheran Church; estimates for the three provinces ran as high as 16,000. Furthermore, 5,391 boys and girls who were officially on the Orthodox Church's registers had been confirmed in the Lutheran Church.[13]

Showing a rare unanimity, the representatives of all four *Ritterschaften* traveled to St. Petersburg in the fall of 1885 to present their religious grievances to Alexander III. Their attempt failed this time because of the dubious value of Baltic German intermediaries at Court. When the emperor refused to receive the representatives personally, Meyendorff asked Adjutant-General Otto von Richter (1830-1903), chief of the emperor's commission on petitions, to deliver the four petitions to His Majesty. Richter, a Livland noble and pious Lutheran who had had a distinguished career at Court and in the military, was most probably the clandestine supplier to Meyendorff of the personal reports to the emperor from the governors of Livland. Nonetheless, on this occasion he showed great caution, asking Alexander whether he, Richter, would be permitted to send him the four addresses from the *Ritterschaften*. Richter added that he had already held onto the petitions for four weeks because he had considered them "untimely" and therefore could not foresee any success.[14]

Alexander sent Richter the gruff message, "Send me the papers." Two days later (November 20, 1885) the emperor categorically rejected the petitions, declaring that "such requests shall not be made again. . . . His Majesty views the Baltic provinces exactly like the rest of Russia and will rule them with the same fairness but also according to the same law, without any privileges whatsoever."[15]

One could hardly have imagined a more total disavowal of the concept of Baltic autonomy. Alexander von Tobien later wrote in an acerbic manner that a denial of the requests was scarcely avoidable after a Lutheran nobleman from Livland had characterized them as untimely and unsure of success. But the episode did not show a weakness in Richter's character. Baltic Germans at Court were influential only as far as they tried to affect *Russian* politics. As soon as they attempted to lobby for provincial interests they became unacceptable, for inevitably they were viewed as foreign elements. Otto von Richter saw this; the Livland *Ritterschaft* and its official historian Tobien did not.[16] At best, the Baltic Germans at Court could mobilize the help of influential Russian statesmen and try to make certain that the complaints of their comrades would come to the emperor's attention. Baltic Germans, however, continued to sit on and influence the decisions of committees in St. Petersburg which in the 1880s worked out laws affecting Estland, Kurland, and Livland.

Meanwhile, government authorities were investigating adults professing the Lutheran faith to learn if, in fact, they had ever been on the Orthodox Church's rolls. These persons—the true "reconverts" in contradistinction to children for whom parents had made the choice of Lutheranism—were often subjected to intimidation by the police.

Late in September 1886 Zinov'ev wrote an official letter to Donat, Orthodox Bishop of Riga, spelling out his position on the reconverts. The governor considered all persons registered in the Orthodox Church's books, no matter what their current practices, to be Orthodox Christians. If they married according to Lutheran ritual their marriages would be unrecognized by law; children of such marriages would be considered illegitimate. If the children were brought up in the Lutheran faith the parents would, according to article 190 of the criminal code, be subject to prison terms of from eight to sixteen months.[17]

The indefatigable Meyendorff protested Zinov'ev's letter to Minister Tolstoi and to Procurator Pobedonostsev, asserting that the only solution would be to remove the reconverts' names from the Orthodox registers.[18] This the government refused to do, because even the resulting large movement to Lutheranism in Livland[19] would have been numerically insignificant compared with the loss in other parts of the empire to schismatic sects and to the Uniate Church, if freedom to convert from Orthodoxy had been allowed.

Like the rest of the tsarist empire, though to a lesser extent, the Baltic Provinces suffered from (or enjoyed!) being undergoverned. Perhaps this lack of manpower explained why, in the main, the imperial authorities refrained from prosecuting the Estonian and Latvian reconverts and preferred to use legal action against them as a threat.

The government's reluctance to prosecute, however, did not extend to the Lutheran clergy. Most pastors, naturally viewing the denial of Protestant religious needs with horror, were drawn inexorably into the same extralegal behavior in which they and their predecessors had engaged twenty years earlier.

All told, between 1884 and 1894 the government instituted 199 proceedings against pastors in Livland and a few in Estland and Kurland. To defend the pastors the Livland *Ritterschaft* engaged two experienced lawyers, a Baltic German for the Riga district court and a Russian Orthodox who declared himself to be a proponent of religious freedom for the court of appeals in St. Petersburg. Although numerous handicaps were imposed upon the defense and verdicts of guilty were the rule, the sentences imposed were somewhat less harsh than the allowable maximum. Most of the pastors were suspended from office for several months, some were permanently removed from office, nine were banished from the Baltic Provinces, but none was imprisoned.[20]

The Russification in the Baltic area, particularly the campaign against Lutheranism, attracted wide attention in Germany. As relations between Germany and Russia cooled after 1887 Baltic German emigrés began soliciting aid for their people. A few extreme voices were impatient for action. The Riga-born lawyer Johann Christoph Schwartz, writing in the *Preussische Jahrbücher* in 1890, called for a preventive war against Russia, or at least, in the event that Russia herself declared war, for the liberation of the old German Baltic colonies and the restoration of Poland as a joint Habsburg-Hohenzollern effort.[21]

Konstantin Pobedonostsev, Procurator of the Holy Synod, became the chief recipient of foreign protests about the Baltic religious situation. One of the most complex and controversial figures in late nineteenth-century Russia, Pobedonostsev was not lacking in knowledge of the Baltic Provinces. His wife was the former Ekaterina Engelhardt, a member of a prominent Baltic German family that had moved to Smolensk Province, and one of his few close friends was Baroness von Rahden. Pobedonostsev's dialogues with a delegation of Swiss pastors, with the Evangelical Alliance, and with Hermann Dalton, a German subject who had served as pastor of the Reformed Church in St. Petersburg for thirty years, all exhibited his iron will and refusal to compromise on the Orthodox Church's special status in the Russian Empire. The issue of freedom of religion, he felt, was merely serving as a smoke screen for a German political campaign against the empire of the Romanovs and an attempt to prevent the amalgamation of the Latvians and Estonians with Russia.[22] Dalton's *Open Letter* to Pobedonostsev was a less eloquent *Livländische Antwort* twenty years later, but one which did make some telling points against the Procurator and was translated and distributed in western Europe and the United States.[23]

The extremely bad name Russia was earning abroad ultimately had an effect on imperial policy. After numerous protests by the Livland *Ritterschaft* had failed, a memorandum they sent through Minister of Justice Murav'ev finally induced Alexander to issue an order in June 1894 directing the minister of the interior to drop the cases against the Lutheran pastors or to let them expire. Two years later, Nicholas II on the occasion of his coronation issued a general declaration of amnesty that included crimes under which the pastors had been sentenced.[24]

The accession of Nicholas II to the throne made no change in the legal status of the reconverts. More than 35,000 persons who considered themselves Lutherans remained on the Orthodox Church's rolls, although a period of milder treatment toward them ensued. Legal change came only with the Edict of Tolerance of April 17, 1905 and the October Manifesto of that same year.[25] Conversion from Orthodoxy was then allowed, and in 1906 in Livland 4,215 individuals went over to Lutheranism. The following year 1,147 converted, and then the rate leveled off to 700-800 annually, a drop which may be explained both as the result of an attempt of the Russian bureaucracy to hinder the exercise of the newly granted freedom and of the growing divisions within the Baltic Lutheran Church between Germans on one hand and Latvians and Estonians on the other. In 1906 the Livland *Ritterschaft* voted to abolish the highly unpopular right of the noble patron to choose the local pastor, but, heeding the opinion of the Livland Synod, it refused to split up the provincial Lutheran Church into German and Latvian branches. By the eve of World War I relations among the three nationality groups within the Baltic Lutheran Church had become acrimonious.[26]

The enforcement of the mixed-marriage pledge, aside from causing the serious dislocations in the lives of thousands of Latvians and Estonians, also was a key factor in the Russification of many Baltic Germans, usually one or two generations after the mixed marriage.[27] Students of this phenomenon have unfortunately failed to explain what they meant by "Russified," so quantification is elusive. The question of when one changes one's nationality is essentially a psychological and sociological problem. In any event the data needed to judge stages of "alinguistication," "acculturation," and "assimilation" are lacking for the Baltic Germans who—to the consternation of the historian—preferred oral to written discussion of this matter.[28]

Historians agree, however, on the general outlines of the process. Russification occurred more frequently among the rural nobility than among the more numerous urban bourgeoisie. Secondly, the most typical individuals who changed their nationality were old conservatives with a strong allegiance to the Russian Empire, ambitious young careerists, and rural nobles with economic ties to the Russian interior. Thirdly, Russification was proportionately greater in Estland than in the other two Baltic Provinces. Finally, the Baltic Germans as a group clung to their nationality more tenaciously than the descendants of people who had emigrated to Russia from Germany in the mid and late nineteenth century.[29]

Interestingly, it took the Revolution of 1905 to generate the formation of Baltic German nationality organizations in Livland, Estland, and Kurland—nearly four decades after the Estonians and Latvians had founded theirs. Led by the nobility and the literati, the German organizations engaged in a variety of educational, financial, cultural, and electoral activities. By 1914 they had enrolled nearly a quarter of the estimated 162,000 Germans of the three provinces.

The imperial government, however, did not allow this awakening ethnic consciousness to get out of hand. In 1908 it forbade the formation of an organization of all Germans in the Russian Empire which had been proposed in Reval. More important, after several years of tolerating the resettlement of over 20,000 Volga and Polish Germans in the Baltic Provinces, the government reconsidered its policy shortly before the outbreak of World War I. It began to present obstacles to further German colonization and considered instead sending Russian farmers in on a large scale.[30]

CHAPTER 11

RUSSIFICATION IN EDUCATION

Senator Manasein believed that the Russian educational program should strive to amalgamate border regions with the center of the empire by instilling respect for and understanding of the Russian language and Russian history and literature among the non-Russian inhabitants. In order to accomplish this aim in the Baltic Provinces he proposed first of all installing effective government control over the elementary schools and making Russian a compulsory subject in them. Andrejs Plakans, in Part Three of this volume, vividly describes how difficult it was to enforce even such modest measures against the opposition of a stubborn Baltic German manor lord. Second, Manasein called for putting the teachers' seminaries under the direct supervision of the Ministry of Education and similarly making Russian the language of instruction in them. Finally, he advocated moving the administrative center of the Baltic educational system from the center of particularism, Dorpat, to Riga where, as we have seen, it had temporarily resided in the 1870s.[1] The Council of the Livland Diet, though not privy to the Manasein Report, saw the handwriting on the wall and in 1884 issued a Russian-language defense of the Lutheran elementary schools in the province, hoping to correct what it saw as misconceptions and to counter recent statements that it considered slanderous.[2]

It was too late, however, for propaganda to be efficacious. In February 1885 an imperial *ukaz* ordered the compulsory instruction of the Russian language in all primary and secondary schools of the Dorpat Educational Region, and Russian soon became the medium for official school correspondence and reports. In 1886 the government transferred the Lutheran rural elementary schools and teachers' seminaries from the sphere of the Ministry of the Interior to the Ministry of Education in order to lessen the control of the nobility and the Church. This functionally logical measure, however, had been applied to the Baltic Orthodox schools a full decade earlier. That same year the imperial authorities definitively removed the seat of Baltic education from Dorpat to Riga.[3] Meanwhile, Mikhail Kapustin, the curator of the Educational Region, set about firing "unreliable" teachers and filling the vacancies in collaboration with the provincial governor. He also explained that children should speak and think in Russian in order to feel spiritual unity with the fatherland.[4]

The Baltic Germans' worst fears were realized on May 17, 1887, when the emperor confirmed a project of the Committee of Ministers entitled "Temporary Supplementary Regulations for the Administration of the Elementary Schools in the Provinces of Livland, Kurland, and Estland." Going beyond Manasein's recommendations, the law introduced Russian in place of Latvian or Estonian as the language of instruction for all subjects except religion and church singing into all but the two lowest grades. (In 1892 the government extended the use of Russian to the very lowest grades with the exception of the same subjects.)[5] The law also gave the curator, through his subordinates, decisive power over the hiring and firing of teaching personnel, texts, and educational programs.

In establishing the "Temporary Regulations" the Russian government was essentially asking the Lutheran Baltic Germans, Latvians, and Estonians to continue financially to support and to share in the administration of their elementary schools which would now, in theory, have a thoroughly Russian character. The provincial Diets reacted by renouncing their responsibilities in building, maintenance, and administration of the elementary schools and by closing their teachers' seminaries.[6] The provincial governors countered by refusing to give the *Ritterschaften* formal release from their school responsibilities, though they could not stop the closing of the seminaries run by the nobles. To compensate for this loss, the imperial government expanded its own seminary facilities in the Baltic Provinces and began allowing Lutheran Latvians, Estonians, and Finns to attend the teachers' seminaries in Gatchina and Pskov.[7] As the serious impact from the departure of the *Ritterschaften*'s voluntary school administrators became apparent, the government expanded its program, begun in the 1870s, of creating Russian-language "ministerial schools" maintained at the expense of the state. These institutions as a rule were better provided with school supplies than the old community schools had been and often were staffed with qualified teachers. Unfortunately, however, their number was insufficient to work a significant change in the Baltic educational system.[8]

The Baltic nobility kept up a steady fire of protests and proposals to try to reverse the "Temporary Regulations," but to no avail. Inevitably, with a premium being put on learning Russian and with either poorly educated Russians or linguistically hampered natives filling most teaching posts, pupil interest fell and school absences rose steadily. Unable officially to renounce their school duties and unwilling directly to challenge the government by simply washing their hands of the whole affair, the *Ritterschaften* steered the rather ungallant middle course of sharply reducing their financial contributions for the upkeep of the schools.[9]

Since the imperial government refused to make up for the decline in *Ritterschaft* support and the Latvians and Estonians were completely unable to do so, clearly something had to give. That something proved to be the quality and extent of education. Before examining the deleterious consequences of the Russification in elementary education, let us first turn from the schools in the countryside to the other types of Baltic educational institutions.

While the rural elementary schools educated the Latvians and Estonian population, the children of the Baltic Germans received their elementary and secondary training in the extensive and highly prized network of gymnasia, municipal, and the private schools. Most Baltic Germans averred that their way of life rested upon the twin pillars of home and school; the former would be difficult for an outside force to disturb, but the schools were clearly vulnerable.

On April 10, 1887, a law ordered the gradual introduction of Russian as the language of instruction in all boys' secondary schools in the Dorpat Educational Region, beginning with the 1887-1888 academic year. The law was to apply not only to all gymnasia maintained by the state, but also to all those maintained jointly by the state, the cities and the *Ritterschaften*.[10] Meyendorff offered a compromise proposal of a postgraduate Russian-language course, and when this was rejected the Livland *Ritterschaft* proposed converting its two provincial gymnasia at Birkenruh and Fellin into private gymnasia without the privileges accorded state schools. Again the nobles' plan was turned down.[11]

In October 1888 the Livland Diet reluctantly began a painful debate on whether or not to close the provincial gymnasia. One party in the Diet favored this drastic step, contending that the *Ritterschaft*, if it acquiesced in the introduction of Russian as the language of instruction in its own gymnasia, would appear to have abandoned its principles in a weak-kneed manner. Another segment of the nobility argued for keeping the provincial gymnasia open despite the introduction of the Russian language. These men noted that the government had promised to allow the *Ritterschaft* to keep the right to name the school directors and teachers, and hence it would still be possible to maintain the old German spirit, especially since they would remain boarding schools with a strong extracurricular life. The choice, these proponents of keeping the gymnasia open asserted, boiled down to German-minded Russian schools or Russian-minded Russian schools.

This argument failed to satisfy the majority of Livland's nobles, including Meyendorff, who considered it naive.[12]

On October 20, 1888, the Livland Diet voted 148 to 75 to close its gymnasia in Birkenruh and Fellin. The following year the government granted permission to close the schools in 1892 and allowed German to continue to be the language of instruction until then. In June 1892 the two Livland gymnasia shut their doors; that same year the gymnasium of the Kurland *Ritterschaft* in Goldingen also terminated its operation. The Estland Diet had received imperial assurances that its venerable *Ritter-und-Domschule* in Reval, if it accepted Russian as the language of instruction, could retain its free choice of faculty members without confirmation by the Ministry of Education. Hence, in 1892 it voted to allow the school to reopen in a Russified form. A few months later the new curator Nikolai Lavrovskii went back on the government's promise, and the Estland Diet, disillusioned and embittered, then voted to close the *Ritter-und-Domschule* early in 1893.[13]

The imperial government also introduced Russian as the language of instruction in municipal and district schools. The Riga school committee tried to evade the Russification by converting its municipal schools into private schools. The question was rendered academic, before final adjudication, by a law which introduced Russian into private boys' schools. The city administration of Windau considered cutting off funds for its Russified municipal school in 1887 but eventually granted partial subsidies. The Baltic *Realschulen* and girls' educational institutions were also compelled to accept Russian as their language of instruction.[14]

After soul-searching debates within the German community, most Baltic private schools, especially the girls' schools, retained their German teaching staffs despite the switch to instruction in Russian. Studying in one of these Russified private schools was no easy task for the pupils. The heavy burden of learning in an insufficiently understood foreign language forced many to repeat their lessons at home in German. Those who managed to complete their course of study were often sent to distant Russian cities to take their state examinations in order to escape the real or imagined anti-German prejudice of Russian bureaucrats in the Baltic Provinces.[15]

Though the majority of Baltic German youth continued its education in the Russified school system, there were three ways of avoiding the Russified schools and yet completing one's secondary education. The first, going to Germany for secondary schooling, was an option exercised by a few. The second, going to one of the German church-schools in Russia (four in St. Petersburg, two in Moscow), was also quite limited since applicants were required to take a stiff entrance examination for a small number of available places. Expansion of enrollments at these schools was impossible for reasons of space and politics.[16] The third path, the so-called instructional circles in private homes, succeeded in educating several hundred Baltic German children. These circles arose spontaneously in many locations and varied considerably in staff and curriculum. Despite the numerous pedagogical handicaps inherent in their clandestine nature, they created a certain *esprit de corps* which the pupils fondly recalled later in their lives. Only after the circles had been functioning for several years did they receive financial aid and a measure of institutionalization from the Livland *Ritterschaft*.[17]

Like most other affairs in the old Russian Empire, government reaction to the instructional circles was erratic, not systematic. Since there was no compulsory school attendance in the empire, private instruction in lieu of going to school was allowed. There was, however, no prescribed policy on the questions of the language of instruction and the permissibility of private instruction in groups. Some Russian school inspectors considered it their duty to suppress all German learning;[18] others tended to look the other way.[19] In any event, such police control as existed was certainly not of the magnitude, for example, of the Prussian control over similar Polish circles in Posen. After various bureaucrats had offered differing opinions on the circles' legality, the tangle was unraveled in the best autocratic fashion. In his administrative report of 1902, Livland's Governor Mikhail Pashkov—perhaps smarting from the personal slights he had received from Marshal of the Nobility Meyendorff and Resident Councillor Arved von Oettingen—strongly condemned the instructional circles and said they should not be tolerated. Nicholas II wrote on the margin of Pashkov's report, "I can't see anything illegal in it." That ended all discussion of the matter; in 1904 the Ministry of Education removed the question from its agenda.[20]

Somewhat earlier, when a Baltic German educator, Ernst Friesendorff, complained to Minister of Education Ivan Delianov about the incompetent teachers whom the Russification had thrust upon the Baltic schools, Delianov answered candidly: "This one generation will suffer damage. There's nothing we can do about it. In return, however, the next generation will completely understand the Russian language, and then all difficulties in instruction will cease."[21] The Russification of the Baltic elementary and secondary schools did not last long enough for one to be able to judge the accuracy of Delianov's prediction, but his prophecy of damage to the first generation of school-age youth seems, on balance, to have been fulfilled. As is mentioned in Part Four of this volume, basic literacy among Estonians increased slightly from 1881 to 1897, though the statistics include only roughly the first half of the period of Russification. The deleterious effects of poorly trained teachers on pupils are difficult to quantify, but the officially accepted data on enrollment, faculty, and number of schools suggest at the very least a significant decline in the delivery of education in less than two decades. The Committee of Ministers agreed in 1905 that the Baltic secondary schools had deteriorated during the Russification process, largely because of the lack of cooperation between government and *Ritterschaft* officials.[22]

Baltic German historians, viewing earlier events through the prism of the revolutionary years of 1905-1906, have blamed the Russification of the elementary schools, especially the influx of teachers from Russia, for a decline in religious belief, a growth of immorality, a brutalization of the peasant youth, an increase in juvenile criminality, and a passion for revolution.[23] The Committee of Ministers, meeting in May 1905 after the first disturbances had begun in the Baltic Provinces but before the first armed clashes and serious fighting occurred, did come to the same conclusion, and the participation of large numbers of Baltic elementary school teachers in the revolutionary activity has been documented.[24] Still, the "outside agitator" theory is far too simplistic to be an adequate explanation for the fury of the Latvians and Estonians in 1905-1906 or the increase in lawlessness in the preceding years. Centuries of German oppression, disillusionment with the Russian government, a rising national consciousness, and rapid urbanization with its accompanying dislocations all played significant roles in the social upheavals of those years.

The partial restoration of the Baltic elementary and secondary school systems was tied to the rapidly changing events of the 1904-1906 period. The assassination of Plehve and the appointment of Prince Sviatopolk-Mirskii as minister of the interior made Meyendorff feel that the time was right to petition for the reopening of the secondary schools. The Russo-Japanese War, meanwhile, was going from bad to worse, and the government was coming more and more to appreciate the stability of the conservative Baltic Germans. After lengthy negotiations the Committee of Ministers declared on May 10, 1905, that "under no circumstances should the schools be made into tools of an artificial execution of Russificatory principles."[25] Six weeks later Nicholas confirmed the usage of the mother tongue as the language of instruction in the elementary schools of the Riga educational region and in April 1906 finally granted permission for the *Ritterschaften* to reopen their provincial gymnasia with German to be the language of instruction for all subjects except Russian language and literature and Russian history and geography. Complaints about imperial officials' disinclination to honor the provisions of these laws, however, did begin surfacing shortly before World War I.[26]

With regard to higher education, the government's attitude toward Dorpat University is not to be understood without reference to the new university policy for the empire decided upon early in the reign of Alexander III. Soon after Delianov's appointment as minister of education student disorders broke out at the universities of St. Petersburg and Kazan. Convinced of the need to strengthen supervision over university students and faculty, Alexander III sided with the minority within the State Council and confirmed a revision of the university statute of 1863. The new statute abolished the university councils which had chosen the rectors, deans, and professors. Henceforth the minister of education would assume these duties and have at his disposal inspectors with greatly increased powers.[27]

This new university statute of 1884 did not apply to Dorpat since in 1865 it had received its own which differed slightly from the general Russian model.[28] Nonetheless, the imperial government was also thinking about reorganizing Dorpat. Manasein in his report had written very negatively about Dorpat's German culture and special status and had recommended the introduction of Russian as the language of instruction, a revision of the faculty of law to conform to the Russian legal system, the replacement of the theological faculty by a new Protestant theological seminary to be located in St. Petersburg, and greater supervision of the student corporations.[29]

At the same time attacks on Dorpat in the Russian nationalist press were becoming increasingly frequent and harsh. In 1884, Ivan Aksakov, writing in the newspaper *Rus'*, railed against the idea of a German university in the Russian Empire and lambasted Dorpat for being the strongest bulwark of Baltic German particularism and the agent for the Germanization of the Latvians and the Estonians. During the summer of the following year *Novoe vremia* began calling for the Russifying of Dorpat and soon escalated its demands to the abolition of the present university and the simultaneous opening of a Russian university in a proximate area, preferably Pskov.[30]

The Russian press, however, was by no means unanimous in its opposition to the existence of Dorpat University. Two weeks after the *Novoe vremia* article appeared, the liberal weekly *Vestnik Evropy* admitted that Dorpat was hostile toward Russia, but it disputed the contention of other Russian papers that the university was having success in Germanizing the Latvians and Estonians. In any case, the periodical continued, "We certainly do not have so many institutions of higher education that we could casually destroy one of them." Finally, *Vestnik Evropy* argued for Dorpat's retention because only by doing that could the idea of true academic freedom be preserved in Russian society.[31]

Baltic Germans were, of course, aware of the clamor in Russia against Dorpat, but the university faculty was not of one mind on the questions of reform and Russification. The various "parties" within Dorpat had long been considered by Russian nationalists to be a hindrance to scholarship. In the mid-1880s, just as the debate over Dorpat's future reached its peak, the faculty's squabbles spilled over into the student body, provoking actions which bordered on the strictly forbidden political demonstrations.[32]

Though the final Russification of Dorpat did not begin until 1889, there were earlier indications of things to come. The university council confirmed a measure in 1884 setting up a commission for testing the Russian-language competence of students in each branch of the university. Although the council soon passed the customary exceptions to the law, the Ministry of Education made it abundantly clear that new chairs at Dorpat would have to be occupied by professors who taught in Russian. Delianov's report to the Committee of Ministers in 1887 exuded distaste for the German character of Baltic education, from Dorpat on down.[33]

As we have seen, in 1888 the imperial government enacted the Baltic police reform and the following year Russified the Baltic judicial system. Hence, it was fitting that the real Russification of Dorpat University began with its faculty of law. According to an *ukaz* of February 4, 1889, old chairs were altered and new ones created in order to conform with legal faculties at the other universities of the empire.[34] Several Russian professors on Dorpat's faculty of law resented the reform, and a German law professor, Johannes Engelmann, led an unsuccessful fight for repeal. As a result, Engelmann incurred official wrath, and there was an attempt to fire him. He fought for his position, taking his case to the Senate in St. Petersburg, but in the end he, too, had to agree to teach in Russian in order to secure a special emeritus appointment.[35]

Several months after the reorganization of Dorpat's faculty of law, the entire university lost its autonomy. In July 1889 the independent university court was dismissed, and in November of that year an *ukaz* deprived Dorpat of the relative freedom which the imperial government had allowed it to enjoy five years longer than the other universities of the empire. The university lost its right to elect its rector, deans, and professors, though henceforth the emperor was to listen to

the opinion of the university council in confirming the rector[36]—
somewhat of a concession, since other Russian universities had lost
their university councils entirely.

With the demolition of Dorpat's autonomy the most important task
remaining to the government reformers was the introduction of Russian as the language of instruction throughout the university. The
minister of education allowed extensions and exemptions to older
professors and to foreigners on the faculty, but by 1895 Russian had
essentially supplanted German as the medium of teaching at the
university, except for the theological faculty which, due to its Lutheran character, was permitted to continue its instruction in German.
The symbolic transformation from a German to a Russian university
had already occurred: in February 1893, Dorpat University was
officially renamed Iur'ev University, a change which corresponded to
the renaming six weeks earlier of the city of Dorpat, Iur'ev, after the
Russian fortress which had stood in the vicinity in the eleventh
century.[37] In addition to changing the language of instruction at
Iur'ev University (as we shall now call it), the government also
passed a series of measures prescribing the Russian language for tests,
dissertations, public debates, formal speeches, other events of academic life, and the internal business of the university.[38]

The Baltic nobility engaged in several actions against the Russification of the area's university. The most widely publicized was a rebuttal to the allegations of Rector A. S. Budilovich that old Dorpat
had been declining as a university since the 1860s. Georg von Oettingen, one of the figures whom Budilovich accused of politicizing
Dorpat, wrote a reply, and a tit-for-tat exchange ensued in which
Oettingen's arguments were severely pruned by the government
censors.[39]

The Russification fundamentally altered student life at Iur'ev. Just
prior to the introduction of Russian as the language of instruction the
Ministry of Education passed rigorous rules concerning student
knowledge of Russian, ending nearly sixty years of half-hearted efforts
and evasions. A decree in March 1894 ordered Iur'ev students to
begin wearing the formal Russian student uniform the following year,
and six weeks later the public wearing of corporation colors after the
conclusion of that academic year was forbidden.[40]

The corporations narrowly missed being banned altogether: Delianov, Kapustin, and Lavrovskii all tried to accomplish this. Governor
Zinov'ev, who increasingly came to respect many Baltic institutions,
may have been responsible for ensuring the corporations' continued
existence by favorable reports on them to the emperor. Although
Zinov'ev did instruct local administrative and police officials to carry

out the orders about student uniforms and the banning of corporation colors, his successors relaxed discipline on certain occasions.[41]
By the turn of the century the corporations began to regain a measure
of official favor. In 1899 student disorders broke out again at the
University of St. Petersburg and quickly enveloped all the other Russian universities. Iur'ev was no exception, and the riots there, many
of which assumed a political character, led to a temporary suspension
of classes in March 1901 and had to be suppressed by the police and
local military. As in the Polytechnical Institute of Riga, members of
the German student corporations at Iur'ev did not take part in these
disturbances. As a reward, in 1904 the government once again allowed
Iur'ev students to wear their corporation colors publicly.[42]

Two results of the Russification dramatically changed the composition of the student body at Iur'ev. First of all, the near-complete
transformation of the university induced many Baltic Germans to
go to universities in Germany. Secondly, there was a huge influx of
Russian students, many of them ill-prepared Orthodox seminarians.
As a result the Baltic German component in the student body of the
university dropped from 82 percent in 1880 to only 16 percent in
1900. During that period the total number of students increased nearly 70 percent from 1,015 to 1,709.[43]

As might be expected, the bitterness of many Baltic Germans who
had studied at the old Dorpat scarcely knew bounds. All were in
agreement that the academic caliber of the university declined with
its Russification, and Roderich von Engelhardt, the chief German
historian of Dorpat-Iur'ev, also accused the new administration, especially Lavrovskii, of lying, deception, and embezzlement of university
funds. In tones reminiscent of Carl Schirren he ascribed to the Russifiers of Dorpat "the symptoms of a Slavic-Asiatic racial instinct, with
only a thin veneer of Europeanization."[44] There is general agreement,
however, that the university gradually emerged from the fundamental
reorganization of the 1890s with enough resiliency to be able to show
a definite professional improvement during the first decade of the
twentieth century.[45]

One private Baltic German institution of higher learning very successfully surmounted the dislocations of Russification. This was the
Riga Institute of Technology, whose administrative council voted in
April 1893 to continue the school's operation in spite of the change
in language of instruction. In protest, the Livland *Ritterschaft* withdrew its two members from the council and terminated its financial
support. In 1895-1896 the school was reorganized and began to receive state support as the Polytechnical Institute of Riga. The government refrained from interfering seriously with courses or faculty,

and the institute managed to cling to its German character, including student corporation life, to a surprising degree. Many exceptions were granted for professors to be allowed to continue to lecture in German, and an outstanding list of chemists, physicists, mathematicians, astronomers and geologists of international reputation was attracted to the faculty. Even the Livland Diet was sufficiently impressed to bury the hatchet and respond affirmatively to the institute's request in 1908 once again to send representatives to the administrative council and to resume its financial support.[46]

A private Baltic German school was actually founded during the Russification. In 1901 the Riga stock exchange opened a commercial school which offered a secondary school education along with business training. Well-endowed financially, the school was immediately put under the supervision of the Ministry of Finance where it was safe from any interference by the Russian school authorities. Officially Russian was the language of instruction, but professors, as at the Polytechnical Institute, used German frequently.[47]

CHAPTER 12

CONCLUDING REMARKS

THE REDUCTION of Baltic autonomy during the period 1855 to 1914 had many aspects and motivations. The administrative and judicial reforms can be seen as part of an attempt to modernize the governing of a huge multinational realm, made imperative by the great increase in the empire's population. The Russification of education and religion was less rational, but was typical of the ethos of a period in which the Germans forced their culture on the Poles of Posen, the Danes of North Schleswig, and the Alsatians, in which attempts were made to Germanize or Magyarize Slavs, Italians, and Rumanians of the Habsburg Empire, and in which several countries through colonial and missionary activities tried to Europeanize important segments of African populations.[1]

Seen in the context of the whole Russian Empire, the government's actions in Livland, Estland, and Kurland were neither unique nor extraordinarily harsh. There was precedent for the abolition of a viceroyalty; Baltic cities were given a seven-year period of grace after the passage of the 1870 Russian municipal statute; St. Petersburg waited a full quarter-century to introduce the 1864 judicial reform; the Manasein Inspection of 1882-1883 was merely one of many senatorial investigations in the empire; and even Dorpat University, a special object of nationalist Russian animosity, was allowed to preserve its autonomy five years longer than Russian universities. The harassment of the Baltic Lutherans, unconscionable though it was, did not compare with the officially sanctioned brutalities against Uniates and Lithuanian Catholics, or with the officially tolerated atrocities against the Jews. While the restrictions put on the German language were an affront to proud sensibilities, they paled in comparison to the severe cultural limitations enforced in Lithuania, Poland, the Ukraine, and Belorussia. All these parallels might well have seemed irrelevant to a Baltic German who considered his autonomy anchored in firmer guarantees than those of other minority nationalities, but it is well to remember that Finland, a Grand Duchy with still stronger autonomy, also saw its privileges violated.

The Russification process, though it caused the emigration of some

Baltic Germans and the conversion to the Russian nationality of others, in the last analysis was a limited phenomenon. There was no general cultural Russification in the Baltic Provinces, perhaps as much because of inept enforcers as by dint of policy. At any rate, the imperial government never made an attempt to flood the area with Russian settlers. The economic dominance of the Baltic Germans in industry, banking, wholesale trade, the professions, and on the large landed estates was left undisturbed. Finally, the government allowed the *Ritterschaften* to survive. Due to the police and judicial reforms this concession was of limited importance before 1905, but shortly thereafter the *Ritterschaften* secured the reinstatement of instruction in the native languages in Baltic elementary schools, and for a brief period during the turmoil after the collapse of the Russian Empire they again played a political role.

Baltic German resistance to Russification in education and religion and the championing of Latvian and Estonian cultural interests has led some historians to glorify them as defenders of the old concept of *Reich* with its broad tolerance of cultural autonomy against the modern idea of the *Nationalstaat*.[2] It is true that it was Baltic Germans who played a major if often patronizing role in the restoration of Latvian and Estonian culture, fought for the native languages in the elementary schools during the Russification process, and ministered to desiring Latvians and Estonians at personal risk to themselves. On the other hand, the Baltic Germans severely circumscribed Latvian and Estonian cultural development by politically and economically repressing the Baltic peasantry for centuries, a fact that is impossible to reconcile with an image of defenders of ethnic cultural autonomy. Indeed, it could be said that the 150-year-long *modus vivendi* between the Russian government and the Baltic Germans had been built upon the backs of the Latvians and Estonians.

The Baltic nobles had always maintained that their privileges contained a mandate to speak for the commonweal. The Latvian and Estonian awakenings made this Baltic German position national, particularistic—and untenable. Just as the myth of Baltic commonweal was breaking up, the Russians were beginning a serious push against the regional autonomy that was retarding rational modern development. Shorn of the moral right to speak for all the people of the area (though many nobles insistently continued to assert it), the Baltic Germans were left with the task of defining their privileges for reason of class or of nationality.[3] National and class interest was in most cases identical, the outstanding exception being the German bourgeoisie in Riga, which profited from the state-supported industrialization and hence was not inclined actively to oppose Russification. The majority of the Baltic Germans who did oppose the government's measures gravitated in its defense toward the idiom of the day, the national. This tack did help to foster by the end of the nineteenth century a new sense of German identity, but also often a concomitant Russophobia.[4]

Might the activist Baltic Germans have defended themselves better against the unwanted changes? Certainly whatever these Baltic Germans did, they could not have prevented most of the modernizing reforms, but it is equally true that they facilitated the work of the more extreme Russifiers in several ways. Their frequent displays of tactlessness offended the Russians, whose behavior toward Germans during the last century resembled the mixture of revulsion and envy which one sees today in the attitudes of many developing countries toward the West. Baltic Germans might have been able to draw the distinction between a spiritual and a political homeland, but the fine points were lost on the Russians who heard Dorpat students sing patriotic German songs. Similarly, though Bishop Walter's 1864 Diet sermon was misinterpreted, his topic and ideas scarcely suited the political climate immediately after the Polish rebellion. Livland's intransigence in the Cathedral Question seemed to the Russian Court to be a personal affront to Alexander II. Even the bitter experience of Russification was not enough to impress upon some leading provincial politicians the wisdom of flexibility; and so the tale went on.

More than simply want of tact, it was Baltic German disunity that hampered their efforts to forestall Russian reforms. The Baltic judicial conference of 1865, the reaction to the language decree of 1867, the Cathedral Question, the "Great Action," and the district government reform proposal of 1886 all showed deep divisions along class and provincial lines. Especially in the 1860s and 1870s while they still had an emperor who was favorably disposed toward them, the Baltic Germans, if they had worked together and passed much-needed reforms, might have taken the steam out of demands for the more extreme measures of the 1880s.

Usually acting without formal coordination,[5] the Baltic German institutions nevertheless functioned fairly efficiently in trying to retain the status quo. This was especially true in the municipal elections after the introduction of the Russian form of city government. The *Ritterschaften* managed to make their views heard at Court, but aside from saving their own corporate identity and helping to restore elementary and secondary education after 1905 they succeeded in little else. The representatives of the nobility were generally talented; some, notably Meyendorff and Ekesparre, were very gifted. Others suffered lapses of judgment, the most serious being the lack of foresight exhibited by Arthur von Richter and Heinrich von Bock in approving of the Manasein Inspection, although Wilhelm von Wrangell's skillful warding-off of Senator Manasein did not spare Estland when reform time came around a few years later.

The extralegal resistance in religion and education had slightly more success. Bolstered by protests from abroad, the Lutheran pastors defied the ban on ministering to reconverts, and eventually Nicholas II dropped charges against them and allowed freedom of conversion. Success in education was basically limited to the contribution of the household instructional circles and the maintenance of a semblance of the German character of some Russified schools and the Polytechnical Institute of Riga.

In the face of Russification, the Baltic nobility still declined to share power with the Latvians and Estonians, offering (except in Estland, where reform was totally rejected) only a half-way administrative reform plan, which by the time it was submitted in 1886 stood no chance of approval by the imperial government. In any case, political equality without economic and social equality would have been unfeasible, and given the history of the Baltic area one could not have expected the German nobility there voluntarily to have given up its centuries-old prerogatives as the Tver' gentry unsuccessfully tried to do in 1862. Even had the Baltic Germans managed to conclude an alliance with the Latvians and Estonians, it is highly doubtful that they could have staved-off Russification.[6] In Finland where the mutually hostile nationalities and classes were able briefly to submerge their differences in 1905 and achieve an apparent halt in the Russification process, the success proved to be only temporary.

The Baltic Germans have also been chided for not having developed ties with Russian intellectuals in their struggle,[7] but it is difficult to see with whom they could have developed these ties. Both the Russian liberals and conservatives in the 1860s favored the national development of the Latvians and Estonians while advocating at least the administrative Russification of Baltic German institutions. Later, when enthusiasm for the national movements waned, sympathy in Russian intellectual circles for the Baltic Germans remained minimal.

A more plausible criticism of the Baltic Germans' one-dimensional resistance to change involves the essentially dual nature of Russification—cultural and political. Need there necessarily have been a conflict between *Nationalstaat* and religious and educational particularism? In nearly every instance of Russification in the tsarist empire political considerations played an important role. The Baltic Provinces and Finland had great strategic importance. The Armenian problem was inextricably tied in to relations with Turkey, as were the Ukrainian and Polish issues with Austria-Hungary. Only in the case of the

Moslem peoples of the empire was Russification mainly a cultural phenomenon.

Might it not, therefore, have been wiser for the Baltic Germans' leaders to have recognized the demands for Russian as the *lingua franca* for administration and for a unified legal and administrative system as legitimate desires of a great power in an age of nationalism, and to have concentrated on defending their religious and educational autonomy?[8] This differentiation between administrative modernization and cultural Russification was, after all, still the main thrust of government policy well into the 1870s. Such a tactic, however, would certainly have been highly unpopular among many Baltic Germans.[9] Most of the leaders of the nobility felt that a concession on any one of the provincial privileges would bring the entire structure of autonomy crashing down.

Meyendorff, who came to exemplify the Baltic German will to resist, showed this unbending aversion to compromise in a letter to Baron Ferdinand Wrangell in 1888. At issue was his opposition to keeping open the newly Russified schools, but his assessment of the Baltic German character transcended educational policies. The question, Meyendorff said, was:

> whether we can dare to appear outwardly as Russians and inwardly to remain German with the entire force of our being. . . . I say: no!!! Other fragments of peoples could perhaps undertake this, like e.g. the Pole and the Jew, because they possess in a special way the ability to put on and wear the coat that one forces upon them. We Balts cannot do it, and therefore our way of acting must correspond to our inner nature.[10]

Here was the essence of the Baltic Germans' quixotic struggle: brave, pathetic, sometimes comical, inevitably in a lost cause. Their privileged position ultimately rested upon imperial sufferance. Once the tsar agreed that the services of this group of his vassals were dispensable in the state's drive toward modernization, no sufficient power base remained for retention of provincial autonomy.

Notes to Part Two

CHAPTER 6. BALTIC PARTICULARISM AND THE BEGINNINGS OF RUSSIFICATION

1. *Soviet Life*, October 1973, p. 56.
2. PSZ, 1st ser., VII, 119, no. 4,309, September 23, 1723.
3. Ibid., IV, 575-77, no. 2,301, September 30, 1710. Latvian historians

have questioned the authenticity of the *Privilegium Sigismundi Augusti*. See Alfred Bilmanis, *A History of Latvia* (Princeton: Princeton University Press, 1951), pp. 127-28, and Arnolds Spekke, *History of Latvia. An Outline* (Stockholm: M. Goppers, 1951), pp. 195-97. The real importance of the *Privilegium* for the eighteenth century is, of course, the fact that the Russian government considered it authentic.

4. PSZ, 1st ser., IV, 519-26, no. 2,279, art. 19, July 4, 1710. Despite the supposedly exclusive nature of this right, the burghers of Riga also received permission to own manors. See ibid., 1st ser., IV, 577, no. 2,302, September 30, 1710. This contradiction caused confusion and disputes until the situation was clarified in the codification of the provincial law in 1845 (art. 876 of the estates law), which gave the right of manor ownership exclusively to nobles in all of Livland except Ösel, and exclusively to registered nobles in Estland and Kurland and on Ösel.

5. For Livland: PSZ, 1st ser., IV, 519-26, no. 2,279, arts. 5, 6, 9, 10, July 4, 1710; IV, 578-80, no. 2,304, October 12, 1710. For Estland: IV, 567-75, no. 2,299, arts. 2, 4, 5, 6, 8, 31, September 29, 1710; IV, 810, no. 2,495, March 1, 1712. For Riga: IV, 515-19, no. 2,278, arts. 2, 3, 4, 5, 7, 9, 10, July 4, 1710. For Reval: IV, 560-67, no. 2,298, arts. 6, 7, 25, September 29, 1710.

6. Ibid., IV, 516-26, 560-75, 578-80, nos. 2,278, 2,279, 2,298, 2,299, and 2,304, July 4, September 29, and October 12, 1710.

7. Ibid., IV, 575-77, no. 2,301, September 30, 1710.

8. R. Baron Staël von Holstein, "Zur Geschichte der livländischen Privilegien," BM, LI (1901), 4-5; PSZ, 1st ser., IV, 810-17, no. 2,496, art. 6, March 1, 1712.

9. PSZ, VI, 420-31, no. 3,819, arts. 9, 10, August 30, 1721; XI, 853-74, no. 8,766, arts. 8, 9, August 7, 1743.

10. Of the nobility of Livland: Catherine I—ibid., VII, 512-15, no. 4,743, July 1, 1725; Peter II—VIII, 89-90, no. 5,330, September 12, 1728; Anne I—VIII, 315-17, no. 5,608, August 23, 1730; Elisabeth I—XI, 618-20, no. 8,573, June 25, 1742; Catherine II—XVI, 132-33, no. 11,727, December 19, 1762 and XVI, 341, no. 11,905, August 27, 1763; Alexander I—September 15, 1801. See Otto Müller (ed.), *Die Livländischen Landesprivilegien und deren Confirmationen* (2nd ed.; Leipzig: Steinacker, 1870), pp. 99-100. The PSZ does not contain Alexander's confirmation for the Livland nobility for the given date. Nicholas I—PSZ, 2nd ser., II, 167, no. 889, February 9, 1827; Alexander II—XXXI, 90, no. 30,185, February 17, 1856. Of the nobility of Estland: Catherine I—PSZ, 1st ser., VII, 512-15, no. 4,743, July 1, 1725; Peter II—VIII, 92-94, no. 5,332, September 12, 1728; Anne I—VIII, 314-15, no. 5,607, August 23, 1730; Elisabeth I—XI, 620-22, no. 8,574, June 25, 1742; Catherine II—XVI, 384-85, no. 11,933, September 21, 1763; Alexander I—XXVI, 787, no. 20,010, September 15, 1801; Nicholas I—PSZ, 2nd ser., II, 166-67, no. 888, February 9, 1827; Alexander II—XXXI, 90, no. 30,186, February 17, 1856. Of the nobility of Ösel: Elisabeth I—PSZ, 1st ser., XI, 706-8, no. 8,653, October 27, 1742; Catherine II—XVI, 646, no. 12,092, March 17, 1764; Alexander II—PSZ, 2nd ser., XXXI,

91, no. 30,188, February 17, 1856. Of the nobility of Kurland: Nicholas I—PSZ, 2nd ser., II, 167-68, no. 891, February 9, 1827; Alexander II—XXXI, 90-91, no. 30,187, February 17, 1856. Paul I never gave formal confirmation of the privileges of the nobility of Livland or Estland but essentially did the same thing in his *ukaz* of November 28, 1796 (PSZ, 1st ser., XXIV, 20-21, no. 17,584), by restoring the rights of Livland and Estland that had been revoked by Catherine's reforms.

11. For detailed discussion of Baltic German provincial institutions and offices, see Georg von Krusenstjern, *Die Landmarschälle und Landräte der Livländischen und der Öselschen Ritterschaften in Bildnissen* (Hamburg: Harry von Hofmann, 1963); Krusenstjern (ed.), *Kurland und seine Ritterschaft* (Pfaffenhofen/Ilm: Ilmgau-Verlag, 1971); Krusenstjern (ed.), *Zur Geschichte der Ritterschaften von Livland und Ösel* (Pfaffenhofen/Ilm: Ilmgau-Verlag, 1974); Georg Hermann Schlingensiepen, *Der Strukturwandel des baltischen Adels in der Zeit vor dem Ersten Weltkrieg*, Wissenschaftliche Beiträge zur Geschichte und Landeskunde Ost-Mitteleuropas, no. 41 (Marburg, 1959), pp. 135-40; Walther Freiherr von Ungern-Sternberg, *Geschichte der Baltischen Ritterschaften* (Limburg/Lahn: C. A. Starke, 1960); Wilhelm Lenz, *Die Entwicklung Rigas zur Grosstadt*, pp. 3-4; Wilhelm Baron Wrangell and G. von Krusenstjern, *Die Estländische Ritterschaft, ihre Ritterschaftshauptmänner und Landräte* (Limburg/Lahn: C. A. Starke, 1967); and Wittram (see List of Abbreviations; other works by this author cited separately), pp. 135-40.

12. See, for example, *Die Rosensche Deklaration vom Jahre 1739: Ein Beitrag zur Geschichte der Leibeigenschaft in Livland und Estland*, ed. Jūris Vīgrabs (Tartu: Akadeemiline Kooperativ, 1937).

13. A. Schwabe, *Agrarian History of Latvia* (Riga: B. Lamey, 1928), p. 100; J. Hampden Jackson, *Estonia* (London: G. Allen, 1941), pp. 70-72; Spekke, *Latvia*, p. 275; Evald Uustalu, *The History of Estonian People* (London: Boreas, 1952), p. 100; Hubertus Neuschäffer, "Der livländische Pastor und Kameralist Georg Eisen von Schwarzenberg: Ein deutscher Vertreter der Aufklärung in Russland zu Beginn der zweiten Hälfte des 18. Jahrhunderts," in *Russland und Deutschland*, ed. Uwe Liszkowski (Stuttgart: Ernst Klett, 1974), pp. 120-43. Other well-known exposés of the exploitation of the Baltic peasantry were written by Garlieb Merkel and Johann Heinrich von Jannau.

14. PSZ, 1st ser., XXI, 907-11, 967-68, nos. 15,724, 15,774, 15,775, and 15,776, May 3 and July 3, 1783. The government further formalized the new administrative organization by creating Riga and Reval Provinces: ibid., XXI, 1058, no. 15,881, November 15, 1783, and XXI, 4-5, no. 15,904, January 15, 1784. The most detailed, if uncritical, account of the period of the Baltic reforms of Catherine the Great is Friedrich Bienemann, *Die Statthalterschaftszeit in Liv-und Estland 1783-1796* (Leipzig: Duncker & Humblot, 1886).

15. PSZ, 1st ser., XXIII, 664-85 and 818-21, nos. 17,319 and 17,411, April 15 and November 27, 1795.

16. Ibid., XXIV, 20-21, 251, nos. 17,584 and 17,681, November 28 and

December 24, 1796. At the same time, however, Paul extended the harsh Russian recruiting law to the Baltic Provinces. As usual, the peasantry suffered the most heavily, now being liable to twenty-five years of military service.

17. The literati (German: *Literaten*) were defined in the Baltic Provinces as those individuals who had received some higher education. They were grouped with the nobility, clergy, and members of the merchants' guilds as privileged classes exempt from personal taxation (*nepodatnye sosloviia*). After the introduction of the Russian form of municipal government in 1877, the literati could vote in city elections if they paid a special tax (*Literatensteuer*). They lost this right in the conservative electoral reform of 1892. See Evgenii Blumenbakh, *Grazhdanskoe sostoianie (soslovie) v Rossii a v chastnosti v Pribaltiiskikh guberniiakh ego prava i obiazannosti* (Riga: E. Plate, 1899), pp. 22-29. On Kurland's literati, see Wolfgang Wachtsmuth, "Adel und Literatentum, ihre Struktur und ihre gegenseitigen Beziehungen: Ein Beitrag zur baltischen Standesgeschichte," BM, 1928, pp. 101-14; Wilhelm Räder, *Kurländische Akademikerfamilien* (Marburg: Johann-Gottfried-Herder-Institut, 1953); and Wilhelm Lenz, *Der baltische Literatenstand*, Wissenschaftliche Beiträge zur Geschichte und Landeskunde Ost-Mitteleuropas, no. 7 (Marburg, 1953).

18. Jakob von Uexküll, *Niegeschaute Welten* (Berlin: S. Fischer, 1936), p. 34.

19. Ibid., p. 46.

20. See Parts Three and Four of this volume.

21. See e.g. the naive opinions of a well-intentioned Baltic German liberal, Theodor Hermann Pantenius, "In Riga. Aus den Erinnerungen eines baltischen Journalisten," in *Baltische Lebenserinnerungen*, ed. Alexander Eggers (Heilbronn: E. Salzer, 1926), p. 118.

22. Theodor Schiemann, *Geschichte Russlands unter Kaiser Nikolaus I*, 4 vols. (Berlin: G. Reimer, 1904-1919), III, 404.

23. PSZ, 1st ser., XXVI, 775-78, no. 20,004, September 9, 1801; Tobien, II, 229-30; Buchholtz (see List of Abbreviations), p. 273; R. Baron Staël von Holstein, "Die Gefährdung der Landesrechte durch den Marquis Paulucci," BM, LI (1901).

24. Buchholtz, pp. 273-83. On Suvorov's entire Baltic career, see A. von Tidebohl, *Fürst Alexander Suworow, Generalgouverneur von Liv-, Est- und Kurland 1848-1861* (Riga: W. F. Häcker, 1863).

25. Baron B. E. Nol'de, *Iurii Samarin i ego vremia*, pp .46-49.

26. PSZ, 1st ser., IV, 578-80, no. 2,304, art. 10, October 12, 1710; R. Baron Staël von Holstein, "Die Kodifizierung des baltischen Provinzialrechts," BM, LII (1901), 190-208, 249-80; P. M. Maikov, *Vtoroe otdelenie sobstvennoi Ego Imperatorskogo Velichestva kantseliarii 1826-1882*, p. 211ff.; Baron A. E. Nol'de, *Ocherki po istorii kodifikatsii mestnykh grazhdanskikh zakonov pri Grafe Speranskom* (St. Petersburg: Senatskaia Tipografiia, 1906), pp. 230-47, 255-82.

27. PSZ, 1st ser., XVII, 442, no. 20,598, January 24, 1803; XXXVII, 283-342, no. 28,303, June 4, 1820.

28. A. Schönfeldt, "Geistiges Leben der Deutschen-Schulwesen," Carl Peterson et al., *Handwörterbuch des Grenz- und Auslanddeutschtums*, 3 vols. (Breslau: Ferdinand Hirt, 1933-1938), II, 211-12; Tobien, I, 279-83.

29. Petukhov (see List of Abbreviations), I, 423-26; PSZ, 2nd ser., X, 841-55, no. 8,337, July 26, 1835.

30. PSZ, XI, 298-99, no. 9,792, December 19, 1836; XII, 53-54, no. 9,883, January 20, 1837; Petukhov, I, 434, 439-49; Buchholtz, pp. 154, 170-81; Engelhardt (see List of Abbreviations), 90-96.

31. Bienemann, *Statthalterschaftszeit*, pp. 434-35.

32. PSZ, 1st ser., XXXVI, 314-16, nos. 27,896 and 27,897, July 20, 1819.

33. Gert Kroeger, "Die evangelisch-lutherische Landeskirche und das griechisch-orthodoxe Staatskirchentum in den Ostseeprovinzen 1840-1918," ed. Reinhard Wittram, *Baltische Kirchengeschichte* (Göttingen: Vandenhoeck & Ruprecht, 1956), p. 180; Erik Amburger, *Geschichte des Protestantismus in Russland* (Stuttgart: Evangelisches Verlagswerk, 1961), p. 100.

34. PSZ, 2nd ser., VII, 956-1022, no. 5,870, December 28, 1832.

35. R. Baron Staël von Holstein, "Zur Geschichte des Kirchengesetzes vom Jahre 1832," BM, LII (1901), 170-74.

36. Kroeger, "Landeskirche," p. 182; Friedrich Wiegand, *Siebenhundert Jahre Baltischer Kirchengeschichte* (Gütersloh: C. Bertelsmann, 1921), p. 55.

37. Kroeger, "Landeskirche," pp. 183-84; Uustalu, *Estonian People*, pp. 107-8; Robert Stupperich, "Motive und Massnahmen in der livländischen Bauernbewegung der Jahre 1845-47," *Kyrios*, IV (1939/40), 41-42. See also the report written in 1845 from the Estonian part of Livland in Adolf von Harless, *Geschichtsbilder aus der lutherischen Kirche Livlands vom Jahre 1845 an* (Leipzig: Duncker & Humblot, 1869), pp. 43-51.

38. Buchholtz, 241-53; Maximilian Stephany, *Konversion und Rekonversion in Livland*, Abhandlungen der Herder-Gesellschaft und des Herder-Instituts zu Riga, IV, no. 8 (Riga: G. Löffler, 1931), *passim*; Kroeger, "Landeskirche," pp. 185-87; Heinrich Thimme, *Kirche und nationale Frage in Livland während der ersten Hälfte des 19. Jahrhunderts*, Schriften der Albertus-Universitat, Geisteswissenschafliche Reihe, XIX (Königsberg und Berlin: Ost-Europa-Verlag, 1938), 94-98; Stupperich, "Bauernbewegung," p. 44; and Harless, *Geschichtsbilder*, pp. 85-99, 125-26, 137-38; Wiegand, *Siebenhundert Jahre*, pp. 58-59.

39. PSZ, 2nd ser., XXXI, 404-549, no. 30,693, July 5, 1856; XXXV, 240-380, no. 36,312, November 13, 1860; XXXVIII, 136-37, no. 40,164, October 28, 1863.

40. Buchholtz, pp. 311-23; Kroeger, "Landeskirche," pp. 192-95; Thimme, *Kirche und nationale Frage*, pp. 113-18; Harless, *Geschichtsbilder*, pp. 138-57.

41. For a perceptive commentary, see Gert von Pistohlkors, "Führende Schicht oder nationale Minderheit?," *Zeitschrift für Ostforschung*, XXI (1972) Heft 4, 607-9.

CHAPTER 7. RUSSO-GERMAN POLEMICS OF THE SIXTIES

1. Isakov (see List of Abbreviations), pp. 8-16; Tobien, I, 27, 126.

2. DBL, pp. 180-81; Julius von Eckardt, *Lebenserinnerungen*, 2 vols. (Leipzig: S. Hirzel, 1910), I, 2-3.

3. The Baltic Germans did not see the Polish case as similar to their own autonomy, which was founded upon special privileges. In June 1863, during the Polish rebellion the Baltic *Ritterschaften* sent a declaration of loyalty to Alexander II. Heinrich Schaudinn, *Das baltische Deutschtum und Bismarcks Reichsgründung* (Leipzig: J. C. Hinrichs, 1932), pp. 52-53.

4. DBL, p. 847; Bischof Dr. Ferdinand Walter, *Seine Landtagspredigten und sein Lebenslauf* (Leipzig: Duncker & Humblot, 1891), p. 93; "Brief des Bischofs Ferdinand Walter an Baron Felix Meyendorff (2/15. Mai 1869)," Marburg, Hessisches Staatsarchiv, Nachlass Alexander Meyendorff (I am indebted to Professor Peter Scheibert for this letter).

5. Katkov, *1864 god*, p. 259, 293-94.

6. Walter, *Landtagspredigten und Lebenslauf*, pp. 374-76.

7. Isakov, pp. 34-39, 86-88, 134-38, 173-75. A few articles praising Dorpat's academic excellence and conservative atmosphere did appear at the end of the decade.

8. Tobien, I, 125, 130-31; Isakov, pp. 106, 163. Buchholtz expounds in detail the Baltic German view of press censorship in *Fünfzig Jahre russischer Verwaltung in den baltischen Provinzen Russlands*, p. 250, and in *Deutsch-protestantische Kämpfe*, pp. 361-85. PSZ, 2nd ser., XL, 1st Section, 396, no. 41,988, April 6, 1865.

9. Tobien, I, 135.

10. DBL, p. 80; Woldemar von Bock, *Livländische Beiträge zur Verbreitung gründlicher Kunde von der protestantischen Landeskirche und dem deutschen Landesstaate in den Ostseeprovinzen Russlands, von ihrem guten Rechte und von ihrem Kampfe um Gewissensfreiheit*, 3 vols. (Berlin: Stilke & van Muyden; Leipzig: Duncker & Humblot, 1867-1871), Band II, Heft 4, p. 370; Tobien, I, 127-29. Bock later converted to Catholicism and lived the rest of his life in Germany. He died in Bamberg in 1903.

11. Nol'de, *Samarin*, pp. 9-17, 30-31.

12. The first two volumes of *Okrainy Rossii* were published in Prague in 1868; the remaining four in Berlin between 1871 and 1876. See Thaden, "Samarin's 'Okrainy Rossii' and Official Policy in the Baltic Provinces," *Russian Review*, XXXIII, 405-15. The following discussion of the Samarin-Schirren polemics appears in slightly different form in Michael Haltzel, *Der Abbau der deutschen ständischen Selbstverwaltung in den Ostseeprovinzen Russlands*, Marburger Ostforschungen, no. 37 (Marburg: J. G. Herder-Institut, 1977), pp. 33-40.

13. Samarin, VIII, 64-70.

14. Ibid., pp. 139-55.

15. Ibid., pp. 108-19.

16. Ibid., p. 23.

17. Ibid., pp. 55, 166-67.

18. Ibid., pp. 157-58.
19. Ibid., p. 174.
20. Ibid., pp. 170-71.
21. Ibid., pp. 172-73.
22. Isakov, pp. 150-52, 152 n. 361.
23. Nol'de postulated that either Alexander never read Samarin's letter or did not have the heart to punish such a person. Nol'de, *Samarin*, pp. 203-4.
24. Reinhard Wittram, *Das Nationale als europäisches Problem* (Göttingen: Vandenhoeck & Ruprecht, 1954), p. 163.
25. DBL, pp. 680-81.
26. Wittram, *Das Nationale*, p. 166.
27. *Livländische Antwort* (Leipzig: Duncker & Humblot, 1869), Introduction.
28. Ibid., p. 110.
29. Ibid., p. 192.
30. Ibid., pp. 114-15.
31. Ibid., p. 155.
32. Ibid., pp. 134-35.
33. Ibid., p. 135.
34. Ibid., pp. 146-49. There is a large literature on the legal questions surrounding the privileges and capitulations. The most objective treatment is the discussion in Baron B. E. Nol'de, *Ocherki russkogo gosudarstvennogo prava*, pp. 331-411.
35. *Livländische Antwort*, p. 194.
36. Ibid., p. 114.
37. Ibid., p. 14.
38. Ibid., p. 103.
39. Ibid., p. 104-5.
40. Ibid., p. 101.
41. Ibid., p. 174.
42. DBL, pp. 373-74, 680-81; Wittram, *Das Nationale*, p. 167.
43. Reinhard Wittram, *Meinungskämpfe im baltischen Deutschtum während der Reformepoche des 19. Jahrhunderts* (Riga: E. Bruhns, 1934), p. 91n.
44. Thaden, *Conservative Nationalism*, p. 135.

CHAPTER 8. QUARRELS AND ACCOMMODATIONS WITH
RUSSIAN OFFICIALDOM, 1855-1881

1. Materialien (see List of Abbreviations), v, 234-35.
2. Ibid., 349-51, 353-454.
3. PSZ, 2nd ser., xxxvii, 2nd Section, 145-74, no. 38,761. For discussions of the Baltic judicial system, see P. A. Zaionchkovskii, "Sudebnye i administrativnye preobrazovaniia v Pribaltike," ed. N. G. Sladkevich, *Problemy obshchestvennoi mysli i ekonomicheskaia politika Rossii xix-xx vekov. Pamiati Professora S. B. Okunia*, pp. 36-41; Tobien, I, 484-87; and Theodor

Richter, "Ländliche Selbstverwaltung. Organisation," ed. Carl von Schilling and Burchard von Schrenck, *Baltische Bürgerkunde*, Erster Teil (Riga: G. Löffler, 1908), p. 178; [Alexander Faltin], "Zur Reform unserer Gerichtsverfassung," BM, xii (1865), 216; and [Philipp Gerstfeld], "Die Reform der Rechtspflege in den Ostseeprovinzen," BM, vi (1862), 562.

4. DBL, pp. 457-58.

5. R. Baron Staël von Holstein, *Fürst Paul Lieven als Landmarschall von Livland* (Riga: W. F. Häcker, 1906), pp. 86-177; Robert von Büngner, *Rechtskraft und Rechtsbruch der liv- und estländischen Privilegien* (Leipzig: Duncker & Humblot, 1887), pp. 64-65; [Faltin], "Zur Reform," 219-31; Tobien, i, 487-88; *Istoriia Estonskoi SSR*, ii, 246.

6. Katkov, *1864 god*, May 30, no. 120, pp. 327-30; August 8, no. 175, pp. 486-89; September 22, no. 208, pp. 580-84; November 18, no. 254, pp. 733-38; December 8, no. 270, pp. 786-91.

7. On the often acrimonious debates about reform, see Pistohlkors, "Führende Schicht," *Zeitschrift für Ostforschung*, xxi, 611-13; Wittram, *Meinungskämpfe*, pp. 120-34; and Tobien, i, 392-401. Dukhanov (*Ostzeitsy*, pp. 83-98) sees the Baltic Germans as a unified camp in the late 1850s to mid-1860s with only insignificant differences between liberals and conservatives, nobles and burghers—all of whom wanted to hold onto provincial autonomy and special rights.

8. PSZ, 2nd ser., xli, 1st Section, 149-60, no. 43,034, February 19, 1866.

9. Arveds Schwabe, *The Story of Latvia* (Stockholm: NLF, 1950), p. 27.

10. Landtagsrezess, from January 15 to June 27, 1870, as cited in Tobien, i, 466n.

11. Pantenius, "Erinnerungen," pp. 94-96. A delightful example of Baltic German thinking on the old patriarchal form of municipal government is found in Elisabeth Hoffmann, "Bilder aus Revals Vergangenheit," *Baltische Lebenserinnerungen*, p. 18.

12. Lenz, *Riga*, p. 4.

13. Ibid., 21-23; Gerhard Masing, *Der Kampf um die Reform der Rigaer Stadtverfassung (1860-1870)* (Posen: Bruhns, 1936), *passim*.

14. PSZ, 2nd ser., lii, 262-66, no. 57,101, March 26, 1877. For the genesis of and provisions of the urban reform of 1870, see Gr. Dzhanshiev, *Epokha velikikh reform*, 9th rev. ed. (St. Petersburg: B. M. Vol'f, 1905), 531-66.

15. Wittram, *Meinungskämpfe*, p. 109n. Masing (*Rigaer Stadtverfassung*, p. 14) gives population figures which differ very slightly for 1881. See also Part Four of this volume.

16. Wittram, *Meinungskämpfe*, pp. 109-17; Heinrich Rosenthal, *Kulturbestrebungen des estnischen Volkes während eines Menschenalters (1869-1900)* (Reval: Cordes & Schenk, 1912), pp. 254-56.

17. Reinhard Wittram, *Peter I. Czar und Kaiser*, 2 vols. (Göttingen: Vandenhoeck & Ruprecht, 1964), ii, 80; Ernst Seraphim, "Riga nach dem Nordischen Kriege," BM, lxx (1910), 65; PSZ, 1st ser., xix, 818-19, no. 14,036, September 9, 1773; xxxiv, 529-737, no. 27,024, August 25, 1817.

18. Buchholtz, p. 300. The Russian text of this article may be found in *Obozrenie rasporiazhenii* (see List of Abbreviations), p. 1.

19. *Obozrenie rasporiazhenii*, p. 1.

20. Ibid.

21. Reinhard Wittram, "Das Scheitern russischer Überfremdungsversuche in den Ostseelanden bis zum Weltkrieg," *Ostland*, i (1942), 4.

22. PSZ, 2nd ser., xxv, 1st Section, 5-6, no. 23,796, January 3, 1850; xlii, 1st Section, 845-46, no. 44,651, June 1, 1867; Buchholtz, pp. 303-7; Tobien, i, 359.

23. *Rigaer Zeitung*, June 14-15, 1867, as cited in Tobien, i, 83n. Alexander had used the term "the great family of the Russian Emperor" in his speech opening the Finnish Diet in 1863.

24. Tobien, i, 363-64; Brokgauz-Efron, v, 437-40; DBL, p. 557; Valuev, ii, 224.

25. Tobien, i, 362-63; Arved von Oettingen, "August von Oettingen," BM, 1928, pp. 134-37.

26. *Obozrenie rasporiazhenii*, pp. 5-7; *Suppliken der Livländischen & Estländischen Ritterschaften an Seine Kaiserliche Majestät Alexander II Kaiser und Selbstherrscher aller Reussen nebst Memorial der Livländischen Ritterschaft* (Bern: Wyss 1870), pp. 17-68.

27. PSZ, 2nd ser., li, 45-46, no. 55,501, January 25, 1876; [Buchholtz], *Fünfzig Jahre*, p. 297; Valuev, ii, 421-34; Isakov, pp. 178-83.

28. See, for example, Eduard Freiherr von Dellingshausen, *Im Dienste der Heimat!*, pp. 156-57; Wolfgang Wachtsmuth, *Wege, Umwege, Weggenossen: Lebenserinnerungen* (Munich: Winkler, 1954), p. 28; Helmut Muskat, *Bismarck und die Balten* (Berlin: E. Ebering, 1934), pp. 90-96, 107-36; Schaudinn, *Reichsgründung*, pp. 106-7; Edzard Schaper, *Die baltischen Länder im geistigen Spektrum Europas* ([Munich]: Baltische Gesellschaft in Deutschland, [1965]), p. 12.

29. DBL, pp. 373-74; On Bismarck's relations with Keyserling, see Muskat, *Bismarck*, pp. 44-80.

30. Alexander Graf Keyserling, *Ein Lebensbild aus seinen Briefen und Tagebüchern*, ed. Helene von Taube von der Issen, 2 vols. (Berlin: G. Reimer, 1902), ii, 544.

31. Samarin, ix, 447.

32. Thaden, "Samarin's 'Okrainy Rossii,'" *Russian Review*, xxxiii, 410-11.

33. Arthur von Villebois, "Die Landvolksschulen," Schilling and Schrenck (eds.), *Baltische Bürgerkunde*, pp. 242-44.

34. Schönfeldt, "Geistiges Leben," *Handwörtebuch*, ii, 112. There were also several specialized schools, most often founded and maintained by private individuals or Baltic German associations.

35. F. Waldmann (compiler), "Schlussbericht über den Bestand und die Thätigkeit des livl. Landesgymnasiums zu Fellin 1875-1892" (Fellin: F. Feldt 1892), pp. 1-9, 17-21; Tobien, i, 280-88.

36. Katkov, *1864 god*, pp. 294-95.

37. *Obozrenie rasporiazhenii*, pp. 22-23; Buchholtz, pp. 395-98; Rozhdestvenskii, pp. 669-70.

38. Engelhardt, pp. 113-39; Keyserling, *Lebensbild*, ed. H. von Taube, I, 475; Petukhov, II, 5-6, 11-13.

39. See e.g. the description of the University of Dorpat in J. G. Kohl, *Die deutsch-russischen Ostseeprovinzen oder Natur- und Völkerleben in Kur-, Liv- und Esthland* (Dresden and Leipzig: Arnold, 1841), pp. 259-60, and the praise given Dorpat by Ivan Delianov, minister of education in the 1880s: Ernst Friesendorff, "Erinnerungen eines alten Pädagogen," *Baltische Lebenserinnerungen*, p. 287.

40. M. Walters, *Baltengedanken und Baltenpolitik* (Paris: Société Générale d'Imprimèrie et d'Edition, 1926), p. 166.

41. It is true, however, that the Dorpat corporations were usually more important to sons of burghers than to the young nobles, who often regarded membership as only one of many episodes of their university days. See e.g. Wachtsmuth, *Lebenserinnerungen*, p. 39.

42. Jackson, *Estonia*, p. 112.

43. The neo-classic style also recalls to mind the ante-bellum American South—and one scarcely need mention the similarities in life style and outlook of the Southern plantation owner and the rural Baltic manor lord.

44. See e.g. P. Krasovskii, *Rodnoi krai. Ocherki, zametki i nabroski* (Riga: V. P. Matveev, 1902).

45. DBL, p. 162.

46. Dellingshausen, *Im Dienste*, p. 14. The meaning of the word "Balt" is confusing, as it has changed over the years. Beginning in the late 1850s it became a designation for a Baltic German, originally with connotations of the hopeful spirit of the "New Era" under Alexander II. After World War I the term began to be applied to members of the three principal Baltic nationalities—Estonians, Latvians, and Lithuanians. Because of these shifting meanings, this author prefers to use the term only when necessary in a direct translation, as in this case.

47. Krasovskii, *Rodnoi krai*, p. 75.

48. P. D. Boborykin, *Za polveka (moi vospominaniia)* (Moscow: Zemlia i Fabrika, 1929), p. 95.

49. The *Rigaer Tageblatt* reported on these differences on April 8 (20), 1887, p. 3. See also Petukhov, II, 199-204; Engelhardt, p. 446, and the reminiscences of the famous surgeon Nikolai Pirogov who studied and later taught at Dorpat: F. Waldmann, "Pirogows Erinnerungen an Dorpat," BM, XL (1893), 28.

50. Wachtsmuth, *Lebenserinnerungen*, p. 78.

51. Georg von Oettingen, "Erinnerungen," *Baltische Lebenserinnerungen*, p. 157. Boborykin, who found *Ruthenia* as mindlessly anti-intellectual as the German corporations, noted that up until the moment the Germans kicked *Ruthenia* out of the student government they had addressed the *Ruthenia* delegates in the familiar "*Du*." Boborykin, *Za polveka*, pp. 95-96.

52. Brokgauz-Efron, VI, 530; Helene Hoerschelmann, "Aus alten Dorpater Tagen," *Baltische Lebenserinnerungen*, p. 249; Erich von Schrenck, "Deutsche Bildungsarbeit in den baltischen Landen," Franz Schmidt and

Otto Boelitz (eds.), *Aus deutscher Bildungsarbeit im Auslande* (Langensalza: Beltz, 1927), p. 339.

53. Brokgauz-Efron, xxviii-A, 20; Petukhov, ii, 14-15; Hoerschelmann, "Aus alten Dorpater Tagen," p. 253.

54. PSZ, 2nd ser., xlii, 1st Section, 845-46, no. 44,651, June 1, 1867; Petukhov, i, 446-47; ii, 77, 84-85.

55. PSZ, 2nd ser., xxxvi, 1st Section, 754-57, no. 37,016, May 16, 1861; Eižens Leimanis, "The Polytechnical Institute of Riga and its Role in the Development of Science," *Journal of Baltic Studies*, iii (1972), 113-14; Tobien, i, 350-52; Wolfgang Wachtsmuth, "Der Rigasche Burschenstaat von 1865 bis zum Ersten Weltkrieg: Beitrag für die Festschrift zum 100. Stiftungstag der Fraternitas Baltica am 13. November 1965" (Eschweiler: Fraternitas Baltica, 1961), p. 5.

56. For further details of the "Cathedral Question," see Tobien, i, 26, 51-62, 509-21; Dellingshausen, *Im Dienste*, pp. 11-12; Walters, *Baltengedanken*, pp. 199-202, 205-6; Keyserling, *Lebensbild*, ed. H. von Taube, i, 572.

57. DBL, pp. 163, 550.

58. Kroeger, "Landeskirche," *Baltische Kirchengeschichte*, pp. 192-93; Buchholtz, 325-27; Harless, *Geschichtsbilder*, pp. 164-70; Wilhelm Kahle, *Die Begegnung des baltischen Protestantismus mit der russisch-orthodoxen Kirche* (Leiden and Cologne: E. J. Brill, 1959), p. 149; Kroeger, "Landeskirche," p. 193.

59. Brokgauz-Efron, iv, 129; Valuev, i, 279. Later, Valuev referred to the reconverts as "pseudo or half-Orthodox." Ibid., ii, 27.

60. *Rapport du général-major à la suite . . . , M. le comte de Bobrinski*, p. 8.

61. Staël, *Fürst Lieven*, p. 58.

62. Brokgauz-Efron, xxxix, 956; Amburger, *Behördenorganisation*, pp. 145, 329, 384, 389, 448; Buchholtz, pp. 328-33.

63. The text of Alexander's order appears in a confidential directive from Governor-General Shuvalov to the Lutheran Consistory of Livland on May 20, 1865, and is reprinted in W. von Bock (ed.), *Livländische Beiträge*, i, zweiter Beitrag, p. 226. Not only does Alexander's imperial command not appear in the PSZ, but, according to Zaionchkovskii, it also cannot be found in any of the *fondy* of the Council of State, Committee of Ministers, Senate, or Holy Synod. Commentary to *Valuev*, ii, 445n32.

64. Buchholtz, pp. 335-37; Kroeger, "Landeskirche," p. 196; Staël, *Fürst Lieven*, p. 66; Arved von Oettingen, "August von Oettingen," BM, 1928, p. 132.

65. Kroeger, "Landeskirche," p. 197; Buchholtz, pp. 353-54.

66. Eckardt, *Lebenserinnerungen*, i, 181-82. The book by Harless was *Geschichtsbilder*, cited earlier.

67. Kahle, *Begegnung*, p. 153. Stöcker had previously lived for several years with a noble family in Kurland. On the Evangelical Alliance's interest in the Baltic region through the 1870s, see Hermann Dalton, *Lebens-*

erinnerungen, III (Berlin: W. Warneck, 1908), 128-29; Tobien, I, 184-88; Leopold von Wurstemberger, *Die Gewissensfreiheit in den Ostsee-Provinzen Russlands* (Leipzig: Duncker & Humblot, 1872), pp. 9-53; W. von Bock, *Evangelische Allianz und Russische Diplomatie*; Samarin, IX, 3-314. Morse was hardly free from personal bigotry himself. In 1834 he had written a book, *Foreign Conspiracy Against the Liberties of the United States*, which gave expression to a Protestant fear that the Jesuits were plotting to deliver America to the Pope.

68. Buchholtz, pp. 356-57.

69. Materialien, II, 401; DBL, pp. 288-89; D. Traugott Hahn, *Erinnerungen aus meinem Leben* (Stuttgart: C. Belser, 1923), p. 214.

Chapter 9. Triumphs and Frustrations of Administrative
Russification, 1881-1914

1. Victor Bérard, *The Russian Empire and Tsarism* (trans. G. Fox-Davies and G. O. Pope) (London: D. Nutt, 1905), p. 62.

2. The anti-German inclinations of Alexander III were shared by the empress, a Danish princess who had seen Prussia seize Schleswig-Holstein from her father.

3. Rudolf Schulz, *Der deutsche Bauer im Baltikum* (Berlin: Volk und Reich, 1938), p. 16. The former figure was based on nationality and did not include Narva, trans-Narva, and Petschur—all later part of independent Estonia—or Lettgallia and the Illuxt district of Livland. The 1897 figure was based on native language but did not count German-speaking Jews in Livland and Estland. It also did not include the above-mentioned Estonian areas, but did include 5,000 Germans in Lettgallia.

4. Hans Handrack, *Die Bevölkerungsentwicklung der deutschen Minderheit in Lettland*, Rechts- und wirtschaftswissenschaftliche Dissertationen, Jena University, 1932 (Libau: Meyer, 1932), pp. 16-17; Schulz, *Der deutsche Bauer*, p. 16.

5. Handrack, *Bevölkerungsentwicklung*, p. 16; Schulz, *Der deutsche Bauer*, p. 16.

6. Schulz, p. 17; Masing, *Rigaer Stadtverfassung*, p. 14.

7. See, for example, the discussion of *Novoe vremia*'s article on the "flooding" of the Baltic Provinces by German immigrants in the *Rigaer Tageblatt*, September 20, 1885.

8. Amburger, *Behördenorganisation*, p. 448.

9. Ibid., p. 517. Another study of the Russian bureaucracy calculated that between the years 1710 and 1914, 3,600 of the 6,300 members of the *Ritterschaften* served the Russian state. Of the 3,600, one-quarter occupied "high and the highest positions." Annelise Nölle, "Zur Wirksamkeit des baltischen Adels in Russland unter Alexander I und Nikolaus I" (Munich University doctoral dissertation, 1940), p. 6. Walter Pintner has shown that in the mid-nineteenth century Lutheran Russian subjects (presumably nearly all Baltic Germans) filled 15 percent of the top-level posts in the central government agencies, and as much as 40 percent of

the total staff in the Ministry of the Interior, economic department. Pintner noted that if the Lutherans " 'set the tone' for the Russian civil service it was through means other than numerical preponderance." Walter M. Pintner, "The Social Characteristics of the Early Nineteenth-Century Russian Bureaucracy," *Slavic Review*, xxix (1970), 438, 438n.

10. Amburger, *Behördenorganisation*, p. 517.

11. On Meyendorff, see DBL, p. 512, including the extensive citations of works on this man who, more than any other, came to symbolize the Baltic Germans' will to retain their autonomy.

12. Tobien, i, 403-16.

13. This standard Baltic German interpretation is most thoroughly expounded in Tobien, i, 416, 440.

14. For a revealing glimpse into the attitudes of a reactionary Baltic German noble of the period, see Hermann von Samson, "Politische Gedanken" (manuscript printed for circles of the Livland *Ritterschaft* in Dorpat in 1882), pp. 16-17, 48 (quoted in M. Walters, *Lettland: Seine Entwicklung zum Staat* [Rome: n.p., 1923], pp. 234-38).

15. DBL, p. 79.

16. I. Depman, "O naznachenii Senatora N. A. Manaseina revizorom Lifliandskoi i Kurliandskoi gubernii," *Toimetised*, x (1961), 145.

17. Georg von Oettingen, "Erinnerungen," *Baltische Lebenserinnerungen*, p. 159.

18. One Baltic German noble later described Richter's thinking in scathing terms as "the naïveté of the disoriented provincial." Adolf Baron Pilar v. Pilchau, "Bilder aus meinem Leben als Landwirt, Verwaltungsbeamter und Politiker von 1875 bis 1920," *Baltische Hefte*, xv (1969), 15.

19. DBL, pp. 890-91; Wilhelm Baron Wrangell, "Zur Geschichte der Russifizierung der Baltischen Provinzen," *Baltische Hefte*, viii (1961/62), 66, 77n.

20. Depman, "O naznachenii Manaseina," p. 145; Brokgauz-Efron, xviii, 524; Thaden, "N. A. Manaseins Senatorenrevision in Livland und Kurland während der Zeit von 1882 bis 1883," *Jahrbücher für Geschichte Osteuropas*, xvii, 46-47.

21. PSZ, 3rd ser., ii, 159, no. 797, April 13, 1882.

22. Ibid., 3rd ser., iii, 6-7, no. 1,307, January 11, 1883.

23. DBL, p. 257.

24. On Shakhovskoi's prior career, see AS, i, v-xxi. On the dispute with Greiffenhagen, see ibid., i, 3-17, 20-21, 28-29, 41-45, 47-48, 50; Otto Greiffenhagen, "Aus den Erinnerungen eines Revaler Justizbeamten an die Reform-und Russifizierungsära," BM, 1930, pp. 469-77.

25. DBL, pp. 126-27; *Obozrenie rasporiazhenii*, p. 15; *Russisch-Baltische Blätter*, i, 46.

26. *Obozrenie rasporiazhenii*, p. 13.

27. DBL, p. 799.

28. PSZ, 3rd ser., v, 413-14, no. 3,194, September 14, 1885.

29. AS, i, 67, 69, 73-75; *Rigaer Tageblatt*, September 18, 28 and October 2, 11, 12, 17, 30, 1885; V. Shenshin (ed.), *Sbornik tsirkuliarov po*

administrativnoi chasti Lifliandskoi gub. za 1888-1895 gg. (Riga: Sost. po raspor. Lifliandskogo Gubernatora, 1896), p. 87, no. 57.

30. PSZ, 3rd ser., IX, 1st Section, 599, no. 6,332, November 9, 1889. For preparatory decrees on this subject, see AS, I, 83-89, 92-93.

31. Georg von Oettingen, "Erinnerungen," pp. 164-65.

32. PSZ, 3rd ser., XIII, 11-12, no. 9,244, January 14, 1893; Marie Steinwand, *Meine Schulerinnerungen aus Dorpat*, ed. Georg von Rauch (Hamburg: Harry von Hofmann, 1968), p. 30.

33. AS, I, 85-90, 93-94.

34. For an intimate and revealing description of the patriarchal character of justice in the Baltic countryside into the 1880s, see the discussion of the Essern incident in Part Three of this volume.

35. Manasein, p. 151; PSZ, 2nd ser., LV, 1st Section, 307-8, no. 60,996, May 28, 1880; 3rd ser., I, 143, no. 241, June 3, 1881; II, 263, no. 923, May 26, 1882; IV, 497, no. 2,442, October 3, 1884; VI, 250-51, no. 3,762, June 3, 1886.

36. Polovtsov, I, 432-33, 436.

37. Georg von Oettingen, "Erinnerungen," pp. 161-63.

38. *Rigaer Tageblatt*, May 9, 1887.

39. PSZ, 3rd ser., IX, 1st Section, 411-506, nos. 6,188 and 6,189, July 9, 1889.

40. *Istoriia Estonskoi SSR*, II, 250; Rosenthal, *Kulturbestrebungen*, pp. 279-80.

41. PSZ, 3rd ser., XIII, 197-202, no. 9,498, April 17, 1893; *Istoriia Estonskoi SSR*, II, 250-51; Jackson, *Estonia*, p. 113; Tobien, I, 429-30; Thaden, "Manaseins Senatorenrevision," p. 57; P. A. Zaionchkovskii, *Rossiiskoe samoderzhavie v kontse XIX stoletiia (politicheskaia reaktsiia 80-kh—90-kh godov)* (Moscow: "Mysl'," 1970), p. 122; Polovtsov, II, 345. See also Zinov'ev's "Untersuchung über die Landschaftsorganisation des livländischen Gouvernements," trans. A. von Tideböhl, BM, XLII (1895), Beilage.

42. *Svod zakonov Rossiiskoi Imperii. Izdanie 1892 goda.* II, 1, art. 3, points 18, 20, 48.

43. PSZ, 2nd ser., XLI, 2nd Section, 251-52, no. 43,868, November 20, 1866; 3rd ser., VIII, 343-47, no. 5,308, June 9, 1888; AS, I, 132; Zaionchkovskii, "Sudebnye i administrativnye preobrazovaniia," pp. 41-44; Polovtsov, I, 408, 539; II, 60-61, 83, 90-91.

44. PSZ, 3rd ser., XII, 1st Section, 430-56, no. 8,708, June 11, 1892.

45. Lenz, *Riga*, pp. 73-74; A. von Wolffen, *Die Ostseeprovinzen Est-, Liv-, Kurland: Ihre Vergangenheit, Kultur und politische Bedeutung* (Munich: G. D. W. Callwey, n.d.), p. 43.

46. Nikolai Carlberg, "Städtische Selbstverwaltung," ed. Schilling and Schrenck, *Baltische Bürgerkunde*, pp. 215-26, is a standard source, although it is slightly incorrect with regard to Estonian areas. See also Toomas Karjahärm, "Eesti linnakodanluse poliitilisest formeerumisest 1870-ndate aastate lõpust kuni 1914. Aastani (linna-ja duumavalimiste materjalide põhjal)," Toimetised, XXII (1973), 255, 256, 260-62.

47. Manasein, pp. 167-72. For example, Polovtsov wrote on February 6, 1891, that Governor Zinov'ev had told him: "The German element has weakened considerably in recent years, but from our side it would be ill-advised to promote the Ests and Letts too much and to give them an independent existence": Polovtsov, II, 345. In 1892, Alexander III concurred with Zinov'ev's judgment that the nationalist movements, although not yet dangerous, were nonetheless undesirable (KM, IV, 224-25).

48. Manasein, pp. 172-75; PSZ, 3rd ser., x, 1st Section, 493-511, no. 6,927, June 12, 1890.

49. DBL, pp. 185-86.

50. Tobien, I, 418-36; Ernst Seraphim, *Führende Deutsche im Zarenreich* (Berlin: Junker & Dünnhaupt, 1942), p. 392. The land-tax reform was finally worked out from 1901 to 1910 and confirmed in 1912.

51. Wittram (*Baltische Geschichte*), p. 232.

52. C. Leonard Lundin, "The Road from Tsar to Kaiser: Changing Loyalties of the Baltic Germans. 1905-1914," *Journal of Central European Affairs*, x (1950). The first thorough and critical study of the political attitudes, tactics, and goals of the Baltic German leadership during the Revolution of 1905 appeared after these chapters on the reaction of the Baltic Germans to Russification were written: Gert von Pistohlkors, *Ritterschaftliche Reformpolitik zwischen Russifizierung und Revolution.*

CHAPTER 10. RELIGIOUS TURMOIL

1. Josef Glazik, *Die Islammission der russisch-orthodoxen Kirche* (Münster, Westfalen: Aschendorff, 1959), pp. 121-60; Josef Glazik, *Die russisch-orthodoxe Heidenmission seit Peter dem Grossen* (Münster, Westfalen: Aschendorff, 1954), pp. 116-44; Bertold Spuler, "Die Wolga-Tataren und Baschkiren unter russischer Herrschaft," *Der Islam*, XXIX, Heft 2 (1949), 165-85; Serge A. Zenkovsky, *Pan-Turkism and Islam in Russia* (Cambridge, Mass.: Harvard University Press, 1960), pp. 27-30, 64; Zaionchkovskii, *Rossiiskoe samoderzhavie*, pp. 128-30.

2. *Otchet o deiatel'nosti sostoiashchego pod Vysochaishim pokrovitel'stvom Ee Imperatorskogo Velichestva Gosudaryni Imperatritsy Pribaltiiskogo pravoslavnogo bratstva Khrista Spasitelia i pokrova Bozhiei Materi za 1885 god* (St. Petersburg: I. N. Skorokhodov, 1886), pp. 5-25.

3. Polovtsov, I, 520; Zaionchkovskii, *Rossiiskoe samoderzhavie*, pp. 123-25; Bernhard Hollander, "Vor 50 Jahren," BM, 1935, pp. 546-47; Helmut Speer, *Das Bauernschulwesen im Gouvernement Estland vom Ende des achtzehnten Jahrhunderts bis zur Russifizierung*, p. 484; *Russisch-Baltische Blätter*, III, 85-88; W. Lööralt, *Baltenhetze: Die Verfolgung von Glauben, Sprache und Recht in den Ostseeprovinzen Russlands* (Leipzig: Duncker & Humblot, 1890), p. 39; Dalton, *Lebenserinnerungen*, III, 110-11; M. Bukšs, *Die Russifizierung in den baltischen Ländern* ([Munich]: Latgalischer Verlag, 1964), pp. 140-41.

4. N. Carlberg, "Statistik des Konfessionswechsels in Livland," BM, XLII (1895), 795-802; Kroeger, "Landeskirche," pp. 202-3. Wittram (*Baltische*

Geschichte, p. 218) and Hollander ("Vor 50 Jahren'," p. 547) both esti-mated that 3,000 peasants converted. Zaionchkovskii (*Rossiiskoe samo-derzhavie*, p. 125), however, accepted a figure of 37,416 converts during the reign of Alexander III, a total which even exceeded that given by the Holy Synod (31,341). Gerhard Simon, *Konstantin Petrovič Pobedonoscev und die Kirchenpolitik des Heiligen Sinod 1880-1905* (Göttingen: Vanden-hoeck & Ruprecht, 1969), p. 220.

5. Simon, *Pobedonoscev*, p. 231; PSZ, 3rd ser., v, 539, no. 3,410, Decem-ber 23, 1885; ibid., 3rd ser., ix, 617, no. 6,378, November 21, 1889; ibid., 3rd ser., xv, 659, no. 12,204, November 27, 1895; AS, iii, li, 139-40, 159; Kruus, *Grundriss*, 156.

6. Lööralt, *Baltenhetze*, pp. 36-37; *Istoriia Estonskoi* SSR, ii, 232; Simon, *Pobedonoscev*, pp. 232-33. For details of the financing, construction, and dedication of the Alexander Nevsky Cathedral, see AS, i, 217; iii, 85-86; Dellingshausen, *Im Dienste*, pp. 311-12; *Pravoslavie i liuteranstvo v pri-baltiiskom krae po noveishim dannym russkoi periodicheskoi pechati* (St. Petersburg: Gosudarstvennaia Tipografiia, 1911), p. 84; PSZ, 3rd ser., xvii, 613, no. 14,586, October 24, 1897; "Baltische Chronik," BM, lii (1901), 176; and Kroeger, "Landeskirche," pp. 201-2.

7. Kroeger, "Landeskirche," p. 200; Hollander, "Vor 50 Jahren," p. 548; Tobien, i, 190.

8. PSZ, 3rd ser., vi, 50-51, 191, nos. 3,506, 3,507, and 3,693, February 10 and May 14, 1886. See also Polovtsov, i, 353-54, 531; AS, ii, 29-35, 40; Staël, *Fürst Lieven*, pp. 20-22.

9. AS, ii, 126; Shenshin (ed.), *Sbornik tsirkuliarov*, p. 13, no. 10.

10. Kroeger, "Landeskirche, p. 201; Staël, "Zur Geschichte des Kirchen-gesetzes," p. 176; Materialien, ii, 714-15.

11. PSZ, 3rd ser., xi, 357, no. 7,798, June 3, 1891.

12. AS, iii, 178-81.

13. *Russisch-Baltische Blätter*, iii, 30; Hollander, "Vor 50 Jahren," p. 547; Polovtsov, i, 520; Materialien, ii, 551; Simon, *Pobedonoscev*, p. 223. For the Russian nationalists' arguments in favor of the reinstitution of the com-pulsory pledge in mixed marriages see *Pravoslavie i liuteranstvo*, p. 27.

14. DBL, p. 631; Materialien, ii, 496-501. For the text of the Livland *Ritterschaft's* petition, see *Russisch-Baltische Blätter*, iii, 20-22; for that of the Estland *Ritterschaft*, see AS, i, 124-26.

15. Materialien, ii, 501-2.

16. Tobien, i, 193. For discussions of Baltic Germans at Court, see Tobien, i, 143-52, and Seraphim, *Führende Deutsche*, pp. 329, 406-22.

17. Zaionchkovskii, *Rossiiskoe samoderzhavie*, p. 126; *Russisch-Baltische Blätter*, iii, 102-4; Polovtsov, i, 520. It is interesting that Pobedonostsev con-sidered Zinov'ev's tactic of publicly threatening the reconverts in the parish churches inexpedient: Zaionchkovskii, *Rossiiskoe samoderzhavie*, p. 127; Materialien, ii, 701.

18. Zaionchkovskii, *Rossiiskoe samoderzhavie*, p. 127; Materialien, ii, 568-69. The text of Meyendorff's petition to Tolstoi may be found in

B. Dobryshin (ed.), *K istorii pravoslavii v Pribaltiiskom krae: Ocherk s prilozheniem nekotorykh ofitsial'nykh dokumentov* (St. Petersburg; Gosudarstvennaia Tipografiia, 1911), pp. 51-64.

19. Orthodox authorities in Riga estimated there were 18,000 reconverts: Zaionchkovskii, *Rossiiskoe samoderzhavie*, p. 127 n. 139. The results of the Livland Lutheran Consistory's questionnaire in 1886 showed 33,095 reconverts in Livland, not counting the island of Ösel and fourteen parishes on the mainland. The discrepancy stemmed from the fact that the Orthodox authorities apparently were counting only the "true" reconverts and not including their children, who would have raised the figure to above 35,000 plus several thousand more in the districts not reporting: Materialien, II, 584. By 1894, according to Meyendorff, their number had risen to 35,220— 18,803 of them reconverts and 16,317 of them the children of those reconverts: Ibid., pp. 828-29.

20. Materialien, II, 684-86, 695-96; Letter from Moritz to Meyendorff, November 16, 1890 as cited in Kroeger, "Landeskirche," p. 328; "Die livländischen Pastorenprocesse," BM, XLII (1895), 31-45, 131-34; *Russisch-Baltische Blätter*, III, 23-37.

21. Schaudinn, *Reichsgründung*, pp. 198-99.

22. *Russisch-Baltische Blätter*, IV, 69, 74-76; Dalton, *Lebenserinnerungen*, III, 138-41; Materialien, II, 614-16; Friedrich Steinmann and Elias Hurwicz, *Konstantin Petrowitsch Pobjedonoszew der Staatsmann der Reaktion unter Alexander III* (Königsberg: Ost-Europa-Verlag, 1933), pp. 78-79.

23. Hermann Dalton, *Offenes Sendschreiben an den Oberprokureur des russischen Synods Herrn Wirklichen Geheimrat Konstantin Pobedonoszeff* (Leipzig: Duncker & Humblot, 1889).

24. Materialien, II, 804-38; PSZ, 3rd ser., XVI, 1st Section, 427-40, no. 12,936, May 14, 1896.

25. Kroeger, "Landeskirche," p. 204; PSZ, 3rd ser., XXV, 1st Section, 257-58, 754-55, nos. 26,125 and 26,803, April 17 and October 17, 1905.

26. For extensive discussions of the tensions within the Baltic Lutheran Church, see: Viktor Wittrock, *In Sturm und Stille: Ein baltisches Pfarrleben in bewegter Zeit* (Schwerin: Bahn, 1940), pp. 129-38; A. Grenzstein, *Herrenkirche oder Volkskirche? Eine estnische Stimme im baltischen Chor.* (Iur'ev: A. Grenzstein, 1899), *passim*, but especially pp. 95-99, 139-48; Tobien, I, 211-14; Walters, *Baltengedanken und Baltenpolitik*, p. 143; Hahn, *Erinnerungen*, 236-37; Kahle, *Begegnung*, 219-20; and Part Four of this volume.

27. Schlingensiepen, *Strukturwandel*, pp. 5, 131. Conversion to Orthodoxy, however, did not always mean abandonment of German nationality. For example, some of the Wrangells and Meyendorffs were Orthodox yet staunchly Baltic German.

28. Reinhard Wittram told this writer that there was only one individual, Baron Johann (Hans) Rosen (see DBL, p. 646), who knew enough details of the philosophies, language capabilities and preferences, and behavior in key situations of most Baltic German nobles to be able accurately

to pass judgment on whether or not individuals were Russified. Sad to say, Rosen, as far as Professor Wittram knew and available records reveal, never committed this information to paper.

29. Schaudinn, *Reichsgründung*, p. 200; interviews with Reinhard Wittram and Hellmuth Weiss.

30. Gert Kroeger, "Zur Situation der baltischen Deutschen um die Jahrhundertwende," *Zeitschrift für Ostforschung*, XVII (1968), 601-32; Wittram, pp. 233-36.

CHAPTER 11. RUSSIFICATION IN EDUCATION

1. Manasein, pp. 180, 212-13.

2. "Materialy k izucheniiu polozheniia Evangelichesko-Liuteranskikh zemskikh narodnykh shkol v Lifiandii" (Riga: Lifliandskaia Landratskaia Kollegiia, 1884).

3. PSZ, 3rd ser., V, 90, no. 2,780, February 28, 1885; VI, 82-83, 99, nos. 3,532 and 3,563, February 19 and March 7, 1886; *Rigaer Tageblatt*, October 18, 1885. Curiously, the region's official name did not reflect the geographical shift until 1893; PSZ, 3rd ser., XIII, 96, no. 9,364, February 27, 1893.

4. *Russisch-Baltische Blätter*, IV, 36-37; Hollander, "Vor 50 Jahren," p. 552.

5. PSZ, 3rd ser., VII, 226-29, no. 4,455, May 17, 1887; Endel Laul, "1880. aastate alghariduskoolide reform Baltimaadel," *Nõukogude Kool*, 1973, no. 8, p. 694. O. Stavenhagen (ed.), "Baltische Chronik," BM, XLIV (1897), 13-14, claims this measure was not effected until 1895.

6. Tobien, I, 251; Rozhdestvenskii, p. 680; Dellingshausen, *Im Dienste*, pp. 54-55; Stavenhagen (ed.), "Baltische Chronik," p. 13.

7. Rozhdestvenskii, p. 680.

8. *Istoriia Estonskoi SSR*, II, 260.

9. Tobien, I, 252, 261, 265, 267; Bilmanis, *Latvia*, p. 248; Rosenthal, *Kulturbestrebungen*, p. 283; Freymann, "Volksschule," pp. 406-7; *Zhurnal komiteta ministrov*, June 18, 1905, German translation from May 10, 1905, session in *Kalender der Deutschen Vereine in Liv-Est-Kurland für 1913* (Riga, n.d.), p. 119; Arveds Švābe, *Latvijas vēsture 1800-1914* (Uppsala: Daugava, 1958), p. 468.

10. PSZ, 3rd ser., VII, 152-53, no. 4,343, April 10, 1887.

11. Tobien, I, 290; Waldmann, "Landesgymnasium zu Fellin," p. 22.

12. Tobien, I, 291-93; Baron Friedrich von Meyendorff to Baron Ferdinand von Wrangell, August 31, 1888, in Wrangell, "Zur Geschichte der Russifizierung," *Baltische Hefte*, VIII, 71-74. See also Wrangell's answer of September 11, 1888: Ibid., pp. 74-75.

13. Tobien, I, 293; Alexander Bergengrün, "Die Abschiedsgrüsse unserer Landesgymnasien," BM, XL (1893), 245; Dellingshausen, *Im Dienste*, pp. 55-57; Paul Blosfeld, *Geschichte der Domschule zu Reval 1906-1922* (Leipzig: F. Wassermann, 1923), p. 12; Alexander Winkler, "Vom Leben und Untergang der Domschule zu Reval, der ältesten deutschen Auslands-

schule," ed. Franz Schmidt, *Deutsche Bildungsarbeit im Ausland nach dem ersten und dem zweiten Weltkriege* (Braunschweig: Westermann, 1956), p. 91; AS, I, 216.

14. Gotthard Schweder, "Das deutsche Schulwesen in den Städten," Schilling and Schrenck (eds.), *Baltische Bürgerkunde*, p. 267; Hollander, "Vor 50 Jahren," pp. 555-56; PSZ, 3rd ser., IX, 1st Section, 227, no. 6,036, May 23, 1889; X, 1st Section, 299-300, no. 6,720, April 17, 1890; *Rigaer Tageblatt*, April 2, 1887; Rozhdestvenskii, p. 674. For a colorful, if not disinterested, picture of the effect Russification had on the Libau *Realschule*, see Fr. Demme, "Vierzig Jahre Schuldienst," BM, 1927, pp. 263-65. For Demme's career, see DBL, p. 163.

15. Steinwand, *Schulerinnerungen*, pp. 16-17, 31-32.

16. Wachtsmuth, *Lebenserinnerungen*, pp. 44, 59-60. Because of their acceptance of Baltic German pupils, for a brief period in the 1890s the German church schools in St. Petersburg also found themselves in danger of being Russified: Friesendorff, "Erinnerungen," pp. 291-93.

17. Steinwand, *Schulerinnerungen*, pp. 18-30; Wachtsmuth, *Lebenserinnerungen*, pp. 52-53, 61; Tobien, I, 295-97.

18. For example, see Oswald Hartge, *Auf des Lebens grosser Waage. Erinnerungen 1895-1939* (Hannover-Döhren: Harro von Hirschheydt, 1968), p. 131 and Wachtsmuth, *Lebenserinnerungen*, p. 52.

19. For example, twice a week in Dorpat, pupils from the instructional circles would go to a physical exercise class in a sports hall used in common with students from regular schools. Steinwand, *Schulerinnerungen*, p. 26.

20. Pilar v. Pilchau, "Bilder aus meinem Leben," p. 17; Meyendorff's diary from March 19, 1904 as cited in Tobien, I, 300n; Seraphim, *Führende Deutsche*, p. 414.

21. Friesendorff, "Erinnerungen," p. 288.

22. *Zhurnal komiteta ministrov*, June 18, 1905; German trans., *Kalender*, pp. 119-20.

23. Tobien, I, 271-72; Villebois, "Landvolksschulen," p. 253; Dalton, *Lebenserinnerungen*, III, 118; *Russisch-Baltische Blätter*, IV, 26-27; Wittram, "Überfremdungsversuche," *Ostland*, I (1942), 6. Actually, the few Latvians who became enamoured of Marxism at this time got their Marxism from western Europe, not from Russia.

24. *Kalender*, p. 119; Villebois, "Landvolksschulen," p. 253.

25. *Kalender*, p. 120.

26. PSZ, 3rd ser., XXV, 1st Section, 548, no. 26,452, June 18, 1905; XXVI, 1st Section, 518-19, no. 27,855, April 26, 1906; Wittram, p. 240.

27. Zaionchkovskii, *Rossiiskoe samoderzhavie*, pp. 318-28; PSZ, 3rd ser., IV, 456-74, no. 2,404, August 23, 1884.

28. PSZ, 2nd ser., XL, 1st Section, 21-30, no. 41,667, January 9, 1865.

29. Manasein, pp. 199-214.

30. *Rus'*, 1884, no. 12, p. 6 (cited in Petukhov, II, 17-18); *Novoe vremia*, September 17, 1885.

31. *Vestnik Evropy*, October 3, 1885. Dorpat University also received

support from publications in Germany, most notably the *Preussische Jahrbücher* and the *Münchener Neuesten Nachrichten*: Engelhardt, p. 481.

32. *Rigaer Tageblatt*, October 22, 1885; Georg von Oettingen, "Erinnerungen," pp. 160-61.

33. Petukhov, II, 78-80; Rozhdestvenskii, p. 670.

34. The *ukaz* also offered considerable financial bonuses to professors who already held chairs and who would henceforth lecture in Russian. PSZ, 3rd ser., IX, 1st Section, 53, no. 5,755, February 4, 1889.

35. Engelhardt, pp. 489-90, 494, 500. On Engelmann's career, see DBL, p. 195.

36. PSZ, 3rd ser., IX, 1st Section, 389, 613-14, nos. 6,163 and 6,369, July 7 and November 20, 1889.

37. Petukhov, II, 80-82; Engelhardt, p. 498; PSZ, 3rd ser., XIII, 11-12, 96, nos. 9,244 and 9,364, January 14 and February 27, 1893. The *ukaz* of January 14 also officially renamed Dünaburg, "Dvinsk," and the same day Dünamunde was renamed "Ust'-Dvinsk." PSZ, 3rd ser., XIII, 12, no. 9,245, January 14, 1893.

38. Petukhov, II, 82-83, 87. According to Hellmuth Weiss, however, after this order went into effect it was a common occurrence for German professors at Iur'ev surreptitiously to allow students to take examinations in German.

39. Georg von Oettingen, "Erinnerungen," 165-68; Tobien, I, 342-46.

40. Petukhov, II, 78-79, 139; PSZ, 3rd ser., XIV, 1st Section, 105, no. 10,413, March 10, 1894.

41. Shenshin (ed.), *Sbornik tsirkuliarov*, p. 493, no. 315. See, for example, the description of the seventy-fifth anniversary celebration of the corporation *Livonia* in 1897 in Hoerschelmann, "Aus alten Dorpater Tagen," p. 260.

42. Engelhardt, p. 505.

43. A. von Engelhardt, *Die deutschen Ostseeprovinzen Russlands* (München: G. Müller, 1916), p. 226. For detailed statistics on the composition of the Dorpat/Iur'ev student body, see E. V. Petukhov, *Statisticheskie tablitsy i lichnye spiski po Imperatorskomu Iur'evskomu, byvshemu Derptskomu, universitetu (1802-1901)* (Iur'ev: K. Mattisen, 1902).

44. Engelhardt (*Die deutsche Universität*), pp. 494-95.

45. Tobien, I, 344; Engelhardt, pp. 515-18; Wittram, p. 225.

46. Leimanis, "Polytechnical Institute," *Journal of Baltic Studies*, III, 115-21; Hollander, "Vor 50 Jahren," p. 558; Tobien, I, 354-56; Wachtsmuth, "Der Rigasche Burschenstaat," pp. 6, 22.

47. Lenz, *Riga*, p. 72; Schönfeldt, "Geistiges Leben," *Handwörterbuch des Grenz- und Auslanddeutschtums*, II, 213; Demme, "Vierzig Jahre Schuldienst," BM, 1927, p. 330.

CHAPTER 12. CONCLUDING REMARKS

1. For an interesting discussion of Russian imperialism, see Dietrich Geyer, "Russland als Problem der vergleichenden Imperialismusforschung,"

Das Vergangene und die Geschichte: Festschrift für Reinhard Wittram zum 70. Geburtstag, ed. Rudolf von Thadden, Gert von Pistohlkors, and Hellmuth Weiss (Göttingen: Vandenhoeck & Ruprecht, [1973], pp. 337-68). The following "concluding remarks" have appeared in slightly different form in my *Abbau der deutschen ständischen Selbstverwaltung in den Ostseeprovinzen Russlands,* pp. 157-62.

2. Hans Rothfels, *Reich, Staat und Nation im Deutsch-Baltischen Denken,* Schriften der Königsberger Gelehrten Gesellschaft, VII, Heft 4 (Halle: M. Niemeyer, 1930), pp. 219-40. Even the wisest among the Baltic German nobility could compartmentalize their thinking to exclude the Estonians and Latvians. In a speech to the Diet after his reelection as marshal of the nobility, Count Alexander Keyserling called Estland, "that unique land in which not wealth, noble birth, nor high rank can grant a man a position, rather only the extent of [his] willingness to work in the service of the homeland" (Dellingshausen, *Im Dienste,* p. 29). Dellingshausen's memoirs take their title from the last part of this quotation.

3. On the question of the primacy of class or nationality as the Baltic Germans' motive for defense of provincial autonomy, see Kroeger, "Jahrhundertwende," *Zeitschrift für Ostforschung,* XVII, 601-32; Reinhard Wittram, "Methodologische und geschichtstheoretische Überlegungen zu Problemen der baltischen Geschichtsforschung," *Zeitschrift für Ostforschung,* XX (1971), 630-31; Pistohlkors, "Führende Schicht," *Zeitschrift für Ostforschung,* XXI, 601-18; Dukhanov, *Ostzeitsy,* pp. 31-32, 327, 348-54; Lenz, *Riga,* p. 58; *Literatenstand,* p. 38; Kroeger, "Jahrhundertwende," pp. 615-17.

4. Wittram, p. 224; Lenz, *Literatenstand,* p. 36; and especially one of the most anti-Russian diatribes ever written: Victor Hehn, *De moribus Ruthenorum. Zur Charakteristik der russischen Volksseele. Tagebuchblätter aus den Jahren 1857-1873,* ed. Theodor Schiemann (Stuttgart: J. G. Cotta, 1892).

5. The lack of face-to-face contact between leaders of the various *Ritterschaften* is astounding to the historian. In 1894, Marshal of the Livland Nobility Meyendorff wrote to Marshal of the Ösel Nobility Ekesparre, expressing how sorry he was that they had not seen each other for years! He added that he hoped to see him more frequently in St. Petersburg. Meyendorff to Ekesparre, February 27, 1894, BM, LXI, 1931, pp. 462-63.

6. The strongest argument for the thesis that a German-Latvian-Estonian sharing of power could have successfully resisted the Russification is found in Walters, *Baltengedanken und Baltenpolitik,* pp. 152, 156-57, 160-62, 187, 211.

7. Ibid., p. 210.

8. The counsellor of the Austro-Hungarian Embassy in St. Petersburg and later foreign minister, Baron von Aehrenthal, tended to concede the Russian government a right to Russify the Baltic police and judicial systems, but he sharply criticized the Russification of the schools. Reinhard Wittram, "Die russisch-nationalen Tendenzen der achtziger Jahre im Spiegel der österreichisch-ungarischen diplomatischen Berichte aus St. Petersburg,"

Walther Hubatsch (ed.), *Schicksalswege Deutscher Vergangenheit* (Düsseldorf: Droste, 1950), pp. 350-51.

9. As Pantenius, who advocated this position, admitted: Pantenius, "Erinnerungen," pp. 118-19.

10. Meyendorff to Wrangell, August 31, 1888, in Wrangell, "Zur Geschichte der Russifizierung," p. 74.

PART THREE

THE LATVIANS

ANDREJS PLAKANS

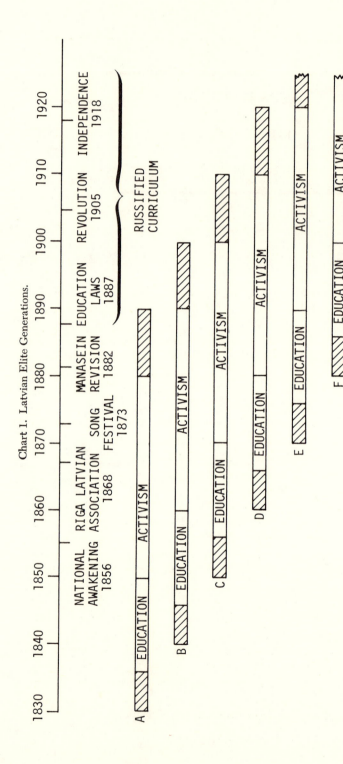

Chart 1. Latvian Elite Generations.

LIFETIME = 60 YEARS

EDUCATION = FROM 8 TO 20

ACTIVISM = FROM 20 to 50

CHAPTER 13

LATVIANS BEFORE THE 1880S

THE POLITICAL EVENTS of the twentieth century have made objectivity in Latvian historical scholarship increasingly difficult, especially in the treatment of topics that are not rescued by their antiquity from association with contemporary issues. Emerging after World War I within the context of newly acquired political independence, Latvian historical writing had little time in these years to break free of the politics of nation building. The same scholars, writers, and artists who had matured intellectually during the last decades of Latvian membership in the Russian Empire—thus during the years of cultural Russification—now dominated the independent Latvian intellectual world in a manner that tended to reflect their earlier experiences. As late as 1937, the journal of the Latvian Historical Institute was urging Latvian historians to interpret the past "in light of nationalism and truth."[1] Since World War II, due to the deep rift introduced by emigration and the appearance of a Soviet Latvia, Latvian-language historical writing has led a schizophrenic existence, producing works by no means bereft of analytical merit but at the same time characterized (as the subject warrants) by either pro- or anti-Russian sentiments.[2]

These remarks are a short explanation of why an examination of Latvian attitudes toward Russification cannot draw upon extensive secondary sources.[3] Up to 1918, the subject was unlikely to be discussed straightforwardly; after that date, it was dealt with in terms acceptable to Latvian nationalism; and, still later, other extrahistorical considerations have normally colored the description of events in the pre–World War I years. Like many deserving problems of Latvian history in the nineteenth century, the subject still awaits a chronicler, an historian with full access to primary sources who will patiently sift through the thousands of pages of the Latvian periodical press, the hundreds of individual biographies, and the many records of local governmental bodies, all of which constitute the *Nachlass* of the Russification period.[4] Such a work is not likely to change significantly the general conclusions that can be drawn on the basis of presently available literature, but not until it appears can the claim be made that the subject has been studied exhaustively.

As the other Parts of the present book show, the phenomenon of Russification had many dimensions. It included administrative proposals that began as far back as the reign of Catherine; cultural policies that were intensively applied only during the last part of the nineteenth century, and then unevenly; and population movements, not planned by anyone, that still involved loss of nationality. Reactions to all of these aspects of Russification among the affected borderland populations varied according to the structural position of each. Latvians, being one of the two major subordinated populations of the Baltic Provinces, had first to change internally before they could express collective views on any subject; until such a change took place, they had neither great interest in nor any say over the shifts of power among the ruling elites. But the "modernization" of the Latvian population, while producing publicly expressed Latvian "viewpoints," did not necessarily give rise to unanimity among Latvians on major issues, so that the historian is still left with the old question of whether the publicly voiced sentiments of the few matched the privately held but unvoiced attitudes of the many. *Latvian* sources are no better than others for solving this problem, and I shall continue to advert to it as an *unsolved problem* throughout the rest of this Part.[5]

At first glance, it seems that the Latvians of Kurland and Livland, and the Lettgallians of Vitebsk *guberniia* (who were ethnically Latvian) sought to accommodate their own lives and those of their children to the new post-1885 circumstances as best they could, in the manner of people who had had long experience in absorbing and adjusting to changes imposed from above.[6] Were the majority of Latvians therefore complaisant recipients of the new policy; participants as it were, in their own denationalization? On this score, it is necessary to take a longer view of the Latvian population. In a relatively decentralized system such as the Russian Empire, policy originating at the center entered a hundred different local milieus, each of which had its own internal history in terms of which the policy was received. These internal, local histories had had their own rhythms, their own peculiar patterns, the timing of which did not necessarily correspond to the periodization we might want to use for the history of imperial policy. As far as serious Russification policy was concerned, it arrived among Latvians during a late phase of their internal development. Several activist generations within the Latvian population had already been popularizing among Latvians the idea of nationality, starting some thirty years before the assassination of Alexander II and the Manasein inspection of 1882. Cultural Russification, which was to affect Latvians more directly than other variants of Russification policy, laid claim to a generation of Latvians whose parents had already lived with the ideal of cultural autonomy for some three decades.

The concept of generations in the Latvian population is of central importance for an understanding of Latvian reactions to cultural Russification.[7] In Chart 1 (q.v.) I have represented abstractly the timing and overlap of generations in the Latvian elite population, that is, those who were likely to respond to policy changes in some overt fashion. The chart assumes for individuals an average lifetime of sixty years, a period of education lasting from about age eight to age twenty, and a period of public activity lasting from age twenty to about age fifty. It was Generation A that launched and supervised the so-called Latvian national awakening, with its call for a new consciousness of nationality and challenge to German overlordship in the Baltic Provinces. From the start of the "national awakening" to the onset of cultural Russification in the mid-1880s, four generations received an education while Latvian nationalism was becoming increasingly more sophisticated and Latvian literary culture increasingly more productive, and the activist period of the last three of these overlapped with the period of cultural Russification. The principal ideas of these generations had therefore been formed *before* the advent of cultural Russification; and it was the members of these three generations, some older and some younger, who challenged existing nationalist ideas in the 1890s, participated in the Revolution of 1905, continued to push for Latvian causes in the four Dumas between 1905 and 1914, and finally entered, as "elder statemen," into the new institutions of the Latvian state after 1918. To a great extent, therefore, the first generation of Latvians whose whole educational experience took place in a Russified school curriculum (Generation *F*) was peripheral to the development of Latvian cultural and political attitudes before 1914, since its members formed but a small proportion of the active Latvian elite of that time. Even though highly schematic, Chart 1 will serve as the basis of our discussion of Russification among the Latvians for the remainder of this Part.[8]

Though Latvians were a subordinated population, the problem was not simply one of master and servant, a government-initiated policy and a passive population receiving it. The same historical currents— summed up with the term "modernization"—that produced Russification also had provoked processes of internal differentiation within the Latvian population.[9] By the 1880s, when with the accession to the throne of Alexander III cultural Russification began in earnest, the Latvian population had undergone social, occupational, and intellectual developments that changed substantially the milieu into which this policy was to arrive. For historians working in retrospect, it is risky to attach the designation of "spokesman" to any one group or individual within the Latvian ranks of this period. To be sure, there was at least one group that wanted to lay claim to that role. The Riga Latvian Association (founded in 1868) promoted for itself the description of *māmuļa* (mother) of all Latvian public activity, which was not altogether unwarranted for the decades before the 1880s.[10] Nonetheless, organizations such as the RLA were not composed of representatives in the strict sense, nor were its widespread activities necessarily an expression of an inclusive understanding of all the "needs" of the Latvian people. These needs were probably much more diverse than the RLA tended to picture them. To point this out is not to fall prey to a "class" interpretation of the decades after the 1850s. It is simply to note that there existed differences in viewpoint between the Riga professionals who dominated the RLA and, for instance, the thousands of small landowners who had acquired their holdings since the 1850s when land could finally be purchased; between those nationalistic intellectuals who were preoccupied with questions of "national culture" and the thousands of landless peasants who after the 1860s began to drift to the interior of Russia in search of land and work; between the urban factory workers whose number had increased since the 1850s and the large peasant landowners of the Kurland and Livland countrysides.[11] The very program of the RLA suggests that there were thousands, perhaps tens of thousands, of Latvian speakers who still did not see themselves as "Latvians" in the same sense that the RLA wanted them to. People to whom "Latvianness" (*latvietība*) was of little concern (even though they might speak Latvian as a primary language) would not have reacted heatedly to policies directed at nationality transformation.

The Latvian-speaking population of the Baltic Provinces had been for centuries a lower order in a hierarchically arranged society of orders, the upper ranks of which—the Baltic Germans—had had to renew their control each time military conflict resulted in a change of sovereigns.[12] As elsewhere in Europe, the peasantry in the Baltic area was the most numerous of the social orders, with the nonpeasant elements of the population seldom exceeding 5-6 percent of the whole. During the premodern era the Latvian population appears to have had the normal demographic characteristics of all preindustrial populations, namely, long-term population gains offset periodically by peaking mortality rates, especially in such events as the disastrous warfare at the beginning of the seventeenth and the beginning of the eighteenth centuries.[13] After the Great Northern War, however, the total population of the Latvian-language areas appears to have increased steadily, from about 465,000 at the beginning of the eight-

eenth century to about 873,000 at its end. Divided by areas in which
Latvian speakers lived, the total of 873,000 was distributed as follows: 293,000 in Livland, 390,000 in Kurland, and 190,000 in Lettgallia.[14] These figures all include the non-Latvian elements of the population, with the Latvian proportion being somewhat over 90 percent
of the total. The least ethnically mixed regions were in the western
areas and contained only Latvian peasants and German-speaking landowners, officials, and rural artisans; in the eastern portions, and
especially in southeastern Kurland, the ethnic mix was considerable,
consisting of Latvians, Germans, Poles, Jews, Russians, Lithuanians,
and Belorussians.[15]

One significant question regarding the Latvian-speaking population has to do with the ties between its different segments in the premodern centuries. Collective designations such as "peasantry" and
"Latvian" tend to be misleading, since they suggest greater cohesion
than may have been present. It is then only a short step to the belief
that this single aggregate had uniform attitudes. Nationalist and
Marxist ideology, both of which have been prominent from the first
in guiding explorations of the Latvian past, confuse the issue further.
On the one hand, nineteenth-century Latvian nationalist thought
contained a strong belief in the concept of the *Volk*, which twen-
tieth-century historians have been loath to abandon; on the other
hand, Marxism introduced the concept of "class consciousness" in the
analysis of even preindustrial populations.[16] Both of these concepts
have served a positive function in the past; the idea of the *Volk*
creating a "Latvian" historiography in contrast to a historiography
that dealt largely with the "Baltic" and the elites thereof; the concepts of "class," "class consciousness," and "class war" forcing the
consideration of socioeconomic divisions within the Latvian population which the nationalists tended to overlook or to consider epi-
phenomenal to "real" unity. At the same time, however, these concepts
promoted the belief in cohesion without considering the effects of
geographic dispersion and the profound localism which Latvian peasants shared with peasants elsewhere in old regime Europe. It has
been pointed out that serfdom, by tying Latvian serfs to the manors
of their fathers, intensified localism; and that the limited movement
that was present was still insufficient to overcome the effects of actual
dispersion.[17] There were, moreover, no major concentrations of Latvians in urban settings in these centuries. Such evidence as we have
concerning the settlement history of the Latvian population strongly
suggests that the term "Latvian" is misleading if used to connote anything other than language similarities. There could not be, in these
premodern centuries, a "Latvian" opinion because there was not a

single, internally coherent "Latvian" population to express and share it.

To geographical dispersion and intense localism as obstacles to the emergence of a "Latvian" opinion in premodern centuries must be added the near-universal illiteracy of the Latvian peasantry. Statistics regarding literacy are sparse in the Baltic area as elsewhere for the preindustrial centuries, and there are none to convince the analyst that the Latvian peasantry differed substantially in this respect from other European peasants. At the end of the eighteenth century, the pastor of Nerft parish in Kurland gathered statistics on the literacy of his parishioners, and these showed that the peasants in his parish may have been somewhat more capable of reading and writing, and may have had in their households more religious literature to read, than was true elsewhere.[18] But it would be misleading to project these statistics backward in time. It is true, of course, that starting with the sixteenth century there came into being a body of written material in the Latvian language, including Pastor Ernst Glück's (1652-1705) translations of the Old and New Testaments, but this for the most part was the product of the pens of the Baltic German clergy. To label it "Latvian literature" as is frequently done, is misleading, since the number of Latvians who actually contributed to its creation could be counted on the fingers of one hand. Moreover, the content of this "Latvian literature" was almost wholly religious; secular topics were not written about in the Latvian language until the eighteenth century when G. F. Stender (1714-1796) began to publish didactic stories for the moral uplift of the peasantry. The biggest gap in our knowledge of peasant literacy is lack of proof that in the premodern centuries these materials were actually widely read.[19] Until more is known, we are forced to conclude that Latvian attitudes, born of experiences within localities, remained local since there was no means of communicating them interregionally.

It has sometimes been held that in the absence of *written* evidence for Latvian attitudes, the historian should turn to folklore materials, to the oral tradition as the "literature of the *Volk*." There have been efforts to deduce legal concepts from folksongs (*dainas*), folktales and proverbs, on the assumption that the surviving oral tradition, collected for the most part in the latter years of the nineteenth century, would yield insights into what Latvians believed as far back as the medieval period.[20] The best of these investigations have been by no means naive, and scholars have paid careful attention to the dating of oral evidence and to the problem of anachronisms. Generally, however, research of this type has proceeded on the basis of assumptions mentioned earlier, namely, that oral traditions in the Latvian language came from one people, and therefore must contain the collective attitudes of this people. To some extent this notion was strengthened by collection techniques: contributions from hundreds of different localities were brought together between the covers of printed volumes, correlated with respect to content, and arranged under thematic headings. The result was a *set* of ideas, perhaps even a primitive philosophical system, purportedly believed in by "the Latvians."[21] In this process the profoundly local nature of most folklore came to be treated as a problem to be overcome by the mechanics of data arrangement. However useful these procedures might have been for the rational study of folklore materials, they also succeeded in hiding some problems of empirical research.

The research on Latvian peasant disturbances in the premodern period has been based on similar assumptions.[22] Here the starting point has been not a *Volk* soul but a uniform consciousness of class among the Latvian-speaking peasants. Court records and political chronicles from the seventeenth and eighteenth centuries document a multitude of grievances as well as the persisting theme of peasant unrest which sometimes involved hundreds of individuals. Subsequent historians have sought to use these individual cases of complaint and disturbance to build theories of centuries-long resistance to the German-speaking upper orders, that is, simmering opposition to the status quo occasionally boiling over into physical destruction and murder. Here, then, would be material for inferring a kind of subterranean public opinion, which expressed itself not in writing but in violent acts. However, if these complaints and acts of violence are examined without an integrating theory of class consciousness, they do not suggest very much uniformity or longevity.[23] They appear as localized phenomena, responsive to short-term deteriorating conditions, with little attitudinal carry-over from one event to the next. Few of them were mentioned in the oral tradition, so that their very existence has had to be brought to light by later historians.[24] In fact, the Latvian nationalists of the 1860s and 1870s were highly conscious of being "new men" and complained always of the real absence of Latvian historical heroes. While it is quite true that there existed a consciousness of landowners as "strangers" who did not speak the peasant language, or spoke it brokenly, there is no evidence to warrant attributing to this sometime characteristic of peasant unrest the status of a primary motive. The approaches which characterize these conflicts as either "national struggles" or "class struggles" must be viewed with great caution and with due respect to their origins in the nationalistic or Marxist ideologies of the nineteenth century.

There have also been attempts to perceive a "national" element in the personal histories of the few Latvians who in the premodern centuries succeeded through their own and their patrons' efforts in leaving the peasantry and becoming, occupationally at least, literati or town residents.[25] The desire to propose nationality as a prime element in the difficulties these people encountered has receded in recent Latvian histories, and their failures or successes have now been attributed to the normal social biases of a society of orders rather than to nationality conflict.[26] What emerges is a picture of able individuals achieving a considerable degree of upward mobility, and suffering little self-doubt in adopting the political opinions of their new peers. The number of these people is small, and evidence about them is scanty, but the phenomenon is marked enough to conclude that the process which some Baltic German historians have termed *Volkstumswechsel* was not unfamiliar to the Latvian peasantry.[27] There were apparently degrees of denationalization. Latvian peasants who became literati adopted German names and became identified so closely with their new professional circles that their earlier identity is frequently unclear even after much arduous research. Latvian artisans and laborers in cities apparently underwent less denationalization, and intermarried largely among themselves. Starting with the eighteenth century, there opened other avenues of denationalization: recruitment into the Russian army was apparently habitually referred to among the peasantry as "becoming Russian."[28] The general point here is that the able, the skilled, the adventurous, and the energetic among the peasants could find at times means of exiting from the peasant *Stand,* and that this process more often than not meant not the formation of a Latvian-speaking elite, which might serve to advance "Latvian" opinions from its new position, but rather the absorption of these upwardly mobile people into other nationalities. Native elites, the original exemplars of which had disappeared during the course of the thirteenth and fourteenth centuries, were a structural element of the Latvian population that would not reappear until the second half of the nineteenth century.

If the ideas of a collective folk soul and a consciousness of class are not used to endow the scanty data of the premodern centuries with special meanings, we are left with a long period of Latvian history during which general Latvian attitudes toward local, regional, and imperial authority can only be guessed at. Presumably attitudes did exist at the individual level. Individual peasants, and perhaps even peasant communities, held opinions about local landowners; and a single generation of peasants may have had the opportunity to draw comparisons between different sovereigns, if a shift took place during that generation. There may even have been unarticulated long-term resentments toward the traditional Baltic German overlords, since language differences between the elites and the peasantry were overt. These conclusions may be *deduced* from the social structural facts of the Baltic littoral, where elite behavior varied greatly from one locality to another, and language groups corresponded to the social orders. But there is very little empirical evidence at this time that such individually and locally held attitudes were identical over large segments of the peasant population, or that they were perpetuated from one generation to the next.[29]

The first opportunity for historians to begin documenting Latvian public attitudes arises with the first decades of the nineteenth century. Even then it was still isolated Latvians who began to participate in the literary life of the Baltic Provinces. The peasant-poet Indriķis Hartmanis ("Blind Indriķis") (1783-1828), with the help of his Baltic German patron, published a book of poetry which to Baltic German provincial culture was something of a *cause célèbre*: "Let us not wonder that this poetry was composed by a blind Latvian," said the periodical *Wöchentliche Unterhaltungen*, "it would have been even more wonderful if it had been done by a Latvian with his eyesight."[30] To the Baltic German literati, Hartmanis was a very different creature from the earlier Latvians who had gained entry into German-language culture by changing nationalities. Then, also, the 1802 peasant uprising in Kauguri was said to have had a leader who had acquired ideas about revolution from reading newspapers about the events in France from 1789 onward.[31] Moreover, in the third decade of the century there began the publication of *Latviešu avīzes*, a weekly newspaper in Latvian containing political information on events outside the provinces.[32] Published by Baltic Germans, the paper nonetheless employed native Latvian speakers to write articles. Though its tone remained didactic and unquestioning as far as local politics were concerned, its significance as a regular Latvian-language publication was probably greater than the publishers ever intended. The appearance of the paper was one manifestation among many of a new attitude among the Baltic German literati toward the culture of the peasantry; another such manifestation was the establishment of the *Lettisch-literärische Gesellschaft* in 1824.[33] Publications and societies of this nature had a double meaning in the Baltic area: on the one hand, they testified to the seriousness with which the dominant language group was now going to approach subordinated groups, as objects of "scientific" investigation; on the other, in the imagination of the Latvian-speaking readers, this new attention had a political meaning, namely that the language of the peasantry was intrinsically valuable, and that it could be used as a vehicle of communication in public media. Without necessarily intending it, the Baltic German literati gave new status to the Latvian language, and the lesson was not lost on the young Latvian men of the 1830s and 1840s who for various reasons had begun to view upward occupational mobility as a distinct possibility.

This shift in Latvian attitudes toward their personal futures appeared in the decades following serf emancipation in the Baltic area. Emancipation has been interpreted variously: as the arrival of "freedom," by those contemporary Latvians who had the opportunity to comment on it; or as a dastardly trick played upon the peasantry by landowners, by later nationalist historians.[34] The emancipation, since it affected the whole Baltic population, had a number of different meanings. Its social-structural meaning was quite clear, however: after the emancipation an increasingly larger number of peasants had the opportunity to leave their order and make their way into other occupations. These number were initially small, consisting of a minuscule proportion of the age groups that could have changed their occupations had *total* freedom been obtained (i.e. freedom of mobility as well as freedom of the person). Thus there were a few Latvians enrolling in Dorpat, other handfuls obtaining the right to teach rural school children through education in the several teachers' institutes (including the famous Cimze seminary), and still others using the help of well-intentioned Baltic-German patrons to acquire self-education.

Serf emancipation in the Baltic Provinces was a drawn-out process, with its last phases concluding some fifteen years after the original edicts. The origins of these emancipatory activities among the Baltic German landowners were in turn tied to earlier reforms in 1804 in Livland; and, in a sense, the whole reform period might be regarded as having reached its final stage when in the late 1850s and 1860s peasants received the right to buy land.[35] No Latvian peasants born after 1800, therefore, lived without experiencing significant changes in their personal status; reform, or at least discussions of reform, had been so spaced as to affect the grandparental, parental, and children's generations. This did not mean, of course, that each successive generation of Latvian-speaking peasants could count on being wealthier than their parents; in fact, the reversion of peasant land to the ownership of Baltic Germans meant in many cases just the opposite. But in the search for the various elements of the "temper of the times" prior to 1850, the restlessness born of ever-increasing expectations of change must surely count as significant.

Among the reforms of the period from 1816 to 1820, the one that placed responsibilities for local affairs in the hands of the peasantry must be counted as a very significant step in the development of

Latvian public attitudes. Landowners willingly gave up their "patriarchal responsibilities," and from this point onward the population of each landed estate was declared to be a township (*Gemeinde; volost'; pagasts*), with its most important offices filled from the ranks of the peasantry. Landowners retained numerous rights, of course, including the right of corporal punishment; but the local solidarity that grew from peasant participation in the township's characteristic institutions—the council, the treasury, the court, the school—was clearly an advance as far as the emergence of Latvian public opinion was concerned. As never before, issues could be discussed, answers to local problems experimented with, and the techniques of local government learned by individuals who had never before had such opportunities. Since local governmental problems tended to be similar over large regions of the provinces, and were confronted in roughly similar forms by each new generation of the peasantry, traditions of expertise could be built up. Complexities of government were thereby brought into the sphere of activity in which the Latvian language was the chief instrument of communication. The language now seemed to its native speakers increasingly less only a peasant tongue; and to some it held substantial promise as a vehicle for expressing high culture.

There is little indication that during the decades between emancipation and the "national awakening" of the 1850s Latvians nurtured hopes about radical changes in Baltic society. Jānis Cimze (1814-1881), whose seminary trained numerous Latvian schoolteachers, defended his institution against charges of radicalism by pointing out that he was teaching his students to link education and Christianity, not to put into practice "radical political principles."[36] That he knew what political radicalism was in the 1830s seems clear from the cosmopolitan education he himself had received. If anything, the publications of Latvian writers of these decades were filled with paeans of gratitude to the "liberator" Tsar Alexander I, to particular Baltic German patrons who had helped Latvians into their nonagricultural careers, and to such historical figures as Martin Luther and Johannes Gutenberg. A number of the pre-awakening Latvians belonged to the *Lettisch-literärische Gesellschaft*, and contributed to its publications. In fact, the acerbic writers of the "national awakening" generally regarded these precursors as too temperate and otherworldly; their apparent willingness to continue working under the stewardship of Baltic German organizations and individuals signaled their acceptance of the old course of upward mobility: from Latvian-speaking peasants to German-speaking literati.[37] Whatever their accomplishments, and their privately held attitudes, publicly there was as yet no clean break with the past.

The appearance of these early Latvian writers was the first phase of a development which became more pronounced later, namely, the separation of a segment of Latvian literary activists from a much larger segment of the inarticulate many. It would be somewhat misleading to talk about this division in terms of an "elite" and the "masses," since the two were still very close structurally, and, if anything, the "elite" was for all intents and purposes absorbed into the German-speaking literati. Nonetheless, even in the pre-1850 period, some differences in outlook can be noted. While the Latvian-speaking men of letters tended toward conservatism, the general Latvian population contained many whose actions suggested a willingness to break with traditional arrangements, even to the extent of departing altogether from the land of their forefathers. During the 1840s and 1850s there took place the so-called movement to the warm lands, which involved thousands of Livland and Kurland peasants and was based on the mistaken notion that with conversion to Russion Orthodoxy free land would be available in the interior of Russia.[38] The roots of this mass phenomenon seem clear: the landlessness of the Latvian-speaking peasants was growing during the decades since emancipation. At the same time, the willingness of so many peasants to convert to the "faith of the tsar" and to abandon the Lutheranism of their forefathers and traditional seigneurs suggests that to many a change of religious loyalties was a fair trade for the promise of economic betterment. Whatever thousands of Latvian peasants felt about the political organization of the Baltic area, or about their subordination to the Russian tsar, these feelings were apparently not an obstacle to the first manifestations of what could be called "unplanned Russification."

With the passage of time, agrarian relations in Livland and Kurland underwent further modernizing changes. By the mid-1850s land could be purchased by peasants in Livland; and in the early 1860s the same became true in Kurland. Labor rents, in existence since the emancipation, were on their way out nearly everywhere.[39] Moreover, a series of internal passport reforms made migration easier within the Baltic Provinces, as well as from the provinces to the interior of Russia. All of these developments, taking place within a single generation, served as the context for a radical alteration of the views of the growing Latvian-speaking intelligentsia, which, according to its own description, began in the second half of the 1850s to preside over the Latvian "national awakening."[40] The exact causes of this change are difficult to isolate: in the final analysis they may have to be looked for in the individual biographies of these nationalistic activists. It appears that in the intellectual development of specific individuals, the idea of Latvian nationality, as the basis of both personal and group identity, became acceptable in the late 1850s in a way that it had not been earlier. As a social type, the "new Latvians" were not so different from the generation of Cimze: both were rooted in the peasant culture, both had to depend on patrons for an education, and both perceived the masses of the Latvian population as objects of education. In the writings of the pre-awakening activists, nationality appeared as only one aspect of the general self-improvement of the peasantry: peasants could achieve enlightenment faster if they were educated via the language they already knew. But with the "new Latvians" nationality moved to a new position: peasants were to be educated not only for the purposes of general enlightenment but also in the full meaning of their basic national membership. The "new Latvians" believed that at this historic juncture the Latvian-speaking peasantry had "evolved" to the point of being able to understand this argument: Krišjānis Valdemārs (1825-1891), one of the most active of the new literati, concluded as early as 1853 that now was the time to "pull our national brothers into the light"; and the new periodical *Mājas viesis* (est. 1856) concluded in 1860 that "the Latvians have now awakened."[41]

All of these metaphors were useful for contemporary activists because they suggested motion, a stirring, a new spirit coming into being; in other words, they were as much wishful thinking as an actual description of what was going on among Latvian peasants. Even the Latvian national historian Arvēds Švābe concluded much later that "it took a long time for most of the Latvian nation to be awakened," and quoted with approval the retrospective characterization of the period by the culture historian R. Klaustiņš, to wit: "The nationalism of the 1860s was by no means a phenomenon of the people at large but of the intelligentsia. . . . The writers of these years were akin to the bright, ambitious and creative Enlightenment rationalists of the end of the eighteenth century."[42] From another perspective, however, these developments seemed full of troublesome implications. "One sees that the people are awakening," wrote Gustav Brasche, a Baltic German pastor who had been long concerned with peasant education, "but the careful observer cannot feel an unqualified enthusiasm for this phenomenon."[43]

There was considerably less unity among the "new Latvians" than might appear from the outside. For some, concern for the Latvian language was uppermost and provincial politics of little moment, while others cared little for literary problems and felt more at home writing critiques of agrarian conditions. Some, apparently, spoke from an attitude of secular liberalism; others were quite pious within the established Lutheran tradition; and still others saw themselves as latter-day exponents of the religious philosophy of the Moravian Brethren, even while their literary activities were not especially religious.[44] Some had undergone traumatic personal experiences that "converted" them to nationalism; some continued to see nationalism as but a tool for overall peasant self-improvement; and some, almost from the very beginning, while deeply concerned with the betterment of their conationals, suspected "nationalism" to be a refuge for charlatans, as they suspected all "philosophies" which spoke in grand concepts far removed from the realities of the Latvian peasant world.[45] There was also a diversity in family situations, a dimension which has never been explored as an element of the group biography of this generation. Some of the nationalists never married; others took German or Russian wives.[46] Some, through their offspring and siblings, established what might be described as "dynasties" of literary activists; the offspring of others intermarried with Baltic Germans or Russians and apparently abandoned their Latvian identity. The siblings of some of the more ardent nationalists were run-of-the-mill business entrepreneurs who worried about the impact on their enterprises of nationalistic excesses. Moreover, this generation of "new Latvians" continued to be bound to the Baltic German world through a variety of personal ties which some tried to keep separated from their literary activities, others renounced in a public fashion, and still others did not perceive as obstacles to holding a well-rounded philosophy of Latvian nationalism.

Other aspects of diversity could be listed, but all of them would speak to the same general point: namely, that the "national awakening" is really an artificial concept, useful perhaps for the internal periodization of Latvian history, but misleading if one wishes precisely to identify public attitudes "typical" of the activists of this period. It is true that now—in the decades between 1850 and 1870—there existed new means of expressing Latvian opinion publicly, and new attitudes to express, but there was also a host of "old" attitudes which did not disappear with the arrival of the new ones, even while the philosophy of Latvian nationalism was receiving increasingly more sophisticated expression and wider currency. Thus, it would be misleading to characterize the period with only the views of the most extreme of the "new Latvians," because the intelligentsia itself contained a variety of views; and it would be equally misleading to characterize the general attitudes of the Latvian population by reference to nationalism only.[47]

These caveats are especially important when we seek to identify the attitudes Latvians held toward constituted authority, be it Baltic

German or Russian. There was, to begin with, an unapologetic animosity to the agrarian conditions of the Baltic area, expressed in such
publications as Andrejs Spāģis', *Die Zustände des freien Bauernstandes
in Kurland*, published in Leipzig in 1860.[48] Systematic questioning of
Baltic German predominance appeared also in the most influential of
the nationalist publications, the newspaper *Pēterburgas avīzes*, which
was published through the efforts of Krišjānis Valdemārs, Krišjānis
Barons (1835-1923), and Juris Alunāns (1832-1864) from 1862 to
1865.[49] Periodical publications such as the *Pēterburgas avīzes*, however, diluted their attacks by placing them in a context of general
information. In addition to these publications, there was the old
Latviešu avīzes, accused by the "new Latvians" as taking a too permissive line toward the Baltic Germans, and the moderate *Mājas
viesis*, which began to appear in 1856.[50]

Except in the few cases of the harsh attacks published abroad, the
nationalistically inclined Latvian-speaking intelligentsia seems in its
literary expressions to have been generally circumspect. Despite their
classification as "awakeners" of the Latvian people by later historians,
and as *"fanatische Nationalisten"* by some Baltic German commentators, the Latvian nationalists appear more as reformers rather than
as "revolutionaries."[51] One element in their strategy, however, contained great potential for trouble, namely, the links they forged with
persons in Russian circles who promised to be truly harmful to Baltic
German interests. A case in point is Krišjānis Valdemārs, one of the
activists who had brought *Pēterburgas avīzes* into being. Valdemārs
had extensive personal contact with the Slavophiles, and appears to
have shared their general attitudes toward Baltic conditions.[52] He saw
no conflict between Russian imperial goals and Latvian self-interest:
the two could be mutually supportive. Judging by his writings,
Valdemārs was uninterested in the philosophical side of nationalism.
An urbane man, moving easily between the centers of the empire
and the Baltic Provinces, he saw no conflict between the use by Latvians of the Russian language and the fight for the Latvian cause.[53]
For Valdemārs, upward mobility entailed eventual entry into a universal community of intelligent men, whose labors on behalf of a
small national culture were not an obstacle to full and continuing
interaction with other nationalities. Economics was the key to Latvian
betterment, and economic development was to be obtained by drawing closer to those with effective power—the Russian government—
and achieving distance from those with waning power—the Baltic
Germans. Valdemārs died in 1894; and though during the last decades
of his life his influence among the Latvian intelligentsia weakened,

he was during his lifetime a symbol of how a heartfelt Latvianness could be combined with complete loyalty to the interests of the crown.

It is not difficult to conceive of Valdemārs' career and attitudes as one kind of response to the opportunities the Baltic area now offered. An ambitious person used avenues of professional advancement and upward mobility, and made such friends and learned such languages as were necessary, without regarding these actions as threats to some deeper national essence. This might indeed entail playing the two dominant nationalities—Russian and German—against each other, which meant that in order to survive, upwardly mobile Latvians needed to be agile politicians. Yet, the scattered evidence that exists about mobility in these decades suggests that seizing the opportunity of the moment could create long-term dangers to the national community. Education frequently meant adoption of a non-Latvian culture later in life.[54] Tendencies toward Latvian-German intermarriage had already been present in earlier periods, when a small proportion of Latvian peasants who had achieved freeman status intermarried with German-speaking rural artisans who had come to the Baltic from Germany proper.[55] There was also movement to the interior of Russia, starting with the 1860s and expanding to a continuous outward flow during the next decades.[56] As a result of this movement, Latvian-speaking "colonies" came into being in distant parts of Russia. Not all of the out-migrating Latvians were located in these. Consequently, for many of these outmigrants intermarriage with Russian-speakers, and probably conversion from Lutheranism to Orthodoxy followed eventually.[57] If modernization of the Latvian-speaking population was to mean movement and occupational diversity, contact with non-Latvian languages was inevitable. Only those who stayed in the localities of their birth, and did not aspire to nonagricultural occupations, could expect to live without close contact with non-Latvians.

Valdemārs' attitudes were not the only ones represented within the intelligentsia. There were also nationalists of a purer variety. It is to these that the Latvians of the decades between 1850 and 1880 owe a systematic exposition of a philosophy of Latvian nationalism. The desire to build a philosophical system was ignited in Atis Kronvalds (1837-1875), whose experiences with nationality problems suggest a pattern that must have been present in the lives of many.[58] During his formative years, Kronvalds was very close to his Baltic German mentor, who made it possible for him to study for a time at the University of Berlin. Kronvalds' account of these years describes how on his return trip from Berlin he was greeted by a Latvian footman as if he (Kronvalds) were a German *Jungherr*, and that that lackey's subservience drove Kronvalds into a period of depression from which he emerged converted to the idea of Latvian nationhood. The contrast between what Latvians were—a "race of subservient peasants"—and what they could be were they to unite and become claimants of what was justly theirs as a nation, spurred him to a brief but productive career as the leading philosopher of Latvian nationalism. Trained as a schoolteacher, he became active among the newer generation of Latvians preparing for this occupation and settled upon education as the one process that would guarantee the emergence of a Latvian nation in the Baltic area.[59] Unlike Valdemārs, Kronvalds restricted his activities to the Baltic area. Like Valdemārs, however, he also needed for practical reasons to publicize his ideas not only in the Latvian language but also in German, so that, in fact, his most important nationalistic tract—*Nationale Bestrebungen* (1872)—was written in German and not translated into Latvian until 1887.[60] According to Kronvalds, the central issue of the nationality question was language. The "spirit" of a people lived in its language, and it was language alone that established a tie between the living Latvians in the 1860s, their deceased forefathers, and the generations that would mature in subsequent decades. Nationality therefore was not so much a matter of economic advancement (as Valdemārs had thought) but a matter of language purity, language growth, and the utilization of the Latvian language from childhood to adulthood in all offspring born of Latvian parents. Kronvalds' writings are full of the standard rhethoric of nineteenth-century nationalistic theory, much of it apparently borrowed from Fichte. What made his theorizing particularly applicable to the current Latvian situation, however, were the dangers implicit in geographical mobility and occupational change. Latvians would be led away gradually from the language of their parents' families, and thus from the language of their forefathers, with the consequence that newly educated Latvians would not be firmly attached to any culture sphere. Such people might be a peripheral part of the dominant German nationality, but if they lost the capability of free and easy communication with their Latvian brothers, they would become unable to serve the educational functions an intelligentsia was supposed to fulfill. Thus, it was the rural school systems and rural Latvian institutions and activities in general that needed to receive the primary attention of the new Latvian activists. The denationalizing potential of modernizing change would be weakened if the primary educational institutions all were made to serve the national purposes of the Latvian people.[61]

There was no irreconcilable conflict between Valdemārs' and Kronvalds' views on these matters, since the former also was concerned with primary schooling and the latter with general economic better-ment.[62] If the two sets of ideas were to find a response within the general Latvian population, however, their legacies for the next dec-ades would be different indeed. Valdemārs' notions fitted in well with the aims of the imperial government: weakening of the Baltic Ger-man influence in the Baltic, coordinating the development of the border provinces with that of the empire as a whole. But Kronvalds' ideas ran counter to the imperial aim of further integrating the Baltic area into the empire. There is not, of course, even a hint in Kronvalds' writings concerning political autonomy for the Latvians, but the drift of his ideas was clearly in the direction of at least cul-tural autonomy. If institutionalized, Kronvalds' uncompromising posi-tion on nationality could very easily become an absolute barrier to cultural Russification.[63]

How certain can we be that by the seventh decade of the nine-teenth century the ideas of Kronvalds and Valdemārs (and lesser na-tionalists) were symptomatic of widespread sentiments among the Latvians, rather than being simply idiosyncratic? To this question there is not likely ever to be a clear answer. Both Valdemārs and Kronvalds, and other members of the intelligentsia, were convinced that they did indeed have a sympathetic audience whose aspirations they were helping to articulate and focus. They were sustained in this belief by the groups of young Latvians who gathered in Dorpat, Moscow, and St. Petersburg to debate—often in German and Rus-sian—the future of the Latvian people.[64] The subscription lists of *Mājas viesis*, *Pētersburgas avīzes*, and other periodicals were impres-sive; and with every decade population shifts were bringing an in-creasingly larger number of people into situations where literacy was necessary, thus enlarging the reading audience.[65] It is likely that the literacy rates of the mid-century increased with every decade in the second half to reach the high levels reflected in the 1897 census.[66] The 1881 provincial census of the Baltic area showed that *adult* literacy among Latvians was already quite high: among Riga Latvi-ans 77.2 percent could both read and write; and in rural areas, judg-ing by the figures from the Latvian *Kreise* of Livland, adult literacy was about 92.9 percent.[67] The reading audience differed in size from city to countryside, and from males to females, but the overall statis-tics favored the nationalists' cause. Among the publications the new audience read, *Latvian*-language materials were now likely to be the most important part. Changes in institutions also revealed the desire among Latvians to engage in activities of a national variety.

The polemical *Pētersburgas avīzes* ceased publication in 1865, but hard on its heels, in 1868, came the founding of the Riga Latvian

Association (RLA) and its newspaper *Baltijas vēstnesis,* a somewhat more moderate vehicle for Latvian ideas, though one quite as independent of Baltic German control and influence as its predecessor had been.[68] The RLA, too, tended toward moderate ideals. The main actors in its controversial founding were Riga professionals who represented the "practical" side of Latvian activism.[69] The networks of friendships, affiliations, and contacts the organization created for the Latvian-speaking bourgeoisie in Riga was in the first instance meant to enhance the economic positions of its members but, through that, the solidarity of the Latvian people as a whole. The organization was soon emulated in provincial centers as well. The RLA, its lesser counterparts, and a host of other Latvian organizations that made their appearance during the years between 1860 and 1880 reflected in a smaller setting a general European impulse to found self-help organizations of various kinds.[70] Not all of the organizations which appeared were nationalistic in intent, but they could not fail to have a meaning for the further development of national sentiments. Since charismatic leaders of the Garibaldi or Mazzini variety had not appeared among Latvians, the consolidation of sentiments, ideas, and future plans fell to an organizational network, and its practical-minded leadership. Each organization worked, by means of regular meetings, bulletins in the Latvian language, celebratory activities such as the Song Festival of 1873 and the like, to acquaint urban and rural Latvians with the mechanics of independent organizational activity, with the benefits of wielding collective power even if only at local levels, and with the expertise of "governing" which they as a traditional order had not acquired until relatively recently.[71] These organizational successes had relatively little immediate impact on Baltic German power, and had even less meaning as far as the imperial government was concerned. But they were part of a constellation of activities which, once started, tended to be self-perpetuating, and could not be expected to wither.

What remains unclear is the extent to which these activists fell into recognizable "camps." Even if at the intellectual level different ideas could be sorted out into "positions," that in itself would not be an argument for the existence of divisions at the level of everyday life. For Latvian nationalists the main battle was with the Baltic Germans: on this point even Valdemārs and Kronvalds were in agreement. But beyond the public confrontations, accompanied by much heated rhetoric on both sides, the issues lost their sharpness in the many compromises that had to be made for everyday life to continue. As mentioned earlier, many nationalists married Baltic German women, and spoke German in their families. The eminent Pastor

August Bielenstein, who applied to the Latvian activists the label of *"fanatische Nationalisten,"* continued a brisk correspondence with other Latvians on scholarly problems he was writing about. A landmark publication, the first full-length Latvian novel *Mērnieku laiki* (*The Time of the Land Surveyors*) (1879) portrayed Baltic German landowners sympathetically while caricaturing rural Latvian nationalists.[72] Attitudes toward the Russian government, emphatically favorable in the thought of activists such as Valdemārs and among the famous Latvian petitioners to the crown in 1871, did not appear to have been focused in the population at large at this point, unless we can interpret all anti-German sentiment as implicitly pro-Russian.[73] The Latvian publications of the period assumed Latvian membership in the Russian state as a given fact; and it is likely that this same attitude was taken by the general population. The potential of anti-government feelings contained in Kronvalds' variant of Latvian nationalism continued to remain latent. Kronvalds and Valdemārs diverged on this point, but the issue was not at the center of the thought of either. Both felt that upward mobility among Latvians no longer required, as it had previously, a loss of nationality; but Kronvalds was more determined than Valdemārs to see this as a moral concern. There is no evidence that the organizational activities engendered by either, or by the men of affairs in Riga, had as their aim autonomy in any but the cultural sense; and, consequently, if there was an enemy, it was the Baltic Germans, and then not all of them. Placed in the larger setting, Latvian activities in these crucial decades were responses more to the increased economic opportunities that land reform had brought with it, than to threats of "Germanization" periodically broached in Baltic German publications. The embryonic national culture which had started to emerge was a byproduct of both the leadership of men such as Kronvalds and Valdemārs, and the interacting economic and political reforms that had allowed public opinion to emerge.

CHAPTER 14

RUSSIFICATION POLICY
IN THE 1880s

MOST OF THE LATVIAN ACTIVISTS who in the mid-1880s could have been expected to hold views on the Russification issue were of a different generation from those who had launched the "awakening."[1] Not all of the pioneers were gone, of course: Valdemārs, for instance, remained moderately influential until his death in 1894; and Krišjānis Barons, another of the founders of *Pēterburgas avīzes*, lived on into the twentieth century. But many of the writers whose pens had created the literary side of the awakening died during the 1870s. The most important loss, from the Latvian viewpoint, was Atis Kronvalds, who died in 1875, at the early age of thirty-eight. Ansis Leitāns, the first editor of *Mājas viesis*, died in 1874; Cimze, the educator, in 1881; Juris Neiķēns, the pastor-poet who wrote from the Herrnhut tradition, died in 1868; and Jēkabs Zvaigznīte, the translator of classics, in 1867. The young poet Miķelis Krogzems (pseud. Auseklis), whose nationalistic poetry played such an important role in the Song Festival of 1873, died in 1879, at the age of twenty-nine.[2] Andrejs Spāǧis, author of one of the first broadside attacks on Baltic agrarian conditions written from a *Latvian* political viewpoint, had already died in 1871. Many lesser writers, too, either passed away or fell into silence, because of the natural workings of mortality or due to the infirmities of old age. It is necessary to add, of course, that the generational shift was taking place in the general population as well; relatively few people who had experienced serfdom were around by the early 1880s, and the parents of those who were schooling themselves in the 1860s and 1870s had grown up in the corvée period (*klaušu laiki*), when the first signs of geographical and social mobility had occurred among Latvian peasants.

The generation in schools during the 1860s and 1870s learned the terms of political debate from the nationalist activists who were then making their views known publicly. It is not surprising therefore that the publicly expressed views of the Latvian intelligentsia from 1875 to 1885 continued the anti-Baltic German theme, as well as the expectation that the reforms the imperial government had sought and was continuing to seek in the Baltic would be "helpful to the Latvian people."[3] Concrete views, of course, came from those publicists and pamphleteers who needed to adopt them; but the formation of a Latvian public opinion was also helped by the continuing appearance of organizations which normally took no stands on political questions. By 1887, for instance, Livland had some 231 Latvian organizations of various kinds, ranging from local literary groups to fire insurance societies.[4] These organizational efforts had substantial meaning for later developments, since in them Latvians learned to work with other Latvians and reaffirmed the belief that the long-term development of the "Latvian nation" was still a going concern. It had been difficult to claim membership in a Latvian nation when that "nation" was still, by and large, a peasantry; but such claims were less fantastic when one could refer to a substantial number of Latvians who were urbanized, a literature expressed in the Latvian langauge, and an organizational network which in at least a minor way was a factor in provincial lower-level politics. In addition to the impassioned rhethoric of Kronvalds, and the fiery poetry of Auseklis, Latvian nationality needed also a concrete basis in the everyday world, and this by the early 1880s was becoming a reality.

The 1870s also witnessed a number of disturbances in Latvian-speaking rural areas, and some minor unrest in the city of Mitau, all of which can be explained by the economic distresses of the decade.[5] These heightened the animosity between the Latvian "movement" and Baltic German officials, and in 1881 the *Lettisch-literärische Gesellschaft* expelled those of its Latvian members who were associated with nationalistic activities: notably Krišjānis Kalniņš (1847-1885), the head of the Riga Latvian Association; and Bernhards Dīriķis (1831-1892), the editor of *Baltijas vēstnesis*. Repeated complaints by the Baltic Germans that the Latvian-language press was contributing to disquiet, that provincial administrators (such as the Governor Alexander Baron von Uexküll-Güldenband) were too permissive with Latvian organizations, and that nationalistic agitation was resulting in murders and arson led the Interior Ministry to propose an inquiry into the truth of these claims. Similar inquiries had just been carried out by the Senate in nine other provinces. The purpose of such an inquiry, the tsar was informed, would be to check the efficiency of the provincial governmental institutions, gather information for the Ministry of the Interior, find out about the political coloration of the provinces, and determine the extent to which the propaganda of "agitators" had had an impact.[6] In May of 1882, Nikolai Manasein, together with seventeen assistants, arrived in Riga to conduct the senatorial inspection that was to cover both Livland and Kurland.

The Baltic German *Ritterschaften* had not expected their complaints to produce such a result, and therefore greeted the idea of an inspection with considerable reserve. On the other hand, Latvian organizations expected from the first that as a result of the inquiry Baltic German autonomy would be weakened and the position of the subordinated nationalities strengthened.[7] The hopes that Latvian complaints would finally reach the ears of imperial officials were heightened by the fact that Manasein had on his staff several Latvians and Estonians who were to translate petitions in those languages sent to the senator from the countryside. The best-known Latvian among these was Andrejs Stērste (1853-1921), who had a degree from St. Petersburg University and was thoroughly familiar with Baltic agrarian problems.[8] Also, it was known that Valdemārs had personally informed Manasein of Latvian complaints.

The Riga Latvian Association took up the task of organizing petitions in the Kurland and Livland countrysides. Though the petitions were formulated by members of the Association, and thus did not really record the *spontaneous* desires of the peasant population, thousands of signatures were obtained, nonetheless. The petitions therefore contained some of the concrete ideas to which the Latvian population was ready to give its assent, and, consequently, were a rare and unprecedented expression of public opinion on the relative merits of existing local arrangements and on conditions envisaged as more desirable.[9] The petitions called for a division of the three Baltic Provinces into two parts based on the real distribution of the Latvian and Estonian populations. These new provinces were to be called Riga and Reval. In addition to such major changes the petitions called for a host of other alterations, some of which (but definitely not all) implied an enlarged Russian presence in Baltic affairs. It was proposed that the existing provincial diets (*Landtage*) be replaced with zemstvos, with elections based on an entirely new voting system. Commissions dealing with peasant questions should all be attached to the governments of the new provinces, rather than being organs of the *Ritterschaften*. An entire reform of the legal system should be carried out, and judges and prosecutors chosen from among Russian officials. The electoral laws of towns and cities should be changed and the class system of voting abolished. But, as far as administration was concerned, the petitions made clear that the native populations should supply personnel at lower levels. Corporal punishment and the private police of the landowners should be abolished, and local police functions taken over by Latvians and Estonians.

Clergymen and local church officials should be chosen by the local church bodies, in which peasants were to have a majority of votes. With respect to education, the petitions showed a clear preference for non-German languages. All schools in the cities and countryside should have either Latvian or Estonian as the languages of instruction, and the University of Dorpat should have chairs in these languages. In the schools the hours for instruction in Russian should be increased and those for German diminished. The task of educating teachers and of appointing school inspectors should be in the hands of the zemstvos. Predictably, the petitions also called for a variety of measures to improve the economic lot of the peasantry. There should be established an agrarian credit bank, through which smallholders would be able to purchase their land outright and pay off mortgages now held by Baltic German landowners. There should be a thorough review of all land purchase agreements signed during the last decade, with the government having the right to lower the agreed-upon price, if excessive. Peasant land which had not yet been sold should be sold in line with the kinds of regulations that governed land sales in Russia proper after emancipation. There should also be a standardization of the cost of renting peasant land, and renters should have the right to have the land they rented sold to them. Landowners should be deprived of special hunting rights and the rights associated with the brewing and sale of alcohol in rural areas; and there should be a just distribution of the public labors needed for the upkeep of roads and the like in rural areas.

There were local variations in all of the petitions on these themes. By the middle of September 1882, Manasein reported that he had already received some 10,200 such petitions and by the end of the revision period their number had reached 20,000.[10] In fact, Manasein and his assistants did not act on the basis of all of these petitions: the actual inspection covered a statistically inadequate sample of all townships and estates (only ten private and thirty crown estates were examined). Whether his final recommendations would have been different had more thorough work been done is a moot question, since the delegation had inadequate manpower and Baltic German office-holders apparently worked hard to frustrate the data-gatherers, and to threaten informants. Even if Manasein had arrived in Riga with a completely objective mind regarding local conditions, the content of the petitions alone would have been enough to inform him that the drift of peasant opinion was in favor of an increased imperial presence in the Baltic area.[11] It should be noted, however, that the desire for increased Russian intervention was expressed for certain areas of activity only: the subjects of cultural activity, schooling, religion, and so forth were mentioned relatively infrequently. This is substantial evidence for the proposition that Latvians at this time were looking to the imperial government for economic betterment, hoping to reserve for themselves a sphere of free activity in matters of schooling and cultural growth.

The Baltic German authorities reacted increasingly more fiercely to all of these activities surrounding the petitions. There was a continuing barrage of polemical articles against Manasein by Baltic Germans in the provinces as well as abroad, and investigations were launched at the local level to determine who had worked to circulate petitions, who had signed them, and who could be accused of agitation and thus of "criminal" activity. But while this continued, there were already warnings from the crown that the petitioners had asked too much and that the inspection should not be expected to result in major changes in agrarian arrangements.[12] The final recommendations of the inspection were drawn up by Manasein in light of these warnings. The recommendations fell into four categories: agrarian conditions in Livland, agrarian conditions in Kurland, legal and political institutions, and popular education. In the first two of these, the report highlighted the inadequacies of existing landholding patterns in comparison with zemstvo institutions, and maintained that the landless segment of the peasant population was growing at an alarming rate. In the third, the report underlined the antagonism Manasein had perceived in the ranks of Latvian and Estonian speakers to the monopoly Baltic Germans had over public offices, and to the use of the German language in the legal process. In discussing the political coloration of the provinces, Manasein also pointed out that he had found no evidence that the Latvian and Estonian peasantry had been infected by revolutionary ideas carried to the Baltic by outside agitators. As far as public schooling was concerned, Manasein recommended that all teacher-training institutes in the provinces should be placed under the Ministry of Education; that the use of the German language be eliminated from them; that Russian be used instead as the teaching language in teacher preparation; and that all other higher intermediary institutions of learning, including the Riga Polytechnic, have Russian as their language of instruction.

Throughout his report Manasein considered the Germanization of the Latvians and Estonians as the most pressing danger that that imperial government faced in the Baltic Provinces. In reality, the 1881 provincial census figures suggest that while processes of denationalization were in fact going on, they were different for city and country, and when seen in light of aggregate figures tended toward negligibility.[13] Speaking of the Latvian population alone, in Livland the census showed that of the 414,000 people who gave "Latvian" as their nationality, 0.3 percent listed "German" as their home language, whereas only 0.03 percent listed "Russian." Of the 55,666 people of Latvian nationality in Riga, 10.3 percent listed "German" as their home language, and only 1.0 percent listed Russian in that fashion. Another way of presenting these figures brings out their meaning more clearly. There were 18,547 people in the Livland countryside who listed German as their nationality, but 21,294 who listed German as the language they spoke at home. Thus, some 2,700 Latvians had started on the path toward denationalization. By comparison, although 15,822 people listed Russian as their nationality, only 15,426 listed Russian as their home language, giving rise to the impression that some 400 "Russian" homes had begun to desert their native tongue. In Riga, the same pattern prevailed, in somewhat more emphasized form. While 52,787 people gave German as their nationality, 66,775 gave German as their home language; 13,988 people (mostly Latvians) in Riga, thus spoke German at home while claiming derivation from another nationality. The Russian language fared no better: though 32,090 of Riga's inhabitants listed Russian as their nationality, only 31,979 listed it as their home language.

These figures are the first for the Baltic area in which the results of the nationality dynamics described earlier in Chapter 13 can be examined. The numbers themselves can be subjected to differing interpretations because of their incompleteness. They do not really reflect the situation in households, and have to be divided by 4 or 5 (putative average household size) to obtain the number of households involved, on the assumption that children were not queried separately but rather fell into categories as stated by their parents.[14] It is nonetheless interesting (using this method of reducing numbers) that of the 80,000 rural Latvian families in Livland about 2,000 (2.5 percent) used German as their home language, whereas of the approximately 1,000 Latvian families in Riga, fully 100 (10 percent) used German. These figures would seem to reflect the adaptation of migrating Latvian families to the German-language dominance in the trades or professions in the urban areas; at the same time, they describe a subpopulation in transition. Fully nine-tenths of the Latvian families living in Riga listed themselves as Latvian-speaking Latvians in circumstances in which the dominance was still held by the German-speaking nationality. As for the other 10 percent, their "Germanization" did not necessarily have to result ultimately in a changed cultural affiliation. Jāzeps Vītols (1863-1948), who was to become a major Latvian composer, related in his memoirs the language division in his own family: "I know next to nothing about my father's kinfolk.

His two brothers visited him from time to time . . . they were prosperous farmers. We children were never introduced to them, and it was just as well since we would not have understood each other. My uncles knew no German; and in our family we did not speak Latvian." Vītols was educated, lived and worked in St. Petersburg, and refrained from meeting with Latvians because "of my tremendously poor Latvian."[15]

In light of total population figures, then, these trends can scarcely be interpreted as promising major changes in the aggregate nationality composition of the Baltic Provinces. The overwhelming bulk of the Latvian population lived in the countryside, where intermarriage between Latvians and Germans constituted only a tiny proportion of all marriages. Moreover, in the countryside the developing network of organizations promised to Latvians an infrastructure in which they would realize their aspirations for upward mobility without coming into contact with German-dominated institutions. However accurate Manasein's report was with regard to the dissatisfactions of the Latvian and Estonian peasantry, widespread denationalization appears to have been adduced by the Russian senator on the basis of his own general political attitudes and his sense of imperial politics rather than out of the empirical proof at hand. The Baltic Germans were still powerful institutionally, but their strength was not likely to be enhanced much by incremental additions of Germanized Latvians and Estonians.

According to Manasein, there were some signs that the Latvian population was tending toward "closeness" with the Russian people through conversion to Orthodoxy. This belief, examined in light of figures for a longer period than the senatorial inspection covered, had some basis in fact.[16] In the twenty-one year period from 1874 to 1894, in Livland, 11,564 persons (or an average of 556 a year) were converted, with the peak years being 1885, when there were 850 converts, and 1887 when there were about 1,000. Similarly, in Kurland the number of conversions peaked with 198 in 1884, 994 in 1885, and 1,120 in 1886. It is not altogether clear whether these figures refer to heads of families, or the total number of people including children who were converted together with their parents; either way, of course, the statistics do not suggest a mass phenomenon, but the continuation within the Baltic provincial Latvian population of a subtheme of their religious history. In addition, Manasein pointed to the presence at the time of the senatorial inspection of 415 Orthodox congregation schools in Livland and Kurland, which together were said to have around 11,000 pupils.

Manasein also recommended that the government react to the Latvian petitions which claimed the existing court system to be unjust.

This could be accomplished by introducing into the Baltic area the reformed Russian court system of 1864. As for the request by Latvians that the provinces be reorganized administratively, Manasein recommended that the three provinces should be divided into two—Riga and Reval—the first of these with about 1,280,000 inhabitants, and the second with about 885,000. Along with these divisions, he also suggested that the southeastern Illuxt area of the province of Kurland be administratively joined to Vitebsk *guberniia*, since in Illuxt the population was "nearly Russian." He was correct with respect to the statistics of the Illuxt area, which showed a majority of non-Latvians as far back as the first Kurland soul revision of 1797. According to Manasein, these new subdivisions would weaken the power of the Baltic German administrative network, help to introduce the zemstvo system, and assist in spreading Orthodoxy, especially among the Lithuanians in southern Kurland.

As is well known, Manasein's recommendations were not implemented as they stood; rather, it was the general tenor of his report that served as the backdrop to the steps that were actually taken. The Baltic German population united in a negative stance toward the report; but the Latvians, judging by some contemporary spokesmen, viewed the proposed changes favorably. *Baltijas vēstnesis*, the newspaper of the Riga Latvian Association, optimistically noted in a Christmas 1885 editorial that "never before has as good a future been promised to us as at the present. The Latvians are now going to have a new day."[17] During the 1886 elections for the Riga city council, the same newspaper warned its Latvian readers not to cast their ballots for "opponents of the government" (i.e. the Baltic Germans) and said further that "the Russian language must now assume in our schools the position that has heretofore been occupied by the German tongue . . . let no one assume a negative position toward the expansion of the Russian language but greet its arrival with friendly feelings." This attitude toward questions of language was adopted by all other Latvian newspapers. By 1890, the two most popular texts for self-instruction in Russian were being published in 60,000 copies, one as a sixth, the other as an eighth printing.[18]

The outcome of the senatorial inspection was to be seen in the administrative and personnel changes which began shortly afterward with the appointment of new governors for Livland and Kurland. At the same time the school systems of the provinces were placed under the control of the Ministry of Education, the first step in a series of changes which were to affect the schooling of Latvian children for the next thirty years. The historian Švābe notes that Latvians acclaimed these actions in the hope that such public expressions of loyalty on their part would convince the government to carry out agrarian reform, the need for which had been documented in Mana-sein's report on the basis of the petitions received from the Latvian peasantry. But agrarian reform was never to come. Instead, the imperial government turned its attention to religion and education and started a series of Russifying edicts by revoking, in July 1885, the existing regulations regarding the children of mixed Lutheran-Orthodox marriages. Henceforth the children born of mixed marriages contracted during the preceding twenty years were to be considered Orthodox, even though in Livland, for example, 6,770 of such children had been baptized in and 5,391 had been confirmed in the Lutheran faith.[19] In October of the same year it was announced that henceforth new church buildings could be erected by Roman Catholics and Lutherans only with the permission of the Orthodox archbishop. Baltic German opposition to these new regulations was fierce, as could be expected, but to no avail. The stream of edicts, decisions, and new regulations continued. In May of 1886 a regulation stated that the Lutheran Church could not require tithing from rural households in which the head was Orthodox. The problem of reconversion from Orthodoxy to Lutheranism was handled in an even more stringent fashion. In September 1886 a letter was read in all of the Orthodox churches in the Baltic Provinces stating that Orthodox parents who were trying to raise their children as Lutherans were risking prison sentences of from eight to sixteen months; and that children of Orthodox parents whose marriages had been contracted in a Lutheran service would henceforth be considered illegitimate, and have their inheritance rights likened to those of illegitimate children. Also, at the same time, Mikhail Zinov'ev, the new governor of Livland, decreed that Orthodox officeholders who had sworn their oath of office in a Lutheran church were serving illegitimately and were to be removed from their posts. This measure was aimed at officials at the county level, as well as at Lutheran clergymen who had presided over such oath taking. This decree affected some 101 clergymen, among them a small number of Latvians. Such directives against the clergy and the consequent loss of their positions attracted the attention of the Evangelical Alliance, which sent its representatives to investigate the situation.

The problems of religious affiliation involved relatively few people, since intermarriage, conversion, and reconversion had always been peripheral to the religious life of the Baltic Christians, who were either staunchly Lutheran or Catholic. But the question of language touched all, since there were few Latvians who did not aspire to educate their children or who did not have, at some time in their adult lives, dealings with the local or regional governmental institutions. A regulation of September 1885 called for the immediate introduction of Russian as the official language of business into all Baltic governmental institutions, with the exception that at the township level business could continue to be carried on in the local "dialects." In November 1885 M. N. Kapustin, the head of the Dorpat school region from 1883 to 1890, was able to accomplish a transfer of all school matters to the supervision of the Ministry of Education.

This opened a new chapter in the administration of schools in the Baltic area. The number of and enrollment in educational institutions in the Baltic area had grown apace since the 1860s. Most of the schools had been under the direction of local congregations, and had served the purpose of general education as well as training children for church membership. In Livland, for instance, school attendance in rural districts was obligatory for all Lutheran children in the age-group 10 to 13 for three winters, thus about eighteen months altogether. The subject matter taught varied among different kinds of schools, but all curricula involved instruction in reading, writing, religious songs, arithmetic, the Scriptures, and elementary geography. The primary language of instruction was Latvian, though both German and Russian were frequently taught as separate subjects. The growth in the number of rural schools was reflected in statistics concerning new school buildings. In the decade 1850-1860, 65 new school buildings were constructed in Livland; in the decade 1860-1870, 252 new buildings; and in the decade from 1870-1880, 399 new buildings.[20] A similar situation obtained in Kurland, with the difference that there Russian was frequently an obligatory subject while the German language was only an elective one. In Kurland, also, Latvian was the primary language of instruction.

The school situation in cities and towns differed somewhat, for here attendance was not obligatory. In comparison to rural districts, urban schools catering to elementary education were few; and in 1883, the few schools that did so all had languages other than Latvian as their primary language of instruction. In 1884 the city of Riga decided to open two schools with instruction of elementary subjects in Latvian, though at that time the Latvian population of the city numbered approximately 50,000.[21] By 1889 only 23.2 percent of all children attending educational institutions in Riga were Latvians.

The conversion of the school system to a vehicle of Russification can be studied from the viewpoint of new regulations; but regulations were only one part of this history. The more important question of how effectively regulations were implemented at the local level has never been answered, and thus we are likely to have to remain in the dark with respect to prevailing *collective Latvian* attitudes at this level. Individual incidents of Russification attempts in localities can be instructive, however; the most famous of these concerns the so-called ministry schools. In 1884 Kapustin announced that henceforth townships would no longer be obliged to support schools and that they could convert existing schools, if they so wished, to ministry schools subsidized by the government and directly under the supervision of school inspectors who were state officials. The first of these ministry schools was established in the Mitau district, in the locality of Essern (Lielezere), and the controversy surrounding its founding is a good illustration of the cross-currents that affected educational change at the local level.[22] It should be noted that in the course of the next twenty years the number of such state-sponsored educational institutions continued to grow: by 1904 there were altogether 98 such ministry schools in the Baltic area (25 in Estland, 47 in Livland, and 26 in Kurland), all established on the initiative of Kapustin and his successors.[23] In 1904 these schools had approximately 10,106 pupils, which in that year was about 6 percent of all rural pupils.

The story of Essern began in March 1884, when the Essern township council decided to ask permission from the Baltic German school supervisors to add another grade in which "more Russian would be taught" to the county school. Permission for this project was denied on the basis that the existing school law did not provide for such a higher grade, and because it would be difficult to find competent instructors to teach Russian. Baron Wilhelm von Nolcken, the *Erbherr* of Essern, apparently supported the addition of a grade but not the new emphasis on Russian in it. Having met with rejection, the council waited and sent a delegation to Kapustin to seek his aid. The official explained that he had no jurisdiction over Lutheran schools, and suggested that the council think about converting its school to a ministry school, which would involve a system of two grades. Subsequently the council sent Kapustin a petition which said:

> As citizens of the Russian state we felt the need to teach Russian to our children not only because this language is needed for everyday life but also because it is useful in military service. The Russian tongue is only barely taught in the local schools, but the present authorities oppose changing our schools for this purpose. Thus the council requests the Curator to establish in place of the existing township school a two-grade ministry school. The township will assume the expenses of upkeep of such a school and will provide for it a stone house of twenty rooms.[24]

As could be expected, the request was quickly approved, and in

August 1885 the township as well as the Kurland School Commission received notification from St. Petersburg that official permission had been granted. The Commission, however, quickly communicated to the council that (1) it forbade the township to close its present school and (2) that the building in which the present school was housed had been built with financial help from Baron von Nolcken and he refused permission for the building to be used for other purposes. The battle was now joined. The township school had to remain open, according to the law; but the ministry school obviously could not be declared illegal by the regional authorities. The question thus revolved around the problem of the building; was it really von Nolcken's, or was he only partially an owner of it? The governor of Kurland directed that the ministry school be allowed to use one room of the building until the question could be settled in court. The problem turned out to be more complicated than appeared at first glance. The building had been constructed on the foundations of an old tavern which von Nolcken had owned, with materials provided by the baron, but with the manpower of the township inhabitants. Moreover the baron had granted for the use of the school twenty desiatins of the surrounding land. But he had never formally signed over to the township either the building or the land and was thus legally empowered to withdraw them.

In the meantime Kapustin had directed that the ministry school begin its activities on September 1 and sent the school inspector of the district to supervise the opening. Upon arrival, the inspector was informed by von Nolcken that the question of the building had not been resolved and thus the ministry school would have to remain inactive. The inspector countered with Kapustin's directive and von Nolcken threatened to arrest him, but did not do so, apparently because a large crowd of peasants had arrived at the school in order to participate in the opening ceremonies. The result of this stage of developments was that the school did in fact open with appropriate ceremonies, but with the baron's representative leaving the site with a warning that the matter was not to rest there. Nor did it. Four days later the township elder, one Zēniņš, received from the district judge a letter saying that he, Zēniņš, had been released from his position and indicted for allowing an illegal meeting, resisting the legal directive of the baron, and disturbing the normal course of operations of the township school. By this time the township population had divided into two camps: one opposing, the other supporting the existence of the ministry school.

On September 4 von Nolcken called together the farmstead heads of Essern and announced to them that he was dissatisfied with their behavior in the ministry school question and therefore was withdrawing the use of the granted land from the school. Moreover, he would not give firewood to the school, even for money. None of the farmstead heads who had supported the ministry school would be allowed to purchase firewood for their own use. And, finally, when the day arrived for farmsteads to make their final mortgage payments, no extensions would be granted and the baron would use all means at his disposal to reclaim land that was legally his. This economic blackmail strengthened the sentiment that perhaps the ministry school had not been a good idea, and a petition was now circulated in the township in opposition to it. This von Nolcken delivered to St. Petersburg personally. The dispute ended with von Nolcken losing out to the ministry: henceforth he would have to allow the school building to be used for the ministry school. Somewhat later, the district court received a directive from the governor of Kurland that the matter of Zēniņš should be terminated immediately without further consequences. This improved the mood of the township considerably, as did the arrival from Kapustin of the sum of 100 rubles for use by the ministry school. Similar local battles were fought later that year over two other ministry schools—in Gulbene and Vietlava—both of which were resolved in favor of the ministry school. Some indication of the purposes of the ministry school policy can be seen in the directive received at the founding of the Dondangen ministry school: namely, that Latvian could not be taught there as an obligatory subject. When Russian was made mandatory in these schools, the pace of their founding appears to have slowed down.

In the study of as broadly conceived a governmental policy as Russification an examination of the interaction between policy and local conditions is of prime importance. Yet the Essern incident is the only one about which sufficient detail has survived to be studied by historians. The incident is revealing, since the actors of this local drama represented the larger elements in the Baltic situation: the Latvian peasantry seeking to accommodate itself to the new conditions, the "helpful" Russian official trying to turn local practical aspirations to benefit the new governmental policy, the antagonistic Baltic German landowner perceiving peasant "ingratitude" and using his not inconsiderable economic power to try to keep the imperial government out of local affairs. How uniform the implementation of policy could have been, given the local opportunities for circumvention of it, is still an open question. Furthermore, in the Latvian areas the implementation of school policy was to be inspected, as it turned out, largely by Latvians themselves. In 1887 there was established in Riga the position of "Director of Schools" who was to supervise four school inspectors. Krišjānis Valdemārs, now sixty-two years of age, recommended to Kapustin that one of these inspectors' positions be filled with his (Valdemārs') protégé Fricis Brīvzemnieks (1846-1907) and the others with other Latvians.[25] It was the hope of Valdemārs and Brīvzemnieks that Latvians in these jobs could be expected to behave with understanding; and on his side, Kapustin believed it to be politic if Russification measures were implemented by Latvians themselves. Valdemārs' general sympathy for the new policy was well known; Brīvzemnieks apparently saw no dangers in it for the future of Latvian culture. Brīvzemnieks had been actively involved in the collection of Latvian folklore materials and was in close touch with the new generation of Latvian literati. Matīss Kaudzīte (1848-1926), himself a rural schoolteacher and co-author (with his brother Reinis) of the brilliant (and first) Latvian-language novel *Mērnieku laiki* (publ. 1879), had sent to Brīvzemnieks an article to be published in a Moscow newspaper in which the novelist had sought to make the point that the government had nothing to fear from the Latvians, since the Latvians knew they had nothing to fear from the government. In a letter commenting on the article, Brīvzemnieks said (at the very height of the new policies): "There are some things now going on about which, to tell the truth, Latvians do not know whether to be sad or happy. This I can say, however, that with every day I am more and more confident about the future course of growing Latvian self-awareness."[26]

The various regulations regarding elementary and secondary schools were codified in laws approved by Alexander III in the latter 1880s. This codified version of school policy was to remain in effect henceforth, though it would be amended from time to time. The existing governing bodies in local school districts were to be left intact, but the schools themselves would also be subjected to the authority of the inspectors, who would have the right to fire teachers. This created jurisdictional confusion, which was to be reflected in hundreds of disputes during the 1890s and after the turn of the century. The 11th paragraph of the elementary school regulations of May 1887 was particularly ominous from the nationalist viewpoint, since it provided for the use of Russian, Estonian, or Latvian in the first two years of rural township schools, whereas in the last year all subjects save religion and church singing were to be taught in Russian.[27] This paragraph was designed to apply to city schools as well. Other laws discussed elsewhere in this study stipulated that gymnasia and *Realschulen* had to convert to the use of Russian gradually, starting in 1887. The next three years witnessed a bitter struggle over the school question between the Baltic German *Ritterschaften*, the imperial bureaucracy, and the government's representatives in Riga. As a result of the implementation of the 1887 codification, Baltic German authorities began to withdraw financial support from local school systems, which hampered but did not stop the widespread introduction of the Russian language in the school systems during the 1890s.

From the Manasein inspection until the codification of school laws in 1887 was but a half-decade, but the changes this short period introduced into the Latvian world seemed momentous. Henceforth, Latvian parents, especially in rural districts, would have to accept the Russian language as an integral part of their children's education and of the provincial institutions with which the parents themselves were likely to come into contact. On the basis of the available evidence, we have surmised that a large part, if not a majority, of the Latvian general population accepted these changes without much ado, even with positive attitudes; and that a segment of the Latvian intelligentsia saw them as a way of diminishing Baltic German control over provincial life. Yet—and here we reiterate a theme stated earlier in the section—it would be a mistake to characterize Russification measures either as the main feature of Latvian history during the 1880s, or as accomplishing at that time a profound reorientation of Latvian cultural developments. Had Senator Manasein integrated in his report the recommendations for agrarian reform requested in the peasant petitions, and had the imperial government acted on these, the course of socioeconomic changes affecting the Latvians might well have been altered; but as the situation stood at the end of the 1880s, the Russification measures that had been effected were too weak to redirect the changes that had begun prior to that decade. Some of these changes resulted in unplanned Russification of segments of the Latvian population, but most of them had results that rendered the relatively weak cultural Russification measures even less effective.

The population shifts that had the effect of helping government-inspired Russification were tied up with changing landholding and occupational opportunities. Ever since the 1860s the Latvian rural population had had the freedom to purchase rural land and to migrate to cities as well as out of the Baltic Provinces. The peasants who were wealthy enough to make a down payment on land could finally realize the age-old dream of owning outright the holdings of their forefathers, however encumbered with mortgage payments in the long run; but significantly large numbers could not avail themselves of the opportunity. Accompanying the shift in landownership there was also a movement out of the countryside, one part of the migrating population seeking its fortune in the major cities of the provinces, another part in the interior of Russia. It has been estimated that during the last four decades of the nineteenth century, some 200,000 Latvian peasants left for Russia proper in search of cheaper land and employment opportunities; and the likelihood is that a majority of these intermarried with the Russian population.[28] Among those who went to the Baltic cities, there appears to have been a significant amount of resentment toward the Latvians who had become landowners as well as toward the cultural institutions in the cities that stressed Latvian nationality.[29] Though they probably remained Latvian speakers, large numbers of these urban migrants also remained unaffected by nationalist ideology, took low-skilled and marginal jobs in factories, and became susceptible, because of their structural position, to ideas of social democracy which gained currency during the 1890s.[30] Very likely, these people were much less hesitant about intermarriage with other nationalities than those who had been "nationalized" through education, or self-instruction. It is also likely that, finding few opportunities in the cities, they continued to move out of the provinces in a second-stage outward migration.

There were, however, many others to whom the new opportunities for landownership and migration meant upward social mobility. The growing number of Latvian-speaking peasant landowners, and city dwellers with relatively secure jobs, provided a continually expanding audience for the growing Latvian literary culture. The institutional base of this culture had continued to expand during the 1880s, by means of additional newspapers, local organizations, periodical journals, and publishing houses. Survivors of the activist generation of the 1860s and 1870s now saw added to their ranks many who had been educated during those decades, and for whom Latvian nationality was no longer an aspiration but an internalized value. The participation of Latvians in municipal elections during the decades starting with 1877 had given to the urban Latvian population a political sense it had not had before; and, in the countryside, sustained participation in various organs of local government had trained Latvian politicians as well.[31] Literary production, here understood to include all writing and not just *belles lettres*, had become multi-faceted and increasingly more sophisticated, so that Latvian intellectuals no longer had to bewail the discontinuity between their own "peasant literature" and the "high culture" of their traditional overlords. Even more importantly, Latvian culture had ceased to be purely oral: books, newspapers, and journals could be stored and circulated. This meant that the parents of the children who in the late 1880s were being educated in schools caught up in the Russification process had concrete evidence that Latvian culture was a successful enterprise deserving their loyalty;

and the children themselves, though having to learn Russian during their formative years, would have when intellectually mature a Latvian culture to attach themselves to.

It is important to keep in mind, then, that by the time school-age groups ("cohorts," in the vocabulary of demographers) in the Latvian population began to receive instruction in Russian, Latvian culture could not have been easily extruded from the cultural world of the Baltic Provinces. A few examples of pre-Russification cultural production will suffice to make this point. The first of these concerns the oral tradition. Latvian intellectuals by the 1870s had achieved sufficient intellectual distance from their peasant origins to conceive of the oral tradition objectively. Gone was the naive belief that the oral tradition—especially the *dainas* (folksongs)—of the Latvians was on equal footing with the culture, however expressed, of older countries; this notion had been replaced by a more realistic appreciation of oral culture as an aspect of the Latvian past that could be studied "scientifically."[32] The first efforts in this direction were made by the same Fricis Brīvzemnieks whom Valdemārs had recommended to Kapustin as a school inspector. Brīvzemnieks' interest in the oral tradition antedated his involvement with the Russification program. Already in the 1870s he had published a small volume of *dainas* (interestingly, in the Cyrillic alphabet). His work as a folklore collector continued during the 1880s, and his philosophy of folklore was formulated before he acquired his job as a school inspector, implementing Russification measures. In 1881 he published a series of articles in the Latvian journal *Pagalms*, in which he recommended that the oral tradition be collected on a widespread scale.[33] This, in his view, was not antiquarian activity; rather, through knowing the contents of its folklore a people deepened its sense of its national belonging, and acquainted itself with the lives its forefathers led. According to Brīvzemnieks, Latvian intellectuals could learn a lesson from the Russian Slavophiles, who had urged a turning inward, a deepening of the sense of what it meant to be a Russian. The job of folklore collecting, however, came eventually to interfere with his official duties and Brīvzemnieks turned his collection and techniques over to two others—Krišjānis Barons, one of the activists of the 1860s, and Ansis Lerchis (1849-1903), a 30-year-old rural schoolteacher with a profound interest in Latvian folklore.[34] These two continued the collecting endeavor through the rest of the 1880s and 1890s, publishing the results of their work, with the financial assistance of the St. Petersburg Academy of Sciences, in the period from 1900 to 1915. During the years of most intense Russification in the educational system, therefore, the foundation was being laid for the study of Latvian folklore in a scientific fashion by later analysts. The measures which made the Russian language an integral part of the institutions in which Latvians were being educated and moved touched in no way the preparation of materials that served later to strengthen among intellectuals and the population at large the sense of national unity and national consciousness.

There were other signs that the earlier naive attitudes toward the oral tradition had been transcended. To some Latvian intellectuals the oral tradition had seemed incomplete, due to the absence of an epic of the *Kalevala* or *Kalevipoeg* type. The tens of thousands of *dainas* recited by Latvian peasants dealt only with mundane and pastoral subjects and in none of them could one find examples of heroic action of past Latvian leaders. This shortcoming of the oral tradition inspired the manipulation of legends with the aim of creating epics. Jēkabs Lautenbachs (1847-1928) wrote three lengthy pseudomythological epics of this nature during the 1880s.[35] But the most successful of these manufactured tales of Latvian heroism came from the pen of Andrejs Pumpurs (1841-1902), who in 1888, at the age of 45, published his *Lāčplēsis* (The Bear-Slayer).[36] The poem threw caution to the winds as far as historical veracity was concerned and raised a minor legendary hero to the status of a symbol of all Latvian people. The internal mood of the poem owed much to Garlieb Merkel, the Baltic German champion of the Latvian people who had come into prominence at the end of the eighteenth century.[37] Written in a highly readable meter and filled with memorable descriptions of pre-German Latvian "tribal" life, the epic took as its central theme the struggle of the Latvian against the German, thus reinforcing social resentments that were very much alive even in the 1880s. Appearing at the very time when the new Russification measures seemed to be becoming permanent parts of the world in which Latvians moved, the epic reminded its thousands of readers of the heroic battles their forefathers had once fought against another "invader." It is significant that the poem remained popular during the 1890s, when an increasingly larger number of Latvians began to attend institutions of higher learning, and that its central theme was later adopted by the social-democratic playwright Jānis Rainis (to be discussed later) for a play that appeared on the eve of the Revolution of 1905.[38]

These examples of folklore investigation and folklore use mark the gradual severance of the Latvian imagination from the common Latvian social past, that is, the peasantry. The peasant past and its typical culture had ceased, by the 1880s, to be as commanding an element in Latvian culture as it had been for the Latvian writers prior to 1850 or even during the decades of the "awakening." In the realm of imaginative creations a distance had been achieved, and the manipulative consciousness of the literary *artist* inserted between the social realities of Latvian existence and the print culture the artist produced. In *belles lettres*, the most persuasive examples of such a development—before the 1880s—was the novel *Mērnieku laiki*, written during the last years of the 1870s and published in 1879 by Reinis and Matīss Kaudzīte.[39] This was a work with many meanings, but its significance for the present discussion lay in its general objectivity in portraying the social world of the Latvians of the 1860s. There was no sign in the novel of nationalistic preoccupations: rather, it contained, among other things, a biting satire of excessive nationalism. Nor was there an attempt, in dealing with the question of Latvian-German relations in the Baltic countryside, to locate virtue on only one side: instead, the Baltic Germans as well as the Latvians were both portrayed sympathetically, as possessing all of the weaknesses and strengths of humankind. The novel contained a realistic attempt to picture the Latvian peasantry in the process of change and of how the changes of the mid-century affected the generations that had matured before the 1850s, those who were maturing during that time, and the new generation of the 1860s. Notably, there was also an excellent caricature of Latvians who sought to take on German culture and manners: a negative portrayal of Germanization, which portrayal was based on the assumption that "being Latvian" had a definite meaning and that self-induced efforts at denationalization produced twisted characters. The novel achieved widespread popularity during the eighties and nineties, leaving in the common parlance of the Latvian population a residue of stereotypes of people inhabiting a multi-national culture. If Latvians during the nineties and thereafter were tempted to "become Russian" as in the past many had been tempted to "become German," in these decades they were likely to be immediately typed in the negative way first laid out by the Kaudzīte brothers.

Finally, the mid-eighties also produced the first philosophical conservative in the figure of Jēkabs Apsītis (1858-1929), a rural schoolteacher and writer of short stories and reflective essays.[40] In his thought the somewhat naive preoccupation of the 1860s' intellectuals with "awakening the people" and "self-improvement through education" came to an end. Apsītis set his sights not so much against Russification, which he never addressed directly, but against all trends that pulled Latvians out of the countryside and away from the traditional Latvian farmstead, which he revered. The basis of his thinking was the still-influential tradition of the Herrnhut: religious piety, poverty as God's will, rural life, and man's irredeemable sinfulness. Rejection of the idea of change did not make him less a Latvian, Apsītis believed, but it did give him a perspective on current events which was unprecedented in the development of Latvian thinking. The changes which Kronvalds, Valdemārs, and others had called for, Apsītis believed to have been instrumental in giving rise to generations of poseurs who thirsted for secular knowledge, and tried to act as if they possessed higher culture. Latvians had eaten from the tree of knowledge and suffered the consequences, namely, departure from Eden, which Apsītis tended to locate in the patriarchal relationships of the landed estate sometime before the 1850s. Such an attitude was a signal that among some of the Latvian literati the energy produced by the nationalism of the sixties had been spent. This nationalism had left a residue of firm convictions about Latvianness, and Apsītis never questioned his own nationality; but the aspirations which had accompanied the growth of the Latvian national consciousness led in this view to national ills, rather than to national development.

To repeat the contention which the foregoing examples of Latvian cultural productivity were meant to support: before cultural Russification had a chance to effect changes in the Latvian cultural world, that world had already matured sufficiently to withstand attacks upon it, whether planned or unplanned. The reimposition of Orthodoxy on reconverts to Lutheranism and on the offspring of mixed marriages; the systematic insertion of the Russian language into primary curricula; the conversion of German-speaking institutions of higher learning such as Dorpat into Russian-speaking institutions; the steady departure of Latvians from the Baltic Provinces to the interior of Russia; and the increased use of Russian in provincial governmental and judicial institutions—all of these manifestations of Russification policy had arrived too late to reverse patterns set in the previous decades among the Latvians. Even if uniformly and efficiently implemented, which they were not by any means, these policies would affect most directly a generation that was to grow up within a context of a Latvian-speaking population that already showed many outward signs of being able to sustain cultural autonomy. And, what is of equal importance, these measures were powerless to affect the thinking of those Latvians who were coming into intellectual maturity during the 1890s, since they belonged to a generation that had been raised and schooled before the late 1880s. Much depended now on this cohort emerging as cultural activists during the 1890s: if it proved unable to sustain the continued effort of Latvian culture building, or showed itself susceptible to adopting the government's goals for the Baltic nationalities as their own, the cultural Russification now in effect would have the opportunity to reorient the next generation of Latvians toward some sort of integration with the Russian nation.

CHAPTER 15

THE EIGHTEEN-NINETIES

BY THE TURN of the decade of the 1890s, Russification measures in Livland and Kurland were well on their way toward seriously diminishing Baltic German control of provincial life. Correspondingly, the most heated public exchanges on these questions took place between Baltic German publicists and representatives of the crown's viewpoint, and these have been described in detail by Michael H. Haltzel in Part Two. As for the Latvian-speaking population, its place in the Baltic scheme of things was being changed not so much by governmental policy as by patterns of movement not initiated by any single individual or law. Historically, the Latvians had been peasants, and the terms *Bauer* and *Lette* had seemed to many—Germans and Latvians alike—to be synonymous. The most significant break with the past, from the Latvian perspective, was not the shift of power from the Baltic Germans to the Russian government, but the move to cities by a large segment of the Latvian population. Since the late 1860s the proportion of Latvians in the major cities of the Baltic Provinces had doubled: in Riga, in 1867, about 24 percent of the people had been Latvians, while in 1897 that figure stood at 45 percent; in Libau the proportion had gone from 16 percent in 1863 to 39 percent in 1897; and in Mitau the change was from 22 percent in 1863 to 46 percent in 1897. For the whole Latvian population, the figures show that in 1863 about 15 percent were urban dwellers, while in 1897 that proportion had reached nearly 30 percent.[1] Not only were changes taking place in the nationality composition of cities but the total city populations were themselves growing. Riga more than tripled its size, increasing from 77,000 inhabitants in 1863 to 282,000 in 1897; and doubled that number again in half the time, growing to a metropolis of 530,000 people by 1914.[2] Mitau increased its size ninefold during the same period of fifty years, expanding from 10,200 people in 1863 to 94,000 in 1914.

Accompanying these shifts was an alteration in the character of the Latvian intelligentsia. The generation which had spearheaded the national awakening had been, as it could not have helped but be, preoccupied with problems of the Latvian peasantry: seeking to help it redefine itself as a nation; showing how it deserved to have more power in Baltic institutions; urging it to educate its sons and daughters. These same problems had occupied the generation which had been educated during the decades of the national awakening and had started to participate in Latvian culture building during the course of the 1880s.

It was the next generation—educated in the latter 1870s and during the 1880s, that is, before the onset of organized Russification policy —which found itself in a unique position with respect to the further development of Latvian culture and attitudes. Having achieved intellectual maturity by the early 1890s, its members moved in a Baltic setting in which urban life was of far greater significance than at any previous time and which was suffused by the new idea—encouraged by the imperial government's representatives in the Baltic Provinces —that personal success was linked to an acquisition of Russian culture and language. Schoolteaching, which involved more professionally trained Latvians than any other occupation, had come to involve special difficulties; teachers suffered if they did not know Russian, but advanced if they showed the correct attitudes and learned the right skills.[3] It should be remembered that it was in the realm of popular education, and the teaching professions, that Kronvalds had located the most significant *national* effort as far as the future of the Latvians was concerned. For the hundreds of young Latvians who had begun higher education at the beginning of the 1890s, a career choice could involve questions of national allegiance. Their collective decisions would in the long run determine the success of the Russification effort.

The implementation of Russification policy continued throughout the 1890s, and there were significant changes in higher personnel. In 1890, the administrator Kapustin was replaced in Riga by N. A. Lavrovskii, who was intent on doing the job more thoroughly than his predecessor. Immediately thereafter Brīvzemnieks and other Latvian school inspectors were attacked for being too lenient, and the question of elementary-school language once more came to the fore. In March 1891 Lavrovskii ordered city schools to teach all subjects in Russian the first two years; and his inspectors, whose number had now been raised to twenty-two, used this order to demand that rural schools do the same. In 1895 he instructed his inspectors to see to it that rural libraries buy only the kinds of books which were recognized as "useful" by the Ministry of Education. The question was a particularly troubling one to local schools since, for example, in the year 1895 there appeared some 450 new books in Latvian, many of them of obvious use to schools. The allocation of annual budget items now caused heated debates at the beginning of every school year.[4] In 1897 it was teachers themselves that appeared to be a problem, since many of them, especially in rural districts, were still unable to use Russian as the language of instruction. In April of that year, a directive allowed graduates of city schools—some as young as seventeen—to become rural teachers if they could show that they knew Russian. In addition, such youths were subject to inquiries about books they read and journals they subscribed to. They were also warned that membership in Latvian organizations could hurt their careers. In 1898, Lavrovskii turned again to the influx of "undesirable" books in rural schools, and instructed that a school could buy only Russian books for the money it received from the government, while half of the books purchased with locally raised funds had to be in Russian as well. Understandably, it was next to impossible to enforce these regulations stringently. Only about half of the rural schools had libraries to which systematic additions were made, and in the rest of them it was difficult for inspectors to determine precisely how funds had been spent. By the time of his death, in 1899, Lavrovskii had significantly expanded the rights of the curator, through having acquired a monopoly on the decisions regarding language use in the early elementary grades.

With respect to the school network, therefore, by the turn of the century Russification policy had created in the Latvian-speaking areas of the Baltic a sizable local bureaucracy, which sought to implement the regulations of the curator without much regard for local sentiments. How far such interference in local school matters could go was shown in the first renewed schoolteachers' conference called by Lavrovskii's successor A. N. Shvarts (or Schwarz; 1848-1915) in Riga in 1899.[5] Such conferences had been banned in 1886, but now they were again to be held regularly under guidelines issued by the Ministry of Education. The first meeting was presided over by Inspector Pravdin in Riga. Similar meetings were held in Libau and Mitau. Accounts of these show that Latvian schoolteachers understood thoroughly the impact Russification regulations were having on their pupils and on pedagogical routines. The changes that Russian administrators asked for were not acquiesced to blindly, and on points of pedagogical principle there was little meeting of minds. In the Riga meeting, for instance, Inspector Pravdin insisted that illiterate children should be admitted to schools, while the teachers argued that they had to be able to read and write before they entered. The problem here revolved around the extent to which children would be taught at home by parents before receiving instruction in the (Russified) school system. Pravdin was clearly arguing for the earliest possible exposure of children to the Russified system; the teachers for considerable training at home (by Latvian-speaking parents) before the child came into contact with the Russian tongue. Similarly, Pravdin argued strongly for the "natural" system of learning Russian, that is, without any translations or explanations in Latvian; while the teachers stood firm on the desirability of Russian instruction in the context of Latvian-language explanations and translations of vocabulary. Pravdin further argued against the active involvement of parents in local school life, against the use of maps with Latvian place names, and against the use of any Latvian language schoolbooks which had not received his approval (he believed that there were only eleven usable books at the moment). The resolutions of this meeting, and others like it, were generally indecisive. Ultimately, the efficacy of Russification measures in the school system depended on the acquiescence of the schoolteachers, and these, as the meetings made clear, could find many different ways to counteract the (to them) negative national impact of the Russifying regulations. In addition, Latvian historians have noted the rise in the popularity of home instruction after the mid-1890s, so that many parents apparently ceased sending their children to school entirely.[6]

There were of course other, less direct, ways to counteract the effects of Russification. The literate segments of the Latvian population fully supported the continued growth of a Latvian language culture, as expressed in newspapers, periodicals, and books. A third Latvian literary magazine—*Austrums*—published in Moscow since 1885 by Valdemārs' friend and protégé Jēkabs Velme (1855-1928) was now in existence, and the quality of its articles showed that the Latvian imagination had gone far beyond the early years of "instructing the peasantry."[7] The reading public was now being informed by four Latvian newspapers that appeared regularly: *Latviešu avīzes*, established in 1821; the two papers that were close to the politics of the Riga Latvian Association, *Baltijas vēstnesis* (est. 1868) and *Balss* (est. 1878); and the recently established *Dienas Lapa* (1887), which by the mid-nineties was showing signs of becoming the first left-oriented paper among Latvians. Efforts to found other periodical publications had failed for a variety of reasons. The writer of epics, Lautenbachs, had sought to establish two literary magazines in the 1880s: *Pagalms* was now defunct, while *Rota* continued to struggle along. A proponent of the interests of the Latvian smallholders (*sīkgruntnieki*), Juris Māters (1845-1885), had tried to establish a newspaper to express their views, but his efforts had come to naught.[8] Success in such endeavors apparently had become a question of mass appeal: special-interest publications failed, while those which appealed to the broadly based reading public succeeded. It was, however, significant that even minority opinions among the Latvians now sought to find expression in print, however short-lived their successes.

Even during the decade of most intense Russification, the Latvian reading public continued to be inundated with books in Latvian in increasingly larger numbers. The number of annual new titles in Latvian rose from 181 in 1884 to 822 in 1904, and the total number of new books printed from about 168,000 (1884) to over 5 million (1904). The latter figures are not, of course, the number of copies actually sold, but one suspects that sales were also on the increase.[9]

The authors among the Latvian intelligentsia did not write with the explicit purpose of fighting Russification, of course; but there is no doubt that the outpouring of Latvian-language materials had that as one of its major consequences. The importance of the printed word in counteracting denationalization was realized, if indirectly, by the Lithuanian nationalists to the south, who at this time were in the middle of a vast book-smuggling effort from Lithuania Minor (Prussian Lithuania); and by the Lettgallians in Vitebsk *guberniia*, who in the 1890s were undergoing their own "national awakening."[10] Among the Latvians of Kurland and Livland, institutionalized nationalistic sentiment, as represented in the age groups that were now enjoying relatively greater wealth and standing, countered the psychological impact of Russification in the school-age generation by expanding the physical evidence of a living Latvian culture: books, newspapers, periodicals, museums, and festivals of various kinds.

During the 1880s the Riga Latvian Association had continued to organize song festivals, and there was another—the fourth—in 1895.[11] In 1886 a "useful book" section was established with the purpose of systematically translating the best foreign writings into Latvian.[12] In 1889 a Music Committee was established, and in 1892 an Ethnographic Museum for the preservation of Latvian material culture. Its first exhibit took place in 1896. In 1899 the Association called a general farmers' congress, and around the turn of the century sections to deal with development of Latvian agriculture, medicine, maritime trade, and the historical profession were added to its internal organization.[13] Earlier sections had been created to subsidize creative writing and the scientific study of the Latvian language. A few years later, in 1903, the Association launched its most ambitious publication to date: a Latvian encyclopedia.[14] As mentioned earlier, starting in 1876, and continuing through the 1880s and 1890s, there appeared the *Raksti* (*Schriften*) of the Association's Scientific Committee, which reprinted the papers given at the Committee's annual congresses by Latvian, as well as Baltic German, men of letters.

The generation of the Latvian intelligentsia active after 1890, then, moved in a Baltic cultural world which had in it not only the Russifying efforts of the imperial government but also a Latvian literary culture of considerable magnitude. The question is how this new generation related to its national heritage, as represented in the efforts of the older generations, and to the Russifying innovations which were of more recent vintage. Judging by its earlier representatives, the new generation was first of all characterized by a Western orientation.

For instance, Teodors Zeiferts (1865-1929), the literary critic who began an intellectual career in the mid-1880s, in his early writings had started by pointing out which aspects of the main currents of Western intellectual life were relevant to the Latvian intelligentsia.[15] He felt that Latvians should turn westward for their literary inspiration, to the great authors of Western literature and literary criticism. Even at an early age Zeiferts read avidly in the writings of the Danish critic Georg Brandes and the Frenchman Hippolyte Taine. He never addressed the question of Russification directly, but ceaselessly drummed the "Westernization" theme. For the censors, writings of this sort, being apolitical, were of little consequence for governmental policy, but to the evolution of Latvian letters they were of magisterial significance. As arbiters of the tastes of an expanding public, men such as Zeiferts were, in a sense, prescribing the content of the Latvian literature the current school generation would read when it came of age. Moreover, through their critical endeavors, Zeiferts and others were underlining the very existence of a Latvian literature: through sifting the good from the bad, the experimental from the accomplished, they were identifying what Latvian literature was and was not; and by judging what acceptable Latvian literature was through the publication of its "classics" in anthologies, they were making it very clear to the reading public that "true" Latvian literature was not being inspired by Russian culture.

Another westward-pointing link between Latvian thought and the outside world showed up in the short-lived publication *Pūrs* (*The Dowry*), issued by a group of Latvian students at the University of Dorpat during the years from 1891 to 1894.[16] The average age of the editors and contributors of this magazine was about 22; thus, some of them had personally experienced the consequences of Russification policy in the final years of their pre-university schooling, and they were all, of course, attending an institution of higher learning which was itself being subjected to Russificatory pressures. These Latvian students were in a contentious frame of mind. The Latvian reading audience, according to *Pūrs*, did not have sufficient exposure to ideas from the West, and therefore the goal of the magazine was to "force the reader to weigh and consider the value of *various* philosophies, so that he would become used to employing his reason critically, and so that he would be able to achieve an independent perspective on all important questions."[17] The key concept here was "critical reason," which linked *Pūrs* to the philosophies of Hegel and Marx. *Pūrs* intended to be "scientifically critical" and combined a mixture of articles on physiology, botany, and other topics in the natural sciences with pieces on the philosophy of history, sociology, and Darwinism. In his seminal article on the "laws of history" Aleksandrs Dauge (1868-1937) used the terminology of Marxism without mentioning Marx, concluding that "when opposing economic forces finally end their struggle . . . men will no longer give in to mysterious external powers . . . and will be able through the use of their conscious reason to make their own history."[18] In an article entitled "The Dialectic," Kārlis Kasparsons (1865-?) discussed the dialectical method of reasoning, mentioned Hegel as its founder, linked the expansion of freedom to the dialectical movement of history, and explained dialectical materialism, again without once mentioning Marx.[19] All of this discussion was quite abstract; there was no effort to reinterpret Baltic history in terms of dialectical materialism. What is more significant for our theme is that in Dauge and Kasparsons and others of the *Pūrs* group Latvian readers were hearing the voices of a new generation that was to become increasingly more prominent as the decade wore on and as the century turned. Dauge was eventually to become a professor in the University of Latvia (est. 1919), and Kasparsons the first Latvian minister of education (1918-1920).

The dissatisfactions of the *Pūrs* group were by no means an isolated phenomenon in this new generation of the Latvian intelligentsia. Among the young, covert Marxism was only one kind of expression of disenchantment with the development of Latvian culture to date. Even more widely read, and possibly more influential than *Pūrs*, was the poetry of Edvards Veidenbaums (1867-1892), which circulated in manuscript form among Latvian students in Dorpat after being denied publication by the censor.[20] Veidenbaums was a close friend of the *Pūrs* group, and had participated in the founding of the magazine. Born in 1867, he had begun his studies in Dorpat in 1887, and by the early nineties had concluded that Latvian culture-building efforts had become too narrow, that is, too tied to the Riga Latvian Association's viewpoint. Cultural homogeneity was stifling "men of genius"; the nationalists were too materialistic; and the RLA was more concerned with the institutions of popular culture rather than with true creativity. Though apparently not a Marxist as were his friends,

Veidenbaums was also concerned with the economic plight of urban industrial workers and the landless agricultural laborers. A cultural critique and social concerns were combined with a fine poetic sense to produce a verse that turned the reader either to the West or to the Greek and Roman classics, but, significantly, not in the direction of Russian culture. A similar though more prosaic statement of these same themes was made by another youthful Dorpat student, the 21-year-old Jānis Jansons (1872-1917), who published in 1893 a booklet entitled *Domas par jaunlaika literatūru* (Thoughts on Present-Day Literature).[21] The book was a combination of polemics and analysis, attacking earlier Latvian writing and the society which it had as its base. What offended Jansons about the pre-1893 Latvian literature was its "blindness" to what he termed the "social questions." Preoccupation with the problems of national cultural growth had blinded Latvian writers to the growing social differentiations of the Latvian population, and the injustices implicit in class divisions. These injustices made Baltic society very similar to that of western Europe and rendered it capable of being analyzed by "philosophies imported from abroad," which the RLA circles claimed were not applicable to the Latvian situation.[22] An expansion of Latvian thinking was in order, and an incorporation of "seminal ideas" from the outside. Jansons admired Ibsen for his interest in "social question"; and he noted that in Latvian literature Apsītis—the conservative social critic—was the only writer to perceive the real problems.

The activities of the *Pūrs* group, Veidenbaums, Jansons, and others coalesced in a "movement" called the "New Current" (*Jaunā Strāva*).[23] There was less inner coherence to this "movement" than subsequent historians have pictured, since it included not only those to whom Western (i.e. German) Marxism had become a guiding philosophy but also many others whose disenchantment was nonideological, and partook of *fin de siècle* characteristics. As could be expected, the writings produced by the New Current were voluminous, spanning the range from incidental pieces in the newspaper that became the voice of the movement, *Dienas Lapa*, to serious *belles lettres*. As could also be expected, the sheer volume of writings had the effect of moving subjects close to the hearts of the New Current to the forefront of everyday discussion among Latvians. Notably, these did not include the topic of Russification, in any direct way. The "problems" of the Latvian population were now being discussed largely in terms of the general social stresses of turn-of-the-century European society rather than in terms of the specific local difficulties created by Russifiers. Concern with the introduction of the Russian language in elementary and higher education, and the conversion of provincial institutions to the use of Russian, remained muted, not to say almost drowned out, by the "large" questions suggested by the New Current.

This generation knew, of course, the local problems Russification had created, since its members moved daily in the institutions the new policies had affected. Yet Russification had not touched all aspects of the Latvian world uniformly, and therefore the Russian language, Russian culture, and the Russians themselves could be avoided easily enough. Fēlikss Cielēns (1888-1965), a writer and politician sympathetic to social democracy, suggested in his memoirs that he knew few Latvians his own age "who became Russified, even though the government promised good opportunities in government service to those who would turn Russian and adopt the Orthodox faith."[24] In a general survey of the Latvian society he experienced during his youth, he listed as the main "opponents" of Russification the family circle, national literature, organizations, and the illegal political groups of the young. Cielēns grew up in a well-to-do Riga family, whose home became a kind of salon for Latvian students of the Riga Polytechnic, many of them participants in the New Current. His mother insisted that her son, and his friends, speak "pure" Latvian at home, and corrected the Germanisms and Russianisms that were naturally present in the language of the young who were growing up in a multi-cultural society. According to Cielēns, student organizations of various kinds also created a countervailing power to Russifying school officials. Though the older Latvian fraternities—Lettonia and Selonia—did not attack Russification publicly, they continued to hold literary and discussion evenings in which the use of the Latvian language was mandatory. Organizational activity among Latvian students in gymnasia was forbidden, which gave rise to several illegal organizations, in one of which Cielēns was a member. This organization—called *Darbs* (*Work*)—had as its goal the widening of their members' education (presumably in a political direction). According to Cielēns:

> The majority of the members were 18-20 years of age. . . . Discussions covered philosophy, psychology, Darwinism, history, literature, and art. The presentations and debates took place in Latvian, which in those circumstances was no easy thing. We knew the Russian and German vocabulary to discuss those topics, but for many of the concepts we wanted to discuss there were as yet no terms in Latvian. . . .[25]

The organization also had its own publication, which initially was circulated in a single handwritten copy. Of the twenty members of Cielēns' illegal group, eleven assumed positions of importance in independent Latvia after 1918: six became deputies to the *Saeima* (parliament), three ministers in various governments, and one a general.

Cielēns' account covers the period from the early nineties to the Revolution of 1905, and suggests that for large segments of the Latvian urban intelligentsia "becoming Russian" was not a decision to be made lightly. One learned Russian (and German) as a matter of course, for reasons that might be based wholly on self-interest. But the Latvian component of Baltic cultural life was too active and lively to allow people from this stratum of the Latvian population to merely drift into different nationalities. One would encounter the nationalistic sentiments of one's peers; the old argument that denationalization was an absolutely necessary step to a successful professional private or governmental career could no longer serve. Even though the public ideology of this generation was in large part directed against the Latvian "establishment" as symbolized in the RLA, its private activities suggest the presence of strong national feeling. The question of national identity had been answered in favor of Latvianness; and from that basis the generation of the 1890s felt free to search outward—largely in a Western direction—for new ideas.

From the sociocultural dissatisfaction on which the New Current based its ideas, several lines of future development were possible. One of these took a number of the Latvian literati into a profound cultural pessimism, which was apolitical, largely egocentric, and innocent of practical recommendations for the solution of Latvian problems. The best example of this trend was Jānis Poruks (1871-1911), who by any measure was the best lyrical poet to emerge on the Latvian scene in the 1890s.[26] Poruks was born in 1871 as the son of a landowning farmer, in a region of Livland where the traditions of the Herrnhuters were still alive. His productive career was relatively short, lasting only from about 1895 to 1905, but even during that time he was able to state a Latvian problem in a new way. The problem was the conflict between the little tradition of the Baltic world and the great tradition of the whole civilization of the West. Poruks had spent some years being educated in Germany, and upon his return to the Baltic Provinces his creative work revealed a continuing tension between localism and cosmopolitanism, between what he felt to be his duty to his Latvian brethren and to his art. He gradually convinced himself that his "interests" separated him from the former, while at the same time he was forced, because of his nationality, to express his creative impulses in the language of his forefathers. In his own mind, he was estranged from his primary public because of his cosmopolitanism; but also from the great traditions of Western creativity because of the language in which he wrote. This he believed to be the fate of all culturally sensitive individuals living in the peripheral cultures of Europe: they were bound not to be recognized for their genius among their own people or in the great tradition. Poruks' inability to resolve this problem eventually led him to madness, and in the final years of his life, he wrote to his wife from a sanatorium that he was planning a play based on Lessing's "Nathan der Weise," in which the Nathan-esque figure would be none other than Pobedonostsev.

Writers such as Poruks lived increasingly in their own fantasy world, which was far removed from the everyday conflicts of Baltic area at the turn of the century. These aesthetes were also of the generation we are describing, of course; and their literary products served to expand the scope of Latvian literary culture, and therefore the cultural legacy which an even younger generation would inherit. But it was the politicized segment of the New Current which created the mainstream of Latvian history after the mid-point of the decade. Central to this political direction was the newspaper *Dienas Lapa*, which since 1891 was published under the guidance of a new editor, Jānis Pliekšāns (pseud. Rainis).[27] Rainis had been born in 1865, during the national awakening era, had received a law degree from St. Petersburg in 1888, and since that time had worked as a writer and publicist in Riga. Already before the age of twenty-six, when he became editor of *Dienas Lapa*, he had been absorbed in the so-called social question, and now he had a platform for his ideas. These received conceptual sharpening by German social-democratic literature which Rainis brought to Riga from abroad, and with the year 1891, the pages of *Dienas Lapa* took on a decidedly Marxist tone. Translations of Western socialist pamphlets, excerpts from socialist classics, and analyses by Western European socialists of current European problems became standard fare, and, surprisingly, the censors did not seriously question this content until 1895, when a series of strikes beset the factories of Riga and Libau. Until that date, the authorities were willing to countenance Latvian social-democratic ideas in print because they were thought to be weakening the strength of the nationalist movement.[28] With the advent of 1895, however, the situation changed, since now it was perceived that social-democratic ideas were likely to disturb the public order. This perception was to some extent true, since even before 1895, the staff of *Dienas Lapa*, and other members of the New Current, had been instrumental in the formation of illegal workers' groups in Riga, Mitau, Libau, and elsewhere, finding fertile ground for their ideas within the dissatisfied urban proletariat which had grown apace in the cities. Strikes and other kinds of agitation, lectures and question-and-answer evenings, pamphleteering and political education—all of these activities by the radical members of the New Current brought the situation to a head in 1897, when the staff of *Dienas Lapa*, the members of left-wing Latvian student groups at Dorpat and the Riga Polytechnic, and other groups suspected of illegal activities were summarily arrested, jailed, and expelled from the Baltic Provinces for a time.[29] Some members of these groups were exiled to the interior of Russia; others went abroad to continue their activities in the United States and in England.[30] Their presence, however, continued to be felt in their homeland, because their activities had attracted followers who had not been affected by the arrests of 1897.

The arrests of 1897, and the subsequent exile of many activists, had the effect of turning large numbers of the Latvian intelligentsia against the government and its policies, which were now perceived by them to be totally beyond redemption. Pamphlets published abroad in the Latvian social democratic circles in Boston called for an unremitting struggle against both "Russian absolutism and the capitalist order" and condemned the "Latvian petty bourgeoisie" for its "dog-like loyalty to the Russian government."[31] Among these intellectuals the oppositional stance had become larger than simple resistance to particular policies, or to the traditional Baltic German landowners; Latvians were now perceived to be living in an exploitative system, which would be broken not so much by means of national unity as by the international unity of all subordinated classes.

The experience of the Latvian Marxists was yet another example of the prevailing pattern of the 1890s: namely the conversion by intellectuals of Latvian problems into problems of greater theoretical import, in light of which Russification seemed but a minor injustice. The tendency of those who had been born and educated before Russification, and who came to intellectual maturity in the 1890s, was to reinterpret the problems of the Baltic littoral in terms of general cultural or political questions, expressed in the vocabulary of Western philosophies. This procedure did not make Baltic problems disappear, of course, nor did it provide solutions. But it did guarantee that the insertion of the Russian language in the educational process of Latvian schoolchildren was not perceived by itself to be a major threat to the survival of Latvian culture. The aesthetes of the 1890s ignored this range of problems because they became absorbed by their individual development as artists. The politicized segments of the New Current, however, undertook to subsume all individual policies deemed unjust to categories of class and national exploitation.

The government modified its Russification policy on the eve of the events of 1905. In the spring of that year, after receiving a long series of petitions on the school and language question, the government agreed that "the Baltic *schools* in no fashion should be made into an instrument of the realization of Russification principles [italics added]."[32] But this retreat from the more adamant position of the 1890s did little to quiet the voices of dissatisfied Latvians. The departure of many of the active Latvian social democrats to foreign lands and to the interior of Russia had not ended the activities of their sympathizers who remained in the Baltic area.[33] The movement had grown, so that by the time of the Russo-Japanese War, the social democratic movement among the Latvians was stronger than ever. The most active groups were in the larger cities—Riga, Mitau, and Libau—and there was a separate group for Kurland as a whole. The problem of the social democrats was not only to channel into appropriate activity the dissatisfactions of the urban workers and rural landless—their primary audience—but also to gather support among those who were better-off and whose concerns included the national question. On this score social-democratic theory was not well developed. But a position had to be taken, so that in 1904, when the movement published a set of demands (probably written by Jānis Jansons) entitled *Ko mēs prasam?* (*What Do We Demand?*), it included the following paragraph:

> We demand that each nationality which is a member of the Russian Empire should have the right to determine its own fate; that each nationality should have the right to maintain its own culture and to develop its spiritual strengths; and that the language of each nationality should have the right to be used in schools, local administrative institutions, and local courts.[34]

Not all social democrats agreed with his position. Fricis Roziņš, the editor of the Latvian paper *Socialdemokrāts*, maintained that autonomy should be granted not to ethnic groups (nationalities) but rather to regions. This kind of disagreement among social democrats on the nationality question was reflected in party congresses.[35] The first of these was held in Riga in June of 1904, and the majority of the delegates, after prolonged debate, decided that membership in the Latvian party should be based on nationality. This exclusive definition would change later, but these pre-1905 actions revealed that, far from being solely the preoccupation of the "bourgeois" RLA, the nationality problem had penetrated even the most internationally minded of the various Latvian political groupings. Though for some social democrats attitudes on the nationality question were a tactical matter, others, less enthusiastic about proletarian internationalism, saw it as inextricably bound up with the assistance the party could render to the Latvian working masses. But disagreements on the nationality question were not restricted to the ranks of the social democrats. The petition presented to the government in March 1905 by the leadership of the RLA was very conservative, citing the fact that the Latvians were not yet ready for nationhood, and asking only that advisory councils on the nationality question be set up, with Latvians represented therein.[36] This petition was opposed by much of the Latvian press. At the same time, another petition submitted by the Central Committee of the Latvian Social Democratic Party in March 1905 called for complete township, district, and provincial autonomy, with government officials elected in a democratic fashion, and all languages having complete equality in all governmental institutions. During the period of petitioning, social-democratic agitation continued in the form of strikes, marches, meetings, and proclamations; and as a result, martial law was declared for Kurland in August 1905.[37]

Latvian history during the months before August 1905 was far more complicated than we have pictured it thus far, the nationality question being only one of many to be discussed across the spectrum of Latvian politics. Yet the history of attitudes toward Russification had now become the history of the nationality question as a whole. A decade-long effort by the New Current, especially the Marxists in it, to up the ante in political discussions by subsuming lesser problems under the all-inclusive question of the imperial system had drawn other Latvian activists into the same rhetorical mode.[38] The public positions of the various Latvian "parties" and political groupings revealed that the development of a political consciousness among Latvians had been far more rapid than the development of nationalist theory. The different positions which emerged during the years surrounding 1905, and during that year itself, left the impression that while Latvians no longer had to wrestle with national identity at the personal level, at the collective level there was considerably more disagreement than unanimity.

Championing a traditionalist stance was the Latvian National Party, founded by Fricis Veinbergs (1844-1924), and working with the slogan of "unifying the cause of the Latvian nation with the cause of the Russian state and government."[39] Veinbergs' position was that the true defender of Latvian interests was the Russian government, and that socialism, imported from Germany, was not applicable to the Latvian situation, because, he claimed, the industrial workers in Livland and Kurland were non-Latvians. This viewpoint was expressed in the newspaper *Rigas Avize*, which was also to be the only Latvian newspaper to approve of the punitive expeditions after the events of 1905. A different position was taken by a segment of the Riga bourgeoisie gathered under the banner of the Latvian Democratic Party, which had been founded by the current editor of *Baltijas vestnēsis*, Arvēds Bergs (1875-?).[40] These people found it possible to cooperate with the social democrats, and in their petitions and programs they called for a constitutional convention, full manhood suffrage, Latvian autonomy within a transformed empire, and the use of the Latvian language in governmental institutions and schools. Somewhat more moderate than this was the Latvian Constitutional Democratic Party, which expressed its viewpoint in the newspaper *Latvija*.[41] This party demanded the union of all Latvian speakers in the Baltic into one autonomous province, and, among other things, the use of Latvian in all judicial institutions. A somewhat more amorphous group was the Latvian Reform Party, which did not mention autonomy, but did ask for, among other things, the use of the Latvian language in schools and judicial institutions.

Yet another group, the so-called neonationalists, sought to deepen Latvian nationalist philosophy by borrowing from the ideas of the social democrats, which tended to weaken its ideological thrust. This group included a number of well-known literati, the most prominent being the novelist Andrievs Niedra (1871-1941).[42] The neonationalists propagandized the same constituency as the social democrats, but believed their main mission to be the creation of another national revival. They accused the older generation of Latvians of trying to become Germans, and of lacking idealism; and called for the uniting of the Latvian "colonies" in Russia proper with the rest of the Latvian people. Andrievs Niedra periodically warned against the dream of full Latvian autonomy.

The most active competitor of the Social Democratic Party was the Social Democratic Union, which had been founded in 1903 and included by 1905 many of the best-known Latvian literary figures.[43] By 1905 it had some 1,000 members. It stressed in its program the issues of nationality autonomy and agrarian reform. The Social Democratic Party had never gone so far as to ask for the complete separation of the Latvian lands from the empire, but the Union was quite adamant on this point. Already in 1903 a prominent publicist of the Union, Miķelis Valters (1874-1970?) had published in the monthly journal of the Union, *The Proletarian*, a piece which had argued that "we must say to each nationality of the empire: break free of Russia, and strengthen the separatist tendencies within Russia."[44] This general line of thought continued strong in the publications of the Union throughout the years from 1904 onward. Its program, adopted in the general congress of December 1905, was in fact less of a document addressing immediate problems than an attempt to lay down the first principles of a separate Latvian state. It stated that:

> all the land presently occupied by Latvians—Kurland, Southern Livland, and Inflanty (Lettgallia)—are to be united into a single self-governing district—Latvia—which has the right to conduct its own internal affairs. These rights are vested in the people collectively, and are expressed in their autonomy to make laws, i.e. in an autonomous parliament and in the autonomy of the executive implementation of such laws.[45]

The Social Democratic Union was not the first to debate the question of the Lettgallians. The problems of who the Lettgallians were, how it came to be that they lived outside the Baltic Provinces, and whether they were to be included in a definition of Latvian nationality had been broached before in both Latvian and Baltic German publications.[46] But these issues had not been as pressing in the past as now, when the concept of Latvian nationality needed a precise definition and the Lettgallians appeared to be undergoing their own national awakening. Beyond the eastern borders of Livland and Kurland, in the adjoining province of Vitebsk, there had appeared a handful of writers and publicists whose claims to participation in Latvian national development had to be listened to seriously.[47]

Disregarding political boundaries, and considering the Catholic Lettgallians as ethnically Latvian, the calculations we can make on the basis of imprecise enumerations show that Lettgallians comprised about a fifth of all Latvians in the Baltic littoral in 1863, about the same proportion in 1880, but already about 26 percent in 1897.[48] It is probable that this trend reflects a continued high fertility rate among the Lettgallians, as compared to a declining rate among the Latvians in Livland and Kurland, who by 1897 showed a fertility pattern closer to Western populations than to, for example, the Russian.[49] In other respects, too, the history of the Lettgallians had differed considerably from that of their western brethren. Emancipation from serfdom had not come until 1861, thus forty years later than among the western Latvians; and the dominant elites in the Lettgallian areas had been Russian and Polish, not Baltic German. Settlement patterns tended to be different: the western Latvians lived in scattered farmsteads, whereas the Lettgallians lived in villages closer to the Russian type. The ethnic mix in Lettgallian areas was also greater than in Kurland and Livland. In fact, ethnographers such as Pastor August Bielenstein, who sought to map out the area of "Latvian" settlement in the Baltic, had considerable difficulties specifying easternmost boundaries, since there were districts in which Lettgallian was heard as frequently as the Russian language.[50] It is possible to speculate on this basis that intermarriage between Lettgallian-Latvians and non-Latvians (i.e. Russians, Poles, and Belorussians) had for years been more extensive than among the western Latvians. It is also probable that inheritance practices among the Lettgallians enhanced contact with other eastern-area nationalities. Partible inheritance had promoted the splintering of holdings, and as a result there were numerous Lettgallian peasants who left their smallholdings to their wives and children to manage and sought to supplement their incomes by becoming raftsmen, road repairmen, and factory workers outside the Lettgallian districts.[51]

There were few signs that before the 1890s most Lettgallians knew or understood the changes taking place among their western brethren. A few Catholic clergymen took an interest in Lettgallian folklore, and published a number of collections, some of them in the Cyrillic script. There were few rural schools: only 28 in 1866, and only 41 in 1881. Most teachers were Russian. There were only two districts of Vitebsk *guberniia* in which the Lettgallians were a majority of the population: Rēzekne (72 percent) and Ludza (64 percent).[52] In other districts government officials had taken to designating the Lettgallians as "Russian Latvians." Concepts of national identity in these areas remained in a confused state. In 1889, the western Latvian journal *Sēta, Daba, Pasaule*, published an article by Vilis Roznieks on "The Latvians of Polish Livland" reporting on his travels in Lettgallian districts, during which he had questioned the indigenous population on its nationality.[53] Some had said that they were Poles, since the Poles were also Catholic, although these peasants spoke not a word of Polish. Some replied that they were not Latvians but Catholics; that Latvians lived closer to Riga. The terms "Lettgallia" and "Lettgallians" were to appear in print for the first time only in 1904.

The pace of social differentiation remained slow even in the 1890s, and individuals who now began to concern themselves with Lettgallian cultural life came largely from the Catholic clergy. Men such as Francis Trasūns (1864-1926), Pēteris Smelteris (1868-?), and Fēliks Laizāns (1871-1931) apparently drew their inspiration from the publications of the RLA, especially the suggestion that a "national" culture should be based on folklore.[54] Folklore collecting was initiated in 1889 and the first results published in collections of Latvian *dainas* at the turn of the century. Greater efforts than this, however, remained a post-1900 phenomenon, so that the Lettgallians entered the twentieth century with only the most tenuous of ties to the literary culture of the western Latvians.

Speaking strictly of literary culture, it is ironic that the inspiration provided by the western Latvian cultural activists did not occasion among the Lettgallian men of letters any great desire to blend their own literary products with those of their western brethren. Instead, during the decade of the 1890s when western Latvian culture was being riven by ideological conflict, Lettgallians were beginning to insist that their own dialect deserved to exist independently of the rest of the Latvian language, and that the writings in it be recognized as a unique "Lettgallian" literature.[55] This development was hardly helpful to the further clarification of Latvian nationality and proposals of political reorganization based upon it. The incorporation of the Lettgallian population, and its historical experience, into the ideological expressions of Latvian aspirations during 1905 rendered these even more confused than they already were. The national development which had brought Latvians to the point of demanding, in 1905, cultural autonomy if not political independence, had been paid for with the disappearance of unanimity at the level of theoretical formulation.

The last months of 1905 were filled with a series of congresses aimed at establishing a common strategy regarding legal and illegal activities, and a common ground for making social, economic, and political demands. In November the Latvian Schoolteachers Congress was held in Riga, and was attended by approximately a thousand people.[56] A leading faction within this organization consisted of the social democratic schoolteachers. On the question of nationality, the Congress adopted the resolution that the Latvian nation should remain autonomous without politically separating from the Russian Empire. On November 18 the Congress of County Representatives began.[57] On the question of nationality, this congress called for an empire-wide constitutional convention, and Baltic autonomy as an article of a new imperial constitution. This Congress also agreed that its future activities would be handled by a network of local committees in the two Latvian-speaking regions; subsequently, 190 such local committees were formed in Kurland and 156 in Livland, which included 80 percent and 60 percent of all of the townships, respectively. Local affairs thereafter were to pass from the hands of the traditional township councils to these local committees. Reacting to these and other events, the government declared martial law in Livland on November 22. Kurland had already had martial law since August.

November was also the month during which there began an almost uninterrupted series of strikes in urban areas and violent incidents in the countryside. A general strike was called in Riga on November 25, to the accompaniment of lesser strikes throughout the rest of the Latvian territories. In fact, striking was not a new activity by this time, but 1905 was a peak as far as the number of strikers involved. The number of laborers engaged in strike activity climbed from only 243 in 1895 to 316,459 in 1905, falling back to 26,165 in 1907.[58] To work stoppages and striking, the peasantry added as well the illegal cutting of lumber in forests to which only the landowning nobles had rights. Much more serious was the illegal occupation and seizure of manorial buildings, an activity which was not generally supported by Latvian national and political organizations. Nonetheless, the amount of property destroyed in 1905 was considerable. In the Latvian sections of Livland, 136 manor farms and 72 landowners' dwellings were put to the torch; in Kurland the numbers were 229 and 45, respectively.[59]

Since both Kurland and Livland were under martial law, these activities by Latvians were answered by the private militia of the Baltic German landowners, working together with units of the imperial army. These so-called punitive expeditions ranged over the countryside, burning farms, hunting various peasant activists who were considered revolutionary, and carrying out drumhead trials and summary executions. Estimates of the number of people who were imprisoned, exiled, or executed differ considerably.[60] The largest estimate is that up to the year 1908 the punitive expeditions had executed 2,041 Latvian peasants. Military tribunals tried and executed 724 others, and 128 were tried by civil courts and executed. Some 713 were sentenced to hard labor, to jail, or to deportation to Siberia. Lighter sentences, including whippings, were meted out to some 2,652. Among all these individuals there had been some 688 people who were members of leftist groups, some 80 percent of them social democrats. The numbers also included throughout the Latvian regions some 600 rural schoolteachers. Approximately 5,000 political refugees had fled abroad as a consequence of the 1905 events. In addition to these, numerous people had fled into forests to become roving bands of terrorists (the so-called forest brothers). They continued their activities during the next few years. In the last six months of 1906, in Kurland, some 643 such acts of terror were recorded.

Historians of the Baltic area have not agreed on the basic nature of the 1905 uprising.[61] Some stress that the events of 1905 were inspired and led by the urban proletariat; others that the leadership role had been assumed by rural masses, whose enemy was not industrial capitalism but the traditional Baltic German landowner and his continued favored position in the Baltic rural economy. Some historians stress the basically economic nature of these events; others that they were basically political in character and were guided by the hope of at least an autonomous, if not an independent, Latvian state. From the perspective of the history of Russification, the 1905 events also had great significance. The activities of the imperial army, at the service of the Baltic German landowners, convinced many that Latvian expectation could not be based on the presumed good will of the imperial government. Thus, a large part of the intelligentsia, by no means all of them of the political left, took up a stance which seriously questioned continued Latvian membership in the empire.

CHAPTER 16

1905-1914: A POSTLUDE

EVEN THE HISTORIANS who have wished to make the Russification period into a major chapter of Latvian history concede that in the decade after 1905 this aspect of Russian rule was singled out for special complaints only rarely. Already before 1905, there had been a few Latvian voices which had placed Russification into a larger context of general Russian maladministration; during the revolution, a condemnation of Russification in petitions of grievances appeared in the context of general proposals of solutions to the nationality question; and after 1905, it continued to be the overall national position of the Latvians, rather than specific policies, that held center stage in the public debate. Political debates had become very public indeed. In the two years between October 1905 and July 1907, the Latvian press had expanded to some 102 periodical publications: 19 daily and 44 weekly newspapers, 20 monthly journals, and 19 satire magazines that appeared sporadically.[1] The desire to make one's views known appeared to have become uncontrollable. Of the mentioned periodicals, during the same period, some 40 were stopped by the censor for a time, and 48 others banned outright. Yet as a newspaper was closed, its technical workers and contributors reorganized quickly and started publishing another paper with a different title but roughly the same content. These skirmishes between the government and the periodical press continued up to the start of World War I, and no doubt confirmed many in the belief that fundamental alterations in the government were an absolute necessity.

If before 1905 the case could be made that Latvian literary culture had limited appeal, the postrevolutionary decade witnessed a number of innovations in literary productivity specifically designed to bring Latvian culture to the masses. Certainly, the widespread circulation in city and countryside of the aforementioned newspapers testified to this. In addition, the printing house which the publisher Ansis Gulbis (1873-1936) had founded in St. Petersburg in 1903 reopened in Riga after the revolution, and began to publish the *Universālā Bibliotēka* (*Universal Library*), a series of cheap editions of literary and political classics in Latvian translation.[2] Some six or seven titles appeared monthly, with the total number of titles growing eventually to 178. Each title was printed in lots of 10,000. The editor of the series was Jānis Rainis, the social democratic activist who had since 1905 turned increasingly to literary matters. Through his position he supplied a large number of the semi-employed intelligentsia with incomes as translators. The historian Švābe has also pointed out, somewhat ruefully, that in the decade after 1905 "the book market was flooded by Marxist political brochures in the form of translations from the German or compilations by Latvian social democrats."[3] By 1910 there were altogether 79 publishing houses in the Latvian areas of the Baltic Provinces, 45 of them in Riga. Books in Latvian, the classics as well as tracts of the times, had become a cheap commodity: an omnipresent aspect of the cultural world in which Latvian schoolchildren educated in Russified curricula were coming of age.

Precisely how many schoolchildren were being educated in the Russified curriculum remains unclear. The statistics used by Latvian historians suggest that there was a drop in primary school enrollment from 168,350 children in 1886 to 113,300 in 1911, and these figures are used to support the assertion that parents were withholding their offspring from schools *because* the curriculum had been Russified.[4] No doubt this was true in many cases. But these statistics are insufficient to show that decreasing school enrollment was a *trend* between 1886 and 1911. Also, as mentioned before, the Baltic nobility had begun to withdraw financial support from rural schools. If in 1880-1881 the nobility of Kurland, for instance, had covered some 27 percent of all rural school costs, by 1897-1898 its share had dropped to 9 percent, and to 4 percent by the year 1904.[5] While part of the difference was picked up by the government, and the townships themselves, there was very likely a diminution of the absolute number of schools, which meant that by the post-1905 period Latvian parents had fewer schools to send their children to. Further, these school attendance statistics do not discuss the loss enrollment due to the out-migration of Latvian families, which continued steadily during these decades, and probably increased after the turn of the century. By 1913, according to the statistician Mārģeris Skujenieks, most of the Latvian "colonies" outside of the Baltic area (comprising about 14.8 percent of the Latvian population in the empire in 1914) had their own schools. He estimated that about 82 percent of these "colonies" had from 1 to 500 Latvians in them, and the remaining 18 percent from 500 to 1,000.[6] While the drain on the school-age population represented by these emigrants is impossible to estimate, it is at least probable that such a drain existed and that it showed up in the aggregated statistics regarding enrollments in the lower grades.

Assuming for a moment that the cumulative impact of parents' negative attitudes did mean a drop in enrollments in lower grades from, say, 1887 onward, the same kind of decrease cannot be detected in enrollment statistics for higher grades and post-elementary education. It appears that more Latvian children than ever before, once enrolled in a school system, were not withdrawn but continued their education, in spite of a Russified curriculum, in gymnasia and the universities. If in the last decade of the nineteenth century there had been some 600 Latvians pursuing advanced education, in 1913 that number had swelled to 1,850; and the estimate is that by the year 1914 there were altogether about 3,000 Latvians with advanced academic degrees.[7] In the light of these numbers it seems impossible to view a Russified curiculum at any level as having been a disincentive of major significance. The "damage" done by Russification to Latvian education would have begun to reveal itself *after* 1914, in the later careers of young people entering the school system after 1897. Those entering the school system between 1887 and 1897, however, contributed more than any previous age cohort to the aggregate number of academically educated Latvians within the whole population.

By the time Latvians born at the beginning of the Russification reached early adulthood, that is, after the turn of the century, the cultural reorientation the policy sought to achieve should have started to show some results. It is certain that it did not diminish Latvian nationalistic sentiments or cultural activity, and there is additional evidence—though not as unequivocal as we would like—that no new trends appeared in the realm of marital choices. An increase in the proportion of mixed marriages (Protestant-Orthodox) especially in such multi-national centers as Riga, would have meant an expansion of the number of households in which children would come into contact with "Russian Christianity," but no such new trends were in evidence. The bulk of all marriages in Riga during the whole Russification period continued to be between Protestants: an average of 90.5 percent during the years between 1886 and 1890 and exactly the same proportion in the year 1919 (with a maximum of 91.4 percent and a minimum of 89.1 percent in the intervening years). There was a slight increase in the years between 1886 and 1909 in the proportion of Protestant males marrying Orthodox females, the average rising from 3.7 percent of all marriages in the years from 1886 to 1905 to 4.0 percent in the years from 1906 to 1909; but a slight drop in the proportions of Orthodox males marrying Protestant women, from an average of 5.3 percent of all marriages in the years 1886 to 1905 to an average of 5.2 percent in the years from 1906 to 1909.[8] Assuming rural marriages to have been even more conservative along religious lines, it can be said that the main characteristics of marriage choices among Latvians remained generally unchanged during the Russification period.

Speaking qualitatively, Latvian cultural endeavors in the post-1905 years could no longer be accused, in the manner of the New Current generation, of being undifferentiated and cleaving to the institutionalized nationalism of the RLA. Since the turn of the century, and especially after 1905, Latvian cultural activity was so variegated as to deserve being called anarchical. The most prosaic as well as the most exalted imaginations among the educated could find therein a sympathetic hearing, and there were few political viewpoints, including those touching on the question of nationality, that could not find one or more journals or newspapers in which to express themselves. At one end of the cultural spectrum, there were apolitical aesthetes continuing the tradition of Poruks: self-absorption, experimentation with poetical form, and admiration for the cultural products of the West.[9] In the middle stood a wide range of writers of prose—novelists, essayists, political commentators—whose attention was riveted to *Latvian* social problems to the extent that the best of them, the novelists Andrievs Niedra and Augusts Deglāvs (1862-1922), became in their novels historians of the Latvian transition from peasanthood to urban life.[10] At the other end of the spectrum were the practical men of affairs, who also wrote, but directed their attention to everyday problems of provincial politics (if they were of the political right) and to the transformation of the Russian imperial system (if they were of the left).

With the Duma in existence, these Latvian men of affairs now had a larger arena for their political activities. Latvians were elected to all four Dumas, more to the first than to the others; of considerable significance to our general theme is the fact that with few exceptions all Latvian deputies had been born and educated before the Manasein senatorial inspection, and hence had experienced in the formation of their political attitudes the disappointments cultural Russification and the Revolution of 1905 had brought to Latvians who had depended on the imperial government for helpful reforms.[11] The main concerns of these men of affairs as well as of their educated constituency in the Baltic area remained twofold. First, and primarily, they were interested in improving the lot of the landowning Latvian peasant through the establishment of agrarian credit banks and other sources of improvement capital, and in achieving further diminution of the proportion of the total arable land (48 percent in 1914) which still remained in the hands of the Baltic Germans. Landownership among the privileged orders had become more concentrated over time, so that 3.5 mil-

271

lion hectares owned by them belonged to 820 families. There were some 1,300 private estates; most of these were owned by persons with no further property, but there were numerous landowners as well who owned more than a single estate.[12]

From the Latvian viewpoint, the continuation of this state of affairs was clearly unsatisfactory, and the desire to own rather than rent from others remained a powerful theme in all Latvian discussions of agrarian matters. But as long as the imperial government was not willing to support wide-scale agrarian reforms, the Latvian deputies in the Duma, and their educated constituency, had to remain satisfied with calling for relatively moderate changes. At the same time, much could be done entirely through private initiative. Latvian farmers' organizations were growing apace, so that in 1906 the Central Organization of Latvian Farmers established in that year had some 106 local farmers' organizations as members. By 1914, there were some 860 farmers' organizations active in the Latvian countryside—a notable continuation of the theme of organization that had begun as early as the national awakening period. Such organizations, as mentioned before, had more than an economic meaning, since they hired instructors in the agrarian sciences, started scientific animal breeding, and set up seed laboratories; in a word, continued to build an infrastructure in the Latvian countryside that called for extensive and continuing interaction between Latvians in their own language.

Moderation also remained the main theme of official Latvian discussions of the nationality question. The opinions on these matters that had found expression during the restless years before 1905 were still represented in the population at large, but within the Dumas, Latvians tended to call for no more than cultural autonomy, all the while pledging loyalty to the imperial system. Indeed, in the best known of these speeches, the Riga lawyer Jānis Zālītis (1874-1919), speaking in the Fourth Duma, achieved a synthesis of the viewpoints of Valdemārs and Kronvalds:

We regard Russia as our motherland and recognize that the basis for our welfare and existence is unification of the Russian nation. Latvians and Estonians have never had, nor do they have now, a desire to separate from Russia: they have never had a significant past, they have never had their own separate countries, and because of their small size they now have little incentive to long after autonomy. . . . All the rumors, whispers, and comments about Latvian and Estonian separatism are spread by people who do not know the conditions of life in the Baltic area, or by those

who are our former lords, who held us in slavery for six hundred
years and who now, when because of the high-mindedness of our
Russian sovereign we have been able to escape from the claws
of our oppressors, still seek to retain us under their overlordship and identify us in the eyes of the government as separatists.
I can testify that the native inhabitants of the Baltic Provinces
are no less loyal than the Baltic Germans. . . . Among the Latvians and Estonians there are no persons who have sympathies
for countries other than Russia. But, being fiery sons of Russia,
we want to preserve and develop our own culture. . . . We are
waiting anxiously for reforms that are being blocked by the
Baltic German landowners through their various contacts in the
government. If only the government would view us with its own
eyes, and not through the eyes of intermediaries, then the government would be able to achieve its goal—to unify the inhabitants of the Baltic with the great Russian nation.[13]

Thus, as late as 1913, when the speech was made, many old themes
were still alive in Latvian political thinking, notably the theme first
established by Valdemārs, namely, that the imperial government had
nothing to fear from the Latvians if only it would deal harshly with
the Baltic Germans. Zālītis, of course, was wrong on a number of
counts: among Latvians and Estonians there *were* separatists, and if
these were not "loyal" to other nations, then at least many of them
(the radical wing of the social democrats) were considerably more
loyal to an international "proletariat" than to the specific institutions
of the Russian Empire. The speech was also disingenuous on the
theme of "unification with the great Russian nation," since Zālītis
could not have helped but know that the cultural development of the
Latvians had made this Russifying goal of the government quite impossible by this late date. At best, only a structural unification could
have been achieved, that is, the co-residence within a loose political
framework of nationality groups, each with a thriving national culture. The de facto autonomy that Latvians had already achieved in
the essence of their cultural activities, and which was now the basis
of the self-confident activities of the Latvian cultural elite, was not
likely to be given up willingly. Even though Russification of the
school curriculum was at the moment affecting the generation just
coming of age, cultural and political activity was being carried out
by people for whom their nationality was no longer an open question
and who were not likely to abandon it even for thoroughgoing agrarian reform.

Notes to Part Three

CHAPTER 13. LATVIANS BEFORE THE 1880s

1. *Latvijas vēstures institūta žurnāls*, I (1937), 3.

2. There are no histories of post–World War II non-Marxist Latvian historical scholarship; for a complete bibliography see Benjamiņš Jēgers, *Latviešu trimdas izdevumu bibliogrāfija 1940-1960* (Stockholm: Daugava, 1968-1976), 2 vols. For an account of the interwar period see Ludwig Karstens, "Die Entwicklung und der Charakter der lettischen Geschichtswissenschaft," *Jomsburg*, III (1930), 45-72. A complete account of Soviet Latvian historical writing (to 1966) can be found in Vasilijs Dorošenko and A. Birons, *Vēstures zinātnes attīstība Padomju Latvijā* (Riga: ZA Vēstures Institūts, 1966); and an updated bibliography of more recent writings appears in Z. Sakare (ed.), *Latvijas PSR Zinātņu Akadēmijas Vēstures Institūta Publikācijas (1946-1972)* (Riga: "Zinātne," 1973).

3. The only systematic account of Russification policy from the Latvian viewpoint that comes close to acceptable standards of historical objectivity is to be found in Arvēds Švābe, *Latvijas vēsture 1800-1914*, pp. 427-78; hereafter cited as Švābe, *LV 1800-1914*. The value of these informative chapters is reduced by the absence of footnotes, however; the literature used by the author is cited in chapter bibliographies. A general treatment of Russian expansion into the Baltic area from the medieval centuries onward appears in Kārlis Stalšāns, *Krievu ekspansija un rusifikācija Baltijā laikmetu tecējumā*. This fact-laden work utilizes the same reference procedures as Švābe, and is colored throughout by strong anti-Russian sentiments. The Soviet Latvian interpretation of the period can be found in K. Strazdiņš et al. (eds.), *Latvijas PSR Vēsture*, II: *No 1861. gada līdz 1917. gada martam* (Riga: Zinātņu Akadēmijas Izdevniecība, 1955), pp. 74-331, particularly in the chapters on nationalism (pp. 74-89), the reforms of the 1870s and 1880s (pp. 89-121), and capitalist development (pp. 121-61). The general attitudes of interwar Latvian intellectuals toward Russification are represented by Kristaps Bachmanis, "Pārkrievošanas politika un tās sekas," IMM (see List of Abbreviations), 1931, pp. 399-411, 525-35.

4. Outside the Soviet Union, the best collection of materials published in the Latvian language from the mid-1850s to World War I is to be found in the "Lettonica" Collection to the Helsingin Yliopiston Kirjasto (Helsinki University Library), Helsinki, Finland.

5. For a further discussion of this problem see Andrejs Plakans, "Peasants, Intellectuals and Nationalism in the Russian Baltic Provinces 1820-1890," *Journal of Modern History*, XLIV (1974), 445-75.

6. The best multi-volume history of the formation of the Latvian population (including the Lettgallians) is the still-incompleted series published by Daugava publishers in Sweden, of which Švābe, *LV 1800-1914* (see Note No. 2) is a part. For the pre-nineteenth-century period see Edgars Dunsdorfs and Arnolds Spekke, *Latvijas vēsture 1500-1600* (Stockholm: Daugava, 1964); Edgars Dunsdorfs, *Latvijas vēsture 1600-1710* (Uppsala:

Daugava, 1962); Edgars Dunsdorfs, *Latvijas vēsture 1710-1800* (Stockholm: Daugava, 1973); Andrejs Johansons, *Latvijas kultūras vēsture 1710-1800* (Stockholm: Daugava, 1975). The counterpart to these volumes representing the Soviet Latvian viewpoint is K. Strazdiņš et al. (eds.), *Latvijas PSR vēsture, I: No vissenākajiem laikiem līdz 1860. gadam* (Riga: Zinātņu Akadēmijas Izdevniecība, 1953).

7. The general biographic information on which the chart is based comes from Arveds Švābe (ed.), *Latvju enciklopēdija*, i-iii; hereafter cited as *Enciklopēdija*.

8. A different schema of the interplay between generational and other kinds of change would obtain for the Lettgallian population of Vitebsk *guberniia*.

9. See Andrejs Plakans, "Modernization and the Latvians in Nineteenth-Century Baltikum," in Arvīds Ziedonis et al. (eds.), *Baltic History* (Columbus, Ohio: Association For the Advancement of Baltic Studies, Inc., 1974), pp. 123-34.

10. See *Enciklopēdija*, iii, 2164-65.

11. These differences in outlook and interests are noted in equal detail by Latvian Marxist and non-Marxist historians; the former, however, portray such divisions as class conflict, whereas the latter stress the continuing linguistic and cultural unity of all Latvians regardless of differing socioeconomic status. Compare, e.g. the treatment of the topic of the rural landless by the Soviet Latvian historian Austra Mieriņa, "Par lauku proletariāta veidošanos Kurzemē," *Vēstis*, 1959, no. 8, pp. 17-62; and by Švābe, *LV 1800-1914*, pp. 549-63.

12. Because such political settlements, if shown to have enhanced Baltic German power, meant continuing and perhaps legitimizing noble control over the Latvian-speaking peasantry, Latvian historians, on their side, have tended to characterize the settlements as "charlatanry": cf. Dunsdorfs, *Latvijas vēsture 1710-1800*, pp. 16-17.

13. See Dunsdorfs, *Latvijas vēsture 1600-1710*, pp. 171-200.

14. See ibid., pp. 275-314.

15. The large proportion of non-Latvians in this region led Senator Manasein in 1882 to recommend that this—the Illuxt-region—be administratively joined to Vitebsk *guberniia*. See Manasein, pp. 175-79.

16. Contrasting accounts of the entry of these concepts into Latvian scholarship can be found in the articles "Historiogrāfija" in *Enciklopēdija*, pp. 758-61, and "Vēstures zinātne" in *Latvijas PSR mazā enciklopēdija* (Riga: "Zinātne," 1970), iii, 671-75.

17. Johansons, *Latvijas kultūras vēsture 1710-1800*, pp. 7-12.

18. Parts of the Nerft parish register, including literacy tabulations, have been transcribed and translated from the original German by Lauma Sloka, *Kurzemes draudžu kronikas* (Riga: Valsts Archīvs, 1930), ix, pt. 2, 19-246.

19. Jānis Andrups and Vitauts Kalve, *Latvian Literature: Essays* (Stockholm: Zelta Ābele, 1954), pp. 47-88.

20. See Arveds Švābe, "Latviešu tautas tiesiskie uzskati," in his *Straumes un avoti* (Lincoln, Nebraska: Pilskalns, 1962; orig. ed. Riga, 1938), I, 9-44.

21. For collecting techniques see A. Švābe (ed.), *Latviešu tautas dziesmas* (Copenhagen: Imanta, 1952), I, 17-25.

22. For a general description see Teodor Zeids, "Formen des bäuerlichen Klassenkampfes in Lettland im Zeitalter des Feudalismus," *Jahrbuch für Geschichte der UdSSR und der volksdemokratischen Länder Europas*, XII (1968), 267-89; and for a chronologically circumscribed treatment Mārģers Stepermanis, *Zemnieku nemieri Vidzemē 1750-1784* (Riga: Zinātņu Akadēmijas Izdevniecība, 1956).

23. A classification of forms of collective violence and their measurement is suggested in Charles Tilly, "Collective Violence in European Perspective," in H. D. Graham and T. R. Gurr (eds.), *Violence in America* (Washington: U.S. Government Printing Office, 1969), pp. 4-56.

24. One of the few uprisings which was to have a "national" reputation throughout the nineteenth century was that at Kauguri, Livland, in 1802. It has been exhaustively researched by A. Kāpostiņš, *Vidzemes zemnieku nemieri Kaugurmuižā 1802. gadā* (Riga: Valsts Archīvs, 1924).

25. See, for example, Jānis Straubergs, *Rīgas vēsture* (Brooklyn, New York: Grāmatu Draugs, 1954), pp. 433-34.

26. Dunsdorfs, *Latvijas vēsture 1710-1800*, pp. 1124-28.

27. Wilhelm Lenz, "Volkstumswechsel in den baltischen Ländern," *Ostdeutsche Wissenschaft: Jahrbuch des Ostdeutschen Kulturrats*, III/IV (1956-57), 181-200. The article poses the problem of assimilation nicely while employing concepts (such as *Volkstum*) which have no precise equivalents in English. Lenz argues that assimilation was a two-way street: Latvians assimilated to the German-speaking population while at the same time "on the other side, almost all peasant immigrants—Russians, Swedes, Finns, Poles, Lithuanians, and also Germans—assimilated to the indigenous peasant populations" (p. 185).

28. Johansons, *Latvijas kultūras vēsture 1710-1800*, p. 405. Latvian involvement in the armed forces of the ruling orders of the Baltic is discussed further in Edgars Dunsdorfs, *Mūžīgais latviešu karavīrs* (Melbourne: K. Goppers Fonds, 1967).

29. The methodology employed by recent research on collective unrest in French industrial areas in the nineteenth century suggests how local evidence can become the basis for generalizations at the national level. See Edward Shorter and Charles Tilly, *Strikes In France* (Cambridge: Cambridge University Press, 1974).

30. Cited in *Enciklopēdija*, II, 1775. See also P. Dreimanis, "Latvju tautiskās atmodas pirmsākums XVIII. g.s. otrā pusē," IMM, 1926, pp. 489-97, for a cursory description of the early Latvian men of letters.

31. See Jānis Zutis, *Latvija klaušu saimniecības sairšanas periodā un Kauguru nemieri 1802. gadā* (Riga: Vēstures Institūts, 1953).

32. See the article "Prese" in *Enciklopēdija*, III, 1997-2009.

33. Jürgen von Hehn, *Die lettisch-literärische Gesellschaft und das Let-*

tentum (Königsberg/Berlin: Osteuropa Verlag, 1938). Almost from the first this organization was known among Latvians as the "Latviešu Draugu Biedrība" ("The Society of the Friends of Latvians").

34. For the attitudes of pre-1850 Latvians toward emancipation see Andrejs Plakans, "The National Awakening In Latvia 1850-1900" (dissertation), pp. 81ff.; cf. Švābe, *LV 1800-1914*, pp. 114-33. For a Soviet Latvian treatment of the emancipation see Jānis Zutis, *Vidzemes un Kurzemes zemnieku brīvlaišana XIX. gadsimta 20. gados* (Riga: Vēstures Institūts, 1956).

35. For additional information on the agrarian reforms in the nineteenth century see Benno Ābers, *Vidzemes zemnieku stāvoklis 19.g.s. pirmā pusē* (Riga: A. Gulbis, 1936); Jānis Zutis, *Vidzemes un Kurzemes zemnieku likumi 19.g.s. sākumā* (Riga: Vēstures Institūts, 1954); and A. Tobien, *Die Agrargesetzgebung Livlands im 19. Jahrhundert*, 2 vols.

36. Cited in Matīss Ārons, "Cimzes seminārs Valkā," *Austrums*, 1898, pp. 259-63.

37. On the other hand, in polemics with the Baltic German press, the Latvian nationalists of the 1860s fought against the designation "jaunlatvieši" (Young Latvians), believing it to have revolutionary connotations. See Švābe, *LV 1800-1914*, p. 362.

38. See Jānis Krodznieks, *Zemnieku nemieri 1841. gadā* (Riga: Valsts archīvs, 1922); Maximilian Stephany, *Konversion und Rekonversion in Livland* and Švābe, *LV 1800-1914*, pp. 191-203.

39. H. Strods, *Lauksaimniecība Latvijā pārejas periodā no feodālisma uz kapitālismu* (Riga: "Zinātne," 1972), pp. 289-321.

40. The secondary literature on the Latvian "national awakening" is considerable: see Plakans, "The National Awakening in Latvia 1850-1900," pp. 361-88. Two differing interpretations of the period can be found in Ernests Blanks, *Latviešu tautas atmoda* (Riga: A. Raņķis, 1927), representing the non-Marxist view; and Strazdiņš et al. (eds.), *Latvijas PSR Vēsture*, II, 74-89, representing the Marxist view.

41. Citations from Švābe, *LV 1800-1914*, p. 360.

42. Citations from Švābe, *LV 1800-1914*, pp. 360-61.

43. Gustav Brasche, "Ein Blick auf unsere lettische Volksliteratur der letztern Zeit, besonders die Journalistik," BM, IV (1861), 455.

44. The history of the Moravian Brethren (Herrnhut) in the Baltic area is described in J. R. Weinlick, "The Moravian Diaspora," *Transactions of the Moravian Historical Society*, XVII (1959), 82-100; and, specifically in Livland, in Matīss Kaudzīte, *Brāļu draudze Vidzemē* (Riga: M. Jakobsons, 1877).

45. Plakans, "The National Awakening In Latvia," pp. 214-29.

46. According to Švābe, "normally, the wives of the 'young Latvians' were German, and for that reason the husbands spoke Latvian in public but German at home." Švābe, *LV 1800-1914*, p. 363.

47. In a retrospective account of the "national awakening" period, the 1890s Latvian novelist Augusts Deglāvs maintained that in the general

population Germanized Latvians were the harshest critics of budding Latvian nationalism: Augusts Deglāvs, *Latviešu attīstības solis no 1843. līdz 1874.g.*, p. 36.

48. For a biography of Spāģis, see Kristaps Bachmanis, *Andrejs Spāģis un viņa laikmets* (Riga: author's ed., 1932).

49. The primary sources pertaining to the founding, publication, and closing of the *Pēterburgas avīzes* can be found in A. Tentelis (ed.), *Dokumenti par Pēterburgas avīzēm*. See also R. Klaustiņš, "Pēterburgas avīzes," *Vērotājs*, 1904, pp. 1433-49, for an assessment of the meaning of this newspaper for Latvian nationalistic development.

50. *Mājas viesis* became the most long-lived of the Latvian publications, lasting until 1910.

51. The term "fanatical nationalists" was applied to them by August Bielenstein in his *Ein glückliches Leben* (Riga: Jonk & Poliewsky, 1904), p. 367.

52. A brief characterization of Valdemārs' nationalism and his Slavophile sympathies can be found in Jēkabs Velme, "Krišjāņa Valdemāra nacionālisms," IMM, 1925, pp. 1-7. See also Antons Birkerts, *Krišjānis Valdemārs un viņa centieni.*

53. See, for instance, his passionate defense of Russification quoted in A. Zandbergs, *Atmiņas par Krišjāni Valdemāru* (Riga: author's ed., 1928), pp. 147-49: "Do you think that it is better for Latvians to become Germanized and remain in slavery than to be Russified and gain freedom?" (p. 147).

54. According to Švābe, Valdemārs claimed that from the beginning of the nineteenth century to 1865, some 117,000 Latvians and Estonians had been "Germanized": Švābe, *LV 1800-1914*, p. 373. This figure must be treated with skepticism, as even Švābe admits.

55. There has been no systematic study of this subpopulation in the pre-emancipation period, but such mixed marriages can be found scattered throughout the first enumerations of the Latvian population, as, for instance, the Kurland revision of 1797.

56. Mārģeris Skujenieks, "Ieceļošana un izceļošana Latvijā," *Domas*, 1913, pp. 1155-62. See also the article "Latvieši: kolonijas," *Rīgas Latviešu Biedrības Zinību Komisijas Konversācijas Vārdnica*, pp. 2327-28; hereafter cited as *Konversācijas Vārdnica*.

57. It has been estimated that very few of these Latvians returned to the Baltic area even after the achievement of independence in 1918: *Enciklopēdija*, II, 1048.

58. The best biography of Kronvalds is to be found in Volume I of Alfrēds Goba (ed.), *Kronvalda kopoti raksti* (Riga: Valters un Rapa, 1937).

59. For a full discussion of Kronvalds' nationalistic philosophy see Plakans, "National Awakening in Latvia," pp. 163-88.

60. Numerous editions of this work exist. I have used the following: Atis Kronvalds, *Tautiski centieni* (St. Petersburg: A. Gulbis, n.d.).

61. The "nationalizing" effect of primary education in the Latvian setting is explored in Ludvigs Adamovičs, "Latviešu tautības veidošana un tautas

izglītība latviešu un vācu apgaismojumā," *Latvijas vēstures institūta žurnāls,* II (1938), 211-25, 337-63.

62. For a comparison, see Margarethe Lindemuth, "Krišjānis Valdemārs und Atis Kronvalds: Zwei lettische Volkstumskämpfer," *Baltische Hefte,* XIII (1967), 84-107.

63. Kronvalds' influence on later nationalists has been studied in Kārlis Kārkliņš, "Kronvalda loma latviešu nacionālās kultūras izveidošanā," IMM, 1937, no. 4.

64. Alfreds Bērziņš, "Kronvalda Atis un Tērbatas latvju rakstniecības vakari," IMM, 1938, nos. 4-6.

65. The number of subscribers of *Pēterburgas avīzes* was 4,200, for instance, and approximately the same number took the newspaper *Latviešu avīzes.* See Švābe, *LV 1800-1914,* p. 381.

66. *Pervaia vseobshchaia perepis' naselenia rossiiskoi imperii, 1897 g.,* 89 vols. (St. Petersburg: Tsentral'nye Statisticheskii Komitet, 1899-1905), XIX, *Kurliandskaia guberniia,* pp. 12-25; XXI, *Lifliandskaia guberniia,* pp. 12-25.

67. For the 1881 statistics see the following volumes of the multi-volume work *Ergebnisse der baltischen Volkszählung von 29. Dezember, 1881*: Teil I, Band I, Lieferung II, *Die Zählung in Riga und Rigasche Patrimonialgebiet* (Riga: Statistische Commission der Stadt Riga, 1883); and Teil I, Band III, Lieferung II, *Die Zählung auf dem flachen Lande* (Riga: Livländisches Landratskollegium, 1885).

68. See the article "Rīgas Latviešu Biedrība," *Konversācijas Vārdnīca,* pp. 3427-52.

69. Švābe, *LV 1800-1914,* pp. 400-1.

70. George L. Mosse, *The Culture of Western Europe* (Chicago: Rand McNally, 1961), pp. 153-96, 245-52.

71. *Konversācijas Vārdnica,* pp. 2324-27, discusses these organizations in detail.

72. See Jēkabs Līgotnis, *Maza latviešu literatūras vēsture* (Riga: D. Zeltiņš, 1911), pp. 72-84.

73. Švābe, *LV 1800-1914,* pp. 348-59. Švābe dismisses as exaggerated Valdemārs' claim that the 1871 petitions to the crown represented the feelings of 200,000 Latvians (pp. 351-52).

CHAPTER 14. RUSSIFICATION POLICY IN THE 1880s

1. A summary of biographical data can be found in Edgars Dunsdorfs, *Latvijas vēstures atlants* (Melbourne: K. Goppers Fonds, 1969), pp. 132, 138.

2. For Auseklis see Jēkabs Līgotnis (ed.), *Auseklā izlasīti raksti* (St. Petersburg: A. Gulbis, n.d.), pp. 1-18.

3. Alfreds Goba, "Leģenda par tautiskās kustības panīkšanu 80-tos gados," IMM, 1930, pp. 230-45.

4. By 1907 Latvians themselves estimated the number of such non-political organizations at about 1,000: see *Konversācijas Vārdnīca,* p. 2327.

5. Švābe, *LV 1800-1914*, pp. 431-32.

6. For a thorough discussion of Manasein, see Part One of the present work.

7. For the Baltic German reaction to the inspection, see Michael Haltzel, "The Reaction of the Baltic Germans to Russification During the Nineteenth Century" (Harvard University Ph.D. dissertation, 1971), pp. 232-37.

8. Jekabs Lautenbachs, "Stērstu Andrejs," IMM, 1922, pp. 30-46.

9. Švābe, *LV 1800-1914*, pp. 434-35.

10. *Enciklopēdija*, II, 1620-21.

11. See Parts One and Four of the present work.

12. Švābe, *LV 1800-1914*, pp. 437-38.

13. The sources for the Riga and Livland statistics are cited in the preceding chapter, n. 67.

14. The mean household size of 4-5 is a rough estimate; such average sizes are likely to be smaller for urban than for rural households. The 1881 census did not present its statistics in terms of clearly defined coresidential units.

15. Jāzeps Vītols, *Manas dzīves atmiņas* (Uppsala: Daugava, 1963), p. 18.

16. Švābe, *LV 1800-1914*, pp. 445-46.

17. This and the following quotation from *Baltijas vēstnesis* cited in Švābe, *LV 1800-1914*, p. 450.

18. Švābe, *LV 1800-1914*, pp. 448-49.

19. Ibid., pp. 446-47.

20. For a survey of statistics regarding educational institutions see *Enciklopēdija* I, 823-32.

21. Edgars Dunsdorfs, "Rigas iedzīvotāju skaita attīstība 1547-1935," in H. Asaris (ed.), *Latvijas Pilsētas* (Riga: Latvijas Pilsētu Savienība, 1938), pp. 156-60.

22. A. Vičš, "Kā Latvijā nodibināja pirmo ministrijas skolu," IMM, 1920, pp. 17-22.

23. Švābe, *LV 1800-1914*, pp. 461-62.

24. Cited in Vičš, "Kā Latvijā nodibināja . . . ," p. 19.

25. Teodors Zeiferts, "Brīvzemnieka loma tautiskos centienos," *Zalktis*, 1908, pp. 23-38. See also Žanis Unams, "Kr. Valdemāra un Fr. Brīvzemnieka sarakstīšanās par Baltijas skolu lietām," IMM, pp. 112-21.

26. Cited in Švābe, *LV 1800-1914*, p. 462.

27. PSZ, 3rd ser., VII, 226-29, no. 4,455, May 17, 1887. Laws concerning the Russification of Baltic education are reprinted in Lembit Andersen (ed.), *Eesti rahvakoolid seadused 18. ja 19. sajandil* (Tallinn: ENSV Korgema ja Kesk-Erihariduse Ministerium, 1973), pp. 134-44.

28. Skujenieks, "Ieceļošana un izceļošana," p. 1156.

29. See A. Birons et al. (eds.), *Latviešu etnogrāfija* (Riga: "Zinātne," 1969), pp. 171-74.

30. Jānis Bērziņš, "Strādnieku streiku kustība Liepājā 1899. gada maijā," *Vēstis*, 1972, no. 6, pp. 35-45.

31. Švābe, *LV 1800-1914*, pp. 543-49.

The Latvians

32. Matīss Arons, *Mūsu tautas dziesmas* (Riga: Pūcīšu Ģederts, 1888).

33. Fricis Brīvzemnieks, "Latviešu tautas gara mantas," *Pagalms*, 1881, pp. 203-4, 210-11, 219, 227-28.

34. Andrups and Kalve, *Latvian Literature*, pp. 98-100.

35. These were based on a complex theory of Latvian mythology: see Jēkabs Lautenbachs, "Ievedums latviešu mitoloģijā jeb veco latviešu ticībā," *Rīgas Latviešu Biedrības Zinības Komisijas Rakstu Krājums*, IV (1888), 33-44.

36. Numerous editions of this work exist. I have used the one published in Fischbach, West Germany, in 1946.

37. For Merkel's influence on Latvian nationalist thought see Plakans, "National Awakening in Latvia," pp. 100-6.

38. The play "Uguns un nakts [Fire and night]" in *J. Rainis: Kopoti raksti* (Riga: A. Gulbis, 1937), v, pp. 11-138.

39. Matīss Kaudzīte, "Par *Mērnieku laiku* izcelšanos," IMM, 1920, pp. 193-202.

40. Apsītis' stories appeared in many different editions and formats during the period 1884-1909. See Pēteris Šmits, "Apsīšu Jēkabs," *Rīgas Latviešu Biedrības Zinības Komisijas Rakstu Krājums*, XX (1930), 7-15.

CHAPTER 15. THE EIGHTEEN-NINETIES

1. Mārģeris Skujenieks, *Latvijas statistikas atlass* (Riga: Valsts Statistiskā Pārvalde, 1938), p. 11. See also Rita Brambe, "Rīgas pilsētas iedzīvotāju skaita dinamika no 1787. līdz 1860. gadam," *Vēstis*, 1972, no. 8, pp. 55-66.

2. Wilhelm Lenz, *Die Entwicklung Rigas zur Grosstadt*, pp. 19, 21, 69; *Rīga: Apcerējumi par pilsētas vēsturi* (Riga: Latvijas Valsts Izdevniecība, 1965), p. 100.

3. A. Vičš, "Latviešu skolotāju sapulces," IMM, 1920, pp. 121-30, 210-15, 311-17, 413-18, 500-14; 1921, pp. 10-18, 113-19, 304-22, 408-15, 508-18.

4. Švābe, *LV 1800-1914*, pp. 464-67.

5. Vičš, "Latviešu skolotāju sapulces," pp. 117-18.

6. There are no reliable statistics to back this contention, however: see Švābe, *LV 1800-1914*, p. 468.

7. Jekabs Velme, "Atmiņas no manas Maskavas dzīves," IMM, 1922, pp. 1233-41.

8. Alfreds Goba, "Māteru Juris un latviešu zemnieku politikas sākums," IMM, 1930, pp. 289-303.

9. *Konversācijas Vārdnīca*, p. 1141 (table).

10. Mikelis Bukšs, *Latgaļu literatūras vēsture*, pp. 346-57.

11. For a history of these festivals see Valdemārs Bērzkalns, *Latviešu dziesmu svētku vēsture*.

12. By 1904 this "Useful Books" series had nearly 10,000 regular subscribers.

13. Švābe, *LV 1800-1914*, pp. 507-8.

14. None of the encyclopedia projects launched before World War II

281

were completed. *Dravnieka Konversācijas Vārdnica* (ed. J. Dravnieks, 1891-1900), did not go beyond the letter K; the Riga Latvian Association's Encyclopedia (1903-1913) reached the letter S, but did not complete it; and the *Latviešu konversācijas vārdnica* (ed. A. Gulbis, 1927-1940), reached the letter T in the twenty-first volume but did not complete it. The two post–World War II encyclopedias that have been completed are cited in notes 7 and 16 of Chapter 13.

15. Teodors Zeiferts, "Devinpadsmitā gadu simtena pēdejais gadu desmits," *Austrums*, 1903, pp. 35-45.

16. The student organization of which *Pūrs* was the organ had been set up by Latvian students at Dorpat as a rival to the Latvian student corporation "Lettonia," which modeled itself on the Baltic German student corporations.

17. "Priekšvārds," *Pūrs*, I (1890), 2-3.

18. Aleksandrs Dauge, "Vēstures likumi," *Pūrs*, II (1892), 1-13.

19. Kārlis Kasparsons, "Dialektika," *Pūrs*, III (1893), 85-105.

20. See A. Vilsons (ed.), *Veidenbauma kopoti raksti* (Riga: "Zinātne," 1961), 2 vols.

21. Jānis Jansons, *Domas par jaunlaiku literatūru* (Riga: Dienas Lapa, 1893).

22. See his critique of the nationalist movement in Jānis Jansons, "Tautiskie centieni un saimnieciska nokārtošanās," *Austrums*, 1903, pp. 182-90; 264-70; 581-87.

23. For differing evaluations of the New Current, see Ernests Blanks, "Jaunā strāva," IMM, 1923, pp. 995-1006; and Pēteris Laizāns, *Jaunstrāvnieku filozofiskie uzskati* (Riga: "Zinātne," 1966).

24. Fēlikss Cielēns, *Laikmetu mainā: Atminas un atzinas*, p. 128. Cielēns comments that "in the first half of the nineteenth century the Baltic Germans with their economic and cultural powers of attraction succeeded in Germanizing tens of thousands of Latvians. The national awakening stopped this process, but even in the last quarter of the nineteenth century it still happened that wealthy Latvian families went over to Germanness" (p. 128).

25. Cielēns, *Laikmetu mainā*, pp. 132-33.

26. Andrups and Kalve, *Latvian literature*, pp. 115-18.

27. See the biography of Rainis by A. Birkerts, "J. Raina dzīve" in *J. Rainis: Kopoti raksti*, I, 9-222.

28. Švābe, *LV 1800-1914*, p. 530.

29. Blanks, "Jaunā strāva," p. 1000.

30. *Enciklopēdija*, II, 1243-58.

31. Švābe, *LV 1800-1914*, p. 534.

32. The Russification question on the eve of the Revolution of 1905 is discussed in *Enciklopēdija*, II, 1860-62.

33. Social democratic sentiment remained especially strong among schoolteachers: see Jānis Ruberts, *Latvijas skolotāji un skolu jaunātne 1905-1907* (Riga, "Zinātne," 1965).

34. Cited in Švābe, *LV 1800-1914*, pp. 586-87.

35. For a short history of the Latvian Social Democrats before 1917, see Andrew Ezergailis, *The 1917 Revolution In Latvia* (New York: East European Quarterly, 1974), pp. 23-37.

36. The economic and political stance of the various Latvian urban groupings is discussed in Švābe, *LV 1800-1914*, pp. 585-636. A Marxist interpretation of the same topic can be found in Indulis Ronis, "Latviešu buržuāzijas šķiriskās organizācijas pirmā pasaules kara priekšvakarā," *Vēstis* 1971, no. 8, pp. 75-88.

37. Švābe, *LV 1900-1914*, p. 599.

38. Cielēns, himself a participant in the events of 1905, suggests that "among us the year 1905 was not the result of social hopelessness, but a political revolution, in which a nation fought for its rights and its freedoms." *Laikmetu maiņā*, p. 148.

39. See *Enciklopēdija*, iii, 2612.

40. See *Enciklopēdija*, i, 242.

41. See *Enciklopēdija*, ii, 1392.

42. A representative expression of neo-nationalist opinions is contained in Andrievs Niedra, "Nazijonālisms mūsu gara dzīvē," *Pēterburgas avīžu literārais pielikums*, 1902, pp. 445-47, 466-69, 491-92, 499-500, 506-7.

43. See *Enciklopēdija*, iii, 2331-32.

44. Cited in Švābe, *LV 1800-1914*, p. 610.

45. Švābe, *LV 1800-1914*, pp. 611-12.

46. See, for instance, the chapter entitled "Polnisch Livland" in Julius Eckardt, *Die baltischen Provinzen Russlands* (Leipzig: Duncker und Humblot, 1869), pp. 83-98.

47. Bukšs, *Latgaļu literatūras vēsture*, pp. 361-78.

48. Edgars Dunsdorfs, "Dažas Latvijas 19.g.s. otrās puses iedzīvotāju skaita attīstības problēmas," *Latvijas vēstures institūta žurnāls*, iii (1939), 241-70.

49. The declining fertility in the Baltic Provinces proper (i.e. Livland, Kurland, Estland) is discussed in Ansley J. Coale, Barbara Anderson, and Erna Härm, *Human Fertility In Russia Since the Nineteenth Century* (Princeton, N.J.: Princeton University Press, 1979), especially pp. 115-17.

50. August Bielenstein, *Die Grenzen der lettischen Volkstamms und die lettische Sprache* (St. Petersburg: Eggers & Co. und J. Glasunof, 1892).

51. It has been estimated that in the period from 1895 to 1902 some 68,000 Lettgallians left the Lettgallian districts for Russia. See Švābe, *LV 1800-1914*, p. 721.

52. Comparative statistics on the Lettgallian districts and the other Latvian-speaking regions can be found in Stalšāns, *Krievu ekspansija un rusifikācija*, pp. 84-95.

53. Švābe, *LV 1800-1914*, pp. 477-78.

54. An illustrative career is that of Trasūns. See Mikelis Bukšs, "Die Rolle Trasūns' bei der Vereinigung Lettlands," in Ziedonis et al. (eds.), *Baltic History*, pp. 175-88.

55. Bukšs, *Latgaļu literatūras vēsture*, pp. 346-57.

56. A. Vičš, "Latviešu skolotāju sapulces," pp. 311-14.

57. George Longworth, *The Latvian Congress of Rural Delegates in 1905* (New York: Northeast European Archives, 1959).

58. Švābe, *LV 1800-1914*, pp. 624-25.

59. Ibid., pp. 628-29.

60. Ibid., pp. 632-33.

61. For a representative interpretation from the Marxist-Leninist viewpoint, see Jānis Krastiņš, *1905. gada revolūcija Latvijā 1905-1907* (Riga: Zinātnu Akadēmija, 1948), a general treatment; and for the Lettgallian districts, Jānis Babris, *1905-1907.g. revolūcija Latgalē* (Riga: Vēstures Institūts, 1960). For a retrospective social-democratic interpretation see Cielēns, *Laikmeta maiņā*, I, 142-275. Švābe's interpretation, *LV 1800-1914*, pp. 637-56, concludes that "it is difficult to clearly establish the consequences these unique events had in the psychology of different social groups" (p. 655).

Chapter 16. 1905-1914: A Postlude

1. *Enciklopēdija*, III, 1997-2009.

2. *Enciklopēdija*, I, 736-37.

3. Švābe, *LV 1800-1914*, p. 706.

4. Mārģeris Skujenieks, *Nacionālais jautājums Latvijā*, pp. 96-97.

5. Švābe, *LV 1800-1914*, pp. 468-69.

6. Skujenieks, "Iecelošana un izcelošana Latvijā," p. 1159. See also *Lavijas PSR Mazā Enciklopēdija*, p. 243.

7. [F. Mīlenbachs], *Latvieši un latvietes Krievijas augstskolās*. This work contains 2,078 short biographies and awaits detailed analysis. The compiler suggests, in a short analytical essay, that of the 1,171 degree-holding Latvians still alive in 1908 wholly 48.1 percent had had to find employment outside the Baltic Provinces.

8. The marriage statistics are from B. von Schrenck, *Rigas natürliche Bevölkerungsbewegung in den Jahren 1881-1911* (Riga: Müllersche Drückerei, 1913), pp. 456-57. See also M. Skujenieks, "Pārgrozības Rīgas iedzīvotāju nazionālā sastāvā," *Domas*, 1915, pp. 286-96.

9. A good summary of the literary trends after 1905 is contained in J. Sarma, "Rakstnieku deklarācija," in E. Dunsdorfs (ed.), *Archivs*, I (1960), 121-48. The title refers to a manifesto signed in 1906 by a group of Latvian writers who declared that artists cannot be understood to have an obligation of serving society.

10. Plakans, "National Awakening in Latvia," pp. 321-33.

11. Švābe, *LV 1800-1914*, pp. 683-84.

12. L. Balēvica, *Lauksaimniecība Vidzemē un Kurzemē pirmā pasaules kara priekšvakarā* (Riga: "Zinātne," 1970), pp. 17-104, contains a detailed analysis of landholding patterns in the Latvian areas of the Baltic prior to World War I.

13. Cited in Švābe, *LV 1800-1914*, pp. 732-33.

PART FOUR

THE ESTONIANS

TOIVO U. RAUN

CHAPTER 17

THE IMPACT OF MODERNIZATION

Tʜᴇ ʜɪsᴛᴏʀɪᴄᴀʟ ᴅᴇᴠᴇʟᴏᴩᴍᴇɴᴛ of the Estonians since late medieval times shows striking parallels with that of other small peoples of eastern Europe,[1] most notably the Latvians and Slovenes, and to a lesser degree, the Slovaks and Czechs.[2] For centuries, these national groups formed the lower orders of *Ständestaaten* dominated by non-native elites; after the French Revolution and the spread of romantic nationalism in Europe, they all experienced similar national awakenings. For the Estonians, the six decades from the mid-1850s to the First World War were a decisive period in their history. From an amorphous peasant society there developed a conscious Estonian nationality with growing economic power, increasing social differentiation, and definite goals for a modern native culture and a participatory political role in the Russian state. By 1905, the Estonian intelligentsia was pursuing the twin aims of cultural and political autonomy. Although not encouraged by the tsarist regime, a modern Estonian culture was emerging by 1914 while the fulfillment of Estonian political autonomy came only with the Russian Revolution. It is within the context of these far-reaching changes—modernization and the development of Estonian nationalism—that the impact of Russification must be viewed. The policy of uniting the borderlands more closely with the interior regions of the empire had significant political and cultural effects in the Baltic Provinces, but the continual economic expansion, which brought about extensive social change throughout this period, remained unaffected by Russification. Furthermore, it will be seen that the historical emergence of an explicitly Estonian nationality had already proceeded too far for cultural Russification to have a lasting impact. Although in some aspects Russification may have been synonymous with modernization (e.g. the administrative realm), its cultural thrust could only seem retrograde to an increasingly self-confident Estonian intelligentsia with a distinctively *Estonian* vision of the future.

In assessing the Estonian response to Russification in the sixty years before 1914, it is thus important to bear in mind the transformation of Estonian society fostered by the process of modernization.[3] Historically, the demographic development of the Estonian areas had been subject to several major shocks, the most powerful of which was certainly the Great Northern War (accompanied by famine and plague). From a nadir of perhaps 80,000-100,000 in 1712, the population grew rapidly to some 485,000 in 1782; in the next eighty years the rate of increase slackened, but by 1858 the number of inhabitants of Estland and northern Livland probably reached 750,000. In the period under consideration here demographic growth continued to be modest, but a significant Estonian emigration, beginning in the 1860s (discussed below), must be taken into account.[4] In 1897, the population of the Estonian areas (including Narva)[5] was 986,000; the Estonians comprised more than 90 percent of the total, with German and Russians forming minorities of 3.6 and 5.1 percent, respectively.[6]

In the rural areas of the northern half of the Baltic Provinces the most striking socioeconomic phenomenon was the emergence of peasant landownership. While the emancipation of the Baltic serfs had taken place in 1816-1819, the Estonian peasantry was still landless and subject to the overlordship of Baltic German estate owners as late as the beginning of the reign of Alexander II in 1855. Not until the 1860s, following reforms forced through by the St. Petersburg government, did a stratum of Estonian landowners begin to appear. The sale of land to the peasantry (the so-called *Bauernland*) proceeded much more rapidly in northern Livland than in Estland; in the former, about half the peasant land was sold by 1882 and 86.4 percent by 1898, with the process nearing completion on the northern Livland mainland (i.e. with the exception of the island of Ösel [Saaremaa]) in the first decade of the twentieth century. In contrast, only 11.6 percent of the peasant land in Estland was sold by 1881; thereafter the pace rapidly quickened, with 50.4 percent sold by 1897 and about 83 percent by the end of 1914.[7] Thus, the wealth of the peasantry in Estland lagged significantly behind that in northern Livland, and this crucial difference was reflected in the geographical base of the Estonian national movement, especially in the 1860s and 1870s.

The newly landed Estonian farmers of northern Livland established agricultural societies in Dorpat (Tartu), Pernau (Pärnu), and Fellin (Viljandi) in 1870-1871 in order to promote technological advancement and the general welfare of their profession; in Estland, the first such institution appeared only in 1888 in Reval (Tallinn). The most intensive period of growth of these organizations began in the latter half of the 1890s, and by 1910, seventy-nine Estonian agricultural societies had been founded. In the decade after 1905, the rapid expansion of agricultural cooperatives strengthened the economic position of Estonian farmers; by 1914, for example, in the Estonian countryside there existed 135 milk cooperatives, 138 consumer cooperatives, and 153 machinery cooperatives.[8] It was the independent Estonian farmers (both landowners and renters) along with rural intellectuals (mainly schoolteachers) who formed the social basis of the national awakening of the 1860s and 1870s; and it was largely their offspring, often urbanized in the following generations, who were able to acquire secondary and higher education in increasing numbers and form the leadership of an expanding Estonian intelligentsia.

Nevertheless, landowners and renters continued to be a minority among the Estonian agricultural population throughout this period. On the eve of World War I, the large estates in Estland and northern Livland still accounted for 58 percent of the total rural land area, much of it in forests, with an average size of 2,113 hectares. However, since a significant portion of the estate land was rented out to the peasantry, the actual disposition of rural land, as the following figures suggest, was somewhat different:[9]

	% of land at the disposal of estates	% of land at the disposal of peasant landowners and renters
Total rural land	44.6	55.4
Agricultural land	25.2	74.8
Forest and non-agricultural land	80.4	19.6

It is striking that while Estonian farmers had the use of nearly three-fourths of the agricultural land in Estland and northern Livland, there were less than 75,000 farmsteads for a rural population approaching 900,000.[10]

As a result of the limited availability of land, two-thirds to three-fourths of the Estonian rural population remained landless laborers on estates or farms until the end of the tsarist regime. After restrictions on freedom of movement were eased with the passport law of 1863, large numbers of landless Estonian peasants emigrated from the Baltic Provinces to the interior regions of the Russian Empire in search of a better livelihood. While economic motivations predominated in the Estonian emigration in the half-century before World War I, the political repression following the Revolution of 1905 contributed to the largest single period of outward migration

(1907-1910). On the eve of the Russian Revolution, there were close to 200,000 Estonians, over half of whom had settled in St. Petersburg province, living in the empire outside the Baltic Provinces. Among these emigrants, unplanned Russification was a common phenomenon; the tendencies toward assimilation were strongest in the central Russian areas, but noticeably weaker in Siberia, the Crimea, and the Caucasus.[11] For much of the Estonian educated elite, many of whose members also faced the problem of unemployment in the Baltic, the apparent loss of some one-sixth of their co-nationals was a matter of serious concern.[12]

Throughout the northern half of the Baltic Provinces communications were revolutionized in the last three decades of the nineteenth century by the railroad. In 1870, the Reval-Narva-St. Petersburg line was opened, while Dorpat was linked to this route in 1876 and to Riga and Pskov in 1889. By the early twentieth century a basic railway network, including the smaller cities, had been completed. In the urban areas of Estland and northern Livland (and Narva) industrialization was effecting economic modernization and social change. The rate of industrial growth was most rapid in the period 1695-1914, when the number of industrial workers more than tripled (from 14,200 to 46,000) and the value of production quintupled (from 24 million to 120 million rubles). In 1914, Reval and Narva were the two noteworthy industrial centers with 40 percent and 32 percent, respectively, of the total number of factory workers.[13] This new working class was drawn mainly from the landless Estonian peasantry in the countryside. As a result of this expansion, Estland and Livland were among the most economically advanced areas of the Russian Empire. In 1908, Estland ranked fourth and Livland fifth in per capita industrial production as well as in the number of industrial workers per 100 inhabitants among the fifty provinces of European Russia.[14]

Urbanization, the social concomitant of industrialization and commercial expansion, increased markedly in this period. From 1862-1863 to 1913, the urban population of Estland and northern Livland (including Narva) nearly quadrupled, from 64,000 to 253,000, the urban proportion rising from 9 percent to 22 percent. In 1913, Reval (116,000) was more than twice the size of Dorpat (45,000) and more than five times that of Pernau (22,000) and Narva (21,000). Urbanization also signified Estonianization since the local countryside provided the major base for urban immigrants at all socioeconomic levels. If the Estonians had comprised about half of the urban population in 1867-1874, by the census of 1897 their share had grown to 68 percent. In 1913, the populations of Reval and Dorpat were 72 percent and 73 percent Estonian, respectively.[15] This growth in numbers was accompanied by the formation of an increasingly stronger Estonian bourgeoisie. In the years 1871-1912 in Reval, the Estonian portion of the total number of property owners rose from 18.3 percent to 68.8 percent. In terms of wealth, Estonians in Reval had owned only 4.5 percent of the real estate in 1871, but by 1904-1908, they constituted nearly 75 percent of the property owners under the value of 5,000 rubles and about one-third of those above this level.[16] Although such figures are not available for other Estonian cities, a similar process in all probability transpired there as well. By the last two decades before World War I, the locus of Estonian public life had shifted to the cities, and it was now this growing bourgeoisie (property owners, merchants, minor officials, artisans, and above all, a professional middle class of lawyers, teachers, journalists, and physicians) who set the tone in Estonian affairs.

In the following discussion of the Estonian response to Russification, expressions of public opinion for which records are available, for example, mass petitions in the 1860s or congresses held in the revolutionary year of 1905, will be noted. However, at best, such evidence is limited. As is to be expected, the most articulate source on this subject is the intelligentsia, here defined as a social grouping distinguished not only by education, but also a conscious desire for Estonian national development. This is not to suggest, of course, that all educated persons of Estonian background were committed to an Estonian nationalist world view. Some continued to assimilate willingly to German or Russian culture while others adopted a cosmopolitan outlook or remained lukewarm to the idea of Estonian nationalism. Although no statistical evidence is available on such persons, it is probable that their numbers declined steadily in the decades before 1914 as the bases of a specifically Estonian culture became firmer; in any case, such individuals have left few discoverable records of their reactions to Russification. It is to be remembered that in the absence of significant political power and higher social classes among the Estonians, the intelligentsia in its role as the educated elite of an emerging nationality not only spoke for itself but to a significant degree also shaped Estonian public opinion.

CHAPTER 18

ESTONIAN ATTITUDES TOWARD
RUSSIFICATION BEFORE
THE MID-1880s

THE ESTONIAN EXPERIENCE under the Russian Empire before the mid-1850s had created a positive mood among the Estonian peasantry toward the tsar and his government. The myth of the "good tsar"[1] was not limited to the Russian masses; it appears to have had strong roots among the lower orders of the non-Russian peoples as well. Since the 1760s the St. Petersburg government had provided the impetus for gradual change in agrarian conditions in the Baltic area; Alexander I, the tsar-liberator for the Estonian peasantry, was held in especially great esteem. Under Nicholas I the seeming fruits of emancipation degenerated into "corvée slavery," leading to widespread unrest and outbreaks of peasant violence in the 1840s. However, the problems were not blamed on the tsar or the Russian government. Instead, the Estonian peasantry consciously turned for the first time to Russian institutions as a solution. In the course of the mid-1840s, about 65,000 Estonians in northern Livland (roughly 17 percent of the total Estonian population of the province) converted to Russian Orthodoxy, not out of religious conviction, but rather in the hope of improving their social and economic condition.[2] Although having no basis in fact, seemingly unstoppable rumors circulated among the peasantry that in exchange for accepting Orthodoxy ("the tsar's faith") they would receive generous land allotments free from the nobility's control. Even when the desired benefits failed to materialize, peasant enthusiasm for the tsar was hardly shaken, for the complement of the myth of the good tsar was the myth of the wicked nobility. For the Estonian peasant, the obvious explanation of his problems was the continuing overlordship of the Baltic German landowners.[3]

Before the late 1850s, the Estonian peasantry referred to itself as simply "the people of the country" (*maarahvas*), and this term was used in all publications in the Estonian language, which in turn was called "the language of the country" (*maakeel*). The term *maarahvas* denoted that the Estonians were both natives to the area as well as rural inhabitants belonging to the peasant *Stand*. In the mind of the Estonian peasant, the environment was not so much divided by nationality as by the social distinction between *maarahvas* and *saks*. Although the term *saks* originally meant (and continued to mean) "German," by the nineteenth century in popular usage a *saks* had also become an individual of whatever nationality (including Estonian) who had more than an elementary education, spoke some German, and did not live by manual labor.[4] More accurately, a *saks* was simply a person from a higher social estate than the peasantry.[5] Before the middle of the nineteenth century, the upper and middle strata of Baltic society were almost exclusively German, and any Estonian who reached these heights (i.e. anyone who became a *saks*) was essentially co-opted into the Baltic German value system. Naturally, the degree of Germanization covered an entire spectrum. Among the urban lower middle classes, there were many Estonians who became only partially Germanized (the so-called *kadakasaksad*—Juniper-Germans). Germanized Estonian intellectuals came to share the Baltic German emphasis on a special Baltic position in the Russian Empire as well as a sense of superiority with regard to Russian culture. Even those who were not Germanized, such as the physicians Friedrich Robert Faehlmann (1798-1850) and Friedrich Reinhold Kreutzwald (1803-1882), could not escape the influence of German culture. Their entire formal education was in German, and both married women from German families. Since the Estonian language lacked development, it was very cumbersome for an educated Estonian to express himself fully in his native tongue, and in any case, there were few other educated Estonians with whom to exchange ideas. It is characteristic that only a tiny fraction of the Faehlmann-Kreutzwald correspondence was in Estonian.[6]

The origins of the Estonian national awakening, which first made itself felt (as would be expected) among the educated elite, reach back into the eighteenth century. Although serfdom reigned supreme, secular literature for the peasantry had appeared by the 1730s, and by the end of the century, mainly as a result of the influence of pietism and a growing tradition of home instruction, perhaps as many as two out of three adult peasants in northern Livland were able to read.[7] One may suspect, however, that the level of this literacy was quite low. Furthermore, there was little available in Estonian for the lower orders to read; in the second half of the eighteenth century an average of only 3.2 books and brochures in Estonian was published annually, not to speak of the nonexistence of a periodical press.[8] In this period and well into the nineteenth century, Estonian literature was written by non-Estonians; Baltic German pastors and other literati,

influenced by the Enlightenment and motivated by "Estophile" sentiments, sought to uplift the peasantry with edifying tracts. Only in the
1840s did native Estonian speakers begin to dominate the production
of literature in Estonian.

If the first third of the nineteenth century witnessed a moderate
growth of Estonian printed matter, from the latter half of the 1830s
the rate of increase rose sharply. Between the 1830s and the 1850s, the
average number of books and brochures published per year nearly
tripled (13.6 to 38.7).[9] At the same time the rural educational network underwent substantial expansion; in the period 1835-1860 the
number of Lutheran rural township (Ger. *Gemeinde*, Russ. *volost'*,
Est. *vald*) schools in Estland jumped from 47 to 230 while in northern Livland (excluding Ösel), where a considerable educational base
already existed, the increase was from 393 to 496 schools.[10] The instructional corps for the township schools was drawn from graduates
of a growing number of parish (Ger. *Kirchspiel*, Russ. *prikhod*, Est.
kihelkond) schools and several teacher-training institutions. As suggested above, by the 1860s this body of rural schoolteachers would
form a major social basis of the Estonian national awakening.

While the emancipation of the Baltic serfs brought few immediate
benefits to the Estonian peasantry, by raising the status of the Estonians to at least theoretical equality with other European peoples, it
laid the basis for the emergence of an Estonian intelligentsia. For the
first time, educated persons of Estonian origin could contemplate the
possibility of a choice in their loyalties. The earliest beginnings of
the Estonian intelligentsia can be dated from the 1820s, when students of Estonian background at Dorpat University first began to
recognize their heritage publicly. However, such individuals were few
and far between, and their lasting impact on Estonian cultural life
began only at the end of the 1830s. The two outstanding Estonian
intellectuals of the pre-awakening era were undoubtedly Faehlmann
and Kreutzwald. Both studied medicine at Dorpat and became practicing physicians, Faehlmann in Dorpat itself and Kreutzwald in
Werro (Võru). Faehlmann was the leading founder of the Dorpat-
based *Gelehrte Estnische Gesellschaft* (established in 1838), a scholarly society dedicated to the study of Estonian folklore and the development of didactic literature for the Estonian peasantry, and later
served as its president in the years 1843-1850. At the same time (1842-
1850), Faehlmann held the lectureship in the Estonian language at
Dorpat University. Although physically isolated in a small provincial
town, Kreutzwald maintained a wide-ranging correspondence and became an active contributor to Estonian *belles lettres* from the beginning of the 1840s. His major literary work was the Estonian epic,

Kalevipoeg (first published, 1857-1861), the compilation of which was actually begun by Faehlmann in the 1830s.[11]

Although Faehlmann and Kreutzwald held similar rationalistic world-views with regard to the future of the Estonian people, there was a crucial difference between the two men. On the one hand, Faehlmann concluded that an independent Estonian nationality was an impossibility and that Germanization would be an inevitable process as the cultural level of the people was raised. On the other hand, Kreutzwald, noting the example of the Finns, felt that a distinctive Estonian nationality and culture could be achieved.[12] However, as products of a German cultural milieu, both men offered a highly negative evaluation of an early aspect of Russification: the Orthodox conversion movement among the Estonian peasantry in the 1840s. Following the first signs of peasant unrest in 1841, Faehlmann published a short story in an Estonian calendar which stressed that peasant hopes for benefits from emigration and religious conversion were entirely illusory. On the contrary, he suggested, the peasant plight could only be ameliorated by improvement in socioeconomic conditions at home and the spread of education. A year later, in a verbal confrontation with the Baltic German landowner Georg von Nolcken, Faehlmann, while again deploring the social and economic state of the peasantry, declared that Russification would be a much more difficult experience for the Estonians than Germanization, because the former involved a totally foreign language, customs, and religion.[13] During the conversion movement itself in the mid-1840s, both men condemned the phenomenon in the strongest of terms in their private correspondence. Blaming the Baltic German nobility and pastors for a failure of leadership and the Moravian Brethren for encouraging proselytism, Faehlmann averred that there could be no progress for the Estonians if they were Russified. Kreutzwald went even farther, and asserted that the conversion of the Estonian peasantry to Orthodoxy would set back its intellectual development a few hundred years.[14]

Decisive changes in Estonian life came with the reign of Alexander II. As elsewhere in the Russian Empire, the spirit of the thaw and various reforms fostered growing anticipation of change. The first sign of a new era was the resurrection of the Estonian language press, which had ceased to exist under the stern censorship policies of Nicholas I. As early as the end of 1856, permission was granted for the publication of two Estonian newspapers.[15] Rising expectations were fed by important reforms in rural administration (granting greater independence of the Baltic German landowners to the peasantry), by enhanced economic opportunities in both town and country, and by the apparent successes of a growing national cultural movement—the First All-Estonian Song Festival (1869), the Society of Estonian Literati (founded in 1872), and the Estonian Alexander School movement (beginning in the 1860s). The crucial element in the national awakening (and one which suggests more than metaphorical significance for this term) was the gradual emergence, beginning with the educated elite, of a positive vision of future Estonian development. In assessing Estonian attitudes toward the Russian government and the possibility of Russification during the national awakening (the 1860s to the mid-1880s), it is essential to bear in mind this mood of growing self-confidence, especially among the articulate segments of the population.

In the three decades before the onset of Russification in the mid-1880s, the Estonians remained overwhelmingly rural. In 1881, 90.4 percent of all Estonians in Estland lived in the countryside, while in northern Livland the figure was as high as 93.3 percent.[16] Although it is difficult to ascertain what the rural Estonian masses were thinking in these years, it is clear that the eastern orientation of the peasantry continued and that it took on new forms during the relatively permissive rule of Alexander II. It is highly instructive that the major mass social movement during the national awakening involved a petition campaign to the Russian government. To the astonishment of the central authorities, several delegations of Estonian peasants from the rural townships of northern Livland appeared in St. Petersburg in 1864-1868, humbly requesting aid against the economic, administrative, and cultural power of the Baltic German establishment. The main delegation, carrying a petition with 251 names representing 15,263 male peasants in twenty-four townships, succeeded in seeing Alexander II himself in November 1864.[17] Pledging their undying loyalty to the tsar, the petitioners stressed the highly negative effects of continued Baltic German overlordship while praising the benefits of the Great Reforms in the interior of the empire. It is noteworthy that the document asked for the extension of Russian peasant and judicial reforms to the Baltic, the placing of rural elementary schools under the Ministry of Education, and the introduction of the Russian language as a subject in the schools. Although drawn up by rural intellectuals (most notably, the brothers Adam and Peeter Peterson), the petitions appear to have been representative of the desires of the peasantry as a whole.[18]

Before Russification, the other major indication of the aspirations of the Estonian peasantry was the response to Senator Nikolai A. Manasein's inspection of conditions in Livland and Kurland in 1882-1883. Manasein collected material from every rural township in great detail, receiving a massive outpouring (over 20,000 items from Livland and Kurland together) of complaints and reform requests despite Baltic German efforts to prevent his communication with the peasantry.[19] As in the 1860s, the recurrent viewpoint was that the central government could and would right all existing wrongs. One of the more important collective memoranda from northern Livland asked for, along with agrarian and other reforms, the following changes in Baltic life: the introduction of Russian judicial and zemstvo institutions, the substitution (for German) of Estonian and Russian as co-equal administrative languages in the Estonian areas, and the abolition of Baltic German control over Estonian education with the replacement of German by Russian as the major foreign language in the Estonian schools.[20]

Thus, during the reign of Alexander II and the early years of Alexander III, the Estonian peasantry actively sought administrative Russification as a means to end Baltic German hegemony in local institutions. At the same time, it favored limited cultural Russification for both practical and tactical reasons. A knowledge of Russian would offer greater economic opportunities to Estonians, while the replacement of German by Russian as the major administrative language of the Baltic would obviate the study of two foreign languages. Furthermore, the Estonian petitioners during the national awakening were not unaware that a request for some cultural Russification would probably gain them a more sympathetic hearing in St. Petersburg.

The Estonian intelligentsia that emerged during the national awakening of the 1860s and 1870s differed fundamentally from earlier intellectuals in two important ways. For the first time this intelligentsia was sufficiently numerous to constitute at least a small social grouping, and furthermore, it was no longer necessarily tied to a Baltic German cultural *Weltanschauung*. The keynote of its attitude in this period was a romantic optimism about the prospects for Estonian development, perhaps best expressed by Carl Robert Jakobson (1841-1882) in the first of his "Three Fatherland Speeches" in 1868. Jakobson divided Estonian history into three periods: an era of "light" before the German conquest, a time of "darkness" under German rule, and the "dawn" of a new era following emancipation under Alexander I.[21] If all the fears relating to the survival of a small people (about 812,000 according to the 1881 census)[22] had not been laid to rest, it was nevertheless an accepted act of faith to believe in the future of the Estonian people. At least three different conceptions of this future emerged, but of these, only two were spelled out and acquired a significant following among the intelligentsia.

The first view, basically represented by Johann Voldemar Jannsen

(1819-1890) and Jakob Hurt (1839-1906), can be called the Baltic
Estonian or Germanophile position. Jannsen, a former sexton and
elementary schoolteacher as well as the founder of Estonian journalism on a permanent basis with his *Perno Postimees* (*The Pernau
Courier*) in 1857, was more a pragmatic leader than a theoretician.[23]
In contrast, Hurt, a man of considerable intellectual achievement,
who was graduated from Dorpat University in 1865 with a degree in
theology and who would later take his Ph.D. in philology at Helsinki
University (1886), proved to be the foremost ideologist of the national
awakening. As head of both the Society of Estonian Literati and
the Estonian Alexander School movement executive committee in the
1870s, he was the dominant figure in Estonian public life in this
decade.[24]

Stressing both the uniqueness of Baltic experience and the common
bonds of the peoples who shared it, Hurt felt that the basis for Estonian culture should be Baltic German culture. To his mind, ". . . the
Estonians are Western with regard to character, religion, and culture,
to the extent that they have any of the latter."[25] This did not mean
that the Estonians should be Germanized, but rather that German
achievements should serve as a model. Having drunk deeply of German romanticism and Herderian ideas, Hurt regarded every nationality as a unique organism with divinely inspired traits such as language, spirit, character, and customs. In spite of its small size, the
Estonian nation, like all nations, had a particular mission in the world.
For the Estonians, Hurt saw this mission as achieving "a different
greatness" in the spiritual and cultural realm, an arena of accomplishment which he regarded as more significant than the potential
political and military successes of larger nationalities.[26]

The advocates of this view essentially accepted Baltic German
institutions and the notion of working within the existing system by
means of a conciliatory relationship between Estonians and Germans.
For Hurt, the most important local institution was the Lutheran
Church.[27] As noted above, he received his university training in theology and later became a practicing pastor in 1872. In the course of the
1870s, he was forced to choose between loyalty to the increasingly
radical national movement and the Baltic Lutheran Church; not surprisingly, he chose the latter. For all his sincere arguments with regard to Estonian culture and the necessity for its development, Hurt
remained very much at home in the Baltic German milieu he found
at Dorpat. He had joined a Baltic German student corporation and
married a Baltic German. More importantly, there was in Hurt himself and in his ideology a strong sense of gradualism and tendency
toward compromise.[28] Since Hurt emphasized a cultural and an apo-

litical program for Estonian development, his premises led, in effect, to a resigned acceptance of Baltic German political leadership.

The other major view, the chief proponents of which were C. R. Jakobson and Johann Köler (1826-1899), can be termed the Russo-phile position. Köler, who rose from a humble family in northern Livland to become a professor at the St. Petersburg Academy of Fine Arts in 1867, spent the great majority of his adult life in the capital. While thus physically removed from Baltic life, Köler nevertheless corresponded widely with other Estonian intellectuals and served as a crucial link to the tsarist government for the Estonian national movement (e.g. the 1860s petition movement and the 1881 memo-randum to the tsar—discussed below).[29] Along with Hurt, Jakobson was the most remarkable Estonian figure in the 1860s and 1870s. At various times in his meteoric career he was a schoolteacher, tutor to the daughter of Alexander II's brother Grand Duke Konstantin, writer, farmer, journalist, and above all, political and social activist. After attending the teacher-training seminary in Walk (Valga), Jakobson spent the better part of his ideologically formative years in St. Peters-burg (1864-1871). Here he met Köler and other Estonian intellectuals as well as Krišjānis Valdemārs, the Latvian activist, and was exposed to a non-Baltic perspective on the problems of Estonian life.[30]

Beginning with a premise directly opposed to Hurt's Germanophile views, Jakobson declared that historical contact with the Baltic Ger-mans had been an unmitigated disaster for the Estonians. Further-more, he argued that all positive developments among the Estonians in the nineteenth century stemmed from the actions of the Russian government, beginning with emancipation in 1816-1819 and con-tinuing into the 1860s with the reform of rural township administra-tion, abolition of most of the patriarchal rights of the German land-owners, and restrictions on corporal punishment.[31] In contrast to Hurt, Jakobson condemned nearly all Baltic German institutions and espe-cially the Lutheran Church, which he felt had been used to keep the Estonians in ignorance and confine them to the lower echelons of so-ciety. Indeed, the major reason for the public break between Hurt and Jakobson in 1878 was the failure to resolve their differences over Jakobson's anticlericalism.[32]

While Hurt emphasized Estonian cultural development, Jakobson contended that this aim could not be fulfilled without first achieving political power for the Estonians. He was the first Estonian intellectual to challenge publicly the political power of the Baltic Germans, call-ing first for equal representation for the peasantry and urban citizens in Baltic Diets (*Landtage*) and later for the establishment of zemstvo institutions. As a theoretical justification for this position, Jakobson invoked Rousseau's concept of the social contract, arguing that the Baltic Germans had broken the contract by their historical subjugation of the Estonian people.[33] In Jakobson's view, the only way to break the deathlike grip of Baltic German control over the Estonians was through the aid of the Russian government with the tsar acting as a kind of patriarchal deliverer. It is important to note that for all his seeming radicalism in Baltic questions, Jakobson was absolutely loyal to the tsar and viewed with horror the activities of such Russian revolutionary groups as the People's Will.

Although the main division in the Estonian intelligentsia was between a moderate Germanophile group and more radical Russophile one, not all intellectuals fell into these two categories nor were the divisions all that clear-cut. Still a third position involved a rejection of the two major views. Two outstanding literary figures, F. R. Kreutzwald and Lydia Koidula (1843-1886, Jannsen's daughter and the one noteworthy woman intellectual of this period), regarded both the German and Russian orientations as fraught with pitfalls and offering only illusory benefits. The now elderly Kreutzwald agreed with the Russophiles that the continued German stranglehold on Baltic education made the establishment of a serious Estonian culture questionable. On the other hand, he considered the Russian orientation dangerous, and compared it to selling a herd of sheep into the hands of a merciless butcher.[34] Both Kreutzwald and Koidula suggested turning to Finland as a model and ally for Estonian development. The potentially subversive nature of this would, Koidula hoped, go unnoticed in a continuing confrontation between the Baltic Germans and the Russians.[35] This reasoned skepticism about both Baltic German and Russian support for Estonian development did not gain a significant following among the intelligentsia. Kreutzwald and Koidula remained a kind of odd couple, and neither was able to or tried to propagate his or her ideas. Although acknowledged as the greatest living Estonian writer, the aged Kreutzwald was no longer capable of active leadership. For all her talents, Koidula, as a woman, was relegated to a secondary position by the values of her society.

In assessing the attitude of the Estonian intelligentsia toward the impending Russification, it will be useful to establish a distinction between administrative (administrative and political institutions) and cultural (linguistic, educational, and religious) Russification. Central government activity in both areas was no secret to Estonian intellectuals; administrative reform began, however haltingly, in the 1860s during which time the example of Russified schools in the Polish provinces was certainly known. To all Estonian intellectuals, with the exception of the moderate Hurt faction, administrative Russification was seen as a useful tool for attacking outmoded Baltic German privileges and attaining political and civil rights.[36]

The clearest expression by the Estonian intelligentsia of its ideas on political and administrative reform in this period came in a memorandum from representatives of seventeen Estonian societies to Alexander III on June 19, 1881. Although it is not clear where the idea of sending a delegation to the tsar originated,[37] in the end the cream of the Estonian intelligentsia was among the delegates, including Hurt, Jakobson, Köler, and the only two Estonian Ph.D.s of the time—Mihkel Veske and Karl August Hermann.[38] Specifically, the memorandum asked for the following Russificatory reforms in administration: extension of zemstvo institutions to the Estonian areas, the confirmation of justices of the peace by the minister of justice in St. Petersburg (in order to avoid domination of local elections by the Baltic Germans), and the introduction of judicial and police reforms according to the Russian standard, with all officials being named by the central government.[39] Fully three of the nine points in the memorandum were directly concerned with administrative Russification. Clearly, the sentiments expressed here were those of the Jakobson faction, and all but one or two of the nineteen delegates signed the memorandum. Indeed, the only representative who did not sign for ideological reasons was Hurt. However, it is not at all clear whether he objected to the administrative Russification called for in the document or to other clauses.[40] If newspaper subscription figures can be used as a guide, the memorandum probably represented the views of the great majority of Estonian intellectuals (and public opinion in general) at this time. In the years 1878-1881 the number of subscribers to Jakobson's *Sakala* rose from 2,300 to about 4,500, while at the same time the figures for *Eesti Postimees* (*The Estonian Courier*—the organ of the Hurt-Jannsen faction) showed a decline from about 4,600 to 1,500.[41]

With regard to cultural Russification, there was universal agreement within the Estonian intelligentsia. The developing national language had first priority, and cultural Germanization and Russification were both anathema. The Germanophile and Russophile factions agreed that as much education as possible should be in Estonian (even up to the university level in certain subjects) and that Estonian should have at least equal rights as an administrative language.[42] Hurt offered the most systematic arguments against purposeful denationalization of the Estonians. Above all, he felt it was morally and historically wrong. An Estonian's innate character and moral fiber would be destroyed if he were alienated from his mother tongue. In addition, Hurt contended that the Estonians could achieve a high cultural level only through "natural" development, that is, by the use of their native tongue. Beyond this, Hurt was convinced by the 1870s that neither Germanization nor Russification of the Estonians was possible. The Estonians, he said, were already too conscious of themselves as a separate nationality to be assimilated. Furthermore, the Russian government would no longer permit Germanization; indeed, Hurt warned the Baltic Germans that any attempts along these lines would encourage the "Eastern neighbors" to implement an analogous policy of their own.[43] However, Russification was even less thinkable because the basis for it simply did not exist. Hurt felt that the geographical location, educational system, and national Church of the Estonians formed an unbreachable barrier to cultural Russification. He also counted on the goodwill and rationality of the Russian government. In fact, he rather naively believed that the central government would withdraw any reforms not acceptable to the Baltic peoples.[44]

In contrast to Hurt, Jakobson still saw a real danger in Germanization and felt that the stranglehold of German culture and educational institutions on Estonian life could be lethal to the development of any native language culture.[45] At the same time, in line with his Russophile tendencies, Jakobson was convinced that there was no danger of cultural Russification for the Estonians. When Koidula expressed fears about denationalization, Jakobson evoked the example of the Finns in Ingria, who had retained their native language and culture for centuries despite living in the midst of a Russian environment. While he was fully aware of the writings of such Moscow polemicists as Katkov and Leont'ev, Jakobson retained a boundless faith in the benevolence of the tsar and his government with regard to their intentions in the Baltic Provinces.[46] In the 1860s, Jakobson had even sent material to Katkov's *Moskovskie vedomosti* in order to expose Baltic conditions, but the increasingly Russifying position of the newspaper led him to discontinue this practice. In any case, Jakobson firmly believed that the policies of the St. Petersburg government would be very different from those advocated by Russian nationalist circles.[47]

Once again, Kreutzwald and Koidula were among the few to sound the alarm regarding cultural Russification. With his long experience and with no pretensions to political leadership, Kreutzwald was able to view the situation with fewer illusions than his younger colleagues. While Hurt and Jakobson tended to dismiss the nationalistic Moscow journalists as insignificant, Kreutzwald pointed out that the ideas of Katkov and others were already being implemented in the Polish schools where instruction was in Russian. With prophetic accuracy, he declared that the Estonian Alexander School would be no more than a means by which "our [Estonian] grain would be ground into Russian flour."[48] However, Kreutzwald's skepticism was disregarded in the prevailing optimism of the national awakening. Certainly the high point of Russophile sentiments among the Estonian intelligentsia (and probably among the general population as well) was reached in the early 1880s with the delegation to Alexander III in 1881 and the hopes engendered by Senator Manasein's inspection in the following two years.

In order to keep the three decades before Russification in proper perspective, it should be stressed that the Russian language and culture were still terra incognita for the Estonian intelligentsia. Estonian social and cultural life were only beginning to emerge from patriarchal Baltic German tutelage. For example, the song festivals in these years (traditionally viewed as great national manifestations) were presided over by Baltic German notables. The *Estonia* cultural society in Reval, founded in 1865, was directed in its early years by Baltic Germans, largely because Estonians lacked the self-confidence to assume the responsibility of leadership.[49] Public opinion was dominated by Jannsen's *Eesti Postimees* (established in Dorpat in 1864), the only Estonian newspaper with a national following before 1878. As suggested above, Jannsen's policy called for progress through gradualism and without confrontation with the Baltic German establishment.[50] The strength of German control over Baltic life was reflected in the virtually continual difficulties Jakobson encountered with the authorities during his brief career as a newspaper editor (1878-1882).[51] On the whole, Estonian intellectuals in this period (and really until around 1900) tended to communicate with each other, both in speaking and writing, in German. This included not only those who were partially or completely Germanized, but also the leading-lights discussed here. Hurt, Kreutzwald, Koidula et al. could express themselves more fully in the "cultured" language in which they had been educated than in their native tongue. At the same time a knowledge of Russian among the intelligentsia was rare before Russification. Jakobson, for example, for all his Russophile sentiments, did not know Russian well and gave his speech in 1881 to Alexander III in Estonian.[52]

The three decades before 1914 witnessed both the height and the gradual decline of Russification as a policy in the Baltic Provinces. The response of the Estonians to Russification can be conveniently divided into three ten-year periods. The first decade, corresponding to the implementation of Russificatory reforms, was dominated by a loss of confidence and sense of helplessness among both the intelligentsia and the masses.[53] However, one should be cautious in attributing the major causal role to Russification itself. Economic problems and the temporary failure of the national cultural movement probably contributed more to the pervasive mood of pessimism. The second decade witnessed both a spiritual and material recovery and renewed rising expectations, culminating in the bold visions of the Revolution of 1905. The tsarist regime under Nicholas II did not pursue Russification with the same vigor as it had under Alexander III. At the same time, economic conditions generally improved, while a new generation which grew up under the Russified system had fewer psychological adjustments to make than the one that had faced its original implementation.[54] In the final decade, the potential dangers of Russification seemed more and more irrelevant to Estonian life as certain improvements grew out of the Revolution of 1905, and Estonian culture began to flourish as never before.

In assessing the effects of Russification among the Estonians, it will again be useful to maintain the distinction between administrative and cultural Russification. These two aspects of the policy continued to be regarded with differing attitudes, especially within the intelligentsia. It must be remembered that the Estonians were only a developing nation (to use mid-twentieth-century terminology) in the mid-1880s. Indeed, it is not an exaggeration to describe them as a colonial people under the tutelage of a nonnative elite. As such, they did not have the economic or political power or social and cultural development to affect the policies of the tsarist regime. Their role during the implementation of Russification was essentially a passive one. It is clear that the major struggle in Russifying the Baltic Provinces was between the Russian government in St. Petersburg and the local German elite. Nevertheless, despite their lack of participation in policy-making, the Estonians certainly stood to benefit from a confrontation between the two ruling elements of the Baltic Provinces.

In order to implement Russification large numbers of Russian officials were sent to the Baltic area for the first time. It was hardly to be expected that these *chinovniki* would be familiar with local conditions in a relatively unknown corner of the Russian Empire. If they had some acquaintance with the Baltic Germans, they knew next to nothing about the Estonians. During his first year in the Baltic Provinces, Sergei V. Shakhovskoi, Governor of Estland from 1885 to 1894, stated that there was simply no basis for an independent Estonian nationality; the Estonians, he alleged, did not have a history, an indigenous musical culture, or a native literature.[55] Furthermore, Russian officials and the Estonians lacked the means to communicate with each other. The *chinovniki* did not know Estonian (indeed, they had no desire to know it), and the Estonians were only beginning to learn Russian. The lack of comprehension of Estonian developments was perhaps best exemplified by Shakhovskoi himself, in large part because of his meager sources of information. One of the oddities of Russification in the Baltic area was occasioned by the fact that the Estonian population lived in two separate provinces, ruled by two governors. The striking differences of opinion between Shakhovskoi in Estland and Mikhail A. Zinov'ev in Livland (governor from 1885 to 1895) meant that Russification among the Estonians could not possibly be carried out with any uniformity. In general, Zinov'ev proved to be far less adamant in pursuing Russificatory policies than Shakhovskoi.[56]

CHAPTER 19

ADMINISTRATIVE RUSSIFICATION

IT IS STRIKING that administrative Russification touched the lives of the Estonians at all levels of government except the provincial one, that is, the Baltic Diets, which remained the nearly exclusive purview of the landowning nobility up to the Russian Revolution. Lack of reform in this area clearly indicated that Russification of Baltic administration was not carried out systematically or to its logical conclusion. It will be remembered that the Estonian intelligentsia actively sought zemstvo institutions for the Baltic Provinces in a memorandum to the tsar in 1881 and that this request was seconded by massive petitions from the rural population in Livland during the Manasein inspection. Why zemstvos were never established in the Baltic area under the tsarist regime needs to be explained principally at the central government level. Manasein himself accepted Estonian and Latvian suggestions that there should be not only Baltic zemstvos, but also administrative unification into two (instead of three) provinces. Had the tsarist government wanted to make an all-out attack on the hegemony of the Baltic German nobility, this would undoubtedly have been an effective step.[1] However, despite the fact that the matter of Baltic zemstvos was raised several times from the 1870s to 1914, the Baltic Germans always managed to find enough support among the upper echelons of the St. Petersburg government to block implementation. Indeed, Alexander III himself decided not to force the issue during his reign.[2] Clearly, the Russian government under the last two tsars was not interested in encouraging participatory politics in the Baltic Provinces or anywhere else; the *Landtage* remained to the end of the tsarist regime.

The most important Russified political institution in the Baltic Provinces was the municipal government, the one fundamental Russificatory reform (1877) carried out under Alexander II. For the Estonian bourgeoisie, which was enfranchised by the reform, it was obviously a highly welcome change and one which it could not have effected with its own still meager power. In place of the previous medieval, estate-based regulations, which had totally excluded the Estonians from participation in municipal government, the 1877 law enfranchised men 25 years of age and over of any nationality who paid a certain level of city taxes, dividing them into curiae according to the amount of taxes paid. In fact, the suffrage was limited to about 5 percent of the total urban population, and virtually all Estonians, that is, the smaller taxpayers, were concentrated in the III or the largest voting curia.

The first municipal election in 1877 witnessed a large turnout in northern Baltic cities in all three voting curiae; however, in the 1880s, the percentage voting declined overall and most dramatically in the III curia. In Reval, for example, in 1877, 70.4 percent had voted in the III curia while by 1889 the figure was only 28.4 percent. The Estonian urban voter had clearly become apathetic, probably because the political power of the Baltic German ruling class had proven too strong to break. At the same time, the Estonian bourgeoisie appeared to lose confidence in itself due to economic reversals, the stagnation of the national movement, and some aspects of the Russificatory reforms.[3] Nevertheless, an Estonian opposition did appear in some of the cities in Estland and northern Livland in the course of the 1880s, the strongest in Reval, where there existed a combined Estonian-Russian block. It is noteworthy that the Reval opposition (in which the Estonians were a majority) continually supported the Russificatory reforms throughout the 1880s.[4]

The new 1892 municipal suffrage regulations were put into effect in the Baltic Provinces at the same time as in the interior regions of the Russian Empire, and the franchise base was changed from taxes to property value. While the value varied according to the size of the city, the level was generally high enough to disenfranchise over half of the previous voters, not only in the Baltic Provinces, but elsewhere in the empire as well. For this reason, historians have generally included the 1892 municipal laws under the rubric of the counterreforms of Alexander III. However, for the Estonian bourgeoisie, the new regulations were a step forward since they eliminated the division into three separate curiae and placed all voters on an equal footing. As the Estonian middle class acquired more property, there would be an increased possibility of challenging Baltic German control of urban government. Nevertheless, in the 1890s, the Estonian voter remained passive, and, if anything, voter participation declined even more. In the Reval City Council, the Estonian-Russian bloc engaged in no oppositional activity whatsoever in the second half of the 1890s.[5] With the turn of the century, however, as their urbanized numbers and wealth grew, Estonians gradually began to outnumber Germans on the lists of eligible voters. At the same time, voter participation increased rapidly, especially during and after the Revolu-

Toivo U. Raun

tion of 1905. By 1914, the Estonian bourgeoisie had won control of six out of ten major cities in Estland and northern Livland: Walk (in alliance with Latvians, 1901), Reval (1904), Werro (1906), Hapsal (Haapsalu, 1909), Pernau (1913), and Wesenberg (Rakvere, 1914).[6] Without question, the Russification of municipal government was a major factor leading to Estonian control of a majority of the cities in the northern half of the Baltic Provinces by beginning of World War I.

In 1888-1889, the two Baltic administrative institutions which most directly affected the lives of the Estonians, the police and the judiciary, were Russified with minor deviations from the Russian model. The police reform essentially emancipated the Estonians from Baltic German overlordship in this area. In the countryside the German landowners lost all police power over the peasant townships (although they retained such power on their estates). On the district level and in the cities, the police system was completely reorganized and placed directly under the governor and the Ministry of the Interior. The crucial change here was that the higher police officials were appointed by the central government, not by the local Baltic German authorities.[7] If the police apparatus was still controlled by non-Estonians, the Russian officials were nevertheless regarded by the Estonian population as more impartial than the previous Baltic German ones. In 1887, for example, *Virulane*, an Estonian newspaper in Reval, credited Governor Shakhovskoi with ending the practice of corporal punishment in the pre-Russification police system. Russification also meant a more rational bureaucratic structure for the Baltic police network as well as a significant increase in the number of police officials.[8]

Russification of the judicial system and procedure (Baltic law was left untouched) also meant modernization, although there continued to be a division between the rural peasantry and the rest of Baltic society. For less serious matters, the peasantry had its own courts—the township court (*volostnoi sud*)[9] with appeals to the higher court for the peasantry (*verkhnii krest'ianskii sud*). Where the issues were more serious, both for the urban population and the rural peasantry, the Russian institutions of the 1864 reform were introduced: the justice of the peace (*mirovoi sud'ia*) with appeals to the conference of justices of the peace (*s"ezd mirovykh sudei*); the circuit court (*okruzhnyi sud*) with appeals to the court chamber (*sudebnaia palata*).[10] In contrast to the 1864 Russian regulations, in the Baltic Provinces justices of the peace were appointed by the central government (rather than elected) and trial by jury was not introduced. The reform undoubtedly signified at least some improvement from the

308

point of view of the Estonian population. As with the police reform, the new judicial system meant the importation of relatively impartial Russian officials and emancipation from Baltic German control. The judicial process became public, and the whole procedure was rationalized (e.g. the number of judicial levels was significantly reduced) and made more uniform.[11] In the peasant courts, Estonian remained as the basic language of administration.[12]

On the other hand, the judicial reform also involved certain negative aspects for the Estonians. The major problem was that the proceedings in the higher courts were conducted exclusively in Russian. The great majority of the judges and court officials were non-Baltic Russians. Even if the officials knew Estonian, the procedural regulations specifically stipulated that all spoken and written communication with the courts should be in Russian (in the pre-Russification courts Estonian had been permitted). The effect of this was to force Estonians who had business with courts to communicate through an interpreter.[13] Unfortunately, the quality of these translators was not high because a person bilingual in Estonian and Russian was still a rarity. However impartial the courts may have been, the problems in communication made the administration of justice very difficult. Because Estonian plaintiffs could not speak for themselves, they were often forced to undertake considerable expense. For example, in a civil suit at a circuit court, a person not knowing Russian was required to hire a lawyer in order to gain a hearing. Even at the justice of the peace level, the court procedure was really too complex for the average peasant to be able to represent himself adequately. Thus, for much of the Estonian peasantry, the higher courts were too expensive and inaccessible.[14]

Simultaneously with the judicial reform in the Baltic Provinces, the office of commissar for peasant affairs (*kommisar po krest'ianskim delam*) was created. Strictly speaking, this was not a Russificatory reform. However, the duties, competence, and jurisdiction of the Baltic commissars for peasant affairs were highly similar to those of the land captain (*zemskii nachal'nik*) in the interior provinces of the Russian Empire, and it is instructive that the two offices were established only three days apart in July 1889. In effect, the commissar for peasant affairs replaced the abolished parish and district courts (*Kirchspielsgericht, Kreisgericht*). His major tasks were to supervise the functioning of peasant government as well as the proper application of Baltic agricultural laws in the countryside, especially with regard to rental and sale contracts. In contrast to the land captain, the commissar did not exercise the role of justice of the peace.[15]

Traditionally, the land captain has been regarded as a reactionary

force who destroyed any semblance of peasant self-government (although George Yaney has recently challenged this view).[16] In the
Baltic case, it would be a misnomer to dismiss the commissars for
peasant affairs as representatives of the class interests of the landed
nobility or as reactionary agents of the central government (like the
land captains, they were appointed from a list drawn up by the
provincial governor). From the creation of the office in 1889, there
was a balance of both non-Baltic and Baltic Russians, Baltic Germans, and even some Estonians. It is striking that during the tenure
of Governor Aleksei V. Bel'gard in Estland (1902-1905) nearly all
eight of the commissars for peasant affairs were Estonians.[17] Among
the *chinovniki*, some acted in an arbitrary manner, but such actions
could be overturned by the governor or other higher officials. Others
gained the sincere respect of the local population.[18] The commissars
could also be viewed as agents of modernization. In the early 1890s,
especially in Estland and on the island of Ösel, they carried out the
consolidation of rural townships, reducing their total number from
over 1,000 to less than 400. Although this meant the loss of jobs for
some, the economic base of the consolidated townships was strengthened and the administrative structure was rationalized.[19]

A major factor that ran through all administrative Russification
(and one which touches on the cultural realm as well) was the gradual introduction of Russian as the language of administration at all
but the lowest levels after 1885. By 1889, municipal government and
higher courts were conducted exclusively in Russian, as was communication among all administrative organs (except among institutions
at the peasant level). It will be recalled that in the early 1880s, the
Estonian intelligentsia and peasantry sought to replace German with
Russian and Estonian as the administrative languages in the northern
half of the Baltic Provinces. Furthermore, it was desired that all officials know both Russian and Estonian.[20] With Russification, educated and established Estonians, especially those who worked as either
rural or urban officials, faced a difficult situation. Very few of them
had any appreciable knowledge of Russian; yet they were expected
almost immediately to correspond and conduct business in Russian.
The effect clearly was one of disorientation. Some Estonian intellectuals who had received their education in German were able to re-
tool themselves; however, it was a long and formidable task, and few
ever learned Russian as well as they had known German. Others simply could not make the psychological adjustment of switching from
German to Russian; they were too rooted in a Baltic *Weltanschauung*
which tended to regard Russian culture as something necessarily inferior.[21]

In order to keep these administrative reforms in perspective, it is necessary to bear in mind that several important Baltic institutions were not Russified. Indeed, what emerged was a kind of motley mixture of old and new. As noted earlier, the *Landtage* remained in complete control of provincial self-government. In Livland, the parish assembly (*Kirchspielskonvent*), a unit of local administration (established in 1870) between the township and district levels, continued untouched by Russification. Although the parish assemblies offered some political participation to the peasantry for the first time above the township level and theoretically called for equal representation for both peasants and large landowners, they were nevertheless under firm Baltic German control because the chairman of these institutions was always an estate owner.[22] In addition, the administration of the Baltic Lutheran Church continued unchanged, and even the Russified educational system retained much of its previous institutional structure.[23] In all these organs, Baltic German landowners and pastors remained in a position of leadership.

It is noteworthy that between the onset of Russification and the Revolution of 1905 there were no programmatic Estonian statements on Baltic administration such as the petitions and memoranda of the 1860s and early 1880s. Superficially, it may have seemed that the tsarist government had satisfied the majority of the requests made during the national awakening. In reality, it appeared to many Estonians that only the letter, and not the spirit, of the reforms had been fulfilled. On balance, the reforms that were adopted were regarded as beneficial, but the potentially most crucial measure, the introduction of zemstvo institutions, was not effected. Even more disturbing was the tsarist government's rejection of equality for Estonian as an administrative language. It is instructive that Russian officials began to refer to Estonian and Latvian as "dialects" rather than languages.[24] The Estonian silence during the first decade and a half of Russification, no doubt, reflected satisfaction with some aspects of the administrative reforms, but it also revealed a consciousness of powerlessness. Psychologically, the Russophile orientation, which had flourished on the eve of the reforms, had now reached a state of bankruptcy, given the important failures to achieve political participation on the provincial level or the use of Estonian in administration.

The mood of resignation began to fade after the turn of the century. Spurred on by ferment throughout the Russian state, the Estonian intelligentsia began to express a bolder vision of its political goals.[25] With the central government thrown off balance and in the heady atmosphere of the Revolution of 1905, the Estonians had complete license to express their views on administrative Russification. While a number of Estonian reform proposals were put forward during the revolutionary year, the most representative statements appeared in the so-called *Bürgermusse* and *Aula* resolutions at the All-Estonian Congress in Dorpat in November 1905, in which some 800 delegates participated. The representatives were selected as follows: four delegates from every city, two each from the working and propertied classes; two delegates from each rural township, one landed and the other landless; one delegate from every Estonian society. Although the franchise clearly fell short of a democratic one, the All-Estonian Congress offered the most broadly based expression of Estonian public opinion in 1905.[26] The *Bürgermusse* and *Aula* documents differed considerably on several political, social, and economic issues, but they entertained remarkably similar views on the administrative changes wrought by Russification.

What was called for in these resolutions was nothing less than a repeal of administrative Russification, to be replaced by Estonian political autonomy, uniting Estland and northern Livland as one self-governing province. There was no longer any thought of introducing zemstvo institutions or subordinating Baltic administrative organs to centralized control in St. Petersburg. An autonomous Estonian self-government, elected by universal suffrage, would have control over such matters as the police, the judicial system, education, health, and the selection of administrative personnel. It is important to note that not only were the Russificatory reforms under attack but also the remaining administrative institutions which afforded the Baltic Germans a privileged position, like the *Landtage* and the parish assemblies. The *Bürgermusse* resolutions specifically called for a new administrative structure to be elected by universal suffrage on three levels: the township, the district, and the entire area of Estland and northern Livland. In spite of previous support, administrative Russification was now under fire because it stood fundamentally against the two major Estonian political demands in 1905—autonomy and democratization.[27]

The experience of 1905 proved to be a turning point for the Estonians; above all, it signified a great escalation of goals. For Estonians of all political persuasions, the centralization implied by administrative Russification was unacceptable, and some form of autonomy remained the ideal. After 1906, the Duma in St. Petersburg provided a political forum for Estonian representatives to unite with other non-Russians in the Union of Autonomists.[28] Although the decade before World War I was dominated by increasing governmental reaction, the fundamental change effected in Estonian political thought by the Revolution of 1905 proved to be an enduring one. The Estonian press continued to advocate modification of the most objectionable aspects of administrative Russification, especially the exclusion of Estonian as the business language in local government and the courts.[29] Nevertheless, Russified political and administrative institutions remained essentially unchanged in the Baltic until the end of the tsarist regime.

CHAPTER 20

RUSSIFICATION IN EDUCATION
AND RELIGION

Cᴜʟᴛᴜʀᴀʟ, as opposed to administrative, Russification posed more serious questions for the Estonians, especially the intelligentsia. Here it was more than simply a question of political and civil rights; the ramifications of cultural Russification raised doubts about the survival of the Estonian nationality. It will be remembered that during most of the national awakening cultural matters dominated over political ones in the mind of the intelligentsia. It seemed to most educated Estonians that before they could compete with the Baltic Germans for political power, they needed a sufficiently strong cultural base in order to wage an effective struggle. Imbued with romantic nationalism, the Estonian intelligentsia set as its major goal the creation of a modern and autonomous Estonian culture. Carried to its logical conclusion, cultural Russification was a head-on assault against that very notion. The following assessment of the effects of Russification on Estonian cultural life in the three decades after the mid-1880s will be divided into two parts. The first section will deal with education and religion, the two areas in which tsarist policies sought to have a specific impact on Estonian culture, while the second will discuss the relationship between Russification and various aspects of the Estonian national movement.

The entire question of educational development was a matter of first priority for the Estonian intelligentsia both before and after the Russifying reforms. It was also recognized by both the Baltic German elite and the St. Petersburg government as the crucial battleground in the struggle for the allegiance of the Estonian people. During the national awakening the rural elementary school system in the Estonian areas witnessed significant expansion in numbers and improvement in quality. From 1860 to 1881, the number of Lutheran rural elementary schools in Estland and northern Livland grew from 923 to 1,291.[1] At the same time, in the 1860s, writing and arithmetic began to be taught to all pupils, and by the end of the decade the principle of compulsory school attendance had been established. In the 1870s, the curriculum was generally made uniform, and new subjects such as geography, history, and the Russian language were added.[2]

It is noteworthy, however, that even before Russification a sizable minority of the rural elementary schools in the Estonian areas (especially northern Livland) were conducted under the auspices of the Orthodox Church. Following the influx of Orthodoxy into Livland in the 1840s, schools linked to the state religion began to be founded. By 1884-1885, 19.5 percent (315 of 1,612) of the rural elementary schools in Estland and northern Livland were associated with the Orthodox Church while the other 80.5 percent (1,297) were Lutheran. Already in 1873 the Orthodox elementary schools were placed under the jurisdiction of the Ministry of Education. Although the language of instruction in these schools was Estonian, the first general curricular directive (in 1860) established Russian as an important subject of study. Some Lutheran parents preferred this emphasis on Russian for their male children who later had to face military service in the empire; in 1885-1886, for example, 23.6 percent of the boys in the Orthodox elementary schools in the Estonian areas were Lutheran.[3] On the whole, however, the educational level of the Orthodox schools was definitely inferior to that of the Lutheran ones.[4]

Before the latter half of the 1880s, the educational system of the Baltic Provinces remained basically under Baltic German control. The administration of the Lutheran rural elementary schools in Estland and northern Livland, attended almost exclusively by the children of the Estonian peasantry, was in the hands of German landlords and pastors although the new Baltic township law of 1866 afforded the peasantry the opportunity to participate in the decision-making process for the first time.[5] Prior to Russification, the language of instruction in both township and parish schools was Estonian, although beginning in the 1860s German was often used as certain Baltic German leaders (such as Carl Schirren and Bishop Ferdinand Walter of Livland) called for the Germanization of the native peoples of the area. However, an opposing school of Baltic German thought argued that the peasantry by virtue of its station should not know German and continued to advocate instruction in Estonian.[6] In the course of the 1870s, the Russian language gradually emerged as a subject in the township and parish schools. In 1875, a new educational statute for Estland specifically called for the teaching of Russian in all Lutheran rural elementary schools within five years. However, in 1880, only 42 percent of the township schools in Estland and 48 percent of those in northern Livland offered Russian as a subject, and it may be presumed that the level of instruction was quite low.[7] In nearly all urban elementary and secondary schools as well as at Dorpat University, German was the exclusive language of instruction, and administration was also controlled by Baltic German notables. However, growing tsarist interest in Baltic education was shown by the establishment in the 1870s and early 1880s of four secondary schools (two each in Reval and Narva) with Russian as the language of instruction.[8]

Russification of the educational system in the Baltic was gradually implemented between the mid-1880s and mid-1890s. On the primary level, the following changes were decreed: (1) In 1885-1886, all Lutheran rural elementary schools, along with their teacher-training institutions, were placed under the jurisdiction of the Ministry of Education; (2) In 1887, as a means of insuring state control of the educational administration, the positions of director (one for each Baltic Province) and inspector (several in each province) were created; (3) In 1887, Russian became the language of instruction (for all subjects except religion and hymn singing) from the third year of rural elementary schools, and by 1892, it was required already in the first year; (4) In the latter 1880s, the urban elementary schools changed over from German to Russian as the language of instruction and adopted the format of similar schools in the Russian areas of the empire.[9] At the secondary level, along with the shift from instruction in German to Russian (1887-1892), the major changes involved the elimination of local differences and the implementation of centralized control. In higher education, Dorpat University lost its previous autonomy and was also placed directly under the Ministry of Education. In 1893, both the name of the city and university was officially changed to Iur'ev. Except for the theology faculty, in which teaching remained in German, the transfer to instruction in Russian occurred in 1889-1895.[10]

There can be no doubt that the loss of elementary education in the native language was regarded as the bitterest blow of Russification by both the Estonian intelligentsia and the masses of the rural population. The educational reform shattered the myth of the benevolence of the tsarist regime and produced a profound pessimism about the Estonian future. At the same time, it should be noted that the shift to instruction in Russian in an area where this language was hardly known was a colossal undertaking and required years to implement. Although Russian obviously gained ground as the 1890s proceeded, there appears to have been a conscious conspiracy by the Estonian population to keep alive instruction in the native tongue. The tradition of education at home now stood the rural population in good stead, and even in the schools many teachers ignored the ban on Estonian as the language of instruction.[11] The enforcement of Russification in the rural Baltic schools was significantly hindered by the relative absence of inspecting officials. In 1891, there were only ten inspectors for all three Baltic Provinces, some of them responsible for as many as 400 schools. While their number increased in the 1890s, there was generally a period of some years between inspections in any given school.[12]

Nevertheless, the use of more and more Russian in the rural elementary schools could not be avoided, and there is much evidence that the quality of instruction suffered greatly from the enforced use of a foreign language as the means of instruction.[13] The Russified curriculum offered no significant improvement over the previous Baltic German one, and the tsarist regime showed little interest in disseminating much secular knowledge to the Estonian peasantry. The confusion involved in the transition to the Russified educational system is suggested by figures on school attendance during the first decade of Russification. In Estland, the number of elementary school pupils declined from 25,646 to 20,565 in the years 1886-1892. Only in the mid-1890s was the pre-Russification attendance level attained. In Livland, the immediate decline was not as marked, and the period 1886-1896 showed an overall increase in elementary school attendance from 75,718 to 86,888. In both provinces, the major causal factors in this temporary decrease were the same. On the one hand, Baltic German landowners and pastors often closed rural elementary schools as a protest against the Russificatory reforms; on the other hand, Russifying tsarist officials dismissed teachers who did not learn Russian with sufficient speed, and new candidates could not always be found immediately.[14]

However, the question remains whether Russification of the elementary schools (which served some 90 percent of the Estonian population) had a disastrous effect on the intellectual development of Estonian youth. While no elaborate statistics are available on this question, literacy figures from the 1881, 1897, and 1922 censuses do provide some useful information. Defining literacy as only the ability to read (in any language), the Estonian population of both Estland and Livland showed a slight improvement between 1881 and 1897 in the already high literacy rate. In 1881, 95.8 percent of the Estonian population 14 years of age and over in Estland was literate while in 1897, the figure for those 10 years of age and older was 96.6 percent. For the Estonians of Livland, the corresponding figures were 94.3 percent (1881) and 95.8 percent (1897).[15] It was to be a full quarter-century before the next general census in the Estonian areas was conducted in the early years of the Estonian republic. Despite the upheavals of war and revolution in the intervening years, in 1922, the literacy rate for those aged 10 and over in Estonia (including non-Estonians and adjusted to the land area of the 1897 census) was 96.9 percent. With regard to both reading and writing ability, a more striking comparison can be made between the 1881 and 1922 censuses. Considering those 14 years of age and over among all nationalities in the Estonian areas, in 1881, 43.1 percent could read and write, while by 1922 (adjusted to the land area of the 1881 census), the rate had jumped to 90.6 percent.[16] If nothing else, these figures indicate that Russification did not halt the advance in the basic educational skills of the Estonian population.

Russification created a difficult situation for Estonian schoolteachers, who held about 70 percent of the positions in the rural elementary schools of Estland in 1881 and probably a comparable share in northern Livland.[17] In order to retain their jobs, they were required to learn Russian through independent and summer study in the space of a few years. For many, especially the older ones, the psychological adjustment from a German to a Russian cultural world proved to be too great to bear. Thus, in the 1890s there was a large turnover in the elementary teaching profession while, at the same time, the preparation of new teachers was greatly hindered by the power struggle between the tsarist regime and the Baltic German elite. Of the six teacher-training seminaries functioning in the Estonian areas in the mid-1880s, only two, those in Dorpat (founded in 1878 with Russian as the language of instruction) and Karmel (Kaarma) on the island of Ösel (which was of only local importance), survived Russification.[18] As a result, the number of rural teachers with professional training declined markedly, with consequently yet another adverse effect on the quality of education.

In the urban elementary and secondary schools, Russification created a widespread turnover in leadership and faculty, including the influx of large numbers of teachers of Russian nationality. Although new, Russified secondary schools were founded in the 1890s, the Baltic Germans closed (either voluntarily or under duress) a significant number of previously existing schools, so that there was an overall decline in this decade. Nevertheless, the number of secondary students grew slightly in the same period, and the Estonian share showed a continual rise, reflecting the increasing socioeconomic power of the Estonian population.[19] At Dorpat University, Russification drastically changed the complexion of the student body in the 1890s. As exact nationality figures on Dorpat students in this period are not available, perhaps we can glean the best information on the changes of the 1890s from statistics on religious background. If the total number of students at the beginning and end of the decade was about the same (roughly 1,800), the number of Lutherans declined from 1,119 to 362 in the years 1890-1900, while the Orthodox share jumped from 104 to 958 in the same period.[20] The Russification of Dorpat University appears to have had little immediate effect on Estonian attendance, which remained relatively stable (at about 70) to around 1900. By the eve of the Revolution of 1905, however, the number of Estonians at Dorpat had risen to some 100-120.[21] At the same time, the transformation of the university into a Russian cultural center opened new intellectual avenues to Estonian students and for the first time brought them into contact with the Russian revolutionary movement.

In spite of its negative effects, the Russification of the educational system also had positive and unforeseen influences on Estonian culture. While the older generations found adjustment to the reforms difficult, the younger ones soon became emancipated from the dominance of Baltic German culture. No longer did German pastors have complete control over Estonian schoolteachers and students. At the same time, teachers of Russian nationality, if usually Russifiers, brought an entirely different, and often radical, world-view to the Baltic.[22] For the tsarist regime, an entirely unforeseen consequence of Russification was the growth, rather than decline, of Estonian nationalism. In effect, the assumption behind linguistic Russification had been that there was no future for the Estonian language, the only choice being Germanization or Russification.[23] However, the tsarist authorities overestimated the power of Russian culture in the Baltic and underestimated the unfavorable reaction to forced Russification. After the initial shock of the reforms was past by the mid-1890s, for many Estonians the pressure of Russification awakened a greater sense of national identity than might otherwise have been the case.[24]

Based on this strengthened sense of national consciousness, a revolutionary change occurred among the Estonian intelligentsia. Although it is obviously impossible to pinpoint the shift exactly, both contemporary and later observers are agreed that Estonian became the everyday language of native intellectuals at the start of the twentieth century.[25] Among the many causal factors involved, there can be little doubt that Russification played a major role. The hegemony of the German language in the Baltic had been based on its unchallenged position as the only highly developed idiom in the area. With the Russification of Baltic education and administration, the Estonians were exposed to two competing cultural influences, neither of which was strong enough to supersede the other. The position of German, while weakened, was not entirely eclipsed since Baltic society was still dominated by the local German elite. At the same time, while Russian had strong official backing from St. Petersburg, there was no significant Russian society in the Baltic which would have made Russian culture attractive to the Estonians. Thus, an unintended byproduct of the Russo-German *Kulturkampf* was the revival of a more confident movement for a modern and autonomous Estonian culture among the rapidly growing native intelligentsia.

In the decade before 1905, as Estonian intellectuals adjusted to Russification, the desire for education in the mother tongue was revived as a cardinal point in the developmental program for Estonian culture. While tsarist censorship remained relatively stringent before the Revolution of 1905, the Estonian press increasingly, if guardedly, criticized the negative effects of the Russified educational system.[26] As the pace of Estonian intellectual life quickened after the turn of the twentieth century, educational reform received more and more emphasis in public meetings and discussion groups. During the Revolution of 1905 itself, with the tsarist regime thrown off balance, the Estonians were able to air demands which had been germinating in recent years. The most specific expression of Estonian public opinion on education came in the *Bürgermusse* resolutions at the All-Estonian Congress in November 1905, the salient points of which can be summarized as follows: (1) instruction was to take place in Estonian in all elementary schools and, in principle, in the secondary schools; at Dorpat University, Estonian lectureships were to be established in all faculties along with professorships in Estonian language and literature, Finno-Ugric languages, and theology; (2) in the elementary schools, Russian was to remain as a subject only from the second year of study; (3) educational administration was to be entirely under the control of an autonomous, Estonian self-government. The radical or *Aula* wing of the All-Estonian Congress was less specific on education, but in essential agreement with these demands. Six months earlier, the newspaper *Uudised* (*The News*) had gone even further on the question of secondary education, calling for the immediate use of Estonian as the language of instruction.[27]

The thrust of these demands was squarely against both cultural and administrative Russification. Both the Russian language and the St. Petersburg government were slated to lose their positions of importance in Estonian education. While the demands were not realized (except temporarily in some areas at the height of revolutionary ferment), significant changes did occur in the Baltic educational system in the aftermath of the Revolution of 1905. To be sure, the tsarist regime's ideal of Russification of the borderlands was not abandoned, but as a safety valve in the face of unrest, concessions were made. In April 1906, private schools with instruction in Estonian, Latvian, or German (without state support) were permitted in the Baltic Provinces, and by 1910, twenty-four such Estonian institutions had been established. Furthermore, in October 1906, the curator of the Riga Educational Region, D. M. Levshin, allowed instruction in the mother tongue during the first two years of Baltic elementary education. For the rural schools, this signified a return to the official status quo of the years 1887-1892, but in the cities (with the exception of Reval), Estonian could be used as the instructional language for Estonian pupils for the first time. This latter concession came under attack by Russifying officials almost immediately and was temporarily revoked in 1913. However, it continued in practice, and was officially reinstated during World War I.[28]

The all-empire elementary school census of 1911 provides the last major indication of the status of Estonian primary education before World War I. In Estland and northern Livland (including Narva), the census showed a total of 1,646 elementary schools with 74,873 pupils; however, it is estimated that 29 percent of the school-age children in Estland and 21 percent of those in Livland remained without elementary education. In the rural areas, where the overwhelming majority of the Estonian population was still located, there were 1,480 schools with 58,906 students. Lutheran township and parish schools continued to predominate in the countryside; the number of Orthodox schools was only slightly higher (320, or 21.6 percent) than a quarter-century earlier. However, in the decades following Russification, there was one significant, if relatively minor, institutional addition to the rural educational system—the so-called ministerial school (*ministerskoe uchilishche*)—subsidized and promoted by the Ministry of Education. By 1911, there were eighty such schools in the Estonian areas with 7,936 pupils (13.5 percent of the total rural student body).[29] A journalistic debate at the turn of the twentieth century reflected sharp differences in Estonian public opinion with regard to the ministerial schools. While the politically and socially moderate *Postimees* (*The Courier*) opposed these new institutions, the more radical *Teataja* (*The Herald*) supported them as an alternative to the traditional Lutheran schools on the grounds that the former received state aid, offered a longer school year, and were allegedly no more Russifying than other rural elementary schools.[30] In any case, as the above figures suggest, the influence of the ministerial schools remained limited, and Russification brought only minor changes in the institutional composition of Estonian rural education.

While the great majority of Estonian private schools founded after 1905 functioned only at the elementary level, four Estonian secondary schools, most notably the Eesti Nooresoo Kasvatuse Selts (Society for the Education of Estonian Youth) high school for girls in Dorpat, emerged during the years 1906-1908. After 1908, as Russifying tendencies again heightened in official circles, the tsarist regime rejected all further attempts to establish Estonian secondary schools. If the four existing schools were only a fraction of the total in the northern Baltic region (fifty in 1914), they nevertheless were viewed as an improvement over the pre-1905 situation and contributed to growing confidence in the possibility of an Estonian secondary school system.[31] In spite of the fact that most high schools in Estland and northern Livland were conducted in Russian (with a substantial minority in German), a notable Estonianization process was taking place among the student body in the decade after 1905. In Estland in 1913, Estonians already formed 53.4 percent of the secondary school students, and for the entire northern Baltic area in 1916-1917, the Estonian share was about 7,000 of 13,000.[32]

At Dorpat University, no concessions were made to the Estonian demands of 1905, and the Russified system continued unchanged. Nevertheless, here the number of Estonian students also increased substantially, growing to 287 in 1910 and 434 (about one-sixth of the overall enrollment) in 1914. At the same time, the total number of Estonian university students, including those in Riga, St. Petersburg, and elsewhere in the Russian Empire, grew three and a half times in the first decade of the twentieth century (about 200 to 700) and further to roughly 1,000 in 1915.[33] In addition, the administration of imperial universities proved to be markedly more tolerant after 1905, and it is from this period that the existence of large numbers of Estonian student organizations can be dated.

Buoyed by the experience of the Revolution of 1905, the Estonian intelligentsia turned to educational activity with a heightened enthusiasm in the following decade. Newly established educational societies supported not only private schools in Estonian but also adult education, libraries, and public cultural forums. If the cultural goals of 1905 were not reached, the Russified school system was no longer perceived as a dire threat to Estonian national existence, even as tsarist policy became increasingly reactionary before 1914. A renewed sense of self-confidence from the 1905 experience could not be eradicated, and the escalated educational aims of that year continued, and indeed grew more firmly rooted in the intelligentsia as well as among broader sections of the entire Estonian population.[34]

Given the significant role assigned to Russian Orthodoxy in the official ideology of the tsarist regime in the nineteenth century, it is not surprising that Russification in the Baltic Provinces also involved the active propagation of the state religion. However, it is noteworthy that this policy was only pursued vigorously from the mid-1880s to the mid-1890s during the heyday of Baltic Russification. At other times, the central government remained cautious or uninterested in supporting a conversion movement among the Baltic masses. Historically, the Estonian peasantry had outwardly followed the religious persuasions of its Baltic German masters—Catholicism before the Reformation and Lutheranism thereafter. However, considering the exclusive German control of the Church and the great social and cultural differences between the clergy and the parishioners, it is likely that Christianity only became rooted among the Estonian population very gradually. Indeed, as late as the eighteenth century, pietism, the one historical phenomenon which appears to have engendered genuine religious enthusiasm among the Estonian peasantry, was actively combated by the Baltic Lutheran establishment as a dangerous phenomenon.

In the sixty years before World War I, the Lutheran Church in the Baltic Provinces remained under virtually complete German control. The Estonians were entirely excluded from the upper echelons of the church hierarchy, and they were able to make only minor inroads at the parish level. As late as 1909, there were only nine (13 percent of the total) Estonian pastors and fifty-nine German ones in Estland while northern Livland had nineteen Estonians (29 percent), forty-six Germans, and one Swede.[35] In nearly all cases, the selection of pastors continued to be in the hands of the large Baltic German landowners, and even after small Estonian landowners were admitted to the local church councils in northern Livland in 1870 (but not in Estland), they were unable to exercise any significant influence on the decision-making process. Furthermore, those Estonians who succeeded in becoming pastors, especially in the early part of this period, had to make certain compromises with the Baltic German establishment in order to be acceptable. In an era of growing Estonian nationalism, the great majority of the population remained unrepresented in the affairs of the Lutheran Church, and part of the success of Russian Orthodoxy in the Baltic must be seen against this background.[36] In contrast to the relatively minor Estonian role among the Lutheran clergy, fully 61 percent of the Orthodox priests in Estland and northern Livland in 1909 were Estonian. Writing in 1870, Jakob Hurt, who would become one of the few Estonian pastors of the national awakening era, attributed much of the success of the state religion in the Baltic area to the linguistic skills of the Orthodox clergy.[37]

As noted above, the emergence of Russian Orthodoxy as a significant force in Baltic life came unexpectedly in the 1840s. While the conversion movement among the Estonian and Latvian peasantry began spontaneously, motivated by socioeconomic conditions rather than religious conviction, it could not have succeeded without some official support by the central government. Although similar conditions existed in Estland and Kurland, it is noteworthy that the conversions took place exclusively in Livland, because only in that province was there an Orthodox prelate willing to register the prospective proselytes. While the government of Nicholas I looked with favor on an increase in the Orthodox fold, it also feared any mass movement among the lower social classes. In spite of this ambivalent attitude, the tsarist regime permitted the movement to develop in the years 1845-1848, and this resulted in the conversion of about 17 percent of the Estonian peasantry in northern Livland and reached the figure of 29.8 percent in the district of Ösel.[38]

With the intrusion of Orthodoxy into the Baltic area, the Lutheran Church began an immediate counterattack. Indeed, the entire Baltic German establishment perceived that its hold over the native masses would be seriously weakened if the conversion movement reached larger proportions. In this effort, the Lutheran Church was significantly aided by the attitude of the tsarist regime from 1848 until the mid-1880s. Throughout this period, the central government offered little active support to the Orthodox movement in the Baltic Provinces. In 1865, Alexander II unofficially permitted children of mixed Orthodox-Lutheran marriages to be baptized in the church of the parents' choice. Although these figures should be treated with caution, Baltic German sources estimate the number of "reconverts" from Orthodoxy to Lutheranism (from among the original Orthodox proselytes of the 1840s as well as their offspring) in the mid-1880s in all of Livland to have been about 30,000-35,000.[39] Overall, however, from the mid-1840s to the early 1880s the number of Orthodox Estonians in the northern Baltic region appears to have remained fairly stable.[40]

In 1883, on the eve of Russification, another spontaneous conversion movement to Orthodoxy among the Estonian peasantry began in the Wiek (Läänemaa) district of Estland. In this case, the motivations, which were more complex than four decades earlier, involved strong anti-German sentiment, some genuine religious conviction, as well as a desire for economic benefits.[41] Before Shakhovskoi became governor of Estland in 1885, this proselytism, while looked on with favor, did not receive active encouragement from central government officials. Indeed, without his energetic intervention, the Wiek movement would probably not have lasted more than two years, and despite Shakhovskoi's efforts, the conversion rate to Orthodoxy slowed sharply by 1888. In contrast to the phenomenon in Livland in the 1840s, the conversion movement in Estland in the 1880s remained geographically and numerically limited. In the years 1883-1884, 3,407

Lutheran Estonians in Wiek were converted to Russian Orthodoxy, while the figure for Estland as a whole in 1885-1887 was 7,266.[42] Nevertheless, these results represented the first important inroads of Orthodoxy in the northernmost Baltic Province.

From the beginning of his tenure as governor of Estland, Shakhovskoi led the active propagation of the state religion in the northern Baltic area. As a confirmed Russian nationalist of conservative persuasions, he shared the views of Konstantin P. Pobedonostsev, procurator of the Holy Synod. In 1886, Shakhovskoi suggested to Pobedonostsev that, given the spiritual dissatisfaction of the Baltic natives under a German controlled Protestantism, the quickest way to unite the Estonians and Latvians with the "great Russian family" was through Orthodoxy.[43] With the support of Governor Zinov'ev of Livland, Shakhovskoi directed successful efforts to secure state aid for Orthodox congregations and schools in the Baltic. Symbolically, his most imposing project was locating the Alexander Nevskii Cathedral on the Domberg (Toompea), the traditional bastion of the Baltic German elite, in Reval. In 1885, reversing the decision of his father, Alexander III retroactively reinstated the requirement that children of mixed Lutheran-Orthodox marriages be baptized only as Orthodox, and the reconverts to Lutheranism (i.e. former Orthodox proselytes) were again considered members of the state church. As a result, a large number of Lutheran pastors came under prosecution by the tsarist regime for ministering to the religious needs of the reconverts.[44]

Active Orthodox proselytism among the Estonian population during the first decade of Russification yielded relatively meager results. A comparison of the 1881 and 1897 censuses indicates that the percentage of Orthodox Estonians in Estland increased only 3.9 percentage points (from 0.7 percent to 4.6 percent) in this period. In Livland, the figures for 1897 show 17.7 percent of the Estonian population as Orthodox, a growth of less than 1 percentage point over the level reached fifty years earlier.[45] Furthermore, Shakhovskoi's hope that acceptance of Orthodoxy would lead to rapid assimilation to the Russian nationality was not borne out in practice. While the Estland governor was able to recruit men like Jakob Kõrv and Jüri Truusmann (see p. 329), they proved to be exceptions, and the great majority of Orthodox Estonians retained a strong sense of national identity, for example, Konstantin Päts, the editor of *Teataja*. Among the Estonian population, there was not so much objection to the propagation of Orthodoxy as there was disappointment over the failure to reform the Lutheran Church. The most vigorous statement on this question came from Ado Grenzstein at the end of the 1890s in his *Herrenkirche oder Volkskirche?*, in which he advocated the creation of three completely separate national churches for the Estonians, Latvians, and Germans in the Baltic Provinces.[46] There is no doubt that Orthodoxy would have been even less successful among the Estonians had the Lutheran establishment shown more flexibility in its policies.

With the beginning of the reign of Nicholas II and the end of the tenures of both Shakhovskoi and Zinov'ev as governors, active Orthodox proselytism as well as the harassment of Lutheran pastors came to an end. During the Revolution of 1905, all Estonian political factions agreed on the principles of freedom of religion and the separation of church and state.[47] In April 1905, Nicholas II's toleration edict permitted all adults to freely choose or change their religion. However, children of mixed marriages (where one parent was Orthodox) had to remain in the Orthodox Church until the age of twenty-one. As a result of this decree, significant defections from Orthodoxy in the Baltic Provinces occurred in the decade before World War I. In Livland, for example, 5,362 converts from Orthodoxy to Lutheranism were recorded in 1906-1907, and the same trend continued at the level of about 700-800 annually in the following years. At the same time, proselytism in the other direction declined even further after 1905. In Livland, the highest number of conversions from Lutheranism to Orthodoxy was reached in 1912, when it was 183, while the annual figures for Estland in 1912 and 1913 were as low as 89 and 99, respectively.[48] Thus, judging by the results in the three decades before World War I, religious Russification was almost completely unsuccessful as a means of uniting the Estonian population with the Russian nationality.

CHAPTER 21

RUSSIFICATION AND
THE ESTONIAN NATIONAL MOVEMENT

ALTHOUGH THE MAJOR CONCERNS of tsarist cultural policy were education and religion, the impact of Russification on Estonian culture and the national movement was considerably more far-reaching. The mere fact of Russification coupled with the failure to achieve the cultural and political aims of the national awakening forced the intelligentsia to reassess its views on Estonian development. As noted above, the first decade of Russification was dominated by a widespread sense of pessimism among the Estonian educated elite. It was also in this period that tsarist bureaucrats actively intervened in Estonian cultural affairs in order to combat what were perceived to be "separatist" tendencies. In the following two decades, however, the Estonian national movement revived and redefined its goals more ambitiously than ever before. The present section will discuss the role of Russification in the following aspects of Estonian development: the movement for an autonomous and modern Estonian culture, journalism, and political and social thought.

The Estonian awakening of the 1860s and 1870s spawned national cultural efforts—the Estonian Alexander School (*Eesti Aleksandrikool*) movement, the Society of Estonian Literati (*Eesti Kirjameeste Selts*), and periodic song festivals—as well as local ones such as musical and theatrical societies. Clearly the most important of these was the movement for the Estonian Alexander School (EAS), a proposed secondary school with instruction in Estonian with the goal of producing a body of teachers to educate the rest of the nation. For a decade and a half after its beginning in 1871, the EAS movement, the first nationwide Estonian organization, carried fund-raising operations into all but the remotest and least-developed parishes in Estland and northern Livland. Above all, the semiannual plenary meetings in Dorpat, including the executive committee as well as representatives from the local areas, provided a kind of parliamentary school for the Estonian people, especially in the absence of actual political institutions.[1] In contrast, the Society of Estonian Literati (SEL)—formed in 1872—was an organization limited to the educated elite, but with aims complementary to those of the Alexander School movement. While the SEL's primary purpose was the development of educational literature in the Estonian language, its activity gradually broadened to include linguistic reform and the collection of Estonian folklore.[2]

In order to assess the effects of Russification on these organizations, it is necessary to note their internal evolution in the 1870s and early 1880s along with certain changes in the Estonian intelligentsia toward the end of the national awakening. In the decade of the 1870s, when the romantic optimism of this era reached its height, the moderate Hurt faction dominated both the Estonian Alexander School movement and the SEL. After 1878, however, when Jakobson finally acquired his public forum, the newspaper *Sakala*, the national movement became increasingly polarized as these two organizations became the battleground of a power struggle between the Hurt and Jakobson forces. In both cases, Jakobson and his followers emerged victorious by 1881, but only at the cost of destructive, internecine warfare. On the whole, the Estonian intelligentsia proved incapable of conducting its own affairs in a statesmanlike manner. The most fateful aspect of the struggle involved the invitation of central government intervention by both sides against their opponents in the early 1880s.[3] The result was a loss of confidence in the future of the national movement among much of the intelligentsia and the masses of the population, fostering a mood of pessimism on the eve of Russification.

At the same time, the leading Estonian figures of the national awakening passed from the scene. A stroke ended Jannsen's public career in 1880. The still young and vigorous Jakobson died unexpectedly at the height of his career in 1882, and the death of the elderly Kreutzwald followed a few months later. Hurt became a pastor in St. Petersburg in 1880 and gradually withdrew from public life as his forces lost control of the national movement. Although still interested in Baltic affairs, Köler, a professor at the Academy of Fine Arts in the capital, could only exercise an indirect influence from a distance. It was an indication of the still meager basis of educated leadership among the Estonian intelligentsia that no one of sufficient stature emerged to replace either Hurt or Jakobson.

By the mid-1880s, when the not inconsiderable sum of nearly 100,000 rubles had been collected for the Estonian Alexander School, the fate of the proposed institution was already in the hands of tsarist officials. If the prevailing sentiment in the preceding years among the Estonian intelligentsia had been for a *Realschule* with instruction in Estonian, Mikhail N. Kapustin, curator of the Dorpat Educational Region, and Governor Zinov'ev of Livland agreed that the EAS should follow the format of a Russian urban middle school (*gorodskoe uchilishche*). In 1887, this view was confirmed by the Ministry of Education, and the following year the Estonian Alexander School opened its doors with Russian as the language of instruction. It differed from a typical Russian school only in that Estonian was a required subject.[4] More than anything else, the fate of the EAS symbolized the shattered hopes of the Estonian population during the onset of Russification.

Nevertheless, the Estonian Alexander School was not a total loss from an Estonian point of view. While Russian dominated in the curriculum, the entire student body and most of the faculty were Estonian throughout the existence of the institution (1888-1906), and thus provided at least a native environment. In January 1906, following the ferment of the previous year, the tsarist authorities closed the Estonian Alexander School as an alleged hotbed of unrest. Although the cessation of study was originally intended to be only temporary, it proved to be permanent. However, almost from the founding of the EAS, following the failure to achieve an Estonian-language secondary school, a movement arose to change the nature of the institution to an agricultural training school. In the 1890s, a consensus emerged on this question among the Estonian population, and even tsarist authorities approved, but lack of both local funds and state support frustrated this plan. Only in 1914, on the eve of World War I, was the Estonian Alexander Agricultural School able to begin operations.[5]

In contrast to the Estonian Alexander School, the Society of Estonian Literati escaped government interference in the 1880s, but nevertheless suffered a continual decline in membership and in the quality of its activities after Jakobson's death in 1882. Internal squabbles, lack of leadership, and the disorientation caused by Russification all contributed to the negative trend.[6] The demise of the SEL should be viewed against the background of the intrigues of the epigone who dominated Estonian public life in the early 1890s. Seeking to swim with the tide of Russification, Jüri Truusmann and Jakob Kõrv in Reval and Ado Grenzstein in Dorpat endeavored to ingratiate themselves with the local representatives of the central government.[7] Truusmann and Kõrv became the confidants of Governor Shakhovskoi of Estland on Estonian affairs, while Grenzstein was less successful in reaching Governor Zinov'ev of Livland. Kõrv and Grenzstein each sought to control the Society of Estonian Literati through official support, but Truusmann appears to have encouraged Shakhovskoi to force the closing of the organization.[8] In any case, the internal struggle in the SEL came to a head in 1892 with Kõrv's temporary expulsion, and both Shakhovskoi and Zinov'ev were actively involved in the affairs of the organization by the end of the year.

As in other areas, Shakhovskoi took the more adamant position with regard to the Society of Estonian Literati. In September 1892, he suggested to the Ministry of the Interior that, as a result of Russification, the organization had lost any reason for existence, but stopped short of recommending drastic action. By January 1893, however, the Estland governor had once to view it as a potentially dangerous center of Estonian separatism and called for its immediate liquidation. Such a movement, said Shakhovskoi, was particularly ominous among the Estonians (whom he described as a coarse and underdeveloped people) because they formed the mass of the population in the area.[9] Recently discovered evidence indicates that in December 1892 Zinov'ev was also advocating its closure, urging, however, that the central government move cautiously in order to avoid creating unrest among the Estonian population. By February 1893, under pressure from Shakhovskoi, the Livland governor was ready to demand the immediate end of the Society on the basis of alleged unconstitutional activity at its January meeting.[10] In April 1893, it was officially liquidated by the tsarist authorities; Shakhovskoi's prediction that no significant reaction among the Estonian people would follow this action proved correct.

The demise of the Estonian Alexander School movement and the Society of Estonian Literati, the two major organized elements of the movement for a modern and autonomous Estonian culture, contributed to a sense of dejection with regard to future Estonian development. However, it would be difficult to maintain that Russification was the only major causal factor in the failure of these efforts. In both cases, it was the internal weakness and ineptness of the Estonian intelligentsia which contributed to the original decline of these movements, affording tsarist officials the opportunity to step in and apply the *coup de grâce*.[11] On the other hand, once Russification of the Baltic education began in earnest, approval of an Estonian language secondary school became extremely unlikely, irrespective of how well the movement was organized. Moreover, once the Society of Estonian Literati was closed down, the intelligentsia's efforts to establish a new society with similar aims (which began almost immediately) foundered on official opposition until after the Revolution of 1905. In 1907, however, the Estonian Literary Society (*Eesti Kirjanduse Selts*) was founded in Dorpat.[12] Concentrating on language and literature, folklore, history, and education, this organization played a central role in the Estonian cultural flowering before World War I, and under its auspices the first professional Estonian cultural journal, *Eesti Kirjandus* (*Estonian Literature*), was published from 1906.

An important link between the Society of Estonian Literati (1872-1893) and the Estonian Literary Society (1907-1940) was provided by the activities of Jakob Hurt in the intervening years. Following his withdrawal from the major organizations of the national movement by the mid-1880s, Hurt turned increasingly to the scholarly study of the Estonian language and folklore. In 1888, he publicly enlisted the aid of his co-nationals in order to collect as many examples of Estonian dialects and folklore as possible.[13] By the end of 1906, on the eve of his death, Hurt had registered 960 co-workers and given 155 public progress reports. Given the absence of an institutional base for the study of the oral tradition during much of the Russification period, the folklore collection effort led by Hurt played a significant role in fostering a continuing interest in the Estonian past as well as maintaining national self-respect.[14] Following Hurt's death, his archives were turned over to the Estonian Literary Society.

More than any other single event during the national awakening the First All-Estonian Song Festival, held in Dorpat in 1869, provided a powerful impetus for the development of a distinctively Estonian culture in the following decades. The subsequent song festivals of this period (1879, 1880) deepened the emerging choral and orchestral tradition. All three occasions were also unique in affording the Estonians opportunities for legal mass gatherings, ranging from about 10,000 to 15,000 people.[15] After the onset of Russification, it is striking that the tsarist regime permitted three Estonian song festivals in five years (1891-1896). As before, the ostensible reasons for these events were tsarist anniversaries or the commemoration of the emancipation of the Estonian peasantry. However, even the Fourth All-Estonian Song Festival in 1891, sponsored by the Society of Estonian Literati at a time when Russophile tendencies were strongest in the organization, did not really become an "official" celebration. The central government presumably expected the song festivals to be "tsarist" in content, but in effect, they proved to be guarded, but important, Estonian nationalist demonstrations.[16] In the song festivals of the 1890s, the number of participants grew continuously, and estimates of the size of the public reached as high as 50,000 in 1894. At the same time, the musical repertoire became increasingly Estonianized.[17]

After a hiatus of fourteen years and in the changed atmosphere of the post-1905 era, the Seventh All-Estonian Song Festival in 1910 offered for the first time a program drawn entirely from the work of Estonian composers. Compared with 1896, the number of active participants more than doubled to over 12,000.[18] Thus, except for a certain superficial control, Russian officials were unable to exercise a significant influence on the development of the Estonian song festival tradition. In particular, the musical domain remained completely outside the purview of the tsarist *chinovniki*.

With the establishment of the *Vanemuine* (mythical god of song) Society in Dorpat and the *Estonia* Society in Reval in the mid-1860s, local Estonian cultural organizations began to emerge in Estland and northern Livland, first in the cities and later in the rural areas. The success of the national song festivals was such that choral and orchestral societies became the most important means of Estonian self-expression on the local level until at least the 1890s.[19] Essentially, the local organizations mirrored the status of the national movement. While they began with enthusiasm in the first two decades of the national awakening, the decline of the Estonian Alexander School movement and the Society of Estonian Literati in the mid-1880s, coupled with the shock of Russification, also led to stagnation and disorientation on the local level. By 1893, for example, the *Estonia* in Reval had lost nearly all its membership, and, seeking to ingratiate itself with Governor Shakhovskoi, temporarily ordered the keeping of minutes in Russian.[20] Furthermore, with the exception of such relatively innocent undertakings as temperance societies, the activity of local Estonian organizations remained highly circumscribed during the tenure of Shakhovskoi and Zinov'ev.

With the recovery from the initial effects of Russification by the second half of the 1890s, local organizations played a crucial role in the Estonian cultural revival before 1905, especially in the absence of national associations, which continued to be forbidden by the central government. Once again, the movement began in Reval and Dorpat, but the geographical dispersion of local societies was now much broader than in previous decades. As the educated base of the Estonian population expanded, it was characteristic that the local groups concentrated increasingly on adult education and enlightenment. Moreover, by 1903, some 200 local organizations were engaged in theatrical pursuits.[21] After the Revolution of 1905, the *Vanemuine* and *Estonia* both established professional theaters in 1906, and growing Estonian economic power was seen in the construction of substantial cultural centers in the smaller provincial cities such as Pernau and Fellin in 1911.[22] In the decade before World War I, the tsarist regime no longer had the means nor the desire to seriously limit local Estonian cultural activities.

As a means of communication, journalism, and the printed word in general, played a decisive role in Estonian public life during the national awakening. Jannsen's *Perno Postimees* (and later *Eesti Postimees*) significantly developed the national consciousness of the Estonian peasantry from the late 1850s through the 1870s, and Jakobson's *Sakala* (1878-1882) was the means by which the first major Estonian political movement was able to acquire mass support. While a relatively lenient official policy toward the Estonian press prevailed during the reign of Alexander II, the central government and its representatives in the Baltic region adopted a repressive line with the beginning of Russification. From the mid-1880s, the governors of Estland and Livland began to stress the allegedly dangerous political aspirations of the Baltic natives, and their negative recommendations to the Chief Press Administration in St. Petersburg led to the curbing of Estonian journalism in the following years. During the late 1880s and the 1890s, nearly fifty requests for new Estonian newspapers and journals were rejected by the central government, usually on the grounds that a sufficiently large Estonian press already existed, and in these years, censorship was more stringent than at any other time in the period 1855-1914.[23] In the years 1888-1892, the number of titles in the Estonian periodical press declined by 37.5 percent (twenty-four to fifteen), and only in 1897 did the figure again reach the 1888 level.[24]

Especially in the first decade of the Russification era, Estonian journalism clearly reflected the disorientation and disillusionment of the intelligentsia. In 1888, Jaan Jõgever (1860-1924), editor of the magazine *Oma Maa* (*One's Own Country*), published a series of articles asserting that the poetic period of Estonian nationalism was over and that the Estonian people were no longer interested in national questions. Furthermore, Jõgever offered a devastating criticism of Estonian public life and the intelligentsia, implying very pessimistic prospects for the future of the Estonian people unless matters improved rapidly.[25] The strongest note of rebuttal was struck in *Virulane*, edited by Jaak Järv (1852-1920) in Reval, who argued that the national movement had merely entered a less active phase. However, in November 1888, *Virulane* (the largest Estonian newspaper at the time) was closed down, and Governor Shakhovskoi ordered Järv administratively exiled from the Baltic for two years for alleged hostility toward the government and the Orthodox Church.[26] Järv's exile had a chilling effect on Estonian journalism, and a tone of obsequiousness toward the government came to dominate the press until the latter half of the 1890s.

The remaining three major newspapers chose differing means in their response to increased state pressure in the heyday of Russification. In *Postimees* (published in Dorpat), K. A. Hermann (1851-1909) declared that all reforms were and should be in the hands of the state, and that political questions were outside the purview of the press. He appears to have felt that the road to survival was through self-prostration, presumably indicating that the government had nothing to fear from his journalistic activities or from the tiny Estonian people.[27] If Hermann was personally successful in this approach (he was able to turn *Postimees* into the first Estonian daily in 1891), his views nevertheless contributed to an erosion of self-respect among some elements of the Estonian population in this period.

Through his newspaper *Valgus* in Reval, Jakob Kõrv was the first Estonian public figure to make a virtue of Russification. Even before it was officially announced by the government, Kõrv was advocating Russian as the language of instruction in the Estonian Alexander School. By 1891, he declared that it would not be a "harmful or difficult matter" if the Estonians were to become Russians.[28] Under the protection of Governor Shakhovskoi, *Valgus* was the only Estonian newspaper to survive the suspicions of the Russian bureaucracy in the 1880s and 1890s. Although he was a consistent supporter of the Russifying reforms in all areas, Kõrv's major concern was not ideological, but rather financial. His brand of yellow journalism, including sensationalist reports of crime and war along with an almost complete absence of editorials, made *Valgus* the most widely read Estonian newspaper in the 1890s (one of the most telling indicators of the disillusionment with the Estonian national movement in this period).[29] However, Kõrv had only very limited support among the intelligentsia because he offered no real ideological program and because his intrigues against his fellow journalists, most notably Järv, did not pass unnoticed.[30]

With important differences, Kõrv's counterpart in northern Livland was Ado Grenzstein, editor of *Olevik* in Dorpat. After Järv's disappearance from the scene, Grenzstein was clearly the most able Estonian journalist until the latter part of the 1890s. In contrast to the opportunistic Kõrv, Grenzstein was a sincere ideological convert to the positive values of Russification for the Estonian people. However, in the cutthroat world of Estonian journalism in the early Russification era, involving secret denunciations and intrigues with the tsarist bureaucracy, he always came out second best to Kõrv. While Grenzstein was generally able to gain the support of Governor Zinov'ev of Livland and his successors (thus assuring his professional survival), at the central-government level he failed to erase the effects of a condemnatory memorandum by Shakhovskoi to the Ministry of the Interior in 1892. If it is highly ironic that the most committed Estonian exponent of Russification in the 1890s should be regarded with suspicion in St. Petersburg, the situation exemplifies the limited and contradictory evidence received by the tsarist bureaucracy on Estonian culture.[31]

By the second half of the 1890s, the fortunes of both Kõrv and Grenzstein, the two dominant figures of Estonian journalism in the previous decade, were already in decline. As state pressure lessened with the departure of Shakhovskoi and Zinov'ev and the Estonian national movement showed signs of revivial, both *Valgus* and *Olevik* began to face shrinking circulations. By 1898, Grenzstein had fallen behind his Dorpat rival, *Postimees*, edited since 1896 by the young and dynamic Jaan Tõnisson (1868-19??).[32] In the summer of 1901, Grenzstein left Dorpat voluntarily for permanent exile in Paris, attempting no doubt to salvage some personal honor before his role as an Estonian public figure was totally eclipsed. For his part, Kõrv managed to hang on until 1906, but after 1901 *Valgus* was completely overshadowed by the new Estonian daily in Reval, *Teataja*, edited by Konstantin Päts (1874-1956).[33]

After a slow increase in the latter part of the 1890s, a period of rapid expansion in the Estonian press began in the early twentieth century as the number of journalistic titles almost doubled between 1900 and 1905 (twenty-seven to fifty-one).[34] At the same time the quality of the press improved considerably as more and more serious issues were handled. Tõnisson's *Postimees* was instrumental in restoring the national self-respect of the Estonian reading public in his editorial debates with Grenzstein. With the advent of *Teataja* in 1901 and *Uudised*, edited by Peeter Speek (1873-1968) in Dorpat in 1903, both of which were more radical than *Postimees*, a lively journalistic competition ensured. It is noteworthy that as the educated Estonian population increased around 1905, the circulations of all three major newspapers (*Postimees*, *Teataja*, and *Uudised*) showed a definite upward trend.[35]

As with other aspects of Estonian culture, the Revolution of 1905 had a liberating effect on Estonian journalism. Although the repression at the end of the year led to the demise of several radical and even moderate newspapers, including *Teataja* and *Uudised*, a lasting consequence of the revolution was the abolition of preliminary censorship in April 1906.[36] Although the press was still subject to fines and closure after 1905, the effective range of expression had significantly broadened. For the first time, Estonian journalism could openly discuss and criticize various aspects of Russification, not only in the Baltic Provinces but in the entire Russian Empire as well. Sharp and continuous attacks were levied on the Russified educational system and on the denial of equal rights for Estonian as an administrative language in the Baltic. In 1909, *Päevaleht* (*The Daily Newspaper*) in Reval flatly declared the policy of Russification to have been counterproductive, citing growing separatist tendencies among the non-Russian nationalities.[37] Moreover, the quantitative growth of the Estonian press continued in the years 1905-1914 as the total number of issues printed more than doubled.[38]

With respect to the number of books and brochures published in Estonian, the effects of Russification appear to have been negligible. Although there were periodic fluctuations in the three decades from 1885 to 1914 (most notably a downturn in the latter part of the 1880s), the overall trend in the total number of titles and pages was strongly upward.[39] No doubt, the tsarist regime was less concerned about books and brochures in Estonian, as opposed to the periodical press, since the audience for the former was more restricted. In any case, with the important exception of journalism during the late 1880s and much of the 1890s, the St. Petersburg government did not place serious limitations on printed matter in Estonian.

No group in Estonian society felt the effects of cultural Russification more deeply than the intelligentsia. This was most clearly seen in the weakness of political and social thought during the first decade of the Russification era. In contrast to the forceful ideologists of the national awakening such as Hurt and Jakobson, the characteristic figures of the later period were men like Hermann and Kõrv. Even a man of firmer principles like Järv was unable to provide strong leadership before his exile in 1888. However, one Estonian public figure—Ado Grenzstein—did try to offer a major ideological statement in the changed circumstances of the new era. Reaching maturity in the latter part of the 1870s, Grenzstein at first associated himself with the Germanophile faction. After becoming editor of *Olevik* in 1882, he continued to follow the Hurt line until Russification. At the same time Grenzstein grew increasingly disillusioned with the slow progress of the national movement, and already by the mid-1880s was expressing guarded doubts about the future of the Estonians.[40]

As the implementation of cultural Russification began, Grenzstein retreated to a position of "neutrality" on all public questions. The shocking exile of Järv and hostile attacks by Russian newspapers on *Olevik* had a very depressing effect on him.[41] At first, as a product of an era when German cultural influence reigned supreme in the Baltic, he simply did not know how to adapt to the new wave. However, seemingly motivated by a personal ambition to retain a leadership role in Estonian public life, Grenzstein, by 1893-1894, was ready to offer a new ideology for the Estonians. He began to draw extremely pessimistic conclusions from the small number of the Estonian people. While Hurt in the 1870s had regarded this to be in some ways an advantage, Grenzstein now saw it as a tragic weakness. The value of a nationality, he said, was proportional to its size. Although implying that Russification of the Estonians was inevitable, Grenzstein suggested that the process could be postponed through quietism. The more nationalistic fervor expressed by a small people, he argued, the more rapidly would it be assimilated by larger ones. In fact, the entire national movement had allegedly done more harm than good for the Estonians.[42]

In the course of the 1890s, Grenzstein came to make the flat assertion that only a nationality of more than ten million could create an independent culture. He did not regard this as a value judgment, but simply as a fact of life. Unlike Kõrv, who glibly advocated Russification for personal profit, Grenzstein felt a sense of tragedy about the Estonian situation, but sincerely believed he was serving the best interests of the people by preparing them for the inevitable. Despite a loss of language by the Estonians in the future, Grenzstein argued that they would not lose their nationality because they would retain a common heritage and consciousness.[43] By the second half of the 1890s, while still declaring that unification with the Russian nationality was the most rational future for the Estonians, Grenzstein offered a more positive contribution to Estonian ideology through strong criticism of continued German hegemony over certain aspects of Baltic life, especially by means of the *Landtage* and the Lutheran Church.[44]

If the national awakening had witnessed an affirmation of the future flowering of Estonian life and culture, based on either Russian or Baltic German support, the first decade of Russification saw the collapse of that faith along with the hope of support from either quarter. While a Russophile viewpoint continued among a segment of the intelligentsia, it was now regarded as a matter of necessity, not of choice, and for that reason, could not evoke much enthusiasm among educated Estonians as a whole. On the other hand, it would seem that Russification might have fostered a drawing-together of Estonians and Baltic Germans, but the historical gap between the two nationalities proved to be too wide to bridge. Both sides were increasingly aware that any new Estonian advances would almost inevitably bring a clash with Baltic German interests. Also in contrast to the national awakening, the early Russification period saw the demise of an Estonian political movement. While Jakobson had offered clearly defined political goals, Grenzstein and others in the late 1880s and early 1890s could only pledge undying loyalty to the Russian tsar and state.

In the last years of the nineteenth century, however, the leadership of the Estonian intelligentsia passed to a new generation, virtually all of which had received some university education. As the educated elite grew in numbers and confidence, the sense of inferiority associated with the consciousness of being a small nation, so evident during Russification, waned, and an Estonian national ideology revived. In a sense the major political orientations of the national awakening were resurrected, but on a more complex and sophisticated level. Jaan Tõnisson, an 1892 graduate in law from Dorpat University, emerged as the foremost ideologist in the decade before 1905, representing a revived Baltic Estonian position. While no longer accepting Baltic German tutelage, Tõnisson believed that the Estonians and Germans could work together for the common aim of Baltic development. For him, the Baltic remained a world apart, and he felt it should continue to develop according to previous historical precedents.[45]

Like Hurt, Tõnisson argued that the Estonian nation had the right and, indeed, the duty to exist. It was morally wrong for an Estonian to become denationalized. At the same time, Tõnisson felt that the size of the Estonian nation imposed certain limits on its freedom of action. The Estonians, he said, could not play a role in policymaking in the Russian state as a whole, and he advocated nonparticipation in the empire-wide political and social movements before 1905. As the leading heir to the Jannsen-Hurt tradition, he emphasized political moderation and gradualism. In 1905, Tõnisson founded the first legal Estonian political party, the Estonian Progressive People's Party (EPPP), which drew its support from the growing urban and rural bourgeoisie.[46]

The other major orientation before 1905, grouped around the newspapers *Teataja* and *Uudised*, involved an updated version of Jakobson's Russophile position. For the men of this wing of the intelligentsia (from which no outstanding ideologue emerged), the fantasy of a benevolent, patriarchal tsar no longer existed, but they regarded the Estonian future as being intimately connected with all-Russian developments. Like Jakobson, they viewed the position of the Baltic Germans as a great roadblock to Estonian development, and in seeking ways to remove it, they wholeheartedly sympathized with the all-empire liberation movement in the years before 1905. In contrast to Tõnisson, men such as Päts and Speek, while Estonian nationalists, were mainly concerned with social and economic questions, and emphasized the poor conditions of the Estonian lower classes.[47] They proved to be highly receptive to radical and revolutionary ideas, imported to the Baltic via Russian and other non-Estonian intellectuals at Dorpat University or by way of western Europe. In 1905, the majority of this group formed a loose, radical opposition to Tõnisson's EPPP. A more revolutionary minority organized two similar social democratic parties: one as a section of the Russian Social Democratic Workers' Party, the other an independent Estonian one, based on a federalist view of the Russian state.

Thus, in the first years of the twentieth century, a fundamental break with the past occurred in the Estonian political movement. For the first time, loyalty to the tsarist regime was undermined among a significant segment of the intelligentsia. By 1905, all Estonian political forces, whether revolutionary or reformist, sought sweeping changes in Baltic life. As we have seen, the most substantive statements of Estonian demands in 1905 came at the All-Estonian Congress in November. Reflecting the major division between moderates and radicals among the intelligentsia, the Congress split into two hostile wings: Tõnisson and the EPPP (meeting in the Bürgermusse) and the *Teataja, Uudised* groups (located in the Aula). While there were important differences on social and economic questions and with regard to tactics, both the *Bürgermusse* and *Aula* resolutions stressed Estonian cultural and political autonomy and signified a frontal assault on the Russification policies of the tsarist regime.[48]

The experience of the Revolution of 1905 proved to be a great watershed for the Estonian intelligentsia. While autonomy was not achieved and various Russified institutions continued until the end of the tsarist regime, the political education of 1905 could not be eradicated, and the modest visions of the pre-1905 era had become obsolete. Moreover, the social changes fostered by modernization as well as growing contacts with the non-Baltic world were increasingly reflected in Estonian political and social thought. In general, the division of the intelligentsia into moderate and radical political wings continued in the decade after 1905. Tõnisson's EPPP remained the only legal political organization in this period. Although his party was now loosely allied with the Russian Constitutonal Democrats, Tõnisson still advocated an isolationist and nonparticipatory position with regard to all-Russian matters. Thus, he continued to emphasize cultural and economic aims over political ones, and despite increasing urbanization, to base his ideology (like both Hurt and Jakobson during the national awakening) on the rural agricultural population.[49]

In contrast, the radical Estonian intelligentsia regarded any further Estonian advances as inevitably tied up with empire-wide developments. For those with a sociopolitical orientation, Marxism and socialism provided the dominant models, and a growing knowledge of Russian laid the basis for increased participation in both factions of the Russian Social Democratic Workers' Party. Cultural radicalism was dominated by the Young-Estonia (*Noor-Eesti*) movement, which utilized a variety of foreign models to modernize Estonian literature and culture before World War I. There were obvious tensions between these differing emphases among the radicals; the most notable attempt to bridge the gap came from Gustav Suits (1883-1956), the ideologist of Young-Estonia, who offered a synthesis of individualism and socialism as the basis for Estonian development.[50] However, in spite of the growing complexity and variety of Estonian political and social thought before 1914, both the moderate and radical intelligentsia continued to reject Russification, and political and cultural autonomy remained the future ideal.

IN THE HALF CENTURY before World War I, the Estonian population reacted to both the possibility and actuality of Russification in a complex manner. Before the Revolution of 1905, the great majority of the intelligentsia and the masses regarded administrative Russification as an important means to break Baltic German hegemony over local institutions. However, after the escalation of Estonian political goals to include outright autonomy in 1905, Russian administrative institutions were considered obsolete. With the exception of the moderate wing of the intelligentsia, the Estonian attitude toward limited cultural Russification, that is, the replacement of German by Russian as the major cultural language of the area, was also decidedly positive. Yet, except during the nadir of Estonian self-confidence in the late 1880s and early 1890s, all segments of the Estonian population strongly opposed extensive cultural Russification, such as the introduction of Russian as the language of instruction at all levels of education and as the exclusive language of administration.

On balance, from an Estonian point of view, the effects of the administrative Russification actually carried out (municipal, judicial, and police institutions) were beneficial because the reforms weakened Baltic German domination of Estonian life. On the other hand, the failure to establish zemstvo institutions and the exclusive use of Russian as the language of administration remained highly negative aspects of tsarist policy for the Estonians. In the cultural realm, there is no question that Russification had a detrimental, short-term effect in the areas of education, the national and local cultural movements, journalism, and political thought. It is noteworthy, however, that certain elements of Estonian culture, such as music and religion, remained relatively resistant to central government interference. In fact, the negative effects of cultural Russification proved to be only temporary, and the goal of a modern and independent Estonian culture began to be achieved in the decade before 1914.

If the ultimate goal of the policy of Russification was to denationalize the Estonians, it failed totally. A comparison of census data both before and after the Russification period affords a graphic illustration of this. In 1881, 98.9 percent of the individuals in Estland and 98.8 percent of those in Livland who declared Estonian nationality also indicated that they habitually spoke Estonian. In 1922, only five years after the fall of the tsarist regime, and with a now slightly larger territory in the new Estonian republic, 99.1 percent of the Estonians by nationality also spoke Estonian as their usual language. Thus, over a period of four decades dominated by the Russification era, what might be called an index of partial denationalization (i.e. abandonment of mother tongue, but not yet nationality) actually decreased among the Estonians.[51]

In assessing the impact of Russification on Estonian life, it is important to keep this phenomenon in proper perspective. Both contemporaries and later observers have tended to overestimate its historical role. Even without Russification, it is clear that the Estonian national movement was in a state of decline in the mid-1880s, mainly because of internal problems in Estonian society as well as unfavorable economic conditions. Furthermore, it is necessary to distinguish the truly Russifying aspects of tsarist policy from those which were motivated simply by the prevailing political reaction; for example, the restrictions placed on the Estonian cooperative movement before 1914 certainly involved the traditional tsarist fear of any grass-roots movement. All this is not to deny the importance of Russification, but rather to argue that it is properly seen as only one of several factors shaping Estonian life in this period.

Finally, there are certain ironies associated with the role of Russification in Estonian life. Because of the peculiar political and social conditions in the Baltic and the lack of development of Estonian culture, Russification, a seemingly negative phenomenon from a non-Russian point of view, elicited a relatively favorable response from the Estonian population during much of this period. However, from the standpoint of the tsarist regime, the policy of Russification backfired. Instead of drawing the Estonians closer to official state ideology, contact with Russian culture and ideas contributed to the breakdown of the traditional Estonian loyalty to the tsar. Moreover, far from transforming Estonians into Russians, the effect of Russification was to heighten the sense of national identity among the Estonian population.

Notes to Part Four

CHAPTER 17. THE IMPACT OF MODERNIZATION

1. Sections of the following Part have appeared, in a slightly different form, in Toivo U. Raun, "National Elites and Russification in the Baltic Provinces of the Russian Empire, 1861-1914: The Case of the Estonians," Don K. Rowney and G. Edward Orchard (eds.), *Russian and Slavic History* (Columbus: Slavica Publishers, Inc., 1977), pp. 123-47.

2. For studies of these nationalities in the nineteenth century, see the following: Andrejs Plakans, "The National Awakening in Latvia, 1850-1900" (Harvard Ph.D. dissertation, 1969); "The Nationality Problem in the Habsburg Monarchy in the Nineteenth Century: A Critical Reappraisal, Part II: The National Minorities," *Austrian History Yearbook*, III, no. 2 (1967); Robert A. Kann, *The Multinational Empire*, 2 vols. (New York: Octagon Books, 1970; first published 1950), I, 150-220, 271-83, 294-304; Peter Brock, *The Slovak National Awakening* (Toronto: University of Toronto Press, 1976); Peter Brock and H. Gordon Skilling (eds.), *The Czech Renascence of the Nineteenth Century* (Toronto: University of Toronto Press, 1970); Miroslav Hroch, *Die Vorkämpfer der nationalen Bewegung bei den kleinern Völkern Europas*, Acta Universitatis Carolinae Philosophica et Historica Monographia XXIV (Prague: Universita Karlova, 1968).

3. This concept is discussed more specifically in Toivo U. Raun, "Modernization and the Estonians, 1860-1914," Arvids Ziedonis, Jr. et al. (eds.), *Baltic History* (Columbus: Association for the Advancement of Baltic Studies, 1974), pp. 135-41.

4. Heldur Palli, "Historical Demography of Estonia in the 17th and 18th Centuries and Computers," *Studia Historica in Honorem Hans Kruus* (Tallinn: Eesti NSV Teaduste Akadeemia Ajaloo Instituut, 1971), p. 211; Sulev Vahtre, *Eestimaa talurahvas hingeloenduste andmeil (1782-1858)* (Tallinn: "Eesti Raamat," 1973), p. 236.

5. Located on the northeastern border of Estland, Narva was administratively part of St. Petersburg province from 1802 until the end of the tsarist regime. From 1897 to 1913, the Estonian presence in Narva grew from 44 percent to 58 percent. Raimo Pullat, *Eesti linnad ja linlased XVIII sajandi lõpust 1917. aastani* (Tallinn: "Eesti Raamat," 1972), p. 60.

6. Pullat, *Eesti linnad ja linlased*, p. 38; the German and Russian percentages for 1897 are calculated from data in N. A. Troinitskii (ed.), *Pervaia vseobshchaia perepis' naseleniia Rossiikoi imperii, 1897 g.* XXI, 78-79, 81; XLIX, 42-43; and Pullat, *Eesti linnad ja linlased*, pp. 37, 60.

7. *Eesti NSV ajalugu*, II, 71; Arno Köörna, *Suure Sotsialistliku Oktoobrirevolutsiooni majanduslikud eeldused Eestis*, pp. 37-40.

8. *Eesti NSV ajalugu*, II, 461, 490.

9. Köörna, *Suure Sotsialistliku Oktoobrirevolutsiooni majanduslikud eeldused*, pp. 37, 41.

10. *Eesti entsüklopeedia*, 8 vols. (Tartu: "Loodus," 1932-1937), V, 806.

11. Viktor Maamiagi [Maamägi], *Estonskie poselentsy v SSSR (1917-*

1940 gg.) (Tallinn: "Eesti Raamat," 1976), p. 47; August Nigol, *Eesti asundused ja asupaigad Wenemaal* (Tartu: "Postimees," 1918), pp. 9-11, suggests that there were nearly 250,000 Estonians living in the Russian Empire outside the northern Baltic area, but this figure appears to be somewhat inflated. Certainly his assertion that there were 1,050,000 Estonians in Estland and northern Livland at the time of the Russian Revolution is not credible. The rapidity with which unplanned Russification occurred among Estonian emigrants from the Baltic Provinces should not be overestimated. As late as 1926, 88.4 percent of the Estonians by nationality in the Soviet Union indicated that they spoke Estonian habitually; see Hugo Reiman, "Eestlaste arv Venes (N.S.V.L.)," *Eesti Statistika*, no. 101 (1930), p. 194.

12. Ea Jansen, "Väljarändamisest 1860-ndate aastate lõpul ja selle peegeldumisest erinevate ideoloogiliste suundade võitluses Eestis," Ea Jansen (ed.), *C. R. Jakobson ja tema ajastu* (Tallinn: Eesti Riiklik Kirjastus, 1957), pp. 3-33; Matthias J. Eisen, "Eesti rahva kasvamine," *Eesti Kirjandus*, v (1910), 57-58. In 1915, nearly 40 percent of all Estonians in the Russian Empire with a higher education lived outside Estland and northern Livland; see Toomas Karjahärm, "Eesti rahvusliku haritlaskonna kujunemisest möödunud sajandi lõpul ja praeguse algul," *Keel ja Kirjandus*, xvi (1973), 629.

13. Otto Karma, *Tööstuslikust revolutsioonist sotsialistlikule revolutsioonile Eestis* (Tallinn: Eesti NSV Teaduste Akadeemia Ajaloo Instituut, 1963), pp. 234, 337.

14. Köörna, *Suure Sotsialistliku Oktoobrirevolutsiooni majanduslikud eeldused*, p. 15.

15. Pullat, *Eesti linnad ja linlased*, pp. 37-38, 60.

16. Raimo Pullat, "Eesti kodanluse kujunemisest Tallinnas aastail 1871-1912," *Toimetised* (see List of Abbreviations), xiii (1964), 51-52, 54.

CHAPTER 18. ESTONIAN ATTITUDES TOWARD RUSSIFICATION
BEFORE THE MID-1880s

1. On the veneration of the tsar by the Russian peasantry, see Michael Cherniavsky, *Tsar and People: Studies in Russian Myths*, 2nd ed. (New York: Random House, 1969), and Daniel Field, *Rebels in the Name of the Tsar* (Boston: Houghton Mifflin, 1976). It is important to note, however, that the great majority of the traditionally Lutheran Estonian peasantry remained unaffected by the Orthodox Church throughout this period, and the religious aspect of the myth, so prevalent among the Russian peasantry, was muted in the Estonian case.

2. Hans Kruus, *Talurahva käärimine Lõuna-Eestis XIX sajandi 40-ndail aastail* (Tartu: Eesti Kirjanduse Selts, 1930), pp. 400, 402; Olaf Sild, *Eesti kirikulugu vanimast ajast olevikuni* (Tartu: Akadeemiline Kooperatiiv, 1938), p. 203.

3. Kruus, *Talurahva käärimine*, pp. 212-17, 408-10; Friedrich R. Kreutzwald to Friedrich R. Faehlmann, September 27, 1848, *Fr. R. Kreutzwaldi kirjavahetus*, i, 212-13.

4. August Kitzberg, *Ühe vana "tuuletallaja" noorpõlve mälestused*, II, 103; Mari Raamot, *Minu mälestused* (New York: Kultuur, 1962), p. 54.

5. Ferdinand Johann Wiedemann, *Eesti-saksa sõnaraamat* (4th ed.; Tallinn: "Valgus," 1973; first published, 1869), p. 999.

6. *Fr. R. Kreutzwaldi kirjavahetus*, I, 8, 13-252.

7. Lembit Andresen, *Eesti rahvakoolid 19. sajandil*, p. 36.

8. Calculated from data in Richard Antik, "Eestikeelse raamatu ja bro-šüüri arvulised kokkuvõtted aastate järgi," Daniel Palgi (ed.), *Raamatu osa Eesti arengus* (Tartu: Eesti Kirjanduse Selts, 1935), pp. 293-94.

9. Calculated on the basis of data from ibid., pp. 294-95.

10. Andresen, *Eesti rahvakoolid*, pp. 53, 58-59, 67, 70-71.

11. For overviews of Faehlmann and Kreutzwald, see *Eesti kirjanduse ajalugu*, 3 vols. (Tallinn: "Eesti Raamat," 1965-1969), I, 471-509 and II, 60-127.

12. Mihkel Kampmann, *Eesti kirjandusloo peajooned*, 4 vols. (Tallinn: G. Pihlakas, 1921-1924; Tartu: Eesti Kirjanduse Selts, 1936), II, 31-32; "Mein Streit mit Nolcken u. Liphart," Mart Lepik, ed., *Faehlmanni ja Kreutzwaldi kirjavahetus* (Tartu: Õpetatud Eesti Selts, 1936), pp. 203-4.

13. "Tühhi jut, tühhi lorri, tühhi assi, tühhi kõik," *Tarto- ja Wõrroma Kalender ehk Täht-ramat 1842 ajastaja päle, perran meie Issanda Jesusse Kristusse sündimist* (Tartu: J. C. Schünmann, 1841), pp. 52-63; *Faehlmanni ja Kreutzwaldi kirjavahetus*, pp. 205, 208.

14. Fr. R. Faehlmann to Fr. R. Kreutzwald, August 10, 1845, *Fr. R. Kreutzwaldi kirjavahetus*, I, 113-14; Fr. R. Kreutzwald to Fr. R. Faehlmann, October 1, 1848, *Fr. R. Kreutzwaldi kirjavahetus*, I, 126.

15. Sergei G. Issakov [Isakov], "Tsaarivalitsuse tsensuuripoliitikast eesti ajakirjanduse suhtes 19. sajandi teisel poolel," Juhan Peegel (ed.), *Läbi kahe sajandi*, pp. 109-10.

16. Paul Jordan, *Die Resultate der ehstländischen Volkszählung vom 29. December 1881 in textlicher Beleuchtung* (Reval: Lindfors' Erben, 1886), p. 56; the figure for Livland has been calculated from data in Friedrich von Jung-Stilling and W. Anders (eds.), *Ergebnisse der livländischen Volkszählung*, III, 148-49.

17. "Polozhenie estov v 1860-kh godakh," *Russkaia starina*, C (1899), 655n.

18. For the text of the November 1864 petition, see ibid., pp. 655-65; for a detailed description of the movement, see Hans Kruus, "Eesti talu-poegade palvekirjadeaktsioonid 1860-ndail aastail," *Eesti ajaloost XIX sajandi teisel poolel* (Tallinn: Eesti Riiklik Kirjastus, 1957), pp. 9-87.

19. Otto Karma and August Traat, "Senaator N. A. Manasseini revisjoni puhul valdadest kogutud ankeetmaterjalidest," *Toimetised*, X (1961), 164, 166-67; *Eesti NSV ajalugu*, II, 214.

20. "Senaator Manasseini revisjonist," Hans Kruus (ed.), *Eesti ajaloo lugemik*, 3 vols. (Tartu: Eesti Kirjanduse Selts, 1924-1929), III, 292-95.

21. Carl Robert Jakobson, "Eesti rahva valguse-, pimeduse- ja koiduaeg," *Valitud teosed*, I, 279-306.

22. Matthias J. Eisen, "Eesti rahva arv," *Eesti Kirjandus*, iv (1909), 339-42.

23. On Jannsen's life and activity, see *Eesti kirjanduse ajalugu*, ii, 128-45.

24. For Hurt's biography, see *Eesti biograafiline leksikon* (Tartu: "Loodus," 1926-1929), pp. 149-51, and *Eesti kirjanduse ajalugu*, ii, 411-13. On Hurt's ideological contribution to the Estonian national movement, see Hans Kruus, "Jakob Hurda pärand eesti rahvuslikule mõttele," Hans Kruus (ed.), *Jakob Hurda kõned ja avalikud kirjad*, pp. 7-32.

25. Jakob Hurt, "Mis keeles ja ulatuses tuleb meie rahvakoolides õpetada?," *Jakob Hurda kõned*, p. 62.

26. Jakob Hurt, "Meie koolitatud ja haritud meestest," ibid., pp. 68, 71, 75-76.

27. Hurt viewed religion as the single most important factor uniting a nationality; see Jakob Hurt, "Esimene üleskutse tööks Eesti Aleksandrikooli heaks," ibid., p. 100.

28. See, for example, Hans Kruus, *Eesti Aleksandrikool* (Tartu: Noor-Eesti, 1939), p. 76.

29. For Köler's biography to 1886, see *Russkaia starina*, xxxiv (1882), 743-54 and lii (1886), 333-78

30. On Jakobson's life, see Ea Jansen and Rudolf Põldmäe, *Carl Robert Jakobson* (Tallinn: "Eesti Raamat," 1968).

31. Jakobson, *Valitud teosed*, i, 295-306; Jakobson, "Kuidas eesti rahvas vaimuharimise teel oma õigusele jõuab," *Valitud teosed*, i, 407.

32. Kruus, *Eesti Aleksandrikool*, p. 104; *Sakala*, no. 27, August 19, 1878.

33. Ea Jansen, *Carl Robert Jakobsoni "Sakala"* (Tallinn: "Eesti Raamat," 1971), p. 208; Jakobson, *Valitud teosed*, i, 398-410.

34. Fr. R. Kreutzwald to Lydia Koidula, October 1, 1869, *Fr. R. Kreutzwaldi kirjavahetus*, v, 308; Fr. R. Kreutzwald to L. Koidula, April 21, 1868, *Fr. R. Kreutzwaldi kirjavahetus*, v, 148, 150n; L. Koidula to Fr. R. Kreutzwald, October 30, 1869, *Fr. R. Kreutzwaldi kirjavahetus*, v, 331.

35. L. Koidula to Fr. R. Kreutzwald, October 30, 1869, ibid., p. 333.

36. L. Koidula to Karl August Hermann, April 25, 1882, *Revisjoni tulekul* (Tartu: "Odamees," 1923), pp. 37-38; C. R. Jakobson to Mart Mitt, November 14, 1871, *Eesti Kirjandus*, i (1906), 177.

37. Friedebert Tuglas, *Eesti Kirjameeste Selts*, pp. 133, 133n.

38. *Sakala*, no. 31, August 1, 1881.

39. "Eesti saadikute märgukiri Vene Keiser Aleksander III-le 19. juunist 1881," *Eesti Kirjandus*, xv (1921), 347-49.

40. Tuglas, *Eesti Kirjameeste Selts*, pp. 136, 136n.

41. Jansen, *Carl Robert Jakobsoni "Sakala,"* pp. 275, 279.

42. See the minutes of a meeting of moderate Estonian intellectuals, held in 1878, *Eesti Kirjandus*, xv (1921), 125-27 and the June 19, 1881, memorandum to Alexander III, *Eesti Kirjandus*, xv (1921), 347-49.

43. *Jakob Hurda kõned*, pp. 78-79, 62; Hans Kruus, "Väikerahvalik tunnetus eesti ühiskondlikus mõttes," *Ajalooline Ajakiri*, xviii (1939), 138-39.

44. Jakob Hurt, "Eesti päeveküsimused," *Jakob Hurda kõned*, pp. 158-59.

45. C. R. Jakobson to L. Koidula, April 28, 1870, *Eesti Kirjandus,* vii (1912), 34; C. R. Jakobson to L. Koidula, December 1, 1869, *Eesti Kirjandus,* vi (1911), 369.

46. C. R. Jakobson to L. Koidula, April 28, 1870, *Eesti Kirjandus,* vii (1912), 34; C. R. Jakobson to Jaan Adamson, March 7, 1870, *Eesti Kirjandus,* viii (1913), 274-75; C. R. Jakobson to L. Koidula, December 1, 1869, *Eesti Kirjandus,* vi (1911), 369.

47. Hans Kruus, "Eesti rahvuslik liikumine 1860-80-ndail aastail Venele lähenemist taotlemas," *Eesti ajaloost XIX sajandi teisel poolel,* pp. 256-57, 257n; Leida Loone, "Jooni C. R. Jakobsoni poliitilise võitluse taktikast," *C. R. Jakobson ja tema ajastu,* p. 97.

48. Fr. R. Kreutzwald to L. Koidula, April 21, 1868, *Fr. R. Kreutzwaldi kirjavahetus,* v, 147-48.

49. Jaan Kärner, *"Estonia" kuuskümmend aastat* (Tallinn: T. E. S. "Estonia," 1925), p. 15.

50. Jannsen received a subsidy for his newspaper from the Baltic Germans throughout the 1870s; this was clearly proven only in 1940. See Voldemar Miller, "Eestikeelne ajakirjandus baltisakslaste teenistuses," *Minevikust tulevikku* (Tallinn: "Eesti Raamat," 1972), pp. 18-19. For an interesting fictional defense of Jannsen, see Jaan Kross, "Pöördtoolitund," *Looming,* no. 1 (January 1971), 3-38.

51. Jakobson had six lawsuits filed against him during his first year as editor of *Sakala,* and the newspaper was shut down by order of the Chief Press Administration for eight months in 1879. See the two articles by Hans Kruus, "Ajakirjanduslikud kohtuprotsessid C. R. Jakobsoni vastu," and "Liivimaa rüütelkonna võitlus eesti rahvusliku trükisõna vastu," *Eesti ajaloost XIX sajandi teisel poolel,* pp. 148-71 and 172-200.

52. Anton Jürgenstein, *Minu mälestused,* 2 vols. (Tallinn: Noor-Eesti, 1926), i, 51; *Eesti biograafiline leksikon,* p. 162.

53. Friedebert Tuglas, *Mälestused* (Tallinn: Eesti Riiklik Kirjastus, 1960), p. 86.

54. Friedebert Tuglas, *Ado Grenzsteini lahkumine,* p. 132; F. Tuglas, "Moodsa kirjanduse algus Eestis," *Raamatu osa Eesti arengus,* p. 277.

55. AS (see List of Abbreviations), iii, 209.

56. Tuglas, *Eesti Kirjameeste Selts,* p. 331.

CHAPTER 19. ADMINISTRATIVE RUSSIFICATION

1. *Sakala,* no. 34, August 22, 1881; Edward C. Thaden, "N. A. Manaseins Senatorenrevision in Livland und Kurland während der Zeit von 1882 bis 1883," *Jahrbücher für Geschichte Osteuropas,* xvii (1969), 55.

2. Karma and Traat, "Senaator N. A. Manasseini revisjoni puhul valdadest kogutud ankeetmaterjalidest," *Toimetised,* x (1961), 165; Eduard Laaman, *Eesti iseseisvuse sünd* (Stockholm: Vaba Eesti, 1964; first published, 1936), p. 24; *Olevik,* no. 44, October 29, 1896; no. 4, January 26, 1889; *Teataja,* no. 229, September 13, 1902.

3. Toomas Karjahärm, "Eesti linnakodanluse poliitilisest formeerumisest 1870-ndate aastate lõpust kuni 1914. aastani (linna- ja duumavalimiste materjalide põhjal)," *Toimetised*, xxii (1973), 252-53.

4. Hans Kruus, "Opositsioon Tallinna linnaomavalitsuses 1877-1904," *Ajalooline Ajakiri*, xvii (1938), 108-9, 111, 113.

5. Karjahärm, "Eesti linnakodanluse poliitilisest formeerumisest," *Toimetised*, xxii (1973), 253-55; Kruus, "Opositsioon Tallinna linnaomavalitsuses 1877-1904," *Ajalooline Ajakiri*, xvii (1938), 116.

6. Karjahärm, "Eesti linnakodanluse poliitilisest formeerumisest," *Toimetised*, xxii (1973), 255-56, 260-62.

7. *Olevik*, no. 1, January 2, 1890; *Eesti NSV ajalugu*, ii, 212-13.

8. *Virulane*, no. 8, February 16, 1887; no. 35, August 29, 1888; no. 36, September 5, 1888.

9. Russian names will be used in referring to Baltic administrative institutions established after the mid-1880s while German names will be applied to those already in existence before Russification.

10. *Olevik*, no. 50, December 11, 1889; no. 51, December 18, 1889; PSZ (see List of Abbreviations), 3rd ser., ix, no. 6,188, 478-87 and no. 6,189, 503-5; Sergei G. Pushkarev, comp., *Dictionary of Russian Historical Terms from the Eleventh Century to 1917* (New Haven: Yale University Press, 1970), pp. 153-54. The township court officials were elected by the peasantry; all other judicial officials were appointed by the central government.

11. *Eesti NSV ajalugu*, ii, 215; *Olevik*, no. 51, December 18, 1889; Juhan Kahk, Endel Laul, and August Traat (eds.), *Eesti NSV ajaloo lugemik*, 2 vols. (Tallinn: Eesti Riiklik Kirjastus, 1960-1964), ii, 201n; Kitzberg, *Ühe vana "tuuletallaja" noorpõlve mälestused*, ii, 82; Heinrich Rosenthal, *Kulturbestrebungen des estnischen Volkes während eines Menschenalters (1869-1900)* (Tallinn: Cordes & Schenk, 1912), p. 280.

12. Although the Baltic judicial reform of 1889 specifically stated that Estonian (as well as Latvian and Swedish) could be used only "temporarily" in the peasant courts, in practice, Estonian continued to be used to the end of the tsarist regime. Eduard von Bodisco (ed.), *Die Estländische Bauer-Verordnung von 5. Juli 1856 und die Bauer-Verordnung abändernden und ergänzenden Gesetze und Verordnungen* (Tallinn: Kluge & Ströhm, 1904), pp. 475-76; *Eesti NSV ajaloo lugemik*, ii, 201n.

13. It should be noted here that a thorough command of Estonian was often lacking among pre-Russification court officials as well, and it was not unusual for Estonian plaintiffs to employ German interpreters; see Jakob Hurt, "Eesti keele õpetamisest kõrgemais koolides," *Jakob Hurda kõned*, p. 90. However, there is no doubt that the post-Russification judicial officials in the higher courts knew far less Estonian than those in the previous system.

14. *Eesti NSV ajaloo lugemik*, ii, 201-2; Johan Kõpp, *Mälestuste radadel*, 3 vols. (Lund: Eesti Kirjanike Kooperatiiv, 1953-1969), i, 223; Rosenthal, *Kulturbestrebungen*, p. 280.

15. *Eesti NSV ajaloo lugemik*, II, 199-200; *Eesti NSV ajalugu*, II, 214-17; Kitzberg, *Ühe vana "tuuletallaja" noorpõlve mälestused*, II, 85; *Liiwi kubermangu Talurahwa Seadus* (Viljandi: F. Feldt, 1899), pp. 153-60.

16. George L. Yaney, *The Systematization of Russian Government*, pp. 365-76.

17. *Olevik*, no. 50, December 11, 1889; no. 52, December 22, 1889; Aleksei V. Bellegarde [Bel'gard], *Minu mälestusi Eestimaa kubernerina* (Tartu: "Loodus," 1937), p. 121.

18. In the early 1890s, the Estonian playwright, August Kitzberg, and Jaak Wink were arbitrarily fired from their positions as township clerk and elder by the local commissar for peasant affairs, V. N. Seleznev. Kitzberg and Wink appealed the decision to the governor of Livland, M. A. Zinov'ev, who reinstated both of them and dismissed Seleznev. See Kitzberg, *Ühe vana "tuuletallaja" noorpõlve mälestused*, II, 93; *Eesti NSV ajalugu*, II, 218.

19. *Olevik*, no. 23, June 4, 1890; Villem Reiman "Kolm tähtsat ajaloohallikat venestamise päivilt," *Eesti Kirjandus*, VI (1911), 198; *Eesti NSV ajalugu*, II, 216-17.

20. "Eesti saadikute märgukiri Vene Keiser Aleksander III-le 19. juunist 1881," *Eesti Kirjandus*, XV (1921), 348-49; *Eesti ajaloo lugemik*, III, 293-94.

21. Villem Alttoa, *August Kitzberg* (Tallinn: Eesti Riiklik Kirjastus, 1960), p. 111; Kitzberg, *Ühe vana "tuuletallaja" noorpõlve mälestused*, II, 81-82. A study published in 1894 indicated that in Estland only 9.2 percent of the township elders and 6.5 percent of their aides knew Russian. See A. Kharuzin, "K statistike volostnykh dolzhostnykh lits Estliandskoi gubernii," in A. Kharuzin (ed.), *Vremennik Estliandskoi gubernii*, 2 vols. (Tallinn: Tipografiia Naslednikov Lindforsa, 1894-1895), I, 352, 355-56.

22. *Liiwi kubermangu Talurahwa Seadus*, p. 255; *Eesti ajaloo lugemik*, III, 297-98.

23. Johan Kõpp, "From Established Church to Free People's Church," *Apophoreta Tartuensia* (Stockholm: Eesti Teaduslik Selts Rootsis, 1949), p. 5; *Eesti NSV ajalugu*, II, 226.

24. Wittram (see List of Abbreviations), p. 218; AS, I, 64.

25. Before 1905, there was no public Estonian criticism of administrative Russification, but see, for example, *Uudised*, no. 53, June 8, 1904 for a statement on the necessity of fundamental reform at the township level.

26. For an analysis of the All-Estonian Congress, see Toivo U. Raun, "The Revolution of 1905 and the Movement for Estonian National Autonomy, 1896-1907" (Princeton Ph.D. dissertation, 1969), pp. 170-79.

27. "Tartu Ülemaalise Rahvaasemikkude Kongressi Bürgermusse koosolekute otsused," Hans Kruus (ed.), *Punased aastad*, pp. 223-24; "Tartu Ülemaalise Rahvaasemikkude Kongressi Aula koosolekute otsused," *Punased aastad*, pp. 227-29.

28. *Postimees*, no. 108, May 16, 1906; no. 216, September 22, 1906.

29. *Päevaleht*, no. 150, July 5, 1907; no. 287, December 14, 1909; no. 183, August 14, 1909.

The Estonians

Chapter 20. Russification in Education and Religion

1. Calculated from data in Andresen, *Eesti rahvakoolid*, pp. 58-59, 70-71, 75-76, 141.

2. Ibid., pp. 113, 126, 128.

3. Elmar Ernits, "Õigeusu koolid 1840. aastatest 1880. aastate reformideni," *Nõukogude Kool*, xxxi (1973), 853-54, 849.

4. Endel Laul, "Kirik ja kool XIX sajandi vahetusel Eestis," *Religiooni ja ateismi ajaloost Eestis*, 2 vols. (Tallinn: Eesti Riiklik Kirjastus, 1956-1961), ii, 264; Andresen, *Eesti rahvakoolid*, p. 76.

5. Andresen, *Eesti rahvakoolid*, p. 46.

6. Reiman, "Kolm tähtsat ajaloohallikat venestamise päivilt," *Eesti Kirjandus*, vi (1911), 194, 196; Andresen, *Eesti rahvakoolid*, pp. 102-3; Bellegarde, *Minu mälestusi*, p. 24.

7. "Seadus Eestimaa kubermangu ewangeli-lutteruse usu maakoolide ja koolmeistrite seminaaride pärast," *Eesti rahvakoolide seadused 18. ja 19. sajandil* (Tallinn: Eesti NSV Kõrgema ja Kesk-Erihariduse Ministeerium, 1973), p. 103; the percentages for the use of Russian as a subject in township schools are calculated from data in Andresen, *Eesti rahvakoolid*, pp. 60-61, 70-71, 132-33.

8. Allan Liim, "Keskkoolivõrgu kujunemine ja areng Eestis 19. sajandi teisel poolel," *Nõukogude Kool*, xxxi (1973), 696.

9. Endel Laul, "1880. aastate alghariduskoolide reform Baltimaadel," *Nõukogude Kool*, xxxi (1973), 692-94; *Eesti NSV ajalugu*, ii, 226-27.

10. On the Russification of the secondary schools, see Allan Liim, "18. [sic] sajandi 80-ndate aastate koolireform Baltimaadel ja keskhariduskoolid," *Nõukogude Kool*, xxxii (1974), 433-37; on Dorpat University, see Evgenii V. Petukhov, *Imperatorskii Iur'evskii, byvshii Derptskii, universitet za sto let ego sushchestvovaniia (1802-1902)*.

11. *Eesti kirjanduse ajalugu*, ii, 365; Karl Ast-Rumor, *Aegade sadestus*, 2 vols. (Lund: Eesti Kirjanike Kooperatiiv, 1963-1965), i, 234, 236.

12. *Postimees*, no. 49-50, February 29-March 1, 1896; *Valgus*, no. 3, January 13, 1898; Märt Raud, *Sulg ja raamat* (Lund: Eesti Kirjanike Kooperatiiv, 1962), p. 29.

13. Tuglas, *Mälestused*, pp. 70-71; Karl Ruut, *Eesti rahvakooli ajalugu* (Viljandi: "Valgus," 1921), p. 66.

14. *Eesti NSV ajalugu*, ii, 229; Sergei G. Isakov, *Russkii iazyk i literatura v uchebnykh zavedeniakh Estonii XVIII-XIX stoletii*, ii, 204-5.

15. Calculated from data in the following: Paul Jordan, *Beiträge zur Geographie und Statistik des Gouvernements Ehstland* (Tallinn: n.p., 1889), p. 60; *Ergebnisse der livländischen Volkszählung*, iii, Tab. 20; *Pervaia vseobshchaia perepis' naseleniia Rossiiskoi imperii*, xxi, 100-3 and xlix, 56-59.

16. *Eesti arvudes 1920-1935* (Tallinn: Riigi Statistika Keskbüroo, 1937), p. 26. In 1881, the Estonians comprised 89.8 percent of the population of Estland and northern Livland while in 1922 (adjusted to the area of the 1881 census) their share was 92.4 percent.

17. Calculated from data in Paul Jordan (ed.), *Ergebnisse der ehstländischen Volkszählung*, III, 28; see also Ea Jansen, "Sakala kaastööliste sotsiaalsest ja kutselisest jagunemisest," *Toimetised*, XIV (1965), 439.

18. *Eesti NSV ajalugu*, II, 228; Andresen, *Eesti rahvakoolid*, pp. 203-7; see also J. Kirotar, "Kaarma seminar kui Eesti kultura tegur 1871-1910," *Eesti kultura*, 4 vols. (Tartu: "Postimees," 1911-1915), I, 37-86.

19. Liim, "Keskkoolivõrgu kujunemine ja areng Eestis," *Nõukogude Kool*, XXXI (1973), 701, 703.

20. Evgenii V. Petukhov, *Statisticheskie tablitsy i lichnye spiski po Imperatorskomu Iur'evskomu, byvshemu Derptskomu, universitetu (1802-1902)* (Iur'ev: K. Mattiesen, 1902), pp. 8-9, 22.

21. Hendrik Sepp, "Üliõpilaskond Tartu vene ülikoolis," Juhan Vasar (ed.), *Tartu üliõpilaskonna ajalugu seoses eesti üliõpilaskonna ajalooga* (Tartu: Tartu Üliõpilaskond, 1932), p. 61; Linda Eringson, *Iz istorii Tartuskogo universiteta v kontse XIX i nachale XX vv.*, TRÜT (see List of Abbreviations), no. 114 (1961), pp. 197-99.

22. Ast-Rumor, *Aegade sadestus*, I, 291; Hans Kruus, *Sajand lõppes, teine algas* (Tallinn: Eesti Riiklik Kirjastus, 1964), p. 236.

23. See, for example, an official government report on the Baltic question in 1870-1871 which suggests that the Estonians and Latvians should not be regarded as independent nationalities, but rather as ethnographic material. From the central government's point of view, the real danger was seen in the possible Germanization of the Baltic natives. Sergei G. Isakov, *Ostzeiskii vopros v russkoi pechati 1860-kh godov*, TRÜT, no. 107 (1961), pp. 178-80.

24. Raud, *Sulg ja raamat*, p. 75.

25. Kõpp, *Mälestuste radadel*, II, 104; Juhan Luiga, "Noor-Suomi-Eesti," *Eesti Kirjandus*, XII (1917), 226; Otto A. Webermann, "Probleme des baltischen Raumes als Forschungsaufgabe," *Ural-Altaische Jahrbücher*, XXXV (1964), 294.

26. See, for example, *Postimees*, no. 7, January 11, 1900; no. 149, July 7, 1907; *Teataja*, no. 106, April 8, 1902.

27. *Punased aastad*, pp. 224, 228-29; *Uudised*, no. 41, May 25, 1905.

28. Allan Liim, "Eesti algkoolide õppekeel kahe kodanlik-demokraatliku revolutsiooni vahelisel perioodil," *Nõukogude Kool*, XXIX (1971), 474-79; Peeter Põld, *Eesti kooli ajalugu* (Tartu: Akadeemiline Kooperatiiv, 1933), pp. 158-59.

29. *Eesti NSV ajalugu*, II, 610.

30. *Teataja*, nos. 137-40, May 22-28, 1902; nos. 168-70, July 3-5, 1902; *Postimees*, no. 124, June 10, 1902.

31. Allan Liim, "Keskkoolivõrgu areng Eestis 20. sajandi algul (kuni 1917. a.)," *Nõukogude Kool*, XXXI (1973), 856-59.

32. *Obzor Estliandskoi gubernii za 1913 god* (Tallinn: Estliandskaia Gubernskaia Tipografiia, 1914), Prilozhenie no. 23; Liim, "Keskkoolivõrgu areng Eestis 20. sajandi algul," *Nõukogude Kool*, XXXI (1973), 860.

33. Karjahärm, "Eesti rahvusliku haritlaskonna kujunemisest," *Keel ja*

Kirjandus, xvi (1973), 628; Sepp, "Üliõpilaskond Tartu vene ülikoolis," *Tartu üliõpilaskonna ajalugu seoses eesti üliõpilaskonna ajalooga,* p. 61.

34. *Postimees,* no. 3, January 4, 1907; no. 10, January 13, 1912.

35. Karjahärm, "Eesti rahvusliku haritlaskonna kujunemisest," *Keel ja Kirjandus,* xvi (1973), 630.

36. Kõpp, "From Established Church to Free People's Church," *Apophoreta Tartuensia,* p. 4; Wilhelm Lenz, "Zur Verfassungs- und Sozialgeschichte der baltischen evangelisch-lutherischen Kirche 1710-1914," Reinhard Wittram (ed.), *Baltische Kirchengeschichte* (Göttingen: Vandenhoeck & Ruprecht, 1956), pp. 127-28; Peeter Põld, "Jaan Tõnisson eesti rahvusliku mõtte arendajana," *Jaan Tõnisson* (Tartu: "Postimees," 1928), p. 43.

37. Karjahärm, "Eesti rahvusliku haritlaskonna kujunemisest," *Keel ja Kirjandus,* xvi (1973), 630; Hurt, *Jakob Hurda kõned,* p. 89.

38. Kruus, *Talurahva käärimine,* pp. 407, 342-44. The conversion movement was strongest in the northern part of Livland. In 1848, there were 65,683 Orthodox Estonians and 40,397 Orthodox Latvians in Livland; see ibid., p. 400n.

39. P. A. Zaionchkovskii, *Rossiiskoe samoderzhavie v kontse XIX stoletiia* (Moscow: "Mysl'," 1970), p. 127n; Wittram, p. 217.

40. It is extremely difficult to arrive at an accurate tally of the number of Orthodox Estonians in this period. Both Lutheran and Orthodox sources tend to be biased in favor of their respective religions and estimates vary greatly. Furthermore, some of the reconverts from Orthodoxy to Lutheranism may have feared reprisals and continued to consider themselves "officially" members of the state religion. Unfortunately, the best potential source on this question, the 1881 census for Livland, does not provide a direct correlation between nationality and religion. However, an approximate estimate for the number of Orthodox Estonians in northern Livland can be reached by calculating the total Orthodox population in the area and then subtracting the total number of Russians. The figure thus arrived at is about 70,000; the data is taken from *Ergebnisse der livländischen Volkszählung,* iii, 148-49, 164-65.

41. Leida Rebane, "Usuvahetuslik liikumine Läänemaal aa. 1883-1885," *Ajalooline Ajakiri,* xii (1933), 91-92, 137-39.

42. Calculated from data in ibid., 203, 205, 205n.

43. AS, iii, 6.

44. Sild, *Eesti kirikulugu,* p. 218; Wittram, p. 217.

45. Calculated from data in the following: *Ergebnisse der ehstländischen Volkszählung,* i, 6; ii, 7; iii, 26-27; Jordan, *Beiträge zur Geographie und Statistik,* p. 25; *Pervaia vseobshchaia perepis' naseleniia Rossiiskoi imperii,* xlix, 44-45; xxi, 80, 82-83.

46. Ado Grenzstein, *Herrenkirche oder Volkskirche?* (Iur'ev: A. Grenzstein, 1899), pp. 136-37.

47. See the *Bürgermusse* and *Aula* resolutions in *Punased aastad,* pp. 222, 229.

48. Tobien (see List of Abbreviations), i, 211; *Obzor Estliandskoi gubernii za 1912 god* (Reval: Estliandskaia Gubernskaia Tipografiia, 1913),

p. 86; *Obzor Estliandskoi gubernii za 1913 god*, p. 90. Another estimate suggests that about 12,000 members of the Orthodox Church in the Baltic Provinces converted to Lutheranism between April 1905 and 1910; see *Pravoslavie i liuteranstvo v Pribaltiiskom krae po noveishim dannym russkoi pechati* (St. Petersburg: Gosudarstvennaia Tipografiia, 1911), p. 54.

CHAPTER 21. RUSSIFICATION AND THE ESTONIAN NATIONAL MOVEMENT

1. Kruus, *Eesti Aleksandrikool*, pp. 233-234.
2. Presumably as a gesture of humility to the St. Petersburg authorities, the Russian translation of the Society of Estonian Literati's charter application read *Obshchestvo gramotnykh estontsev* (Society of Literate Estonians). The inertia of the Russian bureaucracy was such that once the charter was confirmed, the name, despite its curious inaccuracy, remained in use until the end of the SEL in 1893. See Tuglas, *Eesti Kirjameeste Selts*, p. 64.
3. Kruus, *Eesti Aleksandrikool*, pp. 169-70, 176.
4. Ibid., pp. 202, 208.
5. Ibid., pp. 295ff.
6. Tuglas, *Eesti Kirjameeste Selts*, pp. 191, 217.
7. Truusmann (1856-1930) was a censor in Reval (1885-1907) while Kõrv (1849-1916) published the newspaper *Valgus* (*The Light*) in the same city from 1882 to 1906. In Dorpat, Grenzstein (1849-1916) was the editor of *Olevik* (*The Present*) in the period 1881-1902. For biographical information on these men, see *Eesti biograafiline leksikon*, pp. 108-10, 256, 529-30.
8. Tuglas, *Eesti Kirjameeste Selts*, pp. 286-87, 336-37.
9. AS, III, 266, 293-95. Shakhovskoi's limited and biased sources on Estonian affairs (i.e., Truusmann and Kõrv) are highly evident in his recommendation that Grenzstein, as the leader of an Estonian nationalist party, be exiled from the Baltic Provinces at the first opportunity (AS, III, 277). In fact, by this time (1892), Grenzstein was a strong supporter of Russification in Estonian life.
10. Sergei G. Issakov [Isakov], "Uusi andmeid Eesti Kirjameeste Seltsi sulgemise kohta," *Keel ja Kirjandus*, XIII (1970), 290-91.
11. Carl Heinrich Niggol, "Minu mälestused varemast ajast (alates 1851)," *Eesti Kirjandus*, XX (1926), 644; Peeter Tarvel, "J. Tõnissoni rahvuspoliitilisi vaateid," *Jaan Tõnisson töös ja võitluses* (Tartu: koguteose "Jaan Tõnissoni" komitee, 1938), p. 437.
12. Tuglas, *Eesti Kirjameeste Selts*, p. 383.
13. Jakob Hurt, "Üleskutse rahva vaimse vanavara korjamiseks," *Jakob Hurda kõned*, pp. 230, 232-33. The original appeal appeared in Grenzstein's newspaper *Olevik*.
14. *Jakob Hurda kõned*, pp. 8, 229.
15. Rudolf Põldmäe, *Esimene Eesti üldlaulupidu 1869* (Tallinn: "Eesti Raamat," 1969), p. 105; Tuglas, *Eesti Kirjameeste Selts*, p. 17; Rudolf Põldmäe, *Kaks laulupidu: 1879-1880* (Tallinn: "Eesti Raamat," 1976), pp. 99, 208.

16. Tuglas, *Eesti Kirjameeste Selts*, pp. 260, 267; Kõpp, *Mälestuste rada-del*, I, 174.

17. *Postimees*, no. 137, June 27, 1894; *Üleüldine Eesti Rahwa Wabastuse Seitsme-kümne-wiie Aasta Juubeli Tänu-laulupidu* (Tartu: n.p., 1894), pp. 7-8; *Eesti muusika*, 2 vols. (Tallinn: "Eesti Raamat," 1968-1975), I, 89.

18. *Eesti muusika*, I, 135; *Juubelilaulupeo juht* (Tallinn: "Eesti Raamat," 1969), p. 36. By 1910, Russification was perceived by the Estonians as more of a nuisance than a threat, e.g., at the Seventh All-Estonian Song Festival, Governor I. V. Korostovets of Estland required that the tsarist anthem be sung first in Russian and only then in Estonian and that the words *tsar' pravoslavnyi* be included in the translation; see Johannes V. Veski, *Mälestuste raamat* (Tallinn: "Eesti Raamat," 1974), p. 219.

19. Põldmäe, *Kaks laulupidu*, p. 242.

20. Tuglas, *Eesti Kirjameeste Selts*, p. 205; Kärner, "*Estonia*," pp. 24, 30.

21. August Rei, *Mälestusi tormiselt teelt* (Stockholm: Vaba Eesti, 1961), pp. 20-21; Kärner, "*Estonia*," pp. 36-37; *Teataja*, no. 51, March 4, 1903.

22. *Päevaleht*, no. 244, October 25, 1911; no. 250, November 1, 1911.

23. Issakov, "Tsaarivalitsuse tsensuuripoliitikast," *Läbi kahe sajandi*, pp. 127, 134-38.

24. Richard Antik, *Eesti raamat 1535-1935* (Tartu: n.p., 1936), p. 90.

25. *Oma Maa*, no. 5 (1888), pp. 125-26; no. 6, pp. 137-41; no. 7, pp. 161-66; no. 8, pp. 178-83.

26. *Virulane*, no. 26, June 27, 1888; *Eesti biograafiline leksikon*, p. 182; *Postimees*, no. 134, November 22, 1888, cited in *Eesti NSV ajaloo lugemik*, II, 196.

27. *Postimees*, no. 103, September 9, 1889; Peeter Ruubel, *Poliitilised ja ühiskondlikud voolud Eestis* (Tallinn: "Varrak," 1920), pp. 57-58n.

28. *Valgus*, no. 37, September 10, 1887; Tuglas, *Eesti Kirjameeste Selts*, pp. 259-60.

29. From a circulation of 1,600 in 1887 (Jordan, *Beiträge zur Geographie und Statistik*, p. 61), *Valgus* grew to 10,000 by 1895, according to Kõrv's own claim (Tuglas, *Ado Grenzsteini lahkumine*, p. 54). In 1898, central government figures put the circulation of *Valgus* at 8,000, twice that of its nearest competitor (Issakov, "Tsaarivalitsuse tsensuuripoliitikast," *Läbi kahe sajandi*, p. 136).

30. On Kõrv's role in Järv's exile, see Tuglas, *Eest Kirjameeste Selts*, p. 437.

31. Issakov, "Uusi andmeid," *Keel ja Kirjandus*, XIII (1970), 289, 291; Tuglas, *Ado Grenzsteini lahkumine*, pp. 185-87; Issakov, "Tsaarivalitsuse tsensuuripoliitikast," *Läbi kahe sajandi*, pp. 131-32.

32. Issakov, "Tsaarivalitsuse tsensuuripoliitikast," *Läbi kahe sajandi*, p. 136; Friedrich Puksov, *Eesti raamatu arengulugu* (Tallinn: Eesti Raamatu-koguhoidjate Ühing, 1933), p. 38.

33. On Grenzstein's exile, see Tuglas, *Ado Grenzsteini lahkumine*, pp. 139, 145. There are several striking parallels in the lives of Kõrv and Grenzstein. Both were born in northern Livland in 1849, became rural

schoolteachers and later journalists supporting Russification, and died in west European exile in 1916.

34. Antik, *Eesti raamat*, p. 90.

35. J. Roos, "Jaan Tõnissoni elukäik," *Jaan Tõnisson töös ja võitluses*, p. 48; *Veski, Mälestuste raamat*, p. 164; *Uudised*, no. 16, February 25, 1905.

36. Benjamin Rigberg, "The Efficacy of Tsarist Censorship Operations, 1894-1917," *Jahrbücher für Geschichte Osteuropas*, xiv (1966), 331n.

37. On education, see *Päevaleht*, no. 191, August 25, 1907; no. 281, December 7, 1911. On demands for equal rights for Estonian as an administrative language see *Päevaleht*, no. 150, July 5, 1907; no. 287, December 14, 1909. For general criticism of Russification as a policy, see *Päevaleht*, no. 291, December 18, 1909; *Postimees*, no. 36, February 13, 1912.

38. 1,958 in 1905 versus 4,435 in 1914; see Antik, *Eesti raamat*, p. 90.

39. Ibid., pp. 28-29. The number of books and brochures grew from 152 (1885) to 702 (1913—the last full prewar year) while the figure for total pages jumped from 13,338 to 56,639 in the same period.

40. *Olevik*, no. 20, May 14, 1884; no. 42, October 14, 1885.

41. Ibid., no. 1, January 4, 1888. *Moskovskie vedomosti*, citing the exile of Järv as a correct and necessary step, attacked *Olevik* for printing a poem about alleged Estonian plans for autonomy; see *Olevik*, no. 3, January 16, 1889.

42. *Olevik*, no. 32, August 8, 1893; no. 15, April 11, 1894; no. 16, April 16, 1894.

43. Grenzstein, *Herrenkirche*, pp. 129-31; Ado Grenzstein, "Eesti küsimusest" (memorandum to Governor V. D. Suvortsev of Livland in 1896), in Tuglas, *Ado Grenszsteini lahkumine*, p. 204; Kruus, "Väikerahvalik tunnetus," *Ajalooline Ajakiri*, xviii (1939), 142-43.

44. *Olevik*, no. 44, October 29, 1896; no. 2, January 12, 1899; Ruubel, *Poliitilised ja ühiskondlikud voolud Eestis*, p. 58. See also Grenzstein's *Herrenkirche*.

45. Tarvel, "J. Tõnissoni rahvuspoliitilisi vaateid," *Jaan Tõnisson töös ja võitluses*, p. 458.

46. Ibid., pp. 439-41; Hans Kruus, *Jaan Tõnisson eesti kodanluse juhina* (Tartu: "Odamees," 1921), pp. 53-54; Kruus, "Väikerahvalik tunnetus," *Ajalooline Ajakiri*, xviii (1939), 143-44.

47. *Teataja*, no. 226, September 10, 1902; *Uudised*, no. 53, June 8, 1904.

48. *Punased aastad*, pp. 220-30. Of the 801 delegates present, a majority joined the radical (Aula) wing of the congress.

49. Kruus, "Väikerahvalik tunnetus," *Ajalooline Ajakiri*, xviii (1939), 144; Jaan Tõnisson, "Woolud ja püüded 1911," *Oma Maa* i (Tartu: "Postimees," 1911), 42; Kruus, *Jaan Tõnisson*, p. 84.

50. Gustav Suits, *Sihid ja vaated* (Helsinki: Yrjö Weilin, 1906).

51. Calculated from data in the following: Jordan, *Die Resultate der ehstländischen Volkszählung*, p. 61; *Ergebnisse der livländischen Volkszählung*, iii, 166-67; *1922. a. üldrahvalugemise andmed*, vihk 1 (Tallinn: Riigi Statistika Keskbüroo, 1924), p. 34.

PART FIVE

FINLAND

C. LEONARD LUNDIN

SWEDEN

GULF OF
BOTHNIA

OULU

FINLAND

MIKKELI

LAPEENRANTA

PORI

TAMPERE

LAKE
LADOGA

HÄMEENLINNA

UUSIKAUPUNKI

HAMINA

TURKU

PORVOO

HELSINKI

ÅLAND IS.

TAMMISAARI

VIIPURI

GULF OF FINLAND

ST.
PETERSBURG

REVAL

ESTLAND

Map 2. Finland.

CHAPTER 22

CONSTITUTIONAL AND HISTORICAL
BACKGROUND OF THE RUSSIFICATION
DISPUTE IN FINLAND

Iɴ ᴛʜᴇ ᴅᴇᴄᴀᴅᴇs before World War I, of all the borderlands subjected to pressure from St. Petersburg for the remodeling of institutions, Finland offered perhaps the least possibility of success. Every attempt to absorb it into the Russian system, whether in administrative, military, juridical, or cultural aspects, collided with the fact that Finland had grown into a modern country with a high degree of self-awareness and a set of institutions and values that differed markedly from those of Russia.

In the long run, only the Poles offered as stubborn an assertion of the right to go their own way as did the Finns. In the case of Poland, however, the differences between the ruling and the subjected nation were based in large part upon centuries-old historical enmity and upon memories of recent Polish independence and still more recent bloodshed; their social structures were not notably different. In the case of Finland, on the other hand, the country had merely been transferred from one sovereignty to another; there had been no intervening history of national independence. The memories of centuries of warfare and destructive raids had been overlaid with three-quarters of a century of peace and relative contentment. During the nineteenth century, however, the Finns had created, upon the basis of a society already very different from that of Russia, a new nation, increasingly aware of her own identity and preoccupied with the internal strains of rapid modernization.

Before the end of the century the high degree of autonomy granted by Alexander I had developed into the apparatus of a largely self-governing state, with a representative—though before 1905 a far from democratic—parliament and an incomparably higher degree of general political interest and activity than could be found anywhere else in the empire. Well before 1900 the Finns had political parties, through which differing views could not only be expressed (with limitations) but (also with limitations) translated into effective action.

Finland had produced in the course of a few decades a national literature of high quality that in some cases came openly to grips with certain social facts of the contemporary world with a forcefulness for which there seems to have been no equivalent in Russia. Women's rights, for instance, were discussed vigorously, along with frank and eloquent treatments of poverty, bourgeois greed, and religious bigotry, in the writings of the gifted novelist and playwright Minna Canth, who seems to have had no counterpart, male or female, in Russia. The wider social spread of the reading and writing public in Finland is illustrated by the treatment of the peasant in the literature of the two countries. Certainly the life of the peasant was of concern to various Russian authors; but those who presented the subject in novels were writing as well-disposed outsiders, not as persons who had experienced peasant life themselves. Tolstoi, for instance, wrote with sympathy about the peasants; but his sympathy is sometimes mingled with condescension or irritation; he certainly does not write from the point of view of the *muzhik* himself. In Finland, on the other hand, the first great national writer in Finnish, Aleksis Kivi, brought to his pages and to the Finnish stage a real, living peasantry, which he knew from having been born into it; other writers followed his example.[1]

In at least one of the arts, architecture, the Finns were in much closer touch with the new currents of European life than were the Russians: by the 1890s they were entering the period of brilliant creativity that was to put their country among architecture's world leaders.[2] In music and painting Finland's achievement, though less notable than that of its great neighbor Russia, was nevertheless respectable;[3] and at the end of the century one composer who was to achieve world fame, Jean Sibelius, was well launched upon his career.[4]

Class distinctions were considerably less rigid in Finland than in Russia proper and the Baltic Provinces. Finland's peasants had never been serfs (although, as will presently appear, legal freedom did not necessarily mean absence of exploitation). There had always been some degree of social mobility, and the barrier of language and social status between the Swedish-speaking minority and the Finnish-speaking majority was never so formidable as the barrier between German and Estonian or Latvian in the Baltic Provinces.

Thus, by these distinguishing characteristics, Finland was by the end of the nineteenth century a special entity. The question as to whether it constituted a separate *state* was formulated and strongly argued about only as the century drew toward a close. In the ensuing debate it was impossible, because of the confusing and contradictory historical documentation, for either side to convince the other. What is clear, however—at least in retrospect—is that Finland had become what it was not at the opening of the century—a nation. The speculative historian, then, may ask: could the Russian government, by wise and conciliatory policies, have retained the loyalty of the Finns by permitting them to lead their own cultural and political life, and at the same time have modernized the imperial structure in such a way as to protect Russia's own external interests? Such a question is as unanswerable as the more familiar one about the Habsburgs: could they have held their empire together had they followed the counsels of the Czech Palacký and the liberals of the Kremsier constituent convention in 1848 and 1849? The difficulties would have been many; Finnish leaders would have needed a less narrow provincial view and less determination to preserve special privileges than they had, and St. Petersburg a far more statesmanlike vision than in fact it possessed.

Above all, to adjust Russian imperial interests, as seen by the makers of Russian policy, to the Finns' conception of their rights would have required tolerance; and tolerance for differing ideas was a quality not strikingly characteristic of the last two tsars and their advisers. Indeed, it would have been almost impossible to find a basis of discussion, let alone agreement, between the two conflicting societies and their political conceptions. The clash was one of centuries. The idea of absolute monarchy was a product of the seventeenth century. The upper-class Finnish conservatives essentially desired mildly liberal early-nineteenth-century political institutions. Finnish radicals looked forward to a democratic twentieth century.

Unintentionally, the Russian government, by forcing a change in its relationship with Finland, precipitated a fundamental change in Finland itself. Russification did not survive, but neither did the old Finland of the nineteenth century. Russification was a corrosive acid that found all the cracks in Finnish society and widened them.

To a considerable extent the complex and often passionate arguments about Russia's and Finland's respective rights, which proliferated into a formidable literature toward the end of the nineteenth century, are due to the ambiguity of Alexander I in defining the nature of his acquisition in Finland in 1808 and 1809. In a series of proclamations, speeches, manifestoes, instructions, and private utterances between 1808 and 1816, the tsar left room for widely differing interpretations of the way in which he saw his relationship to his newly acquired province. An apparent contradiction between his expressed views in 1809 and his practice in later years adds to the obscurity of the debate. Any attempt to review in detail the arguments about the juridical nature of the Russo-Finnish relationship would exceed the scope of this work and the learning of this writer. In any case, as a

C. Leonard Lundin

recent German scholarly study has convincingly shown,[5] under all the tsars until well into the last quarter of the century that relationship varied greatly from time to time and was determined by pragmatic rather than legalistic considerations. Nevertheless, if we are to understand in some measure the constitutional disputes that arose toward the end of the century it is necessary to cast a glance at what happened at the beginning.

It is clear that Alexander wished to acquire the loyalty as well as the territory of the Finns; and he issued reassuring messages to them during the conquest and in the years that followed. These messages contained two themes: (1) that the conquest was divinely ordained and irreversible; and (2) that the inhabitants would not suffer any loss of their safety, rights, or privileges as a result of it. Both themes appeared in an address to the Finns in June 1808, before the military operations were concluded. "According to the decisions of the Almighty," it declared, "who has blessed Our weapons, We have united the province of Finland for all time with the Russian realm. . . . The inhabitants of now conquered Finland have from this time assumed a place among the nationalities that obey the Russian scepter and with them constitute one realm. . . . From this great whole only the will and decision of the Almighty can separate them. . . . The old constitutions and privileges of your land shall be maintained sacredly."[6]

Five months later, in November, Swedish troops evacuated the territory they still held in Finland, and shortly thereafter the tsar received in St. Petersburg some deputies from Finland's four Estates (nobles, clergy, burghers, and peasants, the groups represented in the Swedish parliament), who were to inform him of the condition of the country. The deputies, in a foretaste of what was going to happen decades later, administered a respectful rebuff. According to the fundamental laws of the land, they pointed out, a general meeting of the representatives of the four Estates was necessary, to discuss in the presence of the ruler the matters presented to them.[7]

To the Finns' clear statement of their belief that Alexander was not free to rule Finland arbitrarily and that Finland was still to be governed by its old constitutional privileges Alexander yielded gracefully. In January 1809 he convoked a meeting of the Estates:

> WE have resolved, conformably with the constitutions of the country, to unite them in a Diet and in consequence have ordered and order by these presents that a general Diet be convoked for the tenth of March of this year in the town of Borgo [sic]. For this purpose the plenipotentiaries of all the Estates will proceed thither in the manner prescribed by the rules of the Diet to dis-

cuss the subjects that WE shall consider suitable to confide to their deliberations.[8]

The Diet met, as commanded, in Porvoo (Borgå). The tsar opened the meeting with a cordial speech in French, saying, among other things, "I have promised to maintain your constitutions, your fundamental laws; your meeting here guarantees my promise."[9] There followed ceremonies in which each of the Estates swore fealty to the ruler. The Estate of the Knights and Nobles was explicit as to the nature of its oath, which could be interpreted as making a distinction between Alexander in his capacity as ruler of Russia and Alexander as ruler of Finland, and as establishing certain expectations or conditions:

> We . . . promise and swear . . . that we will have and hold as our rightful lord the High and Mighty Prince and Lord Alexander the First, Tsar and Autocrat of all the Russias and Grand Duke of Finland, and unshakably maintain the fundamental laws and constitutions of the country, as they are now accepted and valid.[10]

After the Diet had deliberated on various subjects for several months, it was dissolved in July 1809 by the tsar, who returned to Porvoo for a cordial valedictory, once more in the French language:

> . . . I have left perfect freedom to your deliberations. No influences, no authority outside your own, dared to cross these thresholds. . . . I have kept watch over the independence of your opinions. . . . The counsels you have just given bear the imprint of wisdom and love of country. Carry into the hearts of your provinces, imprint into the minds of your compatriots the same confidence that has presided here at your deliberations. Inspire them with the same conviction, the same assurance on the subjects most important to your political existence. . . .
>
> This brave and loyal people will bless the Providence that has brought about the present order of things. Placed henceforth on the level of nations [*placé désormais au rang des nations*] under the empire of its laws, it will remember the past domination only to cultivate relationships of friendship when they are restored by peace. . . . I shall see this nation tranquil externally, free internally.[11]

Alexander did not cease his benevolent assurances with the closing of the Diet of Porvoo. In March 1810 he issued a manifesto declaring: "At the moment that Providence gave Us the fate of Finland, We resolved to govern this country as a free nation, enjoying the rights that its constitution guaranteed it." In a secret instruction to the governor-general of Finland the tsar remarked: "In organizing conditions in Finland My intention was to give this people political existence; so that it should not regard itself as conquered by Russia, but as united with it through its obvious advantage; therefore . . . I have retained not only its civil law but also its political laws." To a prominent Finn, Count Aminoff, Alexander wrote in 1810: "My aim is . . . to see the political existence of the Finnish nation consolidated and the means of its prosperity increased."[12]

These and similar utterances by Alexander I were to furnish powerful ammunition later in the century for advocates of the view that Finland was a separate nation and a separate state, with its own permanently guaranteed freedoms and constitutional protections that had no equivalent in Russia. The tsar's characterization of the Finns as a "people" or a "nation," his repeated references to "constitutions" and "fundamental laws," and his recurrent theme of internal "freedom" came to seem to many Finns irreconcilable with the encroachments on Finnish autonomy by the Russian government after 1890.

What the term nation denoted or implied to the Russians at the Diet of Porvoo has been learnedly discussed by one contemporary Finnish historian.[13] The complex history of the changing Russian and Finnish views on Finland's autonomy or dependency and on the nature of Alexander's guarantees has been traced with lucidity and erudition by two Finnish historians,[14] and in impressive detail by a German scholar.[15]

Although the terms constitution and fundamental laws had been used at Porvoo, there was, of course, no such thing as a separate Finnish constitution at the opening of the nineteenth century, and there never had been one. For nearly seven hundred years most of Finland had been part of the Swedish realm and shared the Swedish political system. The Swedish parliament, the Riksdag, originated in the Middle Ages, and its relationship to the king varied greatly over the course of time. At the end of the seventeenth century Charles XI strengthened the power of the crown so that something resembling absolutism emerged. In reaction to this, in the decades of elected monarchs in the eighteenth century, the so-called Age of Freedom, the crown was reduced to virtual impotence and the Riksdag, more particularly the Estate of the Knights and Nobles, along with the royal council, dominated internal and foreign policy. Since the record of this aristocratic government was a dismal one, King Gustav III had little difficulty toward the end of the century in strengthening the position of the monarch by applying limited violence or threats of violence. The Form of Government of 1772 and the Act of Union and

Security of 1789 substantially increased the freedom of the king to act. By the end of the eighteenth century the Riksdag could be characterized as "law-establishing but obedient to law," and the king as "possessed of power but bound by law." There was a considerable range of guaranteed civil freedoms. The Riksdag was to be summoned when and where the king ordered; it no longer had the right to initiate legislation, but was entitled to petition the monarch. Passage of some kinds of legislation required the agreement of the Riksdag; but control of economic legislation and administration had passed largely into the hands of the crown. In general, the restrictions imposed by ancient Swedish tradition and old laws were not entirely clear.

Evidently, then, even on the debatable assumption that Alexander I understood the word "constitution" to mean the Swedish political system, and not merely certain well-established corporate and individual rights and privileges, he was by no means setting up a parliamentary regime. In practice, in any case, once the tsar had secured a firm basis of popular support, he paid little attention to any possible restrictions on his power. He never summoned the Finnish Estates again. Neither did Nicholas I, his successor; it was to be over half a century before the representatives of the people met again.

On the other hand, Alexander continued to leave most of the administration of Finland in the hands of natives. Shortly after the Diet of Porvoo (acting possibly in accordance with a provision of the Form of Government of 1772 that gave the king the right to decide upon officials of the realm) the tsar established a Government Council to deal with judicial affairs and matters of "public economy." In 1816 the name of the council was changed to Senate of Finland. With some changes, this body continued to be the center of Finnish administration until the end of the nineteenth century.

The Senate was composed of Finns; so was the Committee for Finnish Affairs set up in St. Petersburg, later known as the State Secretariat for Finnish Affairs, headed by a minister state secretary and representing the views of the Senate in dealings with the Russian government. Specifically, Russian authority was embodied in the person of the governor-general of Finland, who was—after the first incumbent—always a Russian, and usually a military man, since he was also commander of the Russian armed forces in Finland until just before World War I. In principle the governor-general might preside over the meetings of the Senate; in practice he usually did not, since that body conducted its deliberations in Swedish.

In summary one may say that, although after 1809 Finns could no longer participate in anything resembling the Swedish Riksdag, they

—or a select group of them—probably received more experience in managing the affairs of their country than had been the case before the transfer of sovereignty. Finnish representatives in the Riksdag had rarely wielded any influence upon policy. Finland had in general been a poor, outlying province, both neglected and exploited by the heartland—considered expendable in war and negligible in peace. Swedish kings had rarely visited it, and their coming was usually an indication that war with Russia, with its accompanying devastation, was at hand.

In contrast, the Russian monarchs showed a keen sense of public relations with respect to their new acquisition. All the tsars visited it frequently, and achieved great popularity, until the time of Nicholas II. Even the dour Nicholas I was respected; a little obelisk, the "Empress Column," still stands in the harbor marketplace in Helsinki to mark the spot where he and his empress landed on one visit. Alexander II aroused enormous enthusiasm from his first visit as heir to the throne; and his great contributions to the political, economic, and cultural development of Finland have never been forgotten, as his imposing statue in the Senate Square attests. Even as tensions between Finns and Russifiers began to mount in the 1880s, affection for Alexander III and his charming empress, Maria Fedorovna, the former Danish princess Dagmar, remained strong. In the summer of 1884 and numerous summers thereafter the imperial yacht made long and leisurely cruises through the Finnish coastal archipelago, stopping now and then at idyllic small towns or to call at the country estates of acquaintances of the imperial family. The illustrious visitors were deferentially received, and refreshed with such unlikely combinations of the luxurious and the homely-folklorish as champagne and clotted sour milk. Day after day the yacht was surrounded by swarms of rowboats, sailboats, and even small steamers, carrying Finns who waved, cheered the imperial tourists, serenaded them, and proffered bouquets.[16]

The popularity of the House of Romanov in Finland was not based, however, primarily on public-relations gestures or the personal charm of the monarchs. First and foremost it was evidently due rather to the substantial benefits that Russian rule had conferred upon the country.

For the first time in centuries invasion and the imminent danger of invasion no longer threatened Finland. Although there were rumblings from across the Gulf of Bothnia from Scandinavianist irredentists (of whom more presently) in mid-century, the danger of Swedish attack was really minimal, and no other power offered a serious threat.

During the Crimean War British and French ships penetrated the Baltic, harried the Finnish coasts in a not very destructive way, and frightened the inhabitants of Helsinki into panic flight with a futile bombardment of outlying fortifications; but there was no real danger of serious invasion.

If Finland was spared the devastation of war, it was also largely spared the costs of war. During the last centuries of the Swedish period Finland had had to supply a considerable proportion of the manpower of Swedish armies. It had been heavily taxed to support military adventures that the realm could ill afford. Its economic development—delayed at best—was seriously hampered by the diversion of manpower and raw materials to military purposes. Now everything was different. Finland was not incorporated into the Russian military system; the Russian military conscription, one of the most cruel burdens weighing upon Russian subjects, had no counterpart in the Grand Duchy. The separate military and naval forces of Finland were negligible; so were the costs of their maintenance. At a Cadet School in Hamina (Fredrikshamn) ambitious young men of good family could be trained to become officers in the Russian army, and there were some volunteer Finnish Guards in the imperial service. In the Russian wars of the nineteenth century—the Crimean War, the campaign in the Caucasus, and the Turkish War of the 1870s—Finns did not participate except as volunteers. Russian military units were stationed at various places in Finland for its protection, but they were separate from the small Finnish forces.

Sheltered at long last from wars and the costs of war, Finland began to blossom internally. Helsinki, which had been an insignificant small town in Swedish times, achieved a new importance when the seat of government was transferred there from Turku (Åbo) in 1812, to be followed fifteen years later by the university. A monumental center in neoclassical style gave it an architectural dignity never before evident in any Finnish town. The new capital symbolized a new era in the development of the country. The first modest beginnings of industrialization appeared in Finland—notably in textiles, tobacco processing, and forest industries. Economic development received a strong impetus in 1812 from a generous gesture in St. Petersburg. So-called Old Finland, the territory in the southeast from the vicinity of St. Petersburg through the Karelian Isthmus to a point west of Viipuri (Viborg) which had been ceded to Russia in the eighteenth century, was reincorporated into Finland. Since Viipuri was an increasingly prosperous exporting center, especially for the lumber products of the interior, and became in time a manufacturing center, and since

Finland had its own customs border with Russia, inclusion of this area in the economic system of the Grand Duchy added to the general prosperity.

Most important of all, the first half-century of Russian rule saw the rise of a Finnish-language culture. The tongue of the great majority of the people, which had already produced a rich folklore, was now refined into an instrument for the transmission and spread of modern civilization. From this beginning there was to occur in the last quarter of the nineteenth century and the opening of the twentieth what can properly be called a national cultural explosion.

These developments did not proceed in an atmosphere free of strain, animosity, or repression. The Swedish-speaking minority, or Suecomans, from whose ranks there had proceeded some of the most important pioneers of the Finnish-language (Fennoman) movement, looked with increasing coolness, or even alarm, at the growing tendency of some Fennomans to claim for themselves the only right to represent the people, and to attack the privileges of the Suecomans. There was also increasingly, as time went on, some chafing at the restrictive attitude of Russian rulers. Nicholas I, in Finland as in Russia, represented the principle of autocracy. Like all the other successors of Alexander I, he took an oath to protect the privileges and rights of the Grand Duchy. Because of the wide latitude of action allowed him by the Acts of 1772 and 1789, he did not, in the opinion of Finnish historians, exceed the powers he believed he might claim, except possibly on one occasion. On the other hand, he made no concessions to the development of Finnish self-government. He saw no need to summon the Diet, and he did not do so. Freedom of speech and of the press had not been among the rights guaranteed the subjects of Gustav III; and censorship continued to weigh heavily upon the printed word in Finnish or Swedish. Severe though he may have been in ruling the Grand Duchy according to what he considered his rights, Nicholas never treated it as an integral part of Russia. Indeed, he approved a codification of the fundamental laws of the Russian Empire which declared in Article 4 that the throne of the Grand Duchy of Finland was indissolubly united with the imperial throne. Clearly, an integrated province could hardly have a separate throne.[17]

The humiliating outcome of the Crimean War, which seriously damaged the prestige of the monarchy, made it inevitable, in Finland as in Russia, that there should be increased pressure from below for greater freedom. To such pressure from Finns the government of Alexander II was for several years no more responsive than that of his father would have been. Alexander unquesionably felt benevolent toward his subjects, and he probably had a particularly warm spot in his

heart for the Finns, who had welcomed him on his first visit with un-
bridled enthusiasm. He did not, however, like to be told what he
should do, and he was faced with such horrendous complexities of
overdue reform in Russia that they presumably claimed most of his
attention and time. Censorship continued in Finland; and as time
went on one of the subjects that might not be discussed in print was
that of Finnish Diets, past or future.

A certain restiveness began to spread among educated Finns. They
were not, despite the censorship, completely cut off from the news of
western and central Europe; and European liberalism, hard-hit by the
general failure of the 1848 revolutions, was beginning by the late
1850s to revive and press for change. Educated Finns, too, felt the
need for freedom and a voice in government; specifically, they desired a revival of their legislative Estates. In various ways—by hints,
by veiled allusions in the press, by the construction of a handsome
assembly hall for the Estate of the Knights and Nobles, and even by
a daring speech by a university professor, Frans Ludvig Schauman,
in September 1856, delivered at the University's ceremony of celebration for the coronation of Alexander II—they gave voice to the desire
for "free and independent, law-making but law-abiding estates, under
a power-exercising but law-bound administration." In the breast of
the Finnish people, Schauman asserted, "there is rising a lively wish
to have soon and often the opportunity to meet, as prescribed in the
constitution."[18]

St. Petersburg was not pleased, and Alexander administered a sharp
rebuke to Schauman through the minister state secretary for Finland.
Nevertheless, by the spring of 1861 the tsar decided to compromise.
Acting upon the advice of some of his Finnish and Russian advisers
and against the advice of some others, he ordered the creation of a
committee consiting of twelve members from each of four Estates, to
meet in Helsinki to work on some problems. "I do not wish to act
against your constitution," he assured his Finnish advisers in St. Petersburg, and his manifesto setting up the committee indicated in a
vague way that sometime there would be a meeting of the Diet.[19]

The indefinite half-promise was far from reassuring to some Finns.
The constitutional tradition of Sweden and Finland, they held, included no warrant for such legislation by committee; and, given
Alexander's demonstrated reluctance to call an election, it seemed
possible that a meeting of the Diet might be indefinitely postponed
while this stopgap sort of legislation was repeated. There were protests, including the first political street demonstration in the history
of Helsinki mostly, it would appear, by university students, school-
boys and apprentices, who uttered the significant cry: "Hurrah for

the constitution!" News of the incident was telegraphed abroad and aroused comment in the European press. For the first time "the Finnish question" was beginning to draw international attention.[20]

Alexander capitulated. Acting upon the advice of Finnish counselors who previously had supported his committee policy but now changed their minds, he issued a rescript giving the assurance that the committee "should, in the questions that can be resolved only in a constitutional way, make recommendations to the Diet in its time, while the reports made by the deputies in other matters are referred to Our gracious decision."[21]

A relatively easy but significant victory for militant public opinion had been won in Finland. The handful of protesters were a far cry from the crowds that had convulsed so many European capitals a few years earlier; but their achievement was more far-reaching and long-lasting than that of some of the violent revolutionists had been. The restoration and recognition of the Diet had been wrested from a rather reluctant monarch; the functioning of the representative body could in a way be regarded as a creation of the people. Perhaps that explains in some measure the stubborn insistence of the Finns some years later on what they regarded as their constitutional rights.

Alexander II acted rather handsomely. "He did not want," as a Finnish statesman of the time wrote, "to make of us a Poland in miniature."[22] A new governor-general arriving in Helsinki announced that a Diet would meet as soon as the committee had finished its work. The committee labored efficiently and the tsar kept his word. Elections to the Diet were held in July and August 1863, and the monarch himself opened the historic session on September 18. His address, delivered in French, seemed to Finns to remove all ambiguity as to his relationship to Finland:

> Representatives of the Grand Duchy of Finland! Seeing You gathered about Me, I am happy to have fulfilled My promise and Your hopes.
>
> My attention has been directed for a long time to a certain number of questions successively raised, touching upon the most serious interests of the country. They remained in suspense in view of the fact that their solution required the cooperation of the Estates. Major considerations, of which the decision is reserved to Me, did not permit Me to bring together the representatives of the four orders of the Grand Duchy during the first years of My reign. Nevertheless, I took timely preparatory measures to arrive at this goal, and today, when circumstances are no longer of a nature to justify a longer delay, I have convoked

you. . . . My intention is to have worked out a legal bill that will . . . be submitted to examination by the Estates at their next meeting, which I intend to convoke in three years. In maintaining the principles of constitutional monarchy which are inherent in the customs [*moeurs*] of the Finnish people and of all its laws and of which all its laws bear the character, I wish to have included in this bill a more extensive right than that which the Estates already possess with respect to the regulation of customs dues and the right of initiative which in older days [*ancienne-ment*] they possessed, reserving for Myself, nevertheless, the right to take the initiative in all questions that concern the changing of the fundamental law. . . . It is for You, representatives of the Grand Duchy, through dignity, courtesy, and calm in Your deliberations, to demonstrate that free institutions, far from being dangerous, are a guarantee for order and well-being for the people, which in consultation with its Ruler and with practical understanding works for the development of its welfare.[23]

This flat commitment to the constitutional authority of the Estates was strengthened in the Diet Ordinance of 1869, approved by Alexander, in which it was provided:

Fundamental law can be enacted, altered, declared or repealed only on the representation of the Emperor and Grand Duke and with the consent of all the Estates. . . . If a question arises concerning a change or repeal of privileges, advantages or rights given to the estates, or concerning the concession of new privileges, what appears in the [1772] Form of Government is to be valid.

The passing reference to the Swedish Form of Government was reinforced in the tsar's confirmation of the ordinance:

While We reserve for Ourselves Our right, as it is guaranteed in the Form of Government of 21 August 1772 and the Act of Union and Security of 21 February and 3 April 1789 and has not been altered by specific wording in the following Diet Ordinance, We wish graciously to approve and confirm this Diet Ordinance as an unalterable foundation.[24]

Thanks to Alexander II, a secure basis for popular participation in the government by elected representatives had apparently been secured. Any ambiguities as to what Alexander I had meant seemed to the Finns to have been removed. Although Finland's government was far from being a parliamentary one, and still farther from being a democratic one, the Finnish political climate was beginning to bear some resemblance to that of western Europe.

How secure were these gains? Could they be reconciled with St. Petersburg's ideas of imperial security and efficiency? Could the Finns' newfound sense of nationhood coexist fraternally with the rising intolerant nationalism of many highly vocal Russians? Part of the answer to these questions would depend upon the personalities of the rulers who followed Alexander II; and, unfortunately for the Finns, neither of the last two Romanovs really understood the Finnish position. Alexander III, it is true, issued shortly after his succession in 1881 a formal confirmation of the Grand Duchy's "religion and fundamental laws, as well as the privileges and rights every estate in the aforesaid Grand Duchy in particular and all its inhabitants in general . . . have hitherto enjoyed according to the constitution of that country." A rescript to the governor-general accompanying the manifesto included a confirmation beginning. "Since we . . . have confirmed the constitution with which His Majesty Alexander Pavlovich of glorious memory endowed the Grand Duchy of Finland, and which Our departed dearly loved Father, His Majesty Emperor Alexander Nikolaevich developed with the consent of Finlands Estates. . . ."[25]

It is doubtful, however, that Alexander III ever understood what his father had intended with respect to Finland, or what the Finns' view of their position was. In the words of one prominent Finn who knew him, he was "intellectually not especially gifted," a judgment from which probably few historians would dissent. He was impatient of theoretical subtleties. His view of authority in the state had been shaped by his tutor, Konstantin Pobedonostsev, who distrusted human nature and declared in a well-known speech: "Constitutions as they exist are weapons of all untruth and the source of all intrigue."[26] Pobedonostsev's influence with the tsar was waning by the time the problem of Russo-Finnish relationships became acute, and Finland had never been a subject of particular interest to him. Alexander III was inclined to get along tolerantly with Finnish privileges on a practical basis and to practice the principle *quieta non movere*.[27] When a confrontation developed, however, between the constitutional principles of his imperial advisers and those of the Finnish Senate, there could be little doubt as to which side would make sense to the Autocrat of All the Russias.

The tsar's view of the Russo-Finnish relationship is perhaps best exemplified in a comment he wrote after reading a memorial from the Finnish Senate pointing out the necessity of getting the consent of the Diet for a unification of the Russian and Finnish systems of tariffs and coinage:

I have read this . . . memorial and am *astonished* as to what it is all about—a part of the Russian Empire or about a foreign state? What is Russia, finally? Does it belong to or is it a part of Finland or does the Grand Duchy of Finland belong to the Russian Empire? I find a unification of the tariff systems *essential*. It is not easy, requires work, but *it can be done*. Concerning the postal and coinage systems it is unforgivable that this distinction still exists, and a unification with the general imperial system is essential. I request that this matter be directed in this sense.[28]

However benevolent the intentions of the tsars toward Finland might or might not be, difficulties were bound to arise with respect to the internal problems of the Grand Duchy because of the divergent values of the Russian and Finnish societies. The two societies were interlocked, and the natural bias of the tsar was toward the Russian rather than the Finnish view.

Conversely, there was a question whether the limited degree of freedom accorded to the Finns would satisfy them in the long run. However privileged they might seem to be in comparison with the tsar's Russian subjects, they were by the 1880s still far behind most west European countries in terms of political and civil liberties; and their leaders were still very much in touch with the West. It was customary for sons of well-to-do families to travel to Scandinavia and the continent, either for formal education or merely for the sake of broadening their acquaintance with the world. They could hardly fail to be struck by the different atmosphere they found abroad.

One should not, of course, overestimate the effects of these foreign contacts. University students in Finland, were, as a whole, far from dangerous to the government. Swedish-speaking students, according to the later recollections of one of them, were for the most part strongly conservative and traditional in their views; in their case the exuberance and enthusiasm of youth were directed by the turn of the century to contemporary *belles lettres*, especially Scandinavian.[29] Finnish-speaking students were likely to be more militant; but their hostility was directed more against the privileged Swedish minority than against the government at St. Petersburg. A musical magazine, *Euterpe*, that some of the younger intellectuals and artists took over and turned into a general organ for literature and arts in 1902 aroused criticism, but mostly for its alleged preoccupation with eroticism and atheism.[30]

As for social radicalism, there seems to have been little of it in either linguistic intellectual camp. There was scant reason for the minister state secretary (who was also *ex officio* acting chancellor of the university) to inquire of the rector, Johan Philip Palmén, in the summer of 1891, whether any students were likely to attend a forthcoming international socialist conference in Brussels. The rector was able to reply with truth:

> I am completely certain that no Finnish student will pay any attention to it. They have never betrayed any interest in socialistic workers' questions and the meeting soon to be held will not tempt any of them from his quiet summer vacation at home in the interior of the country.[31]

 In general, then, for most of the reign of Alexander III, until the government began tinkering with the existing relationship between empire and grand duchy, there was little reason for St. Petersburg to be apprehensive about the Finns. They quarreled bitterly enough among themselves, in all conscience; but their animosities were directed at one another, not at Russian rule. In terms of public order the country seemed remarkably tranquil. The report that the governor-general required every two weeks from each of his district governors concerning noteworthy happenings in his district rarely mentioned anything more exciting than a train accident or the fact that a farmer had fallen off a wagon and had his left hand completely crushed by a wheel.[32]

CHAPTER 23

THE INTERNATIONAL AND MILITARY
BACKGROUND OF RUSSIFICATION

IN PART ONE of this book Edward Thaden has described some of the motivations and the measures involved in the tightening-up of Russian policy toward Finland by the end of the nineteenth century. One aspect which would warrant more detailed treatment than the length of this study permits is that of military considerations, and the Russian perception of a threat from abroad. We cannot fully understand what often seems an almost pathological suspiciousness of Finnish "separatism" on the part of some Russian authorities unless we take account of the peculiar geographical, strategic, and historical relationship of Finland to Russia.

After the reincorporation of "Old Finland" (the Karelian Isthmus and the Viipuri area) into the Grand Duchy, the southeastern border of Finland lay once more only about twenty miles from the Russian capital, St. Petersburg. In the eighteenth century, when it had lain considerably farther to the northwest, Sweden had twice mounted unsuccessful attacks in the direction of the Neva, thereby following a pattern established centuries before. After the Napoleonic Wars, with Sweden reduced to the position of a third-class power or less, a Swedish military threat no longer existed. For some decades the ancient enemy no longer worried military planners in St. Petersburg. There was, however, an exception to this generalization during the Crimean War, when, as we shall presently see, Sweden came close to joining the Anglo-French coalition against Russia. After another relative lull, there was a revival of Russian uneasiness at the end of the nineteenth century and particularly at the beginning of the twentieth, as an increasingly powerful and militant Germany seemed to be moving toward a collision with Russia. Sweden, if she should ally herself with Germany, could furnish a convenient base for an attack on Finland; and conceivably the Finns might rise to help the invaders against Russia.

There is an ironical parallel between Russian treatment of Finland during the last decades before World War I and in the last years before World War II. In each case (more particularly in the second) one of the considerations of Russian policy was to reduce the danger of a German attack through Finland—in the earlier case, with support from Sweden; in the latter, with support from the Finns themselves. In each case the policy was based on a false assumption and created precisely the threat it was intended to parry. There was no real menace from Sweden at the opening of the twentieth century, and certainly no likelihood of mass Finnish defection; but by 1914 the long-established loyalty of the Finns had been so seriously eroded by tactless imperial policies that few of them were inclined to oppose independence when the opportunity came, and by some of the population the German invaders were welcomed in the last year of the war. Similarly, in 1939 the pro-German and intensely anti-Soviet elements in Finnish society did not command enough mass support to bring about an attack on the Soviet Union; but the Winter War precipitated by Moscow and the harsh peace treaty that followed made it certain that when Germany did attack Russia in 1941 most Finns were either willing to cooperate with Hitler's forces or at least disinclined for some time to oppose such involvement. In the period we are surveying here there is an evident relationship between Swedish bellicosity and Russian fear of Finnish "separatism" on the one hand and, on the other, the ultimately self-defeating policies advocated or adopted by such military men as Bobrikov and Kuropatkin.

For some decades after the Congress of Vienna relations between Stockholm and St. Petersburg were characterized by an almost unprecedented cordiality. By the mid-nineteenth century, however, this cordiality had been undermined by the growth of Russophobia in Sweden and of the movement known as Scandinavianism.[1] The Scandinavianists constituted one of the fervent, liberal, nationalistic, and ideologically vague movements of which there were so many in the Europe of the early and mid-nineteenth century. Scandinavianism was created by university students and some liberal journalists, and bears some resemblance, in its idealism, intemperateness, and lack of realism, to the German Burschenschaft of a few decades earlier.

One of the most serious miscalculations by the Swedish Scandinavianists concerned Finland. To the general detestation that European liberals felt toward Nicholas I and Russia the Swedish Scandinavianists added a nostalgia for the vanished Swedish empire; they rekindled the traditional hatred of Russia as the historic national enemy. Finland had to be reconquered for the motherland. As one of the most enthusiastic of the Swedish youths put it during the Crimean War, "With cannon on our backs we shall swim over the Gulf of Bothnia and reconquer Finland." But such a program had little appeal for the Finns. The Scandinavianists failed to take into account two facts of prime importance: the peace and prosperity that Finland had enjoyed under Russian rule for nearly half a century and the rise of a Finnish national consciousness based largely upon the Finnish language.[2] If, however, Scandinavianism was generally based upon false assumptions, it never completely died out in Sweden before World War I, particularly with regard to Finland. To the irredentist yearning there was soon to be added a new preoccupation: the fear of Russian aggression in the northernmost part of the Scandinavian peninsula.

In the early 1850s the British repeatedly warned Sweden about the Russian menace. By January 1854 the Swedish foreign minister for the first time initiated a discussion with the British minister about the possibility of a Russian thrust to the Varanger Fjord. Thereafter, with increasing openness, King Oscar I (1844-1859) spoke of Russia's designs in the far north. To some Swedes this expression of concern seemed to be an excuse for pursuing Sweden's irredentist aims. When the Crimean War broke out in 1854 the Swedish government proclaimed its neutrality, but the neutrality was soon weighted heavily on the side of the Western allies. Even before the outbreak of hostilities the crown prince, soon to become Charles XV, was particularly intimate with the British chargé d'affaires, and gave him maps and useful information about the Russians. He was as passionate a Russophobe as any Scandinavianist, and hoped to avenge the defeat of Charles XII.

What the British tried hard to get from this Swedish cordiality was a Swedish alliance; what King Oscar clearly wanted was a reunion of Finland with Sweden and a reduction of Russia to "proportions that are less threatening to the future of Europe." An alliance proved to be impossible, in part because of British unwillingness to fulfill all of Sweden's conditions, including a commitment to fight indefinitely to reacquire Finland for Sweden. All that Sweden did get out of the war was the November Treaty of 1855, which included a pledge that Norway-Sweden should not cede to Russia any territory or concede any fishing rights, and a guarantee by the Allies that they would furnish whatever military forces might be necessary to support such a refusal. Publication of the treaty made it clear that the King's policy had changed to one of clear hostility to Russia; the agreement was, in the witty words of Metternich, *"défensif et offensant."* The Russians said they were astonished by this official expression of mistrust after forty years of good relations, and disclaimed any thought of expansion in the far north. The possibility that Sweden might be drawn more openly into the Anglo-French camp was obviated by the negotiations leading to the Peace of Paris in 1856, from which Sweden was excluded, to the clear disappointment of King Oscar.[3]

The Crimean War cannot have been without its effect on Russian official opinion. Although the full extent of Oscar's ambitions was not known in St. Petersburg, one could scarcely fail to note that Russophobia had grown in a large and vocal part of the Swedish public, which did not conceal its dissatisfaction with the territorial status quo. This mood was illustrated vividly in 1868, when a statue of Charles XII, the one-man suicide squad of the Swedish Empire, was unveiled in Stockholm. The symbolism of the statue, with a drawn sword extended in the direction of Finland, did not escape the notice of travelers.[4]

However unconcealed Russophobia and irredentism west of the Gulf of Bothnia might be, there was no particular reason for St. Petersburg to be worried about it for some decades; the Franco-British entente began to show cracks soon after the Peace of Paris. It was the appearance of a new great power in the Baltic—first an expanding Prussia and after 1871 a united Germany—that made the question of Swedish foreign policy once more a matter of interest to Russia. King Charles XV (1859-1872) and his brother, King Oscar II (1872-1907) retained the anti-Russian sentiments of their father; and Oscar, in particular, regarded his eastern neighbor as the "hereditary enemy."[5] Gustav V, Oscar's successor, was the son of one German princess and the husband of another.

It was not merely in the royal family that pro-German sentiment was evident in Sweden. Economic relations between Sweden and Germany grew rapidly more important in the last decades of the century, as German industrialization got into full swing. As early as the 1880s Germany displaced Britain as the principal source of imports into Sweden, and the process accelerated in the following decades. One Swedish historian remarks: "German commercial adventure went parallel with a general shift of opinion in favor of Germany."[6] In the cultural sphere German influence became even more pronounced. In 1873 the Riksdag made German the only foreign language in the three lower classes of the schools. Scientific and technical education was drawn largely from books in German. About one-half of the recipients of foreign-study grants in the period from the 1870s to 1914 went to Germany.[7]

Along with Germanophilism went an outspoken Russophobia from the mid-1880s on. A "General Defense Union" founded in 1890, with strong support particularly among upper-class elements, kept up effective propaganda for increased military expenditures. When Gov-

ernor General Bobrikov initiated his far-reaching changes in Finland
at the opening of the century, angry comment in Sweden reached
such a pitch that the Foreign Ministry was obliged by Russian displeasure to announce publicly that the anti-Russian sentiment in the
Swedish press had no official or semi-official character, an assurance
we may regard with some skepticism. "All probability indicates,"
says one historian, "that a large number of Swedes interpreted the
events in Finland as a sure sign that Russia harbored designs against
Scandinavia. In this connection the exiled Finns in Sweden undoubtedly played a rather great role as shapers of public opinion."[8]

If some important civilian sectors of the Swedish population were
pro-German, it hardly needs to be said that the Swedish officer corps
admired unreservedly the Prussian-German military system, which
had recently demonstrated its superiority over the armies of Austria
and France. Even the spiked helmet, the *Pickelhaube*, was adopted
as a symbol of this admiration. Young officers were often sent abroad
to complete their training in the military service of other countries;
and service in Germany enjoyed a decided preference over that in
other countries.[9] By the time of World War I it was reported that the
Swedish socialist leader Hjalmar Branting declared: "With the Swedish officer corps one cannot wage war against Germany."[10]

As the fateful year 1914 approached, anti-Russian sentiment in
Sweden increased. A new source of anxiety after 1905 was the quiet
diplomatic effort by the Russian government to secure the abrogation
of the humiliating provision of the Treaty of Paris that demilitarized
the Åland Islands. One practical reason for the attempt was St. Petersburg's wish to use the archipelago as a base for stopping the
smuggling of weapons by Russian revolutionaries through Finland.
As news of the negotiations leaked out to the Swedish public there
was a storm of alarmed indignation. The Åland Islands were, indeed,
of great strategic importance to Russia; they were of far greater importance to Sweden, because they lie much closer to Stockholm than
to the mainland of Finland. Even Branting, the reasonable, peace-
loving socialist leader, wrote in the newspaper *Socialdemokraten*:

> A newly created Russian fleet and a new Port Arthur six hours
> from the [Swedish] capital—that would be to have the colossus
> on our backs in a quite different way: it would clearly imply that
> the words of the Russian minister in Stockholm would acquire
> an emphasis as in a vassal state.[11]

In this cold-war atmosphere, pressure in Sweden for increased
armaments was so strong and opinions varied so greatly about the
desirable extent of rearmament that a constitutional crisis occurred

early in 1914. The king dismissed his ministers and dissolved the
Riksdag. A new election brought to power supporters of a greatly increased military budget—news that can hardly have caused much
rejoicing in St. Petersburg.

While a substantial segment of the Swedish people was thus moving
in the direction of Germanophilism and Russophobia, Berlin for its
part was making overtures for military cooperation. From 1910 on
conversations were held, on German initiative, between Moltke, Chief
of the German General Staff, and General Bildt, his Swedish counterpart, concerning possible joint military action "in case of an attack
on Sweden from the east." Bildt was interested; but he made it clear
that his country was making no commitments and was reserving its
complete freedom of action. Although apparently some sort of "hypo-
thetical" agreement was reached, Bildt left no doubt that there was no
prospect of a Swedish offensive in Finland; the time for that was
long past. The Germans did not get what they wanted.[12]

For all the widespread Russophobia, then, Sweden was not con-
templating offensive action against her eastern neighbor. Gustav V
believed as late as 1913 that Sweden could not avoid being drawn into
any general war, and that her place was at Germany's side.[13] Important
elements of Swedish opinion, however, were more cautious. Even the
Swedish foreign minister, Albert Ehrensvärd, was by no means certain that Germany would win a general war. He felt strong sympathy
with the Western powers, and wished to avoid any entanglement with
the big Teutonic brother. "Any choosing of sides in favor of one or
the other power group," he told the king, "diminishes the number of
our friends and makes our fate exclusively dependent upon a victorious outcome for the power with which we have joined."[14]

If there was never a real threat to Russia from Sweden, was there
a *perceived* threat in Russian eyes? This was the fateful question so
far as Finland was concerned; and the answer was hardly in doubt
by the decade before 1914. Extreme nationalist Russian newspapers
such as *Novoe vremia* and *Moskovskie vedomosti* seized upon the
offensive utterances from across the Baltic to document their own
propaganda. By the early 1890s *Moskovkie vedomosti* was expressing
distrust of Swedish neutrality. There were many signs, it declared,
that pointed to a rapprochement with Germany and the Triple Alliance. The Swedish armament program, it said, was inspired by Germany and directed only against Russia, as the construction of rail-
roads and fortifications in northern Sweden demonstrated. One means
of frustrating Swedish aggressive plans, the journal pointed out in
1893, would be to send Finnish young men subject to military service
into the interior of Russia for their training. This proposal was a clear

indication that the ultranationalist Russian journal shared with some ultranational Swedish journals the illusion that in case of a Swedish invasion there could be an armed rising of Finns to support the invaders. In an article in March 1895 *Moskovskie vedomosti* characterized Sweden as "a sentry post in the north for Berlin and the Triple Alliance." *Novoe vremia* expressed similar views.[15]

By the opening of the twentieth century the tension elsewhere in Europe was becoming acute. The conflict between Russian and Austrian interest in the Balkans was evident, and sharpening. There could be no doubt which of the antagonists Germany would support if war should break out. In such a case, the Russians believed, they could not discount the possibility of a Swedish attack. It would have seemed reckless to overlook the fact that Sweden's military expenditures had increased from 35.1 percent of her budget in 1880-1881 to 55.1 percent a quarter-century later. The Russian General Staff took seriously the possibility of a combined German-Swedish offensive against St. Petersburg, and by 1910 was working on mobilization plans accordingly.[16]

One of the symptoms—and magnifiers—of Russian distrust of Finnish loyalty in such an emergency was the long-drawn-out discussion about building an extension of the Finnish railways system from Oulu in the northwest to Tornio-Haparanda at the Swedish border, where it would connect with an extension of the Swedish network. The project was considered off and on from 1892, and the highest authorities in St. Petersburg blew hot and cold. The reasons advanced by the Finnish Diet for undertaking the work were economic; but some Russians regarded such justifications as disingenuous. In the spring of 1893 an article in *Russkaia starina* by I. N. Elenev made it clear that the writer was not deceived by specious Finnish talk about economic benefits. There already existed, said Elenev, a suitable route—the sea—for the rather insignificant trade between Sweden and Finland. The real purpose of the railway extension, he charged, was to connect the strategic railways of Sweden with the Finnish network, so that the Swedes could turn over the system to the Germans for a combined offensive into Russia. The whole scheme was a plot by the Swedish party in Finland, directed from Stockholm, to facilitate an invasion in the course of which the Finns would rise and try to rejoin their former motherland.[17]

During the following years the argument spread in all directions, and the controversy increased in bitterness, though Nicholas II approved the proposed Oulu-Tornio extension in 1896. The distinguished Finnish historian Tuomo Polvinen, who has studied the episode thoroughly, sums up his conclusions in these words:

The military circles of St. Petersburg were of the opinion that the policy adopted toward Finland of fitting it into the Empire served the interests of the army. Especial mistrust was felt toward the Swedish party in Finland, which, according to the Russian view, was directed from Stockholm. It was believed that the "Finnish separatists," despite all their assurances, were still, in their hearts of hearts, striving to detach themselves from Russia and reunite themselves with Sweden. On the other hand, as long as there were such currents in Finland, Sweden might experience the temptation to reconquer Finland. Not until Russian administration, language and manner of thinking had become completely dominant in Finland would Sweden be forced to bury finally its dream of revenge, and the northwestern boundary of the Empire would henceforth be secure.

All in all, one can regard it as certain that the fitting-in of Finland into the defense system of the empire was determined by one great question: the security of St. Petersburg. . . . It is certain that the tsar's holders of power in Russia at the time did not comprehend at all to what grave results the shortsighted policy, which judged the mentality of the Finnish people utterly wrongly, would lead.[18]

The urgency of the Finnish problem was perceived, however, in differing degrees as time passed. A Russian military plan drawn up in 1880 did not mention Finland at all. The basic Russian strategy was to hold the Vistula crossings until mobilization was complete and the Russian steamroller could get moving forward toward Berlin and Vienna. By 1899 a mobilization plan for the Finnish military district assumed the possibility that the enemy might land in Finland a force aiming at the capture of St. Petersburg. No real defense could be offered in the southwestern corner of the country; resistance should stiffen as the enemy pressed eastward. The Finnish railway system, which terminated on the north side of the Neva, should be connected with the Russian network by a difficult and expensive link across the watery barrier, to permit reinforcements to be sent to the northern front easily if necessary.

The Russian catastrophe in the Japanese War of 1904-1905 and the Revolution of 1905 brought about a completely new strategic situation in the Baltic. For all practical purposes the Russian army had ceased to exist. The Baltic fleet, which previously had been supposed to be available to harry German lines of communication with Finland, had been sunk at Tsushima. No longer was it possible to assume the inexorability of the Russian steamroller; now even western Poland and

Galicia were endangered. The base of the new Baltic fleet must be Kronstadt, just outside St. Petersburg, instead of undefended Libau, close to the German border. For the time being, until the military and naval forces could be rebuilt, Russian planners were forced to think defensively, and Finland was no longer of merely peripheral significance. The Finnish military district was abolished in 1905 and the commander of the Russian twenty-second army corps, stationed in Finland, was directly subordinated to the St. Petersburg military district. Landings by Swedish troops and a rising in Finland were still considered possible.[19]

This dangerous state of affairs and the sense of urgency it created may have been partly responsible for the second wave of Russification, which began about 1908. Undoubtedly the troublesome set of problems had a connection with Russian insistence on building the long-delayed rail link across the Neva River, an issue that aroused particular bitterness among Finns.

When one has said all that can be said about what might be called the rational motives for Russification, there still remains the irrational factor of intolerant, authoritarian Russian nationalism. It can hardly be an accident that the views of Russian military men who were directly responsible for shaping policy toward Finland were often expressed in journals such as *Novoe vremia* and *Moskovskie vedomosti*. Impatience with and often detestation of what was foreign and unwillingness to consider any other points of view were typical of both newspapers and some of the military men. The complexities of the world and the empire they brushed aside with simplistic analyses.

As Edward Thaden argues, one should not overestimate the influence of the extreme-nationalist press. But perhaps, also, one should not underestimate it, as it reflected a good deal of thinking in influential circles and shaped a number of attitudes. By the 1890s one of the favorite targets of *Moskovskie vedomosti's* and *Novoe vremia's* vituperations was Finland. The repeated charges of "Finnish separatism" were, in general, impossible to substantiate; but the course of action adopted on the basis of the assumption eventually made the assumption self-fulfilling.

CHAPTER 24

THE STORM GATHERS

IF RATIONAL or irrational considerations led some Russians to express dissatisfaction with what they considered Finland's anomalous position, the same ambiguity pushed some liberal-minded Finns up to or even beyond the bounds of prudence in their discussions. One insistent voice of discontent was the country's first modern newspaper, *Helsingfors Dagblad*, which was founded in 1862 and was edited after 1865 for twenty years by Robert Olaf Lagerborg (1835-1882). Although Lagerborg, following in the steps of his father, had begun his career in the Russian military service, he soon moved to civilian life, and was intellectually attracted to western Europe; *Helsingfors Dagblad* became the principal spokesman in Finland for liberal ideas.[1] This almost inevitably implied some degree of alienation from the Russian establishment. Even before Lagerborg became editor, *Dagblad* suggested that in case of a Great-Power conflict Finland should declare itself neutral and Russian troops should leave the country.[2] The idea did not disappear: in 1885 some Finnish newspapers were again speculating that in case Russia and England should go to war Finland might remain neutral.[3]

Before Heiden took office as governor-general in 1881, *Dagblad* declared in advance that he ought to be a complete cipher; thereby the journal prejudiced the new chief functionary against the Swedish party.[4] Nevertheless, Heiden, eager at first to be on good terms with the Finns, spoke of trying to obtain from St. Petersburg freedom of the press for Finland; and he had one of his subordinates sound out Lagerborg about the possibility of a meeting with him. The editor refused to accept any invitation from the governor-general, "since anything of that sort could easily be misinterpreted and arouse all sorts of suspicions and doubts about his paper's independence and freedom from all outside influences."[5]

Such bristly standoffishness was perhaps admirably high-principled; it was certainly unrealistic in the context of political facts. Carl Alexander Armfelt, who served during these troubled years in the Finnish State Secretariat in St. Petersburg, was to write some critical words in retrospect about the attitude of many of his countrymen (in this case officials rather than journalists) in the years before Russification got under way in earnest:

> They were too sure of the inviolability of their own positions even to hit upon the idea that they must be modernized, and whenever such a thought arose and steps were to be taken to carry it out they seemed to forget that they did not hold an independent position that would enable them to act independently of a power, a people, with which they had been brought together. . . . That power was, after all, a Great Power; our country merely a vassal country coming under it.[6]

Senator Karl E. F. Ignatius (1837-1909), a rather liberal Fennoman politician who was a member of the Finnish Senate from 1885 to 1909, writes in his unpublished memoirs about the poor timing and occasional utter tactlessness of some Finnish liberals:

> Although I sympathized in general with liberal ideas, an awareness of what the welfare of Finland required had made me take a more conservative standpoint in the questions of the development of our constitution, of freedom of religion and the press, etc. I had always regarded it as one of the greatest mistakes the liberal party made that at a moment unfavorable for us it pressed for codification of Finland's basic laws. It was clear that in such a codification the Russians would have the decisive word. . . . At a time when we had to summon all our ability in order to maintain Finland's autonomous position it was in my opinion sheer imprudence to try to appropriate still greater liberties. . . . It cannot be denied . . . that our newspapers, in the period when a somewhat freer press regime prevailed, were often guilty of utterances and comments that seriously compromised the whole country. When a Swedish [-language] newspaper in Viipuri, for example, reported a speech given at some celebration, in which Viipuri was compared to an outpost of civilization against the East, this was such an open expression of scorn for Russia that it aroused the greatest bitterness.[7]

With voices of intolerance, intemperateness, or imprudence raised in both the Russian-authoritarian and the Finnish-liberal camps, the tsar-grand duke was confronted by a set of extraordinarily difficult problems. Even an open-minded, well-informed monarch would have been hard put to deal equitably with both sides. Unfortunately for Finland, neither of the last two tsars was open-minded; and their sources of information about Finland were defective.

Aside from officials of the empire, whose bias was almost a foregone conclusion, the tsar had frequent personal contacts with only two individuals concerned with Finnish questions: the governor-general and the minister state secretary for Finland. The governor-general, being always a Russian and a military man and usually unable to converse in either of the two languages of the country he was administering, remained essentially foreign to her people. Even Heiden, who began his governorship with a warm respect for the Finnish people and had some awareness of their special traditions, turned against the principal Finnish spokesmen when the clash of imperial and local interests became sharp. The minister state secretaries in the last quarter of the century were, until Plehve, technically Finns; but all were Russian in their early careers and outlook, and at least one of them was as unperceptive about how Finnish politicians were thinking as any governor of Nizhnii-Novgorod or Saratov could have been.

The minister state secretary who was in office in the first years of Russification was Theodor Bruun (1821-1888). Although born in a manor house in Finland and elevated to the ranks of the Finnish nobility in 1863, he was educated in St. Petersburg, spoke Swedish and Finnish imperfectly, and had a long career in the Russian civil service behind him when he became minister state secretary in 1881, at the age of 60. Bruun was no zealot for absolute monarchy; he was well disposed toward his mother country and, to some degree, her institutions; and he used his influence (especially with Alexander II) in her behalf. On the other hand, he believed that Finland was not a state but a conquered province and had no real constitution; the Diet, in his opinion, was only an advisory body, and far-reaching Finnish constitutional claims were unjustified. In 1883, when the question of press freedom was raised in the Diet, he asserted that the Estates had tried to encroach upon the jurisdiction of the monarch. In the preceding year, when it had been proposed that the Diet should be given the right to initiate legislation instead of merely acting upon the proposals of the tsar, he had urged that the proposal be rejected. Bruun was attacked in the Finnish press as none of his predecessors had been: in 1886 he was denounced simultaneously by the three principal newspapers, which represented quite different political orientations and were usually hostile to one another.[8]

Bruun's successor, Johan Casimir Ehrnrooth (1833-1913) was even more unsympathetic to the aspirations of his compatriots. After a successful career in the Russian army he was sent by Alexander II to Bulgaria, then a Russian client state, where he ran the country with such ruthless disregard of constitutional forms that he became known in some circles as "the Finnish dictator of Bulgaria." Having settled

Bulgarian affairs more or less to his satisfaction, he returned to Russia in 1881; the next year, with no apparent qualifications for the post, he became assistant minister state secretary for Finland; in 1888 he succeeded to Bruun's position.[9]

From such a man no understanding of constitutionalism could have been expected; and none there was. While he was still Bruun's assistant the matter of press freedom for Finland came under discussion in St. Petersburg. Three of the Finnish Estates—the nobility, the clergy, and the burghers—petitioned the monarch for freedom of the press. Far from supporting the request of his fellow countrymen, or even forwarding it noncommittally, Ehrnrooth opposed it in the strongest terms. The supporters of the proposed reform, he declared, were "saturated with so-called liberal tendencies"; a relaxation of censorship would "facilitate extremist attacks";

all the organs of the press . . . would act in united opposition to the press administration; with permissible and impermissible methods they would influence public opinion. . . . Satire, ridicule, insinuation, guile, flattery, threats, intimidation and everything would be let loose. . . . The law about press censorship promises to become . . . the point of departure for greater unrest in society than ever before has been seen.[10]

Ehrnrooth was almost universally condemned by his political contemporaries in Finland. Senator Karl Ignatius asserts in his unpublished memoirs:

Finland probably never had a more happy-go-lucky minister state secretary. . . . Gifted with a good mind, he thought he need never make the slightest effort to familiarize himself with [official] matters. He did everything in the easiest way.[11]

It is not surprising that in the Diet of 1891 a speaker declared:

The men who in recent years have presented our sentiments to the Monarch have, as a result of long-lasting activity outside the boundaries of this country, not been well enough acquainted with our social order—not only its outward contours but also the spirit that permeates it—to be able to conduct their responsible office successfully.[12]

Despite his pro-Russian and authoritarian bias, Ehrnrooth was dismissed from office in 1891, possibly because of his negligent conduct of affairs. His successor, Woldemar von Daehn (1838-1900), was an abler and more conscientious public servant; but in the end he proved powerless to defend his country's interests, even in the restricted sense in which he viewed them. He was born in a manor house in southeastern Finland, attended the Cadet School at Hamina, underwent a course at the Academy of the Russian General Staff, became a captain and then a major, was stationed for several years in Georgia, and ended his military career with the rank of major general. In 1877 he married Princess Nina Sviatopolk-Mirskii, daughter of one of the oldest Russian aristocratic families. She appears to have disliked Finland all her life; and the two von Daehn sons grew up as thoroughgoing Russians. In 1882 von Daehn renewed his acquaintance with his homeland, upon being appointed governor of the Viipuri district. Three years later he was made a member of the Finnish Senate and became chief of its section for civil administration. Twelve years later he was recalled to St. Petersburg to become Ehrnrooth's assistant, and in 1891 he succeeded him in office.[13]

While in the Senate he associated himself with the minority of senators supporting Yrjö-Koskinen, the Fennoman leader, with whom he maintained a frank and friendly correspondence up to his death. Von Daehn's family, like some of the others in "Old Finland" was of German origin and looked with suspicion on the Suecoman upper class that dominated Finnish administration and politics in the nineteenth century. He was convinced that this class could not or would not accommodate itself to the demands of the time and changed circumstances in Russia and Finland. While minister state secretary he attributed to the Swedish party a desire for reunification with Sweden, with which he said it maintained secret connections; it was impossible, he said, for the government to trust it.[14] To Yrjö-Koskinen he wrote that the Suecomans "excel in peddling every sort of lie."[15]

Von Daehn was, as we shall see presently, capable of genuine sympathy with peasants in their misery—a quality none too common among either Russian or Suecoman aristocratic landowners. He was, then, neither the typical Suecoman landed aristocrat, clinging to the interests of his class and, secondarily, of his country, nor the typical Russian administrator, to whom everything that was not Russian was of secondary importance. He was probably the best mediator that Finland could have had in the first difficult years of gathering Russification; but he was not good enough. No one appointed to his office would have been good enough. Some Finns said bitterly that he was not *nearly* good enough.

Shortly after von Daehn became minister state secretary he was faced with the problems caused by the first phase of Russification, which became more acute as the years passed. His attitude was one of caution and conciliatoriness. He never, apparently, believed that the Finns had a good legal case. He did not oppose—in fact, he apparently favored—a decree of 1891 providing that the offices in the governor-general's chancery and the state secretariat should be filled mostly with Russians. He preferred to forego statements of Finland's constitutional rights and concentrate upon stopping, by friendly persuasion, measures he considered particularly dangerous to his country. During Ehrnrooth's illness he countersigned—and apparently even encouraged the tsar to issue—the Postal Manifesto, the first overt measure of Russification. This action exposed him to sharp condemnation in Finland, where he was even denounced as a "traitor to the fatherland."[16]

This was unjust: the minister state secretary worked consistently to retain as much of his country's freedom as could be salvaged. In practical terms he was perhaps hampered by his failure to move about in Russian society and make useful contacts; some of his compatriots criticized him for not finding out in advance about measures detrimental to Finnish interests.[17]

Von Daehn was conscious of his isolation and impotence. "You ask me questions," he wrote to Yrjö-Koskinen, "as if I had in my hand the tiller of the empire, whereas I haven't even the smallest piece of rope. . . . For the moment I don't see what people are doing, either in St. Petersburg or in Helsingfors."[18] In a conversation with Ignatius he characterized perfectly the problem of dealing with a tsar: "When a person regards himself as Providence, there can be no question or discussion. The decrees of Providence are always wise, and against them one can accomplish nothing."[19]

The sharpening conflict between political views in Helsinki and St. Petersburg brought about a marked change in the attitude of Governor-General Heiden. As we have seen, he brought with him to Finland a cordial attitude toward the people, and his first tours of the country confirmed his friendly predisposition. It is true that in a letter published in *Stockholm Dagblad* on October 21, 1884, by an anonymous Finn (probably Baron Viktor von Born), Heiden was accused of being "first and foremost a Russifier of the type traditional in the East."[20] This view, however, was not generally shared in Finland. In 1889, in response to an appeal from the Senate, the governor-general signed his name to a short refutation of anti-Finnish polemics in *Moskovskie vedomosti*, and with the tsar's permission the refutation was published in *Pravitel'stvennyi vestnik*. The delighted Senate offered him a testimonial dinner; but he declined for fear of provoking anger in Russia. Nevertheless, when he left in the summer for vacation on his estate in Russia the whole Senate was assembled at the railroad station to see him off—an unprecedented tribute.

The next few months, however, saw a change in Heiden's attitude.

Moskovskie vedomosti continued its attacks and was joined in them by *Novoe vremia*. In St. Petersburg irritation grew over the resistance of the Finnish Senate to the imperial government's proposals for unifying the Russian and Finnish systems of postal service, tariffs and money. The governor-general was not unaffected by this sharpening of the official mood. Even in the privacy of his home Heiden may not have had much surcease from anti-Finnish propaganda: his wife was reputed to be intensely hostile to Finland and to contribute financial support to *Moskovskie vedomosti*. The nationalist Russian press was now making Heiden one of its targets, and he could scarcely remain indifferent to the danger. He had taken the first steps toward disengaging himself from the more extreme positions of the Senate even before the conflict reached a crisis. Now, under attack, he was forced to abandon his previous plan of becoming a sort of Finnish premier, mediating between the tsar and the Senate. As he faced the necessity of choosing between Russian ministers and Finnish senators, his decision could not be in doubt.[21]

The governor-general presided over the meetings of the mixed Finnish-Russian committee created by the Finnish Senate in 1890 to examine the proposals worked out by the Weissenberg committee for the codification of Finnish laws. From the opening meeting of the committee Heiden showed himself hostile to the Finnish point of view, and the sessions turned into a series of perpetual and fruitless wrangles.[22]

Against the growing policy of asserting Russian prescriptive rights the Finns were almost powerless to do anything. Certainly Ehrnrooth was of no help to them as long as he remained in office, and he was officially in charge of Finnish interests until 1891. News leaked out that a plan for unifying the postal systems of the two countries was being worked out in St. Petersburg without consultation of the Finnish Diet or Senate. The speakers of the four houses of the Diet traveled to St. Petersburg on their own initiative to present to the tsar an address voicing their concern about the direction in which policy regarding Finland seemed to be moving. Since they were not traveling as authorized emissaries of their Estates, however, Alexander III refused to receive any of them except Archbishop Renvall, to whom he granted an audience in his episcopal capacity but whom he refused to let read the text of the address.[23]

It was, as Thaden has suggested, probably the method of procedure on the postal question rather than the intrinsic importance of the subject that troubled the Finns. A protest by the Senate that the matter was one which could not be decided in a purely administrative way but required consultation with the Diet was brushed aside; so was a compromise offered by the Finnish side. On June 12, 1890, Alexander III issued his Postal Manifesto, the first measure taken in St. Petersburg which, in the opinion of Finns, violated their constitution. Von Daehn, who, as Ehrnrooth's assistant, had been a member of the postal committee and had countersigned the manifesto, rejected the storm of criticism that his action had raised. "The question itself," he wrote to Senator Ignatius,

> as it lies before us, is of subordinate importance. If on such a question His Majesty is bothered by an appeal to the Diet, this may (and according to Ehrnrooth's view certainly will) be received as an act of disobedience on the part of the Senate. Thereby the position of the country will be exposed to injury in points that are very much more sensitive than the one in question. Such questions are decided not only on juridical but primarily on political grounds.[24]

A few days later he received word that the Senate was considering a refusal to "promulgate"—that is, to publish in the official gazette and have read in the churches of the country—the tsar's decree establishing the principles on which the postal unification was to be accomplished. "The decision of the Senate has astonished me," he wrote to Ignatius,

> for I really cannot understand the motives that had led to its behavior. His Majesty's decision is made, and thus it is unshakable. It has been communicated to the Senate to be promulgated, and the Senate is an executive authority that has to fulfill His Majesty's commands. . . . The Senate has risked the existence of the institution itself. . . . All these independence ideas have support neither in law nor in history.[25]

In this unqualified espousal of the authoritarian point of view von Daehn defined an issue that was to become acute a few years later. If the tsar violated, or seemed to violate, the constitutional rights of Finland, might the Senate, or any other body, legitimately oppose the imperial will? Von Daehn, for all his love of his native country, had given the answer that some Finns were to follow consistently and others were to reject: to oppose the monarch was not only impracticable; it was illegal, wrong, and dangerous to the institutions of the country.

The Senate promulgated the Postal Manifesto; but there were already clear signs of dissent. Alexander von Weissenberg, who had become Procurator (roughly speaking, attorney general) of the Senate in 1886, now resigned his position. His ostensible reason was a desire to retire to private life; but he let it be known that he was protesting against what he considered the illegality of the Postal Manifesto. Numerous expressions of sympathy came to him from private citizens, and university students serenaded him, to the annoyance of Heiden.[26]

Except for the principle involved, the Postal Manifesto did no damage to Finnish interests; it left the internal postal system of the country unchanged. Other proposals under consideration for unification of the systems of money and tariffs were allowed to drop—mostly, it is probable, because it seemed that the suggested changes would inflict considerable hardship upon Finland. No concern for Finnish sensibilities, however, was evident in St. Petersburg's treatment of a very sensitive subject, the Finnish legal system. The Diet had worked out and passed a code of criminal law. The tsar, after considerable hesitation and after reversing his decision once, approved the code in December 1889; it was to go into effect in January 1891. In the course of the intervening year, under the pressure of his advisers, Alexander had second (or third) thoughts. At the last minute, in December 1890, on the advice of the newly formed Tagantsev committee, he suspended the code until the Diet should have time to make certain changes.[27]

The legislators were reluctant to make the alterations desired by St. Petersburg. They saw in the new terminology a danger of legal absorption of Finland into Russia and the loss of Finland's autonomy, and asserted that the indefinite suspension of the code could not constitutionally take place without the concurrence of the Estates. They worked out a revision which failed to satisfy St. Petersburg. Since nothing could be done until the next meeting of the Diet in 1894, some advisers—notably Heiden and the Russian minister of justice—urged Alexander to proclaim the Tagantsev committee's proposed alteration without the consent of the Finnish representative body. After tactful persuasion reluctantly undertaken by von Daehn, the tsar yielded to Finnish opinion. The matter was postponed until the Diet of 1894 and an agreement was achieved then. Thanks largely to the monarch's forbearance, a showdown between the views of Russian officials and Finnish political leaders, which could have resulted only in catastrophe for the latter, had been averted. Meanwhile a second protest resignation had taken place: Senator Robert Montgomery laid down his office the day the manifesto suspending the law was published.[28]

It was clear that battle had not yet been fully joined on basic constitutional issues, and anxiety in Finland was widespread. Senator Ignatius later described the dismay with which members of the Senate had learned from Heiden, after his return from St. Petersburg in December 1889, that sweeping changes were under consideration:

> It was one of the saddest moments I experienced in the Senate. We all looked with anxiety and pain toward the dark future that threatened the fatherland. The Christmas holidays that followed were for the members of the Senate a difficult time of trial, marked by frequent conferences, taxing work, and sleepless nights.[29]

Ehrnrooth's sister wrote him at about the same time (without apparently, having much effect on his actions):

> [There is] gloom here in the city and, it is reported, it is great in the whole country. There is constant chatter, and no one dares to speak aloud about his political apprehensions, but like a nightmare there lies over every question [the thought]: what is threatening us from the east?[30]

Senator Yrjö-Koskinen, the leader of the Finnish party, who had, on the whole, been getting on rather well with the imperial authorities and who was in later years to become a spokesman for a policy of compliance, assessed the state of affairs gloomily but defiantly in a letter to von Daehn on December 22, 1890. Evidently he was impressed—and depressed—by the Russification measures that had already been applied to the Baltic Provinces.

> That we have committed many mistakes is possible. . . . But the Slavophile party . . . would have flung itself upon us in any case, after having accomplished its task in Poland and the Baltic Provinces. . . . When one is weaker, one is always in the wrong. The sheep always muddies the water for the wolf, even when he is downstream. . . . The national feeling that has developed in Finland is built upon the basis of history and will not so easily crumble. Without doubt, since might overrides right, we can be made rather unhappy—individually and especially as a nation; but to have our life taken from us, in a word, to be Russified— never. . . . [According to] M. Ordin we should abandon our institutions, our language, receive a Russian administration with all that crew of employees whose excellence is so well depicted by Gogol in his *Inspector General*. These Russian amenities ought to be appreciated. And our big fault is to be unwilling to accommodate ourselves to the disinterested wishes of our benefactor. From the beginning we were told, don't worry about what

Moskovskie vedomosti says and writes; it is nothing. But in that case how does it happen that the program of the Slavophile organ is being realized little by little by governmental measures in all its details? *Moskovskie vedomosti*, to judge from the facts, is only the organ of Messrs. Durnovo and Manasein (the latter well known for his frolics in Estonia and Livland), who cover themselves with the sovereign will. This state of affairs is not hard to unravel when one sees . . . [that] all the *agents provocateurs*, Ordin and Co., are taken under the protection of the censorship. . . . How far are they going? What is the ultimate goal of this campaign of destruction? What will be left to us in the end?[31]

Yrjö-Koskinen returned to this same pessimistic theme more than once. For the freshly blossoming culture of his nation he saw a serious threat. "Because of the attacks in part of the Russian press and particularly because of certain measures which seem to prove that the supreme power is strongly influenced by the Slavophile agitation, a feeling of sadness and desolation has taken hold of the entire nation." Everyone is convinced that Finnish culture "will have a dismal end as soon as the country no longer fully enjoys its autonomous institutions and especially if the Russian language is imposed on us as a vehicle of superior culture"—a process that he saw as already beginning. "The Finnish people asks itself . . . why should anyone want to destroy a state of affairs that harms no one?"[32]

Governor-General Heiden soon began to feel the effects of the Finns' alarm and indignation over his changed attitude. A ball that he gave was boycotted by Helsinki society. The only persons who came were those who felt obliged to by their official positions; all the others invited offered some excuse for staying away. It was reported that Senator Lerche, when he appeared at the ball, was asked by his host why he had not brought his wife and daughter. When Lerche replied that they both had caught cold, the governor-general exclaimed with evident irritation: "It is remarkable how many cases of colds have broken out in the city just now." Lerche answered quietly: "Your Excellency, there are such cold winds blowing from the east just now!"[33]

The widespread uneasiness in the country resounded publicly when the Diet met in November 1890. By custom each of the four Estates made a response to the opening speech from the throne. Whereas these addresses were usually bland and stereotyped, in 1890 they constituted unprecedented admonitions to the tsar. Remarkably enough, the most outspoken reply came from the Peasant Estate, usually the least politically minded of all. Its speaker, Carl Johan Slotte, declared bluntly:

Finland's Peasant Estate would not regard itself as fulfilling its duty at this moment if it failed to make known most obediently that the quiet peace that even very recently was dominant in the [people's] state of mind has recently . . . been changed, even in the most lowly huts, to anxiety and grief. But the people of Finland cannot surrender itself to despair about its lawful rights. It knows that Emperor Alexander II, of glorious memory, established, as He himself said, the special form of government of this country for all time. . . . Finland's Peasant Estate and Finland's whole people know that their loyalty and sense of duty have . . . constantly remained unaltered . . . , and therefore they raise their eyes in the time of their distress to His Majesty, seeing in Him the strong Protector of the laws and social order of the land.[34]

Upon receiving translations of the four addresses, the tsar wrote irritably in the margin of the one from the peasants: "I should like to know what is arousing their anxiety and grief, since nothing has been changed and no law has been altered." To avoid a harsh open rebuke to Slotte from the monarch, the Peasant Estate agreed to remove from its minutes everything relating to the distressing incident.[35] In a rescript to the governor-general, which was read to the Diet, Alexander disclaimed any intention of encroaching on the rights and privileges of Finland; "My intentions," he declared, "do not include changing the principles of the order valid in the country for its internal government." The Diet received this message with cheers, despite the fact that the tsar had not defined what he considered the limits of Finland's internal government.[36]

By now Alexander was thoroughly annoyed with those Finns he considered unruly, and particularly with the Senate. He soon found an opportunity to show his displeasure. In the summer of 1891 he went to eastern Finland to review the Finnish troops at Lappeenranta (Villmanstramd). The governor-general and the Senate had traveled to Viipuri to greet the ruler and, decked out in full uniform, stood waiting for him in the district governor's mansion. The tsar, accompanied by von Daehn and others of his suite, entered. He shook hands with all the senators, but spoke only a few words. The empress permitted her hand to be kissed, and the ceremony was over. The imperial party proceeded by train to Lappeenranta, taking along only the governor-general and several other functionaries, including only one senator, Carl Tudeer, who was a favorite of Heiden's and was regarded by his colleagues as a conscienceless careerist. The other senators were left

393

in the lurch, with nothing to do but return to the capital. The affair had been an unmistakable snub.[37]

Meanwhile, one head had rolled. Leo (Leopold Henrik Stanislaus) Mechelin (1839-1914) became in course of time the most irritating Finnish thorn in the flesh of Russian nationalists. Enormously gifted intellectually, very learned, and possessed of apparently boundless energy, he combined a professorship in political science with writing and manifold public activities. From 1872 he was a member of the Diet, first as a representative of Helsinki in the house of the Burghers and, after being ennobled in 1876, as a member of the Estate of the Knights and Nobles. He was appointed to the Senate in 1882. He traveled abroad frequently, was well versed in foreign languages, and made acquaintance with numerous foreigners who were in due course to become eloquent advocates of the Finnish cause. An admirer of Western political institutions, in 1880 he founded a liberal party, which, however, never obtained a strong following.[38]

Mechelin's energy, self-confidence, and occasional tactlessness antagonized a number of influential people, both Finnish and Russian. His controversial political activity from 1886 on increased the number of his adversaries. Tired of the continual attacks on Finland by the Russian nationalist press, he edited in the Russian language a collection of documents about Finland's constitutional law; the pamphlet was suppressed by Heiden. Then in 1886 he published abroad a *Précis du droit publique du Grand-Duché de Finlande*, which was later translated into English and Russian. In this work he developed the thesis that was thenceforth to underlie all his polemical writings and activities: that the union of Russia and Finland did not result in a fusion into one state, but that the two states retained their separate identities and forms of government. He published another treatment of the same subject in Germany in 1889: *Das Staatsrecht des Grossfürstenthums Finnland*, which was part of a respectable scholarly collection of works on public law. In the next few decades he followed these first publications by numerous books and pamphlets on the same subject in five languages.[39]

It was Mechelin who raised the discussion of Finland's relationship from the level of the chauvinistic Russian press to the level of scholarship. His *Précis* stimulated Ordin to write a scholarly refutation; the battle thus joined continued for years. Tagantsev once remarked that Mechelin "has rendered Russia no small service in occasioning in Russia the present discussion about Finland by his juridical-writing and in showing the necessity of formulating its state laws in conformity with the real character of its position as part of the Russian Empire."[40]

By early 1890 Mechelin had undoubtedly aroused irritation in Russian administrative circles. In May he gave occasion for his dismissal. An international conference of penologists was to meet in St. Petersburg. The Finnish senator invited its organizing committee to include in the program an excursion to Finland which would include a visit to the Saimaa Canal and a banquet in Helsinki. He took charge of all the negotiations himself, informing his fellow senators only after all the arrangements had been made and not informing the governor-general at all. Heiden, learning of the plans only when someone asked him about the role he was to play in the festivities, was furious. Summoning Mechelin to his office, he informed him that further cooperation between them was impossible. The senator was obliged to resign, and was widely regarded as a martyr to the cause of Finnish freedom. He was honored with addresses, telegrams, visits from deputations, and serenades, as well as at least one poem.[41] Mechelin's public career was by no means over; indeed, its most important part was still ahead. His forced resignation, however, had served as a clear warning of what might happen to persons, however highly placed, who went too far in defying or ignoring Russian authority.

Against gloomy forebodings von Daehn continued to urge calm, prudence, and tact. He disliked what he regarded as the abrasive, doctrinaire liberalism of Mechelin. "It is regrettable," he wrote Yrjö-Koskinen in July 1890, two months after Mechelin's fall, "that the Senate has identified itself completely with Mechelin, to the point of effacing itself entirely behind his person. . . . You know my opinion of the Lagerborg-Mechelin politics. We are now reaping the bitter fruits of it. If that does not open the eyes of the country, it is Jupiter who has willed it."[42]

The minister state secretary was soon to discover that whether or not the Finns had learned a lesson the Russians certainly had not. In November 1892 the Bunge conference established to work out common law for Russia, and Finland began its meetings in St. Petersburg. Von Daehn, as minister, was the principal Finnish representative on the committee, and within a few weeks he ran into trouble. It became evident that the purpose of the Russian members was to channel all Finnish legislation of any sort through appropriate Russian ministers before it was presented to the tsar; it was no longer the minister state secretary for Finland who would decide whether a particular law affected Russian interests. In short, all effective direct contact between organs of the Finnish government and the monarch should cease. As in the case of the committee on Finnish fundamental law a few years earlier, the conflict grew bitter and the opposing views could not be reconciled. On one occasion, objecting to an exposition by Heiden, von Daehn was silenced by chairman Bunge; he appealed to the tsar and was supported by him.[43]

Von Daehn was still worried about what he regarded as imprudent statements in Finland about the fundamental laws of the state, and wrote to Helsinki to urge caution.[44] He was only partially successful; the Diet did vote to send a petition to the tsar. While conceding the possibility "that not only the needed internal improvements in the Grand Duchy but also the common advantage of the Empire . . . required the alteration of established laws," the legislators urged that in such a case the changes be made in accordance with the procedure prescribed by the fundamental laws of Finland.[45]

When Alexander III died at Livadia in the Crimea in November 1894, von Daehn quickly telegraphed the new tsar, requesting permission to wait upon him to discuss Finnish affairs. Upon receiving a favorable reply, he hastened to Livadia and without difficulty got Nicholas' signature on the traditional guarantee of Finland's rights, as well as an oral declaration by the new ruler that he was thereby carrying out the expressed wishes of his father.[46]

Indeed, Nicholas II seemed at first very well disposed toward the Grand Duchy. Possibly because of his intervention, attacks on Finland in the Russian press ceased for a time. When Bunge presented the recommendations of the conference to him, the monarch told him that the situation did not require any change in the relationship between Finland and Russia. A delegation from the four Finnish Estates arriving to greet the new ruler was granted an audience of special warmth. At the coronation in Moscow, von Daehn was awarded the Order of Alexander Nevskii. In July 1896 the tsar approved a proposal by the Finnish Senate and von Daehn extending the Senate's powers in administrative powers and rejecting a proposal by Heiden that would have restricted those powers severely.[47]

All this was very gratifying; but von Daehn kept his fingers crossed. "It would be a gross illusion," he wrote Yrjö-Koskinen shortly after the new tsar ascended the throne, "to believe that an Emperor of Russia, however well-disposed toward Finland, would wish to place himself in opposition to all his Russian people to please the liberals of Helsingfors and the minister state secretary."[48] Soon there were signs of possible trouble ahead. "His Majesty told me yesterday," the minister wrote in November 1896, "that he hopes there will not be at the [forthcoming] Diet any addresses like the one that was made in 1891 and that caused much pain to his late father. I replied to him that I believe there will not be any, but that there are always people who will say foolish things."[49]

Further signs of mistrust appeared. In the autumn of 1896 Heiden resigned his position. He was seventy-five years old, not in the best of health (he had less than three years to live), and probably weary of his perpetual conflicts with the Senate. The tsar's formal acceptance of his resignation took the form of an open rescript of January 13, 1897, which delivered a scarcely veiled warning to Finland:

> Whatever may be the aims of individual persons or representatives of political parties in Finland or the conceptions into which they have let themselves be misled, I believe in the straightforward honesty and devotion of My faithful Finnish people and remain convinced, in accordance with My dear Father's idea, that this country's deepest interests and its further progress will be based on the country's indissoluble union with the great Empire, the fate of which has been entrusted to Me by divine Providence.[50]

Disquieting as the implications of this utterance might have been, it barely escaped, according to von Daehn, being much worse:

> The rescript was drawn up in its entirety for the minister of war, our most rabid enemy. I don't know how the passage about Finland took form, but I do know that the emperor struck it out and gave it his personal wording. The minister of war was furious, and tried to invoke for the emperor the shade of his father, naturally in his own way, but that didn't work, for the simple reason that the emperor knows and appreciates better than the minister of war the intentions of the departed [monarch], who at bottom loved Finland. . . . From it I augur well for the future.[51]

However hopeful a face the minister might try to put upon the rescript, a change was clearly taking place in Nicholas' attitude toward Finland and especially toward von Daehn himself. Finding that he had lost virtually all his influence at Court, and being wearied with service (he, too, had only about three more years to live), he asked the tsar in November 1897 for permission to resign. His request was granted in the spring of 1898. He left office, and Russia, pessimistic about Finland and disappointed in his former high regard for Russia.[52]

The departure of Heiden and von Daehn from the scene marked the end of the first stage of Russification, the period of residual good will, relative restraint, and the observance of old forms. After an interval of several months Heiden was replaced by the egregious Bobrikov, in comparison with whom Heiden looked almost good to the Finns in retrospect. Von Daehn's office remained open for several months;

his work was carried on for the time being by his former assistant, Victor Napoleon Procopé, who exercised no influence at all.

Within a few months the office of minister state secretary for Finland was given, in violation of all precedent, to the Russian politician Plehve, who was no friend to constitutionalism in any place or form. The tenuous link between the tsar and the Finnish people that von Daehn had struggled to preserve had snapped. Now there was no Finn with the right of access to the monarch. All communications from Finnish officials and representatives reached Nicholas—who was notoriously susceptible to persuasion by those around him—through the channels of Russian advisers who were either indifferent or hostile to what Finns considered their established rights. For Finland, catastrophe was at the door.

CHAPTER 25

FINLAND'S DIVIDED HOUSE

WHEN THE LONG-DREADED full-scale attack of the Russifiers struck Finland the nation was in no condition to adopt a policy of united resistance. Although their dismay over the turn of events was almost universal, the Finns' internal conflicts were so bitter that no agreement on a national policy could be achieved.

Aside from the universal differences of human temperament between the militant and the nonmilitant, Finland was torn by three internal schisms. There was a cleavage between rural landowners and landless peasants. There was a cleavage between industrial workers and their employers. There was a cleavage between the traditional political, economic, and cultural elite of the Swedish-speaking aristocracy and haute bourgeoisie on the one hand and, on the other, a Finnish-speaking coalition of a rising bourgeoisie, a militant intelligentsia, a stratum of zealous politicians, and a class of prosperous peasants.

As the authority of the Finnish Diet was a central issue in the conflict between Finns and Russifiers, so the composition of the Diet was involved in all three of the principal internal conflicts in the Grand Duchy. This body, essentially a continuation of the Finnish part of the eighteenth-century Swedish Riksdag, claimed to represent the nation; but its claim was open to serious question. It retained its thoroughly undemocratic character for decades after Sweden had adopted an extensive parliamentary reform.

In the Estate of the Knights and Nobility the head of each noble family, or his designated representative, participated in the deliberations and voted. In the Estate of the Clergy the two bishops were *ex officio* members; the clergy of the two dioceses elected twenty-eight representatives; the teachers and administrators of the university chose one or two delegates; and the teachers and administrators of the elementary schools sent one or two for each diocese. In all, some 1,000 persons had a voice in choosing representatives to this house.

The two lower houses, those of the peasants and the burghers, ought to have represented the masses of the population; but they did not. Only the owners of land might vote for delegates to the Peasant Estate (by indirect ballot), with the number of votes for each voter varying according to the value of his land. Since the majority of the rural people were landless, they remained without political power. Of the overwhelmingly agricultural population of Finland, only about 100,000 persons enjoyed the vote.[1] Most urban dwellers were excluded from choosing delegates to the Estate of the Burghers—notably women and persons employed by others. Plural votes were accorded up to 25 per voter, on scales that varied from town to town. About 20,000 urban dwellers in all of Finland were permitted to vote for the Burgher Estate.[2]

In the political arena, perhaps the most evident of all the conflicts was that between Fennomans and Suecomans. Swedish speakers constituted the landed aristocracy and completely dominated the Estate of the Knights and Nobles. The wealthier bourgeoisie in the towns was strongly Swedish, though to a diminishing degree, and at the end of the century retained a precarious hold on the Estate of the Burghers. Although St. Petersburg after mid-century showed a generally benevolent attitude toward the Fennomans in its appointments, particularly to the Senate, the long-standing Suecoman advantages of education, wealth, and tradition were by no means destroyed. The inner circle of leading Suecoman families constituted a sort of hereditary club, whose members were appointed as a matter of course to administrative posts and honors. It is not surprising, then, that Swedish speakers were on the whole more determined opponents of Russification than were Finnish speakers. To break down the old system of Finland's autonomy would doubtless mean, whatever the final outcome, the irreversible destruction of a structure of privilege.

The relationship of Swedish speakers to Finnish speakers, however, was a complex one—incomparably more complex than the relationship of Germans to Estonians or Latvians in the Baltic Provinces. From the beginning, many of the outstanding Fennoman leaders were Swedish by birth and genteel upbringing, who became converted to the cause of their Finnish-speaking countrymen after reaching intellectual maturity, sometimes after being exposed to a shaking-up of their ideas at the University of Helsinki. Johan Vilhelm Snellman (1806-1881), who is usually considered the founder of the Fennoman political movement, was born in Stockholm and spent the first seven years of his life there. He learned Finnish with great difficulty after he became a university student and experienced a desire to see a united Finnish nation. This goal could be achieved, he thought, only by having all Finns, including the educated and privileged classes, learn and share the language of the great majority of the people. The

Swedish language, he declared, had been imposed from without, and must be abandoned. Snellman did not envisage or desire a social revolution; he demanded, instead, that the classes traditionally furnishing the leadership of Finland should become Finnish in their speech and in their hearts.

Yrjö Sakari Yrjö-Koskinen (1830-1903), a historian and a disciple of Snellman, became toward the end of the century the leader of the Fennoman party and one of its most doctrinaire members; his name during the first part of his life, however, had been Georg Forsman and his forebears for several generations had been clergymen of Swedish culture. Agathon Meurman (1826-1909), Yrjö-Koskinen's close associate and for years the virtual dictator of the Fennoman-dominated Peasant Estate, came of a Swedish-speaking family of landed gentry. Numerous other prominent members of the Fennoman party came from Swedish-speaking backgrounds, notably Karl Emil Ferdinand Ignatius (1837-1909), historian and senator; Edvard Hjelt (1855-1921), who was for several years rector of Helsinki University and later very active politically; Karl Gabriel Thiodolf Rein (1838-1919), vice-chancellor of the university and member of the Diet; Baron Ernst Gustaf Palmén (1855-1921), a senator, a part-time journalist, and a provisional chancellor of the university; and Otto Donner (1835-1909), a professor of linguistics, a newspaper editor, and a member of the Diet for the Estate of the Clergy.

The degree of Fennoman zeal or fanaticism varied considerably among these distinguished men. Yrjö-Koskinen became so intensely anti-Swedish that in 1890 he refused to use the Swedish language any longer in his correspondence with his friend von Daehn (who was annoyed, and said so).[3] On the other hand, several of these men published their most important works in Swedish. Hjelt's published and Ignatius' immensely valuable unpublished memoirs are written in Swedish, and Swedish was the family language in the Hjelt household.

The varying shades of opinion among the Fennomans embraced more than the use of the Swedish language. By the last two decades of the century considerable progress had been made in the use of Finnish as an official language and in the establishment or improvement of educational opportunities for Finnish speakers. To some Fennomans, therefore, the language question as such, though they were far from indifferent to it, did not appear so all-important as it did to Yrjö-Koskinen; other problems claimed their attention as well. The established leaders of the Fennoman party were intellectually conservative, Lutheran-clerical, and anti-Semitic;[4] they had little sympathy for liberal ideas. Some of the members of the party (particularly the younger ones), influenced in part by ideas from the West, considered it time to pay attention to problems of the modern world of wider relevance than Finnish-Swedish linguistic antagonism. By about 1880 this group had begun to take form, and without separating from the national party it became known as the Young Finnish party. In 1881 it established a periodical, *Valvoja*, and in 1890 a newspaper, *Päivälehti*, which was soon to find itself embroiled in controversies with the older party organ, *Uusi Suometar*, of which Yrjö-Koskinen had been one of the founders.

The intransigence of such Fennoman leaders as Snellman and Yrjö-Koskinen bred resistance among Swedish speakers; and, like their Fennoman compatriots, the Swedish speakers were divided between moderates and extremists. The movement of vigorous opposition to Fennonman demands had its effective origin in the organization called the Nyland (or Uusmaalainen) Section (*avdelning, osakunta*), later called "Nylands Nation," which was composed of the students of the predominantly Swedish-speaking province of Nyland, or Uusimaa. Helsinki is situated in Uusimaa; the area had traditionally produced a large proportion of the country's political, administrative, economic and military leaders, and would continue to do so. What happened in the Nyland Section, therefore, was of significance to the country as a whole. Up to just after the middle of the century the students had shown a warm interest in the Fennoman movement; they were likely to spend their summers in the interior of the country among Finnish-speaking peasants. As late as 1858 the secretary of the organization noted in his minutes that the majority of the members seemed to be Fennoman in sympathy.[5]

Within a few years the spirit of the students changed. In theory, the militant Suecomans merely wished to have equal rights with the Finns to cultivate their ancestral language and culture; but it soon became evident that many of them were inspired by the Orwellian belief that "some animals are more equal than others." In its somewhat more polite form the argument for the Suecoman position was that Finland lay in the border area between two cultural areas, Eastern and Western, between which it must choose; that the slim cultural resources of the Finnish people would not enable them to withstand being drawn into the Eastern orbit; and that therefore the strength of the Swedish-speaking cultural aristocracy was necessary to keep Finland in the Western camp.[6] In the more outspoken Suecoman utterances there was more than a trace of the racism of the Scandinavianists in Sweden.

This attitude was especially noticeable in Axel Olof Freudenthal (1836-1911), the first leader of the Suecoman campaign, professor of the Swedish language and literature at Helsinki University from 1878 to 1904. The son of Swedish immigrants, Freudenthal maintained close connections with scholars in Sweden, including outspokenly Scandinavianist ones. Unlike many of his compatriots, he did not believe that the Finns were one people speaking two languages; on the contrary, he held that there were two nationalities in Finland. It was the duty of the Swedish-speaking population to maintain and strengthen its own nationality and its bonds with Sweden. Freudenthal asserted as early as 1858 that the "ultra-Fennomans" were consciously or unconsciously serving the purposes of Russia. Soon he went further and adopted the view that Finland must separate herself from Russia and rejoin Sweden; he evidently had little interest in the continued development of Finnish-language culture. His views won increasing numbers of adherents in the Nyland Section.

Freudenthal's circle liked to talk and write about the vigor and creative ability of the Indo-Germanic race, and to give it credit for having led the Finns out of the barbarism from which they could not have emerged by their own efforts.[7] By failing to maintain their independence, the Finns had lost the inherent rights of every people to self-determination; and the time had come for the Swedes to stop sacrificing themselves on the Finns' behalf. In *Nylands Dragon*, the handwritten periodical of the still officially illegal Nyland Section, Freudenthal wrote in 1860 that the "Chudic"-Finnish tribes had never had enough intelligence to achieve freedom or civilization, "and they may well, without the slightest need for the guardian spirit of humanity to shed tears at their tomb, disappear from the earth, or they may, as peaceable peasants, be content with the idyllic-patriarchal life which best accords with their faithful and quiet nature."[8]

By 1868 most of the members of the Nyland Section could not speak Finnish, and the summer visits to get acquainted with Finnish peasants had gone out of fashion.[9] When E. G. Palmén, a youth from an aristocratic Swedish-speaking family, joined the Nyland Section in 1868, he was shocked by the narrow Suecoman spirit of the members. They applied the contemptuously intended word "Chud" to Finnish speakers, and the phrase "Better Russian than Chud" was often on their lips. According to Palmén:

Nyland's Swedishness was constantly kept so exclusively in view that the Finnish population of the province and the country was completely forgotten. Every effort for their advantage was assumed to proceed from crass selfishness; the existing power-position of Swedish was regarded as a natural right, inalienable for all time. The Nylanders, who nevertheless prided themselves on their liberalism and Scandinavianism, rivaled in short-sighted one-sidedness the feudal barons south of the Gulf of Finland.[10]

"The conflicts of student life," he remarks, "insignificant in their subjects, may deserve attention in the degree they contributed to creating the presuppositions for the great struggle of life. There already appeared full-fledged in the Nyland Section the spirit that later I often encountered in the [Diet] representation and the officials and in the Suecoman press."[11]

While the Nyland Section was going in one direction, other student groups were following an opposite course; the Pohjanmaa (Österbotten) section, for instance, which presumably included many more Finnish-speaking students, remained intensely Fennoman in spirit. The increasingly bitter differences in attitude between the differing student camps sometimes led to physical violence.

A periodical, *Vikingen* (The Viking), was founded in 1870 by the circle of men around Freudenthal. It was not notably flattering to the Finns: its first number sounded the familiar note that only a "magnanimous and vigorous people" (the Swedes) had led the Finns on the pathway to civilization, and congratulated them on having undergone "a centuries-long schooling for the development of their talents."[12] *Vikingen* lasted for only four years; but it aroused so much antagonism among Finns that the name "Viking" came to be applied by them as an uncomplimentary epithet to any ultra-Suecoman.

Belief in the continuing Swedish mission in Finland persisted for decades. A writer for the Stockholm journal *Aftonbladet*, in the course of a reporting visit to Finland in 1894, interviewed one of the most important Suecoman politicians, Major Kasten Antell, a member of the Estate of the Nobility, who had recently resigned his commission in the Russian army rather than be transferred from service in Finland. He told the reporter:

The educated classes in Finland know that the old Swedish culture *must* be maintained if Finland is to be kept free. It is a fact—no one knows it better than the Russians themselves—that Swedish culture is the greatest obstacle to the work of Russification in Finland. The Swedish party has in its old traditions, in its inherited respect for our country's law and institutions, an inner power of resistance that cannot always be found elsewhere.[13]

A Swedish party was formed in 1882, but it did not correspond to the views of some Suecomans, such as Freudenthal, who had hoped to bridge the gap between the Swedish-speaking upper classes and the Swedish-speaking peasantry. It remained "a party of nothing but generals"[14] until after the Revolution of 1905 introduced universal suffrage. By the mid-1890s the Young Finns were talking seriously about broadening the franchise and there was a desire for complete political democracy among those who would soon be organizing themselves as socialists; but the Swedish party resisted all plans for political reform. The excuse offered on occasion to more democratic foreigners was one familiar in modern history: the principle was admirable, but the present time of crisis was not right for change. A reform of the franchise, Antell informed his interviewer, would lose the Estate of the Burghers to the Fennomans; and it was the Swedish party that offered "the best guarantees of devoted defense of Finland's ancient freedom on the basis of law."[15] Ernst Emil Schybergson (1856-1920), a successful banker and for years an influential representative in the Estate of the Burghers, told his fellow delegates in 1894 that the purpose of a petition for reform of the franchise was simply to strengthen the Fennoman party.[16]

In their opposition to political reform and also in their opposition to the introduction of compulsory public elementary education[17] the Swedish-speaking political leaders made clear their party's role as a supporter not merely of cultural tradition but also of class privilege. The labor newspaper *Työmies* (*The Workingman*) published in 1898 an editorial ridiculing the claims of the Swede-Finns to be the bearers and protectors of liberal Western culture. All liberal Western countries except Belgium, it declared, had become democratized politically; Finland stood "outside the civilized world, in the midst of medieval darkness." But the Finland Swedes wanted no change.

> When that Western culture knocks on the door of their own country, they shut the doors and windows. . . . Thus, to our Suecoman guardians of culture, Eastern darkness and medieval conditions are ideals to defend which they must fight tooth and nail, with their mouths full of words about Western culture. . . . They resist tooth and nail all measures leading in a democratic direction, which aim at obtaining the vote for the basic strata of the people and realizing the principle of one man-one vote.[18]

It would have been unrealistic to expect the readers of *Työmies* to rise enthusiastically, on summons from the Suecoman leaders, to protect the political institutions of the country.

As the critical last decade of the nineteenth century opened, the language strife kept Finland divided in the face of incipient Russification. Consternation over the threat from St. Petersburg led most of the Suecoman leaders to favor measures of resistance, or at least of protest. The Young Finns, too, were alarmed. Although a few years earlier their attitude on the language question had been even more militant than that of the Old Finn party leaders, they now believed that more vital concerns were at issue: liberalism, democracy, and constitutionalism. They were prepared, therefore, to conclude an armistice with the Suecomans.

Eero Erkko, the editor of *Päivälehti*, wrote in another publication in December 1891: "As long as the governmental position and the existence of the *whole* people are at such a point as now, no one has a right to play with fire."[19] Kaarlo Juho Ståhlberg, a young man who was just beginning his political career and who a few decades later was to become the first president of the Republic of Finland, wrote to his fiancée in 1891: "At present the language question, important though it is, . . . has decidedly become a side issue. When it is a question of living or dying, internal quarrels must quiet down in every respect in which they affect this question."[20]

The leader of the party, Yrjö-Koskinen, disagreed with such views. He and the other Old Finn notables had no sympathy, in any case, with the liberal, democratic, and constitutional leanings of the Young Finns, whose opposition they regarded as being impelled by eagerness to get control of the party. Yrjö-Koskinen had declared in 1889: "The language question may not be separated from conservative ideals."[21] Like his mentor Snellman, Yrjö-Koskinen was a Hegelian, and historically Hegelianism seems to have had a strong affinity with conservatism. Some of the Old Finn leaders had made tentative gestures in 1889 toward conciliation with the Swedes, and met with complete failure.[22] Now Yrjö-Koskinen was adamant in his refusal to cooperate with the Suecomans.

As soon as the Diet met in 1891, Yrjö-Koskinen read to the Fennoman delegates a secret memorandum, *What the State of Affairs Demands* (*Mitä nykyinen asema vaatii*). The memorandum proposed that Finnish policy should be based on certain premises: that there were still in Russia some fair-minded persons who had not been alienated by the propaganda of the Russian nationalist press; that the tsar's confidence in the Finnish people had not been shaken and that the Finns could rely upon His Majesty's heart and his feeling for justice; and that a powerful national self-awareness had been aroused in the masses of the Finnish people during the decades of the national awakening. It followed that confidence in the tsar must be increased, and the influence of the tainted Suecoman party in St. Petersburg diminished. Toward the Swedish proposal for achieving unanimity he was cold. Unanimity, he said, was a good thing; but as proposed by the Swedes it would mean the Finnish party's simply following the directions of the Suecomans. In the present delicate situation unanimity could be secured only if the "national party" should take power into its own hands "and the Swedish party willingly go along."

> In the delicate questions that may arise at this Diet only the national party has any significance. . . . Freely granting that in the Swedish party there may be as much patriotic zeal as in the national party; granting, too, that in action there is no difference in loyal willingness and faithfulness;—the inescapable fact, nevertheless, is that the Swedish party at this moment, in these questions that were mentioned above, is without governmental influence, to say nothing of the fact that its very name is not calculated to inspire trust on the decision-making level.[23]

The memorandum created dismay in the Finnish party, not only among the Young Finns but also among moderates, particularly in view of the fact that its goal—Finnish domination of national policy —was unattainable in the foreseeable future, since two houses of the Diet were controlled by the Swedes.[24] The Young Finns refused to go along with their titular leader, and from this time on the party was split into factions. Yrjö-Koskinen had sacrificed party solidarity —to say nothing of a national solidarity that might not have been attainable anyway—in favor of von Daehn's policy of conciliation. Within a few years that policy was to prove itself powerless to accomplish anything; but it is difficult to conceive of any Finnish policy that *could* have achieved anything in the face of Russian determination. In any case, Yrjö-Koskinen remained firmly—and increasingly bitterly—committed to his course to the end.

Opposition to the internal structure of power and influence in Finland was by no means confined to the writers and politicians of the Fennoman party. Before the end of the century they had been outdone in their expressions of dissatisfaction by leaders of the rising socialist movement. Indeed, some of the most militant socialists emerged from the ranks of the Old Finns after they had concluded that the Fennoman program did not go far enough toward improving the state of the nation.[25]

The socialist movement in Finland, like the Fennoman movement, was not without paradoxes in its membership and leadership. For example, the real founder of the Labor Party and the principal theoretician of socialism in the country in the early years was Nils Robert af Ursin (1854-1936), the scion of an intellectually gifted family of Swedish culture which had been ennobled in 1845. He had the probably unique distinction of being a member of the Estates of the Knights and Nobles before 1905 and of serving in the new democratic parliament as a leading member of the Social Democratic party in 1907 and 1908.[26] Other important socialist leaders also came from nonproletarian backgrounds.

Open class conflict in Finland was belated in the European context because industrialization was belated. It was not until the 1880s that rapid industrial growth began. Once under way, however, it proceeded rapidly. In 1885 the number of workers in industry was only 28,600; by 1900 it was 74,700; and by 1908, 91,300. In the years 1895-1900 employment in industry increased by 9.6 percent annually. Nevertheless, in 1910 the proportion of the people that earned its living by industry and handicrafts was only 15.2 percent;[27] a shortage of native capital was in part responsible for the relatively slow and belated results.

In the early phases of industrialization in Finland, as almost everywhere else, the condition of the employees was unenviable. Wages were low, jobs were insecure, hours were long, working conditions were bad, housing was almost indescribably bad, and the health of the workers was poor.[28]

The first efforts to improve the condition of the workers were made not by members of the proletariat but by well-disposed persons of higher economic status. The first organization established for this purpose, the Työväenyhdistys or Arbetareföreningen (Workingmen's Association), was set up in Helsinki in 1883; it was led for over a decade by Viktor Julius von Wright (1856-1934), a manufacturer who had returned to Finland from travels on the continent convinced that socialism would spread to his country unless workers and employers could be induced to cooperate unselfishly. Similar associations were founded in numerous cities and towns; by 1896 there were thirty-four of them, with over 5,000 members.

The workingmen's associations were by no means class organizations. Of the original members in the Helsinki association the majority were workers; but there were also teachers, architects, consuls, veterinarians, druggists, captains, generals, restauranteurs, merchants, and non–working-class ladies. By 1895 the membership included 28 professors and 10 senators. Activities of the Työväenyhdistys included setting-up reading rooms, holding lectures and discussions, the provision of concerts and excursions, the establishment of mutual funds for sickness and death benefits, and the collection of statistics on the condition of the working class.

In the first years there was little political or social militancy within the organization. The rural tradition of a patriarchal relationship between employer and employee persisted under the new economic conditions, especially in the smaller industrial communities such as those gathered around sawmills or wood-pulping establishments.

(More than one-half the industrial workers lived in rural or semi-rural areas until about 1910). Even in Helsinki the workingmen were at first diffident about expressing themselves. When Mechelin was forced to resign as senator in 1890, the Helsinki Työväenyhdystys joined in the evening demonstration to honor him and made him a permanent member. The spokesman for the delegation, however, began his message with an apology:

> We workingmen know very well that in general we ought not to meddle in such sensitive matters as those which at this moment are keeping minds in our country in such suspense, and therefore it is not our custom to meddle in them.[29]

Such notable restraint brought few concessions from the Finnish elites. The working class had neither political nor economic clout; and for years two of its principal requests, for the shortening of the working day and the extension of the suffrage, met with no response. Statistics gathered by the Työväenyhdystys in 1886 showed that the shortest working day in Helsinki was 11 hours, but that a 12- to 13-hour day was more common. Shoemakers worked 14 to 16 hours; in some factories and bakeries a shift might extend to 18 hours. Night work was not limited.[30] Yet when von Wright introduced a motion into the Diet in 1889 to establish a maximum 12-hour day by law, his proposal was defeated. Among those speaking against it was the liberal Mechelin; among the journals opposing it in print was the liberal *Päivälehti*.[31] Von Wright's expressed belief that "good will has inspired the estates and the administration in their treatment of the conditions of workingmen"[32] was clearly unfounded.

Under these circumstances the mood of the Finnish industrial workers changed rapidly in the 1890s, as it was changing in Russia. A new militancy became evident, inspired in part by educated men who were in touch with the socialist movement elsewhere in Europe. The aristocratic Nils af Ursin, mentioned above, had a doctoral degree and taught classical languages and ancient history at secondary schools in Viipuri and Turku; he became interested in contemporary social questions when reading about class struggles in ancient Rome. As a university student he was an ardent Fennoman and a liberal; but as time passed the Fennoman program seemed to him to be insufficient with respect to the welfare of the people as a whole. He was tirelessly active in the Työväenyhdystys in Turku, especially in the educational work of the organization, but concluded that the goals of the workingmen's associations were too modest. By the early 1890s he was a socialist, and he was well-read in the history of the movement. After a labor newspaper, *Työmies* (*The Workingman*) was established in 1895, he wrote for it frequently and forcefully, and by 1896 he was proposing the establishment of a workers' political party.[33]

Ursin's views were shared by numerous representatives of the rising Finnish-speaking intelligentsia. Of these the most colorful was Matti Kurikka (1863-1915), the son of an Ingrian-Finnish peasant. When he came to Helsinki University in 1881, he was—not surprisingly in view of his background—refused membership in the Nyland Section; an event which presumably did not inspire him with affection for the Suecomans. He joined the Savo-Karelian section, in which the liberal views of western Europe were finding adherents in the 1870s and 1880s.[34] After concluding his studies and marrying a wealthy young woman, Kurikka traveled on the continent, where he was drawn more deeply into the radical intellectual currents of the time. On his return to Finland he took over the editorship of *Viipurin Sanomat*, a newspaper which had formerly represented the Old Finn point of view but now became independent. In Viipuri he was one of the directing committee of the local Työväenyhdystys. His views moved in the direction of socialism, but his socialism remained always a rather vague, idealistic, humanitarian attitude; based, he said, not upon the teachings of Marx or Lassalle, but upon those of Jesus of Nazareth. He wrote plays and short stories; he was a fiery literary man rather than a systematic social theoretician, and flung himself into controversies regardless of consequences. He became editor of the recently founded workingmen's newspaper *Työmies* in 1897, and quickly attracted both great friends and great enemies.[35]

More important, probably, than the influence of the educated socialist writers was the growing anger and frustration of the workers themselves. From their ranks emerged leaders whose radical views were shaped primarily by their own experiences. Many of the persons active in the workingmen's associations had been members of the Fennoman party; but by the late 1890s it became clear that this party, at least as long as it was controlled by the Old Finns, was scarcely more inclined to support substantial social and political change than were the Swedes.

For many workers the critical disillusionment happened in 1896. A strike began among the construction workers of Helsinki because the employers refused to reduce the working day to 10 hours or to bargain with the union. Workers in other industries joined the strike, and it spread through the country. The construction workers failed to achieve anything. A shipload of Russian workers was imported as strikebreakers and many unorganized laborers from the countryside were brought in for the same purpose. There was no fund to support the strikers. Within three weeks they had to return to work on terms dictated by their employers. Some of the lesser strikes, on the other hand, were successful; and out of the struggle there began to emerge some of the future leaders of the Social Democratic party.

The press was, in general, with the exception of *Päivälehti* and, of course, *Työmies*, hostile to the strike. As was to be expected, the Swedish-language newspapers, including the liberal *Nya Pressen*, condemned it; but so did *Uusi Suometar*, the organ of the Old Finns. "Both *Uusi Suometar* and *Nya Pressen*," wrote *Työmies*, "go along with letting the worker languish in toil and hunger. It is just that one wants to have us starve in Finnish, the other in Swedish." There was particular bitterness over the importation of strikebreakers from Russia. Strikers burned the barracks housing the Russian workers, and anger persisted. "Good gentlemen," exclaimed *Työmies*, "don't talk to us about the fatherland from now on."[36]

As disillusionment and frustration grew, so did radicalism. A first meeting of workingmen's associations, meeting in 1893 and presided over by von Wright, was very moderate in its requests. A second congress in 1896 was livelier, and witnessed a sharp clash between the conservatives who had previously directed the movement and a more radical, younger wing bearing the scars of the great strike. A proposal by Ståhlberg to work for a one-man/one-vote electoral system was adopted after hot debate.[37] The question of founding an independent labor party was raised and discussed. Although the suggestion was rejected for the time being, there could be no doubt as to the way in which thinking among the workers was moving. Benevolent middle-class persons, finding themselves losing influence in the associations, withdrew during the next few years. As von Wright explained, "I do not belong to the kind of men who strive for reforms that are impossible to carry through. At the [1896] meeting a direction has been taken that I cannot approve, and I do not want to have the responsibility for what it can bring with it."[38] By 1898 workers' local political parties were formed in Helsinki, Turku, and Tampere, and preparations were being made to establish a party on the national level; it was clear that it was going to have a strong socialist bias.[39]

The leaders of the working-class movement were as aware as any other educated Finns of the looming threat of Russification, and they were by no means indifferent to it. In July 1898 *Työmies* published a front-page article by Ursin concerning its inherent danger. Whatever the Russifiers might try to do, said Ursin, "we Finns have developed so far in our national self-awareness that we will *never* change to Russians; we are and wish always to be friends of the Russians, but we remain, as we shall *always* remain, Finns, in accordance with the advice of political wisdom of Alexander II, that, keeping friendly relations with Russia, we wish to be good Finnish patriots."

Against the threat from the east Ursin proposed two defences. The first of these, which one suspects may have been a gesture of political maneuver rather than an expression of belief, and which was certainly not Marxian, was to "rely unshakably on the words given by the tsar." More substantially, the writer urged at considerable length the internal consolidation of the country:

> The upper classes of the people must come much closer to the deep ranks, sacrifice their own self-love, improve the spiritual and physical state of these ranks, and grant them much greater political rights and influence in public affairs. Education must be spread to much wider circles than heretofore. If the deep ranks acquire more knowledge, their self-awareness will also grow; they will understand better what they can accomplish in united concern for the fatherland and humanity.[40]

The appeal to give patriotism a broader basis of political and cultural equity than before seems to have made no impression on the traditional Finnish elites. They drifted toward catastrophe without attempting to strengthen the country's threatened political rights by making the people as a whole participatory in those rights.

Among the unenfranchised and disgruntled people was a much larger group than the industrial workers: the landless peasants, who were voicing their grievances more emphatically as the century approached its end. They were too lacking in political sophistication, organization, and leadership to take an active or even a spoiler's part in the Finnish-Russian quarrels, and they did not resort during the Revolution of 1905 to the extensive violence that characterized the Baltic Provinces. Their discontent, however, was well known; it made Swedish-speaking aristocrats nervous and probably confirmed the upper class in their resistance to political change; peasant unhappiness, moreover, offered one more propaganda weapon to the Russifiers.

In the latter half of the nineteenth century agrarian conditions varied from district to district; but in general the status of the rural poor was bad, and getting worse. The population of Finland increased by nearly a million and a half in the half-century before 1914. Neither industrialization nor the extensive emigration to America was able to absorb the surplus completely; the agricultural population continued to grow until the 1930s.[41]

With the growing demand for wood for export and domestic industry, forests became more valuable. Not only individual landowners but to an increasing extent commercial companies bought up forest tracts. There was less possibility than before of clearing land for new farmers; and the security of tenant farmers and marginal smallholders who lived on partially wooded tracts decreased. A growing urban market for meat and dairy products led to a partial conversion of cultivated farmland to cattle pastures; this process displaced many farm laborers, as had been the case in Ireland a few decades earlier.[42]

The landless agricultural population consisted of two groups: agricultural laborers and crofters (renters of farmland). It is estimated that at the turn of the century about 36 percent of rural families owned their own land, almost 36 percent were crofters, and 28 percent were hired laborers. The condition of agricultural laborers was precarious. Their numbers increased rapidly after the middle of the nineteenth century owing to the growth of rural population, the inability of new industry to absorb it all, the dispossession of many crofters as a result of the economic changes mentioned above, and of natural catastrophes, such as the disastrous harvests of the mid-60s, with which marginal cultivators could not cope. The laborers were in oversupply; they had to accept very harsh conditions of employment from landowners.[43]

The crofters presented a particularly difficult problem. The system of crofts became important in Finland in the eighteenth century; originally it served a useful social purpose by opening new land to cultivation and making it possible for a landless man to obtain the use of farmland in return for service to the landowner. The number of crofts in the country increased from about 4,000 in 1750 to 63,000 in 1865; after a sharp decline in the late sixties following the hunger years it grew slowly to a point of 70,000 in 1895, and thereafter began to dwindle.[44]

Long after most of Europe had abandoned the requirement of labor service to the landlord in lieu of rent, the practice continued in Finland. It furnished the landowner with a dependable supply of workers; but to the crofter it meant growing insecurity and worsening conditions.

As late as 1912 nearly one-third of the agreements between crofters and landlords were oral, and more than a quarter were not for a fixed period of time. The landlords were landowning peasants, clergymen, or nobles. But however ruthless a peasant landlord or clergyman might be in his treatment of his crofters, the most visible oppressor was the noble landowner. "Experience shows," wrote Professor E. N. Setälä, a leader of the Young Finn party, in 1899, "that it is for the most part precisely those great landowners of our country, the most educated in our agricultural class, who have demanded unlimited labor requirement, such as is seldom specified in the contracts with peasant landowners."[45] Since the nobles spoke Swedish and most of the peasants spoke Finnish, the agrarian problem was related to the language conflict.[46] In most of the countryside of Finland, as in the Baltic Provinces, language was a badge of caste. The nobility, which constituted 0.12 percent of the country's population,[47] could hardly fail to be aware of the implications for their economic privileges of a democratically tinged Finnish national movement.

Russian nationalists did not ignore the propaganda possibilities offered by this state of affairs. In February 1891, when the first Finnish-Russian crisis was boiling up, *Moskovskie vedomosti* published a letter signed by "a True Finn," declaring that the Finnish common people had no confidence in their Diet, which represented the gentleman class. Whether or not the letter was actually written by a Finn, there was a considerable measure of truth in it; perhaps for that reason it stung writers in Finland into replying. The Helsinki newspaper *Nya Pressen* declared that *Moskovskie vedomosti* might well have turned its attention to the Russian common people, among whom discontent was general. It expressed the conviction that no "True Finn" had written the offensive letter, and surmised that *Moskovskie vedomosti* had ordered it. The Russian journal retaliated with another letter, purportedly written in the Tavastian dialect of Finnish, denouncing the abuses by the ruling class in Finland and concluding with the assurance that "the heartfelt hope of the united Finnish people is that the Finnish Diet be forever abolished and the laws and rights of Russia be applied here also." The writer claimed to be speaking for "more than a million Finnish slaves." A brief but lively international press squabble ensued; it was clearly the purpose of *Moskovskie vedomosti* to demonstrate the existence of a deep cleft between the Finnish masses and their upper class, and to hope that the Russian government would intervene to improve conditions in Finland.[48]

Governor-General Heiden showed sympathetic interest in Finnish agrarian conditions on tours of the provinces and was clearly concerned about the political and social menace presented by a rural proletariat.[49] His concern was not shared by his aristocratic native advisers, and he never went so far as to threaten the established rights of the landlords. In 1882 he received a number of petitions from crofters urging him to redeem them from the arbitrary abuses by landowners by helping them to acquire land of their own. He replied with a proclamation asserting that there was no legal basis for the changes proposed and warning the peasants against tempters who were trying to make them break the laws of their country.[50]

The peasants' petitions met with a generally hostile reception in the press, and the Finnish government showed little concern with the problem. By 1891, after several years of rather desultory discussion, the Diet enacted a law making some mild improvements in the conditions of crofters; even this was rejected by the Estate of the Peasants, which was dominated by peasant landowners.[51] In 1895 a not very princely sum of 400,000 marks was made available to help in the purchase of farms by the landless. The core of the agrarian discontent remained untouched by this legislation.

The government, indeed, showed a consistently callous attitude toward the woes of the poor, in the country as in the city. In 1892 there occurred one of the crop-failure years with which Finnish history is studded. Although there were no such appalling consequences as there had been during the starvation years of the sixties, hardship was widespread. The Senate appropriated 2.5 million marks as a loan for the importation of grain. Von Daehn, scarcely a social radical, wrote angrily about this to Yrjö-Koskinen:

> The difficulty in times of bad harvests is not to procure a certain quantity of grain in foreign markets and move it to the ports. The real difficulty is the distribution, the art of putting the grain within reach of those who need it. . . . We must remember that most of the needy have neither horse nor cart to come to the distribution center to look for grain, and not enough strength to carry a bag of flour on their backs. . . . In my opinion you have done enough, even too much, for the relatively rich population, which can get out of its emergency by its own strength, but I do not see that you have done anything for the population that will suffer and is already suffering from famine.[52]

Among the Finnish elites blindness to the plight of the poor persisted in time of great public crisis. In April 1899, a few weeks after the February Manifesto had aroused general fear for the future of the country, there was published in Helsinki a volume of brief essays written by forty-two leading Finns to express their ideas about the crisis and what ought to be done about it. The writers included leaders of the Swedish, Young Finn, and Old Finn parties (with the notable exception of Yrjö-Koskinen) and members of almost every prosperous group in the country: nobles, professors, other educators, writers, officials, Diet members, clergymen, and others. There was a good deal of rather vague verbiage about the need of improving education for the masses. Of the forty-two contributors only one, Setälä, dealt with the crofter question. He was factual in detailing the abuses of the system and what he regarded as necessary remedies: not only the transformation of the landless peasant into an independent landowner but also "the granting of political rights to the large part of our people who still lack them. How could one hope that he who has no political rights could harbor strong love for the state institution that for the great majority of our people has become dearer than life itself?"[53] Steälä's question was largely disregarded during the next few years by the leaders engaged in a bitter struggle to preserve the national institutions.

If the mass of the peasants were still too uneducated to compose, sign, and circulate petitions, their lack of education only facilitated certain wishful misconceptions which revealed their hostility to the existing social structure. For several decades in the latter part of the century the land-hunger of the peasants was fed by descriptions, presumably in large part unduly rosy, about the supposedly better conditions of landholding in Russia. The reports were spread, apparently, by the soldiers quartered in Finland and by the itinerant peddlers from Russian Karelia (the so-called Arkhangelites) who were welcomed by peasants in the back-country for providing wares (including smuggled goods) not easily available otherwise. These reports about Russia led to persistent rumors, especially in the districts near the Russian frontier, that a parceling-out of land was about to occur in Finland; the prospect was usually conditional upon extension of Russian law to Finland.[54] In 1884 crofters in Häme Province, where such rumors had long been circulating, greeted with joy the appearance of Russian topographical surveyors preparing maps of the region, since they believed the tsar had sent the surveyors to measure the land of estates in preparation for a distribution. Among the numerous rumors current in the 1880s was one reported in 1889 by a Viipuri newspaper that the tsar had ordered a distribution of land but that the execution of the order was being delayed because his advisers, the gentlemen of Helsinki, lied to him and tried to deprive the poor of their rights.[55]

At the end of the year 1890, when the first Russo-Finnish constitutional crisis was seething, a number of local meetings of crofters, in one case with 500 or so attendants, were held. They drew up programs for improved conditions. At least one of the petitions spoke of "general discontent" and was addressed to "His most gracious Majesty," and one delegation waited personally upon the governor-general. Two of the petitions, on the other hand, specifically rejected the assertions of *Moskovskie vedomosti* that the crofters wished to bypass the Diet and have Russian law extended to the country; in general, the petitioners emphasized that they desired to have changes made in a lawful way. They did, however, demand changes. In general, these meetings did not get a very good press. The liberal *Päivälehti* published one petition as something that "perhaps ought to be taken into consideration," but rejected the demands as unfounded. The liberal Swedish-language *Nya Pressen* accused the petitioners of "agitation"; it conceded, however, that the subject was too important to be brushed aside, and that improvements must be made—though not, certainly, at the cost of the age-old freedom of contract.

Hämeen Sanomat, published in the heart of one of the most discontented districts, dismissed the petition of a local meeting as a "propaganda piece" and did not bother to print the resolutions passed. Some of the Finnish-language journals, notably the Old Finn *Uusi Suometar*, were considerably more friendly.[56] Rumors about land distribution were not a form of action, and the crofters' meetings produced little perceptible change with their orderly and legal mode of procedure. In contrast, there occurred in 1891 an event so bizarre that it is worth recording in some detail as a reflection of the violence latent in some of the rural population.

In October 1891 the governor of Viipuri Province, A. Gripenberg, reported to the Senate about disturbing conditions in the rural parish of Räisälä, where:

> for several years community life has witnessed a series of disturbances and an openly contumacious character that could not help having an injurious effect on the conception of, and respect for, the sanctity of law on the part of some of the people there. . . . The blame for this falls principally upon two persons belonging to the district, namely the former chairman of the parish meeting, land-holding peasant Erik Puputti, and his son, former reserve Matts Lähenniemi [Matti Läheniemi]. . . .[57]

Läheniemi was considered by Gripenberg to be a "ruthless agitator," but arresting and sending him to jail proved to be extraordinarily difficult. The inhabitants of Räisälä hid him and refused to cooperate with the authorities, saying that they would no longer obey the laws of Finland but only those of "His Majesty the Tsar." Läheniemi "incited his partisans to resistance on the grounds that he has the authorization of his Majesty the Tsar to kill anyone who wants to arrest him."

A month later a local police commissioner, Fredr. Ollikainen, reported to the police chief of Viipuri:

> One night last week when I had heard that Matti Läheniemi was supposed to be at the home of his father Erik Puputti, I went with Sheriff Elfving and constables Kaponen and Loikkanen to the aforesaid house, but we were not admitted voluntarily,

so that we had to open the doors ourselves. Just as we were searching the outer rooms we noticed that the hired hand, Juho Katarinpoika Arponen, was beginning to load his gun, so that I thought it my duty to take the gun away from him. The next morning Erik Puputti, who had not been at home during the night search, came with thirteen men first to Unnunkoski and then to Kiislahti Inn, where we were lodging, looking for me, threatening me . . . , and at the same time abusing me as a bandit and a robber; but about half an hour earlier I had happened to leave for the church village, so that they did not meet me.

From the above-mentioned facts it appears that in the parish of Räisälä there are clear indications of rebellion.[58]

On 3 November Gripenberg was asking the Senate for a force of twenty men, "which, in view of the terrorism that Läheniemi and his followers appear to exercise, must be sent from outside Räisälä parish." His request was granted, and by 11 November he had a force of about forty men ready to seize Läheniemi, and issued a proclamation warning all persons that if they concealed or defended Läheniemi they would be subject to severe punishment.[59]

At this point, frustratingly enough, the Läheniemi file in the Finnish State Archives ends, and it seems impossible to discover either what became of the rebel and his followers or what the exact nature of the first illegal agitation was. Läheniemi disappears from history at this point, but Räisälä was to be heard from again before long.

One cannot tell how widely known the Räisälä incident may have been. As part of the cumulative series of rumors, petitions, and congresses it ought to have been a warning to the political leaders of the country that something was rotten in the state of Finland. There was no lack of such warnings; but the eyes of Finland's traditional elite were focused primarily on what was wrong—and perhaps irremediable—in St. Petersburg, and not what was wrong—and possibly remediable—at home.

CHAPTER 26

THE STORM BREAKS AND RAGES

THE DECISIVE ATTACK on Finland's constitutional position arose not from any abstract political theory but out of what were perceived in St. Petersburg as overriding military considerations. Uneasiness about Finland and the protection of St. Petersburg concerned, among other things, both the size and the effectiveness of the Finnish army. For more than half a century after 1809, the military forces of Finland remained negligible, except for a brief build-up during the Crimean War. The country continued to be garrisoned primarily by Russian army and navy units. Qualitatively, on the other hand, Finland's contribution to the tsar's military power was not insignificant. Many sons of upperclass families passed through the Cadet School of Hamina or similar military institutions within Russia and had careers, sometimes distinguished ones, in the Russian service. In 1877 there were 281 Finnish generals or other higher officers in Russia; there were forty more Finnish generals in the Russian army than there were Norwegian and Swedish generals in the service of the two united Scandinavian kingdoms.[1]

Officer quality was not enough to satisfy Russian military planners; abundant manpower for the steamroller seemed desirable. During the Russo-Turkish War of 1877-1878, although the small Finnish Guards' Battalion acquitted itself well, Finland did not have to bear much of the cost of the struggle, in terms of either men or money. Acting upon strong hints from St. Petersburg, the Diet adopted in 1878 a system of universal obligation to military service. The law left the Finnish army separate from that of Russia, and the public and the individual burdens were much less than in the empire. The Finnish military system was entirely unsatisfactory from the Russian point of view.

Chapter 5 of this book has mentioned the two committees set up in 1896 to correct the shortcomings of this system. When Kuropatkin became minister of war in 1898 he pressed for decisive action, and a special session of the Finnish Diet was summoned for 19 January 1899 to consider his proposals. Not surprisingly, there was great unwillingness in the Grand Duchy to assume the very considerable extra burdens involved. Instead of a three-year term of service, with two years in the reserve, there would be a five-year term with thirteen years in the reserve. Previously, the young men chosen by lot to serve were conscripted only in the numbers necessary to complete the total active force of 5,600; now a surplus could be sent to serve with Russian troops in Russia. The number of new recruits each year would rise from 1,920 to 7,200; the active force would increase in time, with lengthened service, from 5,600 to 36,000, and the numbers in the reserve to 83,000. The troops might be used anywhere in the empire.[2]

That the Finns would resist the proposed army changes was a foregone conclusion; and St. Petersburg was not disposed to allow any more dawdling. The ideal instrument for carrying through reforms, civil as well as military, seemed to be the new governor-general, Nikolai Ivanovich Bobrikov, who took office in October 1898. The new appointee, whose career had been entirely military, was not in the slightest degree susceptible to dangerous intellectual influences from outside Russia. Although he had received decorations from seventeen foreign governments,[3] he was anything but a cosmopolitan. He spoke no language but Russian. Bobrikov's thoughts and actions were based upon four fundamentals: complete subjection to the will of the absolute monarch; unquestioning love for Russia; devotion to the army; and a belief that problems could be solved by the application of sufficient force. He had no respect for the dignity of the individual, or for the right to divergent opinions. He never referred to the *rights* of the Finns, but always to their "privileges." When he used such words as "state," "autonomy," "constitution," or "fundamental laws" in connection with Finland he always put them in quotation marks. With the contempt not uncommon among military men for small and weak peoples, he ridiculed the "vanity of a little nationality that has never played any role in history and has not enjoyed independence."[4]

Bobrikov had a passion for petty detail, which was exasperating to the Finns with whom he came into contact. He was concerned about the adoption of Western-style uniforms by the cab drivers of Helsinki, and tried unsuccessfully to get the civic authorities to reverse the change.[5] He was dismayed that the elementary schools did not display pictures of the tsar, and brought the weighty matter to the attention of the Senate.[6] Incurably suspicious (not without reason) of the university students, he harassed the rector, Edvard Hjelt, with perpetual complaints and questions about them.[7]

What the tsar's advisers had in mind for Finland was revealed on 15 February 1899, when Bobrikov returned from St. Petersburg, where, it was reported, he had gleefully told a friend that at last he had the Finns bound hand and foot.[8] The occasion for his enthusiasm was a document he brought back with him: the February Manifesto, a proposal that had been worked out by a committee of seven Russians (including Pobedonostsev and Plehve) and one Finn (the acting minister state secretary, whose views, needless to say, had not been heeded). The manifesto announced a "firm and unshakable procedure . . . concerning the preparation and issuing of general laws of the realm."

> While retaining in force and effect valid procedures concerning the issuing of such local statues as affect the needs exclusively of Finland, We have considered it necessary to reserve for Ourselves the determination of subjects for the general legislation of the Empire.

The basic rules which accompanied the manifesto provided that for legislation affecting the empire as a whole, including Finland, the initiative should be taken by the appropriate Russian minister and the minister state secretary for Finland after consultation with each other. Opinions on the proposals would be sought from the governor-general, the Senate, and, in cases to which its competence extended, the Finnish Diet. These opinions would be considered by the State Council, in cooperation with the governor-general, the minister state secretary, and such Finnish senators as might be specially chosen for that purpose by the tsar. The final decision by the State Council and the tsar would be proclaimed in the empire and Finland.[9]

The perils inherent in the manifesto were clear. The Senate and the Diet could offer only opinions on proposed legislation, and the final decision was made in St. Petersburg. There was no enumeration of the subjects which could fall within the purview of the arrangement; by sweeping interpretation it could entirely subvert Finland's autonomy and render the Diet a nullity. The door, as Mechelin remarked, "stood open to any Russian claims at all."[10]

Faced with the order to promulgate such a potentially disastrous provision, the Senate held a series of meetings from 15 to 18 February to discuss what to do. All the members were agreed that the manifesto was illegal, but all were aware there was no possibility of inducing the Autocrat of All the Russians to revoke it. It was clear that some sort of tactful remonstrance should be sent to St. Petersburg to remind the tsar of the promises he and his predecessors had made to the Finns and to try to obtain some assurance that there would be no serious encroachments on the rights of the Diet. Where the views of the senators diverged was on the question of promulgating the law. Should they make the official announcement at once, as they were commanded to? Should they delay promulgation until they had received from St. Petersburg an answer to their remonstrance? Should they refuse to promulgate at all, on the ground that the manifesto was illegal, and then resign their positions? Obviously, the Senate could not defy the tsar and remain in office. Its members were appointed administrative officials, with only advisory functions, not parliamentary ministers. What course would do the least harm to the Finnish cause? Would a prompt yielding to the imperial command increase good will in St. Petersburg, or would it convince the Russian authorities that the Finns were not serious in their professed attachment to their traditional rights? Would a delay in promulgation play into the hands of Finland's already powerful enemies and stiffen hostility in Russian official circles? Would a refusal to promulgate open the way for administration of the country by compliant tools of the governor-general, or even by Russians?[11] For three days the senators examined the possibilities and the dangers, and some of them changed their minds several times.

While the Senate was debating the problem, news of the manifesto leaked out, with startling results. Helsinki, said the poet Juhani Aho, was like an anthill stirred up by a cane.[12] On the evening of 17 February a mass meeting of citizens filled to capacity one of the largest available auditoriums, the Ateneum, and voted to ask the senators not to promulgate. Similar counsel came from the Swedish party's "club" of members in the Diet. The Fennomans' "club," on the other hand, abstained.[13]

When the final vote on immediate promulgation was taken in the Senate on 18 February, the result was a tie, 10:10. The deadlock was broken when Carl Tudeer, who had already voted for promulgation as a senator, cast a deciding vote as presiding officer.[14] It was clear that Finland was not going to be brought to heel easily.

Perhaps the most significant detail in the decision of the Senate was the position that Yrjö-Koskinen took in support of immediate promulgation. He was the most prominent member of the Senate, and up to 1899 the acknowledged—if sometimes resented—leader of the Fennoman party. His prestige among the people was great. Consequently, his decision on whether or not to yield to the demands of St. Petersburg would be more important than that of any other political figure.

Yrjö-Koskinen's attitude toward the February Manifesto was determined by the development of his thought over the previous decades as a historian, a politician, and an intensely patriotic Finn. He believed that in the new age of Great-Power ruthlessness inaugurated by Bismarck the only salvation for small nations among the colossi was, as he declared in 1889, "to strive to be forgotten, so that no one would notice them and eat them." The Finns, he wrote in an unpublished essay in 1902, had made mistakes in the course of the century in emphasizing their difference and their independence at the same time that excessive nationalism was growing in Russia. For the Finns, the weaker party, it was a matter of life or death to establish lasting peace with the Russians and to accept "a considerable reduction of our rights, if there only remains the possibility of national cultural life and development."[15]

In 1899 Yrjö-Koskinen was convinced, he told an acquaintance, that "in St. Petersburg for twenty years there have been efforts to provoke the Finns to some action that could be labeled rebellion; since this has not succeeded, there has been a resort to violent measures, and this means will succeed in the end. I analyzed the new stage of development in Russia: even the absolute tsar himself cannot limit his absolutism by his own promies."[16]

Yrjö-Koskinen firmly believed that Finland could best defend its national culture and autonomy "by a moderate course of conduct." He was strongly opposed to the various demonstrations and protests that broke out in Helsinki in February 1899. When a delegation from the Ateneum mass meeting presented him with a petition requesting the Senate not to promulgate the manifesto, he replied coldly: "I may inform you that as long as I am in my present office I shall not engage in conversation about state affairs with persons who have no other mandate than their honest faces."[17]

He turned upon members of his own party who did not agree with his tactics and made it clear that he regarded noncomplying party members, such as Ignatius, as mere popularity seekers.[18] In December 1900, refusing a proffered banquet on his seventieth birthday (which would have required a more or less courteous speech from him), he published his "Open Letter" in *Uusi Suometar*, which deplored the divisions within the Fennoman party. "A party that does not breathe, and whose members follow banners of all colors or no banners at all, appears to have ceased to exist." He was intractable in refusing any cooperation with the Swedish party.[19] The Open Letter aroused widespread consternation. Ignatius writes:

> His censure of the senators who resigned because of the Language Manifesto, his insistence that the Fennoman party should blindly support the domestic administration, and above all his demand, dictated by a bitter mood, that all cooperation between the Finnish and Swedish parties in the country should be broken off, evoked a storm of indignation on all sides.[20]

As the years passed, Yrjö-Koskinen clung stubbornly, in the face of increasing Russian repression, to the belief that something could be "rescued" for Finland by compliance. His animosity toward all resisters grew more intense and intolerant; he got into undignified public squabbles, deplored the softness and irresolution of the imperial government toward troublemakers, and branded resistance as "scandalous terrorism." From a stubborn defender of a rational position he became a perpetually furious (perhaps senile) zealot.[21]

Even after his angry resignation from the Senate in March 1899, however, Yrjö-Koskinen exercised great political influence. He continued to enjoy an outlet for his views in the most widely read Finnish newspaper, *Uusi Suometar*, and was able to hold the allegiance of large numbers of his countrymen in pursuing a policy that failed to conciliate St. Petersburg and greatly sharpened the internal dissensions in Finland.

If Yrjö-Koskinen was hostile to those who advocated resistance, he and the senators who shared his views met with equally sharp condemnation from some of their opponents. Despite the agreement of the Senate to keep the voting details secret, the names of the members who had supported promulgation of the February Manifesto became known to the public. Their names were displayed upon lampposts; black crosses were painted on the walls of their houses; old acquaintances snubbed them in the streets; they received written denunciations, sometimes anonymous, and unfriendly telephone calls. Of them all, naturally, Yrjö-Koskinen fared the worst. His house had painted or plastered on it the word "Traitor," and a delegation waited upon him to offer him thirty pieces of silver.[22]

Recriminations were not the only means of showing opposition to what had happened. The February Manifesto could not be promulgated immediately, since the editor of the official gazette in which it was to appear gave in his resignation and the typesetters went on strike.[23] One of the most moving public gestures, and one which the government obviously could not forbid, began late in February, when people began laying flowers at the base of the statue of Alexander II in the Senate Square. By honoring the ruler who had confirmed and extended their rights, the people were implicitly condemning the grandson who was revoking these rights. Week after week, month after month, the flowers appeared; they were piled especially high on 13 March, the anniversary of Alexander's death. At the statue a year later for that same occasion, Sibelius' newly composed piece "Finland Awakes," now known as *Finlandia*, was played.[24]

As various newspapers criticized the manifesto or other government measures, they were warned, suspended, or suppressed. Between the beginning of February and the beginning of November disciplinary measures had been taken against at least twenty-seven newspapers or other periodicals; by 3 November the entire district of Kuopio, for instance, was without a newspaper of its own. As might have been expected, public sympathy went out to the journalists, and from 3 to 5 November public festivals were arranged throughout the country to hold lotteries for the benefit of unemployed members of the press.[25] Bold words were spoken about "the free word," and *Novoe vremia* reacted sourly.[26]

The Finnish Senate sent to the tsar a respectful but determined remonstrance, in care of the vice-chairman, Tudeer, and the procurator, Söderhjelm. Nicholas permitted the acting minister state secretary, Procopé, to read him the memorial, and was deeply moved: tears came to his eyes at the end. He insisted, however, that he was not breaking his oath to preserve Finland's privileges, and he refused to receive Tudeer and Söderhjelm. The four Estates also drafted a memorial and unanimously authorized their speakers to carry the protest to the tsar; he refused to grant the four men an audience.[27]

Most impressive of all the protests was the Great Address, which was drafted by a committee elected at another meeting in the Ateneum. The intention was to get signatures from all over the country, but this was an undertaking of enormous difficulty, especially in view of the necessity to keep it secret from the government. Neither the postal system nor the telegraph nor the telephone was safe, since all were official institutions; printing establishments were not proof against indiscretions. The petition, therefore, was hand-copied by hundreds of young volunteers, directed by the curator of the Nyland Section.

Once the document was ready, it had to be circulated throughout a thinly populated country with poor communications, in the dead of a northern winter. Several hundred volunteers, mostly university students, went on skis across the frozen sea to the coastal archipelago and deep into the woods and the wilderness, even north of the Arctic Circle. On Sunday, 5 March, the petition was carried from door to door for signature in Helsinki; and on the same day open meetings were held throughout the back country and delegates were chosen for a mass deputation to carry the remonstrance to St. Petersburg. Over 500,000 signatures were gathered, representing more than a fifth of the total population of the country; and some 500 delegates were chosen to deliver the petition. The collective action was a striking refutation of Bobrikov's assertion, "All reasonable people in Finland are satisfied with the manifesto."

By 13 March, the anniversary of Alexander's death, the 500 delegates were gathered in Helsinki. Shops were closed. The Senate Square was filled with people, many of them dressed in mourning; the piles of flowers around the base of the late tsar's statue were higher than ever. There were no wordy ceremonies. Someone in the crowd struck up Luther's hymn, "A Mighty Fortress Is Our God," and all joined in. Then all sang the national song, "Our Land," and the meeting was over.

Three days later, in the early evening, the delegates departed by train for St. Petersburg. Throngs of people crowded the long platform of the railway station; but everyone was silent as the train pulled out. It was no moment for theatrical gestures.

The whole undertaking had been concealed with almost unbelievable skill from the authorities. Konni Zilliacus, one of the leaders of the resistance, wrote that the episode demonstrated "how ill-organized his [Bobrikov's] spy system really was." At the very least a million people in Finland know about the address.

> . . . in the capital ten thousand knew that the great deputation had been assembled there a few days; and several thousand knew the very minute the special train would leave for St. Petersburg. But not until an hour after its departure did the governor-general learn that a deputation had left Helsinki for the capital of the empire.[28]

This unprecedented expression of national resentment aroused no sympathy or self-doubt in Russian official circles; consideration for popular will, especially in a non-Russian people, was not the strong point of the tsar or his advisers. Despite some rather cautious efforts by the minister state secretary, no audience was granted to the deputation or its leaders. The tsar informed Procopé: "Naturally, I will not receive them, although I am not angry with them. They must go home and hand in their requests to the [district] governors, who will send them to the governor-general, who, finally, is to deliver them to you to be presented to Me, in case any attention can be paid to them." Nicholas showed Procopé the draft of an order forbidding the handing in of petitions concerning the February Manifesto and the holding of meetings for that purpose and for the election of delegates; but the minister state secretary persuaded him to tear up the document.[29]

If the Great Deputation met with a frigid reception in St. Petersburg, it was welcomed with corresponding warmth on its return to Helsinki. This time there was no need for secrecy. The station was filled with people, who overflowed into the surrounding square. Since this was hardly a festive occasion, silence prevailed at first as the delegates left the building; then the crowd burst into "Our Land" and heads were bared. A banquet awaited the delegates in the leading hotel in the city, and patriotic speeches emphasized, as a welcome change from the recent past, that the Finns had "one mind, though two languages." A copy of the Great Address with its signatures, filling six volumes, was left with the governor-general, who forwarded it to Procopé, who sent it on to the monarch. Nicholas merely noted: "Requires no action."[30] Bobrikov felt much more strongly. In a communication to the Senate on 21 March he suggested that an investigation be made to find those who "were immediately guilty, or [had] shown negligence in the exercise of their power and authority while seeing evident disturbance of general peace and quiet."[31] His proposal was not warmly received.

The Great Address and the Great Deputation were a remarkable expression of national will. That will, however, was not unanimous, and there were both loud and muted discords. On 3 March *Työmies* published a front-page article by Kurikka, mentioning the effort to get "signatures for some kind of petition concerning our present governmental questions." He was angry that the workingmen's leaders, who had not been consulted in the drafting of the petition, were now being asked to circulate it. Pointing out that "the minority in power" was not ready to invite representatives of the working class to meet at a common negotiating table, he warned his readers that the upper class was only looking for "names in wholesale lots, which it could then use for its purposes. . . . Let every enlightened workingman stay away from those secret papers for which there will be a fishing expedition for names next Sunday."[32]

Kurikka's editorial enraged the proponents of the Great Address. The writer was accused of breaking the secrecy of the undertaking and imperiling it. When he attended the Finnish Theater on 15 March he was hooted at, manhandled during an intermission by a crowd, mostly of students, and thrown bodily out of the theater; when he returned the crowd refused to take its seats until Kurikka had been persuaded by the orchestra conductor, Kajanus, to leave.[33] Suppliers of paper refused deliveries to *Työmies*, the electric current for its presses was cut off, and vendors of the newspaper were insulted in the streets. The journal managed, nevertheless, to keep going, with hand power and circuitously purchased paper; and a street demonstration in favor of Kurikka, winding up by flooding the office of *Työmies* with flowers, showed that enthusiasm was not all in one camp.[34]

Kurikka's strong views in the crisis of 1899 widened one division in Finnish society, just as Yrjö-Koskinen's increased another. "The persecutions of Kurikka," says one historian of the socialist movement in

Finland, "thus became the immediate occasion for the complete liberation of the workingmen's movement from bourgeois influence. . . . Perhaps a socialistically-inclined workers' party would not have come into being so easily as the meeting of the workers' representatives in 1899 if the Kurikka episode had not occurred."[35]

Although *Työmies* objected to the method of drafting and circulating the Great Address, it did not deny the importance of the action, which it called:

> . . . the result of an astounding patriotic zeal. . . . The way along which the Finnish people are being driven is foreign to our being —[but] normal in the empire. Our constitutional position would be forgotten, and our country would become one of eight *gubernii*, which the governor-general would represent. There can hardly be a difference of opinion that the fate of the Address is finally decided. But its influence on our own people has been [great]. It brings knowledge and right understanding of the blows struck at our country even to the most remote districts.[36]

By October *Työmies* was protesting the wave of arbitrary dismissals of state servants who refused to conform to new, illegal regulations—the first passive resisters:

> That loathsome and inhumane practice of letting the fate of . . . an employee depend on the will of a governmental or other holder of power is such an old and utterly unreasonable practice that in our present-day life, for natural reasons, it arouses well-deserved resistance. . . . Thus the most sacred duty of the working class, as of all who love freedom of life and justice is to fight against oppression and arbitrariness. We know that a people is on the unhappiest of all courses if its life in one way or another falls into the danger of the arbitrariness of individuals.[37]

This assertion—which by implication denied the rights of a strong monarchy—was bolder language than any of the bourgeois opponents of the regime had used so far. It is not surprising, then, that *Työmies* began to suffer from censorship as early as March, was suspended for a month in August, and was again arousing distrust in the governor-general's chancellery in September.[38]

From the time of the February Manifesto on, then, the Finnish socialists were faced in a particularly acute form with the problem confronting many other European socialists: collaboration or noncollaboration with nonsocialist parties on particular questions against a reactionary regime. The problem was never really resolved in Finland, and occasioned bitter disputes among the socialists through the

Great Strike of 1905.[39] When a Finnish Labor Party was organized in July 1899 the delegates straddled the issue by passing a unanimous resolution: "The Labor Party must always strictly adhere to the party program; but in those matters in which, without disregarding the party program, it can cooperate with other parties, it may do so."[40]

It is impossible to obtain a clear picture about the attitude of one discontented class, the landless peasants, during the crisis of 1899. They had no newspapers of their own, no organizations comparable to what were being rapidly developed among the industrial workers, and no brilliant spokesmen; they were, for the most part, poorly educated and out of touch with the world; and they were at the mercy of their landlords or employers. In general, it is evident, the countryside was less given to protesting the February Manifesto than were the towns. A Major General Friedrichs, reporting to the chief of the Russian gendarmerie in Finland on 20 February about conditions in the Turku-Pori district, goes into considerable detail about the signs of dismay in the towns, and concludes laconically: "The population of the countryside is completely indifferent to what is happening."[41]

This was not entirely accurate, as is shown by the thousands of signatures gathered in the back-country for the Great Address. Concerning these signatures, however, we are left with several difficult questions. What proportion of the signers were landowners, and what proportion were landless? Of the landless, how many signed because of conviction and how many because of pressure from their social superiors and economic masters? How much resistance to signing was the result of propaganda organized in Russia?

One of the most evident results of the manifesto in the countryside was the revival and almost universal spread of the old rumors that the extension of Russian law to Finland would mean redistribution of land to the landless. "All sorts of strange figures," wrote Rector Hjelt's daughter Esther in her diary on 10 March, "are roaming around the countryside and deluding people into believing that now good times are coming. In Gammalby, for example, not a single crofter will sign the list, since they all believe that land will soon be partitioned so that it will be taken from him who had it and given to him who had nothing." Five days later she reports: "The crofters and the landless people are fearfully misled. . . . Now they believe the most fantastic rumors as true, and consider everything else as 'tricks of the gentlemen.' "[42]

On the other hand, there is some evidence of pressure from above to sign the Great Petition. A correspondent of Setälä, writing on March 10 from the countryside, reports that some few people have refused to sign, on the ground that the land is to be partitioned. In a neighboring village the local schoolmaster had collected only ten signatures in two days; but when the landlord took the petition around, asking "playfully": "Do you want your own land from the Russians, or do you trust the old law of Finland?" he got 70 signatures in one village.[43]

One illustration of pressure from above comes from that old center of disaffection, Räisälä. On 15 March—the day before the Great Deputation left Helsinki for St. Petersburg—two peasants from Räisälä went to St. Petersburg and delivered to Kuropatkin a memorial for the tsar, complaining that pastor Relander, after church service in Unnunkoski, had called a meeting at which he read the address to the monarch, urged the people to sign it, and declared that it had been sent out by the Senate. The complainants charged that the petition was rebellious toward the tsar and an attempt of the "gentlemen" to draw the people away from loyalty to their monarch, and that the majority of the Finnish people did not approve the address. They also accused another pastor, Elis Bergroth, who had become pastor at Räisälä the year before, of engaging in agitation against the tsar and Russia. The charge against Bergroth is impossible to believe, since he was a follower of Yrjö-Koskinen, a member of the conservative Estate of the Clergy in the Diet, and certainly not the kind of person to stir up his parishioners to political insubordination. He was soon to become one of the most outspoken advocates of compliance with Russian policy.

Since the memorial taken to Kuropatkin was reported to be unsigned, there is no way of knowing how many of the Räisälä folk approved of it. Of the two men who presented it to the minister of war, one, Matti Warwas, had been one of Matti Läheniemi's merry men in the disturbances of a few years before; he had been described then as "unemployed," and was now called a *loismies*, a dependent farm lodger. The other delegate was Juho Meronen, formerly a landholding peasant. After serving three years as chairman of the local council (the Senate learned from the governor of the Viipuri district) Meronen had been removed from office for embezzling 2,200 marks from the community funds, had gone into bankruptcy, had lost his house and land, and was now busy "stirring up the landless people and the ordinary military conscripts about partition of the land, etc." He was said to have been, for a while, a local representative of Kurikka.[44]

A few open declarations of support for the new imperial policy reached Helsinki from the countryside. On 14 March a deputation of fourteen crofters from the village of Sellinge waited upon Bobrikov to thank the tsar for the manifesto and to express the hope that Russian law would soon be extended to Finland.[45] In Heinävesi district three men (all of them dependent farm lodgers and one of them, David Jääskeläinen, reputed to be a ne'er-do-well debtor) wandered about collecting signatures for a letter to the governor-general opposing the Great Address and asserting that the signatures for the Address had been bought for money. Jääskeläinen was said to have spread the story that land would be distributed free to the landless and that officials would lose their offices and be expelled from the country. The three men, it was said, obtained numerous signatures.[46]

In view of the prevalence of such reports a few years earlier, the recrudescence of rumors about land partition ought not to have surprised anyone in Finland. Nevertheless, a sort of panic seems to have seized upon the upper and middle classes. It was widely believed that the landless were being stirred up by wandering Russian agents, especially the peddlers whose activities were so widespread. The Finnish Senate instituted an investigation of these rumors, and a substantial report was presented on 2 May 1899 by K. J. Ståhlberg. He called attention to the fact that the rumors about land redistribution had been circulating for many years and that:

> . . . the belief seems to have been fairly general that the above-mentioned advantage [getting land] was to be gained by the introduction of Russian law and the Russian form of society; and since the rumors of land partition, as a result of the most recent political events and the depressed state of mind of the country occasioned by them have revived with new strength and great extent among the landless population, these rumors have appeared everywhere in connection with the above-mentioned belief.

The rumors included, besides free distribution of land, the prospect that "either all officials should be abolished or their number reduced to a few, principally a village eldest in every village, and the wages of the remaining ones reduced, and that the clergymen also should cease to be paid by the government and that the possibility should be opened by everyone to become a civil servant even without studying." Thereby the tax burden would be reduced.

Although Ståhlberg did not deny that numerous Russian peddlers, gendarmes, and others were active in spreading rumors, he listed twenty native Finns (including Warwas and Meronen) who had been engaged in the same activity. He pointed out that the rumors were most widely and stubbornly believed in areas where the number of great estates was largest. In Tavastkyrö, he reported, a meeting of laborers and crofters had been held, which had resolved to send to the governor-general a message to express satisfaction with the manifesto and the hope that with His Excellency's help it would be quickly put into execution—"all this," said Ståhlberg, "in the belief that by the Manifesto, the contents of which they did not know in detail, they would get not only land but other economic advantages. . . . In Tyrvis district, too, a similar meeting is said to have taken place, at which it was said that the landless would probably lose something with respect to religion, but gain a good deal more with respect to economic matters."

The spreading of rumors, he said, appeared, "in many cases, perhaps most, to have occurred without a purposeful agitation." After citing various reports that the rumors were being encouraged by highly placed persons in St. Petersburg, he added, with remarkably cautious and tortuous wording:

All this cannot, however, lead to anything but a rather slightly valid occasion for surmise; at present we have no manifest, cogent proof that a planned agitation has taken place, or how it originated. But one thing that, on the other hand, has clearly emerged from the investigation is this: that the landless population in the countryside . . . in many districts has shown itself to a serious degree receptive to the belief that its present position ought to, and can, be improved . . . by the introduction of Russian law and Russian social conditions.[47]

The Russifiers did not neglect the opportunity presented by the rural turmoil in Finland. "Although . . . we may assume," says the historian Rasila, "that rumors of distribution of land were not organized by the Russian government, it is evident that within it the course of events was observed and the spread of rumors concerning distribution of land and the coming of Russian law were noted with pleasure."[48] Bobrikov wrote to the tsar that when the Russian government was able to bring thoroughgoing improvements to the condition of the landless Finnish peasants, it would undoubtedly win over the great majority of the people as "a dependable and firm support, which indeed can facilitate the completion of governmental measures of unification."[49] *Novoe vremia* asserted on 8 April (27 March OS) that conditions in Finland were favorable to the Swedish-speaking barons, but that the greatest part of the people were a landless proletariat living in misery. It was unfortunate that Russia had not intervened before; but it was necessary to do so now. A reformation was inevitable, and when it had taken place "we can see which the people of Finland will more willingly listen to, the Swedish gentlemen and their cat's-paws, or the real benefactor, which does not consider its own interests—the government of Russia.[50]

The trouble with proposing to be a benefactor to the Finnish peasants was that a state and society constructed as Russia was, with millions of dissatisfied peasants of its own, was unlikely to institute thoroughgoing agrarian reform anywhere. A gesture, however, was not long in coming. In the spring of 1899 the tsar, at the suggestion of Bobrikov, decreed that 2 million marks of a surplus in the Finnish treasury should be used for purchasing land for the landless. This sum was characterized by the Russian press as a "gift" from the monarch to the Finnish landless people, to the annoyance of the Finnish newspapers. The assertion was repeated in the first number of a new official journal, *Finliandskaia gazeta* and its Finnish-language supplement, *Suomen sanomat*, in 1900. Before long the *Gazeta* declared further that the leading circles in Finland were trying to keep the crofters in slavery by asserting that they were not landless and therefore not entitled to share in the tsar's gift.[51]

Such rather crude propaganda did not accomplish much. The landless peasants did not need to be told that their landlords exploited them; but when they began to think seriously about action, many of them were less attracted by the vague expressions of benevolence on the part of Russia than by the more drastic proposals of the Finnish socialists. The elections in the new, democratic Finnish Diet after 1906 were to demonstrate this.

The revelation of seething discontent among the peasants was a great shock to middle-class and upper-class Finns, previously complacent about the superiority of their country. In the words of Viljo Rasila, the leading authority on the history of the crofters, "The rumors following the February Manifesto had shattered the romantic view of the people and the feeling of belonging together. They prepared the ground for the socialist doctrine of class struggle, which now began to spread powerfully."[52]

The neglect of any significant work of internal reform continued for a number of years. In the course of a series of long and acrid debates in the Diet in 1900 on a law to attack the crofter question, "it seems," says Rasila, "that the Estates, regardless of the events of the previous year, did not yet realize the social scope of the crofter question, but still regarded the matter from the point of view of the landowner."[53] The law which was finally passed in 1902, to go into effect in 1904, could not possibly satisfy the crofters, since, among other shortcomings, it did not set a minimum time for a lease or establish a maximum workday, or effectively protect the security of a crofter's tenure.[54]

If nothing remotely adequate was done to cure the underlying social ills of the country, there was great activity in trying to remove the
political symptoms and counteract attitudes of indifference to patriotic
concerns. Attempts were made to enlighten the peasants with floods
of pamphlets and newspaper articles. The results of this activity were
questionable, given the low or nonexistent reading level of many of the
disaffected peasants, the difficulty of circulating literature in the back
country, and the widespread lack of receptiveness to abstract political
ideas.

More striking was a form of resistance resembling the activity of
the Russian *narodniki*: the exodus of university students to the countryside to educate and rouse the peasants. There was a well-established Finnish background for this activity: for decades some Finnish students had spent summer vacations in the countryside, giving
courses. Now there was a new impetus, and a new content for the
work. "The February Manifesto," writes Herman Gummerus, who
was a student at the time and who plunged immediately into the resistance movement, "affected youths like the blaring of trumpets."
Quite suddenly the students were galvanized into political activism.
Hundreds of them streamed out to the countryside to explain to the
peasants the meaning of the February Manifesto, to set them straight
on rumors of land redistribution, and to help build up a united front
among the people. Officially, they were to give courses in Finnish
history, law, government, economic resources, elementary schools, and
folk high schools, cooperative movements, and the like. No one, however, seems to have been deceived about their real purpose. Bobrikov
was suspicious, and peppered the rector of the University, Edvard
Hjelt, with unending complaints and questions.[55] By 1900 he was demanding that every student lecture should be given only by a mature
person, should be subject to official supervision, and should confine
itself exclusively to the lecturer's specialty; and that there should be
no lectures on constitutional law. From higher authority the governor-
general obtained an order that he should receive periodic reports on
the lectures permitted, specifying the time, the place, the speaker, and
the title of each. In January 1903 he brought the student lectures to
an end altogether.

It is uncertain how far this official alarm was justified. The results
of the student missionary work seem to have been rather mixed. Gummerus, who spent the summer of 1899 in eastern Uusimaa, "where the
oppression of the estate owners had placed its unmistakable stamp on
the people," believed that he had achieved nothing.[56] In any case the
awakening of the peasant to political thought and activity could not
take place overnight.

Whether the students taught the peasants much or not, some of them learned some hard facts about conditions of life in Finland from which they had previously been shielded by their upper-class or middle-class backgrounds. Gummerus, for instance, discovered "an agricultural proletariat on the edge of minimal subsistence."[57] In any case, a large number of students were now enlisted in the struggle against Russification. In the following years they wrote and circulated forbidden literature, collected signatures for addresses and protests, joined in public demonstrations—sometimes clashing with the police —and took a leading role in the army strike. By the time of World War I hundreds of them were ready to enlist in the special 27th Prussian Jäger Battalion to bear arms against Russia.

Students were not the only part of the intellectual community to engage in resistance activity. Finnish scholars of international reputation used their connections to arouse sympathy for Finland abroad. They wrote to acquaintances in other countries, sent articles to foreign newspapers, or went abroad themselves to meet scholars, politicians and journalists to state Finland's case and obtain publicity. On the whole they were very successful. One of the first fruits of their activity was the international cultural address, a set of memorials signed by over a thousand prominent intellectuals in twelve countries and calling the attention of the tsar to conditions in Finland. The collection was published in facsimile in Berlin and Stockholm[58] and carried to St. Petersburg at the end of June 1899 by a delegation of six well-known scholars.

Nothwithstanding its courteous and circumspect behavior and its distinguished membership, the international delegation was not well received in St. Petersburg, where its arrival caused great embarrassment. Although the appeal was addressed to Nicholas, he would not receive it or the delegates. They had to leave St. Petersburg without having accomplished anything except that the Russian government was left in a very bad light.[59]

If the petitioners were snubbed in St. Petersburg, their reception in Finland on their way home more than made up for the earlier slights. For miles outside Helsinki crowds lined the railroad tracks to see their train pass; and in the city, its usual summer somnolence broken by the crowds of vacationing inhabitants who streamed back to town, they were given a warm public welcome.

Not every Finn, however, rejoiced in the international cultural address. Senator Tudeer called it "a great misfortune for Finland, quite aside from the fact that it was inappropriate and tactless in the highest degree. Presumably a day will come that will prove that the men who arranged it were not friends of the fatherland but immature politicians—who don't understand anything. The result of this deputation will certainly be 'sour' for Finland and every one of us."⁶⁰ Tudeer may have been right. Nicholas was reported to have said: "They have smeared my government. I shall never forgive them for that."⁶¹

Whether or not Finnish and international opposition made the Russian authorities more stubborn, it certainly did not make them more conciliatory. Victor Procopé, tired of the frustrations of his job as acting minister state secretary, asked the tsar for leave of absence; instead, the monarch decided to replace him with a Russian, V. K. Plehve, who became acting minister state secretary on 29 August 1899 and regular minister state secretary on 12 January 1900. There was no longer any Finn, however Russified, with the right of direct access to the monarch. In December 1899 Plehve's opportunities for involvement in Finnish affairs became even greater, in a highly sensitive area, when he was appointed Chancellor of the University at Helsinki.

In contrast to the crude and tactless Bobrikov, Plehve was a polished man of the world, affable in manner and willing to listen to Finns. He hid an iron fist, it was said, in a silken glove. Thus, the newly appointed Chancellor of Helsinki University soon warned Rector Hjelt that the university must not become a hotbed for agitation. How strict a devotion to the monarchy he demanded was shown on a visit he paid to the university in the spring of 1900. After listening for a while to a lecture on Catherine the Great he scolded the professor for daring to pass judgment on her. Her person, more than a century after her death, was still sacrosanct.⁶² The practical results of this ultraconservatism were soon to become evident.

By the end of 1899 the battle lines were drawn for Finland, both internally and externally. The Russian government was committed to breaking Finnish "separatism," at whatever the cost. Neither Bobrikov nor Nicholas was the kind of person to admit to having made any mistake; to have rescinded the February Manifesto would have been almost as humiliating as for a Pope to rescind an encyclical. Indeed, as resistance increased in Finland, it only confirmed the Russian administrators' belief that the Finns must be brought to heel.

In one of his long reports to the tsar in 1902 Bobrikov lamented that:

. . . the representative of Russian power in the country has absolutely no one to lean upon here, no one to trust. All the institutions and the educated classes constitute an unbroken wall against the most natural and justified Russian claims. The people, as everywhere, stand aside from politics, but in most recent times agitation has begun to draw them too into opposition. Besides a national and cultural separation and also a complete absence of an inward tie to Russian society, I must attest to the presence of a highly unfriendly and mistrustful attitude toward the Russian government in general and the representative of Russian power in the country in particular.[63]

That the Russian government's policies might be in part responsible for this alienation seems never to have occurred to the governor-general. Instead, he accused the Finns of trying to dictate policies to the empire, and envisaged the possibility that the monarch, in order to put Finland "into its proper place among the other parts of the empire," might, "in case of need, deprive the Grand Duchy of those peculiarities which are interpreted by the Finns as attributes of their separate 'state,' that is, lay the hand of the Sovereign on Finland in all those cases when that district refuses to follow Russian policy."[64] Bobrikov's basic maxim was to be found in one sentence: "Within the entire area of the Russian Empire there must be found complete and undoubted trust in the autocratic power."[65]

Bobrikov was not the only one to consider drastic interference with Finnish political institutions. Plehve warned two visiting senators in January 1900 that the Estates must not engage in political demonstrations, for "the suspension of the Diet was not an impossible matter."[66]

Against this ruthless program the Finns had now become divided into camps that were to become more and more hostile to one another. Almost all Finns detested the Russian measures and the further ones that might come; but the bitterness between the compliers, the resisters, the increasingly revolutionary socialists, and the gradually awakening peasants increased from year to year.

For example, the Labor party in a convention at Forssa in 1903 made itself officially the Social Democratic Party and adopted a platform with a Marxist preamble and a series of demands for complete political democracy and avoidance of cooperation with bourgeois parties except in those cases "when it can be done without setting aside the party program."[67] On the other hand, such militancy drove many social conservatives to anger, not conciliation. Baron Otto Wrede wrote to a friend from his estate the month after the Forssa convention, declaring that the people "whose unjustified claims to self-indulgence and impossible, socially subversive reforms . . . must be opposed, are the acceptable auxiliary troops the present regime rests upon and notably encourages, to overturn, with their help, our constitutional society."[68]

What happened in the next few years was the logical consequence of all these hostilities. The story of the continued struggle is full of interest and drama; but because of the space limitations of this study we can pick out only the highlights. Since the course of events is recounted in considerable detail in most histories of Finland, few footnote references to sources will be made.

In June 1900 a measure long discussed by Russian officials was finally put into effect: the introduction of Russian as the language of official business in Finland. The Language Manifesto was not prepared in conformity with the procedure outlined in the February Manifesto. Instead of the consultations called for in that document, it was worked out in secret by a committee composed of six Russians (including Heiden, Pobedonostsev, Bobrikov, and Plehve). The committee agreed with Bobrikov's assertion that "The Russian language is the spiritual standard of the empire and the foremost condition for the internal unification of all its parts"; and, while disclaiming any intention to denationalize the Finns "in the area of religion, literature and family life," set the goal of eventually making Russian the official language of Finland.[69]

The Language Manifesto occasioned in the Senate the same sort of agonized debate about promulgation as had the February Manifesto; but this time a decision was delayed until a protest had been sent to St. Petersburg. The tsar responded by commanding immediate promulgation; twelve of the twenty senators resigned.

A more serious crisis arose in 1901. A manifesto was issued that completely changed the military establishment of Finland. Like the Language Manifesto its preparation did not conform to the procedure established in the February Manifesto: it, too, was the creation of a special conference. From the Russian point of view the provisions were very mild. The Finnish army was virtually disbanded. Every male Finn was subject to military duty; but for the time being he would serve in units made up "for the most part" of Finnish subjects. By special arrangement some of the recruits might be sent to join Russian units quartered in Finland or in the St. Petersburg military district. Officers and noncommissioned officers had to know Russian; the Finnish forces were to be subjected to Russian command; Russian officers might be appointed to primarily Finnish units and would thereby acquire Finnish citizenship, without loss of their rights as Russians. For the time being, only 500 men were to be chosen annually for the Finnish battalion of guards and the dragoon regiment—the two existing Finnish units that were retained for the time being while the others were dissolved. The period of service was three years. For the first year, 1902, only 280 men were to be drafted, though over 20,000 were liable to military service.

As Senator Eneberg, who had advance notice of the Army Manifesto, wrote to Yrjö-Koskinen about the plan: "It may be rather lenient in the beginning; but what form it will take in the future no one can divine. For in fact we no longer have any law in the military question, but depend exclusively on the emperor. The law itself allows any military burden at all."[70]

By this time the Senate was fairly well tamed, or filtered: only four senators voted against promulgation, and then resigned. Among the people, however, the effect was different. A new Great Address against the Army Manifesto, written by Mechelin, collected 473,468 signatures. It was sent to the Senate and forwarded to Plehve, who presented it to the tsar. Its only effect was to anger the Russian authorities, because so many of the signers were public servants. Plehve instructed the governor-general to see to it that in the future positions of trust should be filled only by persons who had not taken part in such political expression; if suitable Finns could not be found, the positions might be filled by Russians.

By now a movement of passive resistance against illegal actions by the Russian government had got under way and its most dramatic manifestation was the "Army Strike" of 1902 and 1903. When the young men subject to the draft in 1902 were called to present themselves before their draft boards, fewer than half appeared. According to the statistics of a resistance organization, of the 25,000 summoned, only 10,493 obeyed the command. For once the industrial workers and the educated youth were united. Ursin and the other socialist leaders had come out strongly against acquiescence in the draft, and the university students were also overwhelmingly opposed to it. Crowds gathered at the recruiting places, and were not always polite to the authorities. In Helsinki the onlookers, after watching the embarrassment of the draft board, moved on to the Senate Square, to demonstrate against the compliant senators. After the crowd had refused to disperse, the new Russian governor of Uusimaa province, Mikhail Kaigorodov, summoned Cossacks, who charged the people with drawn sabers and rode over them. New masses of demonstrators kept arriving, however, and made it clear that they would not go home until the Cossacks left. Eventually Kaigorodov was persuaded to withdraw his troops; they were replaced by a contingent of the Finnish guard, and the square became peaceful again. Serious violence had now entered the political struggle. So had mass action by all classes of society; Finnish political life was undergoing a rough process of democratization.

It was difficult for the authorities to punish such an enormous number of resisters. By a combination of fairly light penalties, threats, and offers of pardon, however, the government persuaded about 3,000

young resisters to declare that they regretted their nonappearance, so that by the end of the year the number of persons refusing to appear was reduced to about 45 percent. The Army Strike was not the only means of opposing the new military law. When the Finnish sharp-shooter battalion was disbanded its officers were offered posts in the new force; but all of them preferred to resign. Many local communes refused to elect members for the draft boards, and finally the Senate itself had to appoint them.

The only significant nonopponents of the Army Manifesto were the Russian-appointed officials, the purified Senate, the Old Finn party (and most of its press, including *Uusi Suometar*), and the hierarchy and most of the clergy of the state Lutheran Church. All of these, however, actively and effectively urged compliance with the orders from above. In the second year of the strike, 1903, only about a third of those summoned for possible military service failed to appear. By 1904 the resistance had weakened even more; over 81 percent of the young men summoned put in an appearance. There was little comfort to be had in this, however, for the Russian authorities. An army raised with such difficulty was clearly nothing to rely on. In March 1905, when the Russian government was in desperate trouble with the Japanese War and was having to make concessions to its discontented subjects, the tsar proclaimed a "provisional" suspension of the conscription law. In return Finland should pay the Russian government an annual sum for military purposes. After some debate the Finns agreed, though only for the duration of the year 1905. Conscription was never again enforced in Finland under the Russian regime. Passive resistance had accomplished something after all; it was to spare Finland the fearful bloodletting of World War I. That the Finns had a bloodletting of their own in the brief civil war of 1918 was due to their internal hostilities and tensions.

If the years 1900, 1901, and 1902 were bad for Finland, 1903 was worse. Increasing national resistance led to increasing determination by the Russians, especially Bobrikov, to crush all resistance. In January he got rid of four provincial governors by dismissal or resignation, and replaced them with Russians, despite the remonstrances of the Old Finns. Russians were also appointed to some lower offices. Many justices of the district appeals courts lost their positions because of opposing illegal administrative measures. On 9 April (27 March OS) the tsar issued a rescript granting Bobrikov dictatorial powers for three years. Among the menacing provisions was the authorization for the governor-general to direct teaching in the schools in such a way that the youth should be inoculated with "the spirit of loyalty to His Majesty the Emperor of Russia." In November the Russian gendarmes in Finland were given the same powers as the native police. By virtue of his dictatorial powers Bobrikov expelled from the country fifty-three leaders of the opposition; ten were sent to Russia and the others were permitted to go abroad. The first deportees from Helsinki were seen off at the railroad station by a crowd cheering and shouting "Welcome back!" In November Yrjö-Koskinen, worried about the fate of the country for which his policy had been able to accomplish so little, died.

Whether or not as a result of the country's turmoil, emigration from Finland rose sharply in the first years of the century. From the port of Hanko, the principal departure point, the average annual number of emigrants in the years 1891-1898 was 3,378; in 1899 it rose to 12,357; in 1900 to 10,642; in 1901 to 12,659; and in the period January-September 1902 to 17,270.[71] The number of emigrants per 10,000 of the population rose from 13.2 in 1898 to 83.7 in 1903.[72]

This increase was commonly attributed to discontent with the Russian oppression and fear of conscription into the army; indeed, it had been predicted.[73] Bobrikov disputed this assertion in one of his reports of 1902. He admitted that emigration from Uusimaa, which had been insignificant for several years, had grown sharply, and this change he attributed to "agitation" and the fact that the center of the agitation, Helsinki, was in the province. He pointed out, however, that 52 percent of the emigrants belonged to the landless classes and that, therefore, the determining factors must be economic; and that the principal areas of emigration remained the same: Ostrobothnia, the Åland Islands, and part of the coastal archipelago.[74]

As early as the spring of 1899 Bobrikov—evidently unable to believe in such a phenomenon as a spontaneous popular movement—spoke of a "secret, illegal organization" that was directing resistance. There was no such thing then; but, thanks to his policies, one soon developed. By the summer of 1900, when many Finnish newspapers had been silenced by the censor, the most important of the illegal publications began to appear: *Fria ord* (*Free World*) and its sister organ, the Finnish-language *Vapaisia lehtisiä*. They were printed in Sweden and smuggled into Finland, for the most part with great success. A more comprehensive program of resistance began with the founding in September 1901 of an organization of prominent men, from the Swedish Party and the Young Finns. They were soon called the *Kagal* (Kagaali), from a Hebrew word meaning "gathering." The term was applied at first in scorn by Russian reactionaries to Russian revolutionary groups and resisting Finns, and then proudly adopted by the Finnish malcontents. The Kagal divided the country into forty-five districts, with cells that enjoyed the help of hundreds of volunteers who engaged in propaganda work and obstruction and were partly responsible for the success of the Army Strike.

Passive resistance, however, is condemned by its nature to the defensive. As practiced by a divided Finnish people against the Russian autocracy it required individual acts of moral courage by a large number of people over an indefinite but presumably long time. The attenuation of the Army Strike by 1904 made it all too evident that passive resistance was not accomplishing much. "Our people," says Gummerus, "resembled an army that after a long and forced retreat with unceasing losses was threatened with internal dissolution. It was high time to set a counter-offensive in motion."[75]

This counter-offensive, it seemed clear, must be directed against the absolute monarchy itself. To try to restore the status quo ante, as the passive resisters, the "constitutionalists," desired, seemed useless: a return to the old order would make it possible for a policy of repression to begin again at any time.

The radicalization of the resistance was due in large part to the efforts of the journalist Victor (Konni) Zilliacus, who had been one of the founders of *Fria ord* and soon developed a close relationship with various revolutionary movements in Russia, which with his help were smuggling their subversive literature through Finland. He became convinced that freedom for Finland required cooperation with revolutionists in Russia. When the Russo-Japanese War broke out in 1904, Zilliacus saw new possibilities of combined action. He opened contacts with the Japanese ambassador in London, and was able to convene in Paris in September 1904 a conference of various opposition groups within the empire. Nineteen groups had been invited, and eight sent delegates. The conference approved a set of resolutions encompassing abolition of all measures infringing on Finnish constitutional rights, the replacement of the absolute monarchy by a democratic form of government based on universal suffrage, and the right to national self-determination. The tactics to be used would depend in each case on the "needs, strength and position of the social elements, the classes, and nationalities."

The story of the cooperation between the Finnish opposition and Russian revolutionaries has been told in English, in scholarly and interesting detail, by William R. Copeland.[76] Since a number of the Finnish constitutionalists (notably Mechelin) hesitated to associate themselves openly with revolutionists and "terrorists" inside the empire, Zilliacus and some of his colleagues decided to found a new party, "the Finnish Party of Active Resistance." It emphasized the need to resist the monarchy ruthlessly, to cooperate with freedom movements in other parts of the empire, to spread propaganda, to distribute weapons among the people, and to form a combat organization. The nonsocialist opposition was now split between the constitutionalists and the activists.

Months before the formation of the Activist party, a dramatic gesture of violent resistance had startled Helsinki and Europe. As early as March 1899 one of the traveling goodwill emissaries of Finland, Werner Söderhjelm, had been told by Baltic German expatriate historian and influential journalist in Berlin, Theodor Schiemann, that someone ought to assassinate either Bobrikov or Grand Duke Vladimir.[77]

The same idea had occurred independently to some angry young men in Finland. They worked out several plans (none of which succeeded) for a cooperative assassination of the governor-general; but the deed was done for them single-handedly on 9 June 1904. Eugen Schauman, a young government employee, a member of the Nyland Section, and the son of a senator and former general in the Russian Army, met Bobrikov in the Senate building, shot him three times, and then killed himself. He left a respectful letter for the tsar, which was published in *Fria ord* and reached the world press. "The method is violent," he said, "but it is the only one. With knowledge of Your Majesty's good heart and noble intentions I beg Your Majesty only to find out about the real state of affairs in the Empire—Finland, Poland, the Baltic Provinces."

On 28 July Plehve followed Bobrikov: he was cut to pieces by a bomb thrown into his carriage by a Russian Social Revolutionary. With two of the principal Russifiers of Finland dead, and the third, Kuropatkin, directing a losing war in Manchuria, and with increasing popular discontent at home, the Russian government was unable to pursue its hard-line policy. The new governor-general, Prince Ivan Obolenskii, was a well-educated aristocrat, more patient, though not more liberal, than his predecessor. He had difficult problems to face. The elections to the Diet, held in November 1904, brought bare majorities of constitutionalists to those former citadels of the Old Finns, the Estates of the Clergy and of the Peasants, and an overwhelming majority to the Estate of the Burghers and, naturally, to the Knights and Nobles. For the opening of the Diet on 6 December men who had been expelled from the country but elected to the legislature were allowed to return home; they received tumultuous welcomes. Among them was Mechelin, still opposed to violence and hopeful that right and justice would triumph peaceably.

The violent year of 1905 arrived. As turbulence mounted in Russia, Finland became the scene of heated public debates and street demonstrations about such burning questions as universal suffrage. There were both successful and unsuccessful attempts at assassination of unpopular government officials. The general strike in Russia in October spread to Finland. On 29 October railway workers went on strike, and within a few days the movement had spread over the entire country. A National Central Strike Committee, composed of socialists, and led at first by Kurikka, was set up. Bourgeois groups followed, and soon almost every sort of enterprise was shut down: factories, public utilities, communications, shops, inns, schools, and the university. Even the police, now largely Russified, found it prudent to keep out of sight. The workers organized a protective corps, soon called the Red Guard, to preserve order, and the university students set up another volunteer police corps. The Old Finn Senate resigned on 30 October. The governor-general took refuge on a Russian warship in the harbor, and some of the more nervous Russian civil officials fled to the island fortress of Sveaborg (now Suomenlinna). There were really two strikes going on at the same time. The constitutionalists of various political shades wanted to return to the old legal order and a meeting of the Diet, which could then discuss such matters as electoral reform. The socialists, who now commanded the loyalty of almost the entire industrial working class and who were, not unnaturally, distrustful of the reforming zeal of the constitutionalists, demanded the abolition of the Estates, the establishment of a provisional government, the calling of a constituent national assembly, and the establishment of a parliament based on universal suffrage. In the city of Oulu the strikers proclaimed Finland a republic and drove out the provincial governor and the hated Russian gendarmes.

The struggle turned in favor of the constitutionalists on 4 November (22 October OS), when Nicholas signed his November Manifesto suspending for the meantime (though not rescinding) the February Manifesto and revoking the dictatorial measures taken by Bobrikov, as well as the conscription law. The tsar authorized the Senate to prepare proposals for sweeping reforms, including the adoption of universal suffrage. The manifesto was approved and promulgated by a newly reconstituted Senate. The bourgeois groups were now ready to end the strike, and shops began to open. The socialists, who had been principally responsible for the success of the strike, were embittered, but yielded rather than precipitate a civil war. The new Senate was headed by Mechelin and was composed of Swedish-speaking and Finnish-speaking constitutionalists and one socialist; the formerly dominant Old Finns were now shut out. The Great Strike had won a victory, but not necessarily an enduring one. In St. Petersburg the old guard was licking its wounds but had really learned nothing; in Finland the breach between the classes had been widened.

For the moment, the prospect was hopeful. A new governor-general, the moderate Nikolai Nikolaevich Gerard, and a new minister state secretary, Major General August Langhoff, a Finn with long service in Russia and no political experience, were appointed. While a newly elected Diet was discussing reform of the representational system and hesitating, the Red Guard encouraged celerity of decision by demonstrating outside the building where it was meeting. In June 1906 the Estates adopted a system of political representation that was the most democratic in Europe. A one-chamber legislature was to be elected on the basis of universal and equal suffrage by men and women; the number of voters increased from 125,000 to 1,125,000. The tsar approved the measure in July, and Finland was launched upon a new political course.

The first Diet under the new system met in May 1907. The socialists had by far the largest number of representatives, 80 of the total of 200; they showed great strength among the discontented in the countryside as well as in the towns. Given the animosities that had arisen or been intensified during the past eight years and the difficult social problems inherited from the past, it is not surprising that the new representative body spent more time in wrangling than in achieving positive results.

The most serious trouble, however, came not from internal disunity but from St. Petersburg. The policies of Prime Minister Stolypin in Russia were paralleled by those he adopted in Finland. The dismissal of the Second Duma in June 1907 was followed by the dismissal of the Finnish Diet in April 1908 and the reorganization of the Senate with the exclusion of Mechelin and some of the other constitutionalists and the inclusion of some Old Finns. In bringing Finland to heel, Stolypin now had a useful tool in the Third Duma, which was as narrowly nationalist in sentiment as he was. On the other hand, the Finnish Diet was as intractable as ever: Stolypin could not tamper with the Finnish electoral system as he could with the Russian.

Among the subjects of dispute between Helsinki and St. Petersburg was the continued automatic payment of money to Russia in lieu of military conscript despite the fact that, from the Diet's points of view the Finnish military-service law of 1878 had never been legally repealed and no military agreement had been worked out by the Russian authorities and the constitutionally chosen representatives of Finland.

More serious was the question of the so-called Neva Millions. Because the Finnish railway network terminated at St. Petersburg in the part of the city north of the Neva River, and the Russian system south of the river, troops and military supplies destined for Finland had to be transshipped at the imperial capital. To Russian military men this was a most undesirable circumstance and Bobrikov, in particular, had urged making a rail link across the marshy Neva area—a not inconsiderable engineering enterprise. Finns, on the other hand, were reluctant to share in the expense of the project. The link, they thought, would bring little economic advantage to their country, and its execution would necessitate considerable reconstruction of bridges and other parts of the Finnish system to accommodate the heavier Russian rolling stock. Despite this reluctance, the well-tamed Senate had voted shortly before Bobrikov's death to pay 2.5 million rubles for the building of the link. After 1905 the Russian military authorities believed the building of the connection to be especially urgent, in view of the deteriorating international situation in Europe and what they perceived to be an imminent danger of an insurrection in Finland which would require the prompt dispatch of Russian troops to suppress it. Continued resistance by the Diet to making a contribution as large as the Russians demanded contributed to the growing tension.[78]

If Stolypin and his associates really believed that insurrection was imminent in Finland, they did nothing conciliatory to avert it. In May 1908 the prime minister began to criticize the Finns publicly for cherishing revolutionary designs against the monarchy and striving for independence. The next month the tsar confirmed a decision of the Russian Council of Ministers that all matters concerning the administration and legislation of Finland must be submitted to the Council, which would decide whether or not they affected the interests of the empire. In practice this meant that Finnish officials were now completely subjected to the Council of Ministers, and that the minister state secretary for Finland had lost the traditional right of direct access to the monarch to report on Finnish affairs and submit Finnish proposals.

This policy of a firm hand with the natives had already been displayed in November 1907 when the moderate governor-general, Gerard, suddenly, with no previous consultation, found himself saddled with a new assistant, Major General Frants A. Zein (in Finnish historiography spelled "Seyn"), a former enthusiastic supporter of Bobrikov. After this affront Gerard considered his position untenable, and resigned, to be replaced by a new governor-general, Vladimir Bekman (Boeckman). Within less than two months the Mechelin Senate had been dismissed. Sharp conflict arose between the governor-general and the Diet, especially its indomitable speaker, Per Evind Svinhufvud, an outspoken Young Finn. The Diet that met in February 1909 was dissolved almost as soon as it opened. A Diet newly elected in May was quite as assertive of its rights; and in the autumn the Senate,

Finland

too, refused to accept a decision by the Russian Council of Ministers
about payment of money for military purposes. Even the Old Finn
members of the Senate offered their resignations. The Russian government had succeeded in destroying its one base of support among
the Finnish people; it was clear that there was no longer anything to
be rescued, as Yrjö-Koskinen had hoped against hope. The policy of
compliance was at an end. A new Senate composed of Finns who had
long lived in Russia and were Russified was appointed; it could not
possibly hope for any public support. At the end of 1909 the Diet was
dissolved again; but the new elections brought no change. A sort of
involuntary united front of all the parties against Russification had
been created.

There was still no faltering among the Russian leaders. In November 1909 Governor-General Bekman was dismissed, being considered
too conciliatory to the Finns. He was replaced by Zein, a sort of
Bobrikov redivivus. When the Duma assembled in June 1910 Stolypin
delivered a violent speech against the Finns, and the legislature
passed, by an overwhelming majority, a law which ended Finnish
autonomy, in much the same way as the February Manifesto had
done, but permitted the Finnish Diet to send delegates to the Duma
—a privilege it declined to accept. *"Finis Finlandiae!"* exclaimed the
rightist delegate Purishkevich in the Duma after the measure was
passed, and he was correct—for the time being.

However rational some of the justifications for Russification may
have seemed in the first place, the course of events in Finland had
proved the calculations to be fundamentally wrong. A predominantly
loyal people had been alienated; a sense of Finnish nationality had
been intensified; an enemy had been needlessly created. A state of
mind widely shared by his countrymen was expressed in a letter written by Baron Otto Wrede in April 1912:

> Nothing can rescue us but great European or world events that
> will transform all present power relationships. But these, too,
> must be waited for and bring with them great dangers and in-
> calculable social conflicts.[79]

Notes to Part Five

CHAPTER 22. CONSTITUTIONAL AND HISTORICAL BACKGROUND
OF THE RUSSIFICATION DISPUTE IN FINLAND

1. Jaakko Ahokes, *A History of Finnish Literature* (Bloomingtoi
Indiana University Press, 1973), pp. 73-74.
2. Egon Tempel, *New Finnish Architecture* (New York: Prae

pp. 15-19; Nils Erik Wickberg, *Byggnadskonst i Finland* (Helsinki: Söderström, 1959), pp. 80-112. The impression produced by the bold, experimental turn-of-the-century Finnish architecture upon a British tourist with no special qualifications as a critic is recorded in A. Maccallum Scott, *Through Finland to St. Petersburg* (London: Grant Richards Ltd., 1908), pp. 78-82.

3. Scott, pp. 62-65; Maurice Rheims, *The Flowering of Art Nouveau* (New York: Harry N. Abrams, Inc., n.d.), pp. 31 and 142 and illustration p. 192; Wendy Hall, *Green Gold and Granite, Background to Finland* (London: Max Parrish, 1957), pp. 101-102; Kerttu Niilonen (ed.), *Kalela . . . Wilderness Studio and Home* (Helsinki: Otava, n.d.; with Finnish and English text); Onni Okkonen, *Gallen-Kallela, elämä ja taide* (Porvoo-Helsinki: Söderström, 1961); Sakari Saarikivi (ed.), *Hugo Simberg. . . .* (Helsinki: Söderström, 1947, with English text, pp. xiv-xvi); John Boulton Smith, *Modern Finnish Painting and Graphic Art* (London: Weidenfeld and Nicolson, 1970), pp. 10-20.

4. Harold E. Johnson, *Jean Sibelius* (New York: Knopf, 1959); Hall, chap. 9.

5. Robert Schweitzer, *Autonomie und Autokratie.*

6. Robert Fredrik Hermanson, *Finlands statsrättsliga ställning* (Helsinki: G. W. Edlund, 1892), p. 2.

7. Ibid., pp. 5, 6.

8. Ibid., p. 7.

9. Ibid., p. 8.

10. Ibid., p. 10.

11. Ibid., pp. 11-12, 14.

12. Ibid., pp. 67, 72, 86-87.

13. Aira Kemilainen, " 'Nation'-sana ja Porvoon valtiopäivien merkitys," *Historiallinen aikakauskirja*, 1964, pp. 289-304.

14. Keijo Korhonen, *Autonomous Finland in the Political Thought of Nineteenth Century Russia*; Osmo Jussila, *Suomen perustuslait venäläisten ja suomalaisten tulkintojen mukaan 1808-1863.* Among earlier treatments of the subject one might note the well-documented study by Joonas Vuolle-Apiala, *Die Entwicklung der Verfassung Finlands [sic] bis zum Regierungsantritt Nikolaus' II*, Heidelberg: Rössler & Herbert, 1912.

15. Schweitzer, *Autonomie und Autokratie.*

16. S. R. Malmström, *Dagman Prinsessa av Danmark, Kejsarinna av Ryssland. . . .* (Third printing; Helsinki: Söderström, 1938), pp. 222-36; Estlander (see List of Abbreviations), II, pp. 92-97.

17. Anon., "La Situation politique de la Finlande," *Revue du droit international et de législation comparée*, 2nd. ser., II (1900), 17.

18. Estlander, I, 261-63; M. G. Schybergson, *Politische Geschichte Finnlands (1809-1919)* (Gotha-Stuttgart: Perthes, 1925), p. 180. The mood of restiveness among educated Finns in the late 1850s is well expressed in a series of letters from young correspondents in Finland, published anonymously in Sweden in the journals *Aftonbladet* and *Nya Dagligt Allehanda* between 1857 and 1860 and republished in three little volumes in Stock-

holm by Albert Bonnier under the title *Finska Förhållanden* in the same years.

19. Schybergson, *Politische Geschichte*, p. 185.
20. Ibid., pp. 183-84; Estlander, I, 271-72; IgSj (see List of Abbreviations), pp. 15-16; KanEl (see List of Abbreviations), I, 413.
21. Schybergson, *Politische Geschichte*, p. 184.
22. Estlander, I, 274.
23. Hermanson, *Finlands . . . ställning*, pp. 97-98; printed document, *Utdrag ur handlingar belysande Finlands ställning*, published by the Finnish Senate, 1890.
24. Hermanson, *Finlands . . . ställning*, p. 100.
25. *Utdrag*, pp. 23-24.
26. Estlander, II, 90; Robert F. Byrnes, *Pobedonostsev: His Life and Thought* (Bloomington and London: Indiana University Press, 1968), p. 155.
27. Schweitzer, *Autonomie und Autokratie*, pp. 112-13, 115, 129-30 *et passim*.
28. Estlander, p. 280. A facsimile of the comment, in the tsar's own hand, is in the State Archives, Helsinki, ValAs (see List of Abbreviations), kansio 5, nippu 115.
29. Leo Ehrnrooth, *Från et skiftesrikt liv* (Helsinki: Söderström, 1947), pp. 62-64.
30. Ibid., pp. 137-39.
31. ValAs, kansio 3, nippu 96. One should notice in passing that even after the students became politically militant in the first decade of the twentieth century they did not generally display any sympathetic "interest in socialist workers' questions."
32. For example, KKK, 1898, no. 5, II.

CHAPTER 23. THE INTERNATIONAL AND MILITARY
BACKGROUND OF RUSSIFICATION

1. Allan Jansson, *Den svenska utrikespolitikens historia, III: 3, 1844-1872* (Stockholm: Norstedt, 1961), p. 11.
2. For a fairly typical example of the patronizing attitude of Swedish Scandinavianists toward Finland, see Sven Gustaf Lallerstedt, *Skandinavien, dess farhågor och förhoppningar* (Stockholm: Bonnier, 1856), pp. 279-84. This work, also coming out in English and French versions, then attracted international attention. Its principal conclusion was: "Finland must become Russian or Scandinavian."
3. Paul Knaplund, "Finmark in British Diplomacy, 1836-1855," *American Historical Review*, xxx (1924-1925), 478-502; Sune Jungar, *Ryssland och den svensk-norska unionens upplösning*, Acta Academiae Aboensis, ser. A, vol. 37, no. 3 (Turku: Åbo Akademi, 1969), with English-language summary, "Russia and the Dissolution of the Union of Sweden and Norway"), pp. 45-46; Jansson, *Historia, III: 3, 1844-1872*, pp. 70-75, 87,

101-18; Knaplund, pp. 490-502; C. F. Palmstierna, *Sverige, Ryssland och England 1833-1855* (Stockholm, 1932), p. 373.

4. Anatolii Vasil'evich Nekliudov, *Diplomatic Reminiscences* (London: J. Murray, 1920), p. 262.

5. Folke Lindberg, *Den Svenska utrikespolitikens historia, III: 4, 1872-1917* (Stockholm: Norstedt, 1958), pp. 29-34; Nekliudov, pp. 259-61.

6. Lindberg, *Historia, III: 4, 1872-1914*, pp. 127-28. On the other hand, the capital for industrial expansion in Sweden was borrowed mostly from France (ibid., p. 128).

7. Ibid., pp. 124-37.

8. Ibid., pp. 109-15.

9. Ibid., p. 135.

10. Wipert von Blücher, *Gesandter zwischen Diktatur und Demokratie* (Wiesbaden: Limes Verlag, 1951), p. 113.

11. Lindberg, *Historia, III: 4, 1872-1914*, pp. 198-222.

12. W. M. Carlgren, *Neutralität oder Allianz, Deutschlands Beziehungen zu Schweden in den Anfangsjahren des ersten Weltkrieges*, Acta Universitatis Stockholmensis, Stockholm Studies in History, no. 6 (Stockholm: Almqvist & Wicksell, 1962), chap. 1. See also Folke Lindberg, "De svensktyska generalstabsförhandlingarna år 1910," *Historisk Tidskrift*, LXXVII (1957), pp. 1-28.

13. Lindberg, *Historia, III: 4, 1872-1914*, p. 300.

14. Carlgren, *Neutralität oder Allianz*, p. 19.

15. Jungar, *Ryssland*, pp. 56, 63.

16. Ibid., p. 120; Lindberg, *Historia, III: 4, 1872-1914*, p. 291.

17. Tuomo Polvinen, *Die finnischen Eisenbahnen in den militärischen Plänen Russlands vor dem ersten Weltkrieg* (see Select Bibliography), pp. 50-52.

18. Ibid., pp. 29-30.

19. Tuomo Polvinen, "Rysslands militära plan i Finland," in Nils Herlitz (ed.), *Finlands ofärdsår 1899-1917* (Stockholm, 1963), pp. 32-38.

CHAPTER 24. THE STORM GATHERS

1. KanEl, III, 334-36.

2. Keijo Korhonen, *Autonomous Finland*, p. 57. See Lolo Krusius-Ahrenberg, *"Dagbladsseparatismen" år 1863 och den begynnande panslavismen*, Skrifter utg. av Svenska Litteratursällskapet i Finland, no. 346.

3. Keijo Korhonen, *Autonomous Finland*, p. 85.

4. Theodor Cederholm, *Politiska minnen* (Helsinki: Söderström, 1924), pp. 98-99.

5. Ibid., pp. 110-12.

6. Carl Alexander Armfelt, *Vid finska statssekretariatet i St. Petersburg*, p. 36.

7. IgSj, pp. 47-48.

8. KanEl, I, 338-39; Cederholm, *Politiska minnen*, pp. 127, 191-92; Schweitzer, pp. 105-12.

9. KanEl, i, 546-47; Kari O. Virtanen, *Ahdistettu kansakunta 1890-1917* (see Select Bibliography), pp. 25, 26, 50-53; Cederholm, *Politiska minnen*, pp. 197-98.

10. *Öfversättning av Generalguvernören Grefve Heidens skrifvelse till Ministerstatssekreteraren Geheimrat Bruun* den 17/29 January, no. 170, ValAs 5, nippu 122.

11. Ignatius, notes on "Woldemar von Daehn," IgPo. Similar condemnations of Ehrnrooth were made by Senator Edvard Streng in 1890 (Magnus Ehrnrooth, *Casimir Ehrnrooth*, Porvoo: Söderström, 1965, p. 351) and Robert Montgomery, an official in the state secretariat in St. Petersburg, in the same year (ibid., p. 356). See also Schweitzer, *Autonomie und Autokratie*, pp. 260-65.

12. Estlander, ii, 295.

13. KanEl, i, 467-68; Ignatius, notes on "Woldemar von Daehn," IgPo; Otto Wrede, "Woldemar von Daehn," *Finsk tidskrift*, lxxxvii (1919), 65; Armfelt, section on "Woldemar von Daehn" in *Vid finska statssekretariatet*.

14. Armfelt, *Vid finska statssekretariatet*, pp. 45, 48-49.

15. Von Daehn to Yrjö-Koskinen, 27 November 1891, YKK, 16.

16. Virtanen, *Ahdistettu kansakunta*, pp. 25-26.

17. IgSj, p. 46; Armfelt, *Vid finska statssekretariatet*, pp. 80-81.

18. Von Daehn to Yrjö-Koskinen, January 1, 1891, YKK, 16.

19. Ignatius, notes on von Daehn, IgPo.

20. Cederholm, *Politiska minnen*, p. 195.

21. IgSj, insertion after p. 38; Schweitzer, pp. 207-209, 265-67, 286-90, 373-75.

22. IgSj, insertion after p. 41; *Schweitzer*, pp. 286, 290-99.

23. Virtanen, *Ahdistettu kansakunta*, pp. 21-22.

24. IgPo.

25. Von Daehn to Ignatius, April 20, 1890, IgK, 4.

26. KanEl, v, 587; Estlander, ii, 282-83; IgSj, p. 39.

27. Arvi Korhonen (ed.), *Suomen historian käsikirja*, 2 vols. (Porvoo-Helsinki: Otava, 1949), ii, 265-75; Estlander, ii, 277-79; report of the Senate, copy inserted after p. 37 in IgSj.

28. Ignatius, section on von Daehn, IgPo; von Daehn to Yrjö-Koskinen, January 1/23, 1893, YKK (see List of Abbreviations), 16; [Johan Herman] Edvard Bergh, *Finland under det första årtiondet af Kejsar Alexander III⁸ regering* (Helsinki: G. W. Edlund, 1894), pp. 377-83, 47⁽¹⁾-74.

29. IgSj, insertion after p. 38.

30. Magnus Ehrnrooth, *Casimir Ehrnrooth*, p. 329.

31. Yrjö-Koskinen to von Daehn, December 22, 1890, YKK, 34.

32. "Memoire" in Yrjö-Koskinen's hand, April 23, 1891, YKK, 35.

33. Leo Ehrnrooth, *Från et skiftesrikt liv*, p. 15.

34. Bergh, *Finland*, pp. 353-54.

35. Ibid., pp. 349-56; Virtanen, *Ahdistettu kansakunta*, pp. 49-54.

36. Bergh, *Finland*, pp. 351-58; Virtanen, *Ahdistettu kansakunta*, p. 54.

37. IgSj, p. 42.

38. KanEl, IV, 60-65; Sigurd Nordenstreng, *L. Mechelin, hans stats-mannagärning och politiska personlighet,* 2 vols. (Helsinki: privately printed, 1936-1937); IgPo, section on Mechelin.

39. IgPo, section on Mechelin.

40. Estlander, II, 272-74.

41. Ibid., p. 281; IgPo, section on Mechelin.

42. Von Daehn to Yrjö-Koskinen, July 16, 1891, YKK, 16.

43. IgPo; IgSj, insertion after p. 41.

44. Von Daehn to Yrjö-Koskinen, January 6, 1894, YKK, 16.

45. Pirkko Rommi, *Myöntyvyyssuuntauksen hahmottuminen Yrjö-Koskisen ja Suomalaisen Puolueen toimintalinjaksi,* pp. 150-60.

46. IgPo, section on von Daehn.

47. Ibid.; IgSj, pp. 44-45.

48. Von Daehn to Yrjö-Koskinen, January 1, 1895, YKK, 16.

49. Von Daehn to Yrjö-Koskinen, November 26, (1896?), ibid.

50. IgSj, p. 45.

51. Von Daehn to Yrjö-Koskinen, January 21, 1897, YKK, 16.

52. IgPo, section on von Daehn; Armfelt, pp. 57, 65-73.

Chapter 25. Finland's Divided House

1. Jarl von Schoulz, *Bidrag till belysande av Finlands socialdemokratiska partis historia,* Del I (Helsinki: Söderström, 1924), pp. 94-95; Viljo Rasila, *Torpparikysymyksen ratkaisuvaihe, Suomen torpparikysymys vuosina 1909-1918* (Helsinki: Kirjayhtymä, 1970), p. 15.

2. Schoulz, *Bidrag,* p. 95; Estlander, II, 262-64.

3. Von Daehn to Yrjö-Koskinen, 12/24 April 1890. "I am not yet so strong a Finn that I should be quite so sure of my opinion."

4. For the anti-Semitism, see Santeri Jacobsson, *Taistelu ihmisoikeuksista* (Jyväskylä: Gummerus, 1951), esp. chaps. 11-17, and Th. Rein, *Levnads-minnen,* pp. 238-39. Anti-Semitism was not confined, however, to Fennomans.

5. L. A. Puntila, *Ruotsalaisuus Suomessa, aatesuunnan synty* (Helsinki: Otava, 1944), pp. 74, 187; August Schauman, *Från sex årtionden i Finland,* 2 vols. (Helsinki: Schildt, 1922), II, 174-76, 188, 198.

6. Pirkko Rommi, *Myöntyvyyssuuntauksen hahmottuminen Yrjö-Koskisen ja Suomalaisen Puolueen toimintalinjaksi,* pp. 65-67. This admirable work is a careful study of the political thinking of Yrjö-Koskinen and his associates, and the eight-page summary in German is most useful for persons who cannot read Finnish.

7. Puntila, *Ruotsalaisuus Suomessa,* p. 112; Arvid Mörne, *Axel Olof Freudenthal och den finlandssvenska nationalitetstanken,* Skrifter utgivna av Svenska Folkpartiets centralstyrelse, no. 1, (Helsinki, 1927), pp. 60-61; Axel Lille, *Den svenska nationalitetens i Finland samlingsrörelse* (Helsinki: Schildt, 1921), p. 104.

8. Puntila, *Ruotsalaisuus Suomessa,* p. 214; Lille, *Den svenska,* p. 109.

9. Puntila, *Ruotsalaisuus Suomessa*, p. 187; Mörne, *Freudenthal*, pp. 27, 59-66; Lille, *Den svenska*, pp. 87, 96-97, 124, 126, 139.

10. E. G. Palmén, "Minnen från språkstriden," *Från brytningstider, minnen och erfarenheter*, I, 117-20; Lille, *Den svenska*, pp. 139-40.

11. Palmén, "Minnen," p. 120.

12. Puntila, *Ruotsalaisuus Suomessa*, p. 112; Lille, *Den svenska*, pp. 201-2.

13. Otto v. Zweigbergh, *Finska studier, ögonblicksbilder från Finland januari-februari 1894* (Stockholm: Bonnier, 1894), pp. 71-72.

14. Estlander, III, 105; Lille, *Den svenska*, pp. 201-2.

15. Zweigbergh, *Finska studier*, pp. 75-76.

16. Ibid., pp. 173-74.

17. Ibid., pp. 166-68.

18. Article, "Mies ja ääni," *Työmies*, June 18, 1898.

19. Yrjö Blomstedt, *K. J. Ståhlberg, valtiomieselämäkerta* (Helsinki: Otava, 1969), p. 61.

20. Ibid., p. 63.

21. Ibid., p. 60; Rommi, *Myöntyvyyssuuntauksen*, p. 99.

22. Rommi, p. 97.

23. Ibid., pp. 99-102.

24. Rein, *Levnadsminnen*, p. 322.

25. John H. Hodgson, *Communism in Finland: A History and Interpretation* (Princeton: Princeton University Press, 1967), pp. 7-8.

26. *Kan. El.*, v, 13; R. H. Oittinen, "N. R. af Ursin, Suomen työväen opettaja," Hannu Soikkanen (ed.), *Tiennäyttäjät*, I, 13.

27. Carl Erik Knoellinger, *Labor in Finland* (Cambridge, Mass.: Harvard University Press, 1960), pp. 35, 36; Hannu Soikkanen, *Sosialismin tulo Suomeen, ensimmäisiin yksikamarisen eduskunnan vaaleihin asti*, pp. 4-5.

28. Knoellinger, *Labor in Finland*, p. 39; Schoulz, *Bidrag*, pp. 12-20; Estlander, II, 243-44; Soikkanen, *Sosialismin tulo*, p. 6; Y. K. Laine, *Suomen poliittisen työväenliikkeen historia*, 2 vols. (Helsinki: Tammi, 1945-1946), I, 21-25, 63-75; Martta Salmela-Järvinen, *Alas lyötiin vanha maailma, muistikuvia ja näkymiä vuosilta 1906-1918* (Porvoo/Helsinki: Söderström, 1966), pp. 10, 19-22, 24-26.

29. Knoellinger, *Labor in Finland*, pp. 38-39; Estlander, II, 244-48; Laine, *Suomen*, I, pp. 32-38; Soikkanen, *Sosialismin tulo*, pp. 21-27; Schoulz, chap. 1; Antti Hyvönen, *Suomen vanhan työväenpuolueen historia* (Helsinki: Kansankulttuuri Oy, 1959), pp. 18-25.

30. Laine, *Suomen*, I, 64; Hyvönen, *Suomen vanhan*, p. 15.

31. Estlander, II, 248.

32. Hyvönen, *Suomen vanhan*, p. 24. The Diet did pass in 1889 a law creating factory inspectors; but since there were only two of them (three after 1896) in the whole country, their work did not accomplish much.

33. Oittinen, "Nils af Ursin"; *Kan. El.*, v, 514-15.

34. Erkki Salomaa, "A. B. Mäkelä," in Soikkanen, *Tiennäyttäjät*, I, 210-11.

35. Arvi Hautamäki, "Matti Kurikka, utopistinen sosialisti," in Soikkanen, *Tiennäyttajät*, I; *Kan. El.*, III, 271-73.

36. Estlander, II, 253-56; *Suomen historian dokumenttaja*, II, 199-201; Soikkanen, *Sosialismin tulo*, p. 55.

37. Laine, *Suomen*, I, 57; Estlander, II, 262-64.

38. Estlander, II, 264; Soikkanen, *Sosialismin tulo*, pp. 58, 62-63.

39. Soikkanen, *Sosialismin tulo*, pp. 64-66.

40. *Työmies* (Helsinki), July 9, 1898.

41. Viljo Rasila, *Torpparikysymuksen ratkaisuvaihe* (Helsinki, 1970), p. 385.

42. Viljo Rasila, *Suomen torpparikysymys vuoteen 1909* (see Select Bibliography), pp. 45, 486; "Irtolaiskysymyksiä," *Työmies*, July 9, 1898.

43. Rasila, . . . *Ratkaisuvaihe*, p. 15; Laine, *Suomen*, I, 14-15.

44. Rasila, . . . *Vuoteen 1909*, pp. 17-23.

45. *För Fosterlandet: Tankar och uttalanden* (Helsinki: Söderström, 1899), p. 181.

46. Rasila, . . . *Vuoteen 1909*, pp. 59-60.

47. Ibid., p. 53.

48. Ibid., pp. 144-50.

49. Cederholm, pp. 106-7.

50. Rasila, . . . *Vuoteen 1909*, pp. 88-89.

51. Ibid., pp. 95-98, 106-11, 123-28.

52. Von Daehn to Yrjö-Koskinen, October 2/14, 1892, YKK, v. 16.

53. *För Fosterlandet*, p. 185.

54. Printed report to the civil office of the Senate, *Berättelse om verkstäld undersökning angående utspridande af falska rykten i landet*, signed by K. J. Ståhlberg, May 2, 1899.

55. Rasila, . . . *Vuoteen 1909*, pp. 139, 142.

56. Ibid., pp. 128-35.

57. A. Gripenberg to civil office of the Senate, October 17, 1891, in ValAs, 3, nippu 96.

58. Report by Fredr. Ollikainen to the chief of police of Viipuri, November 18, 1891, ibid.

59. Gripenberg to civil office, November 11, 1891, ibid.

CHAPTER 26. THE STORM BREAKS AND RAGES

1. Lauri Hyvämäki, *Ennen routaa: Esseitä ja tutkielmia* (Helsinki: Otava, 1960), pp. 31-32.

2. [Konni Zilliacus], *Ur Finlands nyaste historia* (Stockholm: Wahlström & Widstrand, 1900), pp. 67-69.

3. *Suomenmaan valtio-kalenteri 1899*.

4. Nikolai Ivanovich Bobrikov, *Vsepoddanneishaia zapiska finliandskogo general-gubernatora 1898-1902* (typed copy in JäK), p. 3.

5. Aina Gordie, *Anmerkningar*, entries for March 1900, GorK; communication from A. von Minkwitz to Bobrikov, January 30, 1900, ibid.

6. Nikolai Ivanovich Bobrikov, *Generalguvernör Bobrikoffs berättelse öfver Finlands förvaltning från September 1898 till September 1902* (Stockholm: Varias Boktryckeri, 1905), p. 89n.

7. Esther Hjelt's diary, HjK, 30, *passim*.

8. IgMi, February 18, 1899; HjK, 30, *passim*.

9. Cederholm, pp. 237-50; *Suomen historian dokumenttaja*, ii, 227-30.

10. Estlander, iii, 20.

11. The complex considerations are discussed at some length in Zilliacus, *Ur Finlands nyaste historia*, pp. 80-87. See also IgMi, February 18, 1899.

12. Estlander, iii, 21.

13. Zilliacus, pp. 89-93.

14. Draft of a statement by Yrjö-Koskinen, *Miksi pyysin virkaeron*, March 4 and 5, 1899, YKK, 35; Zilliacus, p. 96.

15. Juho Kusti Paasikivi, *Paasikiven muistelmia sortovuosilta* (see Select Bibliography), i, 11-13.

16. Yrjö-Koskinen's diary, December 1899, YKK, 34.

17. Signed notation by Yrjö-Koskinen, dated February 18, 1899, on copy of petition to the members of the Senate, February 17, 1899, YKK, 35: Yrjö-Koskinen to Ernst Forsman, July 9, 1900, YKK, 24.

18. IgPo, section on "Georg Forsman," p. 8.

19. Yrjö-Koskinen, *Avoin kirje*, YKK, 34.

20. IgPo, section on "Georg Forsman," p. 12.

21. Ibid., pp. 13-14; Estlander, iii, 113-16; draft of a letter in Yrjö-Koskinen's hand, January 1903, YKK, 35.

22. IgMi, February 20, 1899; Estlander, iii, 25.

23. Estlander, iii, 25.

24. Ibid., pp. 35-36; Harold E. Johnson, *Jean Sibelius*, pp. 89-94.

25. KKK, 42, i and ii; Aina Gordie, *Anteckningar*, November 3, 1899, GorK.

26. KKK, 42, ii.

27. Estlander, iii, 27-28; Zilliacus, *Historia*, pp. 108-16.

28. Zilliacus, *Historia*, pp. 117-45; Estlander, iii, 31-37; IgMi, March 13, 1899.

29. Zilliacus, *Historia*, pp. 151-55; Estlander, iii, 39.

30. Zilliacus, *Historia*, pp. 161-63.

31. "Sub secreto" report to the Senate, March 24, 1899, ValAs, 5, nippu 137.

32. "Haaksirikkoon jouduttua," *Työmies*, March 3, 1899.

33. Esther Hjelt's diary, March 16, 1899, HjK, 30.

34. Estlander, iii, 72.

35. Schoulz, *Bidrag*, pp. 130-32; editorial, "Eripuraisuus," *Työmies*, March 23, 1899; "Se yksimielisyys," *Työmies*, March 22, 1899.

36. "Suomen kansan adressi," *Työmies*, March 20, 1899.

37. "Hänellä olkoon valta eroittaa toimesta," *Työmies*, October 21, 1899.

38. *Työmies*, March 16, 1899; KKK, 42, ii.

39. Upton, pp. 5-12; Hannu Soikkanen, "Arbetarrörelsen och rättskampen," *Finlands ofärdsår*, pp. 108-9; Soikkanen, *Sosialismin tulo*, pp. 67-69, 73.

40. Hyvönen, *Suomen vanhan*, p. 57.

41. *Sub secreto* report of Generalmajor Friedrichs to chief of Gendar-

merie, February 20, 1899, ValAs, 5, nippu 141. See also the angry letter of Georg Schauman complaining about peasant apathy, quoted in Irma Rantavaara, *Yrjö Hirn* (Helsinki: Otava, 1977), pp. 97-98.

42. Esther Hjelt's diary, March 10 and 15, 1899, HjK, 30.

43. H. [Gd.?] to Setälä, March 10, 1899, SetK, Kirjeenvaihto, 24.

44. IgMi, March 18 and 28, 1899; Estlander, III, 36-37; Kan El, p. 232. Estlander gives the name of Warwas' associate as Juho Martonen of Kaukola.

45. IgMi, March 18, 1899.

46. ValAs, 5, nippu 137.

47. K. J. Ståhlberg, *Berättelse om verkställd undersökning angående utspridande af falska rykter i landet*, [Helsinki], 1899.

48. Rasila, . . . *Vuoteen 1909*, p. 193.

49. Ibid.

50. *Novoe vremia*, April 8 (March 27), 1899, quoted in ibid., pp. 193-94.

51. Rasila, . . . *Vuoteen 1909*, pp. 195-96.

52. Ibid., p. 191.

53. Rasila, . . . *Vuoteen 1909*, p. 260.

54. Ibid., pp. 203-22 and 488.

55. HjK, 14 and 30, *passim*.

56. Herman Gummerus, *Aktiva kampår 1899-1910* (see Select Bibliography), p. 17.

57. Ibid., p. 17.

58. *Pro Finlandia*, Berlin: Mertz; Stockholm: Tullberg, 1899.

59. Estlander, III, 44-45; Zilliacus, *Historia*, p. 67ff.

60. Tudeer to Armfelt, July 11, 1899, TuK.

61. Estlander, III, 54.

62. Aina Gordie, *Anteckningar*, GorK, p. 49a.

63. Bobrikov, *Vsepoddanneishaia zapiska*, p. 12.

64. Ibid., pp. 19, 22.

65. Ibid., p. 20.

66. Yrjö-Koskinen's diary, January 23, 1900, YKK, 34.

67. *Suomen historian dokumentteja*, II, 254-57.

68. Otto Wrede to Armfelt, September 5, 1903, CAAK, correspondence, 7.

69. Handwritten *Protokoll, fördt vid den . . . Särskilda Konferensen . . .*, StåK, 68.

70. Waldemar Eneberg to Yrjö-Koskinen, June 19, 1901, YKK, 16.

71. *Fria ord*, October 15, 1902.

72. *Suomen historian dokumentteja*, II, 262.

73. Gustaf Johansson to Bobrikov, August 25, 1899, KKK, 42, II.

74. Bobrikov, *Generalguvernör Bobrikoffs berättelse*, pp. 75-79.

75. Gummerus, *Aktiva kampår*, p. 49.

76. William R. Copeland, *The Uneasy Alliance: Collaboration between the Finnish Opposition and the Russian Underground 1899-1904* (see Select Bibliography).

77. H. Söderhjelm, *Werner Söderhjelm* (Helsinki: Schildt, 1960), p. 119.

78. The complex subject is treated in detail in Polvinen, *Die finnischen Eisenbahnen*, pp. 159-67.

79. Otto Wrede to Armfelt, April 13, 1912, CAAK, correspondence, 7.

An important study tracing the interrelationships of class struggles in Finland and the Russification policies, especially after 1905, is Osmo Jussila, *Nationalismi ja vallankumous veneläis-suomalaisissa suhteissa 1899-1914* [with English summary: "Nationalism and Revolution in Russian-Finnish Relations 1899-1914], Historiallisia Tutkimuksia, No. 110 (Helsinki: Suomen Historiallinen Seura, 1979). Jussila's study appeared after the manuscript of the present work had been completed.

EPILOGUE

IN THE LATTER PART of the nineteenth century few public figures disputed the desirability of consolidating and strengthening the nation-state. Before the Franco-Prussian War France was generally considered to be the model for other nations to emulate. After 1871 France was eclipsed by Germany in Europe. The new German Empire steadily gained in power and influence because of its growing military might and rapidly expanding population and industrial production. Germany was also often admired for her uncompromising nationality policy, which subjected Poles, Danes, Frenchmen, and Alsatians to the German language in government offices, public life, schools, and even the Church. During this same period, on the other hand, the example of Austria was one that hardly anyone wanted to imitate. Austria had failed to impose one nationality on her subjects. This, the Russian publicist Iurii Samarin pointed out, could only result in weakness and serious difficulties for the Austrian state; it was a mistake Russia had to avoid.[1]

Russia, like Austria, was a multinational state. In 1897 Great Russians accounted for only 43.3 percent of the empire's population (including Finland). Although assuredly the empire's dominant national minority, Great Russians often found themselves challenged culturally, economically, and even politically by various groups and nationalities living in both the eastern and western borderlands of the empire. The Russian government, despite its determination to rule firmly after 1881, was again and again obliged to yield to pressure and to make compromises. In Central Asia Khiva and Bukhara retained a considerable degree of autonomy within the Russian Empire until 1917; in the Volga region Russian Orthodoxy was on the defensive in the face of the aggressive tactics used by Tatar religious and educational leaders in building schools, converting heathens, and returning Orthodox converts to the Islamic faith of their forebears; in ethnically Polish and Lithuanian areas the Russificatory policies pursued since 1863 were substantially modified after 1905; cultural Russification in the Baltic Provinces was an abortive experiment Russian officials actively pursued for about a decade and then largely abandoned; and in Finland even administrative Russification went scarcely beyond its very initial stages by the time war broke out in 1914. Only in the predominantly Orthodox Ukraine and Belorussia, where the population was Eastern Slav, socially backward, and without a well-organized and effective national intelligentsia, did Russian officialdom act resolutely and consistently in carrying out a policy of administrative and cultural Russification throughout the period 1855-1914.

On the whole, in the Baltic Provinces and Finland the "German" party, to use the terminology of the 1860s, won a clear victory over the "Democratic" party. In regard to the Baltic Provinces, Alexander II listened above all to Al'bedinskii, Shuvalov, and Valuev, who recommended gradual administrative measures to bring the Baltic Provinces closer to the rest of the empire but to avoid Orthodox proselytism and not tamper with the existing structure of local society. Finland was allowed by Alexander II and his advisers to embark on a course of internal reform that greatly accentuated the differences separating her from Russia. Nicholas II, Stolypin, and their Bobrikovite advisers tried to repair the damage that had been done, but the Russian government hesitated to move full speed ahead with the implementation of Russification in Finland even after promulgation of the law on the "order of promulgating laws of general state significance concerning Finland" on June 17, 1910. Meanwhile, the government gradually and quietly abandoned the most objectionable features of cultural Russification in the Baltic Provinces and accepted a form of coexistence with the leaders of Baltic German, Estonian, and Latvian society.

In the nineteenth century it was mainly privileged elements in Baltic German and Swedo-Finnish society that considered Russification a serious threat. This changed at the beginning of the twentieth century. In Finland some Finnish-speaking leaders became much more inclined than before to cooperate with Swedo-Finnish politicians in resisting Russification. In the Baltic Provinces the position of the Estonians and Latvians had by then been sufficiently strengthened by the economic opportunities arising from industrialization and Russian administrative reform for them to aspire to take over the leadership of local Baltic society. At this point they gradually began to see in Russification as serious an obstacle in the way of their obtaining local cultural and political autonomy as the economic and social power of the Baltic Germans.

Changing Russian official attitudes and policies played a role as well. The officials who made Russian Baltic policy during the sixties, seventies, and eighties all accepted the necessity of reform in both the inner *gubernii* and the borderlands. Baltic Governors-General Al'bedinskii and Shuvalov and Interior Ministers Valuev and Timashev opposed restructuring Baltic society along the lines advocated by Grand Duke Konstantin Nikolaevich, Samarin, and D. A. and N. A.

Miliutin. However, they introduced the administrative reforms that eliminated what Russians considered the most objectionable features of Baltic regional autonomy, thus opening the way to more social mobility and, generally speaking, making possible a more modern pattern of development in the Baltic Provinces. As late as the 1880s Manasein worked to continue this work of modernization by carrying out certain remaining projects of administrative Russification and by seeking to help the Estonians and Latvians to free themselves from the shackles of privilege and provincialism that still seemed to hinder their social and economic development and to isolate them from the rest of the empire.

The officials responsible for Russian Baltic policy between the late 1880s and 1914 were neither social and administrative reformers nor friends of Baltic nationalities, be they Latvian, Estonian, Finnish, or Baltic German. Their view of political authority was a narrow one: firm autocratic authority, centralized government, and Russian as the language of the elementary classroom throughout the empire were the only reliable foundations upon which a strong Russian national state could be built. Autocratic rule and centralized government did not, of course, logically exclude the possibility of further reform, but the new policies associated with counterreform during the last years of the reign of Alexander III made social stability seem more important than the support of wide-scale social and agrarian reforms and the carrying out of administrative Russification to its logical conclusions (e.g. the introduction of zemstvos in the Baltic Provinces and the abolition of the Baltic Diets and *Ritterschaften*).

In the Baltic Provinces the indigenous population had little reason at the beginning of the twentieth century to look to official Russia for salvation. High officials and influential journalists in St. Petersburg and Moscow no longer insisted on the need for social and economic reforms beneficial to Latvians and Estonians. Now, having lost faith in the goodwill of the government, Latvians and Estonians expressed their views on political, cultural, and social questions in the vocabulary provided by western European political ideologies and cultural and social movements. Moreover, having undergone a rapid process of social and economic differentiation and modernization, they had freed themselves psychologically from the tutelage of both the Russian government and the Baltic Germans. They self-confidently identified themselves with their own respective nationalities and formulated Estonian or Latvian visions of the future. The allies they sought inside Russia after 1905 for assistance in realizing these visions were from the political opposition, chiefly Social and Constitutional Democrats, not from the parties that supported the government. Thus, when I. I. Visotskii, the nationalistic editor of *Rizhskii vestnik*, wrote in 1910 of the benefits of Russificatory reform for the indigenous population throughout the borderlands, his words probably had little meaning for most Estonians and Latvians. By that time leaders of the Baltic indigenous population considered cultural Russification retrograde and administrative Russification obsolete and irrelevant to their own goals and objectives.

In Finland the reaction to Russification early in the twentieth century was more dramatic and extreme than in the Baltic Provinces. For almost a century Finland had flourished economically and culturally under Russia, been sheltered from war and the costs of war, and had enjoyed a wide degree of internal autonomy. The first hints of administrative Russification in Finland during the 1880s, therefore, came as a shock to the Finns. The next generation in Finland was profoundly influenced by feelings of outrage provoked by what seemed to be arbitrary rule and violations of Finnish autonomy and her "constitutional rights." It was largely because of this sense of outrage that organized resistance to Russification was a much more sustained and significant movement in Finland than was the case in the Baltic Provinces.

On occasion the Baltic Germans felt equally strongly about violations of what they considered their historical rights and privileges. But these rights and privileges depended on imperial sufferance and were only preserved in 1905 with the assistance of Russian bayonets. The Baltic Germans were, therefore, in no position to resist Russification directly or to engage in the sort of revolutionary activism resorted to, at one time or another, by Finns, Estonians, and Latvians. Even so, the Baltic Germans resented pressure on the Lutheran Church and other arbitrary actions on the part of Russian officialdom.

Baltic Germans, Estonians, Latvians, and Finns all opposed one important principle of Russian policy: namely, that no one in the Baltic borderlands had a moral or legal right to oppose policies decided upon by bureaucrats in St. Petersburg. This principle potentially threatened the human and national rights of all the inhabitants of the Baltic region. The uneasiness that Baltic Germans, Estonians, Latvians, and Finns felt in the face of this danger at least partly explains their inclination in the period 1918-1920 to separate themselves from Russia and to form autonomous or independent states under the protection of either Germany or the Western powers.

In an advanced area of tsarist Russia such as the Baltic borderlands, however, Estonians, Latvians, Finns, and Baltic Germans determined their own destinies to a considerable extent—culturally, socially, and economically. Whatever the long-range implications of Russification (and this is what the Finns objected to primarily), it was not of major consequence as a disruptive force during the period 1855-1914. Russification neither obliterated the cultural identity nor seriously retarded the natural social and national development of the Baltic Provinces and Finland. Moreover, the historical forces associated with the government's policy of Russification gradually brought the 5 million inhabitants of the Baltic borderlands closer to the tsar's other subjects. It was an association that benefited Estonians, Latvians, Finns, and Baltic Germans in many ways, offering them not only security and prosperity but also a degree of local self-determination uncommon in an age that worshipped the nation-state.

At the same time, there were disadvantages for the Baltic nationalities in being included in the Russian Empire. Political authoritarianism, arbitrary police power, and growing national and religious intolerance in Russia toward the end of the nineteenth and at the beginning of the twentieth centuries obviously were of no benefit to the empire's national and religious minorities. This point has been illustrated in a number of ways in the present study: the measures against the Lutheran pastors and reconverts, the Russification of elementary education, and the arrest or exile of Finnish officials and political leaders and of Estonian and Latvian peasants, workers, and intellectuals. The Revolution of 1905 was, of course, a national emergency for tsarist Russia, but it was difficult for Estonians and Latvians to forget the mass arrests, punitive expeditions, and executions that occurred between 1905 and 1908.

The ruling of a large, multinational empire is a difficult task. Problems of tsarist nationality policy persist into the Soviet period. In the USSR there continue to be would-be leaders of nationalities who are proud of their own respective peoples' historical pasts and identities, who criticize official Soviet policies, and who resent the efforts of an all-powerful central authority that seems bent on imposing its will on minorities and simplifying as much as possible the structure of a vast multinational state. The relative efficiency of certain techniques of political control in the USSR makes the position of potential leaders of national movements in that country an unenviable one. Their predecessors in tsarist Russia could act much more freely in a country whose officials tended to lack either the will or the means to control the intellectual life and local organizations of minorities located in the borderlands.

Note to Epilogue

1. Samarin, IX, 483-85.

GLOSSARY

I. FOREIGN TERMS

Chin: a rank of military officers and civil government officials according to the Table of Ranks (1722), which divided military officers and civil servants into fourteen ranks, or *chiny*.

Chinovnik (pl., *chinovniki*): an official or functionary in imperial Russia.

General-gubernatorstvo: the territory, usually consisting of several *gubernii*, under the administration of a governor-general (*general-gubernator*). At the beginning of the twentieth century there were governors-general in Asia, Finland, Moscow, Kiev, Warsaw, and Vilna. The Baltic *general-gubernatorstvo* was abolished in 1876.

Guberniia (pl., *gubernii*): a major administrative division of imperial Russia; a province. At the beginning of the twentieth century there were fifty *gubernii* in European Russia exclusive of Finland, Poland, and the Caucasus.

Landtag: the German term for Diet. See the more detailed entry under "Diet" in Part IV of this glossary.

Ritterschaft: a corporation of the Baltic nobility. See the more detailed entry in Part IV.

Sejm: the general Diet in the Polish-Lithuanian Commonwealth, the Grand Duchy of Warsaw (1807-1815), and Congress Poland (1815-1831).

Szlachta: the Polish term for noblemen, nobles, nobility.

Uezd: a subdivision of a *guberniia*; a district.

II. PLACE AND TERRITORIAL NAMES

Listed are the German or Finnish place and territorial names referred to most frequently in the text. In each case the most commonly used Estonian, Latvian, or Swedish name is also given. During the tsarist period almost all Russian place names for the Baltic area were little more than transliterations from the German or Swedish. The Soviets have preferred to transliterate the currently used Estonian, Finnish, and Latvian forms. In three instances (Dorpat, Dünaburg, and Viipuri) we have also provided the special Russian place names used prior to 1917. Viipuri, which was annexed by the Soviet Union in 1945, has retained the tsarist Russian version of its old Swedish name: Vyborg. Our use of the English form Lettgallia instead of the Latvian Latgale or the German Lettgallen and of the Swedish Åland (Islands) instead of the Finnish Ahvenanmaa should also be noted.

Åland (Sw.) Islands; Ahvenanmaa (Fin.)
Arensburg (Ger.); Kuressaare (Est.)
Dorpat (Ger.); Tartu (Est.); Derpt and (between 1893 and 1917) Iur'ev (Rus.)
Dünaburg (Ger.); Daugavpils (Lat.); Dvinsk (Rus.)
Estland (Ger.); Eestimaa (Est.)
Fellin (Ger.); Viljandi (Est.)
Goldingen (Ger.); Kuldīga (Lat.)
Hämeenlinna (Fin.); Tavastehus (Sw.)
Hamina (Fin.); Fredrikshamn (Sw.)
Hapsal (Ger.); Haapsalu (Est.)
Hasenpoth (Ger.); Aizpute (Lat.)
Helsinki (Fin.); Helsingfors (Sw.)
Illuxt (Ger.); Ilūkste (Lat.)
Jakobstadt (Ger.); Jēkabpils (Lat.)
Karmel (Ger.); Kaarma (Est.)
Kuda (Ger.); Kuuda (Est.)
Kurland (Ger.); Kurzeme (Lat.)
Lappeenranta (Fin.); Villmanstrand (Sw.)
Lettgallia (Eng.); Lettgallen (Ger.); Latgale (Lat.)
Libau (Ger.); Liepāja (Lat.)
Livland (Ger.); Vidzeme (Lat.); Liivimaa (Est.)
Mikkeli (Fin.); St. Michel (Sw.)
Mitau (Ger.); Jelgava (Lat.)
Ösel (Ger.); Saaremaa (Est.)
Oulu (Fin.); Uleåborg (Sw.)
Pernau (Ger.); Pärnu (Est.)
Pori (Fin.); Björneborg (Sw.)
Porvoo (Fin.); Borgå (Sw.)
Reval (Ger.); Tallinn (Est.); Revel' (Rus.)
Tammisaari (Fin.); Ekenäs (Sw.)
Tampere (Fin.); Tammerfors (Sw.)
Tukum (Ger.); Tukums (Lat.)
Turku (Fin.); Åbo (Sw.)
Uusikaupunki (Fin.); Nystad (Sw.)
Viipuri (Fin.); Viborg (Sw.); Vyborg (Rus.)
Walk (Ger.); Valga (Est.); Valka (Lat.)

Weissenstein (Ger.); Paide (Est.)
Wenden (Ger.); Cēsis (Lat.)
Werro (Ger.); Võru (Est.)
Wesenberg (Ger.); Rakvere (Est.)
Wiek (Ger.); Läänemaa (Est.)
Windau (Ger.); Ventspils (Lat.)
Wolmar (Ger.); Valmiera (Lat.)

III. ADMINISTRATIVE AND TERRITORIAL UNITS IN THE BALTIC PROVINCES

English	Russian	German	Estonian	Latvian
Region (court, educational)	okrug	Bezirk	ringkond	apgabals
Province	guberniia	Gouvernement	kubermang	guberņa
District	uezd	Kreis	maakond	apriņķis
Parish	prikhod	Kirchspiel	kihelkond	draudze
Township	volost'	Gemeinde	vald	pagasts

IV. INSTITUTIONS AND OFFICES IN THE BALTIC PROVINCES AND FINLAND

Baltic Committee (*Ostseekomitte*, Ger.; *ostzeiskii komitet*, Rus.). This committee, which met in St. Petersburg between 1846 and 1876, discussed and gave its advice concerning almost all projects of Baltic reform. It was dominated by a majority of Baltic nobles and their sympathizers.

Councils of the Diet (*Landratskollegium* in Estland and Livland; *Ritterschaftskomité* in Kurland). The Councils were executive organs that coordinated and supervised the operation of the *Ritterschaften's* institutions of local self-government. In Livland the *Landratskollegium* consisted of twelve *Landräte* (councillors of the Diet), one of whom (the resident councillor, or *der residierender Landrat*) resided in Riga and was in charge of the Livland Council of the Diet's affairs. In Kurland the *Kreismarschall* was the analogue of the *Landrat* in Estland, Livland, and on Ösel.

Diet (*Landtag*, Ger.; *lantdag*, Sw.; *valtiopäivät*, Fin.). In the Baltic Provinces each of the four *Ritterschaften* in Estland, Kurland, Livland, and on Ösel had its own separate Diet. The

467

city of Riga sent two representatives to the Livland Diet but had only one vote in it; the other Baltic towns were not represented in the four Diets, which functioned both as bodies directing the local affairs of the Baltic Provinces and as assemblies of the provincial nobility dealing with the nobles' internal affairs. In Finland the Diet represented all four estates (including the landed peasants). After 1863 the Finnish Diet enacted, on the initiative of and with the concurrence of the Russian Emperor, legislation concerning the internal affairs of Finland and played an important role in dealing with Finnish financial and budgetary matters.

Marshals of the nobility (*Landmarschall* in Livland and on Ösel; *Landesbevollmächtigter* in Kurland; and *Ritterschaftshauptmann* in Estland). The Baltic marshals of the nobility were more powerful and influential figures than their counterparts in the interior of the empire. One of their most important functions in the second part of the nineteenth century was to defend the interests of their respective *Ritterschaften* at Court in St. Petersburg.

Parish assembly (*Kirchspielskonvent*, Ger.; *prikhodskii konvent*, Rus.; *kihelkonnakonvent*, Est.; *draudzes konvents*, Lat.). In Livland after 1870 civil affairs apart from education in the parish were controlled by the parish assembly. Near-parity between the manor and the peasants within the parish was established in Livland by an act passed by the Diet in January 1870; however, the chairman of the parish assembly was always an estate owner. The parish's religious and school affairs were managed by the church assembly (*Kirchenkonvent*, Ger.). Prior to 1870 there had been a single church assembly in Livland to deal with the civil, religious, and school affairs of the parish. Parish institutions of local self-government were more highly developed in Livland than in Estland and Kurland.

Ritterschaft, Ritterschaften (corporation, corporations of the nobility, Eng.). During the period of this study there were four separate corporations in Estland, Kurland, Livland, and on Ösel.

Senate of Finland (known as the Government Council between 1809 and 1816). The Senate administered the internal affairs of Finland between 1809 and 1917.

State Secretariat for Finnish Affairs (known between 1809 and 1826 as the Committee for Finnish Affairs). Located in St. Petersburg and headed and largely staffed by Finnish citizens between 1811 and 1899, this organ represented the views of

Finnish officials in dealing with the Russian government. It was also a coordinating office through which all matters pertaining to Finland were supposed to go. Between 1899 and 1917 Russians and Finns engaged in a tug-of-war for the control of the Secretariat.

SELECT BIBLIOGRAPHY

PART I: ARCHIVES

Bremen, Germany, Universitätsbibliothek, Welding collection

Staël von Holstein, Reinhold, "Materialien zu einer Geschichte der
Livländischen Landesstaates im neunzehnten Jahrhundert":
1-2. Die religiöse Frage
3. Privilegien und Kodifikation
4. Freiherr Hamilkar von Fölkersahm
5. Der Landesstaat zur Zeit der Regierung Alexanders II
6. Die Grundsteuer-Reform
7. Der Fürst Paul Lieven als Landmarschall von Livland.

Cambridge, Mass., Harvard Law School Library

Bunge, N. Kh., "Zapiska naidennaia v bumagakh N. Kh. Bunge," in
*Materialy i zapiski, razoslannye chlenam Komiteta ministrov na
zasedanniia 15, 22 i 23 marta, 5 i 6 aprelia 1905 goda po delu o
poriadke vypolneniia p. 7 vysochaishego ukaza 12 dekabria 1904
goda v otnoshenii 9 zapadnykh gubernii.* [St. Petersburg, 1905.]
Call number: Russ 700.F04. Also available in the *Kollektsiia pechatnykh zapisok biblioteki TsGIA SSSR*, Leningrad, no. 4.

Helsinki, Finland, Valtionarkisto (VA)

C. A. Armfelt collection
Ivar Gordie collection
L. G. von Haartman collection
Edvard Hjelt collection
Viktor Theodor Homén collection
K. F. Ignatius collection, especially:
Autobiography (*Själfbiografi*)
Correspondence (*Kirjeenvaihto*)
Notes on several political figures (*Anteckningar om några poli-
tiska personligheter i Finland. . . .*)
Notes on negotiations about the codification on Finland's basic
laws, 1892 (*Anteckningar . . . från förhandlingar rörande kodifi-
kation af Finlands grundlager*)
Notes (*Minnesanteckningar*) on political events from 1899 to 1909

A. A. Järnefelt collection

Kenraalkuvernöörinkanslian arkisto (Archives of the Chancellery of the Governor-General)

Leo Mechelin collection

Political Information (*Poliittisia tietoja*)

E. N. Setälä correspondence

K. J. Ståhlberg collection

State documents (*Valtiollisia asiakirjoja*)

Sten Carl Tudeer collection

Valtionsihteerinviraston arkisto (Archives of the State Secretariat)

Yrjö-Koskinen collection

Leningrad, USSR

Gosudarstvennaia publichnaia biblioteka imeni M. E. Saltykov-Shchedrina, otdel rukopisei (GPB):
  f. 208   A. V. Golovnin collection
  f. 379   F. P. Kornilov collection

Institut russkoi literatury Akademii nauk SSSR, otdel rukopisei (Pushkinskii dom):
  f. 16   P. P. Al'bedinskii collection
  f. 9092/L   E. M. Feoktistov collection

Tsentral'nyi gosudarstvennyi istoricheskii arkhiv SSSR (TsGIAL):
  f. 1016   Von der Pahlen family collection

Kollektsiia pechatnykh zapisok biblioteki TsGIA SSSR

Marburg, Germany

Hessisches Staatsarchiv:
  Livländisches Ritterschaftsarchiv, Livländische Landtagsrezesse
  Nachlass Alexander Meyendorff

Moscow, USSR

Gosudarstvennaia biblioteka imeni V. I. Lenina, otdel rukopisei (GBL):
  f. 120   M.N. Katkov collection
  f. 265   Samarin family collection

Stanford, California

Hoover Institution Archives:
  Ts Russ B 197: Misc. materials in regard to
  government of Baltic provinces

PART II: NEWSPAPERS

Den', Moscow, 1861-1865.

Select Bibliography

Finlands allmänna Tidning, Helsinki, 1820-1931.
Moskovskie vedomosti, Moscow, 1756-1917.
Novoe vremia, St. Petersburg, 1868-1917.
Okrainy Rossii, St. Petersburg, 1906-1912.
Olevik, Dorpat, 1882-1901.
Postimees, Dorpat, 1886-1907, 1912-1914.
Päevaleht, Reval, 1907-1914.
Rigaer Tageblatt, Riga, 1882-1914.
Russkii invalid, St. Petersburg, 1813-1917.
Valgus, Reval, 1880-1889, 1893-1900.

PART III: BOOKS AND ARTICLES

(Each of the five authors of this study has provided twenty-five titles for the following list of books and articles. Estonian, Finnish, and Latvian titles have been translated; German, Russian, and Swedish titles have not.)

Amburger, Erik. *Geschichte der Behördenorganisation Russlands von Peter dem Grossen bis 1917*. Leiden: E. J. Brill, 1966.

Andersen, Lembit. *Eesti rahvakoolid 19. sajandil* [Estonian Primary Schools in the 19th Century]. Tallinn: "Valgus," 1974.

Armfelt, Carl Alexander. *Vid finska statssekretariatet i St. Petersburg*. Helsinki: Söderström, 1920.

Bachmanis, Kristaps. "Parkrievošanas politika un tās sekas" [Russification Policy and its Consequences], *Izglītības Ministrijas Mēnešraksts* [Monthly of the Ministry of Education], 1931, pp. 399-411.

Bērzkalns, Valdemars. *Latviešu dziesmu svētku vēsture* [The History of Latvian Song Festivals]. New York: Grāmatu Draugs, 1965.

Birkerts, Antons. *Krišjānis Valdemārs un viņa centieni* [Krišjānis Valdemārs and His Efforts]. Riga: Latvju Kultūra, 1925.

Bobrikov, Nikolai Ivanovich, *Generalguvernör Bobrikoffs berättelse öfver Finlands förvaltning från Sept. 1898 till Sept. 1902*. Stockholm: Varias Boktryckeri, 1905.

———. *Vsepoddanneishaia zapiska finliandskogo general-gubernatora 1898-1902*. [St. Petersburg]: Gosudarstvennaia Tipografiia [1902].

———. *Vsepoddanneishii otchet finliandskogo general-gubernatora po upravleniiu Velikim Kniazhestvom s sentiabria 1898 po sentiabr' 1902 g.* St. Petersburg: Gosudarstvennaia Tipografiia, 1902.

———. *Vsepoddanneishii otchet finliandskogo general-gubernatora po upravleniiu Velikim Kniazhestvom s sentiabria 1902 g. po ianvar' 1904 g.* St. Petersburg: Gosudarstvennaia Tipografiia, 1904.

Borodkin, M. M. *Finland: Its Place in the Russian State.* St. Petersburg: J. Ehrlich, 1911.

――――. *Istoriia Finliandii: Vremia Imperatora Aleksandra I.* St. Petersburg: Gosudarstvennaia Tipografiia, 1909.

――――. *Istoriia Finliandii: Vremia Imperatora Aleksandra II.* St. Petersburg: Gosudarstvennaia Tipografiia, 1908.

――――. *Iz noveishei istorii Finliandii: Vremia upravleniia N. I. Bobrikova.* St. Petersburg: R. Golike and A. Vil'borg, 1905.

[Buchholtz, Alexander]. *Deutsch-protestantische Kämpfe in den baltischen Provinzen Russlands.* Leipzig: Duncker & Humblot, 1888.

――――. *Fünfzig Jahre russischer Verwaltung in den baltischen Provinzen Russlands.* Leipzig: Duncker & Humblot, 1883.

Bukšs, Miķelis. *Latagļu literatūras vēsture* [The History of Lettgallian Literature]. Stockholm: Latgaļu Izdevniecība, 1957.

Cederholm, Arne. *Kagalens uppkomst och andra episoder.* Helsinki: n.p., 1920.

Cielēns, Fēlikss. *Laikmetu maiņā: Atmiņas un atziņas* [In Changing Times: Memories and Realizations]. Lindigo, Sweden: Memento, 1961.

Copeland, William R. *The Uneasy Alliance: Collaboration between the Finnish Opposition and the Russian Underground 1899-1904.* Suomen Tiedeakatemian Toimituksia, Sarja B, Nide 179. Helsinki: Suomen Tiedeakatemia, 1973.

Danielson-Kalmari, Johan Richard. *Finland's Union with the Russian Empire.* Porvoo: Söderström [1891].

Deglavs, Augusts. *Latviešu attīstības solis no 1843. līdz. 1875. g.* [Latvian Development from 1843 to 1875]. Riga: J. Brigaders, 1893.

Dellingshausen, Eduard Freiherr von. *Im Dienste der Heimat!* Stuttgart: Ausland und Heimat, 1930.

Deutschbaltisches biographisches Lexikon 1710-1960. Begun by Olaf Welding and edited by Wilhelm Lenz with the assistance of Erik Amburger and Georg von Krusenstjern. Cologne: Böhlau, 1970.

Dukhanov, M. M. "K voprosu o politicheskoi platforme tsarizma v baltiiskikh guberniiakh," *Zinātniskie raksti,* XL (1961, No. 3), 255-97.

――――. "Ostzeiskoe dvorianstvo i sryv sudebnoi reformy v Pribaltiiskikh guberniiakh v 60=kh gg. XIX v.," *Zinātniskie raksti,* CLXXXV, Germaniia i Pribaltika, no. 2, 1973, pp. 80-98.

――――. *Ostzeitsy, iav' i vymysel: O roli nemetskikh pomeschikov i biurgerov v istoricheskikh sud'bakh latyshskogo i estonskogo narodov v seredine XIX veka.* Riga: "Liesma," 1970.

————. "Rossiia i Baltiiskii vopros v 60-kh godakh XIX veka." Candidate's dissertation, Moscow University, 1962.

Eesti NSV ajalugu [The History of the Estonian SSR]. 3 vols. Tallinn: Eesti Riiklik Kirjastus, 1955-1963; "Eesti Raamat," 1971.

"Eesti saadikute märgukiri Vene Keiser Aleksander III-le 19. juunist 1881 [The Memorandum of June 19, 1881, from Estonian Representatives to the Russian Tsar Alexander III]," *Eesti Kirjandus* [Estonian Literature], xv (1921), 347-49.

Eggers, Alexander (ed.). *Baltische Lebenserinnerungen.* Heilbronn: E. Salzer, 1926.

Engelhardt, Roderich von. *Die deutsche Universität Dorpat in ihrer geistesgeschichtlichen Bedeutung.* Reval: Franz Kluge, 1933.

Estlander, Bernhard. *Elva årtionden ur Finlands historia.* 5 vols. Helsinki: Söderström, 1929-1930.

Federley, B. "Storfurstendömet Finlands författningar och de allmänna rikslagarna," *Historiks tidskrift för Finland,* 1969, pp. 41-61, 127-66.

————. *Till frågan om rikslagstiftningen: Om den tyska doktrinen och dess betydelse för den ryska politiken mot Finland.* Societas Scientiarum Fennica, Commentationes Humanarum Litterarum, no. 37. Helsinki: n.p., 1965.

Från brytningstider. Minnen och erfarenheter. 2 vols. Helsinki: Söderström, 1913-1917.

Gasman, A. G. "Subebnaia reforma v Pribaltiiskikh guberniiakh," *Zhurnal Ministerstva iustitsii,* xx, no. 9, (1914), 146-69.

Goba, Alfreds. "Latgales atmodas sākums" [The Beginning of the Awakening in Lettgallia], *Izglītības Ministrijas Mēnešraksts* [Monthly of the Ministry of Education], 1931, pp. 503-21.

Gummerus, Herman. *Aktiva kampår 1899-1910.* Helsinki: Söderström, 1925.

Hyvämäki, Lauri. *Ennen routaa: Esseitä ja tutkielmia 1880-luvusta* [Before the Frost: Essays and Studies on the 1880s]. Helsinki: Otava, 1960.

Infant'ev, B. F. *Russkii iazyk v natsional'noi shkole Latvii: Istoricheskii ocherk.* Riga: "Zvaigzne," 1972.

Isakov, S. G. *Ostzeiskii vopros v russkoi pechati 1860-kh godov.* Tartu Riikliku Ülikooli Toimetised, no. 107. Tartu: Tartu Riikliku Ülikool, 1961.

————. *Russkii iazyk i literatura v uchebnykh zavedeniiakh Estonii XVIII-XIX stoletii.* 2 vols. Tartu: Tartuskii Gosudarstvennyi Universitet, 1973-1974.

Issakov [Isakov], Sergei G. "Tsaarivalitsuse tsensuuripoliitikast eesti ajakirjanduse suhtes 19. sajandi teisel poolel [On the Censorship Policy of the Tsarist Government with Regard to Estonian Journalism in the Second Half of the 19th Century]." Juhan Peegel, ed., *Läbi kahe sajandi* [Through Two Centuries]. Tallinn: "Eesti Raamat," 1971.

Istoriia Estonskoi SSR. Ed. A. Vassar and G. Naan. 3 vols. Tallinn: Estonskoe Gosudarstvennoe Izdatel'stvo, 1961-1974.

Istoriia Latviiskoi SSR. Ed. K. Strazdiņš et al. 3 vols. Riga: Akademiia Nauk Latviiskoi SSR: 1952-1958.

Jakobson, Carl Robert. *Valitud teosed* [Selected Works]. 2 vols. Tallinn: Eesti Riiklik Kirjastus, 1959.

Jansons, J. A. *Tautiskās atmodas laikmeta darbinieki: Alunāns, Barons, Brīvzemnieks* [The Writers of the National Awakening: Alunāns, Barons, Brivzemnieks]. Riga: A. Gulbis, 1939.

Jordan, Paul (ed.). *Ergebnisse der ehstländischen Volkszählung.* 3 vols. Reval: Lindfors' Erben, 1883-1885.

Jung-Stilling, Friedrich von, and Anders, W. (eds.). *Ergebnisse der livländischen Volkszählung.* 3 vols. Riga: Stahl'sche Buchdruckerei, 1883-1885.

Jussila, Osmo. *Suomen perustuslait venäläisten ja suomalaisten tulkintojen mukaan 1808-1863* [Finnish Fundamental Laws as Interpreted by Russia and Finland 1808-1863]. Historiallisia Tutkimuksia, No. 77. Helsinki: Suomen Historiallinen Seura, 1969.

———. *Nationalismi ja vallankumous venäläis-suomalaisissa suhteissa 1899-1914.* Suomen Historiallinen Seura, Historiallisia Tutkimuksia, 110. Helsinki, 1979.

Karjahärm, Toomas. "Eesti linnakodanluse poliitilisest formeerumisest 1870-ndate aastate lõpust kuni 1914. aastani (linna- ja duuma-valimiste materjalide põhjal) [The Political Formation of the Estonian Urban Bourgeoisie from the End of the 1870s to 1914—Based on Municipal and Duma Election Materials]," Toimetised, xxii (1973), 251-65.

Katkov, M. N. *Sobranie peredovykh statei Moskovskikh vedomostei, 1863-1887 gg.* 25 vols. Moscow: V. V. Chicherin, 1897-1898.

Kirby, D. G. (ed.). *Finland and Russia 1808-1902: From Autonomy to Independence: A Selection of Documents.* New York: Harper & Row, 1976.

Kitzberg, August. *Ühe vana "tuuletallaja" noorpõlve mälestused* [*The Memoirs of an Old "Windbag's" Youth*]. 2 vols. Tartu: Noor-Eesti, 1924-1925.

Köörna, Arno. *Suure Sotsialistliku Oktoobrirevolutsiooni majanduslikud eeldused Eestis* [The Economic Preconditions of the

Great Socialist October Revolution in Estonia]. Tallinn: Eesti Riiklik Kirjastus, 1961.

Korhonen, Keijo. *Autonomous Finland in the Political Thought of Nineteenth Century Russia.* Annales Universitatis Turkuensis, ser. B, no. 105. Turku: Turun Yliopisto, 1967.

Kozins, Mikhailis [M. I. Kozin]. *Latyshskaia derevnia v 50-70-e gg. XIX veka.* Riga: "Zinatne," 1976.

Kratkoe obozrenie pravitel'stvennykh rasporiazhenii o vvedenii v upotreblenie russkogo iazyka v Pribaltiiskikh guverniiakh. St. Petersburg: Gosudarstvennaia Tipografiia, 1899.

Kreutzwald, Fr. R. *Fr. R. Kreutzwaldi kirjavahetus* [The Correspondence of Fr. R. Kreutzwald]. 6 vols. Tallinn: Eesti Riiklik Kirjastus, 1953-1962; "Eesti Raamat," 1976-1979.

Krusius-Ahrenberg, L. *Der Durchbruch des Nationalismus und Liberalismus im politischen Leben Finlands 1856-1863.* Annales Academiae Scientiarum Fennicae, no. 33. Helsinki: Druckerei-A.G. der Finnischen Literaturgesellschaft, 1934.

Kruus, Hans. *Eesti Aleksandrikool* [The Estonian Alexander School]. Tartu: Noor-Eesti, 1939.

————. "Väikerahvalik tunnetus eesti ühiskondlikus mõttes [The Consciousness of Being a Small People in Estonian Social Thought]," *Ajalooline Ajakiri* [Historical Journal], xviii (1939), 136-47.

Kruus, Hans (ed.). *Jakob Hurda kõned ja avalikud kirjad* [The Speeches and Public Letters of Jakob Hurt] Tartu: Eesti Kirjanduse Selts, 1939.

Langhoff, [Carl Fredrik] August. *Sju år såsom Finlands representant inför Tronen: Minnen och anteckningar åren 1905-1913.* 3 vols. Helsinki: Söderström, 1922-1923.

Laul, Endel. "1880. aastate alghariduskoolide reform Baltimaadel [The Baltic Elementary School Reform in the 1880s]," *Nõukogude Kool* [Soviet School], xxxi (1973), 691-95.

Lenz, Wilhelm. *Die Entwicklung Rigas zur Grossstadt.* Kitzingen am Main: Holzner, 1954.

Lenz, Wilhelm. "Volkstumswechsel in den baltischen Ländern," *Ostdeutsche Wissenschaft: Jahrbuch des ostdeutschen Kulturrats,* iii/iv (1956-1957), 181-200.

Liim, Allan. "Keskkoolivõrgu kujunemine ja areng Eestis 19. sajandi teisel poolel [The Development and Growth of the Secondary School Network in Estonia in the Second Half of the 19th Century]." *Nõukogude Kool* [Soviet School], xxxi (1973), 613-15, 696-703.

Lindemuth, Margarethe. "Krišjānis Valdemārs und Atis Kronvalds: Zwei lettische Volkstumskämpfer," *Baltische Hefte*, XIII (1967), 84-107.

Manasein, N. A. *Manaseina revīzijā: Senatora N. Manaseina ziņojums par viņa izdarīto revīziju Vidzemes un Kurzemes guberņās no 1882. līdz 1883. gadam* [The Manasein Inspection: The Report of Senator N. Manasein Concerning the Inspection Carried Out by Him in Livland and Kurland *gubernii* in 1882 and 1883]. Ed. A. Drīzulis. Riga: Latvijas Valsts Izdevniecība, 1949.

Materialy sobrannye osoboiu kommiseiu vysochaishe uchrezhdennoiu 2 noiabria 1869 goda, dlia peresmotra deistvuiushchikh postanovlenii o tsenzure i pechati. 3 pts. St. Petersburg: Tipografiia Vtorogo Otdeleniia Sobstvennoi E. I. V. Kantseliarii, 1870.

[Milenbachs, F.]. *Latvieši un latvietes Krievijas augstskolās* [Latvian Men and Women in Russian Institutions of Higher Learning]. Jelgava: H. Allunans, 1908.

Nol'de, B. E. *Ocherki russkogo gosudarstvennogo prava.* St. Petersburg: "Pravda," 1911.

Ordin, K. F. *Sobranie sochinenii po finlianskomu voprosu.* Ed. V. K. Ordin. 3 vols. St. Petersburg: A. S. Suvorin, 1908; Gosudarstvennaia Tipografiia, 1909.

Paasikivi, Juha Kusti. *Paasikiven muistelmia sortovuosilta* [Paasikivi's Memoirs of the Years of Oppression]. 2 vols. Helsinki: Söderström, 1957.

Parmanen, Eino I. *Taistelujen kirja* [The Book of Struggles] 4 vols. Porvoo-Helsinki: Söderström, 1936-1939.

Petrovskii, S. A. (ed.). *Finliandskaia okraina Rossii: Sbornik statei, ocherkov, pisem, dokumentov i inykh materialov dlia izucheniia tak-nazyvaemogo "finliandskogo voprosa."* 3 vols. Moscow: Universitetskaia Tipografiia, 1891-1897.

Petukhov, E. V. *Imperatorskii Iur'evskii, byvshii Derptskii Universitet za sto let ego sushchestvovaniia (1802-1902).* 2 vols. Iur'ev: K. Mattisen, 1902; St. Petersburg: Senatskaia Tipografiia, 1906.

Pistohlkors, Gert von. *Ritterschaftliche Reformpolitik zwischen Russifizierung und Revolution: Historische Studien zum Problem der politischen Selbsteinschätzung der deutschen Oberschicht in den Ostseeprovinzen Russlands im Krisenjahr 1905.* Göttinger Bausteine zur Geschichtswissenschaft, no. 48. Göttingen: Musterschmidt, 1978.

Plakans, Andrejs. "The National Awakening in Latvia 1850-1900." Harvard University Ph.D. dissertation, 1969.

————. "Peasants, Intellectuals and Nationalism in the Russian Baltic Provinces, 1820-1890," *Journal of Modern History*, XLVI (1974), 445-75.

Polovtsov, A. A. *Dnevnik gosudarstvennogo sekretaria A. A. Polovtsova*. Ed. P. A. Zaionchkovskii. 2 vols. Moscow: "Nauka," 1966.

Polvinen, Tuomo. *Die finnischen Eisenbahnen in den militärischen Plänen Russlands vor dem ersten Weltkrieg*. Studia Historica, IV Helsinki: Suomen Historiallinen Seura, 1962.

Rasila, Viljo. *Suomen torpparikysymys vuoteen 1909: Yhteiskunta-historiallinen tutkimus* [The Crofter Question in Finland to the Year 1909: A Study in Social History]. Historiallisia Tutkimuksia, no. 59. Helsinki: Suomen Historiallinen Seura, 1961.

Rein, [Karl Gabriel] Thiodolf. *Lefnadsminnen*. Helsinki: Söderström, 1918.

Rigas Latviešu Biedrības Zinības Komisijas Konversācijas Vārdnica [The Riga Latvian Association's Scientific Committee's Encyclopedia]. Riga: Rigas Latviešu Biedrība, 1903-1913.

Rommi, Pirkko. *Myöntyvyyssuuntauksen hahmottuminen Yrjö-Koskisen ja Suomalaisen Puolueen toimintalinjaksi* [The Formation of the Compliance Direction into the Line of Action of Yrjö-Koskinen and the Finnish Party]. Historiallisia Tutkimuksia, no. 68. Helsinki: Suomen Historiallinen Seura, 1964.

Rozhdestvenskii, S. V. (ed.). *Istoricheskii obzor deiatel'nosti Ministerstva narodnogo prosveshcheniia 1802-1902*. St. Petersburg: Gosudarstvennaia Tipografiia, 1902.

Russisch-Baltische Blätter: Beiträge zur Kenntnis Russlands und seiner Grenzmarken. 4 vols. Leipzig: Duncker & Humblot, 1886-1888.

Samarin, Iu. F. *Sochineniia*. Vols. 1-10, 12 published. Moscow: A. I. Mamontov, 1877-1911.

Schirren, Carl. *Livländische Antwort an Herrn Juri Samarin*. Leipzig: Duncker & Humblot, 1869.

Schweitzer, Robert. *Autonomie und Autokratie: Die Stellung des Grossfürstentums Finnland im russischen Reich in der zweiten Hälfte des 19. Jahrhunderts*. Marburger Abhandlungen zur Geschichte Osteuropas, no. 19. Giessen: W. Schmitz, 1978.

Seredonin, S. M. (ed.). *Istoricheskii obzor deiatel'nosti Komiteta ministrov*. 4 vols. St. Petersburg: Gosudarstvennaia Tipografiia, 1902.

Sergeevskii, N. D. *Finland: The Question of Autonomy and Fundamental Laws*. Trans. V. E. Marsden. London: Wyman & Sons, 1911.

Shakhovskoi, S. V. *Iz arkhiva kniazia S. V. Shakhovskogo: Materialy dlia istorii nedavnego proshlogo Pribaltiiskoi okrainy.* 3 vols. St. Petersburg: V. Eriks, 1909-1910.

Skujenieks, Mārģeris. "Iecelošana un izcelošana Latvija" [Immigration and Emigration in Latvia], *Domas*, x (1913), 1155-62.

―――. *Nacionālais jautājums Latvijā* [The National Question in Latvia]. St. Petersburg: A. Gulbis, 1913.

Soikkanen, Hannu. *Sosialismin tulo Suomeen* [The Coming of Socialism to Finland]. Porvoo-Helsinki: Söderström, 1961.

Soikkanen, Hannu (ed.). *Tiennäyttäjät* [Pioneers]. 3 vols. Helsinki: Tammi, 1967-1968.

Speer, Helmut. *Das Bauernschulwesen im Gouvernement Estland vom Ende des achtzehnten Jahrhunderts bis zur Russifizierung.* Tartu: J. G. Krüger, 1936.

Staël von Holstein, R. von. *Fürst Paul Lieven als Landmarschall von Livland.* Riga: W. F. Häcker, 1906.

Stalšāns, Kārlis. *Krievu ekspansija un rusifikācija Baltijā laikmetu tecējumā* [Russian Expansion and Russification in the Baltic Region over the Centuries]. Chicago: Jāna Šķirmanta Apgāds, 1966.

Suomen historian dokumentteja [Documents of Finnish History]. 2 vols. Helsinki: Otava, 1968-1970.

Suomen kansanedustuslaitoksen historia [History of the Finnish System of Popular Representation]. 9 vols. Helsinki: Eduskunnan historiakomitea, 1962-1971.

Suomen Sosiaalidemokraatisen Puolueen kolmannen (ylimääräisen) kokouksen . . . pöytäkirja . . . Helsingissä [Minutes of the Third (Special) Conference of the Social Democratic Party of Finland . . . at Helsinki in the Year 1904]. Kotka: Kirjapaino "Kotka," 1905.

Švābe, Arvēds. *Latvijas vēsture 1800-1914* [History of Latvia 1800-1914]. Uppsala: Daugava, 1958.

Švābe, Arvēds (ed.). *Latvju enciklopēdija.* [The Latvian Encyclopedia]. 3 vols. Stockholm: Apgāds Trīs Zvaigznes, 1950-1951.

"Tartu Ülemaalise Rahvaasemikkude Kongressi Aula koosolekute otsused" [The Resolutions of the Aula Meetings of the Tartu Congress of National Representatives]. Ed. Hans Kruus, *Punased aastad* [Red Years]. Tartu: Eesti Kirjanduse Selts, 1932.

"Tartu Ülemaalise Rahvaasemikkude Kongressi Bürgermusse koosolekute otsused [The Resolutions of the Bürgermusse Meetings of the Tartu Congress of National Representatives]." Ed. Hans Kruus, *Punased aastad.* Tartu: Eesti Kirjanduse Selts, 1932.

Tentelis, A. (ed.). *Dokumenti par "Pēterburgas avīzēm"* [Documents Concerning *Pēterburgas Avīzes*]: *Latvijas vēstures avoti.* [The Sources of Latvian History]. Riga: Latvijas Vēstures Instītūta Apgādiens, 1937.

Tobien, Alexander von. *Die Agrargesetzgebung Livlands im 19. Jahrhundert.* 2 vols. Berlin: Puttkammer & Mühlbrecht, 1899; Riga: G. Löffler, 1911.

———. *Die livländische Ritterschaft in ihrem Verhältnis zum Zarismus und russischen Nationalismus.* 2 vols. Riga: G. Löffler, 1925; Berlin: Walter de Gruyter, 1930.

Tommila, Päiviö (ed.). *Venäläinen sortokausi Suomessa* [The Period of Russian Oppression in Finland]. Porvoo: Söderström, 1960.

Törngren, Adolf. *Från Finlands strid för rätt och frihet. Personliga upplevelser och minnen 1901-1914.* Skrifter utg. av Svenska Literatursällskapet, no. 290. Helsinki, 1942.

Troinitskii, N. A. (ed.). *Pervaia vseobshchaia perepis' naseleniia Rossiiskoi imperii, 1897 g.* 89 vols. St. Petersburg: Tsentral'nyi Statisticheskii Komitet, 1899-1905.

Tuglas, Friedebert. *Ado Grenzsteini lahkumine* [The Departure of Ado Grenzstein]. Tartu: Noor-Eesti, 1926.

———. *Eesti Kirjameeste Selts* [The Society of Estonian Literati]. Tallinn: Eesti Riiklik Kirjastus, 1958 (first published, 1932).

Unams, Žanis. "Kr. Valdemāra un Fr. Brīvzemnieka sarakstīšanās par Baltijas skolu lietām" [The Correspondence of Kr. Valdemārs and Fr. Brīvzemnieks About Baltic School Matters], *Izglītības Ministrijas Mēnešraksts,* 1932, pp. 112-21; 215-22.

Valuev, P. A. *Dnevnik P. A. Valueva ministra Vnutrennikh del.* Ed. P. A. Zaionchkovskii. 2 vols. Moscow: Akademiia Nauk, 1961.

Vičs, A. "Ka Latvijā nodibināja pirmo ministrijas skolu" [How the First Ministry School Was Established in Latvia], *Izglītības Ministrijas Mēnešraksts,* 1920, pp. 17-22.

———. "Latviešu skolotāju sapulces" [The Regular Meetings of Latvian Schoolteachers], *Izglītības Ministrijas Mēnešraksts,* 1920, pp. 121-30, 210-15, 311-17, 413-18, 508-14; 1921, pp. 10-18, 113-19, 304-22, 408-15, 508-16.

Virtanen, Kari C. *Ahdistettu kansakunta 1890-1917* [Nation under Attack, 1890-1917]. (Kansakunnan historia, vol. 5). Porvoo-Helsinki: Söderström, 1974.

Wittram, Reinhard. *Baltische Geschichte: Die Ostseelande Livland, Estland, Kurland 1180-1918.* Munich: R. Oldenbourg, 1954.

———. *Liberalismus baltischer Literaten: Zur Entstehung der baltischen Presse.* Abhandlungen der Herder-Gesellschaft und des Herder-Instituts zu Riga, vierter Band, no. 9. Riga: G. Löffler, 1931.

Wittram, Reinhard (ed.). *Baltische Kirchengeschichte.* Göttingen: Vandenhock & Ruprecht, 1956.

Zaionchkovskii, N. Ch. *K istorii sel'skoi inorodcheskoi shkoly v Pribaltiiskikh guberniiakh i ee reform.* Riga: Blankenshtein, 1902.

Zaionchkovskii, P. A. *Rossiiskoe samoderzhavie v kontse XIX stoletiia.* Moscow: "Mysl'," 1970.

———. "Sudebnye i administrativnye preobrazovaniia v Pribaltike," *Problemy obshchestvennoi mysli i ekonomicheskaia politika Rossii XIX-XX vekov pamiati professora S. B. Okunia: Sbornik statei,* ed. N. G. Sladkevich. Leningrad: Izdatel'stvo Leningradskogo Universiteta, 1972.

Zutis, Ia. Ia. *Ostzeiskii vopros v XVIII veke.* Riga: Knigoizdatel'-stvo, 1946.

INDEX

Åbo, Treaty of (1743), 113
Adlerberg, N. V., 29, 30, 76; and military reform of Finland, 80
administrative Russification, 9, 421-23, 460-61; in Baltic Provinces, 9, 33-53, 137-60; Catherine II and, 9, 16, 17; Estonians and, 296-97, 300-301, 306-13, 340; in Finland, 76-87, 387-92, 438-41, 460; Finnish peasants and, 429-34; Finnish workers and, 411-12; Finnish university students and, 434-35; Yrjö-Koskinen and, 391-92
agricultural societies in Baltic Provinces, 288
Aho, Juhani, 423
Aksakov, I. S., 35, 38, 125, 127
Åland Islands, 6, 377
Al'bedinskii, P. P., 25, 37, 140; and Baltic municipal reform, 51; and Baltic state peasants, 41; influence on Baltic policy, 33-34, 460; and Orthodoxy in Baltic Provinces, 45-46; and Russian language in Baltic Provinces, 47-48
Alexander I: and Baltic Provinces, 113, 118; and Finland, 359-62; Latvians and, 217; and Lutheran Church, 121
Alexander II, 9, 24, 31, 38, 43, 54, 142; assassination of, 149; Baltic agrarian policy of, 38; and Baltic Lutheran Church, 147-48, 324; and Baltic Provinces, 33, 112, 124, 126, 133, 134, 139-40, 148, 460-61; and Congress Poland, 24; and Finland, 29, 30, 364, 366-67, 424; and Orthodox Church in Baltic Provinces, 45, 46; and Russian language in Baltic Provinces, 47-48; and Samarin, 129
Alexander III, 9, 15; and Baltic Provinces, 54, 112, 150, 162; and Baltic reconverts, 163; and Baltic zemstvos, 306; and codification of Finnish laws,

77; counterreforms of, 461; and cultural Russification, 56, 57; and Dorpat University, 174; and Estonian and Latvian national movements, 196 n. 47; and Finland, 78, 364, 370-71, 372, 390, 393; and Lutheran pastors, 69; and mixed marriages, 325; and Orthodoxy in Baltic Provinces, 69-70, 162; and Russian language in Baltic Provinces, 154
All-Estonian Congress, 306, 320, 339
Alunāns, Juris, 221
Antell, Kasten, 404
Apsītis, Jēkabs, 245-46; Herrnhut tradition in, 246
Arkhangelites, 416
Armfelt, Alexander, 21, 29, 32
Armfelt, C. A., 382-83
army strike of 1902 and 1903 in Finland, 439-40
assimilation: of Baltic Germans, 166, 199-200 n. 28; of Latvians, 214, 222, 231-32, 276 n. 27, 277-78 n. 47, 282 n. 24
Austrums, 251

Bagration, P. R., 52
Bakunin, M. A., 111
Balss, 251
Baltic agriculture: productivity of, 64, 71
Baltic Committee (*Ostseekomittee*), 22, 37, 39, 41, 467
Baltic Diets: and provincial self-government, 311; and Russification, 306
Baltic *general-gubernatorstvo*: abolition of, 53, 140, 179
Baltic Germans: in army, 151; in bureaucracy, 111, 151-52; disunity of, 152-53, 181; in Duma, 73-74; and Estonian and Latvian national movements, 182; history of, 113-14; in municipal elections, 158, 181;

Library of Congress Cataloging in Publication Data
Main entry under title:

Russification in the Baltic Provinces and Finland, 1855-1914.

Bibliography: p.
Includes index.
1. Baltic States—Foreign relations—Russia. 2. Russia—
Foreign relations—Baltic States. 3. Finland—Foreign relations—
Russia. 4. Russia—Foreign relations—Finland. I. Thaden, Edward C.
II. Haltzel, Michael H.
DK511.B3R77   947.08   80-7557
ISBN 0-691-05314-6
ISBN 0-691-10103-5 (pbk.)